MEDICAL SOCIOLOGY

MEDICAL SOCIOLOGY

Ninth Edition

William C. Cockerham
University of Alabama at Birmingham

PEARSON
Prentice
Hall

Upper Saddle River, New Jersey 07458

Library of Congress Cataloging-in-Publication Data

Cockerham, William C.
    Medical sociology/William C. Cockerham.—9th ed.
      p. cm.
    Includes bibliographical references and index.
    ISBN 0–13–111391–7
      1. Social medicine.   I. Title.

  RA418.C657   2003
  362.1—dc21

                          2003048613

AVP, Publisher: Nancy Roberts
Managing editor: Sharon Chambliss
Project coordination: Interactive Composition
  Corporation
Director of marketing: Beth Mejia
Prepress and manufacturing buyer:
  Mary Ann Gloriande
Cover director: Jayne Conte

Cover design: Kiwi Design
Copy editor: Lupe Garcia Ortiz
Marketing assistant: Adam Laitman
Cover image specialist: Karen Sanatar
Cover photo: Elvee Regine/SIS, Inc.
Image permissions coordinator: Debbie Latronica
Manager, rights and permissions: Zina Arabia
Director, image resource center: Melinda Reo

Photo credits appear on page 407.

This book was set in 10/12 ITC Garamond Light by Interactive Composition Corporation
and was printed and bound by Hamilton Printing Company.
The cover was printed by The Lehigh Press, Inc.

PEARSON
Prentice
Hall

© 2004, 2001, 1998, 1995, 1992, 1989, 1986, 1982, 1978 by Pearson Education, Inc.
Upper Saddle River, New Jersey 07458

Printed in the United States of America
10 9 8 7 6 5 4 3 2 1

ISBN 0-13-111391-7

Pearson Education LTD., London
Pearson Education Australia PTY, Limited, Sydney
Pearson Education Singapore, Pte. Ltd
Pearson Education North Asia Ltd, Hong Kong
Pearson Education Canada, Ltd., Toronto
Pearson Educación de Mexico, S.A. de C.V.
Pearson Education—Japan, Tokyo
Pearson Education Malaysia, Pte. Ltd
Pearson Education, Upper Saddle River, New Jersey

To Cynthia,
and to Geoffrey, Sean, Scott,
and Laura and her family

Contents

PREFACE   **xi**

1   MEDICAL SOCIOLOGY   **1**

Defining Health   2
Contrasting Ideas about Health and Social Behavior   3
The Reemergence of Infectious Diseases   7
The Development of Medical Sociology   12
Summary   17
Medical Sociology Internet Sites   18

2   EPIDEMIOLOGY   **19**

Epidemiological Measures   20
The Development of Epidemiology   22
The Complexity of Modern Ills: Heart Disease   25
Disease and Modernization   29
AIDS   30
Summary   38
Epidemiology Internet Sites   38

3   THE SOCIAL DEMOGRAPHY OF HEALTH   **40**

Age   40
Gender   44
Race   51
Socioeconomic Status   62
Summary   70
Social Demography of Health Internet Sites   70

4   SOCIAL STRESS   **72**

Cooley, Thomas, and Goffman: Symbolic Interaction   73
Durkheim: Functionalism   75
Stress   79
Social Factors and Stress   81
Summary   92
Social Stress Internet Sites   93

5   HEALTH BEHAVIOR AND LIFESTYLES   **94**

Health Lifestyles   95
Preventive Care   112
Summary   116
Health Behavior and Lifestyles Internet Sites   117

6   ILLNESS BEHAVIOR   **118**

Self-Care   119
Sociodemographic Variables   120
Recognizing and Coping with Illness Symptoms   135
Summary and Conclusion   139
Illness Behavior Internet Sites   140

7   THE SICK ROLE   **141**

Illness as Deviance   141
The Functionalist Approach to Deviance   144
The Sick Role   145
Criticism of the Sick Role   152
Labeling Theory   158
Sickness as Social Deviance?   161
Being Sick and Disabled   162
Stigma   164
Summary   165
The Sick Role Internet Sites   165

8   HEALING OPTIONS   **167**

Osteopaths   167
Complementary and Alternative Medicine (CAM)   168
Chiropractors   170
Faith Healers   171
Folk Healers   175
Summary   183
Healing Options Internet Sites   183

9   DOCTOR–PATIENT INTERACTION   **185**

Models of Interaction   186
Misunderstandings in Communication   190
Male Physicians and Women Patients   193
Women Physicians   194
Cultural Differences in Communication   196
Patient Compliance   198
The Future of Doctor–Patient Relations   199
Doctor–Patient Relations and New Technology   200
The New Genetics   202
Summary   205
Doctor–Patient Interaction Internet Sites   205

10   PHYSICIANS   **207**

The Professionalization of the Physician   207
The Socialization of the Physician   215
The Power Structure of American Medicine   222
Summary   227
Physicians Internet Sites   228

11   THE PHYSICIAN IN A CHANGING SOCIETY   **229**

Social Control of Medical Practice   231
Countervailing Power   235
Government Regulation   236
Managed Care   237
The Coming of the Corporation   238
The Changing Physician–Patient Relationship   240
The Deprofessionalization of Physicians   241
The Evolution of the Organization of Medical Practice   243
Summary   244
The Physician in a Changing Society Internet Sites   244

12   NURSES, PHYSICIAN ASSISTANTS, PHARMACISTS, AND MIDWIVES   **246**

Nursing: Past and Present   247
Nursing: Future Trends   258
Physician Assistants   261
Pharmacists   262
Midwives   263
Summary   264
Nurses, Physician Assistants, Pharmacists, and Midwives Internet Sites   265

13   HOSPITALS   **267**

The Development of the Hospital as a Social Institution   268
Hospitals in the United States   272
The Organization of the Nonprofit Community Hospital   274
The Hospital–Patient Role   281
The Rising Cost of Hospitalization   285
Summary   287
Hospitals Internet Sites   288

**14   HEALTH CARE DELIVERY AND SOCIAL POLICY
     IN THE UNITED STATES**   **289**

Rising Costs   290
Equity in Health Services   295
Distribution of Services   296
Overview of Health Care Delivery   298
Social Legislation in Health Care   301
Health Reform   305
Health Care: A Right or a Privilege?   308
Summary and Conclusion   311
Health Care Delivery and Social Policy in the United States Internet Sites   312

15   HEALTH CARE IN DEVELOPED COUNTRIES   **313**

Socialized Medicine: Canada, Great Britain, and Sweden   319
Decentralized National Health Programs: Japan, Germany,
     the Netherlands, and France   329
Conclusion   340
Health Care in Developed Countries Internet Sites   341

**16   HEALTH CARE IN FORMER SOCIALIST, SOCIALIST,
        AND DEVELOPING COUNTRIES**   **343**

Socialist Medicine: Alterations in Russia, Poland, Hungary, and China   344
Socialized Medicine: Saudi Arabia and Kenya   356
Decentralized National Health: Mexico   360
Fee-for-Service: South Africa   363
Conclusion   366
Health Care in Former Socialist, Socialist, and Developing
        Countries Internet Sites   367

REFERENCES   **369**

PHOTO CREDITS   **407**

NAME INDEX   **408**

SUBJECT INDEX   **415**

Preface

The field of medical sociology has undergone considerable change since the first edition of this textbook appeared in 1978. At that time, much of the research in medical sociology was dependent upon the sponsorship of physicians, and a clear division of labor existed between sociologists working in academic departments in universities and those working in health institutions. Today, that situation has changed drastically. Medical sociology is no longer highly dependent on the medical profession for funding or focus—although a strong alliance continues to exist in many cases. Medical sociologists exercise their craft in an increasingly independent manner, either working with a greater degree of partnership with health care professionals or functioning as medicine's critics should the situation warrant it. Furthermore, research and teaching in medical sociology in both universities and health institutions are increasingly similar in the application of theory and usefulness in addressing problems relevant to clinical practice. In sum, medical sociology has evolved into a mature, objective, and independent field of study and work.

Medical sociology has also experienced significant growth worldwide in numbers of practitioners. In many countries, including the United States, Canada, Australia, Great Britain, Finland, Germany, the Netherlands, and Singapore, medical sociologists are either the largest or one of the largest specialty groups in sociology. The European Society for Health and Medical Sociology is a large and active professional society, as are the medical sociology sections of the American, British, and German sociological associations. In 1999, the American and British medical sociology sections held their first joint meeting at London University's Royal Holloway College. Elsewhere, the Japanese Society of Health and Medical Sociology is working to further develop the field in its nation, while medical sociologists in Latin America hold regional conferences on a regular basis and have their own Spanish-language journals.

Numerous books, journals, college and university courses, medical programs, and lecture series in medical sociology now exist in different parts of the world. This textbook, for example, has been translated into Chinese by Yang Hui and Zhang Tuohong of Beijing Medical University and published by Huaxia Publishing House in Beijing. It has also been published in Chinese in Taiwan by Wu-Nan Book Company. Additionally, it has been translated into Spanish by Lourdes Lostao of the Public University of Navarra in Spain and published by Prentice Hall in Madrid. In the United States, several universities offer specialties in medical sociology, while two universities, the University of Alabama at Birmingham and the University of California at San Francisco—both with large medical campuses—offer doctorates in medical sociology. Columbia University in New York City offers a combined Ph.D. program in sociology and public health, while medical sociology is a major focus in sociology departments at the University of Kentucky, Rutgers University, Indiana University, the Kent State and University of Akron Program, Florida State University, and the University of Miami (Florida). Additionally, there are departments of social medicine, which include medical sociologists, at Harvard University and the University of North Carolina at Chapel Hill, as well as McGill University in Montreal.

The principal goal of this textbook since its inception has been to introduce students to medical sociology by presenting the ideas, concepts, themes, theories, and research findings in the field. This edition—the ninth—continues this approach. The intent is to identify and discuss the most current issues, debates, and findings in medical sociology.

ACKNOWLEDGMENTS

The material contained in the pages of this book is my own responsibility in terms of perspective, scope, and style of presentation. Nevertheless, I am deeply grateful to several people for their assistance in preparing the nine editions of this book. I would like to acknowledge the insightful comments of those colleagues who reviewed all or part of this work throughout the revision process. For sharing their views and helping to improve the quality of this book, my appreciation goes to Melvin Barber, Florida A&M University; Paul Berzina, County College of Morris; Deirdre Bowen, University of Washington; Herbert Bynder, University of Colorado; Robert Clark, Midwestern State University; John Collette, University of Utah; Spencer Condie, Brigham Young University; Morton Creditor, University of Kansas Medical Center; Norman Denzin, University of Illinois at Urbana-Champaign; Karen A. Donahue, Hanover College; Barry Edmonston, Cornell University; Eliot Freidson, New York University; Reed Geertsen, Utah State University; Sharon Guten, Case Western Reserve University; Wendell Hester, East Tennessee State University; Joseph Jones, Portland State University; Daniel J. Klenow, North Dakota State University; Sol Levine, Harvard University and the New England Medical Center; Richard C. Ludtke, University of North Dakota; Robert Terry Russell, College of St. Francis; Alexander Rysman, Northeastern University; Jeffrey Salloway, University of New Hampshire; Anne Saunders, College of St. Francis; Neil Smelser, Center for the Advanced Study of the Behavioral Sciences, Stanford; and George J. Warheit, University of Miami (Florida). I would also like to thank two doctoral students in medical sociology at UAB who provided important assistance in the preparation of this edition: Emily Norman and Brian Hinote.

William C. Cockerham
Birmingham, Alabama

CHAPTER 1

Medical Sociology

The purpose of this book is to introduce readers to the field of medical sociology. Recognition of the significance of the complex relationship between social factors and the level of health characteristic of various groups and societies has led to the development of medical sociology as an important substantive area within the general field of sociology. As an academic discipline, sociology is concerned with the social causes and consequences of human behavior; thus, it follows that medical sociology is concerned with the social causes and consequences of health and illness (Cockerham and Ritchey 1997). Medical sociology brings sociological perspectives, theories, and methods to the study of health and medical practice. Major areas of investigation include the social facets of health and disease, the social behavior of health care personnel and people who utilize health care, the social functions of health organizations and institutions, the social patterns of health services, and the relationship of health care delivery systems to other systems.

What makes medical sociology important is the critical role social factors play in determining the health of individuals, groups, and the larger society. Social conditions and situations not only promote the possibility of illness and disability, but also enhance prospects for disease prevention and health maintenance. Many of the greatest threats to an individual's health and physical well-being today stem largely from unhealthy lifestyles and high-risk behavior, and this statement is true

1

for heart disease, cancer, acquired immunodeficiency syndrome (AIDS), and a host of modern-day health problems. Healthy lifestyles and the avoidance of high-risk behavior, however, advance the individual's potential for a longer and healthier life.

Social factors also are important in influencing the manner in which societies organize their resources to cope with health hazards and deliver medical care to the population at large. Individuals and societies tend to respond to health problems in a manner consistent with their culture, norms, and values. As Donald Light (Light and Schuller 1986:9) explains, "medical care and health services are acts of political philosophy"; thus, social and political values influence the choices made, institutions formed, and levels of funding provided for health. It is no accident that the United States has its form of health care delivery and other nations have their particular approaches. Health is therefore not simply a matter of biology, but involves a number of factors that are social, cultural, political, and economic in nature.

DEFINING HEALTH

The World Health Organization (WHO) defines health as a state of complete physical, mental, and social well-being, and not merely the absence of disease or injury. This definition calls attention to the fact that being healthy involves much more than simply determining if a person is ill or injured. To be healthy means also having a sense of well-being. While WHO views health as an absence of disease, injury, or distress, most studies suggest that laypersons tend to view health as the capacity to carry out one's daily activities (Blaxter 1990; Bury 1997). Many individuals consider health to be a state of functional fitness and apply this definition to their everyday lives.

Good health is a prerequisite for the adequate functioning of any individual or society. If our health is sound, we can engage in numerous types of activities. But if we are ill, distressed, or injured, we may face the curtailment of our usual round of daily life, and we may also become so preoccupied with our state of health that other pursuits are of secondary importance or quite meaningless. Therefore, as René Dubos (1981) explains, *health can be defined as the ability to function.* This does not mean that healthy people are free from all health problems; it means that they can function to the point that they can do what they want to do. Ultimately, suggests Dubos, biological success in all of its manifestations is a measure of fitness.

As Thomas McKeown (1979) observes, we know from personal experience that the feeling of well-being is more than the perceived absence of disease and disability. Many influences—social, religious, economic, personal, and medical—contribute to such a state. The role of medicine in health promotion is the prevention of illness and premature death and care of the sick and disabled. Thus, McKeown concludes that medicine's task is not to create happiness, but to remove a major source of unhappiness—disease and disability—from people's lives.

CONTRASTING IDEAS ABOUT HEALTH
AND SOCIAL BEHAVIOR

Attempts to understand the relationship between social behavior and health have their origin in history. Dubos (1969) suggested that primitive humans were closer to the animals in that they, too, relied upon their instincts to stay healthy. Yet some primitive humans recognized a cause and effect relationship between doing certain things and alleviating symptoms of a disease or improving the condition of a wound. Since there was so much that primitive humans did not understand about the functioning of the body, *magic* became an integral component of the beliefs about the causes and cures of health disorders. Actually, an uncritical acceptance of magic and the supernatural pervaded practically every aspect of primitive life. So it is not surprising that early humans thought that illness was caused by evil spirits. Primitive medicines made from vegetables or animals were invariably used in combination with some form of ritual to expel the harmful spirit from a diseased body. During the Neolithic age, some 4,000 to 5,000 years ago, people living in what is today the Eastern Mediterranean and North Africa are known to have even engaged in a surgical procedure called *trepanation* or trephining, which consists of a hole being bored in the skull in order to liberate the evil spirit supposedly contained in a person's head. The finding by anthropologists of more than one hole in some skulls and the lack of signs of osteomyelitis (erosion of bone tissue) suggest that the operation was not always fatal. Some estimates indicate that the mortality rate from trepanation was low, an amazing accomplishment considering the difficulty of the procedure and the crude conditions under which it must have been performed (Porter 1997).

One of the earliest attempts in the Western world to formulate principles of health care based upon rational thought and the rejection of supernatural phenomena is found in the work of the Greek physician Hippocrates. Little is known of Hippocrates, who lived around 400 B.C., not even whether he actually authored the collection of books that bears his name. Nevertheless, the writings attributed to him have provided a number of principles underlying modern medical practice. One of his most famous contributions, the Hippocratic Oath, is the foundation of contemporary medical ethics. Among other things, it requires the physician to swear that he or she will help the sick, refrain from intentional wrongdoing or harm, and keep confidential all matters pertaining to the doctor–patient relationship.

Hippocrates also argued that medical knowledge should be derived from an understanding of the natural sciences and the logic of cause and effect relationships. In his classic treatise, *On Airs, Waters, and Places,* Hippocrates pointed out that human well-being is influenced by the totality of environmental factors: living habits or lifestyle, climate, topography of the land, and the quality of air, water, and food. Interestingly enough, concerns about our health and the quality of air, water, and places are still very much with us today.

In their intellectual orientation toward disease, Hippocrates and the ancient Greeks held views that were more in line with contemporary thinking about health than was found in the Middle Ages and the Renaissance. Much of the medical knowledge of the ancient world was lost during the Dark Ages that descended on

Europe after the fall of the Roman Empire. What knowledge remained in the West was preserved by the Catholic church. The church took responsibility for dealing with mental suffering and adverse social conditions like poverty, while physicians focused more or less exclusively on treating physical ailments. The human body was regarded as a machinelike entity that operated according to principles of physics and chemistry. The result was that both Western religion and medical science sponsored the idea "of the body as a machine, of disease as a breakdown of the machine, and of the doctor's task as repair of the machine" (Engle 1977:131).

A few physicians, such as Paracelsus, a famous Swiss doctor who lived in the early sixteenth century, did show interest in understanding more than the physical functioning of the body. Paracelsus demonstrated that specific diseases common among miners were related to their work conditions. But Paracelsus was an exception, and few systematic measures were employed to either research or cope with the effects of adverse social situations on health until the late eighteenth and early nineteenth centuries.

Modern Medicine and Regulation of the Body

Modern medicine traces its birth to Western Europe in the late eighteenth century. In analyzing the development of French medicine at this time, social theorist Michel Foucault (1973) noted the emergence of two distinct trends in medical practice— what he called "medicine of the species" and "medicine of social spaces." Medicine of the species pertained to the strong emphasis in Western medicine upon classifying diseases, diagnosing and treating patients, and finding cures. The human body became an object of study and observation in order that physiological processes could be demystified and brought under medical control. Physicians perfected their so-called clinical gaze, allowing them to observe and perceive bodily functions and dysfunctions within a standardized frame of reference. Clinics were established both to treat patients and train doctors, with the clinic providing the optimal setting for physicians to exercise authority and control over their patients.

The medicine of social spaces was concerned not with curing diseases, but preventing them. Prevention required greater government involvement in regulating the conduct of daily life—especially public hygiene. Physicians served as advisers in the enactment of laws and regulations specifying standards for food, water, and the disposal of wastes. The health of the human body thus became a subject of regulation by medical doctors and civil authorities as social norms for healthy behavior became more widely established. In such a context, Foucault found that scientific concepts of disease had replaced notions that sickness had metaphysical (religious, magical, superstitious) origins. Disease was no longer considered an entity outside of the existing boundaries of knowledge, but an object to be studied, confronted scientifically, and controlled.

The Public's Health

Awareness that disease could be caused by unhealthy social conditions and lifestyles spread through common sense and practical experience. A most significant development occurred when it was realized that uncontaminated food, water, and air, as well as sanitary living conditions, could reduce the onset and spread of communicable diseases. Prior to the advent of modern medicine, high mortality rates from communicable diseases such as typhus, tuberculosis, scarlet fever, measles, and cholera were significantly lowered in both Europe and North America through improved hygiene and sanitation. Thus, the late eighteenth and early nineteenth centuries are conspicuous for the systematic implementation of public health measures.

Noting the link between social conditions, lifestyles and health, some nineteenth-century European physicians argued that improvement was necessary in the living situations of the poor. They advocated governmental recognition of the social as well as medical nature of measures undertaken to promote health. Rudolf Virchow, for instance, a prominent German physician known in clinical medicine for the development of cellular pathology, insisted that medicine was a social science. Virchow argued not only that the poor should have quality medical care, but also that they should have free choice of a physician. Improved medical care was also to go hand in hand with changed social conditions leading to a better life. However, these proposals had little effect outside Virchow's small circle of colleagues. Virchow's views were simply seen as too liberal by many European rulers and politicians of the period who feared that social reforms would erode their authority and lead to revolution. There was also a widespread bias in Europe among the educated classes in favor of a medical science that failed to acknowledge the possible benefits of health measures that were largely social.

This was rather ironic because several twentieth-century scholars have found that the decline in deaths from infectious diseases in the second half of the nineteenth century was mainly due to improvements in diet, housing, public sanitation, and personal hygiene instead of medical innovations (McKeown 1979; McKinlay, McKinlay, and Beaglehole 1989). McKeown (1979), for example, notes that the decline in infant mortality was due more to improved nutrition for mothers and better care and feeding for infants than to improved obstetric services. Deaths from typhus also fell dramatically without a specific medical cause. A similar drop in mortality from typhoid and dysentery led McKeown (1979:53) to conclude that "the rapid decline in mortality from diseases spread by water and food since the late nineteenth century owed little to medical intervention."

The Germ Theory of Disease

Most physicians in the 1800s were primarily interested in treating their patients and improving the state of medical technology. They were not necessarily concerned with social reform. The success during this century of Louis Pasteur, Robert Koch, and others in bacteriological research that led to the conceptualization of the germ theory of disease, along with tremendous progress in the development of internal medicine, anesthesiology, pathology, immunology, and surgical techniques, convinced physicians to focus exclusively upon a clinical medicine grounded in exact scientific laboratory procedures. The practice of medicine in the twentieth century thus rested solidly upon the premise that every disease had a specific pathogenic cause whose treatment could best be accomplished by removing or controlling that cause within a biomedical framework. Dubos (1959) has pointed out that modern medicine's thinking has been dominated by the search for drugs as "magic bullets" that can be shot into the body to kill or control all health disorders. Because research in microbiology, biochemistry, and related fields has resulted in the discovery and production of a large variety of drugs and drug-based techniques for successfully treating many diseases, this approach became medicine's primary method for dealing with the problems it was called upon to treat.

Return to the "Whole Person"

By the late 1960s, polio and smallpox were largely eradicated and infectious diseases had been severely curtailed in most regions of the world. This situation produced a major change in the pattern of diseases, especially in industrialized nations, with chronic illnesses—which by definition are long-term and incurable—replacing infectious diseases as the major threats to health. Diseases such as cancer, heart disease, and stroke became the leading causes of death. Physicians were increasingly called upon to deal with the health problems of the "whole person," which extend well beyond singular causes of disease. Contemporary medical doctors were required to treat health disorders more aptly described as "problems in living," dysfunctions that involve multiple factors of causation, not all of them biological in origin. Social and psychological factors not only influenced whether or not a person became sick, but also the form, duration, and intensity of the symptoms. Consequently, modern medicine is increasingly required to develop insights into the behaviors characteristic of the people it treats.

Also, it is not uncommon for an individual suffering from a chronic disease to feel perfectly normal, even when irreversible damage to organs and tissues has already occurred. Because of the irremediable damage done to the body by a chronic disease, patients may be required to permanently change their style of living and modify their social relationships. So, as Anselm Strauss (1975) has pointed out, health practitioners should know how patients with chronic disorders control their symptoms, adjust to changes in their physical condition, and attempt to live as normally as possible. This is in addition to all else that physicians need to know about the behavior and lifestyles of individuals that influence whether they are likely to develop chronic disorders in the first place.

According to British social historian Roy Porter, it is not only radical thinkers who appealed for a new "wholism" in medical practice, but many of the most respected figures in medicine were insistent that the mechanical model of the body would not produce true health. Porter (1997:634) describes the situation as follows:

> Diseases became conceptualized after 1900 as a social no less than a biological phenomenon, to be understood statistically, sociologically, psychologically—even politically. Medicine's gaze had to incorporate wider questions of income, lifestyle, diet, habit, employment, education and family structure—in short, the entire psychosocial economy. Only thus could medicine meet the challenges of mass society, supplanting laboratory medicine preoccupied with minute investigation of lesions but indifferent as to how they got there.

It is therefore clear that social behavior and conditions play a critically important role in causing disease. Negative health lifestyles involving poor diets, lack of exercise, smoking, alcohol and drug abuse, stress, and exposure to sexually trans-mitted diseases like AIDS can lead to sickness, disability, and death. Positive health lifestyles—the reverse of the above—help lessen the extent of chronic health prob-lems, better control these problems when they appear, or allow the individual to avoid them until the onset of old age. However, an adverse social condition, namely, poverty, also promotes health problems and reduces life expectancy. Several studies report that the poor are more likely to engage in practices that induce ill health and less likely to engage in practices that forestall illness-inducing situations (Wilkinson 1996; Winkleby et al. 1998).

The poor are exposed to more violence in their daily lives and find themselves in situations where stress, inadequate diets and housing, and less opportunity for quality health care are common. They may also live in areas where industries pollute the environment with cancer-causing agents or other chemicals causing skin and res-piratory disorders, or have greater exposure to communicable diseases because of crowded living conditions, parasites, insects, and vermin. To be poor by definition means to have less of the good things in life; it also means the possibility of having more of the bad things and, with respect to health problems, this seems to be the case. The poor have the highest rates of disease and disability, including heart disease, of any socioeconomic group (Link and Phelan 1995, 2000; Wilkinson 1996).

The need to understand the impact of lifestyles and social conditions on health has become increasingly important in preventing or coping with modern health dis-orders. This situation has promoted a closer association between medicine and the behavioral sciences of sociology, anthropology, and psychology. Medical sociolo-gists are increasingly familiar figures not only in medical schools, but also in schools of nursing, dentistry, pharmacy, and public health, as well as in the wards and clin-ics of teaching hospitals. Medical sociologists now routinely hold joint teaching and research appointments between sociology departments and departments in various health-related educational institutions or are employed full time in those institutions.

THE REEMERGENCE OF INFECTIOUS DISEASES

A surprising development at the end of the twentieth century is the reemergence of infectious diseases as a major threat to human health, both from natural causes and bioterrorism. In the late 1960s there was a widespread belief that some infectious diseases were on the verge of extinction and the remainder were controllable through immunization or treatment with antibiotics. In 1967, the Surgeon General of the United States had, in fact, declared that infectious diseases were no longer a sig-nificant problem for Americans. However, disease-producing bacteria have shown a remarkable ability to resist antibiotics and adapt to changing environmental condi-tions. Some previously unknown and deadly viruses like HIV, Ebola, Lassa fever, and the Marburg virus have emerged from areas of tropical rain forests or savanna experiencing penetration by increasing numbers of humans. Other epidemics are the result of old diseases resurfacing, like cholera, yellow fever, and diphtheria. In the last few years, there have been serious outbreaks affecting humans of Ebola in the Congo (1995, 2002), Gabon (2002), and Uganda (2000–01); Marburg virus in the

Congo (1999); malaria in Kenya (2002); Rift Valley fever (2000–01) in Saudi Arabia and Yemen; the plague (1994) in India; cholera (1995) and yellow fever (1995) in Latin America; meningitis (1995) and yellow fever (1995) in West Africa; a chicken influenza virus in Hong Kong (1997, 2001); diphtheria (1992–94) in Russia; mad cow disease in Great Britain (1994–present); E. coli food poisoning in the United States (1993, 1999), Japan (1996), and Canada (2000); Legionnaires' disease in the Netherlands (1999) and Japan (2002); the West Nile virus in Romania (1996) and the United States (1999–present); and the severe acute respiratory syndrome (SARS) in Asia and North America (2003).

The potential for the spread of infectious diseases has been significantly enhanced in today's world by modern transportation systems. Air travel, in particular, makes it easy for infected people or shipments of diseased animals to move from one continent to another, spreading their virus as they go. A cough or a sneeze from an infected but symptomless passenger could pass a respiratory infection to another passenger or someone else days after that person reaches his or her destination. A bite, scratch, or exposure to an airborne virus from a diseased animal might produce an infection in a human. For example, the Marburg virus (an airborne and less potent relative of the deadly Ebola virus) is named for the old university town in central Germany where it was first identified in 1967. The virus spread to humans from a shipment of laboratory monkeys from Uganda and infected thirty-one people, seven of whom died. In 1989, two shipments of monkeys from the Philippines to a laboratory in Reston, Virginia, arrived with the Ebola virus that kills 90 percent of its victims. In a dramatic series of events, a team of medical scientists and Army personnel contained the virus in the lab facility before it was able to spread to humans in the greater metropolitan area of Washington, D.C. The first shipment of infected monkeys were all killed by lethal injection by a team dressed in space suits although one monkey temporarily escaped within the facility before being caught. The second shipment was allowed to simply die of the disease. Four human caretakers tested positive for Ebola but did not become sick and eventually the virus cleared from their blood. According to Harold Preston (1994:361), "they are among the very, very few human survivors of Ebola virus."

The West Nile Virus

A new infectious disease in the United States is the West Nile virus that unexpectedly appeared in New York City in the summer of 1999 and went on to infect people in five northeastern states. The virus was discovered in Uganda in 1937 and was relatively common in the Nile Delta of Egypt. It made birds sick but did not kill them. Something happened to the virus in the Middle East—most likely a genetic mutation which did kill birds and eventually humans and horses—in the early 1990s. Mosquitos get infected when they bite birds that have the disease and transmit it to humans when they bite them. In most people the disease feels like a mild headache, but in the very young, the elderly, and those with weak immune systems it can turn into encephalitis, causing muscle weakness, seizures, comas, and a cessation of breathing. The mutated strain of the West Nile virus was found in Israel in 1998

Wildlife pathologist examines a dead crow for West Nile disease.

when birds began dying. It found its way to the Queens area of New York City the following year, which was the first time the disease had ever been seen in the Western hemisphere. How the new strain of the disease got to New York City is unknown, but it probably migrated in the blood of a traveler who went to Queens and was subsequently bitten by mosquitos there. The mosquitos, in turn, began spreading the disease. Dozens of people became sick, and six elderly persons died. The first sign of it was sick and dying birds at the Bronx Zoo; then two elderly persons were admitted to a hospital in Queens with fever and muscle weakness. Lab samples were sent to the New York State Health Department and the Centers for Disease Control and Prevention (CDC) in Atlanta. As the number of sick persons increased, CDC indicated that their tests showed that the virus was St. Louis encephalitis (a close relative of the West Nile virus). The West Nile virus was not considered, because it had never been known to occur in the United States. New York City initiated an immediate citywide campaign to kill mosquitos as New Yorkers were growing fearful about a potentially dangerous and unknown virus in their midst. All one had to do was to walk outside and be bitten by a mosquito to get it.

Yet a pathologist at the Bronx Zoo knew St. Louis encephalitis does not normally kill birds; furthermore, another form of encephalitis, which is deadly to emus, was obviously not the culprit because the zoo's emus were healthy. CDC was again alerted, and new samples were sent there and to an army laboratory in Maryland. In the meantime, Central Intelligence Agency officials were becoming concerned about a possible act of bioterrorism, since an unidentified viral agent was obviously active in New York City (Preston 1999). The army lab and CDC both concluded it was the West Nile virus, with confirmation coming a few days later from a lab at the University of California at Irvine that had received brain tissue from some of the people who had died from the disease from the New York State Department of Health. The virus abruptly disappeared, and it remains unclear how it will maintain itself in the North American ecosystem. "In discovering the New World," comments Richard Preston (1999:108), "West Nile has killed a few humans and managed to roil the C.I.A., but now it has more important business—to find a way, somehow, to keep making copies of itself." If the virus migrated south with the birds and found a place to hide for the winter, Preston (1999:108) observes that "the only way we will know is if it comes back next year."

It did come back. By 2002, the West Nile virus had spread to 43 states and over 3,600 Americans became sick from it that year. Some 212 died. About 91,000 birds also died, while 13,000 horses became infected and about a third of them died. Earlier strains of the virus had not sickened horses. Nothing like this has ever been seen before in biological history. Not only did a virus in one hemisphere mutate and jump to another, but in its new environment it finds a host (birds) that has no immunity and spreads via mosquito bites to other species. The epidemic ends with cold weather and whether or not it will return, worsen, or disappear remains a mystery. Most likely it will reach the West Coast of the U.S. in 2003 and then head south into Latin America.

Sexually-Transmitted Diseases

One of the greatest threats worldwide from infectious diseases comes from sexually-transmitted diseases (STDs). Rates of STDs like syphilis and gonorrhea had significantly decreased in the United States and Western Europe during the twentieth century because of the widespread availability of antibiotics. Beginning in the 1970s, however, the prevalence of sexually-transmitted diseases increased dramatically and the, as yet incurable, AIDS virus was introduced into human populations in epidemic proportions. In 2000, the ten most frequently reported infectious diseases in the United States were, in order, chlamydia, gonorrhea, salmonellosis, AIDS, shigellosis, syphilis, Lyme disease, tuberculosis, hepatitis A, and hepatitis B. The STDs of chlamydia, gonorrhea, AIDS, syphilis, and hepatitis B account for nearly 90 percent of cases reported for these ten diseases.

What happened? What caused the prevalance of STDs to soar? According to Laurie Garrett (1994), four factors were primarily responsible: (1) the birth control pill that greatly reduced fears of unwanted pregnancy; (2) an ideology of sexual liberation and permissiveness among young urban adults throughout the world; (3) a new pattern of employment in developing nations in which young males migrate to cities for jobs and return to their villages on weekends to spend time with their spouses and girlfriends, thereby spreading STDs acquired in urban areas to the countryside; and, perhaps most importantly, (4) the availability of multiple sexual partners on an unprecedented scale.

Garrett finds that homosexual men in Europe and North America and young heterosexuals in developing countries, especially in Africa, took greatest advantage of the new sexual climate. Ever-increasing numbers of urban residents, the avail-ability of air travel and mass transit systems allowing people from all over the world to go to cities of their choice, and attitudes of sexual permissiveness all combined to promote the spread of STDs. But the number of sex partners an individual has is the most important risk factor in exposure to infection (Laumann and Michael 2001; Laumann et al. 1994). As Garrett concludes, the world's leading infectious disease amplifier today is multiple-partner sex (1994:610):

> At the top of the list has to be sex: specifically, multiple-partner sex. The terrifying pace of emergences and reemergences of sexually-transmitted diseases all over the world since World War II is testimony to the role that highly sexually active individuals, or places of sexual activity, play in amplifying microbial emergences such as HIV-1, HIV-2, and penicillin-resistant gonorrhea.

Bioterrorism

A relatively new threat of infectious diseases is bioterrorism. Bioterrorism takes place when people knowingly prepare biological agents or gases and use them to deliber-ately induce illness and death among other people. There are two categories of bioterrorism: overt and covert (Butler et al. 2002). In cases of overt bioterrorism, the perpetrator announces responsibility for the event or is revealed by the attack, such as the 1995 release of sarin gas in Japan by the Aum Shinrikyo cult in the Tokyo sub-way. Covert events are characterized by the unannounced or unrecognized release of agents in which the presence of sick people may be the first sign of an attack. An example is the 1985 outbreak of gastroenteritis in Oregon caused by a religious cult contaminating several salad bars with salmonella; another incident of gastroenteritis took place in 1996 when a disgruntled coworker put dysentery bacteria in pastries consumed by staff members in a large medical center laboratory.

A significantly more serious and terrifying covert attack was the use of anthrax sent through the U.S. mail in September through November, 2001. This attack came very soon after Middle East terrorists hijacked airliners and crashed them into the World Trade Center in New York City and the Pentagon in Washington, D.C., killing some 3,000 people including themselves. Someone then mailed anthrax spores in letters from post offices in New Jersey to certain media outlets and congressional offices. Five people were killed and eighteen others became sick—some seriously. The first person infected, a female editorial assistant at NBC in New York City, re-covered, but her illness was not diagnosed for weeks even though she was treated in two hospital emergency rooms. The possibility of anthrax was not considered by doctors who treated the first victims because it was so unlikely. It was a disease that doctors had never seen and never thought they would see. But the first person to die, a 63-year-old male photo editor at a Florida tabloid, was confirmed with inhala-tion anthrax and the investigation of his death turned into a criminal matter when CDC epidemiologists found spores in the mailroom of the company where he worked. In the following weeks, two male postal workers in Washington, D.C. and an elderly woman in Connecticut who were exposed to contaminated mail died, as did a female hospital worker in New York City whose means of infection remains un-known. Measures were taken to protect postal facilities and a massive investigation

Hazardous materials workers prepare to enter the Brentwood Mail facility in Washington, D.C. in October, 2001, to test for anthrax contamination.

was launched to find the person or persons responsible, but to date the case remains unsolved.

The return of infectious diseases, from either natural or bioterrorism sources, forecasts a shift in the perspective of medical sociologists from a relatively exclusive concern with chronic illnesses to a focus on both chronic and communicable diseases. Lifestyles and social behavior play an important role in the transmission of infection, as seen in sexual activities, drug use, travel, dietary habits, and living situations. Social conditions obviously play a major role in disease transmission; therefore, the study of social factors relevant to the prevention and spread of infectious diseases is likely to become an increasingly important area of investigation for medical sociologists in the twenty-first century.

THE DEVELOPMENT OF MEDICAL SOCIOLOGY

Medical sociology was established as a specialized field initially in the United States during the 1940s. The first use of the term *medical sociology* had appeared as early as 1894 in an article by Charles McIntire on the importance of social factors in health. Other early work included essays on the relationship between medicine and society in 1902 by Elizabeth Blackwell, the first woman to graduate from medical school (Geneva Medical College in New York) in America, and James Warbasse in

1909. However, these early publications were produced by people more concerned with medicine than sociology, and it remained for Bernard Stern to publish the first work from a sociological perspective in 1927, titled *Social Factors in Medical Progress*. A few publications followed in the 1930s, such as Lawrence Henderson's 1935 paper on the physician and patient as a social system which subsequently influenced Talcott Parsons's conceptualization of the sick role; but it was not until after World War II that medical sociology began in earnest as significant amounts of federal funding for sociomedical research became available (Bloom 2002).

Under the auspices of the National Institute of Mental Health, medical sociology's initial alliance with medicine was in psychiatry. A basis for cooperation between sociologists and psychiatrists existed because of earlier research in 1939 on urban mental health conducted in Chicago by Robert Faris and H. Warren Dunham. A particularly significant cooperative effort that followed was the publication in 1958 of *Social Class and Mental Illness: A Community Study* by August Hollingshead and Frederick Redlich. This landmark research, conducted in New Haven, Connecticut, produced important evidence that social factors could be correlated with different types of mental disorders and the manner in which people received psychiatric care. Persons in the most socially and economically disadvantaged segments of society were found to have the highest rates of mental disorder in general and excessively high rates of schizophrenia—the most disabling mental illness—in particular. This study attracted international attention and is the best known single study in the world of the relationship between mental disorder and social class. This book played a key role in the debate during the 1960s leading to the establishment of community mental health centers in the United States, as did other significant joint projects involving sociologists and psychiatrists, such as the midtown Manhattan study of Leo Srole and his colleagues (1962).

Funding from federal and private organizations also helped stimulate cooperation between sociologists and physicians in regard to sociomedical research on problems of physical health. The Russell Sage Foundation funded a program in 1949 to improve the utilization of social science research in medical practice. One result of this program was the publication of *Social Science in Medicine* (Simmons and Wolff 1954). Other work sponsored by the Sage Foundation came later and included Edward Suchman's book *Sociology and the Field of Public Health* (1963). Thus, the direction of work in medical sociology in the United States when large-scale funding first became available was toward applied or practical problem solving rather than the development of theory.

This situation had important consequences for the development of medical sociology. Unlike law, religion, politics, economics, and other social institutions, medicine was ignored by sociology's founders in the late nineteenth century because it did not shape the structure and nature of society. Emile Durkheim (1951) analyzed European suicide rates in 1897, and Karl Marx's collaborator Friedrich Engels (1973) linked the poor health of the English working class to capitalism in a treatise published in 1845. However, Durkheim, Marx, Max Weber, and other major classical theorists did not concern themselves with the role of medicine in society. Medical sociology did not begin until after World War II, nor achieve any significant development until the 1960s. The field therefore developed relatively late in the evolution of sociology as an academic subject and lacked major statements on health and illness from the classical theorists. Consequently, medical sociology came of age in an intellectual climate far different from sociology's more traditional specialties with direct links to nineteenth- and early twentieth-century social thought. As a result, it faces a set of circumstances in its development different from that of most other major sociological subdisciplines.

The circumstance that most affects medical sociology is the pressure to produce work that can be applied to medical practice and the formulation of health policy. This pressure originates from government agencies and medical sources, both of which either influence or control funding for sociomedical research and have little or no interest in purely theoretical sociology.

Yet the tremendous growth of medical sociology in both the United States and Europe in recent years most likely would not have been possible without the substantial financial support for applied studies provided by the respective governments. For example, in the United States, where medical sociology has reached its most extensive development, the emergence of the field was greatly stimulated by the expansion of the National Institutes of Health in the late 1940s. Particularly significant, according to August Hollingshead (1973), who participated in some of the early research programs, was the establishment of the National Institute of Mental Health, which was instrumental in encouraging and funding joint social and medical projects. "It was through the impetus provided by this injection of money," notes Malcolm Johnson (1975:229), "that sociologists and medical men changed their affiliations and embraced the field of medical sociology." When Alvin Gouldner (1970) discussed the social sciences as a well-financed government effort to help cope with the problems of industrial society and the welfare state in the West during the post–World War II era, the model social science in this regard was medical sociology.[1]

Parsons

However, a critical event occurred in 1951 that began the reorientation of American medical sociology in a theoretical direction. This was the appearance of Talcott Parsons's book *The Social System*. This book, written to explain a relatively complex structural-functionalist model of society in which social systems are linked to corresponding systems of personality and culture, contained Parsons's concept of the sick role. Unlike other major social theorists preceding him, Parsons formulated an analysis of the function of medicine in his view of society. Parsons presented an ideal representation of how people in Western society should act when sick. The merit of the concept is that it describes a patterned set of expectations defining the norms and values appropriate to being sick, both for the sick person and others who interact with that person. Parsons also pointed out that physicians are invested by

[1]For historical discussions of the development of medical sociology, see: Bird, Conrad, and Fremont (2000); S. Bloom (1990, 2000, 2002); Cockerham (1983, 1988, 2000); Cockerham and Ritchey (1997); and Pescosolido and Kronenfeld (1995).

society with the function of social control, similar to the role provided by priests, to serve as a means to control deviance. In the case of the sick role, illness is the deviance, and its undesirable nature reinforces the motivation to be healthy.

In developing his concept of the sick role, Parsons linked his ideas to those of the two most important classical theorists in sociology—Emile Durkheim (1858–1917) of France and Max Weber (1864–1920) of Germany. Parsons was the first to demonstrate the controlling function of medicine in a large social system, and he did so in the context of classical sociological theory. Some have argued that Parsons's concept of the sick role represents the most important single theoretical contribution to medical sociology to date (A. Fox 1989; Wolinsky 1988). Moreover, having a theorist of Parsons's stature rendering the first major theory in medical sociology called attention to the young subdiscipline—especially among academic sociologists. Not only was Parsons's concept of the sick role "a penetrating and apt analysis of sickness from a distinctly sociological point of view" (Freidson 1970b:62), but it was widely believed in the 1950s that Parsons and his students were charting a future course for all of sociology through the insight provided by his model of society.

This, of course, was not the case, as Parsons's ideas—including his concept of the sick role—were strongly criticized. Parsons nevertheless provided a theoretical approach for medical sociology that brought the subdiscipline the intellectual recognition it needed in its early development in the United States.

The institutional support for sociology in America was in the universities where the discipline was established more firmly than anywhere else in the world. Without academic legitimacy and the subsequent participation of such well-known, mainstream academic sociologists as Robert Merton, Howard Becker, and Erving Goffman, all of whom published research in the field, medical sociology would lack the credentials and professional position that it currently has in both academic and applied settings. Parsons's views on society may not be the optimal paradigm for explaining illness, but Parsons helped make medical sociology academically respectable.

Practical Application versus Theory

The direction taken by medical sociology early in its development is best summarized by Robert Straus (1957). Straus suggested that medical sociology had become divided into two separate but closely interrelated areas: sociology *in* medicine and sociology *of* medicine.

The sociologist in medicine is a sociologist who collaborates directly with the physician and other health personnel in studying the social factors that are relevant to a particular health disorder. The work of the sociologist in medicine is intended to be directly applicable to patient care or to the solving of a public health problem. Some of the tasks of the sociologist in medicine are to analyze the etiology or causes of health disorders, the differences in social attitudes as they relate to health, and the way in which the incidence and prevalence of a specific health disorder is related to such social variables as age, sex, socioeconomic status, racial/ethnic group identity, education, and occupation. Such an analysis is then intended to be made available to health practitioners to assist them in treating health problems. Thus, sociology in medicine can be characterized as *applied research and analysis primarily motivated by a medical problem* rather than a sociological problem. Sociologists in medicine usually work in medical schools, nursing schools, public health schools, teaching hospitals, public health agencies, and other health organizations. They may also work for a governmental agency like the U.S. Department of Health and Human Services or the Centers for Disease Control and Prevention in the capacity of biostatisticians, researchers, health planners, administrators, and advisers.

The sociology *of* medicine, however, has a different emphasis. It deals with such factors as the organization, role relationships, norms, values, and beliefs of medical practice as a form of human behavior. The emphasis is on the social processes that occur in the medical setting and how these contribute to our understanding of medical sociology in particular and to our understanding of social life in general. The sociology of medicine shares the same goals as all other areas of sociology and may consequently be characterized as *research and analysis of the medical environment from a sociological perspective*. Most sociologists of medicine are employed as professors in the sociology departments of universities and colleges.

However, the division of work in medical sociology into a sociology of medicine and sociology in medicine eventually created problems. Medical sociologists affiliated with departments of sociology in universities were in a stronger position to produce work that satisfied sociologists as good sociology. But sociologists in medical institutions had the advantage of participation in medicine as well as research opportunities unavailable to those outside medical practice. Tension began to develop between the two groups over whose work was more important. Although this situation has not been fully resolved, two major trends have emerged to reduce differences among medical sociologists. First, an evolution has taken place in medical sociological work toward research relevant to health practitioners and policymakers. This development is largely due to the willingness of government agencies and private foundations to only fund health-related research that can help solve problems or improve conditions. Regardless of whether a medical sociologist works in a health care or academic setting, much of the research in the field today deals with topics that have some practical utility.

Second, a growing convergence among medical sociology and the general discipline of sociology is emerging. This situation is aided by the fact that all sociologists share the same training and methodological strategies in their approach to research. Theoretical foundations common throughout sociology are also being increasingly reflected in medical sociological work (Annandale 1998; Cockerham 2001; Cockerham, Rütten, and Abel 1997; Cockerham, Snead, and DeWaal 2002; Frohlich, Corin, and Potvin 2001; Karlsen and Nazroo 2002; Nettleton 1995; Scambler 2002; Williams 1995, 1999), while many health issues investigated by medical sociologists call for knowledge of social processes outside of the sociomedical realm (Pescosolido and Kronenfeld 1995). For example, studies of health reform require consideration of the larger sociological literature on social change, power, the political process, socioeconomic factors, and connections between social institutions (Bird, Conrad, and Fremont 2000; Skocpol 1995; Starr 1982, 1994), and research on job-related stress demands familiarity with occupational structure (Tausig and Fenwick 1999). Therefore, as Bernice Pescosolido and Jeanne Kronenfeld (1995:24) point out, medical sociologists "need to understand the general nature of social change and social institutions—to recognize, describe, and draw from these changes and institutions implications for health, illness, and healing." Thus, much of the future success of medical sociology is linked to its ability to utilize the findings and perspectives of the larger discipline in its work and to contribute, in turn, to general sociology.

While the division of medical sociology as outlined by Straus (1957) is losing much of its distinctiveness in the United States, it never really developed elsewhere in the world. In Great Britain, Germany, Finland, and the Netherlands, where medical sociology has developed more extensively than elsewhere in Europe, the subdiscipline is concentrated in medical and public health schools. In Japan, medical sociologists are found in both health institutions and sociology departments, but the majority are faculty members in schools of medicine. A major difference worldwide in comparison to the past is that the field has achieved a state of development that allows it to investigate medical problems from an independent sociological perspective. Contemporary medical sociologists are less concerned with whether work is in the sociology of medicine or sociology in medicine, but rather with how much it increases our understanding of the complex relationship between social factors and health.

At present, medical sociologists constitute the largest and one of the most active groups of people doing sociological work in the United States and Western Europe. Medical sociologists comprise the third largest section of the American Sociological Association and the largest sections of the British and German sociological associations. About one out of every ten American sociologists is a medical sociologist; in Germany, the German Society for Medical Sociology, an organization just for persons working in the field of medical sociology, has had more members than the entire German Sociological Association. In Europe, medical sociologists provided the basis for the European Society for Health and Medical Sociology established in 1983. Earlier, in 1974, the Japanese Society for Health and Medical Sociology had been established. Additionally, the Research Committee (RC 15) on the Sociology of Health of the International Sociological Association has members from all over the world. Not only have the numbers of medical sociologists continually increased, but the scope of matters pertinent to medical sociology has clearly broadened as issues of health, illness, and medicine have become a medium through which general issues and concerns about society have been expressed. One result is that numerous books and scientific journals dealing with medical sociology have been and continue to be published in the United States and elsewhere. The future of medical sociology itself is very positive.

SUMMARY

Throughout history human beings have been interested in and deeply concerned with the effects of the social environment on the health of individuals and the groups to which they belong. Today it is clear that social factors play a critically important role in health, as the greatest threats to the health and well-being of individuals stem largely from unhealthy lifestyles and high-risk behavior. Sociology's interest in medicine as a unique system of human social behavior and medicine's recognition that sociology can help health practitioners to better understand their patients and provide improved forms of health care have begun to bring about a convergence of mutual interest between the two disciplines. More and more, medical sociologists are being invited to join the staffs of medical institutions and to participate in medical research projects. Medical sociology courses and degrees are now more frequently offered by universities and colleges. The extensive growth of sociological literature in academic medicine is further evidence of the rising status of the medical sociologist. Although a considerable amount of work remains to be done, the medical sociologist at this time is in the enviable position of participating in and influencing the development of an exciting, significant, and relatively new field.

MEDICAL SOCIOLOGY INTERNET SITES

1. The American Sociological Association homepage.
   http://www.asanet.org/

2. The American Sociological Association Medical Sociology Section homepage.
   http://dept.kent.edu/sociology/asamedsoc/

   The purpose of the Medical Sociology Section of the ASA is to foster the development of sociology in the field of health and medicine. This site also contains a list with links to all graduate programs in medical sociology in the United States.

3. SocioSite: Sociology of Health.
   http://www.pscw.uva.nl/sociosite/TOPICS/Health.html

   This site contains an extensive list of links dealing with sociology and health, mental health, AIDS, drugs, and death and dying.

4. Homepage of the Medical Sociology Group of the British Sociological Association.
   http://nursing.swansea.ac.uk/bsa/medsoc.htm

   The BSA Medical Sociology Group exists to promote scholarship and communication in the field of sociology of health and illness in the United Kingdom.

5. A Few References to Michel Foucault.
   http://www.synaptic.bc.ca/ejournal/foucault.htm

   Links to bibliographies, interpretative analysis, and excerpts of the work of Michel Foucault.

6. Sociosite: Famous Sociologists, Talcott Parsons.
   http://www.pscw.uva.nl/sociosite/TOPICS/sociologists.html#PARSONS

   Selected writings from Talcott Parsons including *Outline of the Social System*.

7. Homepage of the World Health Organization.
   http://www.who.int/

8. Centers for Disease Control and Prevention, Bioterrorism.
   http://www.bt.cdc.gov

CHAPTER 2

Epidemiology

Many sociologists working in the field of medicine are epidemiologists. Epidemiology is a discipline that has evolved relatively specialized methods for investigating health problems. Depending upon the particular health hazard being investigated, epidemiology draws upon the knowledge and techniques of several scientific fields. Besides sociologists, one will find physicians, public health workers, biologists, biochemists, entomologists, ornithologists, mammalogists, veterinarians, demographers, anthropologists, and perhaps even meteorologists (in studies of air pollution) involved in epidemiological work. In its strictest sense, epidemiology is the science of epidemics; however, present-day epidemiologists have broadened their field to include not only epidemic diseases, but also all other forms of disease and bodily injury such as cancer, heart disease, alcoholism, drug addiction, suicide, and automobile accidents. The epidemiologist is concerned with exploring human ecology as it relates to the health of human beings and their environment.

The primary focus of the epidemiologist is not on the individual, but on the health problems of social aggregates or large groups of people. The epidemiologist studies both the origin and distribution of health problems in a population through the collection of data from many different sources. He or she then constructs a logical chain of inferences to explain the various factors in a society or segment of a society that cause a particular health problem to exist. Epidemiology is one of the most important investigative techniques in the study of health and disease.

The role of the epidemiologist can probably be best likened to that of a detective investigating the scene of a crime for clues. The epidemiologist usually begins by examining the sick person or persons and then extends the investigation to the setting where people first became ill and are likely to become ill again. What the epidemiologist is looking for is the common denominator that links all the victims of a health problem together so that the cause of the problem can be identified and eliminated or controlled.

EPIDEMIOLOGICAL MEASURES

Several important analytic concepts assist the epidemiologist in describing the health problems of human groups. One of these concepts pertains to the definition of a *case*. A *case,* in epidemiological terms, refers to an episode of a disorder, illness, or injury involving a person. Two other commonly employed concepts are those of *incidence* and *prevalence. Incidence* refers to the number of *new* cases of a specific health disorder occurring within a given population during a stated period of time. The incidence of AIDS during a particular month would be the proportion of persons within a population who are reported as having developed the illness during the month in question. *Prevalence,* in contrast, would be the *total* number of cases of a health disorder that exist at any given time. Prevalence would include new cases as well as all previously existing cases. Prevalence rates are sometimes expressed as *point prevalence* (the number of cases at a certain point in time, usually a particular day or week), *period prevalence* (the total number of cases during a specified period of time, usually a month or year), or *lifetime prevalence* (the number of people who have had the health problem at least once during their lifetime).

One way to distinguish between incidence and prevalence is to regard incidence as the rate at which cases first appear, while prevalence is the rate at which all cases exist. To illustrate the difference between incidence and prevalence, consider that the incidence of influenza in a community might be low because no new cases had developed. Yet a measure of the disease's prevalence could be a larger figure because it would represent all persons who are currently sick from the illness. For chronic health disorders like cancer, cases initially reported in terms of incidence for a particular period may be reported later as prevalence because the duration of the disease has caused it to exist for a lengthy period of time. The cases are simply no longer new. The use of data on disease determines whether an analysis should be one of incidence or prevalence. An epidemiologist would use cases denoting incidence if he or she were analyzing the outbreak of a health problem. Cases specifying prevalence would be used to study the overall extent of a disorder.

Regardless of the size of the group under investigation, the epidemiologist is concerned with the computing of ratios. This is done to develop an accurate description of a particular health disorder in relation to a particular population. The epidemiologist accomplishes this task by collecting data from various sources such as face-to-face interviews or reports rendered by various health practitioners, institutions, and agencies. Once the relevant data are gathered, the epidemiologist computes a ratio which demonstrates the incidence and/or prevalence of the health problem. The ratio is always expressed as the total number of cases of a disease compared to the total number of people within a population:

$$\frac{\text{Cases}}{\text{Population}}$$

The simplest ratio computed by the epidemiologist is called the *crude rate,* which is the number of persons (cases) who have the characteristics being measured during a specific unit of time. Typical types of crude rates are birth rates and mortality rates. For example, the crude *mortality* (death) *rate* for a particular year is computed by using the number of deaths in that year as the numerator and the total number of residents in a specific population as the denominator. The results are then multiplied by either 1,000, 10,000, or 100,000 depending on whether the mortality rate being figured is for the number of deaths per 1,000, per 10,000, or per 100,000 people. The formula for computing the crude death rate in the United States for 2004 per 1,000 people would be as follows:

$$\frac{\text{Total deaths, all ages, 2004}}{\text{Estimated U.S. population on June 30, 2004}} \times 1,000 = 2004 \text{ death rate}$$

Crude death and birth rates, however, are usually too gross a measure to be meaningful for most sociological purposes. Sociologists are typically concerned with the effects of specific variables or social characteristics within a population such as age, sex, race, occupation, or any other measure of significant social differences. *Age-specific rates* are an example of rates used to show differences by age. Age-specific rates are computed in the same way as crude rates, except the numerator and the denominator are confined to a specific age group (a similar method can be used to determine sex-specific rates, race-specific rates, and so forth). In order to calculate an age-specific rate, the procedure is to subdivide a population by age and then compare the number of cases in this subpopulation with the total number of persons within the subpopulation. If you wanted to compute the age-specific mortality rate for all infants for a particular year in the United States, for example, you would need to know how many infants there were in that year and the number of deaths that occurred in this age-specific group. The *infant mortality rate,* a measure of the deaths of all infants in a geographical area under the age of one year, is a very common age-specific rate in epidemiology. You would compute the 2004 U.S. infant mortality rate in the following manner:

$$\frac{\text{Total number of deaths in 2004 among persons aged less than one year}}{\text{Number of live births during 2004}} \times 1,000 = 2004 \text{ infant mortality rate}$$

The infant mortality rate has special significance for a society because it is traditionally used as an approximate measure of a society's sanitary and medical standards. For instance, the infant mortality rate in the United States in 1900 per 1,000 infants was

162.4; by 1940 this rate had been reduced to 47.0 as a result of improvement in health care, diet, and living conditions. After World War II further advances reduced infant mortality rates per 1,000 infants to 29.2 in 1950, 27.0 in 1960, 20.0 in 1970, 12.6 in 1980, and 6.9 in 2000. Infant mortality rates during the twentieth century have traditionally been lowest in technologically advanced societies such as Japan, Singapore, Western Europe, North America, and Australia. The highest rates are in the developing countries of South Asia and Africa.

THE DEVELOPMENT OF EPIDEMIOLOGY

As a method of measuring diseases in human aggregates, epidemiology has been a relatively recent development. As long as human beings lived as nomads or in widely scattered and isolated communities, the danger from epidemics and infectious disease was relatively slight. However, once people began to crowd into primitive cities with unsanitary living conditions and an abundance of rats and lice, the probabilities favoring the development of communicable diseases greatly increased. The crowded conditions of urban living also ensured that infectious diseases would spread more quickly and that disease-causing microorganisms would persist within the community for longer periods of time. In addition, the migration of peoples from one region of the world to another spread disease from geographic area to geographic area. Bubonic plague, for example, apparently reached Europe from China during the fourteenth century, cholera entered Great Britain by way of India in the seventeenth century, and Europeans brought smallpox to the western hemisphere during the exploration and settlement of the New World. History reveals numerous examples of explorers and travelers introducing the microorganisms of a dreaded disease to a community of unsuspecting people.

The bubonic plague that ravaged Europe between 1340 and 1750 marks one of the worst epidemic afflictions in all human history. It is estimated that one-third of the population of Europe, about 20 million people, died during its greatest prevalence (Cantor 2001). During one month (September 1665) in one city (London), approximately 30,000 people died from the plague. Describing conditions in the fourteenth century, historian Barbara Tuchman (1978:92) reports: "So lethal was the disease that cases were known of persons going to bed well and dying before they awoke, of doctors catching the illness at a bedside and dying before the patient." What made the disease especially frightening was that no one knew what caused it, how to prevent it, or how to cure it. Yet even though the pestilence affected the rich and poor alike, there was still a *social* difference in the death rates. The poor were much more likely to die from it than the rich. Tuchman (1978:98) says:

> Flight was the chief recourse of those who could afford it or arrange it. The rich fled to their country places like Boccaccio's young patricians of Florence, who settled in a pastoral palace "removed on every side from the roads" with "wells of cool water and vaults of rare wine." The urban poor died in their burrows, "and only the stench of their bodies informed their neighbors of their death." That the poor were more heavily afflicted than the rich was clearly remarked at the time, in the north as in the south.

A Scottish chronicler, John of Fordum, stated flatly that the pest "attacked especially the meaner sort and common people—seldom the magnates." Simon de Covino of Montpellier made the same observation. He ascribed it to the misery and want and hard lives that made the poor more susceptible, which was half the truth. Close contact and lack of sanitation was the unrecognized other half of it.

The cause of the plague was thought by many to be God's wrath upon sinners; however, the realization eventually came that diseases could be transmitted from person to person or between animals and people. The origin of the plague turned out to be the flea of the black rat, but the pneumonic plague, the most deadly form of the bubonic plague, was transmitted from person to person. What actually ended the plague about 1750 was the appearance in cities of the aggressive brown rat. The brown rat tended to avoid humans, had fleas that were less effective carriers, and drove most of Europe's black rats out of urban areas. Another very important factor was the development of improved housing and sanitation.

Although the plague is popularly believed to be a disease of the Middle Ages and no longer a major threat to the world's health, its pneumonic version resurfaced in western India in the city of Surat near Bombay in 1994. Some 6,000 persons were hospitalized and at least 55 died. Many people fled from the area in panic and some infected persons spread the disease to other locales. Curable if treated early by antibiotics, this modern-day outbreak of a supposedly vanquished disease is a sharp reminder of the relationship between health and social conditions. Surat's population had more than doubled to over two million people in recent years, many of them migrants drawn to the area's textile plants and diamond-cutting workshops. About half the population lived in some of the worst and most crowded slums in India. Housing in these shantytowns consisted largely of concrete shells or dwellings made of wood, flattened oil drums, and plastic sheets. There were no sewers, running water, toilets, or garbage removal, and the local river was badly polluted from human waste. Not surprisingly, the densely packed shantytowns were the incubators for the airborne bacteria that was supposedly introduced to Surat by a migrant worker from central India and nurtured into a full-blown epidemic by the social conditions in the city.

Epidemics like the plague have existed for centuries, but the field of epidemiology did not develop as a form of systematic scientific investigation until the nineteenth century. It was not until 1854 that the work of John Snow established the foundation of modern epidemiology. Snow was an English physician who plotted the geographic location of all reported cholera cases in London. He then went out into the neighborhoods of these victims and inquired into their day-to-day behavior. He wanted to know what they ate, what they drank, where they went, and the nature of all their activities. Eventually Snow began to suspect that cholera was transmitted by water, since the common factor in the daily lives of the victims was getting their water from the Broad Street pump. At that time, London obtained drinking water from several water companies, and a few of these companies apparently were providing water contaminated with cholera bacteria. By closing down the pump on Broad Street, Snow was able to stop the epidemic. He not only established a mode of investigation but also demonstrated that research could lead to positive action and that social behavior and the physical environment were both important in the transmission of disease (Brown 2000).

At the time of Snow's research, the development of scientific medicine was well under way. The work of Louis Pasteur and his immediate followers during the latter part of the nineteenth century revolutionized medical thought with the germ theory of disease stipulating that bacteria were the source of infection in the human body. The findings of Snow, Pasteur, and others provided the epidemiologist with a framework of analysis. Recognition that germs were causal agents of disease served as a precursor to scientific determination that people come into contact with a variety of causal agents. These agents include (1) biological agents, such as bacteria, viruses, or insects; (2) nutritional agents, such as fats and carbohydrates as producers of cholesterol; (3) chemical agents, such as gases and toxic chemicals that pollute the air, water, and land; (4) physical agents, such as climate or vegetation; and (5) social agents, such as occupation, social class, location of residence, or lifestyle. What a person does, who a person is, and where a person lives can specify what health hazards are most likely to exist in that individual's life. The epidemiologist then identifies a particular host (person or group of persons or animals) most susceptible to these causal agents. Human hosts are examined in terms of characteristics that are both biological (age, sex, degree of immunity, and other physical attributes that promote resistance or susceptibility) and behavioral (habits, customs, and lifestyle). Next, the physical and social environment of the causal agent and the host is explored. The result is intended to be an identification of *what* is causing a group of people to become sick or suffer injury.

The term *social environment* in epidemiological research refers to actual living conditions, such as poverty or crowding, and also the norms, values, and attitudes that reflect a particular social and cultural context. Societies have socially prescribed patterns of behavior and living arrangements, as well as standards pertaining to the use of water, food and food handling, and household and personal hygiene. For example, the plague epidemic in Surat, India, in the mid-1990s had its origin in unhealthy behavior and living standards. The social environment can cause sickness; therefore, information about it can be used to identify the chain of transmission and assist in ascertaining the most effective means of treatment and prevention.

Since its inception in the 1850s, epidemiology has passed through three eras and is now entering a fourth (Susser and Susser 1996a). First was the sanitary era of the early nineteenth century, during which the focus of epidemiological work was largely on sewage and drainage systems, and the major preventive measure was the introduction of sanitation programs. Second was the infectious disease era that occurred between the late nineteenth and mid-twentieth centuries. The principal preventive approach was to break the chain of transmission between the agent and host. Third is the chronic disease era taking place in the second half of the twentieth century. Here the focus is on controlling risk factors by modifying lifestyles (i.e., diet, exercise), agents (i.e., guns, food), or the environment (i.e., pollution, passive smoking). According to Susser and Susser (1996b:674), the era of the twenty-first century is that of "eco-epidemiology." Preventive measures are multidisciplinary as scientists from many fields use their techniques to deal with a variety of health problems at the molecular, intermediate (social behaviorial), population, or global levels.

THE COMPLEXITY OF MODERN ILLS: HEART DISEASE

Many contemporary epidemiological problems are extremely complex, as the major health threat to contemporary society is from a variety of chronic and degenerative ills related to aging and the effects of man-made environments. The role of multi-causality in disease causation is particularly apparent with respect to heart disease.

Heart disease is the leading cause of death in the United States, accounting for more than one-third of all deaths. As shown in the Framingham, Massachusetts, research project (Sytkowski, Kannel, and D'Agostino 1990), a number of factors are responsible for this disease. Begun during the 1950s, this study has shown that arteriosclerosis does not strike people at random as they age, but that highly susceptible individuals can be identified in advance. Some 5,000 persons initially participated in the study, and 5,000 of their children were added in a second-generation project beginning in 1970. They were all between the ages of thirty and sixty and were free from any form of heart disease at the time of their initial examination. They were given relatively complete physical examinations every two years. The data clearly suggest that sex (specifically males), advancing age, high blood pressure, cigarette smoking, diabetes, and obesity constitute significant risk factors in whether a person develops heart disease.

The proportion of risk that a person assumes with respect to each of these specific risk factors is unknown. For example, about twice as many males die from heart

Smoking and obesity are major causes of heart disease.

disease as females. But even though men have the greater overall risk, they are more likely than women to have a favorable prognosis if they survive the first serious heart attack (Wenger 1982). Furthermore, women with diabetes do not show any special advantage over men when it comes to heart disease. In fact, as the Framingham study indicates, women who are diabetic, obese, and have a high level of harmful low-density lipoprotein cholesterol are particularly prone to heart disease. Therefore, when epidemiologists analyze heart disease, they must contend with a variety of relationships between the various risk factors.

Although heart disease remains America's leading killer, since the mid-1960s there has been a rapid decline in deaths from the disease for both men and women. About 586.8 of every 100,000 persons in the general population died from heart disease in 1950 compared with a rate of 272.4 persons per 100,000 in 1998. Improved medical services and surgical techniques, modified eating habits, increased exercise, decreased smoking, and improved control of blood pressure are the factors most responsible for this decline.

What is encouraging about this development is that the risk of heart disease can be significantly reduced if people improve in just four areas: stop smoking, control high blood pressure, eat to lower cholesterol and avoid being overweight, and exercise. Moreover, in 1988, regular use of aspirin was identified as a possible means to reduce heart attacks through its action in preventing blood clots. It is apparent that heart disease is a complex disorder and that changes in behavior can result in a substantially reduced risk. We see this fact, for example, in studies of diet and exercise.

Diet

A major study conducted in Oslo, Norway, by I. Hjermann and his associates (1981) found exceptionally strong evidence that eating less fat and cholesterol can reduce the chances of a heart attack or sudden death from heart disease. The study also found that benefit could be derived from stopping smoking or significantly reducing the number of cigarettes smoked. The research was begun in 1972 among 1,232 men forty to forty-nine years old who were selected because they faced a high risk of developing heart disease. Their blood pressure was normal, but their cholesterol levels were high, and 80 percent of them smoked cigarettes. An analysis of their normal diets showed that most consumed foods high in saturated fats and cholesterol. Foods like butter, sausage, high-fat cheese, eggs, and whole milk were prominent in their diets. The men were randomly assigned either to an experimental or control group. The experimental group was given advice to give up smoking and eat a cholesterol-lowering diet. The new diet included substituting skim milk for whole milk, eating no more than one egg a week, using polyunsaturated oil for cooking, having fruit for dessert, making sandwiches with high-fiber breads, fish, and low-fat cheese or meat, and using fish or low-fat meat with potatoes and vegetables for main dishes. No drugs were used and no recommendations were made to exercise or lose weight, which changed only minimally during the five-year experiment.

In 1977, cholesterol levels were 13 percent lower for the experimental group. Also, the ratio of protective high-density lipoprotein cholesterol had risen in comparison to potentially harmful low-density lipoprotein cholesterol. Hjermann and his colleagues found that the consumption of less saturated fat, usually animal fat, was the single most influential dietary change. They determined that this change accounted for 60 percent of the difference in the number of heart attacks and deaths from heart disease suffered by the two groups of men. Changes in smoking accounted for another 25 percent of the reduction in heart disease.

Since the early 1980s, several other studies have produced convincing results linking high cholesterol levels to heart disease and encouraging the consumption of heart-healthy foods (LaRosa et al. 1990; Shepard et al. 1995). There is evidence that Americans are eating a healthier diet, but the average intake of fruits, vegetables, and grain products meets only minimum requirements (Krebs-Smith 1998). Virtually all major health organizations now urge people to decrease their consumption of saturated fat, lower their cholesterol, lose excess weight, and give up cigarettes. By changing their eating behavior and not smoking, people at risk for heart disease can improve their prospects for a longer life.

Exercise

Another major study on heart disease dealt with exercise and participation in sports. This study, conducted by Ralph Paffenbarger and his associates (Paffenbarger, Hyde, Wing, and Hsieh 1986) investigated the physical activity and lifestyle characteristics of 16,936 Harvard University alumni, aged thirty-four to seventy-four, for a period of twelve to sixteen years (1962–1978). It was found that exercise (such as walking, climbing stairs, and playing sports) improved life expectancy for all causes of mortality—but especially for heart disease. Death rates were one-fourth to one-third lower among Harvard alumni who expended 2,000 or more calories in exercise per week than among less active men. Risks of death were highest among those who did not exercise and who also had hypertension and smoked cigarettes. By the age of eighty, Paffenbarger estimates that regular exercise has provided an additional one to more than two years of longevity. In a subsequent study of Harvard alumni, Paffenbarger and his colleagues (1993) analyzed changes in lifestyle activities between 1977 and 1985 and determined that beginning moderately vigorous sports activity was associated with lower rates of deaths from all causes and particularly from heart disease. Quitting cigarette smoking, avoiding obesity, and maintaining normal blood pressure were also significant in reducing mortality rates.

However, Paffenbarger and his associates (Paffenbarger et al. 1986, 1993; Lee, Hsieh, and Paffenbarger 1995) found that light sports like golf did not influence the incidence of coronary heart disease; rather, moderately vigorous exercise was required. In general, however, some exercise was found to be better for the health of the men in the study than no exercise, but vigorous exercise made the greatest contribution to reducing heart disease. In sum, the more active the men were, the longer they were likely to live—even if they smoked or were overweight. This same result has been found in several European studies. In Great Britain, for example, analysis of the physical activities and lifestyles of a large group of male factory workers disclosed that only relatively strenuous physical activity (especially cycling) in leisure time was related to fitness (Tuxworth et al. 1986). Light exercise made no significant difference. Other studies in Britain (Morris et al. 1990) and Finland (Lakka et al. 1994) reached a similar conclusion about the value of relatively vigorous leisure time exercise, while, in Germany, other researchers (Hollmann et al. 1985) likewise determined that endurance sports or training during leisure time can have a more positive effect on the cardiovascular system than heavy muscular work on the job.

Studies such as these have led to the conclusion that regular physical activity should be promoted in a heart disease prevention program as much as blood pressure control, diet, lowering of cholesterol levels, and smoking cessation. Whereas vigorous leisure time exercise has the most beneficial effects for the prevention of heart disease,

---

BOX 2-1   Heart Disease and the National Football League

The National Institute for Occupational Safety and Health (NISOH) conducted a study of death rates in 2002 among some 7,000 professional football players in the National Football League (NFL) who played between 1959–88. The study found that former NFL players had a 46 percent lower death rate than men of similar age and race in the current general population and that most players could expect to have a normal life expectancy. Some 189 deaths had been expected and only 103 had occurred. Because the study group contained relatively few men who had reached the age of 50, it will still be several years before researchers can determine their actual average age of death.

However, there was a major exception to the predictions of a normal life expectancy for players at certain team positions. Offensive and defensive linemen were found to have a 52 percent *greater* risk of dying from heart disease than the general population and three times (64 percent) *greater* risk of dying from heart disease than football players at other positions, like quarterbacks, running backs, wide receivers, tight ends, and players in the defensive secondary. Why? The answer is body size. Although obesity has been linked to heart disease in several studies, the NIOSH study provides evidence of one of the strongest associations between body size and heart disease. Offensive linemen in particular were singled out for risk of heart disease as many routinely weigh as much as 300 pounds. And the number of huge football players is increasing. Today there are about 300 NFL players who weigh at least 300 pounds (a few even weigh 400 pounds) compared to only 50 such players in 1990.

Heart disease is only one health problem facing these gigantic men. Their joints are often not able to withstand the strain of their weight, and, after they retire and reach their 40s and 50s, having arthritis becomes likely. Also repeated head trauma from being hit often in the helmet area may cause problems, including depression, in later life. The average NFL offensive lineman's career lasts about 3.73 years, but much of what he has to do to maintain such a huge body and subject it to physical punishment on the playing field is cause for significant health problems in later life. These problems exist apart from the potential for injury while playing the sport. Improved helmet technology and protective padding to absorb shock are among the NFL's safety improvements, but professional football players who carry very heavy weight can be eventually harmed by their body size.

exercise in everyday activities like walking up stairs instead of taking an elevator or walking instead of driving short distances has some health value (Dunn et al. 1999). Yet data collected by the Centers for Disease Control and Prevention in 2000 show that about 39 percent of the adults in the United States live a sedentary lifestyle. A sedentary lifestyle is a way of living that involves no or irregular physical leisure time activity. CDC also reports that the prevalence of obesity rose nationally from 12.0 percent in 1960–62 to 27 percent in 1999, with a lack of physical exercise being a primary risk factor (National Center for Health Statistics 2002). Consequently, a failure to exercise remains a significant public health problem despite the fact that lack of physical activity is a significant risk factor for heart disease.

DISEASE AND MODERNIZATION

Although heart disease joins cancer, stroke, accidents, and mental disorders as the leading causes of disability and death in advanced industrial societies, the underdeveloped nations of the world show somewhat different patterns of major health problems. In these societies, the traditional diseases of human history influenced by poor sanitation and malnutrition often prevail. Developing nations usually are characterized by a high birth rate and a high death rate, with a relatively young population because various diseases do not allow large numbers of people to live a long life.

A major distinction, therefore, in how diseases are distributed among population groups becomes apparent when the health profiles of industrialized societies are compared to those of developing nations. Many epidemiologists insist that there is a regular sequence of health problems corresponding to each stage of a nation's change in social organization from a rural to an urban society and from an agricultural to an industrial producer. For example, Table 2-1 shows the leading causes of death in the United States in 1900 were influenza, pneumonia, and tuberculosis. In 1999 these disorders had been replaced by heart disease, cancer, and cerebrovascular disease or stroke as leading causes of death. Improvements in living conditions and medical technology had all but eliminated disorders such as

TABLE 2-1   The Ten Leading Causes of Death in the United States, 1900 and 1999.

1900	1999
Influenza and pneumonia	Heart disease
Tuberculosis	Cancer
Gastroenteritis	Cerebrovascular diseases
Heart disease	Pulmonary diseases
Cerebral hemorrhage	Accidents
Kidney disease	Diabetes
Accidents	Influenza and pneumonia
Cancer	Alzheimer's disease
Diseases of early infancy	Kidney disease
Diphtheria	Septicemia (blood poisoning)

tuberculosis, gastroenteritis, and diphtheria as major threats to life in 1999, but smoking, excessive consumption of calories and animal fats, stress reactions, and inadequate physical activity had helped promote other health problems, such as heart disease and other disorders like cerebrovascular and pulmonary diseases.

The same type of pattern occurs in other countries as they experience modernization. For instance, Jamaica in 1920 had a level of health similar to that of the poorest country in Africa today. But once development was under way in 1945, Jamaica's traditional pattern of health problems changed. There was a remarkable fall in mortality from infectious diseases and parasitic disorders. There were also declines in other diseases of the digestive and respiratory systems with a communicable component. Life expectancy also increased, and infant mortality decreased. However, death rates from heart disease and cancer rose at the same time. Whereas modernization had been accompanied by greater longevity and a steep decline in infectious diseases, it had promoted more heart disease and cancer.

While modernization usually brings a higher overall standard of living and improved health, it also brings the diseases of advanced civilization. Thus, the struggle against disease never ends. In some ways it becomes even more difficult as disease agents begin operating in more subtle and unanticipated ways—often in relation to certain forms of behavior and lifestyles. AIDS is a major example of this development.

AIDS

The acquired immune deficiency syndrome, known as AIDS, is a disease of society in the most profound sense because of its link to specific ways of life. AIDS is a particularly deadly disease that destroys a person's immunity against infection, thereby leaving the individual defenseless against a variety of afflictions like cancer, pneumonia, and a host of viruses. AIDS is a virus itself—the human immunodeficiency virus (HIV)—transmitted through sexual intercourse, intravenous drug use, or blood transfusions, or passed to newborn infants by infected mothers.

What makes AIDS a disease of society is that it is clearly grounded in the conduct of social life, and its potential for changing norms, values, sex habits, and lifestyles worldwide is enormous. Thus, AIDS is no "ordinary" epidemic; it is a lethal illness with far-reaching implications for individuals, families, communities, health care providers and delivery systems, and societies around the globe (Bosk and Frader 1990; Brooks-Gunn and Furstenberg 1990; Chapman 2000; Dill 1994; Earickson 1990; R. Fox, Aiken, and Messikomer 1990; G. Green and Platt 1997; Kinnell 2001; LeBlanc 1993; C. Levine 1990; Pearlin, Aneshensel, and LeBlanc 1997; Rushing 1995; Wight 1999).

United States

Signs of the disease appeared first in the autumn of 1979. Young homosexual men with a history of promiscuity began showing up at clinics in New York, Los Angeles, and San Francisco with an unusual array of ailments. Some had strange fungal infections and others had rare cancers, such as Kaposi's sarcoma that is found only among elderly men of Mediterranean extraction or young men from equatorial Africa. Some had a deadly pneumonia, *Pneumocystis carinii,* seldom seen except in cancer and organ transplant patients weakened from prolonged treatment with drugs. Information from physicians in Los Angeles and New York City alerted the Centers for Disease Control and Prevention in Atlanta to the problems in early 1981. Some fifty cases were initially identified around the country, and each of these individuals was interviewed. But what caused the disease and how it could be treated remained unknown as the number of victims began to increase at an alarming rate.

By mid-1984, 4,918 persons in the United States had developed AIDS; many of them died. While homosexual organizations complained that the federal government had little interest in solving the outbreak because most of the victims were homosexuals, a task force was formed at the CDC. At first, it was thought that the cause might be an inhalant, known as "rush" or "poppers," containing either amyl nitrate or butyl nitrate, sometimes used by homosexuals to produce a "high" during sex. But this possibility was ruled out after interviews with gay men who used the inhalants did not come down with AIDS. This development directed the attention of the investigators toward a virus or some other infectious agent transmitted by sexual contact or dirty needles, since some of the victims used drugs. Support for this theory began to emerge after a few heterosexual drug abusers and a baby in San Francisco who received blood from a donor with AIDS contracted the disease. The strongest evidence on the means of transmission came from sexual histories obtained in Los Angeles. AIDS was consistently linked with the sexual encounters of the victims, with the agent possibly entering the bloodstream through the anus. Three different men, for instance, none of whom were acquainted with each other, identified a man in New York City as a sexual partner; he was found to have AIDS.

The next clues were somewhat puzzling because AIDS turned up in immigrants from Haiti where homosexuality is considered exceptionally taboo. Many of these victims denied they were homosexual or drug users, but additional investigation showed they may have gotten the disease this way. One theory holds that AIDS may have originated in central Africa and was carried to Haiti where it reached the United States through homosexual contacts. But no scientific evidence has been produced that proves this theory.

AIDS research has confirmed that the disease is a virus, but attempts to find a cure have not been successful to date. It is now known that infection occurs when the virus enters the bloodstream, with anal intercourse and intravenous drug use the most common means of transmission in Western societies. In the United States, CDC data for 1985–2001 show that 47.1 percent of all cases reported were homosexual and bisexual men, 24.3 percent were IV drug users, and 6.3 percent were homosexuals and IV drug users. Of the remaining AIDS cases, 10.5 percent resulted from heterosexual contacts, less than 1 percent were hemophilia cases, 1 percent were blood transfusion recipients, and the remaining 10 percent were from other causes or the origin of the infection could not be determined.

Routine, nonintimate contact in the home or workplace with persons with AIDS does not appear to spread the infection. Much of the fear about AIDS arises from the fact that many people who carry the virus are not aware of it. The virus can remain in the body without causing the disease, but among those who do develop AIDS, the average time between infection and diagnosis can be five years or longer. Thus, AIDS carriers can unknowingly infect other people for a number of years, since the only method to determine if a person is HIV-infected in the absence of symptoms is through a blood test. As a study (Prohaska et al. 1990) in Chicago shows, some people consider themselves at risk for developing AIDS—especially if they have had multiple sex partners and know little about the partners' past sexual behavior.

Between 1984 and mid-2001, the total number of AIDS cases in the United States rose from nearly 5,000 to 767,429. Some 60 percent died. However, 1995 was the peak year for AIDS mortality as the number of deaths fell from 49,895 that year to 37,221 in 1996 and dropped even further to 14,215 in 1999. The incidence of AIDS also fell from 60,620 new cases of diagnosed AIDS in 1995 to 40,230 in 2000. Figure 2-1 depicts the number of reported cases per 100,000 of the population for 2000. The District of Columbia had the highest rates in the nation in 2000 with 153.0 cases per 100,000 population. Puerto Rico was second with a rate of 35.4 cases per 100,000 population followed by New York (32.7), Florida (31.1), Delaware (28.2), the Virgin Islands (28.1), and Maryland (27.7).

For males, CDC data for 2000–01 show that non-Hispanic blacks had the highest rate of 106.7 cases per 100,000 population, followed by Hispanics with 42.8, American Indians/Alaska natives 18.3, non-Hispanic whites 13.5, and Asians/Pacific Islanders 7.4. For females, non-Hispanic blacks also have the highest rates at 46.1 cases per 100,000 population in 2000–01, and Hispanics are next at 11.2, followed by American Indians/Alaska natives (6.1), non-Hispanic whites (2.2), and Asians/Pacific Islanders (1.5). Most women become infected by the AIDS virus (HIV) from

FIGURE 2-1   Acquired immunodeficiency syndrome (AIDS)—Cases per 100,000 population, reported to CDC by state, United States, 2000.

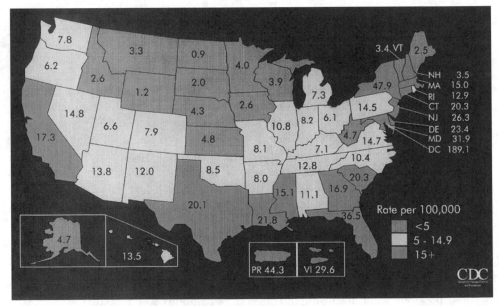

Source: Centers for Disease Control and Prevention, 2002.

TABLE 2-2   Mortality Rates for Human Immunodeficiency Virus (HIV) Disease United States, 1987, 1995, 1999.

	(DEATHS PER 100,000 RESIDENT POPULATION)		
	1987	1995	1999[1]
Males			
Non-Hispanic White	10.7	18.0	4.0
Black	26.2	90.4	37.0
American Indian/Native Alaskan	*	11.6	5.0
Asian/Pacific Islander	2.5	6.3	1.4
Hispanic	18.8	42.0	11.3
Females			
Non-Hispanic White	0.5	1.8	0.7
Black	4.6	24.7	13.3
American Indian/Native Alaskan	*	*	*
Asian/Pacific Islander	*	0.7	*
Hispanic	2.1	9.0	3.1

*less than 20 deaths
[1]Preliminary data for 1999

Source: *Health, United States 2001* (Washington, DC: U.S. Government Printing Office, 2001).

either IV drug use or sexual relations with men who are either bisexual, IV drug users, or both. In the beginning of the AIDS epidemic, in the mid-1980s, those infected in the United States were principally non-Hispanic white homosexual males. That pattern, however, has altered and the magnitude of the epidemic shifted especially to African Americans and also to Hispanics.

Table 2-2 shows the mortality rates for HIV for three selected years: 1987, 1995, and preliminary data for 1999. Table 2-2 depicts mortality rates from HIV for non-Hispanic white males falling from 10.7 deaths per 100,000 in the general population in 1987 to 4 per 100,000 in 1999. The highest death rates belong to black males with a rate of 90.4 in 1995, followed by a steep decline to 37.0 in 1999. While there has been an obvious improvement, black male mortality remains the highest of any gender and racial group. Hispanic males had a mortality rate of 42.0 in 1995, but 1999 figures show a decline to 11.3. The lowest rates for males are among Asians/Pacific Islanders.

For females, Table 2-2 shows that blacks have far higher rates than all other groups even though there was a decline from 24.7 deaths per 100,000 in 1995 to 13.3 in 1999. Female HIV mortality has been negligible among non-Hispanic whites, American Indians/Native Alaskans, and Asians/Pacific Islanders. While the number of new AIDS cases and mortality rates in the United States started to decline in the mid-1990s, the reversal came later and has been much slower for black women, especially those that live in the South. In states like Mississippi and North Carolina, more black women than white men have contracted HIV. The center of the epidemic among women was initially injection drug-using women in the urban Northeast who got AIDS via contaminated needles, but it is now heterosexual black women in the South.

The Joint United Nations Programme on HIV/AIDS estimated in 2001 that 940,000 North Americans were infected with HIV/AIDS, but no one really knows for sure how many persons carry the virus but are not yet ill. Also, no one knows what proportion of those persons who are HIV-positive will ultimately develop AIDS, nor the extent to which it can be contained without a vaccine that still eludes the best efforts of researchers to develop.

Worldwide

On a worldwide basis, the U.N. estimates that 40 million people were affected by HIV/AIDS in 2001, with 28 million in Africa south of the Sahara Desert. At least 25 million people have died since 1981. AIDS is believed to have originated in west central Africa in Gabon in one subspecies of chimpanzee (*Pan troglodytes troglodytes*) that somehow transmitted the virus to humans, possibly through blood in hunting, the preparation of chimpanzee meat to eat or sell, or bites. As long as infections were confined to a few people in remote areas, the virus in humans remained unknown. The earliest infections may have occurred in the 1940s and 1950s, with the earliest confirmed HIV blood sample dating back to 1959 from a Bantu tribesman living in the Belgian Congo (the current Democratic Republic of Congo); it is not known if the man developed AIDS. Migration from rural areas into cities and the increased commercialization of sex in the region apparently caused the disease to spread among Africans, particularly in the eastern and southern parts of the continent, and reach Europe and North America by the early 1980s.

African nations like Botswana, Swaziland, Zimbabwe, Lesotho, Zambia, South Africa, and Namibia have the highest rates per capita of AIDS in the world. Anywhere from 20 to 38 percent of the population in these countries is HIV-infected. The country of South Africa has nearly five million people HIV-infected, which is more than any other country in the world (Rensburg et al. 2002). Both population growth and life expectancy are falling in Sub-Saharan Africa. In Botswana, for example, the average life expectancy has declined from 61 years in 1993 to 39 years in 2001. The effects of AIDS on Africa south of the Sahara are devastating (Barnett and Blaike 1992; Gregson et al. 1998; Lear 1996; MacDonald 1996; Rensburg et al. 2002).

However, in striking contrast to Western society, AIDS is transmitted in Africa primarily by conventional sexual intercourse among heterosexuals. About 80 percent of all AIDS cases in Africa are believed to result from heterosexual relations. AIDS is especially prevalent among prostitutes, migrant workers, and long-distance truck drivers—but reaches up to include significant numbers of people in upper socio-economic groups. The migrant labor system in sub-Saharan Africa plays a particularly important role in the transmission of AIDS (C. Hunt 1989, 1996; Obbo 1993). Whereas African women living in rural areas typically remain in their villages to work and care for their family, African men form a large migrant labor pool seeking greater economic opportunity in mining areas, large commercial farming areas, and some large cities. This system of labor, Charles Hunt (1989, 1996) explains, causes long absences, increased family breakdown, and increased numbers of sexual partners. This situation has created a large population that suffers from epidemics of sexually transmitted diseases, thereby making it especially vulnerable to the AIDS virus. AIDS does seem to affect women in Africa almost as often as men, with women comprising 40 to 50 percent of all AIDS cases south of the Sahara. A particular problem faced by many African women is a lack of power to negotiate safe sex, either in marriage or outside of it, because of their dependent status in relation to men. As William Rushing (1995:66) explains, "In most African societies male dominance is about as extreme as anywhere in the world." Poverty and the widespread lack of employment opportunities in the business sector push many women into prostitution, while men can often have multiple wives or sexual partners and divorce easily (C. Hunt 1996; Jewkes, Levin, and Penn–KeKana 2003; Lear 1996; MacDonald 1996; Obbo 1993; Pitts, Bowman, and McMaster 1995; Rushing 1995).

Why the pattern of AIDS transmission seems to differ so drastically in Africa from that of North America and Europe remains a mystery. The pattern of gender stratification in which women are severely disadvantaged may be a major factor (Barnett and Blaike 1992; Jewkes et al. 2003), along with the high prevalence of sexually transmitted diseases generally (Rushing 1995). It may be that the sores and genital ulcers caused by other widespread sexually transmitted diseases like syphilis enhance the potential for AIDS transmission between men and women.

In Western Europe, the AIDS epidemic has followed the same pattern as in the United States, with the centers of infection found in major cities among homosexual and bisexual men and IV drug users. The U.N. estimated in 2001 that 560,000 people were HIV-infected in Western Europe. Switzerland has the highest rates of AIDS, followed by Spain, France, and Italy. Greece, Norway, and Sweden have the lowest rates. AIDS is principally transmitted by IV drug use in southern European countries like Italy and Spain but is passed in northern European countries like Denmark, Germany, and Great Britain largely through homosexual contact. Germany and France, however, had major scandals in the 1990s when blood contaminated with the AIDS virus was carelessly distributed to hospitals. In Eastern Europe and Central Asia, some one million were HIV-infected in 2001. Cases have more than tripled in this region since 1998. Russia had about 75,000 new cases in 2001, while 1 percent of the population in the Ukraine is infected. This is the first time any European country has reached that level.

AIDS victims in Asia were few until the late 1980s when the disease began spreading rapidly. The U.N. estimates that over 7.1 million people in South and Southeast Asia were HIV-infected in 2001. Like Africa, the major source of AIDS in Asia is heterosexual rather than homosexual. Thailand, which has many prostitutes and drug users, is a major center of AIDS. Some 860,000 people are infected, but the number could reach 1.8 million in the next ten years. However, Thailand is the one Asian country that has mounted a major response to the epidemic with a nationwide program of education, condom promotion, and improved treatment for sexually transmitted diseases generally (Sermsri 1999). And there are signs that the spread of AIDS in Thai society is beginning to slow, as the numbers of new HIV infections are beginning to decrease. Yet other Asian countries like Myanmar (formerly Burma), Indonesia, Cambodia, and Malaysia are now finding that AIDS is entering a new, more visible phase and becoming a major crisis. This is particularly true in China where at least one million people were estimated to be HIV-infected in 2001.

Australia and New Zealand are estimated by the U.N. to have about 15,000 people HIV-infected. In Japan, only some 3,000 people had tested positive for HIV in the mid-1990s, but the government expected this figure to increase rapidly. Sexual intercourse with female prostitutes in Thailand, the Philippines, and other Asian countries by Japanese men is believed to be a major factor in spreading the disease in Japan. Another causal factor, as seen in a 1996 scandal, was the provision of tainted blood to many hemophiliacs. The Japanese public, however, does not view AIDS as a very serious problem, believing it to be associated with other countries and largely confined in Japan to small groups of homosexuals and hemophiliacs (Munakata 1994; Munakata and Tajima 1996).

Elsewhere, in India, AIDS is spreading through the population to a point that the disease may eventually claim more lives there than in any other country. Currently, almost four million people are infected by HIV. Prostitution in large cities like Bombay and Madras and along India's vast system of roadways frequented by some five million truck drivers appears to be the major chain of transmission. Drug use in northeast India also plays an important role in the spread of AIDS. If current trends continue, India may become the world center of the AIDS epidemic in the early twenty-first century, with as many as 25 million infected people by 2010.

Another part of the world in which AIDS is on the increase is Central and South America and the Caribbean. AIDS first appeared among homosexuals and drug users in Haiti, Argentina, and Brazil. It is now spreading throughout the region. Bisexual activity by Latin American men is believed to be important in the infection of a large proportion of females. The U.N. estimates that 1.4 million Latin Americans are HIV-infected with an additional 420,00 cases in the Caribbean. Brazil has the largest concentration of AIDS cases among Latin American countries. About 2.2 percent of the population in the Caribbean has HIV, which is second in the world behind only sub-Saharan Africa, where 8.4 percent of the population has HIV.

AIDS thus stands as an example of how certain types of behavior (especially sexual promiscuity or drug use) provide a particular virus with the opportunity to cause a deadly disease. The sociological implications of the AIDS epidemic are enormous and involve not only the widespread modification of sexual behavior, but also the deeply discrediting stigma attached to AIDS victims, the social rejection of AIDS patients, the subjective distress associated with becoming an AIDS patient, and the moral and religious debate centering on AIDS as a punishment for a deviant lifestyle (Chapman 2000; Ciambrone 2001; R. Fox, Aiken, and Messikomer 1990; G. Green 1995; G. Green and Platt 1997; Nisbet and McQueen 1993; Siegel and Krauss 1991; H. Turner, Hayes, and Coates 1993).

As Renée Fox and her associates (1990:239) observe: "The fact that a large proportion of people with AIDS are homosexual or bisexual men and intravenous (IV) drug users has evoked widespread stigmatizing, shunning, and discriminatory reactions to persons with AIDS." Thus, when one becomes infected with AIDS, that person in many ways becomes a social outcast—avoided by former friends and acquaintances. People often have a "master status," which is a general status that reflects an individual's most important position in society and typically comes from one's occupation. AIDS, however, can take on the attributes of a master status in that it becomes the single most important social characteristic of an infected person. Regardless of income, education, occupation, or other source of status, persons with AIDS will likely find that having the disease will negatively influence the attitudes and reactions of others (Chapman 2000; Green and Platt 1997).

AIDS throws families into crisis as well. Not only do children with AIDS have families, but so do homosexuals and IV drug users. Family relationships can become strained as families cope with the stigma of AIDS, but families also involve themselves in the care and support of the infected member. For all concerned, dealing with AIDS is extremely stressful for families (Levine 1990; Pearlin, Aneshensel and LeBlanc 1997). AIDS is also stressful for the nurses, physicians, and other health care providers who work with AIDS patients (Bosk and Frader 1990; R. Fox, Aiken, and Messikomer 1990; Green and Platt 1997). Health personnel not only risk exposure to the virus, but they themselves may also be shunned by colleagues and friends, mourn the deaths of patients, and become frustrated at their inability to provide a cure. AIDS is clearly a complex social disease.

Since AIDS results from a private act that has extreme social consequences, serious moral and legal questions also arise about the rights of individuals versus the welfare of society. The central public problem is how to alter behavior that occurs in

Friends visiting an AIDS patient.

the most private of settings and whether it can be done in a way that does not violate civil liberties. The current public policy approach to dealing with AIDS is to limit its spread through educational programs stressing safe sex, yet the possibility of quarantines and universal testing remains in the background if the incurable and fatal disease races unchecked through society. However, some state legislatures in the United States have passed laws to protect the public. Several states have laws making it a crime to transmit or knowingly expose other people to HIV/AIDS, as well as requiring mandatory testing of prison inmates and pregnant women and notification of partners of infected people. AIDS has become the major public health issue of our time.

SUMMARY

The epidemiologist is like a detective, investigating the scene of a crime in which the criminal is a disease or some other form of health menace. The epidemiologist is primarily concerned not with individuals but with the health profiles of social aggregates or large populations of people. Important tools of the epidemiologist are the ratios used to compute descriptions of mortality, incidence, and prevalence. These rates can be either crude rates or rates reflecting age-specific data, sex-specific data, and so on.

Many diseases in modern society such as coronary heart disease are very complex; the example of AIDS indicates how challenging health problems can be to the practice of epidemiology. Moreover, it has been noted that as underdeveloped societies modernize, the pattern of their diseases changes accordingly. Communicable diseases are replaced by chronic illnesses like heart disease and cancer. A demanding lifestyle, inadequate diet, smoking, drug and alcohol abuse, obesity, lack of exercise, and exposure to environmental pollution have become the principal risk factors for ill health in modern society. But people can change their behavior and reduce or eliminate their risk of becoming sick.

EPIDEMIOLOGY INTERNET SITES

1. Centers for Disease Control and Prevention, National Center for Health Statistics.
   http://www.cdc.gov/nchs

   National and state data regarding births, deaths, and infant deaths; Healthy people 2000.

2. Centers for Disease Control and Prevention, Chronic Disease Prevention.
   http://www.cdc.gov/nccdphp

   Listings and links dealing with major chronic diseases, risk behaviors, specific populations, and maternal and infant health.

3. Office of Disease Prevention and Health Promotion, U.S. Department of Health and Human Services.
   http://www.odphp.osophs.dhhs.gov

   Announcements, publications, and web links dealing with disease prevention and health promotion priorties within the collaborative framework of the Health and Human Services agencies.

Heart Disease

1. American Heart Association.
   http://www.americanheart.org

   Publications, research, and statistics concerning cardiovascular disease in women and men.

2. American Stroke Association.
   http://www.strokeassociation.org

   News releases and facts concerning stroke and stroke support groups (a division of the American Heart Association).

3. National Heart, Lung, and Blood Institute.
   http://www.nhlbi.nih.gov/index.htm

   A division of the National Institutes of Health.

Diet

Dietary Guidelines for Americans.
http://www.odphp.osophs.dhhs.gov/pubs/dietguid

Published jointly with the U.S. Department of Agriculture (USDA) every five years since 1980, this publication is the statutorily mandated basis for federal nutrition education activities.

AIDS

1. Centers for Disease Control, Division of HIV/AIDS Prevention.
   http://www.cdcnpin.org/hiv/start.htm

   As part of its overall mission of reducing illness and death worldwide, the CDC provides leadership in preventing and controlling HIV infection by working with community, state, national, and international partners.

2. National Institutes of Health, Office of AIDS Research.
   http://www.nih.gov/od/oar/index.htm

   Contains updates, publications, and press releases from the NIH concerning AIDS research.

3. The Journal of the American Medical Association (JAMA), HIV/AIDS Resource Center.
   http://www.ama-assn.org/special/hiv/hivhome.htm

   Contains an easy to use collection of high-quality resources for physicians, other health professionals, and the public.

4. The Joint United Nations Programme on HIV/AIDS.
   http://www.unaids.org

   Contains the most recent country-specific data on HIV/AIDS prevalence and incidence, together with information on behaviors (e.g., casual sex and condom use) that can spur or stem the transmission of HIV.

The Social Demography of Health

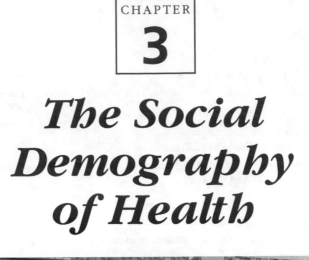

Four of the most important variables employed in epidemiological research are age, gender, race, and social class or socioeconomic status. It has been found that each of these four variables represents important differences between people that can be correlated with health and life expectancy. The purpose of this chapter will be to examine these variables and assess their relationship to health from a sociological standpoint.

AGE

A number of factors including improved medical care, nutrition, sanitation, and housing combined over the course of the twentieth century to help prolong lives for most Americans. In 2000, for example, the average infant at birth in the United States could expect to live 76.9 years. This figure represents an increase in longevity of approximately 60 percent since 1900 when life expectancy was 47.3 years. Less than one-half of all children born in 1900 could expect to reach age sixty-five, whereas today about 80 percent can expect to live to age sixty-five and one-third will live to be at least eighty-five years of age. The rise in life expectancy has brought a corresponding increase in the growth of the elderly population. Men and women are living to 65 years of age and older in greater numbers and proportions than ever before. In 1940, the elderly (those sixty-five and over) constituted 9 million people or about 7 percent of the total population. By 2000, their number had increased to 34.9 million or 12.4 percent of the population.

The twentieth century can be described as a period of rapid growth of the aged population worldwide. In the United States, not only are people living longer, but since 1958 the fertility rate has been in a period of decline. The lower death rate coupled with the lower birth rate has produced a much higher proportion of older Americans in relation to the total population. Table 3-1 illustrates this trend by showing that in 1900 only 4 percent of the total U.S. population was age sixty-five or over. By 2000, however, older Americans constituted 12.4 percent of the total population, and by 2050 it is projected that 20 percent of all Americans will be in this age bracket. That is, persons over age sixty-five will make up one-fifth of the population in 2050. The point is obvious: Americans are living longer, and the percentage of the elderly in the population is significantly increasing.

This trend will undoubtedly bring about a marked change in American society in general and in health care delivery in particular. The aged population will be healthier, better educated, and more affluent than any group of elderly persons in the past. They are likely to have not only a higher standard of living but also increased political power because of their larger numbers and experience with the political process. As a result they will have the clout to bring about legislation for public services to meet their social and health needs. Even though elderly Americans will be healthier than ever before, more pressure is likely to be put on health care delivery systems and public health insurance, namely Medicare, to keep them fit. The need for health services, however, becomes greater as one ages because even minor ailments can more easily develop into serious problems or simply linger longer than usual. Demands for health and other services for the aged are therefore likely to increase in accordance with their proportion of the population.

Pressure also will be put upon the Social Security system to maintain or increase payments for old-age benefits. With relatively fewer children resulting from the baby boom generation in the United States that was born between 1946 and

TABLE 3-1   Percent of Total U.S. Population Age Sixty-Five and Over for Selected Years.

	1900	1930	1950	1970	1980	2000	2050 (projected)
Percent age 65 and over	4.0	5.4	8.1	9.7	11.2	12.4	20.0

Source: U.S. Bureau of the Census, 2002.

1964 and is now passing through middle age, the financing of old-age benefits will require increasingly more money in the future from a smaller working population. In 1955, for example, there were 8.6 taxpayers per Social Security beneficiary; but by 2005 the ratio will be 2.7 taxpayers per retiree. By 2035, the ratio will drop to about 1.9 taxpayers for every retiree. Serious difficulties in the financing and provision of services for the elderly in the United States appear certain.

These trends are important because when people become very old they require a greater share of public services. In developed nations, the care of the elderly has generally shifted from being a family responsibility to being more of a societal responsibility. This change has come about for a number of reasons. One reason is the decline of the extended family, in which multiple generations of a single family continued to live with or near each other, and its replacement by the nuclear family, that is, a family consisting of one couple and their children. Other reasons include the high cost of health and nursing care, the type and degree of care required, and the increase in the number of persons needing such care. Although most old people will be relatively healthy in old age, there will come a time, particularly for the oldest of the old, when their health will fail, bringing about the requirement for extended care and greater public expenditures to meet this need.

Adequate health care for the aged is a particularly significant goal for public policy because the single most important determinant of the quality of an elderly person's life is health (Cockerham 1997a). Older people who are unhealthy lead relatively shorter and less satisfactory lives than older people who are healthy, feel good, and have the physical capability to pursue their chosen activities. Especially among the elderly, health matters affect all other areas of life. Interestingly, older people often rate their health in a positive fashion. But how can this be, since health deteriorates with age? Several studies have investigated this situation and found that many elderly nevertheless rate their health status as very good (Baron-Epel and Kaplan 2001; Cockerham, Sharp, and Wilcox 1983; Ferraro 1980; Linn and Linn 1980; Mechanic and Angel 1987; Stoller 1984). An exception is elderly blacks who tend to be more pessimistic about their health than elderly whites (Ferraro 1993; Mutchler and Burr 1991).

The question thus arises as to whether such self-assessments are accurate measures of a person's health. This is an important question because the accuracy of survey respondents' reports of objective conditions affects virtually all fields of sociology (Ferraro and Farmer 1999). However, extensive analysis of health self-ratings shows that such ratings are indeed valid and reliable and match up as well as or even better than physician evaluations (Ferraro and Farmer 1999; Fillenbaum 1979; Idler and Benyamini 1997; Mirowsky 1999; Ross and Wu 1995). Most people appear to have accurate assessments of their physical state based on how they feel and function. As for the elderly, those who rate their health high are usually older than those who rate their health less positively. Marja Jylhä (1994:988) reports one interview as follows:

Interviewer:	Is it hard for you to compare your own health with that of other people of your own age, would you say it is . . .
Respondent (85-year-old woman):	Well most of them are dead, aren't they?

It may seem incongruent that many older people tend to rate their health positively, in spite of the fact that health declines with age. The reason is that judgments concerning one's health by aged individuals are relative. That is, in assessing their health, aged persons compare themselves with others of their own age and sex, and perhaps also in relation to the expectations others have of their health.

High self-ratings of health by the elderly most likely are rationalized in two ways. First, simply surviving to old age in a condition reasonably free of serious illness or disability would be evidence of relatively good health. Second, subjective responses to a health problem tend to be determined by how much of a person's life is disrupted by the condition, and elderly people usually are not required to maintain a highly active level of functioning. Thus, the aged are able to perceive their health as good enough to perform their daily activities. Therefore, as David Mechanic and Ronald Angel (1987) suggest, the elderly appear to adjust their perceptions of their health as they modify their expectations with age. As people become older, they tend to change their definition of what it is to be healthy in order to fit their circumstances.

Of course, the health of elderly people on the whole is not actually better than that of young adults in general. This fact is apparent when age differences in overall physical condition, stamina, hand and eye coordination, hearing and vision, capacity for healing from disease and injury, and prevalence of chronic diseases are considered. Although there are exceptions, older people generally cannot pursue a highly active physical lifestyle to the same extent as someone much younger. Rather, it is that the health of many older people is quite good for their age. The health of other older people, however, may be poor. The fact remains that health does deteriorate with age, and this deterioration occurs later in some people than in others.

BOX 3-1   The Changing Disease Burden

The aging of the world's population not only means more older people, but it also means that the pattern of diseases and health problems will likely change. While the prevalence of certain diseases will increase, others will decrease. The changes expected to occur between 1990 and 2020 are shown below:

Expected to Decrease	Expected to Increase
Lower respiratory infection	Depression
Diarrhea	Heart disease
Prenatal conditions	Stroke
Measles	Auto accidents
Congenital anomalies	Pulmonary disease
Malaria	War, violence, and suicide
Malnutrition	HIV/AIDS
Anemia	Lung cancer

Adapted from C. Murray and A. Lopez (1996).

But eventually everyone's health declines if one lives long enough. The key to a positive quality of life in old age appears to be that of maintaining one's health as long as possible and as close as possible to the time of one's death.

The most prevalent health problem of persons over the age of sixty-five is arthritis; next is hypertension, followed by hearing impairment, heart disease, cataracts, and orthopedic impairments. With an increasingly older population, these disorders will require greater attention from health care delivery services. So there will be something of a paradox in that the aged will be placing greater demands on the health care system (since there will be more of them), but they also are likely to be healthier than previous generations.

Sociologists concerned with aging usually work in social gerontology, a subfield of gerontology that deals primarily with the nonphysical aspects of aging. These specialists study the ways in which the elderly adjust to their society and how society adapts to the elderly. As larger numbers of people live longer, this area will grow in importance.

GENDER

In preindustrial societies, including those in Europe, the life expectancies of men and women were approximately the same. This was the situation as late as 1850 in England and Wales where fifteen-year-old boys could expect to live another 43.2 years and girls an additional 43.9 years. By 1950, fifteen-year-old girls in England and Wales typically outlived boys of the same age by 6 years. Between 1850 and 1950, life expectancy for women had increased 41 percent as compared with 30 percent among men (Hart 1991). In the 1990s the gap in life expectancy between men and women in England and Wales persisted. The same pattern exists in most of the world. Life expectancy increased for both men and women in the twentieth century, but women live longer on average than men. As British sociologist Nicky Hart (1991) concludes, economic progress appears to have benefited the longevity of women the most.

The only exception worldwide is in a few countries in South Asia such as Bangladesh and Nepal, where men outlive women (Cockerham 1997a). Nutritional deprivation and lessened access to medical care are among the possible reasons for this reversal of the usual female superiority in life expectancy (L. Martin 1988). Outside of South Asia, women have a definite advantage over men in longevity. Males typically exceed female death rates at all ages and for the leading causes of death such as heart disease, cancer, cerebrovascular diseases, accidents, and pneumonia. Women tend to suffer from more frequent illnesses and disability, but their usual health disorders are not as serious or as life threatening as those encountered by men. Yet women, especially in later life, also die from the same illnesses as men. So what should be kept in mind, as Lois Verbrugge (1985:163) observed, is "that men and women essentially suffer the same *types* of problems; what distinguishes the sexes is the frequency of those problems and the *pace* of death." For example, heart

TABLE 3-2   Percent of Males and Females Surviving from Birth in the United States, 1999.

Surviving from Birth	White Males	White Females	Black Males	Black Females
To age 1	99.4	99.5	98.4	98.7
To age 20	98.6	99.0	97.1	98.0
To age 65	79.3	87.4	63.3	77.7

Source: National Center for Health Statistics, 2002.

disease is the leading cause of death for women after age sixty-six, but becomes the number one killer of men after age thirty-nine.

The result is that as of 1999 the average life expectancy in the United States of white females was 79.9 years compared to 74.6 years for white males. The same advantage applies to black females who had an average life expectancy in 1999 of 74.7 years compared to 67.8 years for black males. Table 3-2 demonstrates female superiority in life expectancy. For 1999, the U.S. National Center for Health Statistics projected that 99.5 percent of all white females and 99.4 percent of all white males would survive to age one from birth; by age sixty-five, however, only 79.3 percent of the white males would be alive compared to 87.4 percent of the white females. The lowest level of life expectancy belongs to the black male. Table 3-2 shows that 98.4 percent of the black males will survive from birth to age one compared to 98.7 percent of the black females; by age sixty-five the percentage of surviving black males is 63.3 and the percentage of surviving black females is 77.7. Whereas black females have a definite advantage in longevity over black males, white females have the longest life span in the United States.

Men have a substantial health inferiority in terms of life expectancy because of the combined result of two major effects: (1) biological and (2) social-psychological. The male of the human species is at a biological disadvantage to the female. The fact that the male is weaker physiologically than the female is demonstrated by higher mortality rates from the prenatal and neonatal stages of life onward. Although the percentages may vary somewhat from year to year, the chances of dying during the prenatal stage are approximately 12 percent greater among males than females and 130 percent greater during the neonatal (newborn) stage. Examples of neonatal disorders common to male rather than female babies are such afflictions as hyaline membrane disease (a respiratory disease) and pyloric stenosis (a disorder of the pyloric muscle affecting the emptying of the stomach). Neonatal males are also more prone to certain circulatory disorders of the aorta and pulmonary artery and are subject to more severe bacterial infections. Females are less likely to get childhood leukemia and have a better chance for survival when they do. As an organism, the male appears to be more vulnerable than the female, even before being exposed to the differential social roles and stress situations of later life.

While the evidence is not conclusive, social and psychological influences are nonetheless presumed to play an important part in the determination of life expectancy. Accidents, for example, cause more deaths among males than females, which reflects a difference in sex roles. Men tend to be more aggressive than women in both work and play. High accident rates among males may be attributed to the male's increased exposure to dangerous activities, especially those arising from high-risk occupations. The most dangerous job in the United States (according to the Bureau of Labor Statistics) is commercial fisherman, followed by (in order) logger, airplane pilot, structural metalworker, taxi driver, construction laborer, roofer, electrical worker, truck driver, farm worker, and police officer. Being president of the United States is also hazardous. About one out of three U.S. presidents has lived to enjoy a normal life expectancy.

Another factor contributing to excess male mortality rates may be occupational competition and the pressure associated with a job. The lifestyle of the business executive or professional with an orientation toward "career" and drive toward "success," marks of the upwardly mobile middle-class male in American society, is thought to contribute strongly to the development of stress among such men. Middle-aged professional males in the United States today are noted by life insurance companies as a high-risk group, particularly if they smoke, are overweight, and tend to overwork. It would thus seem that both the male sex role and the psychodynamics of male competitiveness are significant factors affecting male longevity. Alcohol use, particularly heavy use, has also been identified as a risk factor for some diseases (such as cirrhosis of the liver) and deaths from automobile accidents. Men and boys continue to drink more frequently and drink more at one time than women and girls. Driving at high speeds and participating in violent sports is likewise more common for males. Males also tend to have higher levels of blood pressure. Thus, when occupational hazards are added, men are at greater risk in developing major degenerative diseases than women. This situation may change as women move into high-risk occupations and ambitious female executives and professionals experience career pressures.

While men have a higher rate of mortality, women appear to have a higher morbidity or sickness rate. According to the National Center for Health Statistics (2002), females have higher rates of acute illness—namely, infectious and parasitic diseases and digestive and respiratory conditions. The only category of acute health problems in which males had a higher incidence was injuries. Males, however, tended to not stay in bed for injuries as much as females. The rate for acute conditions not related to pregnancy is eleven times greater for females than males.

As for chronic (long-term) conditions, females show higher rates of hypertension, thyroid, anemia, and gallbladder conditions, chronic enteritis and colitis, migraine headaches, arthritis, diabetes and other diseases of the urinary system, and some skin conditions. Males, on the other hand, have more losses of limbs, gout, emphysema, AIDS, and heart disease. Males have higher rates of cancer at the youngest and oldest ages; women have the highest incidence rates between the ages of twenty and fifty-five. Overall, men are more likely to die from cancer. The pattern that emerges from these differences is that women are more likely to have a higher prevalence of chronic conditions that are not a leading cause of death (except for diabetes), while men have more of the chronic health problems that end one's life. Women also exhibit much greater use of health services than men (National Center for Health Statistics 2002). This pattern is consistent even when rates of utilization of maternity services are excluded from analysis. Furthermore, as Judith Auerbach and Anne Figert (1995) explain, women are the primary caretakers for sick people—both in the family and society at large—as well as the major consumers of health care for themselves and others. "Women," state Auerbach and Figert (1995:122), "urge their loved ones to seek medical care; they make the doctors' appointments for their family members; and they purchase and replenish over-the-counter medicines for the family's bathroom medicine cabinet." They are also more likely to leave work to take care of a sick child, monitor the health status of extended family members, and take care of elderly relatives. In sum, women have more physical ailments than men, and spend considerably more time taking care of themselves and others.

It appears there is an inverse relationship between mortality and morbidity when sex differences are considered. Women may be sick more often, but live longer. Men may be sick less often, but die sooner. The possibility exists that women do not have more sickness but are just more sensitive to their bodily discomforts and more willing to report their symptoms to others. The best evidence indicates that overall differences in morbidity are real (Auerbach and Figert 1995; Bird and Fremont 1991; Bird and Rieker 1999; National Center for Health Statistics 2002; Rieker and Bird 2000; Verbrugge 1985, 1986). And, as Lois Verbrugge (1976:401) explains, "Whether the reasons for greater morbidity are mostly social and psychological, or mostly physical, the immediate social outcomes are the same." The outcome is that females report more illness and disability and, consequently, show a greater loss of productivity—whether their work is in the home or outside it. Employers cannot rely on females as readily as they can males to be at work or to feel like working while they are there. Females also spend more days at home in a sick role and thus tend to disrupt more family activities. And, since good health is generally considered to be a highly significant aspect of a good life, females are at a disadvantage compared to males. "Higher female morbidity, compared to males," states Verbrugge (1976:401), "means that females experience a less comfortable and satisfying life with regard to a cherished attribute. They simply do not feel as well as often as males."

While females are more fit biologically at birth, are less often exposed to danger and highly stressful occupations, are more sensitive to their bodily states, and possibly enhance their life expectancy through increased use of medical services, the female advantage in longevity may be a mixed blessing. Women not only appear to feel physically ill more often than men, but many studies confirm that depression and anxiety are more prevalent among women, as is discussed in a later subsection. Female longevity has also resulted in an increasing number of widows faced with important decisions about remarriage, employment, family life, and dealing with loneliness.

There is, however, renewed interest in investigating the health differences of men and women because of changes in the way that people now live. The lives of men and women used to be more predictable in that men typically behaved in certain distinct ways and women in others. Thus, gender differences in activities, goals, and life expectancy were taken for granted and more or less anticipated. But Verbrugge (1985) indicates that important clues are emerging that show Americans may be moving toward greater equality in mortality between the sexes. This suggestion is based upon evidence that sex differences for some major causes of death

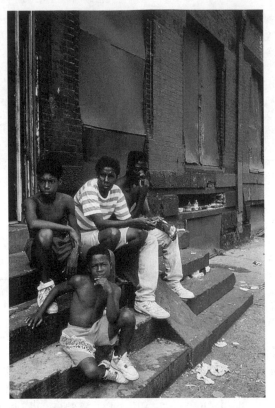

Black males have the lowest life expectancy in
American society. Disadvantaged socioeconomic
circumstances play a key role in this situation.

like lung cancer have either decreased, stabilized, or only slowly widened. Considerable speculation exists with respect to the possible effects on female life expectancy posed by their increased participation in the labor force and changes in lifestyle. Women in recent years, as compared to the 1950s, are more likely to work in occupations that were once almost exclusively male, drink more alcohol, and smoke more cigarettes. It will be several years, until the present cohort of adult women dies, before these effects on women's health can be fully determined.

Lung Cancer

Yet for lung cancer, there is already evidence of change. American women did not begin smoking in large numbers until World War II when they entered civilian workplaces as replacements for men in the military. When women were empowered by the greater equality that came with employment outside the home, their smoking rates increased dramatically (Walsh, Sorensen, and Leonard 1995). Female rates of lung cancer, accordingly, rose from 5.8 deaths per 100,000 in 1950 to 40.8 in 1999.

TABLE 3-3   Percentage of Current Cigarette Smokers by Sex and Race, United States (Selected Years, 1965–2000)*.

	1965	1979	1983	1987	1993	1995	2000
Male	51.6	37.2	34.7	31.0	27.5	26.7	25.2
White	50.8	36.5	34.1	30.4	27.0	26.4	25.5
Black	59.2	44.1	41.3	39.0	33.2	28.5	25.7
Female	34.0	30.3	29.9	26.7	22.7	22.8	21.1
White	34.3	30.6	30.1	27.2	23.7	23.6	22.0
Black	32.1	30.8	31.8	27.2	19.8	22.8	20.7

*18 years of age and over, age-adjusted.

Source: National Center for Health Statistics, 2002.

Lung cancer ranked eighth among cancer deaths for women in 1961, but moved up to first by 1986. The National Center for Health Statistics (1985) attributed this rise to an aging of cohorts with a high prevalence of cigarette smoking. The trend in the United States, however, is toward a decrease in smoking for both sexes, but especially for men. As shown in Table 3-3, the proportion of men who smoke in the United States declined from 51.6 percent in 1965 to 25.2 percent in 2000. The percentage of smokers among both white and black males declined during the period and are now about equal. For females, Table 3-3 shows that the proportion of women smoking dropped from 34 percent in 1965 to 21.1 percent in 2000. Whereas smoking by males began declining in the 1970s, the percentage of female smokers did not decrease significantly until the late 1980s and has decreased much more slowly than that of males. In fact, Table 3-3 shows that between 1993 and 1995, smoking for women *increased* slightly from 22.7 percent to 22.8 percent. This increase was due to greater smoking among young women, especially young black women who are largely responsible for the rise in smoking among black females from 19.8 percent in 1993 to 22.8 percent in 1995. However, between 1995 and 2000, Table 3-3 shows that the percentage of black female smokers has dropped back to 20.7 percent. The percentage of smokers among white females decreased steadily over the years, but still remains higher than that of black females with some 22.0 percent of white women smoking in 2000. Overall, smoking cessation has been more pronounced among men than women. Quitting smoking, even past the age of fifty, tends to increase longevity, but the death toll continues to rise each year as the habits of the past have their effects.

This trend is dramatically depicted in an international study of mortality from tobacco use in developed countries conducted by Richard Peto and his colleagues (1992). Peto and his colleagues projected death rates from smoking for the 1990s by analyzing trends in different countries over the course of several years. They predicted that approximately twenty-one million people would die from smoking between 1990 and 1999 in developed countries alone: five to six million in the United States, five to six million in the European Union, five million in Russia, and two million elsewhere, including Australia, Canada, Japan, and New Zealand. These deaths will not be just from lung cancer but also from smoking-related cancers of the mouth, pharynx, and larynx, diseases of the cardiovascular system, and other diseases. American females were projected to have a dramatically higher mortality rate from smoking than women in Russia, the European Union, and other developed countries.

Mental Health

As for mental health, there are no consistent differences between men and women in clinically diagnosed cases of mental illness, with two exceptions. Women have higher rates of mood (prolonged depression or elation) and anxiety disorders, while men have more personality disorders, which consist largely of impaired personality traits (Cockerham 2003; Kessler et al. 1994; Rosenfield 1999; Simon 2000). Tendencies toward depression and anxiety that fall short of mental disorders in the full-blown clinical sense, but nonetheless cause people to feel psychologically distressed, are also more common among women than men (Mirowsky and Ross 1989, 1995). This is the situation both in the United States and in other countries around the globe (Cockerham 2003; Desjarlais et al. 1995; Fuller et al. 1993; Lai 1995).

These differences appear to be related to both biological and sociocultural factors. Much of the current research in medical sociology focuses on the everyday social roles of women. Women employed outside the home tend to show less psychological distress than housewives but more distress than employed men (Glass and Fujimoto 1994; Mirowsky and Ross 1989). Often working wives have to maintain the house as well as perform satisfactorily on the job; in essence these demands are tantamount to having two full-time jobs. It may be that working wives are under greater strain than their husbands, although both employed men and women generally have fewer health problems than the unemployed. Nevertheless, Catherine Ross, John Mirowsky, and Patricia Ulbrich (1983:681) conclude that "if a married woman gets a job to bolster the family income or find self-expression through occupational achievement, or both, she finds that the wife is now more like a husband but the husband is not more like a wife." There is research that shows the strain of working and doing the majority of work associated with raising children increases psychological distress among married women—particularly those from low-income families (Bird 1999; Lai 1995; Simon 1992, 1995; Thoits 1987).

However, other studies have found that employment outside the home has tended to enhance the overall psychological well-being of women (Glass and Fujimoto 1994; Kessler and McRae 1981, 1982; McLanahan and Glass 1985; Pavalko and Smith 1999; Rosenfield 1992), especially if they are able to exercise some control over what they do on the job (Lennon 1994; Lennon and Rosenfield 1992; Matthews et al. 1998; Roxburgh 1996). Some studies show that women who like to combine a job with that of homemaker show the most positive levels of mental health among women working outside the home (Kessler and McRae 1981). Job satisfaction combined with a positive family life is cited as best for working wives. Unfortunately, many jobs that women perform have low levels of complexity, which reduce the possibilities for satisfaction (Lennon 1987, 1994; Wickrama et al. 1997).

Consequently, the degree to which employment outside the home has resulted in improved mental health for women generally is not clear. What is clear is that increased employment for women has not had a widespread negative impact on the psychological well-being of women working outside the home.

As for marriage, some research suggests that women are more likely to show psychological distress than men regardless of whether they are married (J. Fox 1980; Mirowsky and Ross 1995), but among those who are married (women as well as men) the quality of the relationship with the spouse appears especially important in maintaining a positive level of mental health (Gove, Hughes, and Style 1983). Marriage can carry health benefits—social, emotional, and economic support—that single women do not have (Ali and Avison 1997; Burton 1998; Waldron, Weiss, and Hughes 1998). Marriage, in fact, has mental health benefits for both men and women (Arber and Thomas 2001; Simon 2002). Wives also feel better if their husbands help with the housework (Bird 1999). Yet, whether in the home or on the job, the lives of women are often dependent on what others (usually men) do; hence they cannot control the possibilities for satisfaction as much as men can.

Some women are no doubt content to be wives and mothers; other women may find more satisfaction in establishing a career outside the home or combining a job with being a housewife. But others may experience conflict between being a homemaker or a career person or being both. Married women do have less control over their lives because of the demands of marriage and family and dependence on the careers of their husbands. This lack of control has been found to make women particularly vulnerable to psychological distress (Kessler and McLeod 1984; Mirowsky 1985; Rosenfield 1989; Thoits 1987). Therefore, in comparison to men, women are more prone to psychological distress in general and to anxiety and depression in particular. The social role of the woman appears highly significant in this process. Sarah Rosenfield (1989:77) summarizes the mental health differences between men and women by concluding that these differences exist "across cultures, over time, in different age groups, in rural as well as urban areas, and in treated as well as untreated populations."

RACE

One reflection of social inequality in the United States is the differences among the health profiles of racial groups. Asian Americans have typically enjoyed high levels of health, with blacks being especially disadvantaged. Hispanics and native Americans also have health disadvantages relative to whites. Comparisons of the health of racial minorities with whites in the United States will be reviewed in this section.

African Americans

A comparison of the life expectancy of African Americans and whites shows that black males are especially disadvantaged with respect to longevity. Table 3-4 shows that the black male with a life expectancy of 67.8 years in 1999 lives, on the average, 6.8 years less than the white male (74.6 years) and 12.1 years less than the white

TABLE 3-4 Average Number of Years of Life Expectancy in the United States by Race and Sex, since 1900.

Year	White Males	White Females	Black Males	Black Females
1900	46.6	48.7	32.5*	33.5*
1950	66.5	72.2	58.9	62.7
1960	67.4	74.1	60.7	65.9
1970	68.0	75.6	60.0	68.3
1980	70.7	78.1	63.8	72.5
1990	72.7	79.4	64.5	73.6
1995	73.4	79.6	65.2	73.9
1999	74.6	79.9	67.8	74.7

*Includes all nonwhites.

Source: National Center for Health Statistics, 2002.

female (79.9 years). The white female had a life expectancy in 1999 5.2 years greater than the black female.

Underlying the lessened life expectancy of blacks is a higher prevalence of several life-threatening illnesses, such as AIDS, cancer, heart disease, and hypertension (Braithwaite and Taylor 1992; King and Williams 1995; Polednak 1989). Hypertension or high blood pressure has been a particular health problem for blacks. Some 24 and 20 percent of all white males and females, respectively, over the age of twenty have hypertension compared to over 30 percent of all black males and females in the same age category. The end result is that proportionately more black people than white have hypertension. Various hypotheses have been suggested to explain this situation:

1. The genetic hypothesis argues that blacks are genetically different from whites in ways that predispose them to hypertension.
2. The physical exertion hypothesis postulates that blacks are more likely than whites to be engaged in manual labor, and that greater physical exertion leads to high mortality from hypertension.
3. The associated disorder hypothesis asserts that blacks are more prone to diseases such as pyelonephritis and syphilis that may result in secondary hypertension.
4. The psychological stress hypothesis theorizes that blacks are severely frustrated by racial discrimination and that this stress and the repressed aggression associated with it lead to a higher prevalence of hypertension.
5. The diet hypothesis emphasizes that blacks may have dietary patterns that increase their susceptibility to hypertension.
6. The medical care hypothesis argues that blacks receive poorer medical care than whites and that this results in greater morbidity and mortality from hypertensive disease and perhaps a higher prevalence of secondary hypertension.

The exact cause of the higher rates of hypertension among blacks is not known. Some research suggests that the genetic hypothesis and the psychological stress hypothesis contribute the most to providing an answer, since blacks in general—not just low-income blacks—have higher rates of hypertension than whites

TABLE 3-5   Age-Adjusted Death Rates for Selected Causes of Death, According to Race, United States, 1999*.

	Non-Hispanic Whites	Non-Hispanic Blacks	Hispanics	Asian/Pacific Islanders	American Indian/ Alaska Native
All causes	860.7	1,147.1	601.0	517.5	705.2
Heart disease	263.4	336.7	176.1	154.0	171.4
Cerebrovascular diseases	59.8	82.4	40.0	52.4	39.7
Cancer	199.8	254.4	122.0	125.3	126.4
Pulmonary disease	47.5	33.7	19.9	19.2	30.3
Pneumonia and influenza	23.4	25.6	15.6	15.6	22.0
Liver disease and cirrhosis	9.7	10.2	15.3	3.8	28.2
Diabetes	22.8	50.1	33.6	18.4	50.2
Accidents	35.7	40.9	47.1	17.7	87.6
Suicide	11.5	5.7	6.1	6.4	11.8
Homicide	3.8	20.6	8.4	3.3	10.6
AIDS	3.0	71.4	7.3	0.8	3.1

*Deaths per 100,000 resident population.

Source: National Center for Health Statistics, 2002.

(Hildreth and Saunders 1992). Other research, however, suggests that socioeconomic factors are particularly important because low-income blacks have three times more hypertension than affluent blacks (Polednak 1989). Rates of hypertension among blacks had declined somewhat since 1960 but remained the leading cause of death from kidney failure and a major contributor to deaths from end-stage renal disease, heart disease, and stroke.

Blacks also differ from whites and other races in relation to health problems other than hypertension. The extent of the disparity is shown in Table 3-5, which compares the mortality rate for selected causes of death for non-Hispanic whites, non-Hispanic blacks, Hispanics, Asians/Pacific Islanders, and American Indians/Alaska natives in 1999. For all causes, Table 3-5 shows that non-Hispanic blacks have the highest death rates of 1,147.1 per 100,000, followed by non-Hispanic whites (860.7), American Indians/Alaska natives (705.2), Hispanics (601.0), and Asians/Pacific Islanders (517.5). Non-Hispanic blacks have the highest mortality rates for each specific cause of death shown in Table 3-5, except for pulmonary (lung) disease (non-Hispanic whites), liver disease and cirrhosis, diabetes, accidents, and suicide (American Indians/Alaska natives). Particularly striking are the exceptionally high death rates for non-Hispanic blacks for heart disease, cerebrovascular diseases (stroke), cancer, homicide, and AIDS. Asians/Pacific Islanders, in contrast, have the lowest mortality rates, or close to it, for all causes of death.

Males are more likely to quit smoking than females.

When it comes to infant mortality, blacks are again disadvantaged. Black infants have traditionally had almost twice as high an infant mortality rate as white infants. In 1960, there were approximately 43 infant deaths per 1,000 black infants compared to an infant mortality rate of 22.9 among whites. Although rates of infant mortality have declined significantly for both races since 1960, the gap remains, as 1999 data show an infant mortality rate of 14.6 for blacks versus 5.8 for whites. A major factor causing this difference is poverty. Blacks are overrepresented among the poor, and the poor have the highest rates of infant mortality regardless of race (Hummer 1993; Polednak 1989).

The adverse health situation of African Americans identifies a pattern that is generally produced by socioeconomic, not biological factors (Hayward et al. 2000; Robert and House 2000; Schoenbaum and Waidmann 1997; Williams and Collins 1995). This does not mean that race and biology are unimportant when it comes to disease, as genetic research shows a few notable exceptions. For example, a gene variation usually absent in non-Hispanic whites and Hispanics but found in African Americans increases the risk of developing a rare type of abnormal cardiac rhythm or heartbeat that can be fatal (Splawski et al. 2002). Sickle cell anemia is also more prevalent among people of African origin. However, the concept of race in relation to health does not simply identify homogenous groups linked by a common biological inheritance. Rather, race represents the convergence of biological factors with geographic origins, and cultural, economic, political and legal factors, as well as racism, on health (Williams 1996). There is research showing, for example, that perceptions of racism and racial harassment are associated with poor health (Karlsen and Nazroo 2002). In this situation, the body's physiological defenses against disease are worn down by continuous exposure to adverse social conditions engendered by racism (Hayward et al. 2000).

But the most important overall factor appears to be socioeconomic status. Research by Mark Hayward and his colleagues (Hayward et al. 2000) demonstrates that a racial gap in health between middle-age blacks and whites exists for chronic health problems, with blacks living less longer and having more chronic conditions during their life span. Socioeconomic factors like poverty, marginal employment, low incomes, segregated living conditions, and inadequate education are more common among blacks than whites, and are features of socioeconomic stratification known to contribute to poor health (Link and Phelan 1995). Blacks are more likely than whites, for example, to live in disadvantaged neighborhoods characterized by disrepair, crime, danger, public drinking or drug use, and incivility. The daily stress associated with these neighborhood conditions has been linked to worse health on the part of the residents (Ross and Mirowsky 2001). Living in less safe neighborhoods also explains why adult blacks are less likely than non-blacks to show less participation in vigorous exercise as an outdoor activity (Grzywacz and Marks 2001). Socioeconomic conditions not only reduce opportunities for exercise, but they also promote risk behaviors. There is strong evidence that many blacks are at greater risk because of smoking, alcohol intake, and excess weight that contribute to high blood pressure, high cholesterol levels, and diabetes (LeClere, Rogers, and Peters 1998; Otten et al. 1990; Winkleby et al. 1998).

While factors that contribute to obesity are complex, involving a variety of causes, including genetics, Figure 3-1 shows the connection with race and income. Rates of obesity climbs as poverty rises, especially for racial minorities. Figure 3-1 shows that some 16 percent of whites earning $50,000 a year and over are obese and this rate increases to 19 percent for whites earning under $10,000. For blacks, however, some 22.5 percent are obese in the highest income category, and this rises to 34 percent for blacks who make under $10,000. About the same percentage of Hispanics as blacks are obese at the $50,000 and over level, but Hispanics are about midway (27 percent) between blacks and whites at the lowest income level. Not only do adult blacks get less exercise than whites (Grzywacz and Marks 2001), but consumer research shows they also tend to be heavy purchasers of frozen and canned foods, pork products, and starchy foods (Barboza 2000). Hispanics buy more vegetables than blacks, but additionally purchase large amounts of items high in saturated fats like lard and refried beans. Consequently, the lower an individual's income, the more likely they are to be obese and this is especially true for blacks and to a lesser extent for Hispanics.

Another significant health problem for African Americans is sexually transmitted diseases (STDs), such as syphilis and gonorrhea. There are no known biological reasons why racial or ethnic factors should enhance the risk of STDs and simply being poor and living in disadvantaged neighborhoods is not the entire answer as many Hispanics are also poor, but have lower STDs rates. In addition to poverty, joblessness, minimal access to health care, and a reluctance to seek treatment for

FIGURE 3-1   Race, income, and obesity, United States, 1999.

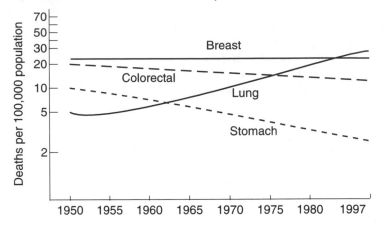

Source: Centers for Disease Control and Prevention, 2000.

STDs because of stigma, segregation is also a factor. Laumann and Youm (2001) find that blacks have the highest rates of STDs because of the "intra-racial network effect." They point out that blacks are more segregated than other racial/ethnic groups in American society and the high number of sexual contacts between an infected black core and its periphery of yet uninfected black sexual partners tends to contain the infection within the black population. Laumann and Youm determined that even though a peripheral (uninfected) African American has only one sex partner, the chance that partner is from a core (infected) group is five times higher than it is for peripheral whites and four times higher for peripheral Hispanics. And finally, it also needs to be noted that the limited availability of medical practitioners and facilities, as well as a lack of financial resources and information about health, are important barriers to health care for low-income blacks. For example, the few cardiac surgeons in predominantly black communities—especially in rural areas—has been cited as one reason elderly blacks receive fewer coronary artery bypass operations than elderly whites (K. Goldberg et al. 1992).

Many African Americans have taken advantage of the increased opportunities provided by the civil rights movement of the 1960s and significantly improved their life circumstances by acquiring the incomes, education, and quality of life of affluent whites. According to William Julius Wilson (1991, 1996), the social conditions available to poor, urban, isolated blacks who inhabit the core of the nation's central cities has worsened; rates of unemployment, out-of-wedlock births, households headed by females, dependency on welfare, and violent crimes have increased to their highest levels ever. While noting the importance of racism and discrimination, Wilson blames this development primarily on the increasing isolation of lower-class African Americans in a changing economy. He points out that both middle- and working-class blacks have moved out of ghetto neighborhoods in the inner city in search of safe places to live and better schools for their children. They have left behind a concentration of the most disadvantaged segments of the African American population—an underclass—whose social and economic isolation is more pronounced than ever before.

At the same time, the American economy has been shifting from manufacturing to a predominantly service and information-oriented base. This situation has produced extraordinary rates of joblessness for those persons (many of them low-income blacks) who lack the education and job skills needed to adapt to these economic changes. Consequently, the inner-city black poor rank among the most disadvantaged groups in American society, and this disadvantage extends to health and longevity. Several studies, as noted, show that differences in life expectancy between blacks and whites can be explained almost entirely by socioeconomic status (Braithwaite and Taylor 1992; Hayward et al. 2000; Polednak 1989). Jan Mutchler and Jeffrey Burr (1991:352) provide the best summary of this situation in their study of health differences between blacks and whites by noting that "most theoretical statements on the association between race and health highlight socioeconomic status as the critical intervening factor between race and health." While the gap between blacks and whites in health cannot be explained solely on the basis of socioeconomic factors, the relationship is particularly strong. According to Stephanie Robert and James House (2000:84): "In sum, race and socioeconomic position are inextricably linked to each other and to health, and hence one cannot be considered without the other."

Hispanic Americans

Because of immigration and high birth rates, Hispanics are the fastest growing minority group in American society and have overtaken blacks as the largest minority. This development represents a profound demographic shift in the United States. In 2000, non-Hispanic whites constituted 69.1 percent of the population, followed by Hispanics (12.5 percent), blacks (12.1 percent), Asians (3.7 percent), and native Americans/Alaska natives (0.7 percent). In 2050, nearly one out of every four Americans (24.5 percent) will be Hispanic. The non-Hispanic white population will have declined to 52.8 percent, with the proportion of blacks remaining stable at 13.6 percent and the Asian population rising to 8.2 percent.

Health data on Hispanics in the United States are limited because, until 1976, federal, state, and local agencies included Hispanics with non-Hispanic whites in the white category. Hispanics were also not included as a separate category on death certificates nationally until 1988. The approximately 15 years of data on Hispanics in the U.S. indicates that, in comparison to non-Hispanic whites, Hispanics have more diabetes, hypertension, tuberculosis, sexually-transmitted diseases, alcoholism, cirrhosis of the liver, homicide, and AIDS (Rogers, Hummer, and Nam 2000; Vega and Amaro 1994). Some 51.3 percent of all Hispanics in the United States, compared to 46.4 and 22.2 percent of non-Hispanic blacks and whites, respectively, are poor or near poor. That is, their incomes are below or just slightly above the poverty line. Despite the fact that many Hispanics live in disadvantaged circumstances, their overall health profile remains better than that of non-Hispanic blacks (Huie et al. 2002).

Moreover, Hispanics have lower mortality rates for heart disease and cancer than either non-Hispanic blacks or whites.

However, Hispanics are more likely than non-Hispanics to not have a regular source of health care and to use hospital emergency rooms as their primary source of medical services. They are more likely than any other racial/ethnic group in American society to not have health insurance, and many face cultural and language barriers in health care settings. Among Hispanics, Puerto Ricans report the worst health status and Cubans the best, with Mexican Americans and other Hispanics in the middle.

Native Americans

Native Americans, consisting of American Indians and native Alaskans, have shown a dramatic improvement in their overall level of health in the last forty years. There is evidence, for example, that the health of elderly native Alaskans is not significantly different from elderly whites in Alaska (Seccombe 1989). Moreover, in 1950, the infant mortality rate for American Indians and native Alaskans was 82.1 per 1,000 live births; in 1997–99, the mortality rate had dropped to 9.1 per 1,000 births. Life expectancy for native Americans in 1950 was 60 years, but stood at 71.1 years in 1992–94. Males lived an average of 67.2 years and females 75.1 years, which was less than whites but much higher than blacks in 1994 (see Table 3-4). Furthermore, American Indians and native Alaskans have the lowest death rates of cancer in the United States. Mortality rates from heart disease are for stroke not exceptionally high, but heart disease is still the leading cause of death for native Americans. Cancer is the leading cause of death for Alaska natives; in fact, native Alaskans have a 30 percent higher risk of dying from cancer than non-Hispanic whites in the United States. About 43 percent of native Alaskan men smoke and, not surprisingly, lung cancer takes the most lives in this population group.

American Indians have high mortality rates from diabetes. The rate of deaths from diabetes are 2.3 times higher among Indians than non-Indians and one tribe, the Pimas, has the highest rates of diabetes in the world. Diabetes among Pima Indians is ten to fifteen times higher than the general American population. The complications of diabetes take a further toll on Indians by increasing the probability of kidney disease, blindness, and heart disease. Indians also suffer more dysentery, strep throat, sexually transmitted diseases, and hepatitis than other Americans. Other significant health problems of American Indians are alcoholism, tuberculosis, dietary deficiency, cirrhosis of the liver, and gastrointestinal bleeding. In addition, chronic otitis media, a severe ear ailment that arises when simple ear infections are not treated, occurs among 10 percent of all Indian children.

So while American Indians have experienced a significant improvement in their overall level of health, important problems remain. The leading causes of death for Indians and Alaskan natives after heart disease are accidents, cancer, liver disease and cirrhosis, stroke, pneumonia, influenza, homicide, and diabetes. More American Indians die from accidents, primarily automobile accidents, than members of any other racial group in the United States.

Another major problem for Indians and Alaska native males is suicide. American Indian and Alaska native male suicide victims are typically younger than those in the general population with suicide peaking at ages fifteen to forty-four, compared with the non-Indian population in which suicides usually occur after the age of forty. For fifteen- to twenty-four-year-old males, the mortality rate from suicide during 1999 was 36.6 per 100,000 compared to 10.7 for the U.S. population (Center for Health Statistics 2002). Non-Hispanic white males were second in suicides in this age group with a death rate of 17.8 per 100,000, followed by blacks (14.4), Hispanics (11.9), and Asian and Pacific Islanders (10.3). In addition to particularly high rates of diabetes, accidents, and suicides, Indians have an exceptionally high prevalence of alcoholism, with most Indian families affected either directly or indirectly by the alcohol abuse of one or more of its members.

Asian Americans

Another example of the importance of socioeconomic factors in relation to health is found by examining data that include Asian Americans. Asian Americans have the highest levels of income, education, and employment of any racial/ethnic minority group in the United States, often exceeding levels achieved by the white population. Consequently, it is not surprising that the lowest age-adjusted mortality rates in the United States are those of Asian Americans. Asians and Pacific Islanders in the United States showed an age-adjusted mortality rate in 1999 of 517.5 per 100,000, which was the lowest of any racial/ethnic group in the nation.

Heart disease is the leading cause of death for Asians, but mortality from this disease is less than that of whites and other minorities. Deaths from cancer, stroke, automobile accidents, AIDS, homicide, and suicide are lowest as well. Overall, Asians and Pacific Islanders are the healthiest racial group in American society.

When infant mortality rates for the United States are reviewed, the health advantage of Asian Americans becomes even more apparent. Table 3-6 shows Japanese and Chinese Americans with the lowest rates. According to Table 3-6, infant mortality in the United States has drastically declined since 1950. The most striking decline, as previously noted, has been that of American Indians from 82.1 deaths per 1,000 live births in 1950 to 9.3 in 1999, the most recent year comparative data are available. The decline for Chinese and Japanese Americans has been almost as great in terms of relative proportion, but the rates were much smaller to begin with and therefore not as dramatic. In 1999, Table 3-6 shows that blacks had the highest infant mortality rates (14.1 per 1,000), followed by Native Americans (10.0), Hispanics (6.1), non-Hispanic whites (6.0), Chinese Americans (5.2), and Japanese Americans (3.2).

Besides illustrating the low infant mortality rates of Japanese and Chinese Americans, with Chinese Americans having the lowest rates of all, Table 3-6 also indicates some other patterns of interest. In 1950, Native Americans had the highest infant mortality rates—almost twice as high as that of blacks. By 1970, Native American infant mortality rates had dropped so sharply that they were lower than the rates for blacks. While infant mortality rates for blacks had declined by more than two-thirds (43.9 versus 14.0) between 1950 and 1999, the black rate was over twice as high as that of

TABLE 3-6   Infant Mortality Rates by Race, United States, Selected Years 1950–1999*.

		RACE				
Year	Black	Native American	Chinese American	Japanese American	Hispanic	White
1950	43.9	82.1	19.3	19.1	—	26.8
1960	44.3	49.3	14.7	15.3	—	22.9
1970	32.6	22.0	8.4	10.6	—	17.8
1977	23.6	15.6	5.9	6.6	—	12.3
1984	18.7	14.3	8.3	6.0	9.3	8.9[†]
1987	17.8	13.0	6.2	6.6	8.2	8.2[†]
1991	16.6	11.3	4.6	4.2	7.1	7.0[†]
1996	14.1	10.0	5.2	3.2	6.1	6.0[†]
1999	14.0	9.3	2.9	3.4	5.7	5.8[†]

*Infant mortality rate is the number of deaths for infants under one year of age per 1,000 live births.
[†]Non-Hispanic whites.

Source: National Center for Health Statistics, 1986, 2002.

non-Hispanic whites (26.8 versus 5.8) in 1999. Hence, the gap between black and white infant mortality rates has not only remained constant, but increased, even though infant deaths from both racial groups have fallen (Singh and Yu 1995).

Although infant mortality rates are only one indicator of health in a society, they are nevertheless an important measure of the quality of life available to a population. Such rates, along with the other data discussed in this section, point toward the fact that Asian Americans enjoy the best health in the United States.

Race: Conclusion

Some afflictions such as hypertension, diabetes, and sickle cell anemia have a genetic basis, but living conditions associated with poverty influence the onset and course of most physical health problems (Hart 1991; Hayward et al. 2000; Marmot 1996; Otten et al. 1990; Wilkinson 1996). Tuberculosis, for example, was nearly extinct in the United States but resurfaced in the late 1980s and early 1990s with the greatest concentration among the poor. Alcoholism, drug abuse, suicide, homicide, lead poisoning, and influenza and pneumonia, along with heart disease and cancer, are more prevalent among the lower class (Braveman and Tarimo 2002; Lahelma 2001; Link and Phelan 2000; Mirowsky, Ross, and Reynolds 2000; Mulatu and Schooler 2002; Robert and House 2000; Wermuth 2003; Winkleby et al. 1992). Race becomes an especially significant variable for physical health in American society because many racial minority persons occupy a disadvantaged social and economic position. This is especially the case for blacks (Braithwaite and Taylor 1992; Ferraro and Farmer 1996; Hayward et al. 2000; Mutchler and Burr 1991; Smaje 2000). As previously noted, the differences in life expectancy of blacks and whites can largely be explained by differences in socioeconomic status.

When it comes to mental health, there is little or no support for the claim that there is a significant difference among races in overall rates of mental disorder, except the relatively low rates for Asian Americans (Cockerham 2003; D. Williams and Harris-Reid 1999). An extensive nationwide study by Ronald Kessler and his associates (1994) finds that there are no mental disorders where either lifetime or active prevalence is significantly higher among blacks than whites. Nor were there significant lifetime or active prevalence differences between Hispanics and non-Hispanic whites.

Social class, however, is an exceptionally strong predictor of mental distress (Cockerham 2003; Kessler et al. 1994; McLeod and Nonnemaker 2000). If race and socioeconomic status jointly influence depression, the effects appear limited to the lower class, with poor blacks possibly more psychologically distressed than poor whites (Kessler and Neighbors 1986; Ulbrich, Warheit, and Zimmerman 1989). Other research shows lower-class white males with higher rates of psychiatric illness than their black male counterparts (D. Williams, Takeuchi, and Adair 1992), or no significant difference between the two groups (Cockerham 1990). Consequently, there is debate concerning the extent of differences in mental health between blacks and whites within the lower class (D. Williams and Harris-Reid 1999). In general, socioeconomic status appears much more important than race in explaining mental disorder.

Furthermore, the time is rapidly coming when racial/ethnic health differences in the United States will no longer be based primarily on comparisons between whites and blacks, but will be multiracial. Both the Hispanic and Asian populations are rapidly increasing. Between 1990 and 1998, the Hispanic population increased by 35 percent and Asians/Pacific Islanders more than 40 percent. Hispanics not only live in large numbers in Texas, California, and New York, but their population literally doubled in Arkansas, Georgia, Nevada, and North Carolina. Totaling 35.3 million people or 12.5 percent of the total population in 2000, Hispanics have surpassed African Americans in overall numbers. Whereas the Asian/Pacific Islander population remains relatively small at almost 10.5 million people or almost 4 percent of the population, their rapid growth increased their numbers twofold in Nevada and nearly doubled in Georgia and North Carolina. This is a major change as Asians/Pacific Islanders had formerly concentrated in Hawaii and the West Coast. The Hispanic population will be an increasingly separate and major comparison group in future studies of health issues, while Asians/Pacific Islanders will represent a much larger and more important racial category than in the past.

SOCIOECONOMIC STATUS

To be poor is by definition to have less of the things (including health care) produced by society. This situation is seen in the experience of the poor in obtaining health services in the United States. Before the 1930s, those who were unable to pay for health care were largely dependent on charity. In addition, many of the urban clinics providing treatment for the poor were established and maintained primarily as teaching facilities for medical and nursing students. In such cases, education was the primary goal of the institution, although the provision of charity care was also important. Since the 1930s, there has been a considerable increase in the number and types of facilities as well as an improvement in the quality of care available to the poor. Yet problems remain. Despite evidence of more frequent visits to physicians made possible by greater health insurance coverage through government-sponsored programs (Medicaid and Medicare), the poor are still treated within the framework of welfare medicine and live on a day-to-day basis within an environment of poverty. Obtaining equal access to care is a major step in improving the health of the general population. However, improved access to health services is only part of the solution for advancing health. The fact remains that people at the bottom of society have the worst health of all, regardless of what country they live in, what type of health insurance they have, and the level of health care they receive.

In the United States and elsewhere in the world, socioeconomic status is one of the strongest and most consistent predictors of a person's health and life expectancy (Braveman and Tarino 2002; Cockerham 1999; Lahelma 2001; Link and Phelan 1995, 2000; Marmot 1996; Marmot, Bobak, and Smith 1995; Mirowsky, Ross, and Reynolds 2000; Mulatu and Schooler 2002; Robert and House 2000; Schor and Menaghan 1995; Wermuth 2003; Wilkinson 1996; D. Williams 1990; Winkleby et al. 1992). As Marilyn Winkleby and her colleagues (1992) determined, this finding persists across all diseases with few exceptions and throughout the life span. Socioeconomic status typically consists of measures of income, occupational status or prestige, and level of education. Although interrelated, each of these measures reflects different dimensions of a person's position in the class structure of a society. In studies of health and illness, income reflects spending power, housing, diet, and medical care; occupation measures status, responsibility, physical activity, and health risks associated with work; and education is indicative of a person's skills for acquiring positive social, psychological, and economic resources (Winkleby et al. 1992:816). While income and occupational status are important, the strongest single predictor of good health appears to be education. Well-educated people are generally the best informed about the merits of a healthy lifestyle and the advantages of seeking preventive care or medical treatment for health problems when they need it. In sum, education promotes healthy living and the ability to solve problems. For example, in a study of health in Finland, Denmark, Sweden, Norway, Hungary, and England and Wales, Finnish medical sociologists Eero Lahelma and Tapani Valkonen (1990) found that education allowed comparisons between countries more readily than income or occupation. In each country, persons with less education had the highest mortality rates.

Elsewhere, in a major study in the United States, Catherine Ross and Chia-ling Wu (1995) found that well-educated people—in comparison to the poorly educated—are more likely to have fulfilling, subjectively rewarding jobs, high incomes, less economic hardship, and a greater sense of control over their lives and their health. The well-educated are also less likely to smoke and more likely to exercise, get checkups from physicians, and drink alcohol moderately. The Ross and Wu study is important because it explains why the relationship between education and health is particularly strong. This relationship, in fact, gets stronger over the life course as less-educated persons have increasingly more sickness and disability, and die sooner than the well-educated (Arber 1993; House et al. 1994; Pappas et al. 1993; Robert and House 2000; Ross and Wu 1996). Sara Arber (1993), for instance, studied chronic illness over the life course and found that by the time lower-class British men and women reached old age, they were significantly less healthy than better educated and more affluent elderly persons. The highest levels of chronic illness were among unskilled workers and the lowest among higher professionals. Class differences in health were more modest below age twenty-five but increased thereafter. The lower class also had greater physical disability, and the difference became especially pronounced among the elderly.

Therefore, as several studies report, lower socioeconomic groups have the poorest health and shortest life spans. These studies have been conducted in different countries in Western Europe (A. Fox 1989; Illsley and Svensson 1986; Kunst et al. 1998; Lahelma and Valkonen 1990; Leclerc 1989; Valkonen 1987, 1989; Whitehead 1998) and in Russia and Eastern Europe (Bobak et al. 1998; Cockerham 1997b, 1999; Shkolnikov et al. 1998), as well as in the United States (Adler et al. 1994; Pappas et al. 1993; Robert 1998; J. Smith 1999; Wray et al. 1998) and other countries like Canada (Frohlich and Mustard 1996; Humphries and Doorslaer 2000; Trovato 1994), Great Britain (Arber 1993, 1997; Borooah 1999; Chandola 2000; Hart 1991; Macintyre 1986; Marmot 1996; Marmot, Bobak, and Smith 1995; Townsend, Davidson, and Whitehead 1990; Wilkinson 1996), Finland (Gissler et al. 1998; Poppius et al. 1999), Britain and Finland (Lahelma et al. 2000; Rahkonen, Arber, and Lahelma 1995; Rahkonen et al. 2002), Finland and Norway (Sihvonen et al. 1998), Germany (Mielck et al. 2000), the Netherlands (Kunst, Looman, and Mackenbach 1990; Spruit 1990), Belgium (Lagasse et al. 1990), Italy (Piperno and DiOrio 1990), Spain (Regidor et al. 2002; Regidor, Gutierrez-Fisac, and Rodríguez 1995; Rodríguez and Lemkow 1990), Spain and France (Lostao et al. 2001); Israel (Shuval 1990), Poland (Wnuk-Lipinski 1990; Watson 1998), Bulgaria (Carlson and Tsvetarsky 1992), Hungary (Carlson 1989), the Czech Republic (Hraba et al. 1998), and even Sweden (Blank and Diderichsen 1996; Diderichsen 1990; Hemström 1999; Lundberg 1986, 1992; Sundquist and Johansson 1997) where social equality in living conditions is among the best in the world.

Additional evidence on the significance of social class for health comes from Europe, where, as in the United States, women have a distinct advantage in life expectancy over men, but lower-class European women live less long than women in higher socioeconomic groups (Arber 1989). Social-class differences in health affect both men and women, although class distinctions appear to influence male mortality the most (McDonough et al. 1999). Regardless of gender, people living in poverty and reduced socioeconomic circumstances have the greatest exposure to risk factors that produce ill health. These risk factors are physical (poor sanitation, overcrowding, extreme temperatures), chemical (pollution), biological (bacteria, viruses), psychological (stress), and lifestyle (poor diets, smoking, alcohol and drug abuse, lack of leisure-time exercise) in origin. Exposure to these factors is generally dependent upon a person's socioeconomic status, since individuals at the bottom of the society confront them significantly more often than people residing higher on the social ladder. "All of us stand somewhere on this ladder," states Helen Epstein (1998:27), "and the nearer we are to the bottom, the sicker we are likely to be and the younger we are likely to die."

Equality of Care: The British Experience

Since many health disorders appear related to poverty, it is a logical assumption that if poverty were not a factor retarding the availability of quality medical care, the incidence and prevalence of illness in the lower social classes would be reduced. Following World War II, socialized medicine was introduced in Great Britain to provide the lower classes with the same medical care available to the upper classes. It should be noted, however, that poverty and social class differences remained—only health care was supposedly equalized. Results have shown that the equalization of health care alone has not reduced the disparity in health between social classes. Mortality rates remained higher for lower classes. Britain's experiment failed to reduce health disparities precisely because living conditions and lifestyles could not be equalized; the physical environment of poverty and poor nutrition continued to adversely affect lower-class health.

Ivan Reid, in his book *Social Class Differences in Britain* (1998), examines the extent to which the British social classes differ with respect to health in a review of data taken largely from the British government's *General Household Survey*. Health in Britain improved significantly for all social classes during the twentieth century, but mostly for the upper classes. The lower classes continue to show several health disadvantages, such as higher infant mortality, lower birth weight, more chronic disability, more absence from work due to illness, lower life expectancy, and higher ratios of risk factors like obesity and smoking. Reid attributes the health differences between the classes to a combination of factors, namely, wealth, personal habits, diet, home environment, exercise, mental stress, and differing occupational hazards. He also points out that the lower classes visit physicians more often than the other classes. This trend, which is similar to that in the United States, is consistent with the fact that the lower classes have more health problems.

Richard Wilkinson (1996) explains that prior to the 1980s it was widely assumed in Britain that society was becoming more egalitarian. Social class differences were believed to be becoming less important because of the growth of welfare services. This assumption was shattered, however, by the publication in 1980 of the Black Report, which not only found that there were very large differences between mortality rates among occupational groups but also that these differences were not declining. British workers in lower-status occupations were clearly not living as long as those persons at the top of the occupational scale, and this trend was not improving.

Among the better studies researching this situation is that of Michael Marmot and his colleagues (1984, 1991), who investigated the mortality of over 17,000 British male civil government employees. Known as the Whitehall studies, this research provided especially strong evidence of social class differences in mortality. The men were classified according to their job, with senior administrators ranked at the top, followed by professionals/executives, clerical, and other (which consisted of jobs lowest in status such as messengers and other unskilled manual workers). In the first study, these men, whose ages at the time ranged from forty to sixty-four, were initially interviewed in the late 1960s with respect to their health habits and then reinvestigated ten years later in relation to mortality. Regardless of the cause, those with the highest occupational rank had the lowest percentage of deaths, and the percentages increased across job categories with the lowest-ranked occupations having the highest percentage of deaths. In other words, the lower the status, the higher the mortality.

Marmot (1996) notes that it seemed unlikely at the time that social class differences in deaths would be as large for the civil servants as they were for the country as a whole. This assumption was made because the jobs were all stable, provided security, and presumably were free of chemical and physical hazards. Yet Marmot (1996:43) indicates that he and his associates were surprised "to discover that the nearly threefold difference in mortality between the bottom and top grades of the civil service was larger than the difference between the top and bottom social classes in national mortality data." They (Marmot et al. 1991) therefore conducted a second Whitehall study to check their results and found the same pattern. As in the first study, each group had worse health than the one above it in the social hierarchy. What Marmot and his associates had uncovered was a social gradient from high to low in mortality. "In the higher grades of the civil service," states Marmot (1996:48), "there is no poverty, yet those who are near the top have worse health than those at the top and the gradient continues all the way down." This pattern is seen in Table 3-7, which shows the mortality rates from the Whitehall I study. Most of the

TABLE 3-7   Percentage of British Civil Government Employees Dying over a Ten-Year Period (1969–1979) by Civil Service Grade and Cause of Death.

Cause of Death	Senior Administrators	Professional/ Executive	Clerical	Other
Lung cancer	0.35	0.73	1.47	2.33
Other cancer	1.26	1.70	2.16	2.23
Heart disease	2.16	3.58	4.90	6.59
Stroke	0.13	0.49	0.64	0.58
Other cardiovascular	0.40	0.54	0.72	0.85
Chronic bronchitis	0.00	0.08	0.43	0.65
Other respiratory	0.21	0.22	0.52	0.87
Gastrointestinal	0.00	0.13	0.20	0.45
Genitourinary	0.09	0.09	0.07	0.24
Accidents/violence	0.00	0.13	0.17	0.20
Suicide	0.11	0.14	0.15	0.25
Other deaths	0.00	0.16	0.26	0.40
All causes	4.73	8.00	11.67	15.64

Source: Adapted from M. G. Marmot, M. J. Shipley, and Geoffrey Rose, "Inequalities in Death—Specific Explanations of a General Pattern," *Lancet,* 83 (1984), 1004.

men died from heart disease, and Table 3-7 shows, for example, that 2.16 percent of the senior administrators died from this cause and the percentage of deaths increased across job ranks with "other" showing a percentage of 6.59. For deaths from all causes, Table 3-7 shows that 4.73 percent of the senior administrators died compared to 8.00 percent of the professional/executives, 11.67 percent of the clerical workers, and 15.64 percent of the other occupations.

An intriguing aspect of this study is the finding of a social gradient in mortality across job positions linked to differences in hierarchy rather than deprivation. As noted, these men all had stable, secure, and hazard-free jobs. They were all white-collar workers, most were Anglo-Saxon, many wore the same dark suits and had similar haircuts, and all were middle-class (Epstein 1998). And they all had access to free health care provided by the British National Health Service. There were some differences, however, as those with the highest-ranked job positions had bigger houses, all owned cars, and they smoked less and were slimmer overall. And, of course, the men in the highest jobs lived longer than those in the next highest, and the same pattern was repeated down the civil service ranks. As Epstein (1998:27) explains:

> Perhaps the most surprising finding of the Whitehall study at the time was that everyone in the hierarchy seemed to be vulnerable to the effects of social status, not just those at the bottom. Even a small increment in social status could be reflected in statistics on life and death. For example, "administrators," those in the civil service who design policies and set the strategies for executing them, were half as likely to have a fatal heart attack as the "executives" who ran the various departments and carried out the policies dictated to them by the administrators. For the clerks, who worked for the executives, the risk of a fatal heart attack was three times as high as it was for the administrators.
>
> The risk of dying of a heart attack increased steadily, right down the chain of command. For the remaining support staff, such as assistant clerks and data processors, the risk was four times as high for the administrators. These were middle-class people, and yet all of them seemed to be part of some mortal gradient. In his book *Unhealthy Societies* [1996], the British economist Richard Wilkinson writes that if a virus or something was killing as many civil servants as the professional hierarchy itself seemed to be, the Whitehall buildings would be evacuated and closed down.

If the social gradient in mortality among British civil servants is extended to modern societies generally, then we find that the highest social strata (the upper class) lives longer than the next highest (the upper middle class) although both are affluent and neither is materially deprived (Evans, Barer, and Marmor 1994). And the upper middle class lives longer than the lower middle class and so on down the social scale until the lower class is reached. So it is not only the case that people at the top of society live longer than those at the bottom, but also that the different classes live less long than those higher than them and have greater longevity than those below them. The reasons for the existence of this gradient are not yet known, but current research centers on differences between socioeconomic groups and classes in self-esteem and stress levels (Evans, Barer, and Marmor 1994), the effects of income inequality (Wilkinson 1996), deprivation through the life course (Power and Hertzman 1997), and health lifestyles and social support (Cockerham, Hattori, and Yamori 2000). The causality debate surrounding the social gradient thesis "is not a boxing match," states James Smith (1999:165), "in which a knockout blow will eventually be delivered." Rather, the answer is likely to be a combination of factors, since the relationship between class position and health is complex and is ultimately to be found in the social environment (Marmot et al. 1998).

What is also suggested by studies such as those of Marmot and his colleagues is that medical care alone cannot counter the adverse effects of class position on health. The evidence is clear that a significant gap in health and life expectancy continues to persist in Britain—despite improved access to medical care (Adonis and Pollard 1997; Annandale 1998; Arber 1993; Bartley, Blane, and Smith 1998; Bartley and Plewis 1997; Blaxter 1990; Borooah 1999; Bury 1997; Chandola 2000; Hardey 1998; Macintyre 1986, 1997; Marmot 1996; Nettleton 1995; Reid 1998; Townsend, Davidson, and Whitehead 1990; Wilkinson 1986, 1996). As indicated by the 1980 Black Report, a government-sponsored assessment of trends in British health, the lower class had the highest rates of illness, disability, and infant mortality and the lowest life expectancy. The lower class also used prenatal and preventive health care services less frequently than members of more affluent classes. So while medical care was equalized and subsequently utilized more often by the poor, the use of services was directed significantly more toward treatment of existing health problems than prevention. The Black Report provided strong evidence that "the lower down on the social scale you are, the less healthy you are likely to be and the sooner you can expect to die" (Abercrombie et al. 1988:352).

The Black Report placed the blame for class differences in levels of health squarely on the socioeconomic environment—smoking, work accidents, overcrowding, poor living conditions, exposure to dampness and cold, and the like. An update of the Black Report for the decade of the 1980s was compiled by Margaret Whitehead (1990). She determined that, while the health of the British population in general and the lower class in particular continued to improve throughout the 1980s, serious social inequities in health remained. Whitehead (1990:351–352) concluded:

> Whether social position is measured by occupational class, or by assets such as house and car ownership, or by employment status, a similar picture emerges. Those at the bottom of the social scale have much higher death rates than those at the top. This applies at every stage of life from birth through to adulthood and well into old age.
>
> Neither is it just a few specific conditions which account for these higher death rates. All the major killer diseases now affect the poor more than the rich (and so do most of the less common ones). The less favoured occupational classes also experience higher rates of chronic sickness and their children tend to have lower birth-weights, shorter stature and other indicators suggesting poorer health status.
>
> The unemployed and their families have considerably worse physical and mental health than those in work. Until recently, however, direct evidence that unemployment *caused* this poorer health was not available. Now there is substantial evidence of unemployment causing a deterioration in mental health, with improvements observed on re-employment.

Equally poor housing, and even worse living situations, exist not only in Great Britain but in other industrialized nations like the United States—not to mention the miserable conditions of the poor who live in underdeveloped countries. The point is that equality in medical care alone cannot change differences in levels of health between social classes.

J. Rogers Hollingsworth (1981) investigated this situation in England and Wales for the period 1891 to 1971 and suggests that societies wishing to equalize levels of health across social classes should consider equalizing income and educational attainment. In a particularly well-designed study, Hollingsworth analyzed changes in technology and structure of the health care delivery systems in England and Wales in relation to changes in health (as measured by mortality) across social classes and geographic regions during the same time span. He hypothesized that as medical technology becomes more effective and the costs increase, there will be a rising public demand that the state increase its responsibility for providing health services. This will result in greater centralization of decision making. As medical care systems become more centralized, medical services will become more accessible to all social classes and regions, thereby suggesting that there should be a convergence in levels of health.

Public demand for greater government involvement in providing medical services (influenced by rising costs) resulted in the centralization of care under a National Health Service (NHS). The NHS made those services more accessible to all social classes. However, there was not a convergence in levels of health across classes though there was some convergence across regions. Mortality rates for all classes declined, but, as noted, the gap between the classes was not significantly reduced. In other words, everyone in Britain tended to live longer, but the upper classes continued to live longer than anyone else. This result occurred even though the lower classes over time began using medical services more than the middle and upper classes.

Hollingsworth notes that income is inequitably distributed in Britain and this inequality is reflected in a wide variation in lifestyles. Education also remains unevenly distributed, and educational levels may be more important than income in explaining differences in health. Hollingsworth (1981:281) concludes "that even though the British National Health Service is the most egalitarian one in the Western world, gross inequalities in levels of health are likely to persist across social classes as long as gross inequities in the distribution of income and education persist."

Modern Diseases and the Poor

The lower class, even in modern nations, suffers more from the typical diseases of past human existence, like influenza and tuberculosis, in comparison to the upper and middle classes. Heart disease, in contrast, has traditionally been associated with an affluent way of life. The incidence was usually high in rich countries and low in poor countries. Yet there have been variations with respect to heart disease between different nations and within countries among people of the same ethnic background with different life experiences. Japan, for example, has shown a relatively lower rate of heart disease despite being one of the most technologically advanced nations of the world. Diet and stress-reducing activities like periodic group vacations and after-work socializing for Japanese males have been thought to contribute to the low mortality rates from heart disease. In recent years, however, heart disease has been increasing in Japan, especially with the spread of Western eating habits. West-ernization of the Japanese diet is considered responsible for the replacement of stroke by heart disease as Japan's second leading cause of death (Powell and Anesaki 1990). This pattern underscores the significance of lifestyle in influencing the distribution of disease. As societies change and environments are modified, the style of living and types of activities available to members of the various social classes also change.

Consequently, in the United States there has been a change in the incidence of heart disease. Rates of heart disease have declined dramatically in the past thirty years for all Americans, but the decline has been greatest among the upper and mid-dle classes. The result is that coronary heart disease is now concentrated more among the poor. The difference is that more obesity, smoking, and stress occur in the lower class, in addition to higher levels of blood pressure, less leisure-time ex-ercise, and poorer diets.

The lower class, therefore, appears to be especially disadvantaged in regard to health. This disadvantage extends not only to communicable diseases associated with unhealthy living situations but also to chronic health problems like heart dis-ease that are more prevalent in modern, industrialized countries and strongly af-fected by how one lives. Clearly, there is more to health than the availability of med-ical care. Lifestyle and social/environmental conditions, along with preventive health measures, primarily determine health status. A healthy lifestyle includes the use of good personal habits like eating properly, getting enough rest, exercising, and avoiding practices like smoking, abusing alcohol, and taking drugs. However, the type of lifestyle that promotes a healthy existence is more typical of the upper and middle classes who have the resources to support it. The most important rela-tionship between social class and health is the manner in which social class affects the opportunities a person has for a generally healthy life. Crowded living condi-tions, poor diet, inferior housing, low levels of income and education, and increased exposure to violence, alcoholism and problem drinking, smoking, and drug abuse—all combine to decrease the life chances of the poor.

The lower class is also disadvantaged with respect to mental health. The basic finding of most studies is that the highest overall rates of mental disorder are found in the lower class, including schizophrenia—the most severely disabling form of mental illness (Cockerham 2003; Kessler et al. 1994). Anxiety and mood disorders, however, tend to be more prevalent among the upper and middle classes, yet the lower class suffers from these problems as well. Why the relationship between mental disorder and social class position exists is not known, but it may be due to genetics or greater stress in coping with the conditions of poverty, or both. Conse-quently, for mental as well as physical difficulties, socioeconomic factors are major determinants of the types and extent of an individual's health problems.

SUMMARY

This chapter has discussed the social demography of health from the standpoint of age, sex, race, and social class. The section on age disclosed that as more and more persons live to older ages in American society, marked changes are likely to occur in society in general and health care delivery in particular. The new generation of the aged, however, is likely to be the most affluent, educated, and healthy in American history. As for sex differences, females generally have a very definite advantage over males with regard to life expectancy. This advantage involves both biological and social-psychological factors. White Americans also have a definite advantage in health over nonwhite Americans, with the exception of Asians. However, the most significant sociodemographic variable affecting nonwhites is that they are likely to be poor, and poverty, as far as healthy living conditions and medical care is concerned, may be equated with second-rate circumstances. In Great Britain, socialized medicine failed to reduce health differentials between the social classes because social class differences themselves were not reduced. Equal access to medical care could not, by itself, overcome the adverse effects of poverty. The lower class suffers not only from more illness and disability, but also shows the highest rates of mental disorder.

SOCIAL DEMOGRAPHY OF HEALTH INTERNET SITES

Age

1. National Aging Information Center; Demographic Trends and Projections.
   http://www.aoa.dhhs.gov/NAIC/Notes/trendsproject.html

   U.S. population statistics, special reports, and demographic links.

2. National Institute on Aging Demography Centers.
   http://www.agingmeta.psc.isr.umich.edu/resources.html

   Provides links to several demographic data sites and ongoing studies dealing with aging and the elderly.

3. United Nations; the Aging of the World's Population.
   http://www.un.org/esa/socdev/ageing/agewpop.htm

   Statistical trends and prediction of world aging as determined by the United Nations Population Division.

4. U.S. Census Bureau:
   a. Age data from the national, state, and county level.
   http://www.census.gov/population/www/socdemo/age.html

   b. Resident population estimates of the United States by age and sex: April 1, 1990, to April 1, 1999.
   http://www.census.gov/population/estimates/nation/intfile2-1.txt

Gender

1. Centers for Disease Control and Prevention, Health Topic: Women's Health.
   http://www.cdc.gov/health/womensmenu.htm

   Statistics regarding HIV, pregnancy-related mortality, and breast and cervical cancer, as well as reproductive health information.

2. Centers for Disease Control and Prevention, Health Topic: Men's Health.
   http://www/cdc.gov/health/mensmenu.htm

   Links to information regarding various diseases affecting men.

3. The National Women's Health Information Center (NWHIC).
   http://www.4woman.org

   A project of the Office of Women's Health, U.S. Department of Health and Human Services. Provides links and information regarding women's health issues.

Race, Socioeconomic Status

1. CDC Wonder, Mortality/Population Data Request.
   http://www.wonder.cdc.gov

   Allows for data searches for mortality by state, race, gender, age, and year (this site is a part of the CDC).

2. Centers for Disease Control and Prevention, Chronic Disease Prevention: Minority and Ethnic Groups.
   http://www.cdc.gov/nccdphp

   Statistics regarding diabetes, infant mortality, cancer, and cardiovascular disease.

3. U.S. Census Bureau, International Database.
   http://www.census.gov/ipc/www/idbnew.html

   Demographic and socioeconomic data for 227 countries.

4. Department of Health and Human Services, Office of Civil Rights.
   http://www.dhhs.gov/ocr

   Descriptions and links to documents and bills dealing with various aspects of health care relative to racial groups, ethnicities, genders, and the like.

5. The Minority Health Network.
   http://www.pitt.edu/AFShome/e/j/ejb4/public/html/min/

   Site developed by an alliance of experts in health and communications that seeks to develop health information structures for the prevention of disease.

CHAPTER

4

Social Stress

Social influences upon the onset and the subsequent course of a particular disease are not limited to such variables as age, sex, race, social class, and the conditions of poverty as they relate to lifestyle, habits, and customs. It is also important to recognize that interaction between the human mind and body represents a critical factor in regard to health. Social situations can cause severe stress that, in turn, affects health and longevity. By way of illustration, an extreme case is "the death of the twenty-seven-year-old army captain who had commanded the ceremonial troops at the funeral of President Kennedy. He died ten days after the President of a 'cardiac irregularity and acute congestion' according to the newspaper report." (Engle 1971:774)

Stress can be defined as a heightened mind-body reaction to stimuli inducing fear or anxiety in the individual. Stress typically starts with a situation that people find threatening or burdensome (Pearlin 1989). Examples of stressful situations include divorce (Aseltine and Kessler 1993; Booth and Amato 1991; Horwitz, White, and White 1996), unpleasant work conditions (Fenwick and Tausig 1994; Pavalko, Elder, and Clipp 1993; Siegrist 2001; Swisher et al. 1998; Tausig and Fenwick 1999), widowhood (Umberson, Wortman, and Kessler 1992), unemployment (B. Turner 1995), migration (Shuval 2001), and high credit card debt (Drentea 2000; Drentea and Lavrakas 2000). A review of selected sociological theories developed by Charles Cooley, William I. Thomas, Erving Goffman, and Emile Durkheim will serve to illustrate how social processes, from the standpoint of both the individual and the wider society, can lead to stress.

COOLEY, THOMAS, AND GOFFMAN: SYMBOLIC INTERACTION

Cooley, Thomas, and Goffman reflect the symbolic interactionist approach to human behavior, which views human group life from the perspective of the individual. Based upon the work of George Herbert Mead (1865–1931), this approach sees the individual as a creative, thinking organism who is able to choose his or her behavior instead of reacting more or less mechanically to the influence of social processes. It assumes that all behavior is self-directed on the basis of symbolic meanings that are shared, communicated, and manipulated by interacting human beings in social situations. Of special relevance to a sociological understanding of stress is Charles H. Cooley's (1864–1929) theory of the "Looking-Glass Self." Cooley (1964) maintained that our self-concepts are the result of social interaction in which we see ourselves reflected in other people. Cooley compares the reflection of our self in others to our reflections in a looking glass:

> Each to each a looking glass
> Reflects the other that doth pass.

Cooley's looking-glass self-concept has three basic components: (1) We see ourselves in our imagination as we think we appear to the other person; (2) we see in our imagination the other person's judgment of our appearance; and (3) as a result of what we see in our imagination about how we are viewed by the other person, we experience some sort of self-feeling, such as pride or humiliation. The contribution of this theory to an understanding of stress is that an individual's perception of himself or herself as a social object is related to the reaction of other people. Quite obviously stress could result from the failure of the observer to reflect a self-image consistent with that of the subject. Thus, stress can be seen as having a very definite social and personal component based on perception of a social situation.

The work of William I. Thomas (1863–1947) is also relevant for its understanding of crisis as residing in the individual's "definition of the situation" (Volkart 1951). Thomas stated that as long as definitions of a social situation remain relatively constant, behavior will generally be orderly. However, when rival definitions appear and habitual behavior becomes disrupted, a sense of disorganization and uncertainty may be anticipated. The ability of an individual to cope with a crisis situation will be strongly related to socialization experiences that have taught the person how to cope with new situations.

Consequently, Thomas makes two particularly important contributions concerning stress. First, he notes that the same crisis *will not produce the same effect uniformly in all people.* Second, he explains that adjustment to and control of a crisis situation result from an individual's ability to compare a present situation with similar ones in the past and to revise judgment and action upon the basis of past experience. The outcome of a particular situation depends, therefore, upon an individual's definition of a situation and upon how that individual comes to terms with that situation. As David Mechanic (1978:293) states, "Thomas's concept of crisis is important because it emphasizes that crises lie not in situations, but rather in the interaction between a situation and a person's capacities to meet it."

Erving Goffman (1922–1982) is noted for the dramaturgical or "life as theatre" approach. Goffman (1959) believed that in order for social interaction to be possible, people need information about the other participants in a joint act. Such information is communicated through (1) a person's appearance; (2) a person's experience with other similar individuals; (3) the social setting; and (4) most important, the information a person communicates about himself or herself through words and actions. This fourth category of information is decisive because it is subject to control by the individual and represents the impression the person is trying to project—which others may come to accept. This information is significant because it helps to define a situation by enabling others to know in advance what a person expects of them and what they may expect of him or her. Goffman calls this process "impression management."

Goffman says people live in worlds of social encounters in which they act out a line of behavior, a pattern of verbal and nonverbal acts by which individuals express their view of a situation and their evaluation of the participants, particularly themselves. The positive social value individuals claim for themselves by the line that others assume they have taken during a particular encounter is termed a "face." This face is an image of self projected by the individual to other people. One's face is one's most personal possession and is the center of security and pleasure, but Goffman is quick to point out that a person's face is only on loan from society and can be withdrawn if the person conducts himself or herself in an inappropriate manner. A person may be in the "wrong face" when information about that person's social worth cannot be integrated into his or her line of behavior or a person may be "out of face" when he or she participates in an encounter without the line of behavior that participants in the particular situation would be expected to take.

Goffman further explains that the maintenance of face is a condition of interaction, not its objective. This is so because one's face is a constant factor taken for granted in interaction. When people engage in "face-work," they are taking action to make their activities consistent with the face they are projecting. This is important because every member of a social group is expected to have some knowledge of face-work and some experience in its use, such as the exercise of social skills like tact. Goffman sees almost all acts involving other people as being influenced by considerations of face; for example, a person is given a chance to quit a job rather than be fired. A person must be aware of the interpretations that others have placed upon his or her behavior and the interpretations that he or she should place upon their behavior. Therefore, Goffman's view of the self is that it has two distinct roles in social interaction: first, the self as an image of a person formed from the flow of events in an encounter; and second, the self as a kind of player in a ritual game who copes judgmentally with a situation. This aspect of Goffman's work identifies the calculative element in dealings between people and presents them as information managers and strategists maneuvering for gain in social situations (Manning 1992).

Goffman's principal contribution to our understanding of stress arises from his claim that the self is a sacred object. The self is more important than anything else to us because it is always with us and represents who we are. For someone to challenge the integrity of that self as a social object is an embarrassing situation. Each self is special, and in social relationships that very special self we have tried to nourish and protect for a lifetime is put on display. Goffman has said that role-specific behavior is based not upon the functional requirements of a particular role, but upon the *appearance* of having discharged a role's requirements. Thus, stress could be induced when people fail in their performance. Otherwise, people might not be so willing to take such great care that they act out lines of behavior considered appropriate to their situation.

The symbolic interaction perspective, as reflected in the work of Cooley, Thomas, and Goffman, contributes to our understanding of stress by identifying the key variable in the stress experience: the perception of the individual. People vary in their interpretation of situations, but ultimately it is the way in which they perceive the strains and conflicts in their roles, tasks, personal relationships, and other aspects of their life situation that causes them to feel stressed. How people feel about themselves (Cooley), define situations (Thomas), or manage impressions (Goffman) can lead to the creation of stressful conditions. People typically cope with stress by trying to change their situation, manage the meaning of the situation, or keep the symptoms of stress within manageable bounds (Pearlin 1989).

DURKHEIM: FUNCTIONALISM

While symbolic interaction theory emphasizes interpersonal forms of interaction, functionalist theory focuses on the influence of the larger society on individuals. Functionalist theory is derived from the initial work of the French sociologist Emile Durkheim (1858–1917). Durkheim was concerned with those social processes and constraints that integrate individuals into the larger social community. He believed that when a society was strongly integrated, it held individuals firmly under its control (Durkeim 1950, 1956). Individuals were integrated into a society as a result of their acceptance of community values reinforced through social interaction with others believing in the same value system. Especially important were participation in events celebrating a society's traditions and also involvement in work activities.

As members of society, individuals were constrained in their behavior by laws and customs. These constraints were "social facts," which Durkheim (1950:13) defined as "every way of acting, fixed or not, capable of exercising on the individual an external constraint." What Durkheim suggests is that society has an existence outside of and above the individual. Values, norms, and other social influences descend on the individual to shape his or her behavior. Social control is, therefore, real and external to the individual.

Among Durkheim's works, the most pertinent to an understanding of the social determinants of stress is his 1897 study *Suicide* (1951). In explaining the differential rates of suicide among various religious and occupational groupings, Durkheim suggested that suicide was not entirely a matter of free choice by individuals. He believed that suicide was a social fact explainable in terms of social causes. Durkheim distinguished between three major types of suicide, each dependent upon the relationship of the individual to society. These three types were (1) egoistic suicide, in which people become detached from society and, suddenly on their own, are overwhelmed by the resulting stress; (2) anomic suicide, in which people suffer a sudden dislocation of normative systems where their norms and values are no longer relevant, so that controls of society no longer restrain them from taking their lives; and (3) altruistic suicide, in which people feel themselves so strongly integrated into a demanding society that their only escape seems to be suicide.

Durkheim's typology of suicide suggests how a society might induce enough stress among people to cause them to take their lives. Egoistic suicide is a result of stress brought about by the separation of a strongly integrated individual from his or her group. Durkheim uses the example of the military officer who is suddenly retired and left without the group ties that typically regulated his behavior. Egoistic suicide is based upon the overstimulation of a person's intelligence by the realization that he or she has been deprived of collective activity and meaning. Anomic suicide is characterized by an overstimulation of emotion and a corresponding freedom from society's restraints. It is a result of sudden change that includes the breakdown of values and norms by which a person has lived his or her life. Sudden wealth or sudden poverty, for example, could disrupt the usual normative patterns and induce a state of anomie or normlessness. In this situation a chronic lack of regulation results in a state of restlessness, unbounded ambition, or perhaps crisis, in which norms no longer bind one to society.

Whereas egoistic and anomic forms of suicide are both due to "society's insufficient presence in individuals" (Durkheim 1951:256), altruistic suicide represents the strong presence of a social system encouraging suicide among certain groups. Suicide in the altruistic form could be characterized as the avoidance of stress by people who prefer to conform to a society's normative system rather than risk the stress of opposing it. Examples of altruistic suicide are the practice of hara-kiri in Japan, where certain social failures on the part of an individual are expected to be properly redressed by his or her suicide, or the traditional Hindu custom of the widow committing ritual suicide at her husband's funeral.

Although altruistic suicide is relatively rare in Western society, stories do appear in the mass media of people killing themselves for reasons that could be considered egoistic or anomic. Yet the significance of Durkheim's orientation toward social processes for the understanding of the stress phenomenon extends well beyond the issue of suicide, since this is only one of many possible ways a person might find to cope with social and psychological problems. What is particularly insightful is

Durkheim's notion of the capability of the larger society to create stressful situations where people are forced to respond to conditions not of their own choosing.

For example, in a series of studies, M. Harvey Brenner (Brenner and Mooney 1983; Brenner 1987a, 1987b) linked increased incidence of heart disease, stroke, kidney failure, mental illness, and even infant mortality in the United States and several Western European countries to downturns in the economy. Brenner's thesis is that there are few areas of our lives not intimately affected by the state of the economy. He argues that economic recession increases the amount of stress on an individual by comparing economic cycles with health statistics. Brenner found that heart attacks increase during periods of recession. Usually the first wave of deaths follows the recession by three years, with a second wave occurring five to seven years after the recession. The lag was thought to be due to the length of time it takes heart disease to cause death. Waves of kidney failure deaths generally lagged two years behind a recession, while death from strokes took about two to four years to follow an economic downturn. Infant mortality rates were particularly striking during periods of recession, according to Brenner. Mothers suffering from the stresses of the recession tended to have higher blood pressure and be less healthy themselves, thereby giving birth to children whose chances for survival had likewise been weakened.

What causes stress during an economic recession was the intensified struggle for the basic necessities of life (food, clothing, shelter, health care, and education for children) and a possible loss of self-satisfaction and social status associated with unemployment while trying to survive on savings and welfare. These stresses were often found to be enhanced by a rise in drinking and smoking at the same time. What is happening, suggests Brenner, is that social stress from economic conditions increases exposure to the major risk factors known to accompany many health disorders.

Earlier, Brenner (1973) focused on the relationship between the economy and mental health. He examined rates of employment and mental hospital admissions in New York over a period of 127 years from 1841 to 1968. He believed that regardless of the number and combination of factors that predispose certain individuals toward becoming mentally ill, a question that needed to be answered was why mental disorder appears *when* it does. Brenner found that rates of mental hospitalization increased during economic downturns and decreased during upturns, thereby suggesting that economic factors may precipitate mental disorder.

Brenner provided two explanations for his findings. He preferred a "provocation" hypothesis that stress resulting from being dislocated from one's usual lifestyle or prevented from improving it during a downward shift in the economy caused vulnerable people to reach the point at which they required hospitalization in a mental institution. Another explanation is also possible and is described by Brenner as an "uncovering" hypothesis. This alternate view suggests that economic downturns do not promote mental disorder but simply "uncover" those people already mentally ill by stripping them of their existing economic resources. These people who are mentally "borderline" may be able to support themselves during periods of economic affluence, only to become the first to lose their jobs when times are bad.

In fact, in a declining economic cycle, mental hospitals may be an attractive source of food and shelter for these marginal individuals.

Although Brenner prefers the hypothesis that economic downturns "provoke" mental disorder, his data also support the finding that such downturns "uncover" mentally disordered people. Additional research is needed to determine whether "provocation" or "uncovering" is actually at work; to a significant degree both hypotheses may be relevant. The import of Brenner's work is that it shows that downward trends in economic activity may stress certain people to the point that they require mental hospitalization, particularly those with the fewest financial resources.

Even though the research of Brenner (1973), Catalano and Dooley (1977; Dooley and Catalano 1984), and others (Fenwick and Tausig 1994; Pearlin et al. 1981; Reynolds 1997; Tausig and Fenwick 1999; J. Turner 1995) demonstrates how large-scale societal processes, specifically those of economic change, can be correlated with adverse physical and mental health, the relationship is not that simple. It is very difficult to substantiate a precise, cause-and-effect relationship between a major social event like an economic depression and health problems of a particular individual because of the wide range of variables that may intervene in the individual's situation and modify the effect. Possible intervening variables could be those of personality, social support, genetics, social class, or socialization. For instance, research on the effects of social support (feelings of being loved, accepted, cared for, and needed by others) on persons subjected to unemployment (T. Atkinson, Liem, and Liem 1986), stressful life events (Ensel and Lin 1991; Haines and Hurlbert 1992; Matt and Dean 1993), sexual assault (Ruch and Chandler 1983), occupational stress (Loscocco and Spitze 1990), homelessness (Schutt, Meschede, and Rierdan 1994), and natural disasters (Haines, Hurlbert, and Beggs 1996) shows that social support can act as a buffer against stress. Social support is typically obtained within families, but can be acquired generally through the community by individuals who live alone by way of social interaction with friends, relationships at one's place of religious worship, and involvement in local groups and clubs (N. Lin, Ye, and Ensel 1999; Rogers 1996). Those persons with the strongest level of social support had fewer health problems than did those with little or no support.

Nevertheless, the fact remains that social and economic conditions beyond the direct influence or control of the average person can create stressful circumstances that force people to respond to them. For vulnerable people, the stressful circumstances may promote ill health.

STRESS

The theories of Durkheim, Cooley, Thomas, and Goffman demonstrate a relationship between social interaction and stress, but they do not explain the effect of stress upon the human body. Embarrassment and psychological discomfort can be socially painful, yet the effects of stress can transcend the social situation and cause physiological damage as well. Hence, a physiological perspective of stress must be considered.

Walter Cannon (1932) believed that the real measure of health is not the absence of disease but the ability of the human organism to function effectively within a given environment. This belief was based upon the observation that the human body undergoes continuous adaptation to its environment in response to weather, microorganisms, chemical irritants and pollutants, and the psychological pressures of daily life. Cannon called this process of physiological adaptation *homeostasis,* which is derived from the Greek and means "staying the same." Homeostasis refers to the maintenance of a relatively constant condition; for example, when the body becomes cold, heat is produced; when the body is threatened by bacteria, antibodies are produced to fight the germs; and when the body is threatened by an attack from another human being, the body prepares itself either to fight or to run.

As an organism the human body is thus prepared to meet both internal and external threats to survival, whether these threats are real or symbolic. A person may react with fear to an actual object or to a symbol of that object—for example, a bear versus a bear's footprint. In the second case, the fear is not of the footprint but of the bear that the footprint represents. Threats in contemporary urban societies could include types of stimuli such as heavy traffic, loud noises, or competition at work, all of which can produce emotional stress related more to a situation than to a specific person or object.

Whether the stressful situation actually induces physiological change depends upon an individual's perception of the stress stimulus and the personal meaning that the stimulus holds. A person's reaction, for instance, may not correspond to the actual reality of the dangers that the stimulus represents; that is, a person may overreact or underreact. Thus, there is considerable agreement that an individual's subjective interpretation of a social situation is the trigger that produces physiological responses (Moss 1973). Situations themselves cannot always be assumed beforehand to produce physiological changes.

Physiological Responses to Stress

Cannon (1932) formulated the concept of the "fight or flight" pattern of physiological change to illustrate how the body copes with stress resulting from a social situation. When a person experiences fear or anxiety, the body undergoes physiological changes that prepare it for vigorous effort and the effect of possible injury. Physiological changes in the body as a result of stress situations primarily involve the autonomic and neuroendocrine systems. The autonomic nervous system controls heart rate, blood pressure, and gastrointestinal functions—processes that occur automatically and are not under the voluntary control of the central nervous system. The autonomic nervous system is delicately balanced between relaxation and stimulation and is activated primarily through the hypothalamus, which is located in the central ventral portion of the brain. It is composed of two major divisions, the parasympathetic and the sympathetic systems. The parasympathetic system is dominant when there is no emergency and regulates the vegetative processes of the body such as the storing of sugar in the liver, the constriction of the pupil of the eye in response to intense light, and the decreasing of heart rate. When there is an emergency, the sympathetic system governs the body's autonomic functions and increases heart rate so that blood flows swiftly to the organs and muscles that are needed in defense. It also inhibits bowel movements and dilates the pupil of the eye in order to improve sight.

Besides the autonomic nervous system, the endocrine glands perform an important role in the body's physiological reaction to stress. The neuroendocrine system consists of the adrenal and pituitary glands, the parathyroids, the islets of Langerhans, and the gonads. They secrete hormones directly into the bloodstream because they lack ducts to carry their hormones to particular glands. The two glands that are the most responsive to stress situations are the adrenal and pituitary glands. The adrenal gland secretes two hormones, epinephrine and norepinephrine, under stimulation from the hypothalamus. Epinephrine accelerates the heart rate and helps to distribute blood to the heart, lungs, central nervous system, and limbs; it also makes the blood coagulate more readily so that as little blood as possible will be lost in case of injury. Norepinephrine raises blood pressure and joins with epinephrine to mobilize fatty acids in the bloodstream for use as energy. The function of the pituitary gland is, upon stimulation by the hypothalamus, to secrete hormones that, in turn, stimulate other endocrine glands to secrete their hormones.

At first, most medical scientists believed that only the adrenal gland was involved in stress reaction; however, in 1936 Hans Selye demonstrated the existence of a pituitary-adrenal cortical axis as having a profound effect upon body metabolism. Selye (1956) developed a theory known as the *general adaptation syndrome*. He believed that after an initial alarm reaction, a second stage of resistance to prolonged stress was accomplished primarily through increased activity of the anterior pituitary and adrenal cortex. If stress continued and pituitary and adrenal defenses were consumed, Selye indicated that a person would enter a third stage of exhaustion. He described this third stage as a kind of premature aging due to wear and tear on the body. However, it now seems that the entire endocrine system, not just the pituitary and adrenal glands, is involved in some manner in stress reaction. Under acute stimulus, hormone secretions by the endocrine glands increase; under calming influences, secretions decrease.

Most threats in modern society are symbolic, not physical, and they do not usually require a physical response. Today the human organism faces emotional threats with the same physical system used to fight enemies, yet modern society disapproves of such physical responses as fighting. Socially the human organism is often left with no course of action, perhaps not even verbal insults. This inability to respond externally leaves the body physiologically mobilized for action that never comes, a readiness that can result in damage to the body.

A number of studies have shown that the human organism's inability to manage the social, psychological, and emotional aspects of life—to respond suitably to a social situation—can lead to the development of cardiovascular complications and hypertension, peptic ulcers, muscular pain, compulsive vomiting, asthma, migraine headaches, and other health problems (House 1974, 2002; Siegrist 1996b, 2001). From Germany, a particularly impressive series of studies by medical sociologist Johannes Siegrist and his associates has documented the relationship between stress and cardiovascular disease among male blue-collar workers and middle managers

(Peter and Siegrist 1997; Siegrist 1996a, 1996b, 2001; Siegrist et al. 1990, 1997; Siegrist and Peter 1996). These studies have demonstrated the effects of stress on the cardiovascular system through measures of quality of life, work load, job security, coping styles, emotional distress, and sleep disturbances and shown how the failure to cope with job-related stressors promotes heart disease. Siegrist suggests that high personal effort (competitiveness, work-related overcommitment, and hostility) and low gain (poor promotion prospects and a blocked career)—the effort–reward imbalance model—are associated with higher risk of heart disease. Research involving blue-collar workers in Germany (Siegrist 1996b, 2001) and civil servants (the Whitehall II study) in Britain (Bosma et al. 1998) confirms the model.

SOCIAL FACTORS AND STRESS

There is a considerable amount of empirical research in medical sociology dealing with stress and stress-related topics. Selected findings will be reviewed here, to include relevant research on social stressors, stress adaptations, group influences, death from overwork, changes in life events, and socioeconomic status. The intent of this section is to show how contemporary sociologists are helping to improve our understanding of stress.

Stressed mother attending crying baby, while trying to get ready to leave for her job at the same time.

Social Stressors

One way understanding is being improved is through the identification of social stressors. Leonard Pearlin (1989) suggests two major types: life events and chronic strains. First, there is the stress of life events like divorce, marriage, or losing one's job. Second are chronic strains that are relatively enduring conflicts, problems, and threats that many people face on a daily basis. Chronic strain includes role overload, such as the strain associated with work and being a parent (Simon 1992) or trying to advance one's career over the life course (Pavalko, Elder, and Clipp 1993). It also involves conflicts within role sets, like those between husbands and wives, interrole conflict where a person has too many roles, role captivity in which a person is an unwilling incumbent of a role like being trapped in an unpleasant job or marriage, or role restructuring in which a person changes relationships within roles (Aseltine and Kessler 1993; Booth and Amato 1991; Burton 1998; Horwitz et al. 1996; Jackson 1997; Simon 1997; Waldron, Weiss, and Hughes 1998). As Pearlin (1989:245) observes, role strains can have serious effects on individuals because the roles themselves are important, especially when they involve jobs, marriage, and parenthood.

Stress Adaptation

Mechanic (1962b, 1978) attempts to explain the stress experience from the standpoint of both society and the individual. He draws on the work of William I. Thomas (Volkart 1951), who pointed out that the meaning of crisis lies not in the situation, but rather in the interaction between the situation and the person's ability to rise above it. The outcome or effect of a crisis depends on how well a person comes to terms with the situation. Stress, therefore, refers to difficulties experienced by the individual as a result of perceived challenges.

BOX 4-1   Stress, Age, and Credit Card Debt

Does high credit card debt cause anxiety? Patricia Drentea (2000) studied this situation in a statewide survey in Ohio. She found that age makes a difference in that younger people were more likely to be stressed over high credit card debt than older people. A major reason as to why this is the case may be that of income. Younger people usually have less money and Drentea found that anxiety increased when the ratio of debt to income is greatest. This was especially likely if the person was in default. Drentea explains that younger people in the United States have come of age during a period of unprecedented growth in materialism, thereby promoting a culture of consumerism. Buying goods and services now and postponing paying for them is common. Moreover, debt anxiety is more typical among younger adults, in part because they are undergoing significant job and family transitions—a situation that is made more difficult by economic hardship. Consequently, anxiety during young adulthood may be associated with the amount of debt that is incurred and Drentea's research helps us to understand the relationship between stress, age, and credit card debt.

Mechanic believes that in social situations people have different skills and abilities in coping with problems; not everyone has an equal degree of control in managing emotional defenses nor the same motivation and personal involvement in a situation. In analyzing any particular situation, an observer must consider not only whether an individual is prepared to meet a threat, but also whether he or she is motivated to meet it.

Extending his concept of stress from the individual to societal components, Mechanic states that a person's ability to cope with problems is influenced by a society's preparatory institutions, such as schools and the family, two organizations designed to develop skills and competencies in dealing with society's needs. A person's emotional control and ability to cope are also related to society's incentive systems—that is, society's rewards (or punishments) for those who did (or did not) control their behavior in accordance with societal norms. As for a person's involvement or motivation in a situation, Mechanic explains that society's evaluative institutions provide norms of approval or disapproval for following particular courses of action.

Hence, the extent of physiological damage or change within an individual depends on (1) the stimulus situation, which includes the importance of the situation to the individual and the extent of his or her motivation; (2) an individual's capacity to deal with the stimulus situation, such as the influence of genetic factors, personal skills, innate abilities, and past experiences; (3) the individual's preparation by society to meet problems; and (4) the influence of society's approved modes of behavior. Mechanic (1962b:8) emphasizes the contribution of society toward an individual's adaptation to stress by stating "that whether or not a person experiences stress will depend on the means, largely learned, that [the person] has available to deal with his [or her] life situation."

Mechanic's model represents an important contribution toward our understanding of stress by showing the importance of adaptation and explaining how that adaptation is based on an individual's perception of life situations, combined with his or her degree of preparation by society to cope with stressful circumstances. Mechanic thus identifies adaptability as the key variable in whether a person will eventually suffer organic damage. This view is consistent with Peggy Thoits's (1994) finding that people are not necessarily passive when faced with stressful situations, but often work to resolve the problems causing them stress.

Stress and the Social Group

People's perceptions of an event may be influenced by their intelligence, past experience, socialization, and awareness of stimuli, but the influence of group membership is also important. Gordon Moss (1973) illustrates the significance of group membership in helping individuals cope with information they find stressful. He suggests that stress and physiological change are likely to occur when people experience information that goes against their beliefs or desires. Moss notes that information processing produces changes in the central nervous system, the autonomic nervous system, and the neuroendocrine system, all of which can alter the susceptibility to disease among certain people. The most vulnerable persons are those whose physiological responses are easily elicited and likely to be more pronounced and prolonged. Moss emphasizes the advantages of group membership in providing social support for the individual. Subjective feelings of belonging, being accepted, and being needed have consistently shown themselves to be crucial in the development of feelings of well-being and the relieving of symptoms of tension. Thus, Moss's work joins that of others (Haines and Hurlbert 1992; N. Lin, Ye, and Ensel 1999; Matt and Dean 1993; Schutt et al. 1994; and Thoits 1995) to show how the social support rendered by families and groups helps reduce the potentially harmful effects of stress upon the body and mind.

Furthermore, there is often a tendency among members of small groups to develop a consensus about how social events should be perceived; this process minimizes individual differences, reduces uncertainty, and maintains group conformity. Conformity to group-approved attitudes and definitions has long been hypothesized in sociology and social psychology as reducing anxiety by ensuring acceptance from persons and groups important to the individual. Much of human behavior is seen as the result of an individual's search for relief from anxiety by conforming to authority and group norms.

Life Changes

Another important factor in the production of stress is the occurrence of significant changes in a person's life experiences. Research in this area has generally focused on the reactions of people both to extreme situations, like wars and natural disasters, and to ordinary life events. This research is reviewed in the next two subsections.

Extreme Situations   Extreme situations like natural disasters would appear to be a likely source of stress because of the great anxiety people usually attach to being caught in such circumstances. But a common misconception about disasters is that people flee in panic from the site of a potential disaster area. In reality, it is usually difficult to get people to evacuate their homes, even when the possibility of damage or destruction is imminent. Some people are even attracted to potential disasters and take risks to see a tidal wave, tornado, or hurricane. Trying to view a disaster and being a victim of one, however, are two entirely different matters. Past research has shown that such extreme situations as earthquakes, tornados, and hurricanes can induce stress (Haines et al. 1996). Mass media reports commonly show or describe people in large-scale disasters as experiencing intense feelings of grief, loss, anguish, and despair.

Thus, there is sound reason for understanding the social and psychological consequences of disasters, especially from the standpoint of developing and implementing programs to assist disaster victims. But few people become severely psychotic in the face of major disasters, and incapacitating psychological reactions are unusual in catastrophes. This is not to say that disaster victims generally escape all psychological trauma—quite the contrary. There is almost unanimous agreement that disasters do promote acute psychological stress, emotional difficulties, and anxiety related to coping with grief, property damage, financial loss, and adverse living conditions. Kathleen Tierney and Barbara Baisden (1979:36) state that "while few researchers would claim that disasters create severe and chronic mental illness on a wide scale, victim populations *do* seem to undergo considerable stress and strain and *do* experience varying degrees of concern, worry, depression, and anxiety, together with numerous problems in living and adjustment in postdisaster." Groups of people with special needs in the aftermath of disasters are usually children and the elderly. Older people, in particular, find it difficult to adjust to life after a disaster. And, as research on elderly flood victims in Kentucky shows, they may also suffer from severe fatigue when great personal loss and high community destruction occurs (Phifer, Kaniasty, and Norris 1988). Low-income groups also present special problems in that often they are left without any material resources and become especially dependent on aid.

A pattern that emerges in studies of natural disasters and psychopathology is that the disaster experience, though severe, is usually short in duration, and the effects on mental health likewise tend to be short-term and self-limiting. The question thus arises about the possible effects of stress in extreme situations lasting long periods of time, such as the experiences of people exposed to the brutalities of Nazi concentration camps and the horrors of war. There is evidence that many concentration camp survivors have suffered persistent emotional problems and are particularly prone to physical illness and early death (Eitinger 1964, 1973). However, as Aaron Antonovsky (1979) notes, other concentration camp survivors adjusted to the effects of having been subjected to a most terrible experience and are now living lives that are essentially normal. Antonovsky (1979:7) states:

> More than a few women among the concentration camp survivors were well adapted, no matter how adaptation was measured. Despite having lived through the most inconceivably inhuman experience, followed by Displaced Persons camps, illegal immigration to Palestine, internment in Cyprus by the British, the Israeli War of Independence, a lengthy period of economic austerity, the Sinai War of 1956, and the Six Day War of 1967 (to mention only the highlights), some women were reasonably healthy and happy, had raised families, worked, had friends, and were involved in community activities.

When considering what differentiates people who are generally vulnerable to stress-related health problems (not just concentration camp survivors) from those who are not so vulnerable, Antonovsky argues that a strong sense of coherence is the key factor. Coherence, in his view, is a personal orientation that allows an individual to view the world with feelings of confidence, faith in the predictability of events, and a notion that things will most likely work out reasonably well. One achieves this sense of coherence as a result of life experiences in which one meets challenges, participates in shaping outcomes (usually satisfactory), and copes with varying degrees of stimuli. Hence, the person has the resources to cope with unexpected situations if they arise. However, people whose lives are so routine and completely predictable that their sense of coherence as previously defined is weakened will find it difficult to handle unpleasant surprises and events. They are likely to be more susceptible to stress-induced health dysfunctions as they are overwhelmed by events. What Antonovsky appears to be saying is that people who have the capability to come to terms with their situation rather than to be overcome by it are those who are most likely to emerge in a healthy condition.

A similar conclusion can be made about soldiers fighting in combat. Environmental stresses faced by combat infantrymen are among the hardest faced by anyone. These stresses include the overt threat of death or injury, the sight and sounds of dying men, battle noise, fatigue, loss of sleep, deprivation of family relationships, and exposure to rain, mud, insects, heat, or cold—all occasioned by deliberate exposure to the most extreme forms of violence intentionally directed at the soldier by the opposing side. Charles Moskos (1970) has compared combat with the Hobbesian analogy of primitive life—both can be nasty, brutish, and short. Yet somehow men generally come to terms with the circumstances, since most combat soldiers do not become psychiatric casualties. Two factors may be largely responsible. First is the existence of external group demands for discipline and efficiency under fire. Observing helicopter ambulance crews and Green Berets in Vietnam, Peter Bourne (1970), a psychiatrist, found these soldiers were subject to strong group pressures to be technically proficient regardless of friendship ties. This finding was particularly true of the Green Berets, who urged their detachment leaders to prove themselves in combat in order to be worthy of their role. Although at times this social pressure added to the stress of the leaders, when the entire group faced an enemy threat there was unusual group cohesion and considerable conformity in the manner in which the threat was perceived and handled.

Second, Bourne suggests that there is a further psychological mobilization of an internal discipline in which the individual soldier employs a sense of personal invulnerability, the use of action to reduce tension, and a lack of personal introspection to perceive his environment in such a way that personal threat is reduced. Whether Bourne's findings are representative of other types of combat soldiers is subject to question, since helicopter ambulance crews and Green Berets are highly self-selected volunteers for hazardous duty. Nevertheless, Bourne's study supports the conclusion of others (Kellett 1982; Rado 1949) that one of the most efficient techniques that allows soldiers generally to adjust to battle is to interpret combat not as a continued threat of personal injury or death but as a sequence of demands to be responded to by precise military performances. In failing to find significant physiological change (excretion of adrenal cortical steroids) occurring among most soldiers during life-threatening situations, Bourne suggests that the men allowed their behavior under stress to be modified by social and psychological influences that significantly affected physiological responses to objective threats from the environment.

Some research has shown relatively long-lasting effects of stress on a few Vietnam combat veterans, such as posttraumatic stress disorders (intense feelings of demoralization, guilt, anger, active expression of hostility, perceived hostility of others) among soldiers exposed to particularly abusive violence usually involving civilians (Laufer, Gallops, and Frey-Wouters 1984) or, in the case of depression, among those who were predisposed to depression in the first place (Helzer 1981). For most people, however, the effects of stress resulting from exposure to extreme situations are that such situations are relatively rare, and whatever stresses are generated among those persons are usually temporary and disappear after a while. Many people are not emotionally affected at all, even though the circumstances are exceedingly stressful. Consequently, as Bruce Dohrenwend (1975:384) pointed out, if stressful situations play a major role in causing mental disturbance, the relevant events must be more ordinary and frequent experiences in the lives of most people, such as marriage, birth of a first child, death of a loved one, loss of a job, and so on. Though such events are not extraordinary in a large population, they are extraordinary in the lives of the individuals who experience them.

Life Events   Life events research does not focus on one particular life event (for example, exposure to combat) and claim that it is more stressful than another life event (for example, unemployment). Rather, it is based on the assumption that the *accumulation* of several events in a person's life eventually builds up to a stressful impact. Current research suggests, for example, that accumulated effects of stressful events over time is harmful to health (R. Turner and Lloyd 1995; R. Turner, Wheaton, and Lloyd 1995). However, what types of events, in what combinations, over what periods of time, and under what circumstances promote stress-induced health problems is not at all clear at the present time.

An important area of contention in life events research, for example, is the issue of whether any type of change in one's life, either pleasant or unpleasant, produces significant stress, or whether stress is largely a result of unpleasant events only. Considerable evidence supports the idea that any type of environmental change requiring the individual to adapt can produce a specific stress response (Selye 1956). Barbara Dohrenwend (1973) concluded from her research on heads of families in the Washington Heights area of New York City that stressfulness is best conceived as emanating from life change itself rather than from just the undesirability of certain life events.

Most research, however, clearly comes down on the side of unpleasant events as being of prime importance (Thoits 1995). Lloyd Rogler and August Hollingshead (1965) compared a matched set of twenty "well" families with twenty "sick" families (defined as having either the husband or wife or both diagnosed as schizophrenic) of lower-class status in Puerto Rico. Based upon recall of life events by the subjects and others in the community, the study found no significant differences in the family lives of the normals and schizophrenics during childhood and adolescence. Members of both groups were exposed to the same conditions of poverty, family instability, and lower-class socialization. There was also a lack of difference in their respective adult lives, with the notable exception that for those persons who became schizophrenic, there was a recent and discernible period—*prior to the appearance of overt symptomatology*—during which they were engulfed by a series of insoluble and mutually reinforcing problems. Schizophrenia thus seemed to originate from being placed in an intolerable dilemma brought on by adverse life events largely stemming from intense family and sexual conflicts related to unemployment and restricted life opportunities.

Robert Lauer (1974) investigated whether the rate or speed of change and the type of change, either positive or negative, were the most important variables in stress produced by change. Though stress was directly related to the perceived rate of change, his findings indicated that the effect of rapid change can be moderated by whether the change was perceived to be desirable. Rapid change and undesirability were the most stressful conditions. Still other research by John Mirowsky and Catherine Ross (Mirowsky and Ross 1989) found that the undesirability of events predicts distress better than change alone does. Ross and Mirowsky observed that the effects of desirable events, ambiguous events, change per se, and the number of events experienced are not especially significant. They conclude that undesirability is *the* characteristic of life events most associated with increased psychological distress. Moreover, research by George Brown and Tirril Harris (1978) on depression among women in London found that long-term depression results from negative circumstances, not positive ones. Losing one's job is an undesirable life event that can also have potentially harmful effects on a person's physical and mental well-being (Hamilton et al. 1990; Kessler, Turner, and House 1989; Turner 1995). Reemployment, however, produces positive emotional effects, leading to the conclusion that the worst psychological effects of job loss can be minimized if opportunities exist for reemployment (Kessler, Turner, and House 1989).

When it comes to health in general, research by Allan McFarlane and his colleagues (1983) in Canada found that undesirable life events cause the most stress, which, in turn, causes poorer health. What determined the impact of life events on health was the perception of the nature of the change by the individual. Events considered to be undesirable and not controllable by the respondents were consistently followed by an increase in reports of distress, symptoms of illness, and physician visits. Many people are particularly prone to seek out the services of a physician after experiencing a stressful life event as observed by several researchers (Gortmaker, Eckenrode, and Gore 1982; Tessler, Mechanic, and Dimond 1976).

Besides the type of change and the speed with which it occurs, the extent to which change affects a person's life may also be important. Libby Ruch (1977) investigated this and suggests that life change actually has three dimensions: (1) the degree of change evoked, (2) the undesirability of change, and (3) the aspect of one's life that is affected (for example, personal, occupational). But Ruch found that the degree of change is more significant than either desirability or the area of life affected. That is, the greater the change, the more likely stress will result. In subsequent research, Ruch (Ruch, Chandler, and Harter 1980) found that women with changes in their lives prior to being raped had significantly more problems adjusting in the aftermath of the assault than rape victims with little or no changes in their lives before the attack. Although too much change may indeed be stressful, too little change in a person's life also may induce stress (Wildman and Johnson 1977). It is not at all clear, however, that too much or too little change is a determining factor in stress-related health problems. Thomas Rundall (1978), for instance, found that patients with higher levels of life change prior to surgery did not have appreciably more difficulty or sickness when recovering than patients lacking changes in their lives. In sum, the research pertaining to life events is contradictory and in need of clarification.

Life events research also entails serious problems of accurately measuring the presumed relationship between stress and particular life experiences. The most influential instrument at present is the Social Readjustment Rating Scale developed by Thomas Holmes and Robert Rahe (1967). This scale is based on the assumption that change, no matter how good or bad, demands a certain degree of adjustment on the part of an individual: the greater the adjustment, the greater the stress. Holmes and Rahe have carried their analysis one step further and have suggested that changes in life events occur in a cumulative pattern that can eventually build to a stressful impact. Thus, the type of change does not matter so much; the extent to which change disrupts normal patterns of life is important.

The Holmes and Rahe Social Readjustment Rating Scale, an adaptation of which is shown in Table 4-1, lists certain life events that are associated with varying amounts of disruption in the life of an average person. It was constructed by having hundreds of people of different social backgrounds rank the relative amount of

TABLE 4-1   Life Events and Weighted Values.

Life Event	Value	Life Event	Value
Death of spouse	100	Son or daughter leaving home	29
Divorce	73	Trouble with in-laws	29
Marital separation	65	Outstanding personal achievement	28
Jail term	63		
Death of close family member	63	Wife beginning or stopping work	26
Personal injury or illness	53		
Marriage	50	Beginning or ending school	26
Fired at work	47	Revision of habits	24
Marital reconciliation	45	Trouble with boss	23
Retirement	45	Change in work hours	20
Change in health of family	44	Change in residence	20
Pregnancy	40	Change in schools	20
Sex difficulties	39	Change in recreation	19
Gain of new family member	39	Change in social activity	18
Change in financial state	38	Loan for minor purchase	17
Death of close friend	37	Change in sleeping habits	16
Change of work	36	Change in number of family get-togethers	15
Change in number of arguments with spouse	35	Change in eating habits	15
Mortgage or loan for major purchase	31	Vacation	13
Foreclosure of mortgage	30	Christmas	12
Change of responsibility at work	29	Minor violations of law	11

Source: Adapted from T. H. Holmes and R. H. Rahe, "The Social Readjustment Rating Scale," *Journal of Psychosomatic Research,* 11 (August 1967), Table 3-1, 213. Reprinted with permission from the authors and Pergamon Press Ltd.

adjustment accompanying a particular life experience. Death of a spouse is ranked highest, with a relative stress value of 100; marriage ranks seventh with a value of 50, retirement is tenth with a value of 45, taking a vacation is ranked forty-first with a value of 13, and so forth. Holmes and Rahe call each stress value a "life change" unit. They suggest that as the total value of life change units mounts, the probability of having a serious illness also increases, particularly if a person accumulates too many life change units in too short a time. If an individual accumulates 200 or more life change units within the period of a year, Holmes and Rahe believe such a person will risk a serious disorder.

Although used extensively and found to measure stress and life events about as well as or better than other scales, the Holmes and Rahe Social Readjustment Rating Scale nevertheless contains some serious flaws that need to be overcome in future research if the scale is going to be continued as a major research tool. Some studies have found that the scale does not adequately account for differences in the relative importance of various life events among ethnic and cultural subgroups (Askenasy, Dohrenwend, and Dohrenwend 1977; Fairbanks and Hough 1981; Hough, Fairbanks, and Garcia 1976; Rosenberg and Dohrenwend 1975). In other words, the Holmes and Rahe scale measures the quantity of change rather than the qualitative meaning of the event (Ruch 1977). Other research suggests that some life events, such as divorce, can be regarded as a *consequence* of stress instead of a *cause*. For example, events such as "change in sleeping habits," "change in number of arguments with spouse," "sex difficulties," and "fired at work" may result from stress rather than cause it (Holmes and Masuda 1974). This situation confounds the relationships being measured. Some respondents also have difficulty recalling past life events (Funch and Marshall 1984).

Another problem is that the scale does not account for intervening variables, such as social support, that might modify the effects of stress for many individuals. While interpersonal influence can be stressful in itself because of discrepancies, conflicting expectations, or excessive demands to achieve or maintain a certain level of performance (Meitlin and Woelfel 1974), there is little doubt that supportive interpersonal influences help reduce stressful feelings (A. Dean, Kolodny, and Wood 1990; Ensel and Lin 1991; Haines and Hurlbert 1992; Matt and Dean 1993; Thoits 1995).

Furthermore, as R. Jay Turner and William Avison (1992) and Peggy Thoits (1994) discovered, life events that are successfully resolved may not be stressful. That is, it may be the case that mastery of an event provides a buffer to stress because successful resolution constitutes a personally meaningful positive experience. This situation, as Turner and Avison explain, can substantially counterbalance the stress associated with the event.

Obviously, life events research is in need of more extensive development. The relationship between stress and life events as a precipitating factor in causing or contributing to the onset of physical and mental disorders is a highly complex phenomenon and not easily amenable to a simple cause-and-effect explanation. Nevertheless, considerable progress has been made in improving measures of stressful life events, and work in this regard continues today. Current findings indicate that per-

The Holmes and Rahe Social Readjustment Rating Scale ranks the death of a spouse at the top of its list of stressful life events, while the death of a close family member is also ranked high.

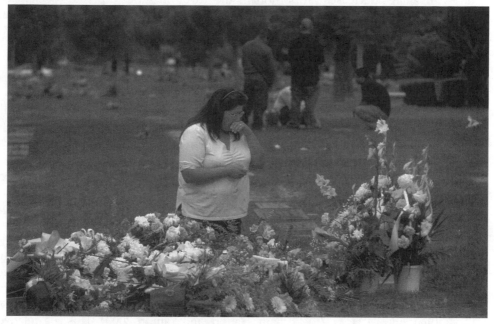

sons at the lower end of the socioeconomic scale are particularly vulnerable to the emotional effects of undesirable life events (Gore, Aseltine, and Colten 1992; McLeod and Kessler 1990; J. Turner 1995; R. Turner et al. 1995). There may also be important differences between men and women, with men more likely to be distressed by work and finances and women by negative events in the family (Conger et al. 1993). Consequently, there is general recognition in the behavioral sciences that psychological distress is a negative influence on health (Thoits 1995). Strong support comes from research in genetics where evidence has been accumulated that stressful situations trigger genetic predispositions toward mental disorder and other psychological problems (Weiner 1985). Debate is no longer centered on whether life events are important in influencing health; rather, the focus now is upon determining in which specific ways they are important.

Stress and Socioeconomic Status

Socioeconomic status also plays an important role in the stress process. The lower class is characterized as being subject to the most stress and having the fewest resources to cope with it (N. Adler et al. 1994; Cockerham 2003; Evans, Barer, and Marmor 1994; R. Turner and Lloyd 1999). After reviewing numerous studies of both humans and primates, Evans (1994) determined that social rank can be correlated with the ability to handle stress. The higher one's position in a social hierarchy, the better one deals with stressful situations and the effects of stress on the body. This advantage decreases proportionally the lower one goes down the social ladder.

Consequently, Evans and his colleagues (1994) suggest that stress is the principal cause of the social gradient in mortality. As discussed in Chapter 3, the Whitehall studies of Michael Marmot and his associates (1984, 1991) provided strong evidence that the association of socioeconomic status with health occurs at every level of the social hierarchy. The upper class was found to live longer than the upper middle class who, in turn, live longer than the lower middle class and so on—until the lower class is reached who have the lowest life expectancy of all. What is important is not just the difference between the top and bottom of society, but the fact that people at the top enjoy better health and longevity than those just below them, even though both groups are affluent.

In Evans's (1994) view, stress is the culprit in that the levels of stress experienced, the amount of resources available to cope with stress, and the degree of control over one's life situation vary by social class position. Evans therefore concludes that it is the quality of "microenvironment" (defined as relations at home and work) that facilitates the transfer of strain from stressful life events. It is the ability to transfer or buffer the effects of stress, not simply being wealthy, that ultimately determines the extent of the effects of stress on the body. It is not certain, however, whether the social gradient in life expectancy is caused by stress or other factors like class differences in health lifestyles and social support, or some other factor or combination of factors (Cockerham, Hattori, and Yamori 2000). This is a relatively new line of inquiry in stress research that requires more investigation.

SUMMARY

The study of the relationship between social factors and stress-related diseases has advanced significantly in the past fifteen years, but the precise nature of this relationship is not yet fully understood. It is clear from existing studies, however, that the experience of stress is a subjective response on the part of an individual as a result of exposure to certain social experiences. Before an assessment can be made of the effect of stress upon an individual, it will be necessary to know (1) the nature of the threat itself; (2) the objective social environment within which the threat appears; (3) the psychological style and personality of the individual involved; (4) the subjective definition of the threat by the individual; (5) the social influences acting upon the individual, particularly the psychological supports offered by group membership; and (6) the duration of the threat. Obviously, stress research represents a very complex investigative effort. But the potential contribution of such research to both the social and medical sciences is great. As House (1974) pointed out, stress research offers opportunities to learn more about a phenomenon that has implications not only for understanding disease processes but also for understanding a wide range of human behavior, such as suicide, delinquency, social movements, family violence, child abuse, mental health, and many other important social problems.

SOCIAL STRESS INTERNET SITES

Social Theory*

1. Sociosite: Famous Sociologists.
   http://www.pscw.uva.nl/sociosite/TOPICS/Sociologists.html

2. SocioRealm, Social Theory.
   http://24.266.88.121/sociorealm/subjects.asp

3. Society for the Study of Symbolic Interaction.
   http://sun.soci.niu.edu/~sssi

*All the listings under this heading have information and links regarding Charles Cooley, William I. Thomas, Erving Goffman, Emile Durkheim, functionalism, and symbolic interaction.

Stress/Mental Health

1. National Institute of Mental Health, Mental Illness in America.
   http://www.nimh.nih.gov/publicat/states.cfm

   Statistical reports of the prevalence of mental disorders among Americans.

2. American Psychological Association (homepage).
   http://www.apa.org

   a. Discussion of the different kinds of stress.
   http://helping.apa.org/work/stress4.html

Health Behavior and Lifestyles

Before discussing the behavior of people who feel sick and in need of medical treatment, we will examine the behavior of healthy people who try to remain that way. This is an important area of investigation in medical sociology because health-oriented behavior does not pertain just to those activities concerned with recovering from disease or injury, but also involves the kinds of things that healthy people do to stay healthy. Living a healthy lifestyle and promoting one's own health in the process has become an increasingly important component of life in modern societies. Consequently, medical sociologists divide health-oriented behavior into two general categories: health behavior and illness behavior.

Illness behavior is the activity undertaken by a person who feels ill for the purpose of defining that illness and seeking relief from it (Kasl and Cobb 1966). Health behavior, in contrast, is defined as the activity undertaken by individuals for the purpose of maintaining or enhancing their health, preventing health problems, or achieving a positive body image (Cockerham 2000a). This definition of health behavior does not limit participation to healthy people trying to stay healthy (Kasl and Cobb 1966). Rather, it includes people in good health, as well as the physically handicapped and persons with chronic illnesses like diabetes and heart disease who seek to control or contain their affliction through diet, exercise, and other forms of health behavior. It also includes persons whose primary motivation in regard to health behavior is their desire to look and feel good and for whom being healthy is secondary. For example, we know from studies of business corporations that the health goals of some people are focused on enhancing their bodily appearance and physical condition to appear attractive and successful (Conrad 1988a, 1998b, 1994; Kotarba and Bentley 1988). For most other people, however, their health behavior is primarily intended to prolong their lives and maintain their health (Goldstein 1992). Yet regardless of the underlying motivation, it is clear that health-promoting behavior and lifestyles are spreading in advanced societies (Cockerham et al. 1988a; Conrad 1988a, 1988b, 1994; Goldstein 1992).

In this chapter we will review the research pertaining to health behavior and lifestyles. The focus in medical sociology is not on the health behavior of an individual, which is more appropriately defined as self-care (K. Dean 1989), but on the transformation of this behavior into its collective form: health lifestyles. The first part of the discussion will focus on the health lifestyles that people pursue on their own more or less independently of the medical profession. The second part will review the health behavior of people that places them in direct contact with medical doctors and other health professionals for preventive care intended to maintain their health and reduce the risk of illness.

HEALTH LIFESTYLES

Health lifestyles are collective patterns of health-related behavior based on choices from options available to people according to their life chances. A person's life chances are determined by his or her socioeconomic status, age, gender, race, ethnicity, and other factors that impact on lifestyle choices. The behaviors that are generated from these choices can have either positive or negative consequences on body and mind, but nonetheless form an overall pattern of health practices that constitute a lifestyle. Health lifestyles include contact with medical professionals for checkups and preventive care, but the majority of activities take place outside the health care delivery system. These activities typically consist of choices and practices, influenced by the individual's probabilities for realizing them, that range from brushing one's teeth and using automobile seat belts to relaxing at health spas. For most people, health lifestyles involve decisions about food, exercise, relaxation, personal hygiene, risk of accidents, coping with stress, smoking, alcohol and drug use, and having physical checkups.

According to the World Health Organization (WHO) (1986), significant improvements in health in the nineteenth century were brought about by what might be called "engineering methods"—the building of safe water supplies and sewers and the production of cheap food for urban areas through the use of mechanized agriculture. These methods continue to improve the health of people in underdeveloped areas of the world. The first sixty years of the twentieth century was the "medical era" in which the dominant approach to health was mass vaccination and the extensive use of antibiotics to combat infection. At present, however, WHO suggests that advanced societies are entering into a "postmedical era" in which physical well-being is largely undermined by social and environmental factors. These factors include certain types of individual behavior (such as smoking, overeating), failures of social organization (loneliness), economic factors (poverty), and the physical environment (pollution) that are not amenable to direct improvement by medicine. WHO (1986:117) concludes: "Whereas in the 'medical era' health policy has been concerned mainly with how medical care is to be provided and paid for, in the new 'post-medical' era it will focus on the attainment of good health and well-being."

While the provision and financing of medical care remains a critically important health policy issue today, the role of health lifestyles as a means to improve the health of people in a postmedical situation is gaining in significance as the twenty-first century begins. Robert Crawford (1984) helps us to understand why this is the case. First, as Crawford points out, there has been a growing recognition among the general public that the major disease patterns have changed from acute or infectious illnesses to chronic diseases—like heart disease, cancer, and diabetes—that medicine cannot cure. Second, numerous health disasters, such as AIDS and cigarette-induced lung cancer, are caused by particular styles of living. Third, there has been a virtual campaign by the mass media and health care providers emphasizing lifestyle change and individual responsibility for health. The result has been a growing awareness that medicine is no longer the automatic answer to dealing with all threats to one's health. Therefore, strategies on the part of individuals to adopt a healthier lifestyle have gained in popularity. As Crawford explains, when threats to health persist in the environment and medicine cannot provide a cure, self-control over the range of personal behaviors that affect health is the only remaining option. This means the person will be confronted with the decision to acquire or maintain a healthy lifestyle, or disregard the situation and perhaps be at greater risk for poor health.

Weber: Lifestyles

Before proceeding to a discussion of health lifestyles, it is useful to review the work of German sociologist Max Weber (1864–1920). Weber is one of the most influential sociological theorists of all time, and his views on lifestyles in general help place the concept of a "health lifestyle" in perspective. Weber's notion of lifestyles appears in his discussion of status groups in his classic work *Economy and Society* (1978), originally published in 1922. Karl Marx had earlier suggested that a person's social class position is determined exclusively by his or her degree of access to a society's means of production. In other words, Marx claimed that one's location in a class structure results strictly from how much of society's goods and services that person is able to command. However, in Weber's view, Marx's concept of class is not the whole story in determining someone's social rank; rather, status (prestige) and power (political influence) are also important. Weber focused primarily on the difference between class and status in his analysis. He pointed out that while class was an objective dimension of social life signified by how much money and property a person has, status was subjective in that it consists of the amount of esteem a person is accorded by other people. Typically, a person's occupation, income, and level of education are the basis of such esteem.

A status group refers to people who share similar material circumstances, prestige, education, and political influence; moreover, members of the same status group share a similar lifestyle. In fact, a particular lifestyle is what distinguishes one status group from another. People with high socioeconomic status clearly lead a different style of life than those at the bottom of society and those somewhere in the middle. Weber also made the pertinent observation that lifestyles are not based upon what one produces, but on what one consumes. That is, one's lifestyle is a reflection of the types and amounts of goods and services one uses or consumes. Thus, for Weber, the difference between status groups does not lie in their relationship to the means of production as suggested by Marx, but in their relationship to the means of consumption.

This view applies to health lifestyles because when someone pursues a healthy style of life, that person is attempting to produce good health according to his or her degree of motivation, effort, and capabilities. Yet the aim of this activity, as Weber's insight suggests, is ultimately one of consumption. People attempt to maintain or enhance their health in order to use it for some purpose, such as a longer life, work, sexual attractiveness, or enhanced enjoyment of their physical being. A. d'Houtaud and Mark Field (1984), for example, found in a study in France that health was conceptualized as something to be cultivated for increased vitality and enjoyment of life among the upper and middle classes, and for the ability to continue to work among lower-class persons. The lower class viewed health largely as a means to an end (work), while persons with higher socioeconomic status regarded health as an end in itself (vitality and enjoyment). In both situations, however, health was something that was to be consumed, not simply produced. Futhermore, in producing a healthy lifestyle, the individual often *consumes* various goods and services, such as athletic clothing and equipment, healthy food and drink, vitamins, possibly sport club memberships, vacations for rest and relaxation, and the like.

Weber did not ignore the socioeconomic conditions necessary for a specific lifestyle. Weber deliberately used three distinct terms to express his view of lifestyles: *"Lebensstil"* (lifestyle), *"Lebensführung"* (life conduct), and *"Lebenschancen"* (life chances). As shown in Figure 5-1, *Lebensführung* and *Lebenschancen* are the two components of *Lebensstil* (Abel 1991; Abel and Cockerham 1993; Cockerham, Abel, and Lüschen 1993). *Lebensführung*, or life conduct, refers to the choices that people have in the lifestyles they wish to adopt, but the potential for realizing these choices is influenced by their *Lebenschancen*, or life chances. Ralf Dahrendorf (1979:73) notes that Weber is ambiguous about what he really means by life chances, but the best interpretation he found of what Weber meant is that life chances are the "probability of finding satisfaction for interests, wants, and needs." For Weber, the notion of life chances therefore refers to the probability of acquiring a particular lifestyle, which means the person must have the financial resources, status, rights, and social relationships that support the chosen lifestyle. One's life chances are shaped by one's social circumstances.

FIGURE 5-1   Weber's Lifestyle Components.

Stilisierung des Lebens
(Stylization of Life)

Lebensführung
(Life Conduct)

Lebenschancen
(Life Chances)

Of course, the life chances that enhance participation in a healthy lifestyle are greatest among upper and middle socioeconomic groups who have the best resources to support their lifestyle choices. Yet it was Weber's contention that lifestyles frequently spread beyond the groups in which they originate (Bendix 1960). A good example is the spread of the Protestant ethic (a lifestyle emphasizing thrift, effort, and the value of work as a good in itself) into the general culture of Western society. One result is that, in the modern world, the Protestant ethic is no longer distinctive to Protestants, nor the West (Jaspers 1988). While lifestyles set people apart, Weber suggests that lifestyles can also spread across society. And there is evidence that health lifestyles, emphasizing exercise, sports, a healthy diet, avoidance of unhealthy practices such as smoking and the like, which had their origin in the upper middle class—are beginning to spread across class boundaries in Western society (Featherstone 1987). It has become increasingly clear that most people try to do at least something (even if it is just eating sensibly, getting enough sleep, or relaxing) to protect their health (Harris and Guten 1979).

Weber's ideas about lifestyles are important for several reasons. First, his work led to the development of the concept "socioeconomic status," or SES in sociology, as the most accurate reflection of a person's social class position. Where a person is located in the social hierarchy of society is determined not by income alone, but typically by a combination of three indicators: income, education, and occupational status. Second, lifestyle is a reflection of a person's status in society, and lifestyles are based on what people consume, rather than what they produce. Third, lifestyles are based upon choices, but these choices are dependent upon the individual's potential for realizing them. And this potential is usually determined by one's socioeconomic circumstances. Fourth, although particular lifestyles characterize particular socioeconomic groups, some lifestyles spread across class boundaries and gain influence in the wider society.

Therefore, when it comes to health lifestyles, Weber's work suggests that, while such lifestyles are oriented toward producing health, the aim of the activity is ultimately toward its consumption as people try to be healthy so they can use their health to live longer, enjoy life, be able to keep on working, and so forth. Furthermore, while health lifestyles seem to be most characteristic of the upper and middle classes, the potential exists for them to spread across social boundaries. The quality of participation may differ significantly, but the level of participation in advanced societies may be spreading nonetheless. Regardless of one's particular socioeconomic position, an important feature of modern society appears to be the tendency for many people to adopt a healthy lifestyle within the limits of their circumstances and opportunities.

Of all the socioeconomic groups, however, the poor are especially disadvantaged in relation to positive health lifestyles. As K. A. Wickrama and associates (1999:260) explain, "socially disadvantaged individuals have less access to health information and resources; they have less control over sleeping hours, and food choices; and they are more likely to live in a social environment where unhealthy eating, smoking and heavy drinking are normality, making the formation of risky lifestyle more probable." Figure 5-2 shows the relationship between smoking and family income in the United States for adults age 18 and older in 1995 to illustrate one way in which the health lifestyles of the poor are negative. Among the behavioral practices affecting health, smoking cigarettes and cigars has the largest number of adverse consequences (Rogers and Powell-Griner 1991; Ross and Wu 1995; Wray et al. 1998). Heart disease, stroke, atherosclerosis, and respiratory diseases, along with lung, throat, and other cancers, are all directly associated with smoking. Figure 5-2 depicts the income gradient in smoking for both men and women, with the poor showing the highest proportion of smokers followed (in descending order) by the near poor, middle-income groups, and high-income groups. About twice the proportion (nearly 40 percent) of poor persons smoke compared to persons (nearly 20 percent) with high incomes.

A major study of the relationship between social class and health lifestyles was that of French sociologist Pierre Bourdieu (1984) who investigated class competition and reproduction, as expressed in cultural tastes and styles. Bourdieu analyzed eating habits and sports preferences that described how a *habitus,* or class-based set of durable dispositions to act in particular ways, shaped particular facets of health lifestyles. People from the same social class tended to share the same habitus because they typically have the same life chances. The habitus operated to align individual aspirations and expectations with the objective probabilities for realizing them typical of people in the same social class. The working class enjoyed soccer, while people in the professions (upper middle class) liked tennis. As for food, the working class typically favored foods that were cheap, nutritious, and abundant, while professional people were more concerned about body image and opted for foods that were light, tasty, and low in calories.

Although socioeconomic status is perhaps the major factor in lifestyle selection and participation, it is not the sole determinant of lifestyles. Since Weber's time other research has shown that more is involved in lifestyle selection than social class, and this generalization is particularly true of health lifestyles. Numerous studies identify dietary, exercise, and drinking and smoking patterns as characteristic of several groups regardless of their class position (Marang-van de Mheen, Smith, and

FIGURE 5-2   Cigarette smoking among adults eighteen years of age and over by family income, United States, 1995.

Source: National Center for Health Statistics, 1998.

Hart 1999; Ross and Bird 1994). High religiosity, for example, has been found to promote healthy lifestyle practices (Dwyer, Clarke, and Miller 1990; Idler 1995; Musick 1996). There is also strong evidence that people tend to take better care of their health as they grow older by showing more careful food selection, more relaxation, and either abstinence or reduced use of tobacco and alcohol (Backett and Davison 1995; Lüschen et al. 1995). Exercise, however, declines significantly at older ages, causing one major health lifestyle activity to be largely curtailed over time.

As for gender, Catherine Ross and Chloe Bird (1994), found that men are more likely than women to exercise strenuously and walk, but are also more likely to smoke and be overweight. Men are particularly at risk for health problems if their advantaged position in the economy (higher salaries and leadership roles) is accompanied by smoking, regular consumption of high-fat foods, and a lack of exercise. Therefore, while men have advantages in their relationship to the means of production, Ross and Bird suggest that the relationship to the means of consumption that comes with this advantage may worsen their health. Other research shows that men consistently consume more alcohol and cigarettes than women, and women are more careful generally about their diet (Abel et al. 1998; Cockerham et al. 1988a; K. Dean 1989; Lüschen et al. 1995; Marang-van de Mheen et al. 1999; Roos et al. 1998). Furthermore, in adolescence, males tend to adopt the health lifestyles of their fathers and females those of their mothers (Wickrama et al. 1999). What is suggested by these findings is that any concept of health lifestyles needs to go beyond an emphasis on socioeconomic status and also focus on alternative status variables like age and gender that influence health practices.

Health Lifestyle Motivation

An emphasis upon a healthy lifestyle is not a new development in the United States. What is new is the reawakened interest in health lifestyles that occurred in the mid-twentieth century because of the profound decline in infectious diseases and increase

Exercise is one of the most important components of a positive health lifestyle.

in chronic diseases associated with certain behavioral practices like smoking, over-eating, and lack of exercise (M. Becker and Rosenstock 1989; Goldstein 1992). Prior to this time, as Harvey Green (1986) shows in an extensively documented history of health and fitness activities in the United States between 1830 and 1940, a long-term interest had existed on the part of Americans to be healthy. Green found that in the early nineteenth century, a strong religious sentiment was associated with health. Various Protestant reformers argued that the Second Coming of Christ might be advanced if humankind could achieve a state of grace and perfection, which included a healthy body. "Good health—the avoidance of disease, debility, and 'premature' death—thus took on extraordinary importance," states Green (1986:10). Sickness was therefore regarded by some people as a spiritual as well as a medical or physiological problem.

Other developments of the nineteenth and early twentieth centuries identified by Green included linking good health with the vitality of the nation; associating health with beauty; depicting athletics as a foundation for a "muscular Christianity" and a means to instill "team spirit" and an outlook necessary for success in business and war; and projecting health as vital to upward social mobility for new immigrants because of its close association with Americanism. Some groups and individuals also advocated good health as a means to avoid illness, reduce the chances of dying early, and gain an "edge" on competition in the workplace; but practical health goals were often not emphasized as much as idealistic values. The dominant view was that good health was an idealized end state that people should achieve for moral, religious, and patriotic reasons or as part of an overall effort to be a success in life (Gillick 1984; H. Green 1986).

Religion remains an important aspect of health lifestyles today for many people. Several studies suggest that religious attitudes and behaviors can have a positive effect on numerous health-related activities (Dwyer, Clarke, and Miller 1990; Musick 1996). These include prohibitions on smoking, drinking, and multiple sexual relationships and the promotion of nutrition, hygiene, and exercise. In one study, Jeffrey Dwyer, Leslie Clarke, and Michael Miller (1990) observed lower mortality rates from cancer among religious groups emphasizing doctrinal orthodoxy and behavioral conformity. They suggest this development is due to the disapproval in such groups of behavior related to cancer mortality, like smoking.

In an extensive review of the literature, Dwyer and his associates found other research supporting the positive effects of religion on health, such as the high life expectancy of Mormons in Utah, which, in the case of lung cancer, appears to extend to the non-Mormon population as well because of the prevalence of social situations in which smoking is strongly disapproved and fewer smokers causing secondary smoke for nonsmokers to breathe. Victor Fuchs (1974), in an earlier study, compared the death rates in Utah and Nevada, and observed that better health existed in Utah because of the lifestyles of a majority of its residents. People in Nevada had significantly higher rates of cigarette and alcohol consumption and family instability, along with less religiosity than was found in Utah.

While religious values remain influential in regard to health lifestyles, most research on contemporary participation in a wide range of fitness activities shows that individual self-control over one's health is emerging as perhaps the principal rationale behind such participation (Crawford 1984; Harris and Guten 1979; Hayes and Ross 1987; Ransford 1986). This theme is also found in literature reviews and essays on fitness and the postmodern self (Glassner 1988, 1989). "By becoming fit," states Barry Glassner (1989:187), "persons are said to achieve a degree of independence from medical professionals and medical technology." Thus, the majority position in American literature today is that health lifestyles are pursued in modern society because they allow a person to assume some personal control over his or her health. A similar pattern appears to exist in Germany as well, where two concepts of health as a social value have developed. The predominant concept views health as a form of efficiency; the second concept, becoming more prevalent in recent years, depicts health as a form of individual emancipation (Rodenstein 1987).

Studies of wellness programs sponsored by American business corporations uncover a related theme. Relevant research shows most people participate in fitness activities provided by their employers because they want to stay in shape or lose weight largely just to look better (Conrad 1988a, 1988c, 1994; Kotarba and Bentley 1988). That is, their health goals were limited to participating in workouts that would result in a positive body image and level of physical conditioning that would allow them to get more out of life (Conrad 1988a). A desire on the part of the individual to look and feel good through exercise and dieting was given priority over physical health.

Crawford (1984) suggests that health has indeed become a metaphor for consumption; that is, good health is a form of release in that it provides a person with the freedom to consume in order to satisfy individual needs. Furthermore, Crawford claims that the abundance of news and commentary in the media on lifestyles and health has reduced complacency about staying healthy; in fact, he notes that the media has declared health and fitness activity to be a lifestyle in itself. An important response to this situation is the virtual flood of commercial products in American society to help the individual "manufacture" health. Thus, states Crawford (1984:76), "the complex ideologies of health are picked up, magnified, and given commodity form by the image-makers." Commercial products associated with fitness not only produce profits, but also reinforce the general idea that health and fitness constitute a practical goal to be achieved through the use of these products.

Consequently, it appears that modern Americans wish to pursue health lifestyles largely for practical, not abstract, reasons. They want to be healthy in order to avoid disease, live longer, feel good, and look good. In other words, as suggested by Max Weber's (1978) work, health is something to be achieved (produced) so that it can be used (consumed) for some practical goal. As Joseph Kotarba and Pamela Bentley (1988:558) explain, workplace wellness programs "illustrate a more general trend in our culture that is transforming health from a status—something an individual has—to an accomplishment—something an individual does." Kotarba and Bentley point out that health becomes an accomplishment to the degree that an individual can rationally and systematically attempt to seek, nurture, and prolong it. Bryan Turner (1995, 1996) notes that religion dominated ideas about the physical use of the body in past Western history, but rationalization and secularization have produced a modern emphasis on the use of the outer surface of the body for desirable feelings and personal significance.

Therefore, as Glassner (1988) points out, greater self-control over one's quality of life through the medium of the body has emerged as a major component of modernism. The rationality underlying this development is what Weber (1978) refers to as "formal rationality." Formal rationality is the purposeful calculation of the most efficient means to achieve a goal. Weber made a major contribution to the development of social thought by explaining how formal rationality became the dominant mode of thinking in Western society and joined with the Protestant ethic to stimulate the rise of capitalism in the West. In the context of formal rationality, health is valued not so much as a substantive, idealized state; rather, health is valued because it has a practical function to perform. As Eugene Gallagher (1988a) notes, a distinctive feature of modernity in the health sphere is a more widespread and penetrating awareness of the value of health and individual efforts to achieve it—which stands in sharp contrast to the more fatalistic and passive attitudes about health prevailing in many non-Western cultures.

Health Lifestyles in Western Society

Health professionals and the mass media have spread the message that healthy people need to avoid certain behaviors and adopt others as part of their daily routine if they want to maximize their life expectancy and remain healthy as long as possible. These statements are supported by ample evidence that a lack of exercise, diets high in fat and cholesterol, stress, smoking, obesity, alcohol and drug abuse, and exposure to chemical pollutants cause serious health problems and early deaths (I. Lee, Hsieh, and Paffenbarger 1995; Otten et al. 1990; Paffenbarger et al. 1986; Shepard et al. 1995). It is also well known that lifestyles involving unprotected and promiscuous sexuality and intravenous drug use increase the risk of AIDS, while smoking is linked to lung cancer, alcoholism to cirrhosis of the liver, and high-fat diets to atherosclerosis and heart disease.

On the positive side, there is evidence that pursuing a healthy lifestyle can enhance one's health and life expectancy. Exercise has been found to reduce the risk of dying from heart disease (I. Lee et al. 1995; Ornish et al. 1990; Paffenbarger et al. 1986), as have reductions in cholesterol levels, blood pressure, and cigarette smoking (Shepard et al. 1995; Sytkowski, Kannel, and D'Agostino 1990). In other research, an extensive ten-year survey of the health lifestyles of nearly 7,000 adults in Alameda County, California, identified seven good health practices: (1) seven to eight hours a night of sleep; (2) eating breakfast every day; (3) seldom if ever eating snacks; (4) controlling one's weight; (5) exercising; (6) limiting alcohol consumption; and (7) never having smoked cigarettes (Berkman and Breslow 1983). People reporting six or seven of these health practices were found to have better health and longer lives than people reporting fewer than four of them.

Such developments suggest that health lifestyles should be important for many people. Health lifestyles also should be more common in advanced societies where people have greater choices in their selection of lifestyles and a better opportunity

BOX 5-1   The Healthiest States

Trying to lead a healthy lifestyle? According to the Government Guide (www.statestats.com/hc02fact.htm), where you live makes a difference. The healthiest state in 2002 was Vermont, followed by Minnesota. The least healthiest was Mississippi. The state rankings are based on 21 factors: percent of low birthweights, teenage birthrates, percent of mothers receiving late or no prenatal care, age-adjusted death rate, infant mortality rate, age-adjusted death rates for cancer and suicide, percent of population not covered by health insurance, health care expenditures as percent of state Gross Domestic Product, per capita personal health expenditures, estimated rate of new cancer cases, AIDS rate, sexually-transmitted disease rate, percent of population lacking access to primary care, percent of adults who binge drink, smoke, and are overweight, number of days in past month when physical health was "not good," number of beds in community hospitals per 100,000 population, percent of children aged 19–35 months not fully immunized, and auto safety belt usage rate. State rankings for 2002 and 2001 are shown below:

2002 Rank	State	2001 Rank	Change	2002 Rank	State	2001 Rank	Change
1	Vermont	1	0	26	Wisconsin	24	−2
2	Minnesota	2	0	27	Michigan	27	0
3	Iowa	5	2	28	Indiana	29	1
4	New Hampshire	3	−1	29	Alaska	37	8
5	Nebraska	6	1	30	West Virginia	30	0
6	Hawaii	4	−2	31	Illinois	32	1
7	North Dakota	9	2	32	Oklahoma	36	4
8	Connecticut	14	6	33	Kentucky	31	−2
9	Massachusetts	10	1	34	North Carolina	35	1
10	Utah	12	2	35	Arizona	28	−7
11	Maine	8	−3	36	Tennessee	39	3
12	Kansas	7	−5	37	Maryland	33	−4
13	California	17	4	38	New York	34	−4
14	Washington	11	−3	39	Missouri	38	−1
15	New Jersey	16	1	40	Arkansas	40	0
16	Rhode Island	15	−1	41	Georgia	41	0
17	Montana	13	−4	42	Texas	42	0
18	Oregon	18	0	43	Delaware	43	0
19	Virginia	18	−1	44	Florida	44	0
20	South Dakota	23	3	45	South Carolina	49	4
21	Colorado	21	0	46	Nevada	46	0
22	Idaho	26	4	47	Alabama	47	0
23	Pennsylvania	20	−3	48	New Mexico	45	−3
24	Ohio	22	−2	49	Louisiana	48	−1
25	Wyoming	25	0	50	Mississippi	50	0

A cyclist smokes a cigarette while passing a cigarette advertisement on a building. Smoking cigarettes is a highly negative health lifestyle practice because it promotes heart disease, lung cancer, and several other serious ailments.

to be healthy than in developing nations with relatively low standards of living and fewer health options. This appears to be the case as shown in research conducted in the United States and Western Europe.

The United States and Germany   Earlier research (Abel et al. 1989; Cockerham, Kunz, and Lueschen 1988a, 1988b; Cockerham et al. 1986b; Lüschen, Cockerham, and Kunz 1987, 1989) compared the health lifestyles of Americans living in Illinois to Germans in Northrhine–Westphalia and found a distinct lack of difference between social classes, races, and occupational groups in health behavior. Although the quality of participation may vary, health lifestyles in these studies appeared widely accepted and practiced.

One study (Cockerham et al. 1988a) examined whether there were significant differences between people with comprehensive health care benefits provided by their government (Germans) and those generally lacking such coverage (Americans) in regard to participating in health lifestyles. Germany has an extensive system of national health insurance that covers 93 percent of the total population (the most wealthy are excluded and required to obtain private health insurance), while in the United States only some 20 percent of the population—the aged and the poor—have government-sponsored health insurance through Medicare and Medicaid. The study sought to determine whether Americans, who do not have the security of a national health insurance program, worked harder to stay healthy than Germans, who have their health care costs covered by a national health plan. The data showed a general lack of difference between Americans and Germans, as well as between social strata in the two countries, with respect to participation in health lifestyles. The more paternalistic German system of health insurance coverage did not appear to undermine personal incentives to stay physically fit in comparison to the American system, where people are more on their own in obtaining health insurance and covering their costs for health care.

These studies would suggest that—at least in the United States and Germany—health lifestyles are spreading across class boundaries in a manner similar to that suggested by Weber (1958) for the Protestant ethic. This observation does not mean that everyone is trying to live in a healthy manner, but many people are, and they include persons in all social strata. Several other studies in the two countries support this conclusion. For example, in the United States, H. Edward Ransford (1986) found in a national sample that lower-class black adults were especially likely to adopt health-protective measures because of particular concern about heart disease. Well-educated whites were found to participate in health lifestyles because of a concern about their health in general. But the result was the same: Health behavior cut across class and racial lines. In Ohio, Daniel Harris and Sharon Guten (1979) found that practically everyone in their survey did something to protect their health. Other research in South Carolina found a lack of socioeconomic differences in health practices in a sample of state government employees in a health promotion program; most participants, regardless of class background, made positive changes in their health habits (Kronenfeld et al. 1988).

In Germany, the pattern of participation in health lifestyles shows signs of becoming increasingly similar to patterns in the United States. The number of Germans involved in sport and exercise has risen substantially, while diets have become more healthy and healthy work conditions have received more emphasis (Scheuch 1989). Moreover, the number of male smokers has significantly declined. With the exception of sports, where participation remains greater among members of the upper and middle classes, there do not appear to be significant class differences in health lifestyles among Germans (Cockerham et al. 1988a; Lüschen et al. 1995).

Other Western Countries   The situation in other Western countries has not been fully established because little research on health lifestyles has taken place to date. Among the existing studies is a major comparative survey conducted in Belgium, France, Germany, and the Netherlands by Günther Lüschen et al. (1995). This study found considerable similarity in health lifestyles across social classes and nationalities. The Germans and Dutch showed almost identical patterns of health lifestyles, and their health practices did not differ significantly from the Belgians and French. An exception was the high level of alcohol consumption (wine) among French persons. Overall, these data show an expansion of health lifestyles across class and national boundaries.

However, in Great Britain, a nationwide survey of health lifestyles conducted by Mildred Blaxter (1990) found that important differences existed between the classes in the things they do to stay healthy, with the upper and middle classes taking better care of themselves than the working class and lower class. The health lifestyle differences between the classes were both strong and persistent. Smoking was by far the greatest among male blue-collar workers in industrial areas, along with heavy alcohol consumption. More frequent drinking, but lower amounts, was found among higher-status males. Sports participation and good dietary habits were significantly more common at the upper end of the social scale. Blaxter suggested that the social conditions within which a person lives could be more important for health than health-related behavior. That is, health lifestyles were most effective in positive social circumstances and least effective under negative conditions like poverty. This finding has important policy implications because it suggests that ultimately social conditions may be more effective than behavior in changing levels of health.

An attempt to replicate Blaxter's results in Denmark and Norway, however, failed (Kooiker and Christiansen 1995). Of course, it can be argued that socioeconomically disadvantaged groups in Denmark and Norway are relatively better off than in Britain, so the material circumstances they find themselves in do not outweigh the effects of their health-related behavior. It is clear that class boundaries in Britain are relatively rigid and that class differences and inequalities in a wide range of British life, including health, are large (Adonis and Pollard 1997). The upward mobility of young males with working-class backgrounds in the late twentieth century was due more to education and changes in the economy through an expansion of jobs in the financial, computer, and information areas of the service sector than to a more open class system (Reid 1998). The material circumstances of the lower and working classes are undoubtedly a major risk factor for poor health in Britain and perhaps more of a causal agent for poor health than in some of the more prosperous countries of the European Union. But there is also strong evidence that the gap in Britain between the classes in morbidity, mortality, and life expectancy is persistently large and caused to a significant degree by differing health lifestyles (Adonis and Pollard 1997; Reid 1998). The decline in smoking, for example, has been greatest among the affluent and reached the point that it is predominantly a habit of the British poor (Adonis and Pollard 1997).

Yet Mike Featherstone (1987) suggests that physical fitness activities are spreading increasingly through British society. Michael Calnan (1989), for example, found little difference between socioeconomic groups in a survey of health behavior in southern England. And there is evidence of a large decline in smoking and the consumption of fats (Coleman and Salt 1992; Reid 1998). In other research involving a group of middle- and working-class women living on the outskirts of London, Calnan (1987) found that both groups agreed that the best way of keeping healthy was a good diet and physical exercise. However, there were different interpretations concerning diets and exercise that apparently resulted from differences in education and class-based life experiences. The middle-class women emphasized that diets should be high in fiber and low in fats and carbohydrates, while the working-class group placed greater emphasis upon having regular substantial meals that included meat and two vegetables. Both groups valued regular exercise, but the working-class women were most likely to regard household duties as meeting this requirement.

On balance, it appears that health lifestyles are spreading in British society, but distinct differences between the social classes remain. Such lifestyles are largely practiced by the middle class (Bunton and Burrows 1995). This finding is not too surprising because class divisions in Britain remain more rigid than in the United States and Germany (Reid 1998). In France, few current data are available on health lifestyle participation, but existing studies suggest relatively positive health practices with the exception of alcohol consumption which is the highest in the world (Corbett 1994; Lüschen et al. 1995). However, moderate (one glass daily) consumption of red wine has been beneficial for preventing heart disease, and the French people have relatively low rates of heart disease mortality despite their rich diet (D. Goldberg 1995; Renaud and de Lorgeril 1992). Both smoking and wine consumption have declined in recent years, and cigarette advertising has been banned since 1993 (Corbett 1994). Moreover, the French have significantly less obesity in their population compared to Americans (Laurier et al. 1992). There are also reports of increased spending on personal health care items and a significant increase in participation in sport and exercise generally in French society (Ardagh 1987). In fact, John Ardagh (1987:425) observes that "the French have become far more fussy about their health."

Claudine Herzlich and Janine Pierret (1987) identify a shift in French thinking toward a norm of a "duty to be healthy." Herzlich and Pierret find that this norm is strongest in the middle class, but they provide accounts of less socially advantaged persons espousing the same orientation and imply that this norm is spreading in French society. They describe health as a necessity for both society and the individual, and the means by which people achieve self-realization. Herzlich and Pierret (1987:231) maintain that "the 'right to health' implies that every individual must be made responsible for his or her health and must adopt rational behavior in dealing with the pathogenic effects of modern life."

In Denmark, it was found that income failed to predict significant differences in some health-protective behaviors, except for greater routine physical exercise among higher-income persons (K. Dean 1989). The Danish study found few differences between socioeconomic groups overall, but many persons in the study indicated they took no particular action with respect to their health. Other research in Italy found that less-educated persons smoked more and drank more wine, while higher-educated persons were more likely to have quit smoking and be involved in physical exercise (Piperno and Di Orio 1990). However, it was also observed that, on the whole, relatively few Italians exercise for reasons of health and persons in the lower classes are even less likely to do so.

The case cannot be made that health lifestyles have spread completely throughout Western society on the basis of the existing studies. The most extensive participation appears to be in the United States, Germany, and the Netherlands; in Britain and France, health lifestyles show signs of spreading, but elsewhere in Western society little or nothing is known about the extent of health practices in the general population. Clearly, more research is needed to determine national, regional, and global patterns of health lifestyles. However, an emphasis on healthy living is an important part of modernity; and while it seems that persons in the upper and middle socioeconomic groups pursue this lifestyle more extensively in Western countries, data from America and Germany in particular show that participation also includes members of the lower social strata.

Health Lifestyles in Russia and Eastern Europe

Other research highlighting the importance of the social class–health lifestyle relationship is the author's (Cockerham 1997b, 1999, 2000; Cockerham, Snead, and DeWaal 2002) investigation of the decline in life expectancy in Russia and Eastern Europe. Although health policy in Europe's former socialist states was ineffective in curtailing the dramatic rise in mortality from heart disease in the region and stress had a role (most likely indirect in fostering negative health habits), health lifestyles were the primary social determinant of the downturn in longevity that generally began in the mid-1960s. The rise in mortality was primarily due to premature deaths among middle-aged working-class males whose health lifestyles were characterized by extremely heavy drinking and smoking, disregard of their diet, and an absence of leisure-time exercise. Dependence on a deteriorating state health care delivery system also promoted a false sense of security, while the state, for its part, assumed responsibility for health and failed to promote responsibility on the part of the individual (Cockerham et al. 2002). As Vladimir Shkolnikov and France Meslé (1996:145) describe the situation in Russia:

> The priority of state aims and interests over personal needs and wishes taught people that their individual values were of minor importance. According to this ideology, there was no reason to pay much attention to one's future health. Many people believed that the state would help them in case of a serious health problem or any other disaster. Their resulting careless lifestyle has become especially dangerous under the new circumstances, when the general weakness of the Russian state has made its social and health efforts even more inadequate than in previous years.

In the case of Russia and Eastern Europe, poor health lifestyles on the part of working-class males were reflected in group norms for social interaction and shaped by limited opportunities to exercise choice in the structure of the society (Cockerham 1999). Alcohol and cigarettes were cheap and readily available, fresh fruits and vegetables were in short supply in winter months, diets were high in fat, and leisure-time exercise was rare. The heavy drinking, smoking, fatty food, and lack of leisure-time exercise promoted high rates of mortality from cardiovascular diseases, especially heart disease. While the decline in life expectancy was primarily a male phenomenon that affected all social categories, age (middle age) and class (working class) were also key variables. The life expectancy of women mostly stagnated between 1965 and 1995 in the former Soviet bloc countries. Male life expectancy either stagnated (East Germany), declined but recovered slightly (the former Czechoslovakia and Poland), or consistently fell without recovery (Bulgaria, Hungary, Romania, and Russia) during this period. The Baltic states of Estonia, Latvia, and Lithuania, along with Ukraine and Belarus, suffered decreases in male life expectancy as well. But the downturn was greatest in Russia where male longevity fell 6.5 years between 1965 and 1994.

It can therefore be concluded that the relationship between class and health lifestyles remains significant, although such lifestyles can extend across class boundaries and the effects of class on health lifestyles can vary in relation to material conditions in a society. Yet the fact remains that even though health lifestyles can penetrate different socioeconomic strata, significant differences in the quality of participation and the consumption of resources persist (Cockerham et al. 1988a). Affluent people can command the best resources in dieting and exercise, and find it easier to give up smoking, since cigarette use is less common in the upper and upper middle classes. Moderate drinking, routine physical exams, and preventive care by physicians are also more prevalent. And day-to-day living conditions at home and work are likely to have fewer health risks.

Moreover, people in higher social classes have experienced greater life chances and acquired a stronger sense of control over life situations than individuals in the classes below them (Mirowsky and Ross 1989). A major outcome of these cumulative experiences and the perceptions associated with them is that planning and effort typically produce the desired result. While many lower-class people may try to live a healthy lifestyle, others may be less likely to expect that their efforts to maintain their health will be successful and be either passive or less active than the classes above them in practicing good health habits. When disadvantaged life changes reduce the opportunities for positive health behaviors and lifestyles or reduce their effectiveness, the impact of agency or choice on the part of individuals is minimized. Consequently, class more than just matters when it comes to health lifestyles; it remains the dominant variable.

A Critique of Health Lifestyles   Marxist-oriented scholars like Howard Waitzkin and Vicente Navarro claim that an emphasis on individual responsibility for leading a healthy life excuses the larger society from direct accountability in health matters. Waitzkin (1983) maintains that capitalism puts the burden of being healthy squarely on the individual, rather than seeking collective solutions to health problems. The emphasis in capitalist societies on healthy lifestyles is seen as an effort to displace the responsibility for health from the social system and its health sector down to individuals. That is, capitalism promotes the philosophy that it is up to the individual to keep healthy by exercising, eating right, avoiding smoking and alcohol abuse, and obtaining medical care when needed. While not denying that individual lifestyles are important determinants of health, Waitzkin explains that individuals often lead unhealthy lives as a result of social inequality. But when the responsibility for staying healthy is shifted to the individual, the social and medical system is not at fault if people become sick or die early deaths because of adverse social conditions.

Navarro (1986) also claims that the strategy of individual responsibility for health assumes that the fundamental cause of an individual's health problem is the individual, not the social system. Navarro argues that an emphasis on individual lifestyles assumes a degree of independence and freedom for the individual that is an illusion. He bases this view on his contention that a person's lifestyle is determined by one's work position. Navarro (1986:34) states, "Here I am not only stressing what is obvious, that in our consumer society what *you have* depends on what *you do,* but even more important, that one's psychological framework—which determines one's level of expectation and behavior and pattern of interpersonal relations—is very much determined by one's work." Yet in capitalist society, the argument continues, workers do not have control over their work or their lives, including their health. Consequently, lifestyles are not left to the individual's discretion but are determined by one's work situation, which is controlled by the upper class and organized to protect their socioeconomic advantage.

The merit of the Marxist perspective on health responsibility, as advanced by Waitzkin and Navarro, is that it calls our attention to the fact that many health problems (the most obvious being those that stem from poverty) can have roots in the structure of society that cannot always be overcome by individual lifestyles alone. Therefore, societal-level responsibility for the health of individuals is an important component in the formulation of health policy. However, choice is important because people also need to decide whether they want as healthy a life as possible given their circumstances. Decisions about smoking, alcohol use, diet, and exercise ultimately are made by the individual. To blame either society or the individual separately for poor health fails to recognize the interdependence of the two.

PREVENTIVE CARE

As noted earlier in this chapter, health lifestyles generally take place outside of the formal health care delivery system as people pursue their everyday lives in their usual social environment. However, an important facet of health behavior includes contact by healthy people with physicians and other health personnel for preventive care. Preventive care refers to routine physical examinations, immunizations, prenatal care, dental checkups, screening for heart disease and cancer, and other services intended to ensure good health and prevent disease—or minimize the effects of illness if it occurs.

Preventive Care and the Poor

While there is evidence that participation in health lifestyles that do not involve contact with physicians and other health personnel is spreading across social class boundaries in American and German society (Cockerham et al. 1988a), there is other evidence from both countries showing that the poor remain least likely to use preventive care (Dutton 1986; Siegrist 1988, 1989; Snead and Cockerham 2002). As Johannes Siegrist (1989:359) points out for Germany, the most striking class differences in the use of health services are present in the field of prevention and screening programs. In the United States, Diana Dutton (1986) observes that, while the lower class visits physicians more frequently than members of other socioeconomic groups, their need for care is greater because of relatively poorer health and underutilization of preventive care. Regardless of the benefits from public health insurance programs, Dutton finds that the poor receive less preventive care whose utilization is at the discretion of the user. Recent research in the American Deep South, for example, confirms this finding for low income and less educated persons (Snead and Cockerham 2002).

Low-income women receive less prenatal care, low-income children are significantly more likely to have never had a routine physical examination, and other measures like dental care, breast exams, and childhood immunizations are considerably less common among the poor (Wilkinson 1996). The reason for this situation is that many low-income persons do not have a regular source of medical care, health facilities may not be near at hand, and costs not covered by health insurance may have to be paid out of the individual's own pocket—and this factor can be a significant barrier in visiting the doctor when one feels well. Moreover, for those 41.0 million people or 16.8 percent of the American population without any health insurance in 1997, going to the doctor for preventive care may be an unaffordable luxury.

The underutilization of preventive care among the poor is common not just in the United States and Germany but also in several countries of Western Europe where the lower class has been found to use preventive medical and dental services significantly less frequently (Macintyre 1989). In Great Britain, for example, it is well established that persons at the lowest end of the social scale make considerably less use of preventive services than do those higher up the social ladder (Townsend, Davidson, and Whitehead 1990; Wilkinson 1996).

Consequently, it can be argued that preventive care is a behavior pattern most characteristic of the upper and middle classes in advanced societies. When explanations are sought for the significant disparity in health and life expectancy between the affluent and the poor in the world today, the conditions of living associated with poverty and the lack of preventive care among the lower classes are major factors.

The Health Belief Model

One of the most influential social-psychological approaches designed to account for the ways in which healthy people seek to avoid illness is the health belief model of Irwin Rosenstock (1966) and his colleagues (M. Becker 1974). The health belief model is derived to a great extent from the theories of psychologist Kurt Lewin, who suggested that people exist in a life space composed of regions with both positive and negative valences (values). An illness would be a negative valence and would have the effect of pushing a person away from that region, unless doing so would cause the person to enter a region of even greater negative valence (for example, risking disease might be less negative than failing at an important task). While people are pushed away from regions with negative valences, they are attracted toward regions of positive valences. Thus, a person's behavior might be viewed as the result of seeking regions that offer the most attractive values.

Within this framework, human behavior is seen as being dependent upon two primary variables: (1) the value placed by a person upon a particular outcome and (2) the person's belief that a given action will result in that outcome. Accordingly, the health belief model, shown in Figure 5-3, suggests that preventive action taken by an individual to avoid disease "X" is due to that particular individual's perception that he or she is personally susceptible and that the occurrence of the disease would have at least some severe personal implications.

FIGURE 5-3   The Health Belief Model.

Source: Marshall H. Becker, ed., *The Health Belief Model and Personal Health Behavior* (San Francisco: Society for Public Health Education, Inc., 1974), p. 334. Reprinted with permission of Marshall H. Becker.

Although not directly indicated in Figure 5-3, the assumption in this model is that by taking a particular action, susceptibility would be reduced, or if the disease occurred, severity would be reduced. The perception of the threat posed by disease "X," however, is affected by modifying factors. As shown in Figure 5-3, these factors are demographic, sociopsychological, and structural variables that can influence both perception and the corresponding cues necessary to instigate action. Action cues are required, says Rosenstock, because while an individual may perceive that a given action will be effective in reducing the threat of disease, that action may not be taken if it is further defined as too expensive, too unpleasant or painful, too inconvenient, or perhaps too traumatic.

So despite recognition that action is necessary and the presence of energy to take that action, a person may still not be sufficiently motivated to do something. The likelihood of action also involves a weighing of the perceived benefits to action contrasted to the perceived barriers. Therefore, Rosenstock believed that a stimulus in the form of an action cue was required to "trigger" the appropriate behavior. Such a stimulus could be either internal (perception of bodily states) or external (interpersonal interaction, mass media communication, or personal knowledge of someone affected by the health problem).

The health belief model has been employed successfully in several studies of (preventive) health behavior, such as the seeking of dental care (Gochman 1971), dietary compliance among obese children (M. Becker et al. 1977), quitting cigarette smoking in Australia (Knight and Hay 1989), engaging in self-care in the United States and Japan (Haug et al. 1989), and ethnic differences in managing hypertension (C. Brown and Segal 1996). Help-seeking behavior was observed in each of these studies to be based upon the value of the perceived outcome (avoidance of personal vulnerability) and the expectation that preventive action would result in that outcome. For example, the Gochman (1971) study found that if children are motivated to have good health in general, their perception of vulnerability to tooth disease and the benefits of visiting the dentist will result in their intentions to seek future dental care. Conversely, those children with low health motivation are not as likely to have the future intention of seeing a dentist. In the Becker et al. (1977) study, 182 pairs of mothers and their obese children were divided into three groups while the children participated in a weight reduction program. The groups consisted of (1) a high-fear group (shown alarming material about the potentially unfavorable consequences of being fat in later life), (2) a low-fear group (shown similar but less threatening information), and (3) a control group (shown no additional information). Children in the control group did not lose weight. Children in the low-fear group lost some weight initially but also tended to put some of it back on. The high-fear group lost the most weight and did not put any of it back on. The intervention of a fear-arousal cue in the high-fear group had a marked effect on the mothers' notions of the perceived susceptibility, seriousness, and benefits of compliance for their children.

Unfortunately, the usefulness of the health belief model is limited in that it has been applied mostly to preventive situations in which the behavior studied is voluntary. Obviously, however, many people who seek health services are motivated to take action only by the appearance of clear and definite symptoms.

Nevertheless, the health belief model has demonstrated considerable utility in the study of health behavior (M. Becker 1979; Janz and Becker 1984; Mullen, Hersey, and Iverson 1987). The merit of the model is that even when an individual recognizes personal susceptibility, he or she may not take action *unless* the individual also perceives that being ill will result in serious difficulty. Thus, the individual's subjective assessment of the health situation becomes the critical variable in the utilization of health services. In fact, a person's subjective assessment may be more important than an objective medical diagnosis. Several studies show no (sometimes even a negative) correlation between medical estimates of health and patient compliance (M. Becker and Maiman 1975). David Mechanic (1972) has noted that the difficulty in preventive medicine is that commonsense approaches do not necessarily match clinical approaches, and common sense often determines whether health services are sought. Furthermore, once a patient subjectively feels well, physicians may be faced with the additional problem of encouraging the patient to continue to follow medical advice.

SUMMARY

Health behavior is the activity undertaken by a person who believes himself or herself to be healthy for the purpose of preventing health problems (Kasl and Cobb 1966). Health lifestyles, in turn, are ways of living that promote good health and longer life expectancy. Health lifestyles include contact with physicians and other health personnel, but the majority of activities take place outside of formal health care delivery systems. These activities include a proper diet, weight control, exercise, rest and relaxation, and the avoidance of stress and alcohol and drug abuse.

Max Weber, one of the most important theorists in the history of sociological thought, analyzed the general role of lifestyles in society and found that, while particular socioeconomic status groups are characterized by their own lifestyles, some lifestyles spread across social boundaries. He also observed that lifestyles are based on what people consume, rather than what they produce. There is evidence from the United States and Germany, and to a lesser extent from Great Britain and France, that health lifestyles are spreading throughout the class structure of these societies— although the quality of participation in the lower classes is undoubtedly less than that of the classes above them. And, while health lifestyles help produce good health, the aim of such lifestyles is ultimately one of consumption as health is used to avoid disease, live longer, feel better, work, or have a pleasing physical appearance.

Another important facet of health behavior is preventive care that involves contact by healthy people with health care providers. Preventive care consists of routine physical examinations, dental care, cancer and heart disease screening, immunizations, and the like intended to prevent or reduce the chance of illness or minimize its effects. Throughout the world, it appears that lower-class persons are significantly less likely to receive preventive care. The chapter concludes with a discussion of the health belief model, which is one of the most influential approaches to the study of health behavior.

HEALTH BEHAVIOR AND LIFESTYLES INTERNET SITES

Preventive Care and Health Lifestyles

1. Centers for Disease Control, Social Statistics Briefing Room: Health Behaviors, Prevention and Risk.
   http://www.cdc.gov/nchs/SSBR/025para.htm

   Access to surveys and studies dealing with the prevention of disease and risk factors associated with disease.

2. Healthy People 2000.
   http://www.odphp.osophs.dhhs.gov/pubs/hp2000/default.htm

   Organization developed to identify the most significant preventable threats to health and to focus public and private sector efforts on addressing those threats.

3. CDC, the CDC Prevention Guidelines Database.
   http://aepo-xdv-www.epo.cdc.gov/wonder/PrevGuid/PrevGuid.htm

   A comprehensive compendium of the entire official guidelines and recommendations published by the CDC for the prevention of disease, injuries, and disabilities.

4. CDC Wonder, Prevention Guidelines Search Criteria.
   http://wonder.cdc.gov./prev00.shtml

   A CDC database with access to guides and recommendations relative to various diseases and risk factors.

5. CDC, Chronic Disease Preventive Database.
   http://www.gov.cdc/index.htm

   A CDC database for chronic diseases.

6. CDC, Chronic Disease Prevention: Risk Behaviors.
   http://www.cdc.gov/nccdphp/risk.htm

   Statistics and information dealing with risks stemming from tobacco use, physical activity, and nutrition.

7. The National Institutes of Health, Office of Behavioral and Social Sciences.
   http://obsst.adinih.gov

   Numerous links to sites dealing with the prevention and onset of new illnesses, as well as enhancing health-promoting behaviors and decreasing health-damaging ones.

Max Weber

SocioSite: Max Weber.
http://www.pscw.uva.nl/sociosite/TOPICS/Sociologists.html#weber

Descriptions of the life and works of Max Weber.

CHAPTER

6

Illness Behavior

Illness behavior, in comparison to health behavior, is the activity undertaken by a person who feels ill for the purpose of defining that illness and seeking relief from it (Kasl and Cobb 1966). As David Mechanic (1995a:1208) explains: "Illness behavior refers to the varying ways individuals respond to bodily indications, how they monitor internal states, define and interpret symptoms, make attributions, take remedial actions and utilize various sources of informal and formal care." Some people recognize particular physical symptoms such as pain, a high fever, or nausea and seek out a physician for treatment; others with similar symptoms may attempt self-medication or dismiss the symptoms as not needing attention.

We know that bodily changes—symptoms of illness that are disruptive, painful, and visible—are the basic determinants of medical help seeking, and this is especially the case if the discomfort is severe. But sometimes physical changes are not obvious, particularly the early stages of chronic diseases. As Susan Gore (1989:311) explains, "the timing of the detection of diseases such as diabetes, heart disease, and cancer is determined by factors outside the disease process itself—social and psychological factors that shape the individual's response to the often subtle bodily changes that are experienced in daily living." Subjective interpretations of feeling states thus become highly medically significant.

For those individuals and groups concerned with the planning, organization, and implementation of health care delivery systems, the identification of social factors that encourage or discourage a person from seeking medical treatment is of great significance. An understanding of the help-seeking process in medicine can have a tremendous impact upon the structuring of health services for people living in a community, both in terms of providing better medical care and making that care more accessible to the people who need it.

The focus of this chapter is on reviewing the social factors influencing the decisions of the ill to use professional medical services. First, self-care will be examined. Next, selected sociodemographic variables are discussed. These, however, explain only that variations in health services utilization exist, rather than *why* they exist. Thus, our third topic will be selected social-psychological models of medical help-seeking. Only when certain conditions are satisfied in a person's mind can we expect him or her to go to the doctor.

SELF-CARE

Self-care is the most common response to symptoms of illness by people throughout the world (Haug et al. 1989; Segall and Goldstein 1989). Self-care includes taking preventive measures (like consuming vitamin supplements), self-treatment of symptoms (such as taking home remedies or over-the-counter drugs), and managing chronic conditions (for instance, use of insulin by a diabetic). Self-care may involve consultation with health care providers and use of their services. As a way of acting in relation to one's health, self-care consists of both health and illness behavior. It essentially consists of a layperson's preventing, detecting, and treating his or her own health problems. What makes self-care distinctive is that it is a form of care that is self-initiated and self-managed (Segall and Goldstein 1989).

In modern societies, a number of factors have promoted interest in self-care on the part of laypersons. According to Alexander Segall and Jay Goldstein (1989:154), these factors include (1) the shift in disease patterns from acute to chronic illnesses and the accompanying need to displace medical intervention from an emphasis on cure to care; (2) growing public dissatisfaction with medical care that is depersonalized; (3) recognition of the limits of modern medicine; (4) the increasing visibility of alternative healing practices; (5) heightened consciousness of the effects of lifestyle on health; and (6) a desire to exercise personal responsibility in health-related matters. Thus, it would appear that self-care is becoming increasingly important and commonplace.

Several sociological studies conducted in different countries have explored self-care practices. In Canada, Segall and Goldstein (1989) found that women, younger persons, and the well educated were more likely to treat their own symptoms than men, the elderly, and those with less education. In Denmark, Kathryn Dean (1989) likewise found women more likely than men to take care of their health; when illness struck, social networks of family and friends became influential sources of information about self-care. In the United States and Japan, Marie Haug and her associates (Haug et al. 1989) found that self-care was common among both Americans and Japanese. However, the Japanese were especially likely to use self-care when they were sick, even for serious symptoms. Haug and her colleagues surmised that self-care gave the Japanese greater autonomy in matters of health. Japanese doctors tend to be authoritative and do not necessarily provide their patients with full information—even to the extent of not informing them they have cancer (Hattori et al. 1991). Japanese doctors believe disclosure of terminal cancer will cause unnecessary grief, so they typically inform the family but not the patient. Self-care therefore was a method by which the Japanese controlled their own health. Once they visit a doctor, the doctor assumes control and the patient is expected to follow orders.

Yet self-care is not an action that is completely independent of the medical profession. People engage in self-care in a manner consistent with medical norms, values, and information. Often medical advice guides the actions taken. When laypersons lack knowledge, competence, or experience to proceed, or are simply more comfortable in allowing professionals to handle matters, they turn to doctors. The remainder of this chapter will discuss the social processes involved in seeking help from a physician.

SOCIODEMOGRAPHIC VARIABLES

A significant portion of past research in medical sociology has concerned itself with the effect of sociodemographic variables on the utilization of health care services. The reader should keep in mind that help-seeking behavior often involves interaction between several variables acting in combination to influence specific outcomes in specific social situations. Nonetheless, attempts to isolate some sociodemographic variables have resulted in studies of such factors as age, sex, ethnicity, and socioeconomic status, explaining how they relate to the behavior of people seeking medical care.

Age and Sex

The findings for age and sex have been consistent: Use of health services is greater for females than for males and is greatest for the elderly. As indicated in Chapter 3 on the social demography of health, it is clear from existing data that females report a higher morbidity and, even after correcting for maternity, have a higher rate of hospital admissions (National Center for Health Statistics 2002; Verbrugge 1989; Weiss and Lonnquist 2000). If extent of knowledge about the symptoms of an illness is considered, it also appears that women generally know more about health matters than men and take better care of themselves (K. Dean 1989). In addition, the proportion of females in a household appears to be strongly related to the number of physician visits for that household. It has been shown, for instance, that the larger the proportion of females in a particular household, the greater the demand or requirement for physicians (Wan and Soifer 1974).

Perhaps it is obvious that people more than sixty-five years of age are in poorer health and are hospitalized more often than other age groups. It is also clear that elderly people are more likely to visit physicians than younger people. Since older people were more likely both to be physically disabled or ill, and to have public insurance (Medicare) coverage, they tend to visit doctors fairly often. Studies of the utilization of medical services by the aged indicate that such use is determined more by actual need than any other single factor (Cockerham 1997a). It is therefore not surprising that persons age sixty-five or older in the United States visited physicians an average of 11.7 times in 1996, much more than any other age group (National Center for Health Statistics 2002).

As for gender, males averaged 5.0 physician visits, compared to 6.5 visits for females in 1996. Females exhibit a lifelong pattern of visiting doctors more often than do males. There are three peaks in the visitation pattern for females. Initially, there are high rates during childhood, followed by a decline until a second rise during the childbearing years. After thirty-five, there is once again a decline, but physician visits by females steadily increase after age forty-five. For males, there are high rates of visits during childhood, followed by comparatively low rates of physician visits until a gradual increase begins at age forty-five.

Pregnancy and associated conditions do result in especially high rates of visits to physicians for women between the ages of fifteen and forty-four, but the woman's reproductive role accounts for less than 20 percent of all doctor visits. The higher visit rates by women are primarily the result of their greater number of ailments (Lorber 1997; Verbrugge 1985, 1986, 1989). More frequent utilization of physicians may have a substantial benefit for women in that they receive, on the average, earlier diagnosis and treatment for illness than men.

Ethnicity

Several early studies in medical sociology attempted to relate a person's utilization of health care services to his or her cultural background. One of the most systematic studies has been Edward A. Suchman's (1965a) investigation of the extent of the belief in and acceptance of modern medicine among several ethnic groups in New York City. Suchman sought to relate individual medical orientations and behaviors to specific types of social relationships and their corresponding group structures. He believed the interplay of group relationships with an individual's personal orientation toward medicine affected his or her health-seeking behavior.

Suchman categorized people as belonging to either cosmopolitan or parochial groups. Persons in a parochial group were found to have close and exclusive relationships with family, friends, and members of their ethnic group and to display limited knowledge of disease, skepticism of medical care, and high dependency in illness. They were more likely than the cosmopolitan group to delay in seeking medical care and more likely to rely upon a "lay-referral system" in coping with their symptoms of illness. A lay-referral system consists of nonprofessionals—family members, friends, or neighbors—who assist individuals in interpreting their symptoms and in recommending a course of action. The concept of the lay-referral system originated with Eliot Freidson (1960), who described the process of seeking medical help as involving a group of potential consultants, beginning in the nuclear family and extending outward to more select, authoritative laypersons, until the "professional" practitioner is reached. Freidson suggests that when cultural definitions of illness contradict professional definitions, the referral process will often not lead to the professional practitioner. The highest degree of resistance to using medical services in a lay-referral structure is found in lower-class neighborhoods characterized by a strong ethnic identification and extended family relationships. The decision to seek out a physician is based not just on professional standards of appropriate illness behavior but also on lay norms, and the two may be in conflict.

By contrast, the cosmopolitan group in Suchman's study demonstrated low ethnic exclusivity, less limited friendship systems, and fewer authoritarian family relationships. Additionally, they were more likely than the parochial group to know something about disease, to trust health professionals, and to be less dependent on others while sick.

Social Networks   What is suggested by Suchman's (1965a) study is that, under certain conditions, close and ethnically exclusive social relationships tend to channel help-seeking behavior, at least initially, toward the group rather than professional health care delivery systems. Yet Reed Geertsen and associates (1975) replicated Suchman's study in Salt Lake City and found an opposite trend. They observed that the Mormon community, with its strong value on good health and education and its emphasis upon family authority and tradition, demonstrated that group closeness and exclusivity can increase, rather than decrease, the likelihood of an individual responding to professional health resources. They concluded that people who belong to close and exclusive groups, especially tradition- and authority-oriented families, are (1) more likely to respond to a health problem by seeking medical care if it is consistent with their cultural beliefs and practices or are (2) less likely to seek medical care if their cultural beliefs support skepticism and distrust of professional medicine.

Geertsen and colleagues focused on the family rather than the ethnic group as the critical social unit in determining help-seeking behavior; the family is the person's first significant social group and usually the primary source of societal values. Thus, knowledge of disease and family authority appear as the key intervening variables in a person's medical orientation, as knowledge assists in recognition of symptoms, while family authority impels the sick person into the professional health care system. Alternatively, low knowledge about disease and/or weak family authority could act as inhibiting factors in obtaining professional treatment.

What is suggested here is that the family represents a social experience that influences how a particular person perceives his or her health situation. Individuals are born into a family of significant others—significant because they provide the child with a specific social identity. This identity includes not only an appraisal of physical and intellectual characteristics but knowledge concerning the social history of a particular family and group with all that means in terms of social status, perspective, and cultural background. As the child becomes older and takes as his or her own the values and opinions of the immediate family or group, or those of the wider society as presented through the mediating perspective of the family, the child is considered to be properly socialized in that he or she behaves in accordance with group-approved views.

Admittedly, children can either accept or reject the social perspective put forth by their family as representative of their own social reality; yet the choices offered to them in the process of their socialization are set by adults who determine what information is provided and in what form it is presented. Thus, although children may not be entirely passive in the socialization experience, what is important, as Peter Berger and Thomas Luckmann (1967) explain, is that they have no choice in the selection of their significant others so that identification with them is quasi-automatic. This further means that children's internalization of their family's interpretation of social reality is quasi-inevitable. While this initial social world presented to children by their significant others may be weakened by later social relationships, it can nevertheless be a lasting influence on them. Parental influence, for example, has been found to be the most important and persistent influence on the preventive health beliefs of their children (Lau, Quadrel, and Hartman 1990) and significant in shaping their health lifestyles as well (Wickrama et al. 1999).

Therefore, it is not surprising that a person's family or social group often guides the perceptual process or signals the perspective from which the total society is viewed. For this reason some studies in medical sociology have emphasized the social network as a major factor in help-seeking behavior (Geertsen et al. 1975; Gore 1989; Pescosolido 1992). A social network refers to the social relationships a person has during day-to-day interaction that serve as the normal avenue for the exchange of opinion, information, and affection. Typically, the social network is composed of family, relatives, and friends that comprise the individual's immediate social world, although the concept of a social network can be expanded to include increasingly larger units of society.

The role of the social network and its specific values, opinions, attitudes, and cultural background act to suggest, advise, or coerce an individual into taking or not taking particular courses of action. While developing a theory of help-seeking behavior, Bernice Pescosolido (1992) stressed the importance of social networks in obtaining medical care. Table 6-1 depicts a list developed by Pescosolido of the various options and choices that people in virtually all societies can potentially turn to for consultation when ill. The most obvious choice is the modern medical practitioner, especially M.D.'s. But the realities of the marketplace, such as insufficient income or health insurance, may push the individual elsewhere. Therefore, alternative medical practitioners, like faith healers or chiropractors, may be a possibility. Nonmedical professionals like social workers, clergy, and teachers represent another option, along with lay advisers like family members, or self-care, or perhaps no choices are available.

Pescosolido points out that people often seek advice and help from a variety of sources until the situation is resolved. She finds that it is through contact with other people that individuals deal with their illnesses and obtain support for medical and emotional problems. "Individuals in social networks," says Pescosolido (1992:1113),

TABLE 6-1   The Range of Choices for Medical Care and Advice.

Option	Adviser	Examples
Modern medical practitioners	M.D.'s, osteopaths, allied health workers	Pysicians, podiatrists, optometrists, nurses, opticians, psychologists, druggists, technicians, orderlies
Alternative medical practitioners	"Traditional" healers	Faith healers, folk healers spiritualists, herbalists, acupuncturists
	"Modern" healers	Chiropractors, naturopaths, nutritional consultants
Nonmedical professionals	Social workers Clergy Supervisors	Bosses, teachers
Lay advisers	Family Neighbors Friends Coworkers, classmates	Spouse, parents
Other	Self-care	Nonprescription medicines, self-examination procedures, home remedies, health foods
None		

Source: Adapted from Bernice A. Pescosolido. 1992. "Beyond Rational Choice: The Social Dynamics of How People Seek Help," *American Journal of Sociology,* 97:1113.

"are more than an influence on help seeking, they *are* caregivers and advisors, part of a 'therapy managing group.'" Consequently, the strategies that people employ for seeking health care are socially organized around the opportunities they have for interacting with people in a position to help.

As for ethnicity, its influence on physician utilization appears largely limited to its role in providing a cultural context for decision making within social networks. A variable that particularly confounds the effects of ethnicity on help seeking is socioeconomic status. The higher an individual's socioeconomic position, the less ethnic the person often becomes (Hollingshead and Redlich 1958). In other words, middle-class Americans of European, African, Hispanic, Asian, and native-origin descent tend to reflect the same middle-class norms and values as part of their mutual participation in middle-class society. Included in this pattern are similar perspectives toward the utilization of health services. This situation suggests that the direct effects of ethnicity on decision making concerning health care are largely confined to the lower class as Suchman's (1965a) work indicated. Studies of racial/ethnic minorities in the United States, such as blacks and Hispanics, seem to support this conclusion. The next three sections will discuss some of this research.

Health Insurance Coverage   To place this discussion of medical care for blacks and Hispanics into perspective, we should first note the extent of health insurance

TABLE 6-2   Health Insurance Coverage for Persons Under 65 Years of Age, Hispanic Origin, and Race, United States, 2000.

Insurance Type	Total U.S.	White Non-Hispanic	Black Non-Hispanic	Mexican American	Puerto Rican	Cuban American
Private	71.7%	79.3%	57.0%	46.6%	52.6%	63.6%
Medicaid	9.4	6.3	19.3	12.5	27.6	9.7
Other public	2.1	1.9	3.7	1.0	3.4	1.5
Uninsured	16.8	12.5	20.0	39.9	16.4	25.2

Source: National Center for Health Statistics, 2002.

coverage in the United States by race. Persons age sixty-five and over are covered by Medicare. The major type of health insurance for the remainder of the American population (under the age of sixty-five) is private insurance paid for by the individual, the individual's employer, or some combination thereof. The lowest income families may qualify for Medicaid, the public health insurance program for the poor. Table 6-2 lists the proportion of health insurance coverage for persons under age sixty-five according to race for 2000. Some 71.7 percent have private health insurance; 9.4 percent have Medicaid; 2.1 percent have some other type of public health insurance, such as military or Veterans Administration health benefits; and 16.8 percent have no health insurance. Table 6-2 also shows that 79.3 percent of all non-Hispanic whites have private health insurance compared to 57.0 percent of non-Hispanic blacks. Among Hispanics, Cuban Americans have the highest percentage of private health insurance (63.6 percent), followed by Puerto Ricans (52.6 percent) and Mexican Americans (46.6 percent).

For Medicaid, the public health insurance provided the poor, some 27.6 percent of all Puerto Ricans are covered along with 19.3 percent of all non-Hispanic blacks. Only some 6.3 percent of all non-Hispanic whites receive Medicaid. For those persons without any type of health insurance coverage, Table 6-2 shows that, among non-Hispanics, some 12.5 percent of whites and 20.0 percent of blacks fall into this category. However, the most striking disclosure is that the proportion of Mexican Americans without health insurance is 39.9 percent, the largest percentage by far of any ethnic group in American society.

The figure of 16.8 percent without health insurance for the nation as a whole in 2000 compares to the figure of 13.9 percent for 1990 and 11.6 percent for 1980; thus, it can be surmised that the proportion of persons in the total U.S. population lacking insurance coverage for health care is continually increasing. The uninsured are typically persons working in low-income jobs whose employers do not provide health insurance benefits for their employees. This would include many Mexican Americans, as well as people from all other racial and ethnic groups. These are near poor who have a job and make enough money to be disqualified from welfare programs like Medicaid but who nevertheless are unable to purchase private health insurance because it remains too expensive for their low level of wages. As Karen Seccombe and Cheryl Amey (1995:179) point out, the working poor "are playing by the 'rules' of the health insurance coverage scheme in this country by possessing employment and they are productive members of our economic system, yet they are without coverage for themselves and for their families."

African Americans Many years ago preventive medicine was largely a white middle-class concept that provided a patient with an elaborate structure of routine prenatal and postnatal care, pediatric services, dental care, immunizations, and screening for the presence of disease. Ralph Hines (1972) blamed the failure of blacks to use preventive health facilities on a lack of value orientation regarding such services. It can probably be attributed to a lack of financial resources as well. For those living at a subsistence level, the only options seem to be welfare medicine, which by its very nature is often bureaucratic and impersonal, or no professional care at all.

However, while some blacks, namely those without any type of health insurance coverage, remain underserved with respect to professional medical care, the pattern of physician utilization by blacks in general has changed dramatically in the last few decades. Prior to the mid-1970s, blacks tended to visit doctors significantly less often than whites and showed more negative attitudes toward seeking help from physicians (Dutton 1978). Since then it has been found that blacks have relatively positive attitudes toward doctors and visit physicians often (Sharp, Ross, and Cockerham 1983).

Hispanics Recent studies on the illness behavior of Hispanics in the United States are lacking, but many older studies of Mexican Americans in rural communities found a strong reliance on folk medicine and a reluctance to visit physicians (Andersen et al. 1981; Madsen 1973). However, other research determined that Mexican Americans were not exceptionally different from non-Hispanic whites in their utilization of health care (Welch, Comer, and Steinman 1973). The key variables appear to be education and income, with educated and more affluent Mexican Americans, Puerto Ricans, Cuban Americans, and other Hispanics having family doctors, going regularly to dentists, and utilizing other health services in the same manner as their non-Hispanic white counterparts.

Several studies investigating the utilization of professional health services in the United States show that Mexican Americans have the lowest rates of any racial/ ethnic minority group (Angel and Angel 1996a, 1996b; Roberts and Lee 1980). Mexican Americans appear to have somewhat lower rates than non-Hispanic whites and blacks for visits to physicians and substantially lower rates for routine physical examinations and eye examinations. Mexican Americans have higher rates for visits to dentists than African Americans, but these rates are markedly lower than those for non-Hispanic whites. Lower utilization rates for Mexican Americans seem to be largely a function of socioeconomic status (lower income and education) rather than ethnicity (Roberts and Lee 1980).

Mexican Americans are among those most likely to report that they could not afford health insurance as the main reason they did not have coverage. The low rates of private health insurance among Mexican Americans (who have the lowest level of health insurance of any ethnic group) result from low income, education, and employment in businesses that generally do not provide such coverage (Angel and Angel 1996a, 1996b). Uninsured Hispanics are less likely to have a regular source of health care, to have visited a physician in the past year or had a routine physical examination, and to rate their health as excellent or very good in comparison to Hispanics with private health insurance (Treviño et al. 1991). Another factor in the low rates of physician utilization by Mexican Americans in particular is the paucity of Hispanic health professionals; only some 5 percent of all American physicians are of Hispanic origin, and the percentage of Hispanic dentists, nurses, pharmacists, and therapists is even lower—about 3 percent of the national total.

Socioeconomic Status

Another major approach to the study of help-seeking behavior has been its correlation with socioeconomic status. Several years ago, it was generally believed that lower-class persons tended to underutilize health services because of the financial cost and/or culture of poverty. The culture of poverty, as summarized by Thomas Rundall and John Wheeler (1979), is a phenomenon in which poverty, over time, influences the development of certain social and psychological traits among those trapped within it. These traits include dependence, fatalism, inability to delay gratification, and a lower value placed on health (being sick is not especially unusual). This, in turn, tends to reinforce the poor person's disadvantaged social position. The seminal study showing how the poor had developed a different perspective concerning their interpretations of symptoms was Earl Koos's *The Health of Regionville* (1954). Koos conducted his study in a small community in New York where he found it possible to rank the local residents into three distinct socioeconomic classes. Class I consisted of the most successful people in town in terms of financial assets. Class II represented middle-class wage earners who were the majority of citizens, while Class III represented the least skilled workers and poorest members of the community.

Members of each socioeconomic class were asked to indicate whether certain easily recognized symptoms were considered to be significant enough to be brought to the attention of a doctor. Class I respondents demonstrated a much higher level of recognition of the importance of symptoms than either Class II or Class III. Only two of the symptoms, loss of appetite and backache, were reported by less than three-fourths of Class I as needing medical attention. Otherwise, almost all Class I respondents were prepared to go to a physician if a symptom appeared. For only one symptom, persistent coughing, did Class I respondents not have the highest percentage, and this difference was negligible.

Class III respondents, in contrast, showed a marked indifference to most symptoms. Seventy-five percent of the lower-class respondents considered ten of the seventeen symptoms not serious enough to warrant medical attention. Only three symptoms (excessive vaginal bleeding and blood in stool and urine) achieved a response of 50 percent or more, and all of these were associated with unexplained bleeding.

Thus, in Regionville at the time of Koos's study in the early 1950s, symptoms did not necessarily lead to seeking medical treatment among the lower class. In addition, Class III persons were inhibited from seeking treatment because of cost, fear, and relative need as related to age and the role of the sick person. The very young, the elderly, and breadwinners were most likely to receive medical attention among the poor. Another important factor in help-seeking behavior for Class III persons was group expectations about symptoms, further suggesting the importance of the social network. Backache, for example, was a symptom the poor commonly defined as not being a serious ailment. For the poor, having a backache was nothing unusual.

At the time, Koos's study helped establish the premise that lower-class persons are less likely than others to recognize various symptoms as requiring medical treatment and that these beliefs contribute to differences in the actual use of services. This premise was supported by the conclusions of surveys by the National Center for Health Statistics in 1960 and 1965, which found that higher-income persons were visiting physicians to a much greater extent than lower-income persons.

In 1968, however, the National Center found a changing pattern of physician utilization. It was now the middle-income group who had become the underutilizers. Highest rates of physician visits were either persons with the lowest level of income or the highest level. The higher rate for the low-income group was largely due to Medicaid and Medicare health insurance programs. Medicaid, administered at the state level, provides coverage intended to help pay the cost of health care for the poor. Medicare, a federal program, provides coverage for the elderly, who are overrepresented in the low-income group.

Between 1963 and 1970, as the effects of Medicaid and Medicare became evident, the use of physician services by low-income persons increased to the point that the significance of the relationship between income and utilization was greatly diminished. In fact, by 1970, it could be demonstrated that the poor had higher rates of physician use than any other income group. For example, according to data collected by Ronald Andersen and Odin Anderson (1979) for selected years between 1928 and 1974, the low-income group had the lowest rates of physician utilization from 1928 to 1931. The middle-income group ranked in the middle, and the high-income group had the highest number of visits. This pattern remained until 1970, when the low-income group emerged with the highest rates, followed by the high-income group and the middle-income group. The present pattern indicates the lowest income group visits physicians most often, followed by middle-income groups. The highest income group visits doctors the least.

Even though the poor are visiting doctors in greater numbers, this fact does not mean that they use the same sources of medical treatment in proportions equal to those of higher-income groups. Differences between income groups in regard to where they seek care are obvious and consistent. People with higher incomes are more likely than those with lower incomes to have received medical services in private doctors' offices and group practices or over the telephone. However, the reverse situation is true for other sources of care. People with lower incomes are more likely to contact hospital outpatient clinics or emergency rooms. Although people of

The poor have the highest rates of physician utilization. They are most likely to not have a personal physician and to routinely seek care in hospital outpatient clinics and emergency rooms.

all income groups use each source, a pattern emerges of a dual health care system—a "private" system with a greater proportion of the higher-income groups and a "public" system with a preponderance of lower-income groups. In the public system, the patient is likely to receive less quality medical care, spend longer amounts of time in waiting rooms, not have a personal physician, cope with more bureaucratic agencies, and return after treatment to a living situation that is less conducive to good health.

Furthermore, when actual *need* for health services is taken into account, low-income persons appear to use fewer services relative to their needs (Dutton 1978, 1986). Diana Dutton (1978) pointed out many years ago that statistics showing increased use of health services by the poor can be misleading. She argued that the poor have higher rates of disability due to illness and that the poor also tend to be more likely to seek symptomatic care. The nonpoor, in turn, are more likely to seek preventive care, which is aimed at keeping healthy people well, instead of waiting to seek help when symptoms appear. Thus, the poor appear to have more sickness and, despite the significant increase in use of services, still do not obtain as much health care as they actually need. Using data collected in Washington, D.C., Dutton tested three different explanations concerning why the poor would show lower use rates in relation to actual need than the nonpoor: (1) financial coverage, (2) the culture of poverty, and (3) the systems barrier.

The financial coverage explanation consists of the claim that the poor cannot afford to purchase the services they need—the cost is high, income is low, and insurance programs are inadequate. Dutton found this explanation to be weak. Public health insurance, notably Medicaid, had stimulated use of services by the poor to a much greater extent than private health insurance had done for the nonpoor. Unlike many private insurance plans, Medicaid paid for most physician services and thereby promoted physician utilization. Conversely, private insurance, with the exception of prepaid plans, had less impact on seeking physician services.

The culture of poverty explanation is derived from the premise that attitudes and norms characteristic of poor people tend to retard use of services. For example, the poor may view society and professional medical practices as less than positive as a result of their life experiences. The poor also may be more willing to ignore illness or not define it as such because they must continue to function to meet the demands of survival. Dutton found the culture of poverty explanation to have some validity when combined with measures of income. As income decreased, belief in preventive checkups and professional health orientation also decreased, while degree of social alienation increased. "Of course," says Dutton (1978:359), "these differences may not reflect cultural variation so much as realistic adaptation to economic circumstances; preventive care may well be less important than paying the rent, and purchasing a thermometer may be viewed as an unaffordable luxury." Nevertheless, Dutton argues that attitudes related to the culture of poverty do play an important role in explaining differences in the use of health services between income groups, particularly the use of preventive care.

In Dutton's view, the strongest explanation for low use of services by the poor in relation to need was the systems barrier explanation. This explanation focused on organizational barriers inherent in the more "public" system of health care typically used by the poor, such as hospital outpatient clinics and emergency rooms. This type of barrier not only pertains to difficulty in locating and traveling to a particular source of care, but also includes the general atmosphere of the treatment setting, which in itself may be impersonal and alienating. For example, as Anselm Strauss (1970:14–15) comments:

> The very massiveness of modern medical organization is itself a hindrance to health care for the poor. Large buildings and departments, specialization, division of labor, complexity, and bureaucracy lead to an impersonality and an overpowering and often grim atmosphere of hugeness. The poor, with their meager experience in organizational life, their insecurity in the middle class world, and their dependence on personal contacts, are especially vulnerable to this impersonalization.
>
> Hospitals and clinics are organized for "getting work done" from the staff point of view; only infrequently are they set up to minimize the patient's confusion. He fends for himself and sometimes may even get lost when sent "just down the corridor." Patients are often sent for diagnostic tests from one service to another with no explanations, with inadequate directions, with brusque tones. This may make them exceedingly anxious and affect their symptoms and diagnosis. After sitting for hours in waiting rooms, they become angry to find themselves passed over for latecomers—but nobody

explains about emergencies or priorities. They complain they cannot find doctors they really like or trust.

. . . To the poor, professional procedures may seem senseless or even dangerous—especially when not explained—and professional manners impersonal or brutal, even when professionals are genuinely anxious to help.

Dutton (1978, 1986) found from her research that low-income patients in public health care systems confronted a lack of preventive examination (physicians had little time for counseling patients or providing preventive care), high charges for services, long waiting times, and relatively poor patient–physician relationships. Dutton's (1978:361–362) position was that this situation posed a highly significant barrier that discouraged low-income patients "from seeking care, *above and beyond* the deterrent effects of inadequate financial coverage and negative attitudes toward professional health care." Low utilization was therefore seen as a normal response to an unpleasant experience.

The majority of people in the Dutton study were black. Subsequent research by Rundall and Wheeler (1979) on the effect of income on use of preventive care involved a sample of respondents in Michigan, who were mostly white. Dutton's findings were confirmed. There was no support for the financial coverage explanation. There was some support for the culture of poverty explanation in that the poor perceived themselves as relatively less susceptible to illness (they could tolerate unhealthy conditions) and therefore were less likely to seek preventive services. However, there was strong support for the systems barrier explanation. People with relatively high incomes were more likely to have a regular source of care, and those individuals with a regular source of care were more likely to use preventive services.

Having a regular source of care has been identified as an important variable in help-seeking behavior. This situation implies that the patient is relatively comfortable with the relationship and has some trust in the physician's skills at diagnosis and treatment. Low-income people receiving medical care in the public sector are less likely to have a personal physician and must be treated by whichever physician happens to be on duty in a hospital or clinic. If they have to maneuver between several clinics and public assistance agencies to obtain either treatment or authorization for treatment, low-income people are subject to even more fragmented pathways to health care.

Future Patterns of Physician Utilization by Social Class

Studies conducted in the 1950s and 1960s suggest that the culture of poverty produces beliefs and values inhibiting the use of physician services. According to this argument, disadvantaged groups hold beliefs that are not consistent with scientific medicine; the poor are skeptical about medical care and less sensitive to the meaning of symptoms (Koos 1954; Strauss 1970; Suchman 1965a; Zola 1966). The potential strength of these attitudes is evident in research reported by Mervyn Susser and William Watson (1971) on physician utilization in Great Britain during the first ten to fifteen years after the introduction of socialized medicine. Even though improved medical care was available at no cost, the poor continued to persist in using self-treatment and to delay seeking professional care. Susser and Watson suggested that despite the change in the availability of services, cultural change lagged behind. Thus, it appears that beliefs can have an impact on the use of physician services that is independent of financial constraints and the structural organization of services.

One would expect, however, that removing the financial barriers to health care might eventually alter the attitudes of people in the lower social classes accordingly. With increasing opportunities for the less privileged to receive health care, such as socialized medicine in Great Britain and the availability of Medicare and Medicaid in the United States, it seems likely that the attitudes of the less privileged would become more positive. Since the utilization rates of the poor have increased significantly over the past thirty years, their attitudes about going to the doctor should have changed also.

The author and his colleagues (Sharp, Ross, and Cockerham 1983) investigated this situation and found that blacks and people with less education have positive attitudes toward visiting physicians and are more likely than whites and people with more education to think that various symptoms are serious enough to warrant the attention of a doctor. These data suggest that as blacks and those with less education have gained more equitable access to the health care system with the advent of Medicare and Medicaid, their beliefs did change in a direction that encourages physician utilization. At the same time, the well educated may be taking more responsibility for their own health and feeling less inclined to visit the doctor. Better educated persons may be more discriminating in deciding which symptoms warrant seeing a physician.

What is suggested by this finding is that there is more of a consumer orientation toward health among socially advantaged persons. In a free-market situation, health consumers typically have more freedom to choose their source and mode of health care than is the case in a system of socialized medicine. Laypersons, as Freidson's (1960) discussion of the lay-referral system made clear, do judge technical performance and the quality of service provided by physicians regardless of whether they are trained to do so. And they make decisions about doctors based upon these evaluations, usually in consultation with their friends and relatives.

The trend toward consumerism in medicine is similar to consumerism in other aspects of American life in which people make informed choices about the services available to them. This orientation is more likely a feature characteristic of middle- and upper-class persons than the socially and economically disadvantaged. Dutton (1978) has suggested that the United States has a two-track system of health care delivery—one private and the other public. What we may be seeing is that those persons at the bottom of society, who are the major participants in the public track, may have a much greater willingness to turn the responsibility for their health over to the health care delivery system itself. This development is consistent with research investigating Talcott Parsons's (1951) concept of the sick role where it was found that persons on the lower level of income are most likely to agree that people have a right not to be held responsible for their illnesses (Arluke, Kennedy, and Kessler 1979; Wolinsky and Wolinsky 1981).

Arnold Arluke and his associates (1979:34) suggest that acceptance of the notion that illness is not the responsibility of the sick person may be related to broader social class differences in imputation of responsibility. That is, lower-class persons may tend to have a more passive orientation toward life in general and less willingness to take responsibility for problems. Certainly this is what is shown by research using locus-of-control measures in which it is reported that members of the lowest socioeconomic group have more fatalistic attitudes and are more accepting of external forces controlling their lives (Wheaton 1980).

Among those studies that have used a locus-of-control measure in relation to physical health, the work of Melvin Seeman and his colleagues appears to be the most relevant. Seeman and J. W. Evans (1962) found that tuberculosis patients with an internal locus of control (belief that one can master, control, or effectively alter the environment) knew more about their illness and took a more active role in coping with it than those with an external locus of control (belief that one is more or less at the mercy of the environment). Seeman and Teresa Seeman (1983) found that a low sense of internal control could be significantly associated with less self-initiated preventive care, less optimism about the effectiveness of early treatment, poorer self-rated health, more illness and bed confinement, and greater dependence on physicians.

In other research, the author and his colleagues (Cockerham et al. 1986a) found important differences between socioeconomic groups with respect to symptom perception, physician utilization, and sense of control over one's health situation. Persons with higher socioeconomic status were more consumer minded and expressed greater personal responsibility for their own health. The poor were less discriminating in deciding which symptoms warranted a doctor's attention. When ill, the poor reported they visited doctors more or less routinely, even for minor ailments, while the more affluent appeared more likely to engage in self-treatment or to recognize minor ailments as self-limiting and likely to disappear in a day or two without a physician's services. The poor also expressed a decreased sense of personal control over their health. Thus, the poor seemed to be relatively passive recipients of professional health services with a significantly greater likelihood of investing responsibility for their own health in the health care system than in themselves.

Consequently, when it comes to the self-management of one's health, studies such as the one just mentioned point to an interesting contrast in the health practices of the poor. Persons in lower socioeconomic groups may be attempting to participate in middle-class health lifestyles in accordance with their level of capability, but adopting a distinctly more dependent posture in interacting with physicians and the health care system. If middle-class values have spread to the lower class in regard to health-advancing behavior, why have they not also spread in relation to coping with medical doctors and institutions?

The answer seems to lie within the cultural context of both poverty and medical practice. The culture of poverty tends to promote feelings of dependence and fatalism. Thus, the poor are especially disadvantaged when they interact with physicians as authority figures and are confronted with modern medical technology.

The development of a large array of medical equipment and procedures has increasingly taken away the self-management of health from laypersons, but particularly from those at the bottom of society with their more limited levels of education and experience with technology. When direct collaboration with medical practitioners is required, the poor become even more dependent.

However, other better educated persons have reacted to the professional dominance of physicians with increased skepticism of physicians' service orientation and an emerging belief that physicians should not always be completely in charge of the physician–patient relationship (Crawford 1984; Haug and Lavin 1981, 1983). They have assumed more of a consumer position with regard to health care. That is, they are making decisions on their own about which steps are most appropriate for them in dealing with doctors and maintaining their health. In doing so, they are becoming less dependent on physicians and rejecting the traditional physician–patient relationship for one of provider–consumer.

This leads us to consider the influence of the culture of medicine. The culture of medicine does not promote equality among laypersons when direct physician–patient interaction is required, nor provide a context within which such an orientation can grow within the medical environment. Instead, physicians are portrayed as powerful individuals with the training and intellect to make life or death judgments and patients as completely dependent on those judgments. Consumerism and equality are not promoted because of the physician's need to have leverage over the patient. In the medical view, leverage is needed because treatment may be painful and discomforting and the patient typically lacks the expertise to treat the disorder (Parsons 1951).

This situation suggests that the culture of medicine is particularly important in explaining the health and illness behavior of the poor. One consequence of the increased frequency of contact between the medical profession and the poor appears to be that medical values have spread to the lower class. Accepting responsibility and self-management for diet, exercise, smoking, and other health-advancing behavior is strongly encouraged by the mass media and the medical profession. Physicians actively promote and reinforce the practice of health-advancing behavior. But consumerism in dealing with doctors and the health care system are not similarly encouraged or reinforced.

The trend for the immediate future in the use of physician services seems to be one in which the more affluent and better educated are likely to be more discriminating in their use of doctors. They likely will take a consumer approach, shopping for the appropriate services, making their own decisions about their symptoms and what they mean, and dealing with physicians on a more equal basis than before. Conversely, the poor appear likely to continue seeing doctors more frequently than members of the other social strata, both because they have more illness and disability and because they have more of a tendency to invest responsibility for their problems in the health care delivery system itself. In doing so, they appear less likely to question the authority or judgments of doctors, while assuming doctors will alleviate their symptoms or cure them.

RECOGNIZING AND COPING WITH ILLNESS SYMPTOMS

Studies in the United States, Great Britain, France, and the Netherlands suggest that laypersons generally conceive of health as either the relative absence of the symptoms of illness (Calnan 1987; R. Williams 1983), a feeling of physical and mental equilibrium or well-being (d'Houtaud and Field 1984, 1986; Herzlich 1973; Herzlich and Pierret, 1986, 1987; Joosten 1989), being able to carry out one's daily tasks (Apple 1960), or some combination of the preceding (Baumann 1961; Twaddle 1969). Conversely, to be ill means the presence of symptoms, feeling bad and in a state of disequilibrium, and functional incapacitation (not being able to carry out one's usual activities).

Thus, what laypersons recognize as illness is in part deviance from a standard of normality established by common sense and everyday experience. David Mechanic and Edmund Volkart (1961) have suggested that a given illness manifests specific characteristics with regard to symptom recognition and the extent of danger. Illness recognition is determined by how common the occurrence of the illness is in a given population and how familiar people are with its symptoms. Illness danger refers to the relative predictability of the outcome of the illness and the amount of threat or loss that is likely to result. When a particular symptom is easily recognizable and relatively devoid of danger, it is likely to be defined as a routine illness. When a symptom occurs infrequently, making identification more difficult, and is combined with an increasing perception of danger, there is likely to be a greater sense of concern.

Yet, as Mechanic (1978) has noted, recognition of a symptom, while certainly a necessary condition to motivate help-seeking behavior, is not in itself sufficient for a definition of illness. Some illnesses, such as appendicitis, may have obvious symptoms, while other illnesses, such as the early stages of cancer, may not. Also there are cases of persons who, despite symptoms, delay seeking health care. Cancer patients have been known to avoid cancer screening procedures because of their anxiety about learning the truth and being forced to confront what it means to have cancer (M. Becker and Maiman 1975). Therefore, the characteristics of illness recognition and illness danger can be significant influences on the manner in which people perceive a disease.

Mechanic (1978:268–269) suggests that whether a person will seek medical care is based on ten determinants: (1) visibility and recognition of symptoms; (2) the extent to which the symptoms are perceived as dangerous; (3) the extent to which symptoms disrupt family, work, and other social activities; (4) the frequency and persistence of symptoms; (5) amount of tolerance for the symptoms; (6) available information, knowledge, and cultural assumptions; (7) basic needs that lead to denial; (8) other needs competing with illness responses; (9) competing interpretations that can be given to the symptoms once they are recognized; and (10) availability of treatment resources, physical proximity, and psychological and financial costs of taking action. In addition to describing these ten determinants of help-seeking behavior, Mechanic explains that they operate at two distinct levels: other-defined and

A boy with asthma recognizes his symptoms and uses a
Nebulizer machine to help him breathe.

self-defined. The other-defined level is, of course, the process by which other people attempt to define an individual's symptoms as illness and call those symptoms to
the attention of that person. Self-defined is where the individual defines his or her
own symptoms. The ten determinants and two levels of definition interact to influence a person to seek or not seek help for a health problem.

The central theme that forms a backdrop for Mechanic's general theory of
help-seeking is that illness behavior is a culturally and socially learned response. A
person responds to symptoms according to his or her definition of the situation. This
definition may be influenced by the definitions of others but is largely shaped by
learning, socialization, and past experience as mediated by a person's social and cultural background. The role of culture in shaping our understanding of illness and responses to it is profound (Quah 2001). This is seen in studies showing that the cultural beliefs of patients are important in coping with cancer (Remennick 1998).
Marjorie Kagawa-Singer (1993), for example, found Anglo-American men had more
difficulty coping with cancer than Japanese-American men who obtained greater social support and maintained the belief that they were healthy despite awareness of
their condition. Even pain and the attempt to prove it exists as an objective condition within the body are grounded in cultural meanings and understandings about
what pain is and how it should be dealt with (Kugelmann 1999; Radley 1994;

BOX 6-1   Anorexia Nervosa as a Culture-Bound Syndrome

One study that illustrates the role of culture in influencing health problems is Sing Lee's (1996) research on anorexia nervosa as a Western culture-bound syndrome. Anorexia nervosa is a condition characterized by food refusal and severe weight loss in young women that can be fatal. It typically results from a generalized aversion to "fatness." "Among Western people," states Lee (1996:24), "slimness has come to symbolize not only attractiveness but also self-control, youth and efficiency in both social and work-related domains." In the past, anorexia nervosa has been linked directly to Western cultural values and confined to Western countries. However, Lee finds that modernization and the spread of Western values to Asia promoted the increased prevalence of the disease in Japan, China, Singapore, and Taiwan. In this case, cultural values (slimness) and the psychosomatic illness it produced, migrated from the West to the East.

Zborowski 1952; Zola 1966). As Alan Radley (1994; Radley and Billig 1996) points out, a person's beliefs about health and illness are based upon that individual's understanding of the world one lives in and one's place in it. "This means," states Radley (1994:62), "that they draw upon a stock of knowledge about sickness, and about its bodily signs, that owes much to their cultural setting."

Suchman's (1965b) analysis of the stages of illness experience demonstrates how individuals draw upon their knowledge and experience of their bodily states to recognize symptoms of illness and do something about it in Western culture. According to Suchman, when individuals percieve themseves becoming sick they can pass through as many as five different response stages, depending upon their interpretation of their particular illness experience. These stages, shown in Figure 6-1, are (1) the symptom experience, (2) the assumption of the sick role, (3) medical care contact, (4) the dependent-patient role, and (5) recovery and rehabilitation.

The illness experience begins with the symptom stage, in which the individual is confronted with a decision about whether "something is wrong." The decision of the person involved may be to deny the symptoms as not needing attention, to delay making a decision until the symptoms are more obvious, or to accept the symptoms as evidence of a health disorder. The person may also attempt to treat himself or herself through the application of folk medicine or self-medication.

If the decision is made to accept the symptom experience as indicative of an illness, the person is likely to enter Suchman's second stage of the sick role. Here the person is allowed to relinquish normal social obligations provided permission is obtained from the person's lay-referral system. The lay-referral system can grant the individual provisional permission to assume the sick role. "Official" permission to adopt the sick role, however, can come only from the physician, who acts as society's agent as the authority on illness. Thus, while lay remedies may continue, the individual is again faced with a decision to deny the illness and abandon the illness experience or accept the provisional sick role and perhaps seek medical treatment.

FIGURE 6-1 Suchman's Stages of Illness Experience.

	I Symptom Experience	II Assumption of the Sick Role	III Medical Care Contact	IV Dependent-Patient Role	V Recovery and Rehabilitation
Decision	Something is wrong	Relinquish normal roles	Seek professional advice	Accept professional treatment	Relinquish sick role
Behaviors	Application of folk medicine, self-medication	Request provisional validation for sick role from members of lay-referral system—continue lay remedies	Seek authoritative legitimation for sick role—negotiate treatment procedures	Undergo treatment procedures for illness—follow regimen	Resume normal roles
Outcomes	Denial (flight into health) → Delay → Acceptance	Denial → Acceptance	Denial → Shopping → Confirmation	Rejection → Secondary gain → Acceptance	Refusal (chronic sick role) → Malingerer → Acceptance

Source: Rodney M. Coe, *Sociology of Medicine* (New York: McGraw-Hill Inc., 1970, 1978), p. 108. Reprinted with permission of McGraw-Hill, Inc.

If professional assistance is sought, the person enters the third stage of medical care contact. At this stage, the person attempts to obtain legitimation of his or her sick role status and to negotiate the treatment procedure. The illness experience may be confirmed or denied by the physician. If there is a disagreement between physician and patient, the patient may go "shopping" for another physician's diagnosis that might prove more acceptable.

If both patient and physician agree that treatment is necessary, the person passes into the dependent-patient stage. Here the person undergoes the prescribed treatment, but still has the option either to terminate or to continue the treatment. Sometimes patients settle for the "secondary gain" of enjoying the privileges accorded to a sick person, such as taking time off from work, and do not seriously try to get well. Or both patient and physician may cooperate to allow the patient to enter the fifth and final stage of recovery and rehabilitation. In this stage the patient is expected to relinquish the sick role and resume normal social roles. This may not happen, as in the case of a chronic illness or when the patient chooses to malinger in an illness experience even though technically well.

Although an illness experience may not involve all of the stages described by Suchman and can be terminated at any particular stage through denial, the significance of Suchman's model is that each stage requires the sick person to take different kinds of decisions and actions. In evaluating the experience of illness, the sick person must interpret not only his or her symptoms but also what is necessary in terms of available resources, alternative behaviors, and the probability of success.

SUMMARY AND CONCLUSION

This chapter has reviewed the major theories and findings of medical sociology concerning the process of seeking medical care and the utilization of health care services. While there is no single theory or approach that has earned general consensus, the existing literature reveals the two most important variables in health care utilization to be the perceived severity of symptoms and the ability to pay for the rendering of services.

Social-psychological models of help-seeking behavior have emphasized the importance of self-perception as it relates to a person's understanding of a particular symptom. Especially important is whether the person perceives himself or herself as able to perform normal social roles. Studies concentrating on ethnicity as a factor have pointed to the role of the social network in influencing the perceptual process according to the network's own sociocultural orientation. Although some patients, notably cancer patients, may delay seeing a doctor because they are fearful about having their perceptions confirmed, the generalization can be made that the more symptoms are perceived as representing a serious illness, the more likely it is that a person will seek professional services.

The ability to pay for health services has traditionally accounted for significant socioeconomic differences in health care utilization. Today it appears that public health insurance and social welfare monies have enabled the poor to visit physicians more frequently than the upper-income groups. However, whether increased physician visitation has resulted in a corresponding rise in the quality of health care provided the poor remains to be determined. Then, too, the poor still reside in an environment of poverty that perpetuates their increased risk to health hazards. Among those persons without public health insurance—those covered by private health insurance plans that still leave considerable cost for the individual consumer, or those without any health insurance—the ability to pay remains an important obstacle to help-seeking behavior. This chapter also discussed the sociodemographic variables of age and sex, which were found to be consistent predictors of seeking medical care. Elderly persons and females generally report more illness than younger persons and males and tend to consult physicians more readily.

ILLNESS BEHAVIOR INTERNET SITES

Sociodemographic Variables

1. Centers for Disease Control and Prevention, National Center for Health Statistics.
   http://www/cdc.gov/nchs

   Contains a search engine with access to many studies dealing with sociodemographic variables.

2. U.S. Department of Health and Human Services: Initiative to Eliminate Racial and Ethnic Disparities in Health.
   http://raceandhealth.hhs.gov

   Resources, links, and other information dealing with infant mortality, cancer, cardiovascular disease, HIV, and immunizations in minority groups.

3. U.S. Department of Health and Human Services: Office of Minority Health Resource Center.
   http://www.omhrc.gov

   This is the Department of Health and Human Services' premier source for minority information including literature, funding, and statistics.

4. The Minority Health Network.
   http://www.pitt.edu/~ejb4/min

   Resources, statistics, and links dealing with diseases among minority groups.

Medicare and Medicaid

1. Health Care Financing Administration—Medicare Information.
   http://cms.hhs.gov/medicare/default.asp

   Information on the Medicare Health Insurance Program.

2. Health Care Financing Administration—Medicaid Statistics and Data.
   http://cms.hhs.gov/medicaid/mcaidsad.asp

   Medicaid National Summary Statistics.

The Sick Role

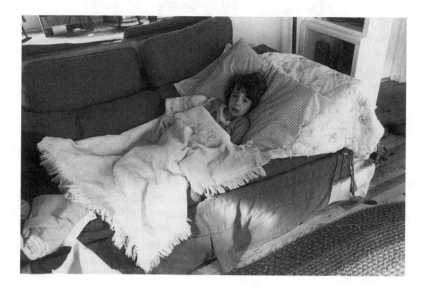

Each society's definition of illness becomes institutionalized within its cultural patterns, so that one measure of social development is a culture's conception of illness. In primitive societies illness was defined as an autonomous force or "being," such as an evil spirit, that attacked people and settled within their bodies in order to cause them pain or death. During the Middle Ages some people defined illness as a punishment for sins, and care of the sick was regarded as religious charity. Today illness is defined as a state or condition of suffering as the result of a disease or sickness. This definition is based upon the modern scientific view that an illness is an abnormal biological affliction or mental abnormality with a cause, a characteristic train of symptoms, and a method of treatment.

ILLNESS AS DEVIANCE

The medical view of illness is that of deviance from a biological norm of health and feelings of well-being. This view involves the presence of a pathogenic mechanism within the body that can be objectively documented. The diagnosis of a disease, for example, results from a correlation of observable symptoms with knowledge about the physiological functioning of the human being. Ideally, a person is defined as ill when his or her symptoms, complaints, or the results of a physical examination and/or laboratory tests indicate an abnormality. The traditional identifying criteria for disease are (1) the patient's experience of subjective feelings of sickness; (2) the finding by the physician that the patient has a disordered function of the body; and (3) the patient's symptoms conforming to a recognizable clinical pattern. The clinical pattern is a representation of a model or theory of disease held by the diagnostician. In diagnosis, logic is the basic tool.

The physician's function in the treatment of illness involves, first, arriving at a diagnosis and, second, applying remedial action to the health disorder in such a way as to return the patient to as normal a state as possible. The evaluation of illness by the physician contains the medical definition of what is good, desirable, and normal as opposed to what is bad, undesirable, and abnormal. This evaluation is interpreted within the context of existing medical knowledge and the physician's experience. On this basis the medical profession formulates medical rules defining biological deviance and seeks to enforce them by virtue of its authority to treat those persons defined as sick.

In medical sociology, *disease* is considered an adverse physical state, consisting of a physiological dysfunction within an individual; an *illness* is a subjective state, pertaining to an individual's psychological awareness of having a disease and usually causing that person to modify his or her behavior; while *sickness* is a social state, signifying an impaired social role for those who are ill. Although a major area of interest in medical sociology is illness behavior, the concept of sickness is of special interest because it involves analysis of factors that are distinctly sociological—namely, the expectations and normative behavior that the wider society has for people who are defined as sick.

Sickness has typically been viewed by sociologists as a form of deviant behavior. This view was initially formulated by Talcott Parsons (1951) in his concept of the sick role—characteristic behaviors a sick person adopts in accordance with the normative demands of the situation. Parsons saw being sick as a disturbance in the "normal" condition of the human being, both biologically *and* socially. Previously, the sociological study of health and illness had relied upon the medical perspective; efforts were in fact limited to correlating social factors with biological factors based on references provided solely by the health practitioner. This medically oriented approach emphasized the physiological reality of the human organism but neglected the sociological reality that a person is sick when he or she *acts* sick.

The basis for describing illness as a form of deviant behavior lies in the sociological definition of deviance as any act or behavior that violates the social norms within a given social system. Thus, deviant behavior is not simply a variation from a statistical average. Instead, a pronouncement of deviant behavior involves making a *social judgment* about what is right and proper behavior according to a social norm. Norms reflect expectations of appropriate behavior shared by people in specific social settings, or they may be more general expectations of behavior common to a wide variety of social situations. Conformity to prevailing norms is generally rewarded by group acceptance and approval of behavior; deviation from a norm, however, can lead to disapproval of behavior, punishment, or other forms of social sanctions being applied against the offender. Norms allow for variations of behavior within a permissible range, but deviant behavior typically violates the range of permissible behavior and elicits a response from other people intended to control that behavior. Most theories of deviant behavior in sociology are concerned with behavior common in crime, delinquency, mental disorders, alcoholism, and drug addiction. These forms of behavior typically *offend* someone.

It is important to note that not all forms of deviant behavior produce undesirable consequences for a society. Deviance from the usual norms in such fields as art, music, theater, literature, and dance often provides very positive rewards both for the creative deviant and the society. However, sickness as deviance is typically regarded as an undesirable circumstance for both the sick person and for society. For the sick person, an illness obviously can mean discomfort and either permanent or temporary disruption of normal biological and social functioning, including death. Illness also entails the risk of economic hardship for the sick person's family. For society, illness can mean a reduction in the ability of a social group or organization to carry out its usual tasks and perform its normal social functions.

While sociologists have suggested that the explanation for sickness as a social event can be found outside of biology and medicine by including sickness within the general category of deviant behavior, this approach has been relatively recent. The early causal theories of deviance in sociology were essentially biological models that defined the source of deviance as something inherent in certain individuals. Undesirable behavior was thought to be caused by the genetic inheritance of criminal traits or perhaps a capricious genetic combination. The biological view of deviance has been generally rejected by contemporary sociologists as concentrating exclusively on the physiology of the individual and completely overlooking the implications of social norms and social judgments about an individual's behavior.

In turn, these social judgments are influenced by various aspects of social change. For example, in our past agrarian society, illness occurred largely in small-group contexts such as the family. It was a common occurrence, and the roles of being sick or attending sick people were part of a role-set that included expectable variations in behavior as well as "normal" behavior. However, far-reaching changes have occurred in industrialized society: the decline of large families, changing theories in the treatment of disease, and the evolution of complex medical techniques that often require hospitalization. These developments have tended to draw disease out of the area of the expectable into a highly specialized, institutionalized context. Similarly, our methods of dealing with sick people have changed, often transferring them to the care of specialists who operate outside the context of the familiar and over whom ordinary people have few powers of control. This transfer itself, coupled with our submission to hospital routines and medical procedures, creates a specialized set of circumstances that lead to a definition of sickness as deviance. The physically sick, like the insane and criminals, represent a social category of people removed from the mainstream of society if their illness is judged severe enough. Of course, the insane and criminals are generally much more stigmatized by society than the physically sick, but the point is that the pattern of treatment (removal from society and treatment by specialists) allows the person who is physically sick to be similar—though not identical—to an insane person who goes to an asylum or a criminal who goes to prison. Since the methods for dealing with the ill, the criminal, or the insane are in certain respects similar, we can see a basis for defining sickness as deviance.

THE FUNCTIONALIST APPROACH TO DEVIANCE

While sociologists reject biological models of deviance, present-day functionalism, stressing societal-level processes, systems, equilibrium, and interrelationships, represents a modern version of a homeostatic theory of deviance. This model is not organic or physiological. It does not find the causes of deviant behavior in individual needs, drives, instincts, genetic combinations, or any other purely individual patterns. It does find the source of deviant behavior in the relationships between individuals and social systems. This approach is based on the view that society is held together in a state of equilibrium by harmonious patterns of shared norms and values. What makes social life possible is the expectation that people will behave in accordance with the norms and values common to their particular social system. This process is "functional" because it results in social harmony and counterbalances "dysfunctional" processes, like crime and mental illness, that disrupt the social order. The tendency of a society toward self-maintenance through equilibrium is very similar to the biological concept of homeostasis in which the human body attempts to regulate physiological (internal) conditions within a relatively constant range in order to maintain bodily functioning. A person may suffer from warts, indigestion, a broken leg, or perhaps even from a nonmalignant cancer and still be generally healthy. Likewise, a social system is viewed in the functionalist perspective as maintaining social functioning by regulating its various parts within a relatively constant range. A social system may have problems with crime and delinquency but be "healthy" because of its overall capacity to function efficiently.

Because functionalist theorists perceive social systems as composed of various closely interconnected parts, they argue that changes, decisions, and definitions made in one part of the system inevitably affect to some degree all other parts of the system. Thus, a person's position within the social system subjects him or her to events and stresses originating in remote areas of the system. Behavior that is adaptive from one's own perspective and peculiar circumstances—like turning to crime—may be regarded as deviant by society at large. The individual then has the choice of continuing the adaptive behavior and being defined as deviant or trying to change that behavior even though the person sees it as necessary for his or her own survival. Many people, not surprisingly, continue the disapproved behavior and are therefore pressured by society into being deviant. Such people run the risk of confrontation with those authorities, such as psychiatrists, the police, and the courts, charged with controlling or eliminating dysfunctional social processes. Deviance in a social system is thus reduced through the application of social sanctions against the offender. These sanctions include the use of jails, prisons, and mental hospitals to remove the deviant from society to ensure social order and cohesion.

According to functionalist theory, sickness is dysfunctional because it also threatens to interfere with the stability of the social system. The medical profession functions to offset the dysfunctional aspects of sickness by curing, controlling, or preventing disease and by establishing technology by which handicapped persons can assist in self-maintenance and in maintenance of the social system. This analytical approach is the basis for Parsons's theory of the sick role, a central concept in medical sociology today.

THE SICK ROLE

Talcott Parsons (1902–1978) introduced his concept of the sick role in his book *The Social System* (1951), which was written to explain a complex functionalist model of society. In this model, social systems were linked to systems of personality and culture to form a basis for social order. Unlike other major social theorists preceding him, Parsons included an analysis of the function of medicine in his theory of society

According to the sick role, a patient should try to get well and seek technically competent help. This photo shows a physical therapist working with a patient.

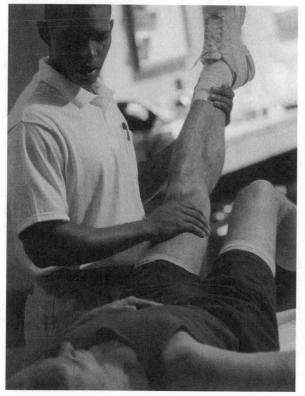

and, in doing so, was led to consider the role of the sick person in relation to the social system within which that person lived. The result is a concept that represents the most consistent approach to explaining the behavior characteristic of sick people in Western society.

Parsons's concept of the sick role is based on the assumption that being sick is not a deliberate and knowing choice of the sick person, though illness may occur as a result of motivated exposure to infection or injury. Thus, while the criminal is thought to violate social norms because he or she "wants to," the sick person is considered deviant only because he or she "cannot help it." Parsons warns, however, that some people may be attracted to the sick role in order to have their lapse of normal responsibilities approved. Generally, society accounts for the distinction between deviant roles by punishing the criminal and providing therapeutic care for the sick. Both processes function to reduce deviancy and change conditions that interfere with conformity to social norms. Both processes also require the intervention of social agencies, law enforcement or medicine, in order to control deviant behavior. Being sick, Parsons argues, is not just experiencing the physical condition of a sick state; rather, it constitutes a social role because it involves behavior based on institutional expectations and is reinforced by the norms of society corresponding to these expectations.

A major expectation concerning the sick is that they are unable to take care of themselves. It thus becomes necessary for the sick to seek medical advice and cooperate with medical experts. This behavior is predicated upon the assumption made by Parsons that being sick is an undesirable state and the sick person wants to get well.

Parsons insists that sickness is dysfunctional because it represents a mode of response to social pressure that permits the evasion of social responsibilities. A person may desire to retain the sick role more or less permanently because of what Parsons calls a "secondary gain," which is the exemption from normal obligations and the gaining of other privileges commonly accorded to the sick. Hence, medical practice becomes a mechanism by which a social system seeks to control the illnesses of its deviant sick by returning them to as normal a state of functioning as possible.

The specific aspects of Parsons's concept of the sick role can be described in four basic categories:

1. *The sick person is exempt from "normal" social roles.* An individual's illness is grounds for his or her exemption from normal role performance and social responsibilities. This exemption, however, is relative to the nature and severity of the illness. The more severe the illness, the greater the exemption. Exemption requires legitimation by the physician as the authority on what constitutes sickness. Legitimation serves the social function of protecting society against malingering.
2. *The sick person is not responsible for his or her condition.* An individual's illness is usually thought to be beyond his or her own control. A morbid condition of the body needs to be changed and some curative process apart from personal will power or motivation is needed to get well.
3. *The sick person should try to get well.* The first two aspects of the sick role are conditional on the third aspect, which is recognition by the sick person that being sick is undesirable. Exemption from normal responsibilities is temporary and conditional upon the desire to regain normal health. Thus, the sick person has an obligation to get well.

4. *The sick person should seek technically competent help and cooperate with the physician.* The obligation to get well involves a further obligation on the part of the sick person to seek technically competent help, usually from a physician. The sick person is also expected to cooperate with the physician in the process of trying to get well.

Parsons's concept of the sick role is based on the classical social theory of Emile Durkheim and Max Weber and the psychoanalytic theory of Sigmund Freud and especially Franz Alexander (Gerhardt 1989a, 1989b, 1989c; Lupton 1997). Psychoanalytic theories of the structure of the personality (id, ego, and superego) and the unconscious assisted Parsons in developing his thoughts on individual motivation. The sick person is presumably motivated to recover (as a result of socialization and the influence of the superego) and yet may perhaps also be motivated, either consciously or unconsciously, to desire the "secondary gain" of privileges and exemptions from daily tasks that accompany the sick role.

Durkheim's ideas on the function of moral authority and Weber's views on religious values are utilized by Parsons in describing the role of the physician. The physician, according to Parsons, is invested with the function of social control. This function, which is similar to that provided historically by priests and which originated in religion, is intended to control deviance. In this case, illness with its dysfunctional nature is the deviance. The designation of illness as an undesirable and illegitimate state is considered by Parsons to have the greatest implications for the healthy in that it reinforces their motivation to stay well. All of this is reflected in the position of health as an important social value in American society and the manner in which people are socialized to accept this value. By incorporating a consideration of health and illness into his analysis of social systems, Parsons was the first to demonstrate the function of medicine as a form of social control and did so within the parameters of classical sociological theory.

The Physician–Patient Role Relationship

A major contribution of Parsons's concept of the sick role is its description of a patterned set of expectations that define the norms and values appropriate to being sick in Western culture, both for the individual and for others who interact with the sick person. The sick role thus views the patient–physician relationship within a framework of social roles, attitudes, and activities that both parties bring to the situation. This approach allows us, with some exceptions, both to understand and predict the behavior of the ill in Western society. The patient–physician role, like all other roles, involves a basic mutuality; that is, each participant in the social situation is expected to be familiar with both his or her own and others' expectations of behavior and the probable sequence of social acts to be followed. *The sick role evokes a set of patterned expectations that define the norms and values appropriate to being sick, both for the individual and for others who interact with the person.* Neither party can define his or her role independently of the role partner. The full meaning of "acting like a physician" depends on the patient's conception of what a physician is in terms of the social role. The physician's role is, as Parsons tells us, to return the sick person to his or her normal state of functioning.

The role of the patient likewise depends on the conception the physician holds of the patient's role. According to Parsons, the patient is expected to recognize that being sick is unpleasant and that he or she has an obligation to get well by seeking the physician's help. The patient–physician role relationship is therefore not a spontaneous form of social interaction. It is a well-defined encounter consisting of two or more persons whose object is the health of a single individual. It is also a situation that is too important to be left to undefined forms of behavior; for this reason, patients and physicians tend to act in a stable and predictable manner.

The patient–physician relationship is intended by society to be therapeutic in nature. The patient has a need for technical services from the physician, and the physician is the technical expert who is qualified and defined by society as prepared to help the patient. The goal of the patient–physician encounter is thus to promote some significant change for the better in the patient's health.

Although the patient–physician relationship involves mutuality in the form of behavioral expectations, the status and power of the parties are not equal. The role of the physician is based upon an imbalance of power and technical expertise favorable exclusively to the physician. This imbalance is necessary because the physician needs leverage in his or her relationship with the patient in order to promote positive changes in the patient's health. Accomplishment of this goal sometimes requires procedures that can be painful or discomforting to the patient, yet the patient must accept and follow the treatment plan if the physician is to be effective. The physician exercises leverage through three basic techniques: (1) professional prestige, (2) situational authority, and (3) situational dependency of the patient. A physician's professional prestige rests upon technical qualifications and certification by society as a healer. The physician's situational power refers to the physician's having what the patient wants and needs. By contrast, the patient is dependent because he or she lacks the expertise required to treat the health disorder.

The role of the physician is also enhanced by a certain mystique reflecting faith in the power to heal. This aspect of the physician role results from the dependence of the patient on the physician for life-and-death decisions. Since the physician has the responsibility to "do everything possible" and because the survival of the patient may be at issue, the patient may be likely to regard the physician with a strong emotional attachment in the hope or belief that the physician has a "gift" or natural skill in the healing arts. Since medical practice is sometimes characterized by uncertainty, a physician's presumed talent can be a very important dimension in the patient–physician relationship. Exact proof of the existence of many minor ailments and most chronic diseases may not be possible, or attempts to establish such proof may not be justifiable because of the hazards to the patient involved in the investigation. Despite the great advancement of the science of medicine during the twentieth century, the physician must still sometimes act on the basis of a hunch.

An interesting analogue to the patient–physician relationship is the child–parent relationship. For some people an illness can foster a childlike state of dependency. However, while the role of the child is an immature role, the role of the patient represents a "disturbed" maturity (R. Wilson 1970). Both the child and the sick person lack the capacity to perform the usual functions of the adult in everyday life, and both are dependent on a stronger and more adequate person to take care of them. Also the physician can be like a parent figure in that he or she provides support and controls rewards significant to the dependent party. The primary reward for the child would be approval, while the primary reward for the sick person would be to get well. Yet the physician and the parent are unlike in the magnitude of their involvement with the dependent party and the depth of their emotional feelings. Obviously, the states of childhood and patienthood are not totally similar, yet the similarity is a striking one because the extremely sick person who is helpless, technically incompetent in treating his or her disorder, and perhaps emotionally disturbed over his or her condition of illness can be very dependent and fully capable of acting in childlike ways.

According to Eliot Freidson (1970a:206), physicians create the social possibilities for acting sick because they are society's authority on what "illness really is." They decide who is sick and what should be done about it. In essence, physicians are "gatekeepers" to most professional health resources, since these resources (such as prescription drugs and hospitals) cannot be used without their permission. Thus, Freidson argues that the behavior of the physician and others in the health field constitutes the embodiment of certain dominant values in society. These dominant values were described by Parsons (1951, 1979) and include the idea that health is positive and should be sought after. Stipulated in his concept of the sick role is that the sick person is expected to cooperate with the physician and *work* to achieve his or her own recovery and return to normal functioning.

Medicine as an Institution of Social Control

Besides Parsons's analytical insight into the ramifications of the patient–physician relationship, implicit in his concept of the sick role is the idea that medicine is (and should be) an institution for the social control of deviant behavior. Some medical sociologists (Conrad 1975; Conrad and Schneider 1980; Freidson 1970a; Twaddle 1969; Zola 1972) have expressed concern that medicine is indeed an institution for the control of deviance and is taking responsibility for an ever greater proportion of behaviors defined as deviant. In other words, acts that might have been defined as sin or crime and controlled by the church or the law are increasingly regarded as illnesses to be controlled through medical care. Thomas Szasz (1974:44–45) explains this trend as follows:

> Starting with such things as syphilis, tuberculosis, typhoid fever, and carcinomas and fractures we have created the class, "illness." At first, this class was composed of only a few items all of which shared the common feature of reference to a state of disordered structure or function of the human body as a physical-chemical machine. As time went on additional items were added to this class. They were not added, however, because they were newly discovered bodily disorders. The physician's attention has been deflected from this criterion and has become focused instead on disability and suffering as new criteria for selection. Thus, at first slowly, such things as hysteria, hypochondriasis, obsessive-compulsive neurosis and depression were added to the category of illness. Then with increasing zeal, physicians and especially psychiatrists began to call "illness". . . anything and everything in which they could detect any sign

of malfunctioning, based on no matter what the norm. Hence agoraphobia is illness because one should not be afraid of open spaces. Homosexuality is an illness because heterosexuality is the social norm. Divorce is illness because it signals failure of marriage.

If Szasz's view is correct, there appears to be a long-term trend toward making sickness and deviance not only synonymous but also toward treating deviance exclusively in a medical mode. Eliot Freidson (1970a) has argued that medicine has established a jurisdiction far wider than justified by its demonstrable capacity to "cure." Nonetheless, the medical profession has been highly successful in gaining authority to define deviant behavior as illness—behavior properly handled only by the physician. Andrew Twaddle (1973:756) points out that "today there are few, if any, problems of human behavior that some group does not think of as medical problems."

According to Bryan Turner (1992, 1995, 1996), regulation of the human body is in the interest of society because of the need to protect public health, the economy, and the social order. Turner notes that disease can be contained through social hygiene and education in appropriate lifestyles. Yet people can also knowingly jeopardize their health through habits like drug addiction, overeating, smoking, lack of exercise, and alcoholism. These behaviors, he continues, are either already regarded as socially deviant or are well on the way to becoming regarded as such. When certain behaviors threaten the health of people and the well-being of society, the state may be required to intervene, such as banning cigarette smoking from public places. Consequently, it is Turner's (1996:214) position that "medicine is essentially social medicine, because it is a practice which regulates social activities under the auspices of the state." Therefore, to the extent that the control of human behavior is the basis of social organization and to the extent that the control of deviant behavior is becoming the function of the medical profession, Parsons's concept of the sick role helps us understand contemporary mechanisms of social stability.

Research Applications of the Sick Role

Parsons's concept of the sick role, as Freidson (1970a:228) has explained, represents "a penetrating and apt analysis of sickness from a distinctly sociological point of view." This comment is particularly appropriate when it is recognized that the sick role has stimulated a considerable body of research in medical sociology. To mention only a few such studies, Paul Chalfant and Richard Kurtz (1971) utilized Parsons's sick-role concept in explaining social workers' denial of the sick role to alcoholics. Social workers in this study felt that drinking was motivated behavior and that alcoholics could avoid their disorder if they desired to do so. Hence, the alcoholic was not entitled to exemption from normal responsibilities.

Another application of the sick role is found in Stephen Cole and Robert LeJeune's (1972) study of welfare mothers. Cole and LeJeune observed that among welfare mothers in New York City the general norm was to accept the dominant cultural view that being on welfare is a result of personal failure. Welfare mothers who had given up hope of getting off welfare were prone to adopt the sick role in order to legitimize their self-defined failure. This study concluded that the sick role may provide a "substitute" status by way of exemption from normal role responsibilities for persons who lack other socially approved statuses. What is implied here is that certain people may use the sick role because it is less stigmatizing than being regarded a failure.

A similar finding was noted in a study by Arnold Arluke, Louanne Kennedy, and Ronald Kessler (1979) of 1,000 patients discharged from two large New York City hospitals. Arluke and his colleagues found that low-income and elderly patients are most likely to agree that a person has the right not to be held responsible for his or her illness. For some elderly people, it was believed that the sick role provided an excuse for being dependent. Consequently, these elderly people were most unwilling to give up the role. Younger people were most likely to agree that a person has the duty to try to get well. In other research, Fredric and Sally Wolinsky (1981) found in a rural North Carolina county that those who expect sick-role legitimation are older, have relatively lower socioeconomic status, and perceive themselves as in poor health. In Illinois, the author and his associates (Cockerham et al. 1980) studied the manner in which physicians treated their own minor ailments. The doctors tended to adopt aspects of the sick role by engaging in actions requiring a physician (or, in this case, being one), such as taking prescription drugs or ordering diagnostic

---

BOX 7-1   The Sick Role in an Intensive Care Unit

David Rier (2000), a medical sociologist, was admitted to an intensive care unit suffering from a severe case of pneumonia. He woke up one morning so weak, he said he could not think clearly and had a high fever, chills, and difficulty breathing. Two days later he entered the hospital. "For a medical sociologist, being ill offers a priceless opportunity to engage in the most intimate manner possible, with the subject of my life's work," Rier (2000:71) commented. Only a few days earlier in class, he had criticized Parsons's concept of the sick role by claiming Parsons's view of physicians was too paternalistic, assumed too readily that patients should place their trust in doctors, and paid insufficient attention to the patient's perspective and ability to challenge, negotiate, collaborate, or circumvent physicians. Parsons's model of the doctor-patient relationship seemed to reflect the 1950s, not the twenty-first century.

Rier almost died. In fact, he said that he could feel himself slipping away, as he became sicker and weaker and had to be put on a respirator to breathe. At this point he thought about dying ("*There's* something I've never done before," he told himself) and it did not seem to him to be all that difficult. He could just relax and let go. But he thought of his family and told himself he was going to make it. All he had to do was lie there and keep breathing, and rely on the medical staff to get him out of this situation. Rier survived. As for the sick role, he had a much better opinion of it. He found that, as Parsons suggests, he had to trust his doctors, his perspective on his treatment was unimportant at the time, and challenging or negotiating was senseless. He was completely in the hands of his physicians and cooperated with their procedures as best he could in order to get well.

tests on themselves. Elsewhere, in Israel, David Rier (2000), a seriously ill medical sociologist who had previously been critical of Parsons's concept of the sick role in his lectures, found that the doctor–patient relationship in intensive care was much as Parsons described. "As for myself," states Rier (2000:75), "in what is the most lasting result of my unaccustomed passivity in the ICU [intensive care unit], my illness provoked me to reassess the critique of Parsons I had been teaching only weeks before."

CRITICISM OF THE SICK ROLE

Although Parsons's concept of the sick role has demonstrated research utility as a framework for explaining illness-related behavior and has become a basic concept in medical sociology, the model has some serious defects that have led some sociologists to suggest that it should be abandoned. Parsons's sick-role theory can be criticized because of (1) behavioral variation, (2) types of diseases, (3) the patient–physician relationship, and (4) the sick role's middle-class orientation.

Behavioral Variation

Much of the criticism of the sick-role theory has been directed toward its lack of uniformity among various persons and social groups. In a random sample of people living in New York City, Gerald Gordon (1966) found at least two distinct and unrelated statuses and complementary role expectations associated with being sick. When a prognosis was believed to be serious and uncertain, expectations of behavior generally conformed to Parsons's description of the sick role; however, when a prognosis was known and not serious, the notion of an "impaired role" emerged from Gordon's data, which required normal role responsibilities and rejected role exemptions despite sickness.

Twaddle (1969) reported at least seven configurations of the sick role, with Parsons's model being only one, in a study of Rhode Island married couples in late middle age. The exact configuration of the alternative sick roles discovered by Twaddle depended in part on cultural values and whether a person defined himself or herself as "sick." Not only were there differing personal definitions of "being sick," but also not all of the respondents stated they expected to get well and not all of them cooperated with the physician. Twaddle found that the sick role, as defined by Parsons, was much more applicable to Jews than to either Protestants or Italian Catholics. Jews were more likely to see themselves as being sick, as expecting to get well, and as cooperating with the physician. Protestants were the most resistant to seeing a physician, and Italian Catholics were generally the least cooperative with the physician. There were also other important ethnocultural differences in the Twaddle study. Protestants, for example, were much more likely to regard functional incapacity (usually an inability to work) as the first sign of illness, while Italian Catholics were more likely to emphasize changes in feeling states such as pain. Jews, however, tended to emphasize fear of eventual outcomes rather than feeling states or functional incapacities.

A well-known study by Mark Zborowski (1952) demonstrated important group differences pertaining to pain. While pain is clearly a biological phenomenon, Zborowski observed that responses to pain are not always biological but vary among ethnocultural groups. Zborowski's sample consisted of eighty-seven male patients and sixteen healthy males in New York City who were primarily of Jewish, Italian, and "Old American" ethnic backgrounds. The so-called Old Americans were defined as white, native-born, and usually Protestant patients whose families had lived at least two generations in the United States; they also did not identify with any particular foreign nationality. All of the patients suffered from neurological ailments, such as herniated discs or spinal lesions, which represented disorders where the pain involved would vary only within fairly narrow limits.

Although the level of pain was thought to be generally similar, Zborowski found significant variation in the responses to pain. Jews and Italians tended to be more sensitive to pain and more prone to exaggerate the experience of pain than Old Americans. While Jews and Italians were similar in responding to pain in the hospital, the two ethnic groups differed in the home setting. At home the Italian acted strong and authoritative, but in the hospital he was highly emotional. The Jewish patient was emotional in both settings. Zborowski observed that Jewish patients also used their suffering as a device for manipulating the behavior of others. But once satisfied that adequate care was being provided, the Jewish patient tended to become more restrained in his response.

In contrast, the Old American patients tried to conform to the medical image of the ideal patient. They cooperated with hospital personnel and avoided being a nuisance as much as possible. The Old American patients also avoided expressing pain in public, and when examined by the physician they tended to assume the role of a detached observer by becoming unemotional and attempting to provide an efficient description of their internal state to aid in a correct diagnosis. If their pain was too much for them to control, they would withdraw to their rooms and express their pain privately.

The attitudes toward pain also varied. Zborowski reported that Italians were more concerned with the discomfort of the pain itself and were relatively satisfied and happy when immediate relief was provided. The Italian patient also tended to display a confident attitude toward the physician. The Jewish patient, however, was not particularly confident about his physician, and he seemed to be more concerned about the significance of his pain for his general state of health rather than about any specific and immediate discomfort. While Italian patients sought pain killers, Jewish patients were reluctant to take drugs because they were apprehensive about the habit-forming characteristics of the drugs. The Old Americans, like the Jews, were also primarily concerned about what pain signified for their general state of health, but unlike the Jews, they were optimistic about the power of medicine and its ability to provide a cure. Hence, they displayed great confidence in the decisions made by the physicians.

In an effort to explain these ethnocultural differences, Zborowski offered the opinion that Jewish and Italian mothers demonstrated overprotective and over-emotional attitudes about their sons' health and that this socialization experience fostered the development of anxieties regarding pain among the Jewish and Italian patients. Zborowski believed that Jewish and Italian parents had tended to prevent physical injury to their sons by discouraging them from playing rough games and sports, whereas Old American parents, on the other hand, had socialized their sons to expect to get hurt in sports and to fight back. Old American boys were taught "not to be sissies," "not to cry," and "to take pain like a man." If such a child were actually injured, he was expected not to get emotional but to seek proper treatment immediately.

Research by John Campbell (1978) involving a sample of 264 children and their mothers in Washington, D.C., supports Zborowski's findings in regard to the responses of the Old Americans. Although Campbell did not focus on the role of ethnicity, his data showed that those children who were older and whose parents were of higher socioeconomic background tended to take a "stiff-upper-lip" or "business-as-usual" approach to illness. "This Spartan orientation," says Campbell (1978:46), "bears more than a passing resemblance to the responses to pain that Zborowski described as typifying his 'Old American' subjects—responses that tended to be approved by members of the medical profession—who themselves, perhaps not coincidently, would be assigned to higher SES [socioeconomic status] levels." According to Campbell, parents *do* make a difference when it comes to socializing their children to handle their emotions and reject the sick role.

As for other studies of ethnic variation, Irving Zola's (1966) comparison of American patients of Irish, Italian, and Anglo-Saxon descent at two hospitals in Boston also supported Zborowski's findings. In general, the Italians tended to dramatize their symptoms, while Zola found that the Irish would often deny their symptoms and the Anglo-Saxons would speak of their health problems in a detached and neutral manner lacking in anxiety. Zola concluded that there were indeed distinct differences between cultural groups and the way in which they communicated complaints about their health.

Besides ethnic variation, there may be other ways in which people interpret the sick role. One study has shown that, among heart patients having surgery, women tend to adopt the sick role more frequently than men and to be less ready to resume their work roles after surgery (Brown and Rawlinson 1977). Thus, there may be differences by sex in regard to acceptance of the sick role as well. Emil Berkanovic (1972) studied sick-role conceptions among Los Angeles city employees. Although his sample cannot claim to be representative of city employees generally, his findings do suggest that some people feel they are able to define appropriate illness behavior under certain circumstances. These people do not reject medical theories of illness, but simply feel competent to decide what is the correct behavior for the sick person, provided the symptoms are recognized and the outcome of the illness is known. Berkanovic points out that often the physician is consulted only as a last resort and only after all other sources of health information fail to provide an adequate explanation.

What is indicated by all of these studies is that Parsons's concept of the sick role does not account for all of the considerable variations in the way people view sickness and define appropriate sick-role behavior for themselves and others.

Type of Disease

The second major category of criticism regarding Parsons's concept of the sick role is that it seems to apply only to acute diseases, which by their nature are temporary, usually recognizable by laypersons, and readily overcome with a physician's help. Yet chronic diseases, such as cancer and heart disease, are by definition not temporary, and often the patient cannot be expected to get well as Parsons's model suggests, no matter how willing the patient may be to cooperate with the physician. Therefore, temporary exemptions from normal role responsibilities for the chronic patient are both inappropriate and perhaps impossible.

Research on patients with chronic disorders (Kassebaum and Baumann 1965; Radley 1994) has shown that they perceive the sick role differently from patients with acute illnesses. Chronic patients were faced with the impossibility of resuming normal roles and the necessity of adjusting their activities to a permanent health disorder. However, in a reconsideration of the sick role, Parsons (1975) argued that even if the goal of a complete recovery is impractical, many chronic diseases can be "managed" so that the patient is able to maintain a relatively normal pattern of physiological and social functioning. While diabetes, for example, cannot be cured in the sense that pneumonia can, Parsons insists that a chronic disease like diabetes should not be placed in a totally different category from that of "curable" diseases if the patient can be returned to a normal range of functioning. True, this explanation may allow the sick-role concept to account for some chronic disorders; still it cannot be applied to a wide range of illness situations such as the bedridden patient, the terminally ill patient, and the HIV-infected patient (Crossley 1998).

Problems also arise in applying the sick role to the mentally ill, in that while the sick role stipulates a person should seek professional care, people who go to psychiatrists for help may be stigmatized for doing just that (Segall 1976). People who admit to a history of mental illness often have problems finding jobs, and a considerable body of research literature describes the difficulties former mental patients have in coping with rejection from other people. In addition, many mental hospital patients refuse to accept the idea that they are mentally ill, and most patients, rather than voluntarily seeking help, are admitted to mental institutions involuntarily (Cockerham 2003).

Patient–Physician Role Relationship

A third major area of criticism of Parsons's sick-role model is that it is based upon a traditional one-to-one interaction between a patient and a physician. This form of interaction is common because the usual setting is the physician's office, where Parsons's version of the sick role is conceptualized. It is the setting where the physician has maximum control. Yet quite different patterns of interaction may emerge in the hospital, where perhaps a team of physicians and other members of the hospital staff are involved. In the hospital the physician is one of several physicians and is subject to organizational constraints and policies. If the patient is at home, the patient–physician relationship may also again vary because the patient and his or her family can much more clearly influence the interaction.

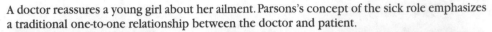

A doctor reassures a young girl about her ailment. Parsons's concept of the sick role emphasizes a traditional one-to-one relationship between the doctor and patient.

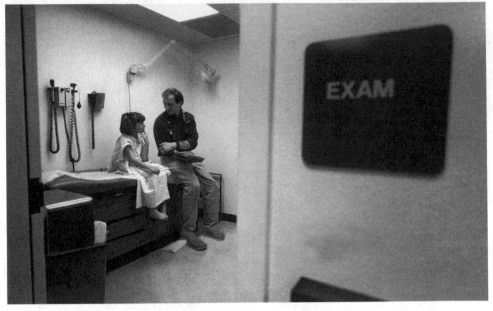

In addition, the pattern of relationships outlined in Parsons's sick role is modified if the client is a target of preventive techniques rather than strictly therapeutic measures. A considerable portion of contemporary medical practice is concerned not with restoring a single patient to normal social functioning but with maintaining and improving public health. The patient–physician relationship is different when the target is a group of individuals, particularly if the health problem is not a disabling illness but a behavioral problem such as smoking cigarettes or an environmental problem such as water or air pollution. In this situation the physician or health practitioner must usually be persuasive rather than authoritative, since he or she lacks the leverage to control the client group. The physician must convince the group that certain actions, such as physical examinations or X-ray examinations for tuberculosis, are good for them. In defense of Parsons's sick role, however, it should be noted that the behavior needing to be changed in such cases is often "normal" rather than "sick."

Middle-Class Orientation

Finally, it should be noted that Parsons's sick-role model is a middle-class pattern of behavior. It emphasizes the merits of individual responsibility and the deliberate striving toward good health and a return to normality. It is oriented to the middle-class assumption that rational problem solving is the only viable behavior in the face of difficulty and that effort will result in positive gain. It fails to take into account what it is like to live in an environment of poverty where success is the exception to the rule.

Also, many people in the lower socioeconomic classes may tend to deny the sick role, not only because they may not have the opportunity to enjoy typically middle-class secondary gains but also because the functional incapacity of the poor person may render him or her less likely to be able to earn a living or survive in conditions of poverty (Kassebaum and Baumann 1965; Kosa, Antonovsky, and Zola 1969). Therefore, people living in a poverty environment might work, regardless of how sick they might be, as long as they feel able to perform some of their work activities.

Yet it should be noted that even though the notion of "striving toward good health" reflects a middle-class orientation, the lower class uses the sick role to justify their disadvantaged social position (Arluke, Kennedy, and Kessler 1979; Cole and LeJeune 1972). That is, some poor people claim they are poor because they are sick, and being sick (and poor) is not their fault. While being sick and working to get well may be typical of the middle class, being sick and using the sick role to excuse one's circumstances in life appear frequently among the lower class.

Parsons's Sick Role: Conclusion

Despite the considerable criticism of Parsons's sick-role concept found in sociological literature, the reader should note that this model represents a significant contribution to medical sociology. Parsons insists that illness is a form of deviance and that as such it is necessary for a society to return the sick to their normal social functioning. Thus, Parsons views medicine as a mechanism by which a society attempts to control deviance and maintain social stability. In light of the trend toward classifying more and more social problems as medical problems, Parsons's explanation of the function of medicine has broad implications for the future treatment of deviants in our society.

While recognizing that some criticisms of Parsons's theory are valid, we should note that at least some of this criticism is based upon a misunderstanding of Parsons. Apparently some critics incorrectly assume that Parsons viewed the sick role as a fixed, mechanical kind of "cage" that would produce similarities of behavior among sick people regardless of variant cultural backgrounds and different personal learning experiences. Instead, what Parsons has given us is an "ideal type" of the sick role. By definition, ideal types do not exist in reality. They are abstractions, erected by emphasizing selected aspects of behavior typical in certain contexts, and they serve as bases for comparing and differentiating concrete behaviors occurring in similar situations in different sociocultural circumstances. Perhaps Eugene Gallagher (1976) said it best when he pointed out that whoever acquires a sociologically informed understanding of health and illness in contemporary society soon realizes how significantly sociological analysis has benefited from Parsons's formulation of the sick role and how, in comparison, many criticisms of it seem petty.

Therefore, it can be concluded that Parsons's model is a useful and viable framework of sociological analysis within certain contexts. Although the theory is an insufficient explanation of all illness behavior, it does describe many general similarities and should not be abandoned. In fact, writing in a later article, Parsons (1975) admitted that he did not believe it was ever his intention to make his concept cover the whole range of phenomena associated with the sick role. Two possibilities exist: (1) using the model as an "ideal type" with which various forms of illness behavior can be contrasted or (2) expanding the concept to account for conditions generally common to most illness situations.

LABELING THEORY

By failing to account for the behavioral variations within the sick role, the functionalist approach to illness has neglected the various aspects of acting sick. Chapter 6, on illness behavior, pointed out that two people having much the same symptoms may behave quite differently. One person may become concerned and seek medical treatment, while another person may ignore the symptoms completely. Z. Lipowski (1970) has noted that individual strategies in coping with illness vary from passive cooperation to positive action to get well and from fear at being diagnosed as ill to actual pleasure in anticipation of secondary gains. Several writers, Freidson (1970a) in particular, have taken the position that illness as deviant behavior is relative and must be seen as such; this is the perspective of labeling theory.

Labeling theory is based on the concept that what is regarded as deviant behavior by one person or social group may not be so regarded by other persons or social groups. Howard Becker (1973), one of the leading proponents of labeling theory, illustrates the concept in his study of marijuana users. His analysis reveals a discrepancy in American society between those people who insist that smoking marijuana is harmful and that use of the drug should be illegal, and those who support a norm favoring marijuana smoking and who believe that use of the drug should be legalized. While the wider society views marijuana smoking as deviant, groups of marijuana smokers view their behavior as socially acceptable within their own particular group.

Becker's position is that deviance is created by social groups who make rules or norms. Infractions of these rules or norms constitute deviant behavior. Accordingly, deviance is not a quality of the act a person commits, but instead is a consequence of the definition applied to that act by other people. The critical variable in understanding deviance is the social audience, because the audience determines what is and what is not deviant behavior.

The applicability of labeling theory as a vehicle for explaining illness behavior is that, while disease may be a biological state existing independently of human knowledge, sickness is a social state created and formed by human perception. Thus, as Freidson (1970a) has pointed out, when a veterinarian diagnoses a cow's condition as an illness, the diagnosis itself does not change the cow's behavior. But when a physician diagnoses a human's condition as illness, the diagnosis can and often does change the sick person's behavior. Thus, illness is seen by labeling theorists as a condition created by human beings in accordance with their understanding of the situation.

For example, among the Kuba people of Sumatra, skin diseases and injuries to the skin are quite common because of a difficult jungle environment. A person suffering from a skin disease would not be considered to be sick among the Kuba because the condition, while unhealthy, is not considered abnormal. In parts of Africa, such afflictions as hookworms or mild malaria may not be considered abnormal because of their prevalence. Margaret Clark (1959) points out that among the Mexican Americans in her study conducted in the southwestern United States, such disorders as diarrhea and coughing were so common they were considered "normal," though not necessarily good. Examples such as these have led to the realization that an essentially unhealthy state may not always be equated with illness when the people involved are able to function effectively and the presence of the disorder does not affect the normal rhythm of daily life. Therefore, judgments concerning what is sickness and what is deviant behavior are relative and cannot be separated from the social situations in which people live.

Labeling Theory and Illness Behavior

Labeling theory has so far failed to develop a theory of illness behavior comparable to Parsons's model. The closest equivalent deriving from the symbolic interactionist view (labeling theory) is that of Eliot Freidson (1970a). Freidson indicates that the key to distinguishing among sick roles is the notion of legitimacy. He maintains that in illness states, there are three types of legitimacy, which involve either a minor or serious deviation. (1) *Conditional legitimacy,* where the deviants are temporarily exempted from normal obligations and gain some extra privileges on the proviso that they seek help in order to rid themselves of their deviance. A cold would be a minor deviation and pneumonia serious in this category. (2) *Unconditional legitimacy,* where the deviants are exempted permanently from normal obligations and are granted additional privileges in view of the hopeless nature of their deviance. Terminal cancer falls in this category. (3) *Illegitimacy,* where the deviants are exempted from some normal obligations by virtue of their deviance, for which they are technically not responsible, but gain few if any privileges and take on handicaps such as stigma. A stammer would be minor and epilepsy serious.

Freidson's classification system implies that there are different consequences for the individual and that his or her treatment by other people depends on the label of definition applied to the deviant's health disorder by others. Freidson's model accounts for the problematic aspects of illness relative to social situations. A person with a skin disease in the Kuba tribe or a person with hookworms in Africa could be classified as unconditionally legitimate, for example, because the afflicted person would gain no special privileges or changes in obligations, since the disorder would be common to most people who functioned normally in their society. A person with cancer, in contrast, would gain a permanent exemption from normal obligations because of his or her condition.

Freidson's concept, however, is strictly theoretical and has not been extensively tested. Whether it can account for variations in illness behavior is therefore still a matter of speculation. While Freidson's model is useful in categorizing illness behavior, it fails to explain differences in the way people define themselves as being sick and in need of professional medical care. The merit of Freidson's model, however, is that it does go beyond Parsons's concept of the sick role by describing different types of illness and by pointing out that illness is a socially created label.

Criticism of Labeling Theory

The labeling approach stresses that judgments of what is deviance are relative, depending upon the perceptions of others. Therefore, the critical variable in understanding deviant behavior is the social audience that has knowledge of the act in question because the audience determines what is and what is not deviance. But despite its merits in providing a framework to analyze the variety of perceptions people may hold about deviance, labeling theory contains some shortcomings.

First, labeling theory does not explain what causes deviance other than the reaction of other people to it. Few would deny that groups create deviance when they establish norms. Admittedly, the reaction of an "audience" to variant types of behavior influences the individual's self-concept and also influences society's response. But a label in itself does not cause deviance. Some situations—murder, burglary, drug addiction, and suicide—are generally defined by most people as deviant, yet people do these things regardless of how they are labeled, and their reasons for doing so may have nothing to do with the label that is attached to them. Second, if deviant acts and actors share common characteristics other than societal reaction, these common characteristics are not defined or explained. Yet people committing deviant acts may share many similarities such as stress, poverty, age, peer group relations, and family background. These characteristics may be as important as, if not more important than, the reaction of the social audience. Jack Gibbs (1971) thus raises the important question of *what* is being explained by labeling theory—deviant behavior or *reactions* to deviant behavior? Third, labeling theory does not explain why certain people commit deviant acts and others in the same circumstances do not. All this seems to pose the question of whether societal reaction alone is sufficient to explain deviant behavior; the answer seems to be that it is not. In a later reconsideration, Becker (1973:179) agreed that labeling theory "cannot possibly be considered as the sole explanation of what alleged deviants actually do."

Labeling Theory: Conclusion

When compared to Parsons's concept of the sick role, labeling theory does address itself to the specific variations in illness behavior that seem to be present among differing socioeconomic and ethnocultural groups in American society. It also provides a framework of analysis for illness behavior according to the definition and perception of particular social groups and allows the social scientist to account for differences between social settings and types of illnesses as well. Over and against these advantages, labeling theory suffers from vagueness in its conceptualization, namely, what causes deviance other than societal reaction—which has little or nothing to do with disease. While Freidson's model has potential, it has not attracted the attention accorded to Parsons's sick role. But most important, there is serious doubt whether societal reactions in and of themselves are sufficient to explain the generalities of behavior occurring among the sick.

SICKNESS AS SOCIAL DEVIANCE?

This chapter has discussed the various approaches to sickness as deviance. The question remains whether this perspective of sickness is useful or adequate for sociological studies. The conceptualization of sickness as deviant behavior does make sickness a sociologically relevant variable, but it also restricts the analysis of sickness to the framework of a social event. This is in accord with the major intention of the sickness-as-deviance perspective in sociology—to focus exclusively on the social properties of being ill and thus to exclude biological properties definable only by the physician. Yet by dwelling exclusively on the social properties of sickness, the deviance perspective severely limits its capacity to deal with the biological aspects of sickness as a condition of suffering.

It can also be argued that, while deviance is behavior contrary to the normative expectations of society, sickness itself does not counteract social norms. The members of any society are expected to become ill now and then during their lives. Accordingly, if sickness is deviance and since deviance is regarded as a violation of expectations of behavior, it would be necessary to assume that society expects people not to become ill, just as it expects them not to commit a crime or become a homosexual or drug addict. People who are sick are different from the norm of wellness, but this situation does not make them bad, as the concept of deviance implies.

However, when people are sick they are not themselves. They are different (abnormal) in a negative sort of way that most people would prefer to avoid—just as they would like to avoid going to prison. Not only do sick people feel bad, but they may be physically disabled as well. They may also experience mental dysfunctions. According to Eric Cassell (1985), people with serious physical illnesses often lose their sense of perspective and are unable to think about situations from more than a single viewpoint. Their ability to reason and make decisions may change and they may become heavily dependent upon doctors and others to take care of them. They may also become so self-absorbed and childlike that they focus exclusively on themselves and ignore the outside world.

Kathy Charmaz (1983, 1991) has suggested that the chronically ill also experience a negative sense of self because their illness restricts their activities, isolates them from other people, discredits them by lessening their sense of worth, and causes them to be a burden to others. Some persons may, in fact, feel stigmatized as a result of their illness as seen in accounts of persons with physical handicaps (Zola 1982), Parkinson's disease (Lefton 1984), epilepsy (Scambler and Hopkins 1986), AIDS (Chapman 2000; Ciambrone 2001; Ezzy 2000), and other problems like diabetes, end-stage renal disease, and multiple sclerosis (Roth and Conrad 1987). Effects such as these would seem to place the ill in a position of deviance with respect to their sense of self, relations with other people, and role in society.

Therefore, when the sick role is considered along with society's method of dealing with the sick (that is, placing them under the control of doctors, putting them in hospitals), the concept of sickness as deviance may well apply. In the absence of other theoretical concepts in medical sociology that would provide a better approach to understanding the sociological aspects of illness, the illness-as-deviance perspective still remains the best sociological thinking on the subject.

BEING SICK AND DISABLED

Everyone becomes ill at some time. Susan Sontag, in her book *Illness as Metaphor* (1978:3), puts it this way:

> Illness is the night-side of life, a more onerous citizenship. Everyone who is born holds dual citizenship, in the kingdom of the well and in the kingdom of the sick. Although we prefer to use only the good passport, sooner or later each of us is obligated, at least for a spell, to identify ourselves as citizens of that other place.

As citizens of that other place—the realm of sickness—we typically feel bad or weak or both. We are unable to feel normal because we experience a sense of being less than our usual self. As Peter Freund and Meredith McGuire (1999:132) explain, "illness is upsetting because it is experienced as a threat to the order and meanings by which people make sense of their lives." What Freund and McGuire mean by this statement is that illness disrupts our daily routine, causes various degrees of suffering, and threatens our ability to plan for the future and control our activities. To be sick is to envy those who are well or envy our own past periods of wellness and hopefully be able to look forward to their return. The latter may not be possible if one has an incurable chronic condition. For example, in a study of HIV-positive homosexual men in New York City, Karolyn Siegel and Beatrice Krauss (1991) found that having AIDS meant having to confront the possibility of a curtailed life span, dealing with reactions to having a highly discrediting and stigmatized illness, and developing strategies for maintaining physical and emotional health. Being sick is clearly an undesirable state despite the exemption from one's usual activities that are an inherent feature of the sick role.

As previously noted, there are two types of illness conditions. One is acute illness, which typically refers to the sudden onset or sharp increase in pain, discomfort, or inflammation; usually such problems last only a relatively short time and either disappear after a few days or are moderated or cured by medical treatment. An acute illness is often communicable and can be passed from one person to another, such as colds, flus, measles, and chicken pox. The other form of sickness is chronic illness, which is usually slow in developing, long in duration, and typically incurable. Chronic illnesses are not usually communicable, although there are exceptions, such as AIDS. Chronic disorders develop within the individual rather than being passed directly from someone else and are usually associated with genetic, environmental, and lifestyle influences. If the chronic disease is life-threatening, like cancer, diabetes, or heart disease, the afflicted person is likely to eventually die from it. Other chronic conditions, like arthritis, are uncomfortable but not life-threatening.

Regardless of whether one's affliction is acute or chronic, when people suffer, their sense of personal competency can be adversely affected. Freund and McGuire (1999) point out that an illness can be particularly damaging to a person's concept of self when it is experienced as overwhelming, unpredictable, and uncontrollable because it paralyzes the ability to act and manage one's life normally. Very sick people often sense a degree of alienation or psychological separation from their body because it no longer feels normal or functions adequately (Ezzy 2000; Freund and McGuire 1999; Kelly and Field 1996). People who are sick often withdraw from others because they feel bad and are unable to pursue normal social relations. They often lose the ability to find pleasure, appreciate beauty, or be frivolous (Radley 1999).

Persons with chronic disorders, particularly those who are physically handicapped, are faced with additional problems of altered mobility, a negative body image, and stigma (S. Bell 2000; P. Brown 1995; Bury 1991, 1997, 2000; Chapman 2000; Ciambrone 2001; Ferraro, Farmer, and Wybraniec 1997; Radley 1989, 1993, 1994; Schieman and Turner 1998; S. Williams 1999, 2000; Yoshida 1993). Consequently, Zola (1982, 1989) points out that the problems facing someone with a physical impairment are not just medical, but include social, attitudinal, economic, and other adjustments. Simply moving about can be a major challenge. Scott Shieman and Heather Turner (1998), for example, found in a study in Canada that disabled persons, as they age, lose their sense of mastery and being in control of their lives. Being both old and disabled is characterized as a "double disadvantage." "As age increases," state Schieman and Turner (1998:171), "age and disability jointly combine so that the disabled become even more disadvantaged in mastery relative to the nondisabled."

Elsewhere, Kathy Charmaz (1983, 1991) observed in a study of chronically ill persons in northern California that such individuals frequently experience a deteriorating former self-image and are unable to assume an equally valued new one. As a result of their illness or disability, they live restricted lives, are socially isolated, are devalued as less than normal, and feel they are a burden to others. All the factors combined to reduce their sense of self-worth, unless some alternative means of satisfaction could be found. Most disabled and many chronically ill individuals are forced by their physical condition to reconstruct their sense of self and personal history—owing to what Michael Bury (1997:123) calls a "biographical disruption"—in order to account for themselves as physically impaired persons (S. Bell 2000; Bury 2000; Radley 1994; G. Williams 1984; S. Williams 1999, 2000). As Bury (2000:177) concludes: "Alterations in the body interact with the wider society in cultural and structural contexts that go beyond practical consequences to issues of appearance, social performance, and thus identity."

Anselm Strauss (1975; Strauss and Corbin 1988) explains that the chief business of a chronically ill person is not just to stay alive or keep his or her symptoms under control but to live as normally as possible. A lifelong illness, in Strauss's view, requires lifelong work to control its course, manage its symptoms, and live with the disability. In this context, the sick role that the person assumes is a permanent condition.

STIGMA

Some sick or physically handicapped people may be stigmatized if their affliction is unpleasant for other people because of how they appear, smell, or behave. Stigma, as defined by Erving Goffman (1963:3), is "an attribute that is deeply discrediting." Goffman explains that the term *stigma* originated with the ancient Greeks, who used it to refer to marks on the body that represented something bad or immoral about the people having them. Usually, the marks were brands cut or burned into the body to identify the bearer as a criminal, slave, or traitor. People encountering such a person were expected to avoid them. In contemporary society, Goffman explains there are three main forms of stigma: (1) abominations of the body, such as various types of physical disformities; (2) blemishes of individual character—that is, mental disorder, sexually-transmitted diseases (STDs), alcoholism, and suicidal tendencies; and (3) the tribal stigmas of race, religion, and nationality. People with such attributes are those who are different from the majority of other people, but different in a negative way and are subjected to discrimination because of it.

People who are physically handicapped typically fall into the first category of "abomination of the body." They may be stigmatized and excluded from the company of the non-handicapped because their physical deformity makes others around them feel uncomfortable. Persons with STDs can also be characterized as having an abomination of the body, but physical evidence of their disease can usually be concealed by clothing. Persons with STDs, however, are often stigmatized as having "a blemish of character" as people often think such diseases are usually acquired through immoral sexual acts (that is, outside of wedlock, with disreputable persons, etc.). As Goffman points out, stigma represents a rupture between an individual's *virtual* and *actual* social identity that is regarded in some way as failing. This failing places the person in a social category of people whose body and perhaps character are tainted. Stigmatized people may try to compensate for their stigma by "passing" as normal as much as they can. Goffman, for example, notes the situation of a badly burned real estate salesman who arranges to meet his clients by approaching them from a distance so they can have time to adjust to his appearance by the time he arrives in their presence.

However, stigma, even though it is imposed on the individual by other people, can obviously have a negative effect on the self-concepts of those stigmatized. People so stigmatized feel devalued and less than normal in public situations. Betsy Fife and Eric Wright (2000) investigated this situation by examining the impact of stigma on self-esteem and body image by type of illness, namely, HIV/AIDS and cancer. They found clear evidence that stigma is a central force in the lives of people with both types of illnesses. Persons with HIV/AIDS reported somewhat stronger feelings of stigma, which is not surprising considering the adverse public characterization often applied to those infected through IV drug use and homosexuality. But persons with cancer also felt stigmatized and sensed social rejection as well as an impaired body image. The more severe the illness, the greater the difficulty in concealing it and, hence, the stronger the feelings of perceived stigma in both groups. Stigma is an example of how feelings about one's illness by the individual and other people negatively affect the self-esteem of those afflicted.

SUMMARY

Two major theories have been advanced to date to explain the relationship between illness and society. Parsons's concept of the sick role has had the greatest impact on sociological perspectives thus far, but Freidson's labeling theory approach also represents an important contribution.

Parsons's concept of the sick role includes the following postulates: (1) An individual's illness is grounds for exemption from normal responsibilities and obligations; (2) an individual's illness is not his or her fault and he or she needs help in order to get well; (3) the sick person has an obligation to get well because being sick is undesirable; and (4) the obligation to get well subsumes the more specific obligation of the sick person to seek technically competent help. Parsons also demonstrates the utility of medicine as an institution of social control by virtue of its mission of treating the deviant sick.

Although Parsons's concept of the sick role has provided a useful framework for understanding illness behavior, it has not been generally sufficient because of its failure (1) to explain the variation within illness behavior, (2) to apply to chronic illness, (3) to account for the variety of settings and situations affecting the patient–physician relationship, and (4) to explain the behavior of lower-class patients. Nonetheless, if we realize the limitations of Parsons's sick-role theory, we can continue to apply it to behavior as an ideal-type model.

The labeling approach to illness, as formulated by Freidson, provides a useful orientation for analyzing the problematic aspects of illness behavior and the social meaning of disease. However, a definitive sick-role theory using labeling theory has yet to be developed. Both Parsons's sick-role concept and Freidson's labeling theory are formulated within the framework of an illness-as-deviance perspective, and currently this view contains the best work on the sociological aspects of being sick. For the chronically ill, the sick role can be a permanent state.

THE SICK ROLE INTERNET SITES

Deviance

1. Allyn and Bacon's Sociology Links: Deviance.
   http://www.abacon.com/sociology/soclinks/deviance.html

   Numerous links to all aspects of deviance.

2. Social Deviance Page, University of California, Santa Barbara.
   http://www.soc.ucsb.edu/honors/deviance/Index.html

   Numerous links and information regarding various categories of deviance.

3. Sociosite: Crime and Social Deviance.
   http://www.pscw.uva.nl/sociosite/TOPICS/Right.html#CRIMI

   National and international information and links regarding all aspects of deviance.

Talcott Parsons

1. Sociosite: Sociologists Dead and Very Much Alive, Talcott Parsons.
   http://www.pscw.uva.nl/sociosite/TOPICS/sociologists.html#PARSONS

   Selected writings from Talcott Parsons.

2. Classical Sociological Theory, Talcott Parsons.
   http://www.spc.uchicago.edu/ssr1/PRELIMS/theory.html

   Links to the complete works of Talcott Parsons.

Labeling Theory

Howie's Homepage: The Homepage of Howard S. Becker.
http://www.soc.ucsb.edu/faculty/hbecker

Links to the recent papers of Howard Becker.

CHAPTER

8

Healing Options

The majority of persons in American society turn to medical doctors for help when they are sick or injured. Other people, for reasons that may be religious, financial, or cultural, or simply because no doctors are available or because modern medicine may not meet their needs, seek treatment elsewhere. To complete our discussion of help seeking, this chapter examines healing options in the United States. These healers exist because they provide a service to their clients. What these services are and why they are sought is our focus. First we will discuss the *osteopath,* who is a physician. Next, we will expand our discussion to include a consideration of *complementary* and *alternative medicine* (CAM), *chiropractors, faith healers,* and *folk healers.*

OSTEOPATHS

Osteopathy began in the 1860s in Kirksville, Missouri, (Baer 2001; Lesho 1999). Its founder, Andrew Taylor Still, a physician, believed that illness was caused by a dislocation of one or more bones in the spinal column and that a pathological condition in one of the body's organs affect other organs. Because of the close relationship between the spinal vertebrae and the autonomic nervous system, the

167

neuromuscluar system is considered to play a vital role in the healthy functioning of the body. For many years, osteopathy was viewed by the medical profession as a form of quackery. But gradually professional respectability was achieved by moving away from the exclusive focus on spinal manipulation techniques to treat most health problems. By the mid-twentieth century, osteopaths were receiving scientific medical training in such areas as surgery and drug therapy. Training for osteopaths takes place at twenty osteopathic colleges in the United States, whose graduates are awarded the Doctor of Osteopathy degree (D.O.). Further training as an intern and resident is required. Osteopaths have also formed their own professional organization, the American Osteopathic Association, which serves to promote professionalism.

In 1953 the American Medical Association recognized osteopaths as another medical specialty, and they now enjoy the rights and privileges of medical doctors. To date, osteopaths have been able to maintain their separate identity, yet the trend is toward absorption into medicine. Osteopaths, for example, can specialize in surgery, anesthesiology, psychiatry, pediatrics, radiology, and other medical specialties. A hotly debated question in osteopathy is whether "classical" osteopathy has given itself over totally to medicine as practiced by medical doctors. This argument remains unresolved at present as the osteopathic profession continues to resist complete assimilation into traditional medicine. Since osteopaths are trained to practice manipulation of the musculoskeletal system, they see themselves as able to provide this service as an added dimension of health care. However, some observers find that the therapeutic practices that originally distinguished osteopathy from traditional medicine have become less and less important to the majority of its practitioners (Baer 2001). In 2000, 44,605 osteopaths were licensed in the United States. They represent about 5 percent of the physician population (Lesho 1999).

COMPLEMENTARY AND ALTERNATIVE MEDICINE (CAM)

Complementary and alternative medicine (CAM) is the use of treatments that are not commonly practiced by the medical profession. CAM includes visits to chiropractors, faith healers, and folk healers, as well as to acupuncturists, homeopaths, and naturopaths, and the use of dietary supplements to prevent or cure disease. Acupuncture is an ancient Chinese technique of inserting fine needles into specific points in the body to ease pain and stimulate bodily functions, while homeopathy is the use of microdoses of natural substances to bolster immunity. In large amounts, these substances could cause an illness, but tiny doses are intended to promote prevention or provide a cure by stimulating the body's defenses. Naturopathy is based on the idea that disease arises from blockages in a person's life force in the body and treatments like acupuncture and homeopathy are needed to restore the energy flow.

Other types of therapists may provide aromatherapy (the use of aromatic oils for relaxation), ayurveda (a centuries-old Indian technique of using oils and massage to treat insomnia, hypertension, and digestive problems), shiatsu (Japanese therapeutic massage), crystal healing (based on the idea that healing energy can be obtained from quartz and other minerals), and biofeedback (the use of machines to train people to control involuntary bodily functions). CAM also includes the use of dietary

Acupuncture is a form of complementary and alternative medicine (CAM).

supplements like algae to enhance alertness, shark cartilage to cure cancer, fish oil capsules to reduce the threat of heart attacks, garlic to prevent blood clots, and the consumption of megadoses of vitamins and herbs to ward off or treat illnesses.

Up to now it is not clear whether many of the techniques actually work, cause harm, or are useless. Some procedures like acupuncture appear effective and are moving into mainstream medicine (Baer 2001; Baer et al. 1998), but most evidence supporting the various types of alternative medicine is based upon personal observations or testimonials from satisfied patients, not scientific testing. The Office of Alternative Medicine, now the National Center for Complementary and Alternative Medicine, was created in 1992 by Congress as part of the National Institutes of Health. The mission of the Center is to facilitate research and the evaluation of CAM techniques and make this information readily available to practitioners and the public.

Despite the lack of scientific research, the rise in the number of CAM practitioners has been accompanied by surprisingly broad acceptance of many of their therapies by the general public (Goldstein 2000; Hafferty and Light 1995; Kelner, Wellman, Pescosolido, and Saks 2000). Some CAM practitioners are even allowed to provide their services in hospitals, but are typically not part of the regular staff and occupy only a marginal position in relation to the hospital's other practitioners (Shuval, Mizrachi, and Smetannikov 2002). The acceptance of CAM therapies by the general public, however, is so extensive that it is estimated that Americans spend more than $27 billion annually on its services and products (Kelner et al. 2000). The dietary supplement industry alone has sales of over one billion dollars annually. This business has flourished since the passage by Congress in 1994 of the Dietary Supplement Health and Education Act. This legislation allows food products to be sold as cures for disease as long as claims that they can actually enhance health are not on the label. Such claims, however, can be displayed in books, pamphlets, and store signs where the products are sold.

While little sociological research has been conducted on these phenomena, it appears that many persons who use some form of alternative or "new age" medicine have middle- or working-class social backgrounds (Schneirov and Geczik 1996). They also consult regularly with medical doctors and use these techniques because they are dissatisfied with physician care, want to be in control of their own health, enjoy the experience, and believe it can actually help them be healthier and live longer. Other people, those who use faith and folk healers, typically come from a lower-class background and use these practitioners because they are inexpensive and culturally similar. What both groups have in common is that professional medicine has not met all their needs (Sharma 1990).

CHIROPRACTORS

The chiropractic approach to healing also involves manipulation of bones in the spinal column. This type of treatment originated with Daniel Palmer in Davenport, Iowa, in 1895. It is based on the idea that manipulation of the spine can relieve pressure on the nerves and thereby alleviate illness and pain. While there is some dispute over whether the osteopathic and chiropractic approaches evolved independently of each other in terms of initial conceptualization, chiropractors today are restricted solely to nonmedical techniques. In 2000 there were seventeen chiropractic colleges in the United States. There are also chiropractic colleges in Canada, England, and Australia. Training is four years in duration, three in the classroom and one in practice at the college. There are no internships or residencies to serve.

While there is evidence that chiropractic techniques can help patients with back, shoulder, and neck pain (Baer 2000), the medical profession has traditionally opposed the extension of professional status to chiropractors. This opposition is based on the assertion that chiropractic methods are derived from inaccurate theories, chiropractic educational standards are low, and the techniques are of little or no therapeutic value to patients. Rather than attempt to absorb the chiropractor into medicine, some physicians have preferred to eliminate the field altogether. In 1987, a federal court ruled that the American Medical Association had conspired to destroy chiropractic medicine in violation of antitrust statutes. The AMA was ordered to cease undermining the public's confidence in chiropractic procedures.

Chiropractors are licensed to practice in all fifty states, are authorized to receive Medicare payments for treatments rendered to patients over the age of sixty-five, and provide services covered by major private insurance carriers. In 2000 more than 50,000 chiropractors nationwide provided services to their clients. Chiropractors may be favored because they charge less than physicians, are friendly, give more time to patients, and explain difficulties in words easily understood.

However, chiropractors have been hampered in their attempts at professionalization not only by physicians but also because of conflicts among themselves. Some chiropractors favor a more expanded role, using a variety of techniques, in which a wider range of health problems would be treated. Others prefer a more "pure" approach, in which chiropractors would limit themselves to spinal manipulation.

Chiropractors must often strongly compete among one another for patients and have little control over who should be licensed to practice.

Physicians rarely refer patients to chiropractors. Yet most people who visit chiropractors also visit a physician for treatment. Therefore, it appears that the majority of people who use chiropractic services do not depend entirely on this method of care. Instead, they use chiropractors and physicians in a complementary manner. Because physicians do not typically refer their patients to chiropractors, it must be assumed that most people visit chiropractors on their own initiative. Many people go to chiropractors for treatment in addition to that received from physicians, but some seek help from both chiropractors and physicians for the same conditions. Chiropractors are the second largest category of primary health care practitioners in the United States, following medical doctors, when the number of providers and patients is taken into account. Nevertheless, chiropractors remain outside the mainstream of medicine.

FAITH HEALERS

Faith healers are people who use the power of suggestion, prayer, and faith in God to promote healing. According to John Denton (1978), two basic beliefs are prevalent in religious healing. One form of belief supports the idea that healing occurs primarily through psychological processes and is effective only with psychophysiological disorders. The other belief is that healing is accomplished through the intervention of God and constitutes a present-day miracle. Denton offers five general categories of faith healing: (1) self-treatment through prayer; (2) treatment by a layperson thought to be able to communicate with God; (3) treatment by an official church leader, for whom healing is only one of many tasks; (4) healing obtained from a person or group of persons who practice healing full time without an affiliation with a major religious organization; and (5) healing obtained from religious healers who practice full time and are affiliated with a major religious group, such as Christian Science healers. A common theme running through each of these categories is an appeal to God to change a person's physical or mental condition for the better.

An example of faith healing is found in the study conducted by Gillian Allen and Roy Wallis (1976) of members of a small congregation of a Pentecostal church, the Assemblies of God, in a city in Scotland. Members of the church subscribed to a belief that the devil caused illness and that even for such afflictions as mental illness, blindness, dumbness, and epilepsy a person could be possessed by evil spirits. Accepting the Bible as the literal truth, the Assemblies of God officially support the idea of *divine healing* based upon Biblical passages indicating that (1) some people have the power to transmit the healing forces of the Holy Spirit or to exorcise demons, and (2) healing can be obtained through faith the same way as salvation from sin. The healing procedure was described in this manner:

> Prayer for healing in the Assembly of God occurs at the end of normal services when those who need healing or help and advice, are asked "to come out to the front." There

the pastor and the elders perform the laying on of hands and sprinkling with holy oil and pray simultaneously: "Oh Lord, heal this woman! Yes, Lord. We know you can heal her." The occasional case of demon possession is dealt with in a similar way when the pastor or evangelist addresses the demon along these lines: "Get out, foul demon! In the name of Jesus, leave her!" (Allen and Wallis 1976:121)

Although the Pentecostal church used divine healing as a central aspect of church dogma, it did not prohibit members from seeking professional medical care. Use of divine healing, however, was preferred because it offered the advantage of providing both spiritual and physical healing. It was also believed to work in many cases where orthodox medical practices failed. The members had a fund of knowledge attesting to spectacular cures, either through the specific effect of the emotional healing services or through the power of prayer in general. Yet since church members also believed that "God's methods are sometimes through men" and that "God put doctors in the world and gave them their skills," it was permissible to seek physician assistance. For serious illnesses in particular, divine healing was used in conjunction with professional medicine. Hence, church members held both religious and scientific beliefs about the causation and treatment of illness simultaneously, without any apparent conflict. "In serious illnesses," state Allen and Wallis (1976:134–135), "members were not faced with the choice between breaking their religious principles by fetching the doctor and refusing medical treatment altogether." Consequently, Pentecostalists were usually able to avoid the dilemma of whether to use *either* a religious *or* a medical curing process.

Deborah Glik (1990) interviewed several people who participated in spiritual healing groups in Baltimore, Maryland. The majority of respondents claimed they had experienced some type of healing and attributed it to their participation and belief in spiritual healing. Rather than cures, however, the most common form of healing was alleviation of symptoms, followed by relief from psychological distress, acceptance of one's health or life situation, or adoption of another perspective about one's situation. In some cases, people redefined what was wrong with them to better fit the outcome of their healing experience; that is, they redefined their ailments as less serious and less medical after religious healing. "While few persons claimed their healing had been complete," states Glik (1990:161), "most cited improvements in some health or life situation." Glik's data suggest that the benefits of religious healing primarily lay in relief from stress, enhanced feelings of support from God, and the adoption of a different viewpoint about the meaning of their health problem in their lives. For example, as two of the respondents in the Glik (1990:157) study reported:

> A 61-year-old female teacher going through a divorce and dealing with depression and arthritis said: "Faith and belief has made me accepting of problems. I have been able to fill up with God, and He will not let my problems get to me."
> A 34-year-old male real estate broker suffering from stress and lower back pain noted, "I am now relaxed. I have learned to let go and let God be alive in my body, mind and all my affairs. Life has changed dramatically for the good."

In the United States, some faith healers hold services in a church or in their homes; others travel from city to city holding meetings, perhaps in tents, and some appear on television or radio. The number of people who frequent such healing services and who are actually helped by this method is not known. But faith healers tend to be readily available, and most cities and towns are visited by such healers at least once a year.

Most religious groups in the United States favor a combination of religious practices and professional medical care in treating health problems. The doctrines of a few religious groups, however, prohibit their members from seeking modern medical treatment. These groups utilize faith healing, laying on of the hands, and individual and communal prayers in treating illnesses. Sometimes there are accounts of "miracle" cures in which a deadly affliction like cancer is overcome. Other times there are tragic cases in which children die unnecessarily because their parents refuse to obtain medical care because of their religious beliefs.

The most prominent group in American society advocating religious healing in place of medical treatment is the Christian Science Church. Founded in 1866 in Boston by Mary Baker Eddy, the Christian Science Church maintains that sickness and pain are an illusion. Disease is not God-given but is believed to be produced by a distorted view people have of their spiritual nature. All forms of disease are considered symptomatic of an underlying spiritual condition that can be healed only through prayer. The key to life and health is thus obtained through spiritual discovery. Christian Scientists are believed to possess the capacity to heal themselves, although the assistance of a Christian Science practitioner, licensed by the church, is also available. Practitioners are not considered to be the equal of medical doctors but are intended to help the sick person find a cure through prayer. Healing consists of prayers meant to convey to individuals a deeper understanding of their spiritual being. This understanding is held to be the crucial factor in eliminating the mental attitudes from which all diseases are thought to originate. There are certain medical problems that are considered more mechanical than spiritual, such as broken bones or a need for surgery, that can be legitimately treated by a doctor. But generally speaking, Christian Science healing is thought to be incompatible with medical treatment.

In 1988 and 1989, however, four court cases resulted in convictions of manslaughter or neglect for Christian Science parents in the deaths of their children because of a failure to seek conventional medical care. One 1989 case involved the death of a two-year-old boy from a bowel obstruction in Boston when the parents relied exclusively on prayer to help the child find relief. In another case in Florida in 1989, a judge rejected a charge of manslaughter against a Christian Science couple after a jury found them guilty of allowing their seven-year-old daughter to die from diabetes. Instead, the judge accepted the more stringent conviction of third-degree murder, along with child abuse, and sentenced the parents to suspended four-year prison terms and fifteen years of probation, and ordered them to provide medical treatment for their surviving children. A Florida appeals court upheld the sentence in 1990 and stated that the right to practice religion freely does not include the liberty to expose a child to ill health or death and added that, while parents may be free to become martyrs themselves, they are not free to make martyrs of their children. In 1950, there were about 11,000 Christian Science healers in the United States alone; by the late 1990s, there were fewer than 2,000 worldwide because of legal and other problems (Fraser 1999).

A faith healer touches a baby's head in a healing ceremony.

The legal issues in cases such as these are clear: On one side is the issue of religious freedom and parental autonomy and on the other is the state's right to protect children. The current trend in court decisions in this matter appears in a 1991 finding by the State Supreme Court in Massachusetts involving Jehovah's Witnesses who refused blood transfusions for their children in two separate cases, one where the child had leukemia and the other hemorrhage of an ulcer. The court held that, while adults have the right to refuse medical care, parents may be forced to have their children treated for life-threatening illnesses.

When it comes to faith healing, however, there is also considerable controversy about whether it actually works. Moreover, questionable ethics on the part of some leading television evangelists, including sex scandals, cannot have helped the overall image of faith healing among the general public in past years. Moreover, the medical profession does not hold faith healing in high esteem, nor do large segments of the general public (Wolinsky 1988). The future of this mode of health care delivery in the United States is uncertain—at least with respect to its electronic version.

Nevertheless, the relationship between health and religion is an important area that needs to be studied in greater detail. Such studies should not be limited to faith healing, but should include the manner in which religious beliefs have an impact generally on health and medical care. It is clear that an appeal to a spiritual or divine being promotes a sense of psychological well-being in the individual (Abrums 2000; Ellison 1991; Idler 1995; Idler and Kasl 1992; Musick 1996; Pollner 1989). Among the few existing studies is that of Ellen Idler (1987), who investigated the health and degree of religious involvement among a sample of elderly persons living in New Haven, Connecticut. Idler found that those persons with the highest levels of religious involvement showed the least depression and physical disability. In a subsequent study, Idler (1995) noted that religiousness can also be associated with poor health as sick people use their religion to help them cope with their illness.

BOX 8-1   The Storefront Church

Mary Abrums (2000) interviewed a group of poor and working-class African American women belonging to a storefront church in Seattle, Washington. She found these women were skeptical about their encounters with the health care system; for example, if they participated in clinical trials to test new drugs and procedures, they rarely felt the research was for their benefit. Nevertheless, they developed a meaning system that enabled them to understand their experiences and feel in control over their own healing. They believed that the body was a gift from God and that only God, not doctors, had the ultimate authority over what happened to their health. They knew who was *really* in charge and that belief made them more comfortable with their illnesses and physicians. As one woman (Abrums 2000:104) reported:

> I admire doctors but they don't know it all. Doctors don't accept nothing they don't understand! Doctor said he was ready to sign my death certificate [the woman had a body temperature of 60 degrees], but I said "Doctor, you don't know, because I'm not yours!"

Studies such as this demonstrate that religion can be a major resource in coping with health problems.

Another study is that by Jeffrey Dwyer and his colleagues (Dwyer, Clarke, and Miller 1990), who determined death rates from cancer were lower in those areas of the United States where there was a high concentration of religious persons. Dwyer and his colleagues suggest that the lifestyles associated with high religiosity emphasize activities that promote health, such as the avoidance of cigarettes, alcohol, and multiple sex partners and an emphasis on nutrition, hygiene, and—for most religions— preventive medical care.

FOLK HEALERS

Folk healers are not used to any significant extent in the United States except by some low-income persons usually belonging to racial and ethnic minority groups. Apparently few non-Hispanic whites go to folk healers, although some elderly persons living in poverty and rural areas may be prone to use "folk remedies" in treating ailments. Common ingredients in folk remedies are such substances as ginger tea, whiskey, honey, sugar, lemon juice, baking soda, aspirin, peppers, garlic, kerosene, salt, butter, mustard, and sassafras (Baer 2001). Practicing folk healers are most likely to be found among African Americans, Hispanics, and American Indians.

Folk medicine is often regarded as a residue of health measures left over from prescientific historical periods (Bakx 1991). Yet folk practices have persisted in modern societies, and the major reason appears to be dissatisfaction with professional medicine and a cultural gap between biomedical practitioners and particular patients (Baer 2001; Bakx 1991; Madsen 1973). These patients, typically low-income persons, may view folk medicine as a resource because it represents a body of knowledge about how to treat illness that has grown out of the historical experiences of their family and ethnic group (Thorogood 1990).

African American Folk Healers

The tendency of some low-income black people to seek the services of lay practitioners rather than physicians is illustrated in the work of Loudell Snow (1978), who studied black folk healers in Chicago. African American folk healers and their patients, according to Snow, subscribe to a belief system that—unlike modern medicine—does not differentiate between science and religion. All life events, including illness, are viewed in relation to the total environment as either natural or unnatural, good or evil. Being healthy is an instance of good fortune like having a good job or a faithful spouse. Being sick is an example of misfortune like unemployment and marital strife. Thus, life is *generally* good or bad, and the cure for *one* problem, says Snow, might cure *all* problems.

Additionally, Snow notes that folk diagnosis of a health problem emphasizes the *cause* of the problem, not the symptoms. Having a body rash might initially be seen as stemming from a lack of cleanliness but come to be defined as the result of black magic. In this belief system, what is important is not the rash, but what or who brought on the rash. Snow (1978:71) gives the following example:

> Even when a direct cause-and-effect relationship is known which is equivalent to the professional view this may be supported by religious or magical overtones. The sister of one of my informants died of bacterial meningitis, an etiology clearly understood by the family. But why did the organism invade her system at all? In their view to punish the father for "drinking and running around with women."

Another prominent belief is that all illnesses can be cured, if not by medicine, then by magic. This belief is supported by the idea that illnesses are either natural or unnatural. Natural illnesses are those maladies caused by abusing the natural environment (staying out too late, eating too much, failing to wear warm clothing) or brought on as a punishment by God for sin or for not living up to the Lord's expectations. Thus, in the case of divine punishment, the afflicted person must make contact with God either directly or indirectly through an intermediary such as a faith healer. "Prayer and repentance," reports Snow (1978:73), "not penicillin, cure sin."

Unnatural illnesses are outside of "God's plan" and beyond self-treatment or treatment prescribed by friends and relatives. And if the mind is affected, unnatural illnesses are thought to be beyond the capabilities of physicians, who are usually associated just with the treatment of natural illnesses that have obvious physical symptoms. The cause of an unnatural illness can be worry or stress, but often the etiology is ascribed to evil influences or acts of sorcery. When black magic is suspected, it is necessary to find a healer with unusual magic or religious powers who can successfully intervene for the victim.

Snow observed that the term *healer* in Chicago's black community included a bewildering array of persons performing different healing roles. The variety of healers is reflected in the number of names used to describe them, such as healer, root doctor or root worker, reader, adviser, spiritualist, or conjure man or woman. If voodoo is practiced, a male healer may be called *houngan* or *papaloi*, a female healer would be a *mambo* or *maraloi*. Few of them refer to themselves as "doctor," since healing is only part of their services. Instead, their given name is likely to be prefaced by a kinship, religious, or political title, such as Sister, Brother, Mother, Reverend, Bishop, Prophet, Evangelist, or Madam. These healers depend on word of mouth for patient referrals, or they may advertise by newspaper or leaflet. They claim to have received their ability to heal (1) as a result of learning (which confers little status since almost anyone can be expected to learn); (2) during an altered state of consciousness, such as a profound religious experience or a divine "call" to healing; or (3) at birth. Snow states (1978:79), "they will probably have in common only the assertion that the abilities are a gift from God."

Many healers do not require direct personal contact with the recipient of services but will conduct business over the telephone or by mail. If the individual's complaint involves sorcery, the use of some substance (such as oils, potions, or perfumes) will be required and may need to be purchased; if witchcraft is at work, a thought, prayer, or verbal spell is necessary. In the case of witchcraft, it might be necessary to purchase candles to assist the healer in effecting a solution. For example, when Snow (1978:99) complained in a letter to "Sister Marina" that she had problems sleeping and eating, was losing weight, and did not seem to enjoy life any more, Sister Marina replied in writing:

> I am so sorry I took so long to write but I had to take your letter into my church to see if what I suspected about your case was true. I had suspected an unnatural problem and I was right. But writing everything to you that I have learned would have to fill 10 pages of paper and maybe you still would not fully understand so I am asking you to phone me so that I can explain to you better the history of your case and let you know what will be needed to help you. I have lit a special candle for you and my spirits have told me since you have written to me you have felt slightly better. But if you want to be helped call me.

Snow wrote back asking if Sister Marina could help her by mail and she received a warning by return mail that if she did not hurry it might be too late to save her. Sister Marina (Snow 1978:99) wrote:

> In order for me to take your case I must burn 9 candles for you to find out just what it is I must do to get rid of this UNNATURAL PROBLEM and remove this EVIL! And each candle costs $10.00 so it would come up to $90.00 to help and if you do not either bring it to Chicago or send it within a week and 1/2 which would be about 11 days I cannot except [sic] your case because you might get too bad off and then no one will be able to help if you decide to come to see me please call me a day ahead of time and let me know.

How effective black folk healers like Marina are in treating their clients is not known. Some of these healers are likely to be frauds. Yet the advantage they offer to their clients is that they are readily available, results are usually quick and sometimes guaranteed, and they claim to be able to solve any problem. Their abilities are supposed to be derived from divine authority and, if they fail, they can attribute the failure to the will of God. In essence, what black folk healers appear to accomplish is to reduce the anxieties of their clients, and they are most effective in dealing with health problems that have some emotional basis. What is particularly significant in the reduction of anxiety, and what distinguishes their practice is the recognition that health problems are an integral part of such other problems of daily life as lack of money, a strayed spouse, loss of a job, or envious relatives or neighbors. Consequently, black folk healers treat the whole person, not just a single symptom, which is often the case with a physician. Moreover, physicians tend to charge significantly higher prices for their services, are not as readily available in low-income areas, and may be unable to show quick results because of the patient's delay in seeking treatment or the severity of the disorder or both.

While the Snow study dealt with low-income black Americans living in an urban area, other data on similar blacks living in a rural setting point toward the same kind of pattern. Julian Roebuck and Robert Quan (1976) compared the health practices of fifty black and fifty white lower-class households in a small town in Mississippi. Although the white households tended to have a somewhat higher average income, practically all of the households received supplemental income from public assistance and welfare programs. Overall educational levels for both black and white households were between the fifth and sixth grades, and those household members who were employed held jobs that were either semiskilled or unskilled. There were important differences, however, when it came to seeking treatment for health problems. More white (68 percent) than black (48 percent) households sought health care only from physicians. More black (42 percent) than white (24 percent) households obtained care from a combination of practitioners— physicians, marginal healers, and illegal healers. Somewhat more whites (8 percent) than blacks (4 percent) went to marginal healers (defined as chiropractors, pharmacists, podiatrists, nurse-midwives). As for illegal healers (defined as folk practitioners, spiritualists, sorcerers), 6 percent of the black households used this source only, compared to none of the white households.

In general, Roebuck and Quan found that lower-class blacks usually waited longer than lower-class whites before seeking the services of a healer when sick. Blacks were less oriented toward Western scientific medicine than whites and believed more in the effectiveness of illegal healers (who were sometimes used along with physicians). One black respondent, for example, stated: "The doctor thought I had a stroke because I couldn't move, but the hoodoo man said someone had placed stumbling blocks in front of me and he chased it away" (Roebuck and Quan 1976:157). Another black respondent said: "I saw Sister Cherokee [spiritualist] and she rubbed some olive oil on the back of my neck and told me I was suffering from high blood—exactly what the doctor told me!" (Roebuck and Quan 1976:157). Many of the blacks not only believed in the effectiveness of the illegal healers but had a corresponding lack of faith in physicians as well. None of the whites used the illegal healers in any capacity, nor expressed confidence in their methods.

Other research conducted by Snow (1977, 1993) among lower-class blacks in a community in the southwest United States showed health practices similar to those found by Snow in Chicago and Roebuck and Quan in Mississippi. Sick people were typically channeled through a lay-referral system of family and neighbors to a source of medical treatment, which in many cases was not a physician. Sometimes physicians were consulted only as a last resort. Health in low-income African American communities was seen as the "ability to 'keep on keeping' on" (Snow 1993:73).

There are two distinct types of black folk healing in the United States: traditional and Caribbean. The traditional form has been discussed in this section. The Caribbean form consists of several variations, such as *Voodoo* (Haiti), *Santeria* (Cuba), and *Obeah* (West Indies). What each of these Caribbean approaches to folk healing have in common is that they are based on native African beliefs and are part of the Caribbean's past slave culture. Each uses rituals, charms, herbs, concoctions, and prayer to prevent or cure illness by healing the mind and spirit, along with the body (Baer 2001; Holloway 1990; Robinson 1990; Thorogood 1990). These healing practices are all part of a larger system of religious and spiritual beliefs that are limited in the United States to small numbers of black Americans with ties to the Caribbean. Miami, New Orleans, Chicago, Philadelphia, and New York show the largest concentrations of these practitioners.

Curanderismo

Male Mexican American folk healers are known as *curanderos* and females as *curanderas*. Like black folk healers, curanderos and curanderas blend religion and folk medicine into a single therapeutic approach. They likewise classify illnesses primarily on the basis of *what* causes the disorder rather than the symptoms, and they do not separate the natural from the supernatural when it comes to diagnosis and treatment. Most of their patients are lower class. Also unlike black folk healers, they do not charge for their services, or they charge very little. They may ask for a small donation (perhaps a dollar or two) for expenses or they may accept a small gift such as vegetables or a chicken.

Curanderos and curanderas also appear to use religion to a much greater extent than black folk healers. Ari Kiev (1968) points out that religion, based upon a Spanish Catholic tradition, is central to the curandero, who believes life is ordained by the divinity, and good health and happiness can be achieved only by those who keep God's commandments. A patient who suffers, therefore, is seen as helping God's plan for the universe, since it is believed that God allows people to suffer in order to learn. The example of Christ suffering on the cross is often used to illustrate that suffering and illness can be a worthwhile experience. Thus, the curandero views helping the patient accept suffering as a major task. In this context, suffering is explained as being part of the patient's burden for the world's sin and ignorance and a necessary role in God's plan for the universe. The more religious the curandero appears to be and the more convincing he or she is in influencing others to accept the will of God, the more highly regarded the curandero is as a healer. One effect the curandero uses to help accomplish this task is to establish a work setting that supports his or her image. Kiev (1968:129–130) describes it like this:

> Each curandero works in his own unique setting, depending usually upon his degree of affluence. The basic atmosphere created is invariably the same. In general, the curandero sees patients in part of his home set aside for treatment. These rooms, even in poor slums, are distinctive because of the great number of religious objects contained in them. The presence of numerous pictures and statues of the Virgin Mary and Jesus, of various sized crosses and religious candles, which are often arranged around an altar in a corner of the room, creates an atmosphere of religious solemnity which makes one forget the poverty of the slum or the humble shack of the curandero. Indeed, in such treatment rooms one feels as if in a church, and cannot help but view the curandero with awe and respect.
>
> The therapeutic effect of this "temple in the home" cannot be minimized. The quiet calm can invoke a feeling of security and protectiveness in the frightened and anxious. . . . Perhaps most important is the authority the curandero derives through his relationship to the setting. It makes him the object of respect and awe and puts him in command of much of the power that derives from the patient's response to the setting and the symbolism. By relying upon religious symbols and objects that have great meaning for the patients, he can immediately establish himself as a man of wisdom and authority, which undoubtedly increases the patient's willingness to cooperate and his expectations of relief.

Besides prayer and religious counseling, the curandero or curandera employs a variety of folk drugs and herbs to produce a cure (rattlesnake oil, mineral water, garlic, sweet basil, wild pitplant, licorice, camphor). To a very large extent this approach is based on sixteenth-century Spanish medicine, derived largely from Greek and Arabic sources, and influenced by beliefs of the Mayans and Aztecs. Prevalent in this view is the Hippocratic notion of bodily equilibrium. Hippocrates, the famous physician of ancient Greece, believed that good health resulted from the equilibrium within the body of four humors of blood, phlegm, black bile, and yellow bile. Important, too, was the harmony of the body with living habits and the environment. As long as the four humors were in balance, the body was healthy. If an imbalance occurred, however, and more of one type of humor than another was present, a person was sick. Because the body is perceived as being a mix of cold and hot conditions, curanderos and curanderas use "hot" foods and medicines to treat "cold" conditions (drowsiness, chills) and "cold" foods and medicines to treat "hot" conditions (fever, hypersexuality).

The most dreaded form of disorder, either physical or mental, is that caused by witchcraft. Witches, or *brujas,* are evil persons who supposedly have made pacts with the devil and use supernatural powers in the form of curses, magic, herbs, or ghosts to harm other people. According to William Madsen (1973), who studied Mexican Americans living in south Texas, conservative lower-class Mexican Americans showed an almost universal acceptance of the existence of witchcraft, even though belief in witchcraft is more strongly denounced than other folk theories of disease by the churches and in newspapers and schools. Hence, curanderos were needed to provide "good" power to offset "evil" influences.

Kiev (1968) points out that curanderismo persists in the American Southwest because it works in many cases. The advantage the curandero brings to the treatment setting is that he or she works in a subculture supportive of beliefs in the effectiveness of the curandero's methods. Especially important is the anxiety-reducing approach of the curandero, carried out within the context of family and friends, that defines the treatment as therapeutic and positive according to the norms and values of the Mexican American community. While Anglos may view illness as impersonal and unemotional in origin and caused by germs, lower-class Mexican Americans may see illness as related to one's interpersonal relationships, community life, and religion.

American Indian Healers: The Navajos and the Cree

There are few studies of American Indian healers. Exceptions, however, are Jerrold Levy's (1983) research on Navajo health beliefs and practices in Arizona and that of Janice Morse, David Young, and Lise Swartz (1991) among the Cree in Canada. Levy notes that the rituals associated with traditional Navajo religion are predominantly health oriented and stem from an emphasis upon enhancing the well-being of the hunter. The principal figure in these rituals is the *singer,* whose knowledge of ceremonies is obtained through several years of apprenticeship with another practitioner. The singer, who is the most prestigious person among Navajo healers, is the ceremonial leader in rituals that may last several days and are intended to drive out of the body whatever is causing the illness. Diseases, according to traditional beliefs, are thought to be caused by soul loss, witchcraft, spirit possession, or improper behavior such as violating a tribal taboo. The singer is assisted by the *diviner* (or the singer may fill both functions), whose role is to diagnose illness and whose ability is believed to be a special gift. Upon making a diagnosis, the diviner may refer the patient to the singer, who performs the ceremony appropriate for the diagnosis. There are also *herbalists* and *bone setters* in Navajo communities who have knowledge of a practical nature about how to treat various common ailments and injuries.

Levy found that the number of singers has been declining over the years because fewer men (healers are males) are able to devote their time to learning the chants, since they also must earn a living. The demands of a wage work economy and education about modern health practices may cause traditional healing to disappear, in Levy's view. Furthermore, the large traditional healing ceremonies last from five to nine nights and involve many guests; therefore, the practice is expensive for families with limited incomes. Some Navajos have substituted the peyote rituals of the Native American church for traditional ceremonies, since these rituals serve the same purpose, last only one night, are more economical, and are consistent with basic Navajo beliefs about harmony with nature and the supernatural.

Like black folk healers and curanderos, Navajo healers are primarily concerned with the cause of an illness rather than its symptoms. In fact, Levy found it difficult to determine precisely what role symptoms play in diagnosis. Levy (1983:132) states:

> No Navajo disease is known by the symptoms it produces or by the part of the body it is thought to affect. Rather, there is bear sickness and porcupine sickness, named for the agents thought to cause them; or there is "that which is treated by the Shooting Chant," so named by the ceremonials used to cure it. Because the traditional health

culture does not rely upon a knowledge of symptoms in the diagnostic process, Navajo patients often have difficulty understanding the purpose of history taking and physical examination, a circumstance that often leads to misunderstanding in the clinical setting.

Nevertheless, Navajos do recognize illness by personal discomfort and some symptoms have meaning for them. Also certain types of healing ceremonies are associated with certain symptoms and not others; some ceremonies are used to treat a broad range of symptoms. So knowledge and logic linking causes to solutions are an inherent feature of Navajo medicine, and symptoms play a part in deciding which ritual is to be used.

Levy indicates that Navajos will often use both native healers and physicians because of the belief that modern medicine will remove symptoms and Navajo medicine will remove the cause of the illness. Among Christian Navajos, the tendency is to combine modern medicine with prayer and not go to native healers. Levy suggests that about half of the Navajo population uses physicians exclusively, about 40 percent use a combination of native healers and physicians, and 10 percent use native practitioners only. Fractures, cuts, and childbirth were treated most often by doctors, while fainting, vague symptoms, or culturally defined illnesses without symptoms were never treated by physicians alone. Since use of native healers conjointly with physicians was common, it was difficult to determine the effectiveness of traditional medicine, but Levy maintained that utilization of native healers was due more to a lack of access to medical facilities and poor communication with doctors than to adherence to native beliefs. The major factor affecting frequency of hospital use, for example, was distance from the hospital on a reservation the size of West Virginia. The declining number of singers, the growing tendency to shorten traditional ceremonies, the gradual replacement of herbalists by physicians among the population, and health education in the schools all point toward a demise in native healing for the Navajos.

In Canada, Morse and her colleagues (1991) identified five phases in the healing ceremony of the Cree tribe. First was an initial ritual in which the healer, other people serving as the healer's spiritual helpers, and the patient participated. A ceremonial pipe was passed around three times to all who were present, and smoke from a smoldering fungus, sage, or sweetgrass was carried around the room four times in a clockwise direction. This activity was a process of purification intended to open channels of communication to the spirit world and attract the attention of the Great Spirit. Purification is intended to foster a receptive attitude among the participants and place the healer in a position of control. All movements by the healer are clockwise, and like rituals in other native American tribes (Avery 1991; Baer 2001) are oriented toward maintaining harmony with nature. Second came a contract phase in which the patient formally requests healing and the healer agrees to mediate with the Great Spirit on behalf of the patient.

Third was the treatment component. This phase consisted of the patient drinking herbal tea and having an herbal solution applied to his or her skin. Throughout this stage, the healer provides vivid descriptions of what the medicine is doing to the cause of the disease, thereby providing visual imagery intended to facilitate the healing process in the patient's mind. Furthermore, the healer constantly offers reassurance to the patient that the treatment is effective and many people in worse condition have been healed in the past. The final treatment consists of a sweat-lodge ceremony in which the patient sits in the dark around a pit of heated rocks and absorbs steam from herbally medicated water that is sprinkled on the stones. The healer sings and occasionally conveys messages to the patient from the spirit world. The fourth phase, which Morse and her colleagues call didactic, consists of the healer educating the patient about the healing process and the effectiveness of the treatment. And, finally, in the fifth phase, closure, the healer ends the healing but assures the patient of the continued healing and support of the Great Spirit.

Cree healing, like folk healing generally, treats the whole person, not just particular symptoms. It is probably very effective at reducing anxiety as the methods are consistent with Cree cultural beliefs. Moreover, the sweat-lodge ceremony may be especially helpful for some respiratory ailments. Morse and her colleagues found, however, that the Cree have low rates of physician utilization and relatively poor health.

SUMMARY

This chapter has examined the role and function of alternative healers and alternative medicine in American society. Other than osteopaths, such healers continue to maintain themselves because there is a demand for their services. Chiropractors, in fact, represent the second largest category (behind medical doctors) of primary health care practitioners in the United States, but they are not generally accepted by the medical profession. Folk healers work generally among persons from low-income backgrounds and racial minority group status. They provide a service consistent with the cultural beliefs of the people who go to them. Many people combine medicine with prayer, but faith healers actively work to achieve recovery from illness and injury through spiritual means. Some religious groups believe in working with doctors, while a few reject medical treatment as incompatible with their beliefs. Excluding osteopaths, the role and function of alternative healers are to meet the health needs of those persons not helped by professional medicine. Generally, these are persons who are not affluent or well educated, with the exception of middle- and upper-class individuals who utilize so-called "new age" therapies and diet supplements.

HEALING OPTIONS INTERNET SITES

Osteopathy

1. American Osteopathic Association (homepage).
   http://www.aoa-net.org

2. American Association of Colleges of Osteopathic Medicine.
   http://www.aacom.org

   Publications, updates, and data relevant to the nineteen member osteopathic medical schools in the United States, as well as information regarding the practice of osteopathy.

Alternative Medicine

1. National Institutes of Health, National Center for Complementary and Alternative Medicine (NCCAM).
http://nccam.nih.gov

2. Alternative Medicine Homepage.
http://www.pitt.edu/~cbw/altm.html

   A site that includes unorthodox, unproven, unconventional, or alternative therapies.

3. Alternative Medicine, Shiffman Medical Library, Wayne State University.
http://www.libraries.wayne.edu/shiffman/altmed/altmed.html

   Includes databases, fact sheets, and directories of alternative medicine organizations.

Chiropractic Medicine

1. American Chiropractic Association (homepage).
http://www.amerchiro.org

2. International Chiropractors Association (homepage).
http:www.chiropractic.org

3. National Association for Chiropractic Medicine.
http://www.chiromed.org

   A consumer advocate association of chiropractors who seek to expand the utilization of chiropractic care in mainstream health care delivery.

Doctor–Patient Interaction

Talcott Parsons's (1951) concept of the sick role provided some basic guidelines for understanding doctor–patient interaction. Parsons explains that the relationship between a physician and his or her patient is one that is oriented toward the doctor helping the patient to deal effectively with a health problem. The physician has the dominant role because he or she is the one invested with medical knowledge and expertise, while the patient holds a subordinate position oriented toward accepting, rejecting, or negotiating the recommendation for treatment being offered. In the case of a medical emergency, however, the options of rejection or negotiation on the part of the patient may be quickly discarded as the patient's medical needs require prompt and decisive action from the doctor.

Parsons's concept of the sick role details the obligations of patients and physicians toward each other. Patients cooperate with doctors, and doctors attempt to return patients to as normal a level of functioning as possible. When people visit doctors for treatment and medical advice, doctors usually (but not always) take some type of action to satisfy the patient's expectations. Eliot Freidson (1970a) suggests that physicians tend to have a bias in favor of finding illness in their patients.

He cites the *medical decision rule* as the guiding principle behind everyday medical practice. The medical decision rule, described by Thomas Scheff (1966), is the notion that, since the work of the physician is for the good of the patient, physicians tend to impute illness to their patients rather than to deny it and risk overlooking or missing it. Although this approach may promote tendencies to prescribe drugs and order laboratory tests and X-rays, such consequences should not be surprising. Patients desire and demand services, and physicians are trained to meet these demands. As Freidson (1970a:258) points out: "While the physician's job is to make decisions, including the decision not to do anything, the fact seems to be that the everyday practitioner feels impelled to do something when [patients] are in distress."

Richard Tessler and his associates (Tessler, Mechanic, and Dimond 1976) remind us that the role of the physician in meeting the needs of patients is quite broad and that physicians should be attentive not only to a patient's complaints but also to whatever factors caused the patient to come to a doctor at a particular point in time. The distress may not be only physical; purely psychological needs can trigger a visit to a doctor as well (Cockerham, Kunz, and Lueschen 1988b; Tessler, Mechanic, and Dimond 1976). Therefore, to assume that interaction between physicians and patients always follows a preset course in which all parties work together under the same set of mutual understandings overlooks the potential for misunderstanding, uncertainty, or disregard of the physician's method of treatment by the patient. The quality of physician–patient interaction is sometimes problematic, yet the process is important because of its potential for affecting the care being provided. This chapter will review models of interaction, misunderstandings in communication, cultural differences in presenting symptoms, and problems in patient compliance. These topics are of interest to sociologists because physician–patient interaction constitutes a structured relationship and mode of discourse that are inherently social.

MODELS OF INTERACTION

Since Parsons formulated his concept of the sick role, two additional perspectives on physician–patient interaction have added to our understanding of the experience. These are the views of Szasz and Hollender and of Hayes-Bautista. Thomas Szasz and Marc Hollender (1956), both physicians, take the position that the seriousness of the patient's symptoms is the determining factor in doctor–patient interaction. Depending on the severity of symptoms, Szasz and Hollender argue that physician–patient interaction falls into one of three possible models: activity–passivity, guidance–cooperation, and mutual participation.

The *activity–passivity model* applies when the patient is seriously ill or being treated on an emergency basis in a state of relative helplessness because of a severe injury or lack of consciousness. Typically, the situation is desperate as the physician works in a state of high activity to stabilize the patient's condition. Decision making and power in the relationship are all on the side of the doctor, as the patient is passive and contributes little or nothing to the interaction. The *guidance–cooperation model* arises most often when the patient has an acute, often infectious illness, like the flu or measles. The patient knows what is going on and can cooperate with the physician by following his or her guidance in the matter, but the physician makes the decisions.

The *mutual participation model* applies to the management of chronic illness in which the patient works with the doctor as a full participant in controlling the disease. Often the patient modifies his or her lifestyle by making adjustments in diet or giving up cigarettes and is responsible for taking medication according to a pre-scribed schedule and seeking periodic checkups. The patient with diabetes or heart disease would be in this category. What Szasz and Hollender accomplish is to show how the physician–patient relationship is affected by the severity of the patient's symptoms.

David Hayes-Bautista (1976a, 1976b) focuses on the manner in which patients try to modify treatment prescribed by a physician. Hayes-Bautista finds that they ei-ther try to convince the physician that the treatment is not working or they counter the treatment with action of their own, such as deliberately reducing the amount of medication they are supposed to take or increasing it. Physicians respond by point-ing out their expertise, that the patient's health can be threatened if the treatment is not followed, that the treatment is correct but progress may be slow, or simply ap-peal to the patient to comply. The relevance of the Hayes-Bautista model for un-derstanding doctor–patient relations is that he views the interaction as a process of negotiation, rather than the physician simply giving orders and the patient following them in an automatic, unquestioning manner. The model is limited, however, to those situations in which the patient is not satisfied with treatment and wants to per-suade the doctor to change it.

What is suggested by the Szasz and Hollender and Hayes-Bautista models is that in nonemergency situations, patients do not necessarily act passively when in-teracting with their doctors in health matters. Patients ask questions, seek explana-tions, and make judgments about the appropriateness of the information and treat-ment physicians provide. But the interaction that takes place appears to be strongly affected by social class differences. Lower-class persons tend to be more passive in dealing with doctors as authority figures and show a decreased sense of personal control over health matters; people with middle and upper socioeconomic status, however, tend to be more consumer oriented and active participants in the physician–patient encounter (Cockerham et al. 1986a). This circumstance suggests that it is middle- and upper-class patients who are most likely to try to negotiate with doctors and involve themselves as partners in decision making about their medical problem, while lower-class persons stand as more or less passive recipients of professional health services.

In their study of consumerism in the doctor–patient encounter, Marie Haug and Bebe Lavin (1981, 1983) found that better educated and younger adults tended to be more skeptical of physician motives in providing treatment. They were more likely to question whether the physician was ordering tests and providing services primarily to help the patient or to make money. These persons strongly believed that decision making in the doctor–patient relationship should not be left entirely to the doctor.

However, it should be noted that despite the general trend toward greater patient equality with the physician in making decisions about one's own health, there are clearly times when patients do not desire to accept responsibility or are unable to do so. There are also times when physicians exert their authority and make decisions regardless of the patient's desires and those of the patient's family to have some say in the treatment. In these situations the activity–passivity model overrides the mutual participation model. For example, David Rier (2000), a medical sociologist critically ill from an acute respiratory and kidney failure, found that Parsons's concept of the sick role was highly applicable to his condition of dependency on doctors in an intensive care unit (ICU). He was so seriously ill, and perhaps near death at one point, that he simply had to trust his doctors. Rier (2000:88) found that notions of negotiation and partnership have only limited relevance to critically ill patients and notes that "such patients often lack the strength and clarity either to challenge or to collaborate with the physician" and that their condition may vastly constrain treatment options.

In another study, Rose Weitz (1999) found that ICU doctors, treating her brother-in-law, Brian, who was badly burned in an industrial accident, were unwilling to share decision-making authority. These doctors defined informed consent (a one-word assent given by the barely conscious Brian) as giving them complete authority to make all decisions and initiate aggressive procedures without informing the

The doctor-patient relationship is moving away from the guidance-cooperation model toward the mutual participation model.

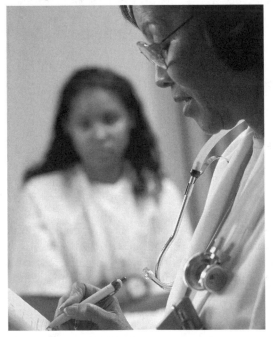

family. Brian never regained consciousness and died three and one-half weeks later. Although Brian's wife Lisa, was acknowledged by the physicians as having the authority to give them permission before beginning various treatments, they generally ignored her. When they did speak to the family, they favored talking to Brian's father, who was a confident and wealthy businessman. Yet the father did not receive more information than the others, nor was he offered any greater involvement in decision making. "Not surprisingly," states Weitz (1999:219), "this experience left family members cynical about and even fearful of medical care, by suggesting that doctors might be more interested in their own careers or egos than in their patients' welfare."

Besides ICU physicians, surgeons are also known for trying to retain decision-making authority for themselves and to present information to their patients and their families that justifies action (Katz 1999). Patients can feel pressured to just go along with what the surgeon orders. But in some instances, patients and/or their families opt for the decision-making role instead. Pearl Katz reports on an eighty-eight-year-old woman who was diagnosed with gallstones. Her surgeon offered to make the decision himself to approve an operation ("If you want to leave the decision to me," stated the surgeon, "I'll make it"; Katz 1999:120). But the woman's son took the decision-making authority away from the doctor. According to Katz (1999:120):

> The son responded, "I don't think that you, me, or my wife has the right to make that decision for her. It's not proper for anyone to make that decision. Whatever needs to be discussed should be discussed with her and decided by her."

When a patient is extremely ill or there is an emergency, doctors sometimes have to make life-saving decisions about patients quickly, and there is no time for consultation. In such circumstances the professional power and authority of physicians is fully exercised, and this may be the case regardless of what the patient or the family might eventually say—since the doctor can assert that he or she has a "moral imperative" to treat the affliction (Weitz 1999). And some physicians may just be generally unwilling to involve patients and their families in decision making, even if the circumstances warrant it (Katz 1999; Weitz 1999). However, despite such exceptions, mutual participation is the norm in most doctor–patient interaction (Cockerham et al. 1986a; Frank 1991; Haug and Lavin 1981, 1983; Lowenstein 1997; Warren, Weitz, and Kulis 1998). Mary Warren, Rose Weitz, and Stephen Kulis (1998) found in a study of physicians in Arizona that the context in which they practiced medicine has changed dramatically in the last twenty years. Among the changes was greater equality in the doctor–patient relationship. Warren and her colleagues (1998:364) state:

> Our data suggest that this context has changed to such an extent that regardless of age or years in practice, many physicians accept a somewhat more collaborative relationship with patients as the norm rather than invidiously comparing their position to those of physicians in some ideal past. . . . Similarly, physicians now accept that patients will seek medical knowledge and desire to participate in medical decisions and thus do not find such patients an impediment to work satisfaction.

MISUNDERSTANDINGS IN COMMUNICATION

The interaction that takes place between doctor and patient is an exercise in communication. Medical treatment usually begins with a dialogue. As is the case in any face-to-face situation, the effectiveness of doctor–patient interaction depends upon the ability of the participants to understand each other. However, a major barrier to effective communication lies in the differences between physicians and their patients with respect to status, education, professional training, and authority. Several sources report that a failure to explain a patient's condition to the patient in terms easily understood is a serious problem in medical encounters (Allman, Yoels, and Clair 1993; Clair 1993; Fisher and Todd 1990; Rier 2000; Waitzkin 2000; Weitz 1999). Physicians, in turn, state that an inability to understand or the potentially negative effect of threatening information are the two most common reasons for not communicating fully with their patients (Davis 1972; Howard and Strauss 1975). Consequently, as Fred Davis (1972) found in a study of the interaction between the parents of children who were victims of paralytic poliomyelitis and their doctors, the most common form of communication was evasion; the doctors tended to answer the questions of parents in terms that were either evasive or unintelligibly technical.

Yet some doctors are very effective communicators and, as Eric Cassell (1985) explains, information can be an important therapeutic tool in medical situations if it meets three tests: (1) reduces uncertainty, (2) provides a basis for action, and (3) strengthens the physician–patient relationship. Cassell (1985:165–166) provides an example of this situation in the following dialogue between a male physician and a female patient:

DOCTOR: Now, first I want you to start off by listening—listen to me, carefully. With your ears, not your fears. I'm very straight with people, as you know. What I tell you is everything, uh—right. Now, on your skull x-rays there is a place where the pituitary gland sits. I'll show it to you. That place right here—

PATIENT: Mm-hm.

DOCTOR: —is larger than it's supposed to be.

PATIENT: I see.

DOCTOR: The pituitary gland sits in there. Now the pituitary gland has a lot—does a lot of work in the body. It's very teeny and makes a lot of little hormones that tell the other glands of your body what to do.

PATIENT: Mm-hm.

DOCTOR: When it's large, like that, we think it has a tumor. The kind of tumor that it has is not a cancer tumor. That is not what makes that kind of tumor.

PATIENT: Mm-hm. . . .

DOCTOR: That would give you the headaches that you complain of. 'Cause tumors cause headaches, they grow very slowly. They're not cancer. They grow very, very slowly. . . . Where we sit right now is, there is a suggestion that you have a tumor of the pituitary gland.

PATIENT: Mm.

DOCTOR: The most common one—ah, name, is called chromophobe adenoma. You know, but the name is not important, except, as I say, it's not cancer.

PATIENT: Mm.

DOCTOR: Now. If that's what you have, you're going to be operated on for it.

PATIENT: Mm.

DOCTOR: Now, as scary as it may be when somebody points at your head and talks about tumors, this is NOT a scary tumor.

PATIENT: I see.

DOCTOR: I don't mean to say that on the way, you ain't going to get scared and worry and be frightened, and have things go on, doctors and all that, because you are. Until this is all settled, you're going to get frightened, and nothing I'm going to tell you is going to make you less frightened, except, I'm telling you the truth. You're going to come out all right, if that's what it is.

PATIENT: Mm-hm.

DOCTOR: All right? I don't mean come out all right, I mean alive, I mean all right.

PATIENT: Mm-hm.

DOCTOR: You know? Able to do your exercises, work, have sex, cook food, get mad at your children, and grow to be one hundred and ten years old like your mother. Nasty. With a nasty disposition.

PATIENT: (Laughs) OK.

Other doctors do poorly when it comes to communicating with patients. Cassell provides further examples of physicians telling their patients they were not going to explain a disease because they would not understand what they were told, or being vague and ultimately frightening the patient. In the following example from a British study, a woman with a neck problem resulting from a car accident sought reassurance that no serious difficulties existed. However, she was clearly not reassured as shown in this conversation with her doctor:

PATIENT: Could you tell me Doctor X, is it all right that my neck clicks now and then?

DOCTOR: Yes.

PATIENT: Is that all right?

DOCTOR: Yes, it may do. Yes.

PATIENT: Fine. Thanks.

> She continued to express her concern to the interviewer. "The doctor just asked if my neck was all right and dismissed it, although I would like to have discussed it—the pain I'm having. I mean, I don't know if it's all right." (Fitton and Acheson 1979:75)

Another example of poor communication by physicians is found in the Weitz (1999) study on the refusal of ICU doctors to share decision making about treatments for Brian, her fatally burned brother-in-law. Lisa, Brian's wife, reported that "when I would try to get more info [from the doctors], their reactions ranged from 'this does not compute'—as if they had never heard questions like these before—to almost animosity" (Weitz 1999:214). The social workers, pastoral counselors, and psychologists on the hospital staff were not helpful in getting information but seemed focused instead on "cooling out" or calming down the family. The doctors did agree to have a weekly family meeting. As Weitz (1999:218) described the situation:

> . . . when Brian's mother asked in a family conference if Brian would retain his ears, the doctor replied it would not matter, given recent advances in plastic surgery. Similarly, according to several family members, Dr. Thompson told them that "so long as Brian's

lungs begin working, we can fix everything else"—a statement that was patently untrue, as the greatest danger to burn patients comes from infections. When Brian, who had been hooked to a ventilator from the start, began taking an occasional breath, the doctors claimed that he was now "breathing on his own." When asked, however, the nurses (who always proved far more forthcoming than the doctors and were much more helpful to Lisa than any other hospital staff) showed us on the monitor how his breaths were both too shallow and too infrequent to sustain life.

This, of course, is the type of situation that promotes misunderstandings between doctors and patients and leaves the patients dissatisfied with the relationship. Two groups in society, the lower class and women, have been identified as having the most communication problems with physicians.

Communication and Class Background

It has been found, for example, that poorly educated persons are the most likely to have their questions ignored and to be treated impersonally as simply someone with a disease instead of an individual to be respected (Atkinson 1995; Ross and Duff 1982). Upper- and upper-middle-class persons tend to receive more personalized service from physicians (Anspach 1993; Link 1983; Taira et al. 1997). They are also more active in presenting their ideas to a doctor and seeking further explanation (Boulton et al. 1986; Weitz 1999).

Howard Waitzkin (1985, 1991, 2001), a physician and medical sociologist, studied information given in medical care and found that social class differences were the most important factors in physician–patient communication. Noting that information often provides a basis for power by those who have it in relation to those who do not, Waitzkin determined that doctors did not usually withhold information to exercise control over their patients. Rather, doctors from upper-middle-class backgrounds tended to communicate more information to their patients generally than doctors with lower-middle- or working-class origins. Moreover, patients from a higher class position or educational level usually received more information. Socioeconomic status thus emerged as a determining factor in both providing and receiving medical information.

According to British medical sociologist Paul Atkinson (1995), a major characteristic of the clinical consultation is the physician's dominant role in the encounter. Atkinson notes that a key feature of the consultation is the assertion of control in which the physician takes over the patient's problem and sets about controlling or guiding what should be done. The focus is typically limited by the doctor to medical issues, and social situations are relegated to marginal topics of conversation (Waitzkin, Britt, and Williams 1994). The doctor's emphasis is on finding out what is medically wrong and doing something about it, so he or she can move on to the next patient. In this circumstance, lower-class patients in particular have difficulty holding the doctor's interest to anything other than brief comments about their specific health problem.

Mary Boulton and her colleagues (Boulton et al. 1986:328) explain that the influence of social class on the doctor–patient relationship is best understood in terms of social distance. Those patients who are similar to physicians in social class are more likely to share their communication style and communicate effectively with them; those with dissimilar class backgrounds are likely to find communication more difficult because their communication style differs from that of the doctor and they lack the social skills to negotiate the medical encounter effectively. The effects of social distance apply not only to class differences, but race as patient satisfaction is greatest when both doctor and patient are of the same race (LaVeist and Nuru-Jeter 2002; Malat 2001).

MALE PHYSICIANS AND WOMEN PATIENTS

As for women, Sue Fisher (1984:1–2) studied doctor–patient communication in a family practice clinic in a small southeastern American city staffed by white middle-class men. She found that many women patients were not satisfied with the explanations given them by their doctors. Fisher claimed that treatment decisions for women were not always in their best interest. She provided the following example:

> One quiet evening my phone rang. It was a fellow graduate student and she was in distress. For the past several years she had used an intrauterine device (IUD) as her method of contraception. Recently she developed a pelvic inflammatory disease (PID) and was treated with antibiotics. The first regimen of antibiotics was unsuccessful and the doctor then recommended a hysterectomy. Faced with the doctor's recommendation my friend, Andrea, felt helpless. She didn't know how to determine whether or not the hysterectomy was necessary. She called to see if I could help. I suggested that she tell the doctor that she was engaged to marry a [physician] who wanted a family, and ask the doctor if there were any other ways to treat her problem.
>
> Several weeks later my phone again rang. Andrea had followed my advice. Once the doctor learned of her impending marriage his attitude changed. He assured her that there were alternative treatments available and they would work hard to avoid a hysterectomy. She was treated with another course of antibiotic, her infection cleared up, avoiding unnecessary surgery.
>
> Andrea's is a distressing, but not an isolated, tale. Repeatedly, while doing research in the Departments of Reproductive and Family Medicine, I saw physicians recommend treatments and patients, usually unquestioningly, accept them. My research gave me access to behind-the-scenes information typically reserved for physicians. Hardly a week passed without someone calling, as Andrea had, to tap into that stock of knowledge. The women who called were often well educated and articulate, yet they did not feel they had the information with which to make reasonable decisions or they felt they did not understand or could not trust the recommendation their physician made. Their feelings were exacerbated when their medical problems were related to reproduction. The women's questions were always of the same kind—How do I evaluate whether the treatment or procedure being recommended is really in my best interest?

Fisher's basic message is to call for greater insight on the part of male doctors in dealing with female patients and their complaints. One example of male physician misperceptions about female patients is a tendency to misdiagnose heart attacks as stomach or anxiety problems. Estrogen is believed to protect women from heart attacks until after menopause when estrogen levels drop; consequently, heart disease is often overlooked or undetected in premenopausal women (McKinlay 1996). An example of this situation is reported by Henig (1993:58) who states:

> Paula Upshaw was a 36-year-old respiratory therapist from Laurel, Maryland. In 1991 she had a heart attack; as a health professional she was more knowledgeable than most about her symptoms—they were the so-called "classic" signs of a heart attack (terrible chest pain, numbness on her left side, sweating, and nausea). She says, "they never ever considered my heart . . . they were all sure it was my stomach." At her insistence (she was an assertive patient) she received three separate electrocardiograms. But, she reports, the emergency room physicians said her symptoms were normal (for stomach problems) and they sent her home to take antacids and ulcer medications. Her heart condition was not diagnosed until she made a third visit to the ER on a Friday evening and refused to go home. Even though she was eventually admitted to the hospital, she says no one was even thinking about her heart. The following day, a cardiologist on weekend duty was flipping through a stack of Saturday's electrocardiograms, which included Paula Upshaw's. Paying no attention to gender, he asked, "Who's the 36-year-old with the massive heart attack?"

The lack of male sensitivity to women patients was a major factor in the formation of the women's health movement to combat sexual discrimination in medicine. As part of this movement, feminist health organizations have evolved that advocate natural childbirth, midwifery, home deliveries of babies, self-help, and recognition of the rights and intelligence of patients (A. Clarke and Olesen 1999). A particular focus has been on the manner in which some male physicians treat women patients and health workers as inferior because of their sex. Reviews of past medical literature have found images of women patients that depict them as being naturally frail, sickly, incompetent, submissive, and in need of physician consultation fairly regularly. In examining the relationship between male physicians and female patients in the early twentieth century, Barbara Ehrenreich and Deirdre English (1979:127–128) noted:

> The doctors' view of women as innately sick did not, of course, *make* them sick, or delicate, or idle. But it did provide a powerful rationale against allowing women to act in any other way. Medical arguments were used to explain why women should be barred from medical school (they would faint in anatomy lectures), from higher education altogether, and from voting. . . . Medical arguments seemed to take the malice out of sexual oppression: when you prevented a woman from doing anything active or interesting, you were only doing this for her own good.

WOMEN PHYSICIANS

Sometimes, for women doctors in a work situation, being a woman is a more meaningful status than being a physician. Candace West (1984) reports that some patients may perceive women physicians as less of an authority figure than male physicians. In one instance, West (1984:99) notes that a male hospital patient was asked by a woman physician if he was having difficulty passing urine and the patient replied,

"You know, the *doctor* asked me that." In this case, indicates West, it was difficult to tell who "the doctor" was because "the doctor" was evidently not the female physician who was treating him. And Judith Hammond (1980) suggests that women medical students deliberately develop personal biographies about themselves that show them as being no different than any other medical student. They do so in order to gain acceptance as colleagues from male students who question their motivation, skills, and potential for medicine. As one woman medical student described the attitude of a male counterpart:

> This guy had this theory . . . if you're a woman, obviously you're going to be the one to bring up the kids. . . . You know, maternal instinct and all that? Like you shouldn't spend all your time being a doctor. You can't do *both*. Well, that's what most of them think: you can't do both. (Hammond 1980:39)

There is evidence, however, that adverse attitudes and stereotypes about women are beginning to be modified among members of the medical profession. Visible changes are occurring in the approaches of some physicians and hospitals toward treating women. A particularly significant source of change is found in the increasing numbers of women physicians. The first American woman to graduate from medical school was Elizabeth Blackwell in 1849, but her experience was atypical. Women have historically been underrepresented in medical school classes. Differences in the socialization experiences of boys and girls (Cole 1986) and a greater degree of persistence among males whose academic records are marginal (Fiorentine 1987) have contributed to this situation. It was not until the 1970s that women accounted for at least 10 percent of all first-year medical students. But in 1999–2000, 44.4 percent of all students entering medical schools were women.

This is not to claim that sexism in medicine is no longer significant because several accounts of women medical students and physicians detail the problems women have in being recognized as equal colleagues by male physicians and as "real" doctors by male patients (Elston 1993; Hammond 1980; Lorber 1984, 1993, 1997; Riska and Wegar 1993; West 1984). Sexism is most evident in the top posts in academic medicine where women physicians are rare, but women doctors are especially hindered in combining a demanding career with motherhood—especially if they have young children. Usually one or the other suffers, unless the mother as doctor can find a position with flexible hours or fewer hours on the job. The pay is lower, but fewer hours allow time for a family life. Susan Hinze (1999) investigated the prestige hierarchy in medicine from the standpoint of gender and found that the top specialties like surgery and internal medicine were characterized as masculine with traits like "toughness," "macho," and "demanding," while those at the bottom like family practice, pediatrics, and psychiatry were considered "soft." The top specialties were open to women, but women moving into these fields tended to take on the masculine traits in order to be successful. Here is an example:

> One male surgeon described the female "chairman" of a surgery program as "a competent surgeon, an impressive woman." He continued, "She started off as, yeah, everyone called her a bitch, she's a bitch, *but attractive, dresses well,* professional, is competent,

and her surgical skills were good, above average I think, at least average or maybe a little better than average" (emphasis added). He insisted, "If you are a female in a male profession, *you maintain your femininity* but you assert yourself as a professional. . . . You will be respected and you will advance yourself" (emphasis added). One female surgeon claims that the only women she knew in surgery were "not very warm and were not feminine." (Hinze 1999:230)

Another female doctor described "how horrified her peers were when she turned down an extremely high status specialty—neurosurgery—for the lower status specialty of obstetrics-gynecology because, to paraphrase, she loved the daily miracle of birth" (Hinze 1999:236). This doctor admitted that she had some difficulty accepting a "girl" specialty because she was one of the top students in her class and could have specialized in anything she wanted. Regardless of the choices women doctors make concerning their career in medicine, it is obvious that they will comprise nearly half of all physicians in numbers in the future and that their impact on the doctor–patient relationship will be significant. For example, Judith Lorber (1984) found that when male doctors assessed their accomplishments, they tended to speak only of their technical skills and choices of appropriate treatment. The personal side of the physician–patient relationship was rarely mentioned. Women doctors, on the other hand, stressed their value to patients and did so using words like "help" and "care." Steven Martin and his associates (Martin, Arnold, and Parker 1988) determined that men and women physicians have similar diagnostic and therapeutic skills, but there appear to be differences in their communication styles: Female physicians tend to be more empathic and egalitarian in their relationships with patients, more respectful of their concerns, and more responsive to patients' psychosocial difficulties. Recent research shows that patients feel more of a partnership with a doctor when the doctor is a woman, most likely because of better communication skills (Cooper-Patrick et al. 1999).

Today, women physicians are not only entering specialties that have traditionally attracted them—namely, pediatrics, obstetrics-gynecology, and general practice—but also increasingly in male-dominated specialties like surgery, urology, and orthopedics. Thus, women physicians are adopting more specialties than before and are now entering areas of medicine where they deal with a wider range of patients. Consequently, we have the beginnings of a new trend in medicine that may not only affect the physician–patient relationship (in terms of improved communication and willingness to relate to patients as people) but may also have an impact on the general image of women held by the medical profession.

CULTURAL DIFFERENCES IN COMMUNICATION

Physician–patient interaction can also be influenced by cultural differences in communication. A major study in this area is Irving Zola's (1966) comparison of Irish and Italian American patients in the presentation of symptoms at an eye, ear, nose, and throat clinic. Zola found that Irish patients tended to understate their symptoms, while Italian patients tended to overstate them. That is, the Irish made short, concise statements ("I can't see across the street"), while Italians provided far greater detail

---

BOX 9-1   Will Medicine Remain a Masculine-Dominated Profession?

Finnish medical sociologist Elianne Riska (2001) asks whether medicine will remain a masculine-dominated profession given the increasing number of women entering its ranks. This is a question that women's health advocates and others have also raised in the past few years. At present, the answer is that change is unlikely. While there are more women doctors than ever before in Western societies, men still fill the vast majority of leadership positions and this has changed very little. Moreover, there is a highly conspicuous segregation of medical work by gender in the United States, Great Britain, and the Nordic countries. That is, women physicians tend to practice in medical specialties consistent with the female gender role, namely, primary care, and those specialties concerned with children and the elderly—such as pediatrics and geriatrics. Male doctors, in contrast, opt for male-dominated and heroic fields like surgery, sports medicine, and internal medicine. Female physicians may be entering these specialties, but they are much fewer in numbers and also less likely to occupy the most powerful positions.

Riska explains that two explanations have been given for gender segregation in medical practice: structural and voluntaristic. The structural explanation holds that barriers, such as a lack of mentors, keep women from advancing to top positions in medicine. Men already in the top positions tend to mentor other men who wish to follow in their footsteps, not women. The voluntaristic view is that women are socialized to follow stereotypical gender expectations and consequently tend to make occupational choices that fit those expectations. They choose specialties that allow them to practice the type of medicine they prefer and are best able to use their gender-specific skills. It may be that the most immediate effect of the large number of women entering the medical profession will be to change the culture of the profession as a whole and soften its masculine image, rather than make medicine a feminine field of work.

("my eyes seem very burny, especially the right eye. . . . Two or three months ago I woke up with my eyes swollen. I bathed it and it did go away but there was still the burny sensation")—for the exact same eye problem. The doctors were required to sort the differences in communication styles in order to help them arrive at the appropriate diagnosis.

In contemporary American society, a particular problem in medical interviews is found among low-income and poorly educated Hispanics who speak little or no English, feel uncomfortable in impersonal social relationships, have no regular source of care, and find it difficult to negotiate their way through an Anglo health care delivery system (Andersen et al. 1981; Madsen 1973).

William Madsen provides an example of cultural misunderstandings in the following exchange with a Mexican American man who took his wife to see a physician in south Texas. The man (Madsen 1973:94) stated:

> We saw the doctor in his office after a long wait while many Anglos went in first. The doctor asked my wife, "What is wrong?" I told him. I said my wife had no energy and often no appetite. I told him how she had bad dreams and cried in her sleep. I

explained she must have *susto* but had not responded to the treatment of a *curandero*. Therefore, she must have *susto pasado*. I said I had come to him because my brother thought he could probably cure this disease. The doctor sat there smiling as I talked. When I finished, he laughed at me. Then he sat up straight and said sternly, "Forget all that nonsense. You have come to me and I will treat your wife. It is my job to decide what is wrong with her. And forget about those stupid superstitions. I don't know how a grown man like you can believe such nonsense!" He treated me like a fool.

The doctor then asked the husband to go to the waiting room and the wife to disrobe for an examination. The husband refused to let his wife be examined in this manner and took her away—never to return. Madsen (1973) reported that increasing reliance on physicians had eased some social barriers as a few doctors explained illnesses in simple terms and treated their patients with respect. But others remained disrespectful of them and the culture surrounding folk medicine.

Other lower-class minorities, including blacks, can have communication problems with doctors as well. Beverly Robinson (1990:211) reports on one black woman who, when asked how she was feeling, told her doctor that "the pain gone." The physician thought the woman was recovering until someone else informed the doctor that the woman meant the pain had only left temporarily. The woman's use of English was influenced by an African dialect in which "gone" meant a temporary absence, "done gone" and "done been gone" meant something had indeed left but could return and "gone gone" meant a complete absence.

Modern-day medical practice is provided within the context of middle-class norms and values emphasizing scientific beliefs, the application of sophisticated technology, and cooperation with physicians. For patients with a different cultural perspective, interaction with doctors can be difficult and subject to misunderstanding on both sides.

PATIENT COMPLIANCE

Another important aspect of physician–patient interaction is patient compliance with medical regimens (Svarstad 1986; Thompson 1984). Physicians prescribe medications, diets, and the like and expect patients to follow them faithfully. Many, perhaps most, patients comply with a physician's instructions, but other patients do not; in fact, some patients may pay little attention to a doctor's guidance, and this is especially the case when they begin to feel better or when symptoms are not obvious.

For example, in a study in Scotland, Mildred Blaxter and Richard Cyster (1984) found that a majority of patients with liver problems caused by alcoholism in an outpatient clinic continued to drink—despite being advised by their physicians to reduce or give up alcohol intake. Either the physicians had not adequately communicated the danger associated with continued drinking, or the patients had misunderstood. One male patient had been told to drink no more than two glasses of sherry a day as an example of how much he could drink, but since he drank whiskey not sherry, he gladly gave up any thought of drinking sherry and proceeded to pursue his normal drinking pattern. Other patients refused to believe their doctors or simply did not want to change their drinking habits, since it meant changing a preferred lifestyle.

Compliance requires comprehension by the patient, and communication is the key for avoiding noncompliance. The motivation to be healthy, a perceived vulnerability to an illness, the potential for negative consequences, effectiveness of the treatment, sense of personal control, and effective communication are the strongest influences on compliance (Thompson 1984).

THE FUTURE OF DOCTOR–PATIENT RELATIONS

Edward Shorter (1991) has traced the social history of the doctor–patient relationship. First, he explains how the medical profession evolved from being a relatively low-status occupation to a highly respected scientific field. The image of the ideal doctor–patient relationship—the caring physician and the trusting patient—was not lasting; it had ended, in Shorter's view, by the 1960s. Doctors had become increasingly distant in interacting with patients, while patients, in turn, had evolved from being willingly passive to active, informed clients who wanted to participate more equally in their care. The high cost of care, high salaries of many doctors, and superior attitudes on the part of some, along with organized opposition to health reform, caused some patients to become disillusioned with the medical profession. Doctors, on their part, became resentful about patients and others who questioned their commitment. As a result, Shorter concludes, doctor–patient relationships in the United States have seriously eroded in recent years.

Not all patients, however, are dissatisfied to the same degree and, as previously noted, social class differences appear to be the key variable in this situation. According to Freidson (1989:13):

> Those of lower status than the doctor, who lack the resources of a higher education, who are not exposed to a broad range of media information, and who are not forced to make calculated choices are not likely to become troublesome for the doctor. On the other hand, those who consider themselves to be of equal or higher status than the doctor, who consider themselves to be well informed about the latest diagnoses, prognoses, and treatments for what ails them, and who are experienced in reading the language of contracts and dealing with bureaucratic procedures have the potential to become serious problems of management.

Therefore, as Cassell (1986) explains, the belief among laypersons that the "doctor knows best" is no longer virtually accepted. Americans have become more knowledgeable about medicine and while they do not believe they are doctors, they do believe that they can understand and perhaps apply a piece of knowledge that is the same as the doctor's in their own health situation. Yet Cassell observes that simply having some knowledge about medicine is not enough to displace physicians from their previous preeminent status. Rather, he notes that during the 1960s, with the social turbulence associated with the civil rights movement and the Vietnam

War, the relationship of individuals to authority began to change in the United States. Americans became more individualistic and questioning about the motives of those in authority, including physicians. Cassell (1986:196) states:

> During this era, the nature of the relationship between the doctor and patient has come under scrutiny, and it has become apparent that the relationship itself is a powerful force in medical care, that it can be endangered, and that it can change as a result of social as well as personal forces. From being seen as effectively passive in relation to the physician (except that patients have always been expected to be active in the sense of "fighting to get well"), patients now frequently believe themselves to be active partners in their care. They want to take part in decisions formerly reserved for the doctor; they want to exercise choice in therapy and they have high expectations about the outcome.

Consequently, when it comes to health care, the evolving pattern among many Americans is one of consumerism in which the consumer wants to make informed choices about the services available and not be treated as inferior. The future direction of doctor–patient relations is one of greater mutual participation in decision making about the patient's health.

DOCTOR–PATIENT RELATIONS AND NEW TECHNOLOGY

An important factor having profound implications for the doctor–patient relationship is new medical technology. The development of computerized information highways connecting a patient's personal home computer to those of doctors, hospitals, drug companies, medical suppliers, health insurers, and medical databases will allow patients to obtain health information directly from their own computer rather than visiting a physician. Electronic monitoring devices will allow the patient to keep track of his or her physical and mental state and report these to physicians or databases by computer. Physicians may be consulted by means of home computers, electronic mail, or teleconferencing rather than in person. A computer can be used to diagnose the patient's ills and determine treatment. Prescription drugs may be ordered electronically and delivered to the patient. Moreover, physicians themselves can obtain current on-line clinical information, including new procedures and data on drugs, that can be used to improve patient care. Questions by patients can also be answered. Consequently, we see medicine adopting many technological features of an information science as it generates vast electronic libraries of health knowledge for those that seek it.

Medical practice in advanced societies has therefore become more and more dependent on increasingly sophisticated technologies from other fields like computer science and bioengineering (Webster 2002). This expanding reliance on new technologies has promoted a shift away from "biographical medicine" with its focus on the patient's oral account of his or her medical history. Instead, "techno-medicine," involving the extensive use of advanced technology for testing, diagnosis and the scientific determination of treatment in a more differentiated world of health care delivery is rapidly developing (Pinkstone 2000).

Internet Medicine

The Internet has already become a major source of medical information for many lay people. Although the information varies in terms of quality and expertise, currently there are about 10,000 sites on health problems ranging from minor ailments to life-threatening afflictions. Articles published in leading medical journals are included as well. This information is available to anyone who has an Internet connection. As Michael Hardey (1999) points out, this development changes the doctor–patient relationship as patients acquire access to information that was previously limited to doctors. Hardey studied households who used the Internet as a source of medical knowledge in Britain. He found that it is the *users* of the Internet, not physicians, who decided what information is accessed and used, as they educated themselves about various ailments and the drugs and procedures considered effective. Many of them negotiated with their physicians about treatment for themselves or children as a result of what they found on the Internet. According to one respondent:

> I was diagnosed as having high blood pressure and they gave me these pills. OK I was told that I might get some effects but I felt pretty bad sometimes after taking them. Anyway I found this place in the States [USA] that had a whole lot of information about this drug. Turns out that my symptoms happen to some people and there was this other pill that works better. . . . When I got to see my GP [general practitioner] she was surprised about what I knew about the prescription and put me on this other drug which works fine. I actually showed her some print outs from the Web that clearly show these tests that had been run on the drug and the symptoms that people in my circumstances had as a result. She was a bit taken aback but took me seriously and spent longer than I have ever had going through the details with me. (Hardey 1999:289)

Shu-Fen Tseng and Liang-Ming Chang (1999) compared doctor–patient relationships in Taiwan on the Internet and in face-to-face visits in a community hospital. For both groups of patients, mutual participation was the most common form of interaction with physicians. However, those patients who visited doctors in person expressed more confidence in physicians and relied on doctors more to treat their ailments than on-line users. The on-line users, in contrast, showed less confidence in doctors, less compliance with a physician's instructions, and a greater willingness to use alternative medicine. On-line users also indicated a strong preference for continued use of the Internet for physician consultations and medical information. However, on-line users did not rely exclusively on the Internet, but visited physicians when necessary. The Internet often served as a "second opinion" on their health problems.

In a survey of women in three southern New Jersey counties, Sanjay Pandey and his colleagues (Pandey, Hart, and Tiwary 2003) found that the Internet had become a major source of health information for the study's participants. There was evidence of the so-called "digital divide" where women with high incomes and education were more likely to use the Internet for health information than those at the lower end of the social scale who lacked Internet access. However, those with access actively used the Internet, primarily to supplement information provided by physicians. For this group, the availability of health information had changed dramatically and empowered the women to interact more knowledgeably with their doctors.

Other Developments

Not only is computer technology emerging as a major educational tool for laypersons and thereby changing the manner in which many persons interact with physicians, but medications are also likely to be different as various drugs become available in a variety of forms—pills, injections, patches, and nasal sprays or inhalers. And treatments normally available only in hospitals, like chemotherapy, may be reconfigured into pills and taken at home. Other measures like the use of robotics and computer-guided imagery may increase efficiency and precision in surgery and reduce the need for extensive hospitalization. Doctors may have little direct involvement in certain surgeries as robots and teams of surgically trained nurses handle most of the tasks.

Moreover, it may be the patient who discovers the requirement for treatment through self-monitoring and computer-assisted analysis of his or her medical history and symptoms. This situation also significantly changes the traditional doctor–patient relationship because patients, not doctors, will cause health care to take place. Doctors will be responding to what patients themselves decide they need, rather than the other way around. Doctors and patients will still have contact, but much of that contact may be through computers. Thus new technology is changing care-giving relationships as providers and consumers of health care obtain diagnostic precision and treatment options that previously have not existed (Timmermans 2000).

THE NEW GENETICS

Breakthroughs in genetics may also change doctor–patient interactions as patients learn through genetic screening what diseases they are likely to get and what measures are needed to treat them. Not only will such screening anticipate an individual's susceptibility to various diseases, but gene therapy also has the potential to eliminate many afflictions before they happen. The idea behind gene therapy is simple: to treat or cure disease by giving patients healthy genes to replace defective ones.

Genetic or genomic information may also furnish the basis for "designer" drugs tailored to match the DNA of a particular individual and provide more precise healing with fewer side effects. The potential of gene therapy and genetically based drugs has yet to be realized, but the completion of the Human Genome Project provides researchers with a map of the human genetic code. This development is likely to bring about an age of "new genetics" in which genetic testing may be the basis of a considerable portion of medical practice. At first, genetic testing will probably be used to refine drugs for common problems like migraine headaches and heart disease, but at some point gene therapy is likely to become commonplace.

Researcher preparing a genetic probe which will bind to the same genetic material in a person's DNA sequence, allowing it to be visualized on an X-ray film. Genetic probes are primarily used in antenatal diagnosis of genetic disorders.

The social use, control of information, risks, and ethics of genetic research has also promoted the birth of a new field in medical sociology: the sociology of genetics (Conrad 1999, 2000; Conrad and Gabe 1999; Cox and McKellin 1999; Cunningham-Burley and Kerr 1999; Ettorre 1999; Hallowell 1999; Kolker and Burke 1998; Martin 1999; Pilnick 2002). Interest by medical sociologists in genetics is in its infancy, but already questions with serious social implications are being examined. For example, can genetic testing become a form of social control, and, if so, what are the consequences for the individual and society? Currently there is no answer. But such testing could lead to new forms of stigma and discrimination as people are classified according to their genetic traits and potential for a healthy life.

Privacy and Gene Ownership

Important social disputes about genetic research also include issues of privacy and gene ownership. As Margaret Everett (2003) explains, genetic testing makes it possible to learn about someone's likely health future that even that person does not know. Genetic information therefore has unique implications for families and groups, and this information is potentially valuable to employers, insurance companies, researchers, and pharmaceutical firms who would use it for their own purposes. This situation opens the possibility of discrimination with respect to employment and insurance, and Everett notes that, as of 1999, some thirty-three states prohibit discrimination in health insurance based on genetic testing and nineteen states have similar laws regarding employment.

Given the potential for the commercialization of information about an individual's DNA, informed consent also takes on an especially high level of importance. Everett reports, for example, about a situation in Miami, Florida, where families affected by Canavan's disease (a fatal and rare recessive gene disorder) allowed their children's tissue samples to be used by hospital researchers to develop a prenatal diagnostic test and new treatment for the disease. The families were outraged when the test was developed and the hospital charged them a fee for administering it. The hospital argued that it needed to recover the costs of its research, while the families claimed that they had not given informed consent in writing, not been informed that hospital would get a patent on the test and limit its availability, and charge them a fee if they needed to be tested. The question thus arises as to whether or not genes are commodities and have property rights. Do they belong to the individual or to others who would use them for research and/or commercial purposes? Oregon is one of the few states that has examined the legal aspects of this question and assigned property rights to the individual, but this area of the law generally remains unresolved.

Prenatal Genetic Screening

Another major area of controversy is that of prenatal genetic screening with the option of abortions available for fetuses identified with gene defects. A study in Finland found considerable tension between the medical staff and the mothers of the unborn children found with such defects (Jallinoja 2001). The staff expected the mothers to behave in responsible and health-conscious ways with the goal of preventing genetic diseases by volunteering to have abortions. The mothers, however, refused and the screening program was eventually terminated. The mothers felt that a life with genetic disabilities was better than no life at all, and opted against having abortions. Research in the United States shows that public attitudes toward abortion in the case of genetic defects has become increasingly negative (Singer, Corning, and Antonucci 1999). The negative attitudes appeared to be primarily related to the abortion question, rather than the genetic testing itself, although racial minority persons were more pessimistic about such testing which was possibly due to fears that the tests could be used as a basis of discrimination.

Human Cloning

Another major controversy is that of cloning. Cloning refers to making a precise genetic copy of a molecule, cell, plant, or animal. Cloning techniques have been used successfully in agriculture in the selective breeding of crops and less successfully in the cloning of animals whose death rates are twice as high as animals conceived through sexual reproduction (Pilnick 2002). The cloning of a human has—to date—not been achieved, although some researchers claim it will happen soon. Human cloning is characterized as either "therapeutic" (the cloning of human organs for transplantation in sick people) or "reproductive" (the cloning of people themselves). As Alison Pilnick (2002) reports, reproductive cloning has been widely criticized as immoral and unnatural, and made illegal in some countries like the United States. Elsewhere, experiments in human cloning are nevertheless taking place as reported in the media. Pilnick observes that the creation of life in the laboratory represents the ultimate scientific power and potentially offers more control over populations than any previous technology as clones would be expected to display particular characteristics as a result of their genetic makeup. At this point in time, the extent to which human cloning is possible and the ways in which it could be successful are unknown. However, as Peter Conrad and Jonathan Gabe (1999:514) point out, "issues around genetics are not limited to those with genetic disorders or identified genetic susceptibilities, but rather the new genetics is likely to affect us all."

SUMMARY

This chapter has examined various social factors that affect doctor–patient interaction. The most likely model of interaction in future medical encounters is the mutual participation model suggested by Szasz and Hollender (1956). This model depicts the doctor and patient working together as more of a team than the patient simply following the doctor's orders in a more or less automatic fashion. However, it was found that a particularly significant barrier to effective interaction is differences in social class. Doctors from upper- and upper-middle-class backgrounds are likely to be better communicators than doctors from lower-middle- and working-class backgrounds, while patients from higher socioeconomic levels are more likely to demand and receive adequate information about their condition than patients with lower status.

Two groups in society are the most likely to have communication problems in medical encounters: one group is the lower class and the other is women, who sometimes do not receive what they consider to be adequate information from male doctors. Cultural differences can also affect doctor–patient interaction and, in the United States, differences between Hispanic patients and non-Hispanic health care providers have been cited as a negative circumstance. Finally, patient compliance with a physician's directions is not always automatic, and some patients fail to comply because of poor communication or other reasons. The doctor–patient relationship typically begins with dialogue, and the quality of that dialogue is often affected by social factors. New technology is undoubtedly bringing additional changes in the relationship as well.

DOCTOR–PATIENT INTERACTION INTERNET SITES

Doctor–Patient Communication

Center for Communication Programs, Johns Hopkins University.
http://www.jhuccp.org

Information, databases, and links regarding all aspects of communication as it relates to behavior change and health promotion.

Cultural Differences in Communication

1. U.S. Department of Health and Human Resources, Race and Health Homepage.
   http://www.omhrc.gov

   Databases, information, and other resources regarding ethnic/racial issues and health.

2. U.S. Department of Health and Human Services, Office of Minority Health.
   http://www.omhrc.gov

   Contains a search engine with access to dozens of articles dealing with minority communication strategies.

3. Multiethnic Healthcare.
   http://www.closing-the-gap.com

   Links, information, and other resources dealing with multiethnic health care.

4. Cross-Cultural Healthcare Program (CCHP).
   http://www.xculture.org

   A site devoted to broad cultural issues that impact health in ethnic minority communities. Emphasis is placed upon effective communication and interpretation.

5. Diversity Rx.
   http://www.diversityrx.org

   Promotes language and cultural competence in order to improve communication between ethnic minority patients and health care providers.

Medical Information

1. U.S. Department of Health and Human Services.
   http://www.healthfinder.gov

   Lets users search by subject and provides links to information from government health agencies, public health and professional groups, universities, support groups, medical journals, and news sites. Information about enrolling in clinical trials for cancer and AIDS is included.

2. Medscape.
   http://www.medscape.com

   Provides access to medical journals, news reports, and links to medical specialties and drugs. Has a medical dictionary and a link to Medline, the medical database at the National Library of Medicine. Also offers technical material for doctors and a special section for laypersons.

3. American Society of Health-System Pharmacists.
   http://www.safemedication.com

   Information about prescription drugs.

Physicians

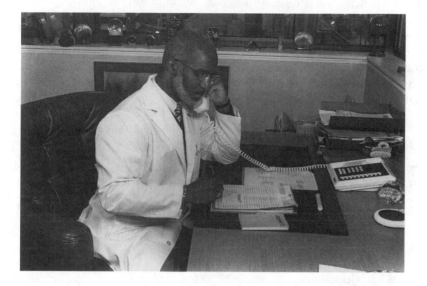

In 2000 there were 690,128 doctors actively practicing medicine in the United States (National Center for Health Statistics 2002). This comes to 22.7 physicians for every 10,000 Americans. Doctors constitute less than 10 percent of the total medical workforce, yet the entire health care industry in the United States is usually subordinate to their professional authority in clinical matters and research. Physicians generally control the conditions of their own work and the work of most of the other members of the health profession as well. Consequently, the status and prestige accorded to the physician by the general public is recognition of the physician's expertise concerning one of society's most essential functions: the definition and treatment of health disorders. As shown in comparisons of countries in North and South America, Europe, and Asia, as well as Australia, the medical profession is highly prestigious throughout most of the world (Quah 1989).

THE PROFESSIONALIZATION OF THE PHYSICIAN

The social importance of the medical function and the limited number of people with the training to perform as physicians are not the only criteria explaining their professional dominance. A particularly important factor is the organization of the medical profession itself. William Goode (1957, 1960) noted that two basic characteristics are sociologically relevant in explaining professionalism: prolonged training in a body of specialized, abstract knowledge and an orientation toward providing a service.

Moreover, once a professional group becomes established, Goode indicates that it begins to further consolidate its power by formalizing social relationships that govern the interaction of the professionals with their clients, their colleagues, and official agencies outside the profession. Recognition on the part of clients, outside agencies, and the wider society of the profession's claim to competence, as well as the profession's ability to control its own membership, is necessary if professional decisions are not to be reviewed by outside authorities. Once this situation (public acceptance of claims to competence and the profession's control of its membership) occurs, Goode (1960:903) believes that additional features of the profession can be established:

1. The profession determines its own standards of education and training.
2. The student professional goes through a more stringent socialization experience than the learner in other occupations.
3. Professional practice is often legally recognized by some form of licensure.
4. Licensing and admission boards are staffed by members of the profession.
5. Most legislation concerned with the profession is shaped by that profession.
6. As the occupation gains income, power, and prestige, it can demand high-caliber students.
7. The practitioner is relatively free of lay evaluation and control.
8. Members are strongly identified by their profession.

What Goode has accomplished, for our purposes, is the development of guidelines for analyzing the development of the medical profession in American society. While physicians in the United States have traditionally shared a basic service orientation, the second requirement, that of lengthy training in a specialized and abstract body of knowledge, was initially lacking. Most American medical practitioners in the period before the American Revolution were ship's surgeons, apothecaries, or clergy who had obtained a familiarity with medical knowledge in Europe. Few practitioners had been educated in either a university setting or a medical school. Anyone who wanted to practice medicine could do so and could claim the title of "doctor," which in Europe was reserved exclusively for persons educated at a university. The most distinguished early American physicians were those trained at the University of Edinburgh, Great Britain's foremost medical school in that era. From this small group of British-trained physicians came the impetus for establishment of the first American medical school in 1765 at the College of Philadelphia. This medical school, which later became part of the University of Pennsylvania, was subsequently joined in the years prior to 1800 by the organization of other medical schools at King's College (Columbia), Harvard, and Dartmouth.

After 1800, American medical schools virtually mushroomed, as school after school was established. But the quality of medical education in the United States remained low, and physicians themselves had little prestige as late as 1850. Not only did the doctors of the day offer little hope in curing disease, but sometimes their methods were either unpleasant or fatal. Often patients were bled, a practice that tended to weaken their condition, or they were administered purgatives, which caused them to vomit. By the middle of the nineteenth century, states E. Richard Brown (1979:62–63), "cholera victims were given an even chance of being done in by the disease or by the doctor."

The best medical training at this time was in Europe, especially in France and Germany where medical research was flourishing. In France, Louis Pasteur's germ theory of disease advanced during the mid-1800s, revolutionized medicine, and provided the foundation for the discovery, classification, and treatment of numerous diseases. By the last quarter of the century, however, Germany assumed the leading role in the scientific development of medicine. Medical scientists in Germany like Rudolf Virchow, who unveiled a general concept of disease based on cellular pathology (1858), and Robert Koch, whose work in bacteriology led to the discovery of the bacillus for anthrax (1876), tuberculosis (1882), and cholera (1883), became important figures in medicine. Their work, and the work of their colleagues, stimulated the growth of clinics and university-affiliated laboratories and promoted high standards of admission for medical training in Germany and Austria. Beginning in 1870, large numbers of American students flocked to the famous clinics and laboratories of German and Austrian universities. First Vienna and then Berlin became *the* centers of medical knowledge. It is estimated that between 1870 and 1914 approximately 15,000 American doctors received at least part of their training in German-speaking universities (R. Stevens 1971). Most of these doctors returned to the United States to set up lucrative private practices by introducing into their work the latest scientific techniques, which, as Brown (1979:73) explains, "at least *seemed* effective in reducing suffering and ameliorating the symptoms of disease." Brown (1979:73) describes the situation as follows:

> Physicians who had the money to take an extra year's study in Europe were able to build more prestigious practices than the ordinary American-trained doctor. Usually they would take themselves out of direct competition with the majority of physicians by specializing in gynecology, surgery, ophthalmology, or one of the other new branches of medicine. They quickly formed a new elite in the profession with reputations that brought the middle and wealthy classes to their doors.

Other European-trained physicians returned to develop medical laboratories and pursue the scientific investigation of disease. Henry Bowditch, for example, founded the first experimental physiology laboratory in the United States at Harvard University in 1871, while William Welch, who discovered staphylococcus in 1892, began the first pathology laboratory in America at Bellevue Hospital medical school in New York City in 1878. By 1900, the entire medical school faculties of Harvard, Johns Hopkins, Yale, and Michigan had been trained in Germany.

In the meantime, medical science continued to record impressive technical achievements. During the 1800s these achievements included René Laennec's (1816) invention of the stethoscope; the work of Crawford Long (1842), Robert Liston (1846), and William Morton (1846) on ether as an anesthetic; Claude Bernard's (1849) discovery of glycogen and the development of a theory of hormonal secretions providing the basis for endocrinology; Joseph Lister's (1866) use of antiseptic proce-dures in surgery; William Welch's discovery of staphylococcus (1892); Wilhelm Roentgen's (1895) development of the X-ray; and Ronald Ross's (1895) research on the cause of malaria. Thus, by the beginning of the twentieth century, American med-ical doctors were clearly able to claim the two core characteristics of a profession as outlined by Goode—a service orientation and a body of specialized knowledge.

Moreover, at the beginning of the twentieth century, medical research in the United States began to surpass that of Europe. American medicine had been influ-enced by the British until 1820, the French until the American Civil War, and then the Germans. By 1895, however, the Americans were ready to forge ahead thanks to the vast sums of money poured into medical research by private American philanthropic foundations, such as those funded by the Carnegie and Rockefeller families. Ac-cording to Brown, physicians in America strongly supported the rise of scientific medicine because it gave them greater effectiveness in a rapidly industrialized soci-ety and provided them with higher status, prestige, and income. Wealthy industrial-ists supported scientific medicine because it appeared to be a good investment in maintaining the moral, social, and economic order of corporate capitalism. Never-theless, the result was, to quote Rosemary Stevens (1971:135), that "under the impact of new knowledge, the rapid improvement of medical schools, and the proliferation of hospitals and clinics which in turn generated new information, medicine was be-coming vastly more efficient."

The American Medical Association

Another important step was necessary before American physicians could take ad-vantage of their evolving professional status—the organization of physicians into a professionally identifiable group. With the founding of the American Medical Association (AMA) in Philadelphia in 1847 physicians could mark the beginning of a new era in medicine. Dues were $3 a year, and immediately 426 physicians joined. Weak and ineffectual in the beginning, the AMA gradually extended its authority to become the single greatest influence on the organization and practice of medicine in the United States.

Two internal organizational measures were highly significant in this process. First, in 1883 the *Journal of the American Medical Association* (*JAMA*) appeared. This journal not only disseminated the latest medical knowledge and contributed to the prestige of the association, but also developed an awareness among the mem-bers of the AMA of their allegiance to the medical profession. Second, in 1902 an important reorganization took place when the AMA was divided into component so-cieties on the local level (district or county medical societies), constituent societies (state or territorial medical associations), a national House of Delegates, a Board of Trustees, and national officers.

As a result of this change, the basic unit of the AMA had become the local so-ciety. Most important, it had the authority to set its own qualifications for member-ship. In theory, all "reputable and ethical" licensed physicians were eligible to join the local society, but final approval of membership was dependent upon the local society's arbitrary discretion. The power of the local society was further enhanced because AMA organizational structure permits no formal right to a hearing or right to appeal the local society's decisions. Thus, threats of denial of membership or of expulsion from the local society represented powerful sanctions, since there is no alternative medical association and AMA membership can be important to a physician's career. Often such membership influences patient referrals, consultations, specialty ratings, and other professional and social contacts important to a highly successful medical practice.

In 1999 the AMA had a membership of 292,700 physicians. This figure represented 45 percent of all active doctors. Nonmembers include those who have retired, who have not satisfied local residence requirements, and who are employed by the government, the armed forces, research agencies, or universities and thus believe they do not need the benefits of membership. Other physicians may not belong because for some reason they are unacceptable to the local society, because they themselves disapprove of the AMA's policies, or because such membership is not important to them. Only about one-fourth of all women doctors belong to the AMA, suggesting a lack of appeal by the organization for female practitioners. Women doctors also have their own professional organization—the American Medical Women's Association—which addresses issues of interest to them.

Local societies have the power to enforce conformity at their level because they determine membership qualifications. However, despite the strength of local societies, there is little dispute within the AMA concerning its national objectives. As Eliot Freidson (1970a) and others have pointed out, the actual exercise of power in the American Medical Association is concentrated in the hands of a relatively limited number of physicians. Many members have either not been interested in the association's internal politics or have been too busy with their own medical practices to devote time to professional problems. The vast majority has usually been content to let the AMA represent the medical profession with Congress and other governmental agencies. The association in turn keeps its membership informed about significant medical and health legislation on both state and national levels.

Additionally, there is no forum for effective dissent within the AMA because public debates are disapproved in order to project an image of a united profession in the association's interaction with outside agencies. Dissenting issues within the AMA must first win major support at the local level or they are not considered further. And the *Journal of the American Medical Association* seldom publishes views other than official policy. Opposition groups within the AMA are further prevented from gaining power because of the indirect system of elections for national officers. Only the House of Delegates, which consists of representatives from each state, elects people to the top offices and to the Board of Trustees, which exercises day-to-day control over the association. Many influential appointments to AMA councils and committees are made directly by the Board of Trustees and are not voted upon by either the general membership or the House of Delegates.

In an examination of the American Medical Association by David Hyde and Payson Wolff in the *Yale Law Journal* (1954), the overall power base of the AMA was described as resulting from three primary sources: (1) power over the medical profession, (2) a strong economic position, and (3) the social status of the physician. The power of the AMA over the medical profession was described as the power of *consent, monopoly,* and *coercion.* Hyde and Wolff speculated that the AMA did have the consent of many physicians to represent organized medicine. This consent was derived from awareness that a formal organization was needed to enforce professional integrity, to advance professional interests, and to resist lay attempts to control medical matters. Monopoly resulted from the AMA's position as the only nationally recognized professional association available to the physician. The AMA's power of coercion was due to its authority to ostracize offending physicians and also to the incorporation of AMA guidelines into state medical practice laws and licensing procedures.

One of the most significant guiding principles of the AMA had been its view of the physician as an independent practitioner largely free of public control who engages in private medical practice on a fee-for-service basis. Since the 1920s a considerable portion of the AMA's energies has gone toward maintaining this situation. One major result is that the public image of the AMA has become that of a protective trade association seeking to ensure that the position of the physician as an individual entrepreneur of health services is not undermined. Yet the AMA's claim that it speaks for the majority of medical doctors is somewhat misleading as less than half of all physicians are members. In 1963, 79 percent of all doctors belonged to the AMA; in 1999, the figure of 45 percent represented a substantial decrease.

Consequently, there appears to be considerably more variation in the political attitudes of medical doctors in the United States than has previously been assumed. If this is the case, then the reputation of the AMA as a powerful lobby in Washington, D.C., may, to some extent, be spurious. David Mechanic (1972:28) finds for a weaker AMA when he explains that the idea of any particular political group's being able to dominate health policy is not consistent with the history of social legislation in health care. Although the AMA opposed both Medicare and other federal medical programs, these programs became law. The AMA was also excluded from direct participation in the planning of health reform by the Clinton Administration in 1994, with President Clinton referring to the AMA as just another "special interest group" (Hafferty and Light 1995:138). "Long accustomed to a privileged seat at the policy table," state Frederic Hafferty and Donald Light (1995:138), "the AMA and other major physician organizations found themselves unexpectedly, purposefully, and pointedly excluded from direct task force participation" and the AMA was warned by Vice-President Gore "that it would no longer dominate health reform."

Therefore, while it cannot be claimed that the AMA no longer yields influence in health legislation, its traditional role in maintaining the best possible policy and financial outcomes for medical doctors—regardless of whether or not it is in the public's interest—seems to have finally eroded its credibility with lawmakers and the public. With its organization, financing, and claims to expertise, the AMA will likely remain an important organization in formulating policy recommendations and guiding the medical profession on public issues. Yet, as Hafferty and Light (1995:138) explain, the AMA's "ability to exert its influence in an increasingly crowded policy environment appears greatly diminished."

The Control of Medical Education

The professionalization of medicine would not have been possible without control over the standards for medical education (Ludmerer 1985; Stevens 1971). At the beginning of the nineteenth century, the United States had seen the emergence of a vast number of proprietary medical schools. These schools, in the absence of any educational controls, were designed to offer medical degrees as a profit-making venture. It is estimated that about 400 proprietary medical schools existed during the 1800s; generally they had low standards of instruction and poor facilities, and admitted any student who could pay the required tuition. Since proprietary schools competed with other schools of this type and with schools affiliated with universities, they attempted to make their programs as attractive as possible. One school, for example, gave free trips to Europe upon graduation to any students who paid fees regularly and in cash for three years (Stevens 1971). Anyone who had the financial resources could obtain a medical degree and practice medicine, especially in the developing American West.

In 1904 the AMA established the Council on Medical Education to originate suggestions for the improvement of education and to become the association's agency for implementing educational change. The council eventually became an important regulating agency that operated both to establish high standards in medical schools and to strengthen the AMA's influence in medical education. The

Medical students attending an anatomy lecture. The medical profession is a service occupation supported by prolonged training in a specialized body of knowledge and determines its own standards of education and training.

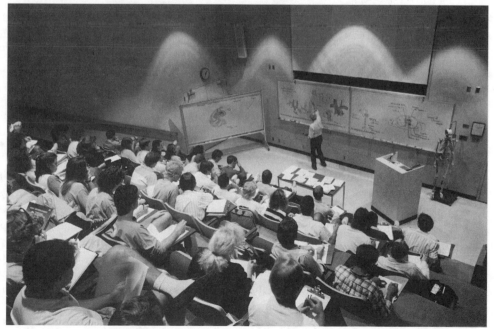

subsequent success of this effort was stimulated by one of the most important events in the history of medical education: the Flexner Report.

Sponsored by the Carnegie Foundation for the Advancement of Teaching, Abraham Flexner visited every medical school in the country and issued his famous report in 1910. Hoping to obtain funds from the prestigious Carnegie Foundation, most medical schools were anxious to discuss their problems and shortcomings while extending their full cooperation to Flexner in assessing their particular situation. The Flexner Report came out as a devastating indictment of the lack of quality medical education in the United States. Only three medical schools—Harvard, Western Reserve, and Johns Hopkins—were given full approval; many other schools were characterized by Flexner as "plague spots," "utterly wretched," "out-and-out commercial enterprises," "wholly inadequate," and so forth (Stevens 1971:67).

Flexner strongly recommended that medical schools consist of a full-time faculty and that both laboratory and hospital facilities be made available to medical students. He also urged that standards concerning the admission of students to medical schools be established and that the qualifications of medical school faculty be raised significantly. He likewise believed that medical education should be conducted by universities on a graduate level and that teaching and research functions be integrated within the institution offering the instruction. The example of a model medical school was Johns Hopkins University, with its medical education system containing a medical school, a nursing school, and a university hospital. Johns Hopkins required the bachelor's degree or its equivalent for admission as well as specific premedical college-level courses. According to medical historian Roy Porter (1997:530–531):

> Flexner was convinced that the key to medical progress and medical education was science. Critical of the French system (too clinical), the British system (decentralized and too clinical in its focus), and of most existing American schools (grossly commercial), Flexner wanted the medical school to be part of a university, with medical students receiving a sound grounding in natural sciences. The medical school of the future should have its own biomedical departments to encourage research; it had to have a teaching hospital and stiff entrance requirements and end with the doctoral degree; and, finding existing lab provision "wretched," Flexner insisted that the new medical schools must have good scientific facilities.

Although widespread protests arose from the affected schools, the Flexner Report induced considerable improvement in medical education. The better schools improved their programs, and the lesser schools eventually closed because of the bad publicity, financial adversity, and failure to meet the requirements of state licensing boards. Many states refused to certify the graduates of inferior medical schools, and money from various foundations was usually channeled only into those schools with good reputations. Since the sole source of medical school ratings continued to be the AMA's Council on Medical Education, the medical profession was able to retain an effective monopoly over educational regulation.

In summary, by the mid-1920s, the medical profession had consolidated its professional position to the point that it clearly had become the model of professionalism. According to Goode's analysis of the characteristics of a profession, the medical profession had not only met the basic criteria of being a service occupation supported by prolonged training in a specialized knowledge, but furthermore, it had determined its own standards of education and training, had successfully demanded high-caliber students, had staffed its own licensing and admission boards, had shaped legislation in its own interests, had developed stringent professional sanctions, had become a terminal occupation, and was free of formal lay evaluation and control. Although threatened by social legislation regarding reforms in health care, physicians constitute, and will in all probability remain, the dominant professional group in the rendering of medical service in the United States.

THE SOCIALIZATION OF THE PHYSICIAN

To understand the perspectives of physicians as a professional group, it is important also to consider the manner in which physicians are selected and trained as medical professionals. In 2000, 16,856 students were selected annually out of 37,092 applicants to begin training at 125 accredited medical schools in the United States. The number of applicants to medical schools declined from 36,727 in 1981 to 26,721 in 1988; however, applications to medical schools shot up dramatically as 45,365 students applied in 1994, only to drop to 37,092 in 2000. Some 55.6 percent of first-year students in 1999–2000 were male; the remaining 44.4 percent represents a significant increase for females. In the 1970s only about 10 percent of all first-year medical students were female. There has also been an increase in the percentage of racial minority students. Since 1969, the percentage of racial minorities in first-year classes has risen from 3 to 35.9 percent in 1999–2000.

Typically, first-year medical students will be between the ages of twenty-one and twenty-three and will have at least a bachelor's degree with a 3.57 (on a 4.0 scale) premedical grade point average. Most likely the undergraduate college major will be in biology, chemistry, zoology, premedical, or psychology. Because these students are motivated and committed to a well-defined, terminal career goal, they have a high probability of successfully completing medical school once accepted; about 95 percent of all entering medical students currently attain the M.D. degree.

Studies on the social origins of American medical students show that most are from upper- and upper-middle-class families. Although increasing numbers of lower-middle- and lower-class students are entering medical school, most medical students are homogeneous in terms of social class affiliation. For example, Howard Becker and his associates (1961), conducted what has become a classic study in medical sociology of students at the University of Kansas Medical School in the late 1950s using participant observation. They found that lower-class medical students, by virtue of their undergraduate education and commitment to becoming successful physicians, assimilated middle-class norms and values.

Oswald Hall (1948) pointed out several decades ago that the decision to study medicine is largely social in character; that is, it originates in a social group that is able to generate and nurture the medical ambition. Family influence is an especially important variable in encouraging and reinforcing the ambitions of the future recruit to the medical profession, and having a parent, close relative, or family friend who is a physician also seems to be a distinct advantage promoting the desire to be a doctor (S. Bloom 1973).

The reason given by many medical students for choosing a career in medicine has been generally that of wanting "to help people." Becker and his associates, for example, found that first-year medical students had idealistic long-range perspectives about why they selected medicine as a career. These perspectives were summarized as follows (Becker et al. 1961:72):

1. Medicine is the best of all professions.
2. When we begin to practice, we want to help people, have enjoyable, satisfying work while upholding medical ideas. We want to earn enough money to lead comfortable lives, but this is not our primary concern.

Some medical students may enter medical school in order to make money or for the prestige of the M.D. degree or both. According to John Columbotos (1969), physicians from a lower-class social origin were more likely than upper-class doctors to emphasize success values as reasons for going into medicine. But once in medical practice, social class background became less significant. Those physicians who were initially success oriented became less so after commencing their practices, while the reverse occurred with those who were less success oriented. Columbotos suggested this trend was most likely due to socialization by colleagues. Success-oriented physicians were probably encouraged to be less obvious about their ambitions, and the less success oriented were most likely encouraged to strive for the level of status indicative of their professional group. Becker and his associates noted that most entering medical students *assumed* they would be well paid. Hence, making money was apparently secondary to helping patients. Many resented the notion that they were solely out to make money.

Once the medical student begins training, he or she is expected to acquire a foundation of knowledge in the basic medical sciences and the techniques employed in the actual practice of medicine. Included in this process is the internalization of ethical and moral principles that are essential if the physician is to be trusted by patients, colleagues, and the community and is to maintain his or her professional status. Most courses of study range from thirty-two to forty-five months, and the educational experience is usually divided into basic medical science studies and clinical studies. Basic medical science studies consist of courses in anatomy, biochemistry, physiology, pathology, pharmacology, microbiology, physical diagnosis, clinical laboratory procedures, and often behavioral science. The clinical programs consist of learning to use basic medical science to solve clinical problems by working with patients under the supervision of the faculty. The students also rotate through clerkships in various medical services, such as medicine, surgery, pediatrics, obstetrics-gynecology, psychiatry, and other specialties.

Much of the sociological research concerning medical education has focused on the consequences of that experience other than mastery of medical knowledge. Among the major studies, Renée Fox (1957) found that medical students at Cornell

Medical School acquired basically two traits as a result of their medical training: ability to be emotionally detached from the patient and to tolerate uncertainty. Fox, whose work was part of an extensive study of student physicians (Merton, Reader, and Kendall 1957), noted that the medical student experienced three types of uncertainty. First, there was uncertainty resulting from an awareness of not being able to learn everything about medicine. Second, there was the realization that limitations existed in current medical knowledge and techniques. The first two uncertainties led to a third type of uncertainty in which medical students had problems distinguishing between personal ignorance and the limits of available knowledge. However, Fox observed that as the student acquired medical knowledge and gained experience, along with a sense of personal adequacy in medicine, he or she learned to cope with the uncertainty and to assess conflicting evidence objectively in arriving at a diagnosis. This process was assisted by the realization that other medical students were coping with the same problems and that the faculty also experienced uncertainty in their everyday work.

One method medical schools have employed to reduce uncertainty among students in the application of medical knowledge is an emphasis upon a technique known as *evidence-based medicine* (EBM). EBM utilizes clinical practice guidelines providing highly detailed step-by-step instructions on medical care that the students can refer to in clinical situations. These instructions are based on "proven" (supported by research and clinical trials) diagnostic and therapeutic procedures. Stefan Timmermans and Alison Angell (2001) investigated the use of EBM among physicians undergoing residency training in pediatrics at Brandeis University Medical School. They found that, while EBM is a major improvement in reducing uncertainty, uncertainty is still attached to many aspects of medical practice. Timmermans and Angell suggest that the strength of a doctor's clinical judgment depends on how well he or she confronts the uncertainties that persist in medical knowledge.

At the University of Kansas Medical School, Becker and his colleagues (1961) determined that the students developed a strong appreciation of clinical experience (actually working with patients rather than reading about disease and studying it in the laboratory) and that they acquired a sense of responsibility about patients. They also learned to view disease and death as medical problems rather than as emotional issues. The focal point of their passage through medical school was to graduate; since they could not learn everything they needed to know to practice medicine, they directed their efforts toward finding the most economical ways of learning. Generally, they tried to guess what the faculty wanted them to know, and then they studied this material for the examinations. Even so, they found that they put in an eight-hour day of classes and laboratories. They also studied four to five hours on weeknights and continued studying on the weekends.

One aspect of medical training that appears in several studies of medical students in the United States (Baker, Yoels, and Clair 1996; Broadhead 1983; Conrad 1988b; Coombs 1978; Hafferty 1991, 2000; Parsons et al. 2001; A. Smith and Kleinman 1989), Canada (Haas and Shaffir 1977, 1982; Shapiro 1978), and Israel (I. Adler and Shuval 1978) is the finding that the experience tends to promote emotional detachment from patients. Robert Coombs, for example, found that in a California medical school the faculty gave little real guidance in how to manage patients except to serve as role models for emotional control and a businesslike demeanor. In Canada, Jack Haas and William Shaffir found the students to be initially dismayed by how the teaching faculty and other hospital staff members treated patients. One student reported:

> What I do remember about Phase II that really got me when I did go to a cancer clinic at the Fensteran and I saw the way they were just herding in ladies that had hysterectomies and cancer, and just the way the doctors would walk right in and wouldn't even introduce us as students, and just open them up and just look and say a lot of heavy jargon. And the ladies would be saying, "How is it?" "Am I better, or worse?" And they say in this phony reassuring tone, "Yes, you're fine," and take you into the hallway and say how bad the person was.
>   They hardly talked to the patient at all. Like this was a big check up after waiting three months or six months and then the doctor whips in for two minutes to take a quick look and then they're gone. We would get in there and he'd hold the speculum and we'd all take a look and we would just herd right out again into another room and have a look and herd out again. I thought the dehumanization was awful. (Hass and Shaffir 1977:82)

In trying to cope with the situation, the students began to rationalize that the large number of patients seen by the physicians precluded them from doing anything more than attending to the patient's medical condition. There were just too many patients and not enough time to deal with psychosocial problems. In fact, in their own work, the students found themselves depersonalizing patients so they could concentrate on learning what was medically important. A student described the situation this way:

> I think you realize that there is a structural problem, and there are a lot of demands made on you and you are forced to act in certain ways just to accomplish your work. But right now in the training phase, I find if the clinical preceptor takes me around to listen to six patients with heart murmurs and I only have five minutes with each patient, I don't get concerned that I'm not getting it on with the patient, because I'm trying to learn about heart murmurs. (Haas and Shaffir 1977:71)

Another study of medical students quoted one who told of residents who were really great with patients, but still occasionally made insensitive remarks about them: "I guess it's something that happens when people are under stress," the student said (Parsons et al. 2001:549). A different student pointed out that one clinical service referred to its patients as "The Toad Service." The student stated:

> They told me someone had named it that a couple of months ago because the patients are all just old people in contractures [bent, weak limbs], and they looked like toads. Which is pretty revolting. It was appalling to me. I was so shocked at the way doctors talked about people in the beginning. But having just finished a month of being tired and sleep deprived, and being up all night for really stupid things, I can see where the frustration comes in. I still don't think it is right, but I can understand it a little. Now it is no longer inconceivable to me why people talk that way about patients and their families. (Parsons et al. 2001:548)

BOX 10-1   Medical Slang and Its Functions

There have been several studies of medical slang (the special vocabulary used by a person in particular situations) as an informal tool of communication between physicians (Coombs et al. 1993; Parsons et al. 2001). Men and women physicians tend to be similar in their use of the terms. Slang use typically begins during the third year of medical school when students rotate among various clinical services, and peaks during their residencies. It is at this time that the medical trainees experience firsthand the stressful circumstances of hospital life: death, terminal illness, troublesome patients, and demanding instructors. According to Robert Coombs et al. (2001) medical slang serves the purpose of (1) creating a sense of belonging, (2) establishing a unique identity, (3) providing a private means of communication, (4) creating opportunities for humor and wit, and (5) softening tragedy and discharging emotions. Some of the common slang terms identified by Coombs et al. are listed below:

Term	Meaning
Doc in the Box	Walk-in Clinic
Gomer Ranch/Gomerville	Veterans Administration Hospital
Death Star	Hospital transport helicopter
Cage	Operating Room
Rock Garden	Unit for chronically ill patients
Doom Tomb	Unit with comatose patients
Vegetable Patch	Coma rehabilitation center
Cooler	Morgue
Shark	Attending physician who attacks and "shreds" medical trainees without provocation
Liver Rounds	Going out for an alcoholic drink
Rear Admirals	Proctologists
Blades	Surgeons
Bone Bangers	Orthopedists
Fruit Loop	Mentally ill patient
Groupie	Patient who routinely uses the Emergency Room without a real emergency
Toad	Troublesome, demanding patient
Trainwreck	Patient with many medical problems
Disasteroma	Horribly ill patient
The Big A	AIDS
The Big C	Cancer
Howdy Rounds	Physician simply waves at the patient from the door and moves on
Bug Juice	Antibiotic
Vitamin V	Valium
Deep Sea Fishing	Exploratory surgery without much to go on
Cut 'N Paste	To open up a patient in surgery, see there is no hope and close
Lazarus	A dying patient who recovers

Previously, the Becker study had attempted to assess the general impact of such attitudes by exploring the charge that medical students become cynical as a result of their medical education. In reply, Becker and his colleagues noted that medical students did appear to enter medical school openly idealistic, but once in medical school, their idealism was replaced with a concern for getting through. Becker observed that medical students may in fact become cynical while in school, but he also pointed out that attitudes are often situational. Thus, when graduation approached, idealism seemed to return as the students could set aside the immediate problem of completing their program of study. What had happened was that medical students had been isolated in an institutional setting and forced to adjust to the demands of that setting. But once the medical student was ready to return to the mainstream of society, the student again became concerned about service to humanity. In an earlier article, Becker and Blanche Greer (1958) had argued that cynicism on the part of medical students represented growth toward a more realistic perspective. What appeared as a harmful change of attitude was actually part of a functional learning process fitted to the physician's role of maintaining an objective perspective of health and disease.[1] The Coombs (1978) study likewise found that medical students' cynicism did not develop into a generalized personality trait. The students in this study learned to balance emotional attitudes with sensitivity toward patients. Elsewhere in two midwestern schools, Bebe Lavin and her colleagues (Lavin et al. 1987) found medical students developing more egalitarian attitudes toward patients in order to deal effectively with them.

For some physicians the possibility still remains that medical training has focused their attention more on technical procedures than on dealing with patients as people. As Donald Light (1979) points out, in emphasizing clinical judgments and techniques physicians run the danger of becoming insensitive to complexities in diagnosis, treatment, and relations with patients. The result can be errors and malpractice suits. Light (1979:320) explains: "Their emphasis on techniques can make them oblivious to the needs of clients as *clients* define them; yet it is clients' trust that professionals will solve their complex problems which provides the foundation of professional power." Zeev Ben-Sira (1980), for instance, has found in Israel that, especially for lower-class patients, some emotional support by the

---

[1]Some physicians do not need to spend a lot of time with patients. Consider, for example, the report of William Nolen (1970:191–192), who was undergoing training as a resident in surgery at a hospital on Long Island, New York:

> Steele was no slouch as a diagnostician. He was one of those surgeons who have a sixth sense about symptoms and could learn more about a patient in five minutes than most doctors do in an hour. I took him to see one of our rare service cases, an eight-year-old boy admitted for possible appendicitis. Steele spent two minutes with him and we stepped back into the corridor.
>
> "Did you notice the way he kept his right knee bent? Did you see that he wasn't moving his abdomen at all when he breathed? Did you get a look at how dry his tongue was? That kid's got peritonitis. Put him on [surgery] schedule."
>
> "But his white count is only nine thousand and his temperature is normal," I objected.
>
> "Nolen, let me tell you something," Steele said. "Try looking at the patient instead of the chart. The chart isn't sick."
>
> The boy had a ruptured appendix with peritonitis.

Medical students develop a strong appreciation for clinical experience that comes with working with patients instead of just reading about disease or learning about it in a laboratory or lecture hall.

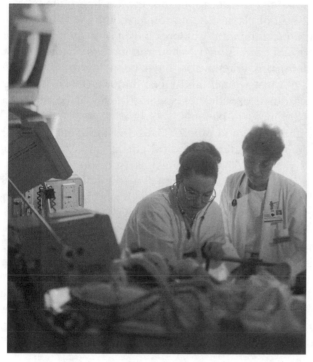

physician will not only reduce the patient's uncertainty about the type and outcome of treatment but will also have a significant impact on the patient's evaluation of treatment.

While much of the older literature on socialization in medical schools finds tendencies on the part of students to depersonalize patients, more recent accounts of medical training show a different situation. Ellen Lerner Rothman (1999) reported on her experiences as a student at Harvard Medical School and found numerous situations where she and her fellow students, as well as staff physicians, developed serious personal concerns about the well-being of their patients and worked hard to help them. She comments on a classmate who was initially annoyed by a sixty-five-year-old man who kept complaining about abdominal pain despite a lack of evidence for a cause of the pain. However, after further tests, it was determined the man had widespread cancer. The classmate felt awful and that somehow her team of doctors was responsible. "I mean," stated the classmate (Rothman 1999:155), "he came in a healthy man, and if we hadn't gone mucking around, we never would have found the cancer in the first place." The classmate was determined to do as much as she could for the man. Rothman herself told of how much joy and excitement she felt when her trauma team saved a man's life on the operating table.

"For the first time," states Rothman (1999:167), "I understood what it was like to care for hospitalized patients and become emotionally invested in their care."

As medical education heads into the twenty-first century, significant changes are taking place. The number of male applicants has declined almost 50 percent since 1975, and medical school classes are no longer composed almost entirely of white males. Females and racial minority students have taken their place, indicating that the image of the medical profession as white and male is changing toward one of greater diversity. Admissions criteria also have been broadened to include a greater mix of students, not just women and racial minorities, but students whose background and undergraduate experiences suggest they will be likely to take a humanistic approach in dealing with patients.

Furthermore, as Light (1988) and others (Gallagher and Searle 1989; Hafferty 2000; Kendall and Reader 1988) indicate, medical education is having to adjust to new realities in medical practice. These realities, as Light points out, include the transition in American health care delivery from (1) a system run by doctors to one shaped by the purchasers of care and the competition for profits; (2) a decline in the public's trust in doctors to greater questioning and even distrust; (3) a change in emphasis on specialization and subspecialization to primary care and prevention; (4) less hospital care to more outpatient care in homes and doctors' offices; and (5) less payment of costs incurred by doctors' decisions to fixed prepayments, with demands for detailed accounts of decisions and their effectiveness. Even though the medical profession and medical schools have a long tradition of conservatism, medical education is adjusting to the realities of medical practice in order to better prepare medical students for the changing environment they will face in the twenty-first century, including medical practice in managed care systems where physicians are employees (Hafferty 2000).

THE POWER STRUCTURE OF AMERICAN MEDICINE

Like any other profession, medicine has its own power structure. One of the early, but still relevant, studies concerning the power structure of the medical profession was conducted by Oswald Hall (1946, 1948) in an eastern American city. Hall identified three factors important in establishing prestige within the medical profession: (1) hospital affiliation, (2) clientele, and (3) the inner fraternity.

The Hospital

A most significant factor in a successful urban medical career, according to Hall, was affiliation with a prestigious hospital because the more important hospital positions were usually associated with the more financially rewarding medical practices. Therefore, gaining an appointment at a prestigious hospital represented a crucial point in the career development of the urban physician.

Of particular significance was the initial appointment because, as Hall (1948:330) explains, the hospital residency "that a doctor has served is a distinctive badge; it is one of the most enduring criteria in the evaluation of his [or her] status."

In a study of the Harvard Medical Unit at Boston City Hospital, Stephen Miller (1970) found that the "best" residency was not necessarily determined by the quality of teaching, the type of patient, or the range of responsibility residents were allowed to assume, though these factors were important. The "best" referred to the reputation of the program and its location.

The reputation of a residency in major medical and research institutions assists the candidate's entry into academic medical circles. For those physicians wishing to become general practitioners, the optimal setting for an internship would be in communities where they hoped to build a medical practice. Even at the local level, the initial hospital appointment was important in that it facilitated the formation of friendships and professional relationships that could help to enhance a career. Usually the location of a residency determines the system of medical institutions and group of physicians the new doctor will be associated with in the future.

For example, Miller observed that the Harvard program of graduate medical training was much more than a way to meet licensing requirements; it was a means by which an academic appointment at a "name" medical school could be secured. As one of the Harvard interns explained to Miller (1970:81):

> I'm going into academic medicine, and I wanted the internship which was the best or very good; I think of the word "prestige," a great deal of prestige in being part of this group. It just has a very good reputation, you know. It will look good on paper.

Many of the interns in the Harvard program were graduates of "name" medical schools. About 50 percent had graduated from Harvard, and another 30 percent were from schools like Cornell, Yale, and Johns Hopkins. The remaining 20 percent were from other medical schools. Thus, it was possible for the graduate of a "lesser" school to begin a residency with the Harvard group in order to acquire the background for an academic appointment at higher-level medical institutions. As Miller explained, there were not enough "name" medical school graduates for all the residencies available; then, too, the Harvard Medical Unit limited the number of Harvard graduates it would accept in order to avoid the "inbreeding" of its faculty.

Yet the process of selection for the Harvard Medical Unit was not entirely democratic. Since many graduates of the program had gone on to the faculties of other medical schools, a large number of schools featured alumni of the unit, in effect a "colony" of physicians with the same medical background. Their letters of recommendation as former students, graduates, and people known to the Harvard Medical Unit greatly assisted the acceptability of applicants. Miller noted that all of the residents from lesser known schools in his study of the Harvard Medical Unit program were graduates of medical schools where Harvard alumni constituted a colony. Miller (1970:70) stated: "Most learned about the program from, discussed it with, and were advised to choose it by Harvard Medical Unit alumni." So not only were initial appointments important for the future careers of the residents, but also the gaining of these appointments was influenced to a certain degree by having recommendations from the "right" people. Hall found a similar trend in his study of the medical career.

Paul Starr (1982) adds that in the decades since World War II there has been a steady extension of the power of medical schools into the hospital systems of metropolitan areas. Noting that some critics depicted these schools as "empires," Starr found that the schools held a powerful position in medical affairs because of their control over academic appointments, hospital privileges, and hospital equipment and labor. Such medical centers, states Starr (1982:361), "typically would not only have a medical and dental school but also schools in pharmacy, public health, nursing, and other paramedical occupations; research institutes for heart disease, mental illness, cancer, rehabilitation, and other fields; several general teaching hospitals, perhaps a women's hospital, a children's hospital, a psychiatric hospital, various clinics, doctors' office buildings, and so on."

Consequently, universities became the hubs for the nation's regional medical centers even though their primary orientation was toward research and training rather than patient care. The most powerful figures in these medical centers were the professors who chaired the major medical school departments and were chiefs of medicine, surgery, psychiatry, obstetrics-gynecology, and pediatrics in the teaching hospitals. They were the ones who controlled policy-making boards and determined the careers of residents. As one administrator put it, "It is inconceivable that the university would try to carry out a policy contrary to the wishes of the department chairmen of the Medical School and damned difficult for the hospital to carry out a policy contrary to the wishes of the chiefs" (Duff and Hollingshead 1968:46). Such a situation, as Starr observes, is practically a textbook definition of power.

The Clientele

The next stage described by Hall is that of acquiring a clientele and retaining and improving it. Hall likened this process to that of a commercial enterprise in that the physician needed to play the role of a promoter. In other words, the physician was required to interact with patients so as to secure their approval of the services provided. Freidson (1960) has pointed out that the lay-referral system not only channels the patient to certain doctors, but also helps the patient to make a decision about returning to a particular doctor. Freidson notes that the first visit to a doctor is often tentative, especially in a community large enough to support more than one doctor. Freidson (1960:378) states: "Whether the physician's prescription will be followed or not, and whether the patient will come back, seems to rest at least partly on his retrospective assessment of the professional consultation." Thus, the patient not only passes through the lay-referral system on the way to the physician, but also on the way back by discussing the doctor's behavior, diagnosis, and prescription with family and friends. In a given community, certain doctors are often chosen more frequently than others merely because they are fashionable or popular. Most physicians become aware of lay expectations and learn to deal with them if they expect patients to return.

Furthermore, Hall observed that success in medicine involves improving the practice by attracting the desired type of patient and discouraging those patients who do not fit into the physician's conception of his or her practice. It may also be true that more affluent patients desire to be treated with others of their kind, so a physician who treats both the rich and the poor in the same setting and under the same circumstances would run the risk of offending the rich. Michael Miller (1973) has observed that upper-class patients will change physicians sooner than lower-class patients.

Although the evidence is not conclusive, existing studies generally suggest that physicians tend to favor upper- and middle-class patients. Physicians who routinely treat more affluent patients tend to have greater status among their colleagues (Link 1983). Besides being perceived as more likely to pay their bills, upper- and middle-class patients also reflect values, norms, and attitudes similar to those of the physician. Duff and Hollingshead (1968), for example, found that physicians tended to be more attentive to upper-class patients by "overidentifying" with them.

The best medical practice in Hall's study was the specialized practice because Hall believed the specialist was accorded superior status by others in the medical profession. Other observers (Stevens 1971; Mechanic 1972) have also pointed toward the trend in specialization, which resulted in the decline in number of general practitioners and the domination of the medical profession by speciality groups. A specialized practice, however, is dependent on having a group of colleagues who refer patients to the specialist. Generally, referring physicians are reciprocated by fee sharing or by the referral of patients back to the general practitioner. A specialized practice also requires access to hospital facilities, and hospital connections in themselves facilitate the development of referral relationships between physicians.

In a study of internists (specialists in internal medicine) in private practice in Chicago, Stephen Shortell (1973) found that they tended to refer their patients to other specialists on the hospital staff where they held a primary appointment. The influence of the hospital appointment was such that it provided both formal and informal channels of communication about who was available in the various specialties and what relative advantages they had to offer. Furthermore, the ability to follow up on a patient after care had been turned over to another specialist or specialists depended on the internist's being on the same hospital staff.

Shortell's study traced the informal organization of medical practice by extensively examining the referral process. He found that patterns of referrals were related to the professional status of the physicians and operated according to the relative rewards and costs perceived by physicians at different levels of the status hierarchy. High-status internists, for example, tended to refer their patients to other high-status colleagues, while lower-status internists also more often referred their patients to higher-status physicians than to their peers. Higher-status physicians thus tended to be the major recipients of referrals. High-status physicians primarily choose each other as referral partners because the exchange helps validate their own personal status and maintains the status structure of their own group as well. Lower-status physicians, however, tend to refer patients outside their group because of the prestige rewards of dealing with higher-status physicians and because of a potential loss of clientele to fellow low-status competitors. The reasoning was that low-status physicians were much more likely to be concerned about building their medical practice and thereby might tend to retain patients sent to them. High-status physicians, on the other hand, would already have a successful practice and would not be so desirous of acquiring more patients on a regular basis.

The "Inner Fraternity"

Hall's study pointed toward the existence of an "inner fraternity" in medicine that operated to recruit new members, to allocate these new members to positions in the various medical institutions, and to help them secure patients through referrals. Hall believed that the urban power structure of the medical profession consisted of four major groups of physicians. The first group was the "inner core," which Hall described as the specialists who have control of the major hospital positions. Immediately outside this inner core were the new recruits at various stages of their careers who were intended to inherit positions in the inner core at some time in the future. Next were the general practitioners who were linked to the inner core by the referral system. Women physicians tend to fall into this second group of "friendly outsiders"—that is, not members of the inner core (Lorber 1993). Besides these two groups were the marginal physicians, those who would remain on the fringes of the system because the inner core had its own methods of selecting recruits. According to Hall, the key to understanding the power structure of the medical profession was found in the system of control exercised by the inner core. The inner core displayed three major characteristics that enabled it to control the medical profession. First, it was a highly cohesive group of specialists with relatively identical educations and socioeconomic backgrounds, technical interdependence, and daily working relationships. Second, the social bonds between different specialists allowed these powerful physicians to integrate the various specialties into a cohesive body. And third, the inner core was able to organize the medical market by controlling the process in which patients were referred from one physician to another.

What Hall's analysis has provided in terms of understanding the power structure of the medical profession is the realization that a doctor's career takes place in a system of formal and informal relationships with colleagues. Formal relationships develop as a result of a physician's position within the prevailing medical institutions in a particular community. The control of the dominant posts within these institutions, especially hospital appointments, is the critical variable that distinguishes influential from noninfluential doctors. Informal relationships also develop over time as physicians interact with one another frequently and arrive at definitions of the quality of each other's work and personal characteristics. Thus, claims to position, status, and power become recognized and are perpetuated within the profession, and mechanisms for recruitment into the inner core become established in both formal and informal ways.

However, a relatively recent development within the inner core of the medical profession's power structure is its division into two major groups: a knowledge elite (physician-researchers) and an administrative elite (physician-administrators). The knowledge elite, according to Freidson (1989), exercises extensive technical and cognitive influence over medical work through its research productivity. This group has been associated with academic medical centers since the time of the Flexner

Report in the early twentieth century. Yet in the last decade, Hafferty and Light (1995) point out, the knowledge elite has shifted much of its attention from individual diagnosis and treatment to conducting clinical trials and assessing entire systems of health care, including their organization and financing. Members of the administrative elite, in turn, have established themselves on a long-term basis in major bureaucratic posts in medical centers, such as deans of medical schools, department chairs, or heads of clinics and hospitals. They wield considerable power over budgets and staff appointments.

Hafferty and Light predict that, as the physician-researchers and physician-administrators establish power and influence, they will move away from the everyday concerns of rank-and-file physicians. They will be more concerned with important research topics or institutional issues. Not only will there be increased professional distance from physicians outside the inner core, but there will also be greater separation between the two elite groups as they go in different directions in pursuit of their particular interests. "Rather, these new elites," state Hafferty and Light (1995:141), "will not only fail to identify with the rank-and-file or with broader professional values but they themselves will evolve in disparate directions, with the administrative elite becoming the more dominant of the two as it develops closer working and ideological ties with corporate interests and bureaucratic structures."

The most significant variable to emerge from this discussion of the power structure of the American medical profession is that of institutional position. The medical profession is based upon a variety of institutions—hospitals, clinics, medical schools, the AMA, and so forth. The policies and practices of these institutions are determined by those individuals who occupy decision-making positions within them. Power and influence among physicians (as in any other professional group) derive from being in a position to direct or at least share in decision making at the highest organizational levels.

SUMMARY

This chapter has examined the professional development of physicians by highlighting the manner in which an initial service orientation and development of a specialized body of knowledge resulted in power and status in American society. Instrumental in this evolution was the organization of the American Medical Association, which expanded and protected the rights and privileges of doctors. In recent years, however, the AMA has sometimes been perceived as a protective trade association for physicians rather than having public welfare as its central interest. Although still influential, the AMA has lost power. There are increasing signs of changed attitudes toward their professional position on the part of many physicians, which suggest that greater attention to the needs of society may be ahead. The power structure of American medicine was also discussed from the standpoint of hospitals, clientele, and the "inner fraternity." The most powerful positions in medicine are those associated with prestigious academic appointments in the university medical centers of large urban areas.

PHYSICIANS INTERNET SITES

1. The American Medical Association (homepage).
   http://www.ama-assn.org

2. The American Medical Association, Section on Medical Education.
   http://www.ama-assn.org/ama/pub/category/2155.html

3. Association of American Medical Colleges, Liaison Committee on Medical Education.
   http://www.lcme.org

   Provides links and detailed descriptions of the accreditation procedures for medical schools in the United States and Canada.

4. The Association of American Medical Colleges, Curriculum Management and Evaluation.
   http://www.aamc.org/meded/curric/start.htm

   Includes a curriculum database to enhance understanding and management of medical student education programs.

5. American Medical Student Association.
   http://www.amsa.org

   Homepage of the largest independent national medical student organization in the United States.

6. The Association of American Medical Colleges.
   http://www.aamc.org

   Excellent links to medical schools and all aspects of medical education.

7. Yahoo! Health: Medicine.
   http://dir.yahoo.com/Health/Medicine/Education

   Complete links to all of the United States' major medical schools.

The Physician in a Changing Society

Public attitudes toward the medical profession have shifted away from the unquestioning acceptance of physician authority as seen in the mid-twentieth century to a more questioning and critical view of doctors today (Pescosolido, Tuch, and Martin 2001). Bernice Pescocolido and her colleagues (Pescosolido et al. 2001:13) found in a nationwide study that while Americans still have high regard for medicine as a social institution, "the movement of public opinion has been toward less confidence in physician authority."

Public dissatisfaction with the medical profession and its provision of health care in the United States is generally viewed as having largely economic and social origins. The specific issues usually cited are those of the rising financial costs of services and the failure to provide quality care for all Americans despite the medical profession's claims of excellence and technological achievement. Both of these issues are based on the organization of medical practice around the concept of financial profit in a free enterprise system. Advocates of this system, notably physicians, claim that the profit motive leads to enhanced efficiency in providing services, increased incentive for research and development, and greater responsiveness to patients. Opponents argue, in rebuttal, that the present system should be changed because the profit motive discriminates against the poor, fosters the unnecessary duplication of services (thereby increasing costs), and introduces a dehumanizing connotation to a service intended to relieve human suffering. Nevertheless, economic considerations have become a primary motivation among physicians and hospitals (Waitzkin 2000, 2001). The profit motive, in turn, has bred increasing resentment among consumers and demands that the professional power of doctors be reduced.

Part of the blame for this situation may lie in medicine's development as a profession. Professionalism in American medicine resulted in at least three undesirable consequences (Rasmussen 1975). First, it fostered the development of a view of disease that is largely confined to specific organs or physiological systems but that fails to consider a more holistic view of patients as people. This conflicts directly with a major societal demand that contemporary practice come to terms with a wide spectrum of disorders related more to problems of living than to specific biochemical and physical abnormalities of the body. Second, professionalism led to the development of a highly rigid stratification system in medical practice that promoted an increasingly large gap between physicians and nonphysician medical personnel. And for certain functions the nonphysician health worker may have a more important service to provide the patient than the physician. Third, professionalism resulted in the separation of professional training so that a common educational base is lacking between physicians and paramedicals that might allow a health care team to

---

BOX 11-1   The Aims of Medicine?

British social historian Roy Porter (1997:717) asks if the aims of medicine have become muddled after doing so much good in the last fifty years. "What are its aims?" he asks. Is its primary duty to keep people alive regardless of the circumstances? Is it to require people to live healthy lives? Or is it a service industry to fulfil whatever fantasies people may have for themselves such as designer bodies or the wishes of postmenopausal women to have babies? Who is going to decide? The questions await an answer. Yet in the meantime, Porter finds that the healthier Western society becomes, the more medicine it craves and the greater the tendency on the part of the public to demand maximum access to it. Medicine, in turn, faced with a healthier population, expands its jurisdiction to include medicalizing even normal events like menopause. The root of the problem is structural, says Porter, in that the public demands more medicine and medicine feels pressured to respond—even if the response means over-doctoring, unnecessary lab tests, more extensive and expensive treatments, and treatments for trivial complaints. In many ways, Porter concludes, medicine has become a prisoner of its own success and needs to define its limits.

work more effectively as a cohesive group. Overall, the physician emerged in the role of a "super-physician" in a "super-hospital" with ultimate responsibility for the patient. But, as individuals, some physicians may not have the time, interest, training, or ability to master the entire range of modern patient care. Thus, while the health care needs of American society are those of the early twenty-first century, organized medicine continues to favor a pattern of professional behavior based upon the image of medical practice in the early twentieth century when the physician worked on a solo basis as an independent, fee-for-service, private practitioner.

SOCIAL CONTROL OF MEDICAL PRACTICE

The social control of medical practice has traditionally presented special problems for American society. It has been argued that since physicians themselves have established the medical standards enforced by governmental regulating agencies and since laypersons are generally unable to judge technical performance, the two most common forms of social control in an industrial society—bureaucratic supervision and judgment by the recipient of services—are lacking (Rueschmeyer 1972). However, the argument continues that the problem of controlling organized medicine is solved by the medical profession's emphasis on the strong self-control of the individual physician, an ethical stance reinforced by both the formal and informal sanctions of a community of colleagues. Society is thus justified in granting the physician professional autonomy because he or she is a member of a self-controlled collectivity providing a vital function for society's general good. This argument contains three serious defects.

First of all, it is important to note that laypersons do judge technical performance regardless of whether they are competent to do so. Eliot Freidson's (1960, 1989) discussion of the lay-referral system made it quite clear that lay avenues of influence and authority exist independently of the physician and operate to guide the patient either toward or away from the services of a particular physician. This activity may not only determine the physician's success in attracting patients but also affects the physician's mode of medical practice. As Freidson (1960:379) has stated, "in being *relatively* free, the medical profession should not be mistaken for being *absolutely* free from control by patients." The choices of clients act as a form of social control over professionals and can mitigate against the survival of a group as a profession or the career success of particular professionals (Goode 1957:198).

Several studies show that patients do terminate their relationships with physicians and actively shop around for other doctors who are more able to meet their expectations (Ben-Sira 1976, 1980; Hayes-Bautista 1976b; Kasteler et al. 1976). Besides lack of confidence in a physician's technical competence, other factors commonly identified as influencing patients to change doctors are the unwillingness of doctors to spend time talking to them, the high cost of services, the possible inconvenience of a particular doctor's office location and hours, and unfavorable assessments of the doctor's personality.

A second major defect in the argument legitimizing the medical profession's autonomy has to do with physicians' efforts at peer regulation. In a study of a medical group practice, Freidson (1975, 1989) found indeed that rules and standards existed to define the limits of acceptable performance by physicians associated with the group. However, norms governing colleague relations, essentially *rules of etiquette,* restricted the evaluation of work and discouraged the expression of criticism. Etiquette was a more important norm than accountability, and it undermined attempts at critical evaluation and control by overlooking fault in order to maintain group harmony. Confrontation with a colleague was considered distasteful even in private and was unthinkable in public. In this medical practice setting, the norms of etiquette had not only seriously limited the exercise of professional control, but had also reduced the scope of procedures colleagues were willing to review.

Marcia Millman (1977a, 1977b) noted a similar situation in her study of three private, university-affiliated hospitals. Many doctors in this study were willing to criticize their colleagues for errors in small group discussions and behind the other's back. But they were strongly reluctant to criticize another doctor's mistakes at any official meeting because of what Millman termed "a fear of reprisal" and "a recognition of common interests."

Millman's examination of medical mortality and morbidity conferences, in which patient deaths were reviewed as a regular hospital procedure, was particularly illustrative of the collective rationalization of mistakes. The atmosphere of these conferences was likened to such social events as weddings or funerals, in which the participants were expected to show tact and restraint in order to remain on friendly terms. Restricted to members of the hospital's medical staff, the conferences were intended to be educational, not punitive. Only certain cases (conspicuous was the absence of cases involving patient deaths by gross medical mismanagement) were picked for review because, as one hospital chief of medicine stated, "it's got to be a cordial affair." Millman (1977a:17) described the meeting as follows:

> At Lakeside Hospital, the chief of medicine stands on the stage and presides as a master of ceremonies. As one member of the staff after another testifies about how he or she was led to the same mistaken diagnosis, the responsibility for the mistake is implicitly spread around. As in a good detective story, the case is reconstructed to show that there was evidence for suspecting an outcome different from the one that turned out to be the true circumstance. Responsibility for the error is also neutralized by making much of the unusual or misleading features of the case, or by showing how the patient was to blame because of uncooperative or neurotic behavior. Furthermore, by reviewing the case in fine detail, the physicians restore their images as careful, methodical practitioners, and thereby neutralize the sloppiness and carelessness that are made obvious by mistakes.

Millman contended that a "gentlemen's agreement" existed among the hospital physicians to overlook each other's mistakes. According to Charles Bosk (1979), in a study of physicians in a surgical training program at a major university medical center, there was a general recognition that honest errors exist and all physicians make them. Technical errors, if they were made in "good faith," were less serious than moral errors. A moral error was making the mistake of being unreliable,

Hospital staff attending a meeting to review procedures and determine causes of problems.

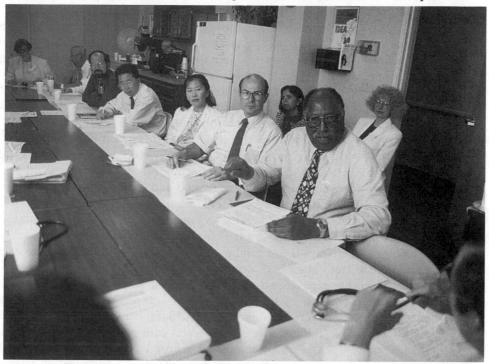

uncooperative, lacking in responsibility to patients, and failing to acknowledge subordination to superiors on the staff. Technical errors, on the other hand, could be forgiven and often had the result of motivating the offending physician to work harder, spend more time with patients, double-check procedures, and learn from the mistake. By admitting mistakes and trying to make up for them, the physician remained a good colleague. Moral errors, conversely, resulted in unfavorable letters of recommendation for those seeking jobs and social isolation from other physicians in the hospital.

Other studies (Grey 1991) suggest that the lack of physician peer control described by Freidson and Millman and the rather weak control studied by Bosk are typical of most medical practice settings. Furthermore, if lawsuits for malpractice can be regarded as any kind of valid indicator, it would appear that incompetence in medicine, or at least a greater public awareness of medical malpractice, is common. Certainly physicians can be the victims of malpractice suits that have no merit in fact. Yet malpractice suits rose dramatically from a few hundred in the 1950s to more than 10,000 a year in the 1980s until 1988 when claims began to drop. There is evidence that doctors have adopted improved standards to reduce patient injuries, as well as develop better rapport with patients, share decision making, and persuade patients to take more responsibility for their health (Annandale 1989; Frank 1991; Lowenstein 1997). Rates for malpractice insurance have declined as states have set limits on the amount of money awarded in malpractice lawsuits and physicians have become more careful in dealing with patients.

These developments do not mean that there are not incompetent or dishonest doctors. A national data bank was established in 1989 to identify incompetent physicians, dentists, and other licensed health practitioners. The data stored consist of suspensions and other serious disciplinary actions and malpractice settlements or judgments. The action to establish the data bank represents one of the most important efforts by the federal government to discipline doctors. Hospitals can be fined or subjected to lawsuits for failing to report disciplinary actions, while other information comes from court decisions, insurance companies, and medical societies. In addition to malpractice, another sign of ineffective control over medical practice is the high cost to the government of Medicare and Medicaid due to physician corruption. Some physicians have been arrested and sentenced to prison for misrepresenting care they supposedly gave Medicare and Medicaid patients.

This discussion is not intended to convey the impression that physicians are generally untrustworthy. Instances of corruption and fraud appear to be rare. In fact, Freidson (1975) argues that it can be assumed that physicians are dedicated to their patients. State medical societies do cooperate with state licensing agencies to remove the medical licenses of demonstrably incompetent physicians, thus preventing them from legally practicing medicine. Furthermore, professional standards review organizations (PSROs) were established in 1970 in conjunction with Medicaid and Medicare to review and evaluate the medical care given to patients eligible to use these services. PSROs are composed of licensed physicians and osteopaths who determine if the services rendered are medically necessary, meet professional standards of quality, and are provided as efficiently and effectively as possible. Although some latitude in the interpretation of standards is likely in any diagnostic category, Freidson (1975:251) points out that a consensus of opinion will at least exclude "the blatant, gross, or obvious deviations from common knowledge and practice."

Nevertheless, medical standards and practices continue to be regulated by the practitioners themselves. Thus, it is generally difficult to find a physician who will be openly critical of another physician or who will publicly testify against a colleague. Mistakes and errors in medical practice, either through neglect or ignorance, can sometimes be defended as "a difference of opinion." Millman (1977a) suggests that possibly all doctors have at some time made a terrible mistake in their careers and realize that they may do so again. Therefore, in matters of peer regulation, they tend to follow the Golden Rule: "Do unto others as you would have them do unto you."

The third major defect in the professional autonomy argument arises from the fact that the autonomy granted the medical profession is granted *conditionally,* on the assumption that it will resolve significant issues in favor of the public interest. However, traditional AMA resistance to cost controls that threaten the fee-for-service pattern has been cited as an example of greater professional concern with matters of self-interest than with public welfare (Stevens 1971). This situation has reduced public confidence in medicine more than any other single issue, since physicians as a profession are often viewed as placing the desire for financial profit ahead of the desire to help people (Light 2000). The AMA in 1984 sued the federal government for its cost-containment measures for Medicare, claiming that the government did not have the authority to impose limits on physicians' fees and that such action interfered with the right to contract for services. This legal challenge was unsuccessful, but it underscored the AMA's opposition to cost controls in a losing battle.

COUNTERVAILING POWER

At the mid-twentieth century, the medical profession in the United States stood at the height of its professional power and prestige and enjoyed great public trust. This was a time that John McKinlay (1999) refers to as the "golden age" of doctoring, and Eliot Friedson (1970b) formulated his "professional dominance" theory to account for an unprecedented level of professional control by doctors over health care delivery that no longer exists. It was also a time of escalating prices and overcharging to a degree previously unknown in the West; a proliferation of unnecessary tests, hospitalizations, prescriptions, and surgical operations; provider-structured insurance that paid for almost any mistakes and poor investments in technology or facilities; and a neglect of the poor in the name of "autonomy" (Light 2000:202). Health, observes Roy Porter (1997:658), had became one of the major growth industries in America, encompassing the pharmaceutical industry and manufacturers of sophisticated and costly diagnostic apparatus, laboratory instruments, and therapeutic devices, in addition to the large number of medical personnel, hospitals, and various lawyers, accountants, and insurers. Porter adds that health expenditures were approaching 15 percent of the GDP in 1966 and were generally unchecked as insurers boosted costs as high as the market could bear, physician incomes were seven times higher than the national average, and hospitals added costly technology that was often duplicated in nearby facilities.

The problem with a professional dominance thesis is that it does not allow for decline; rather, dominance brings greater dominance, making a profession even more powerful (Light 2000). At the beginning of the twenty-first century, however, we are witnessing a profession in decline, and professional dominance is no longer an adequate theory (McKinlay 1999). Donald Light (2000; Light and Hafferty 1993) used the term "countervailing power" to show how the medical profession was but one of many powerful groups in society—the state, employers paying for health insurance for their employees, patients as consumers of health care, and the medical-industrial complex as producers of products and services for profit—maneuvering to fulfill its interests in health care. Health insurance companies are also a major power in health care delivery as they determine who gets insurance coverage and what health conditions are covered (Light 1992, 1994). Over time, the medical profession's control over its market faltered as these countervailing powers established powerful positions as well and ended the profession's monopoly. "Dominance," states Light (2000:204), "slowly produces imbalances, excesses, and neglects that offend or threaten other countervailing powers and alienate the larger public." And this process is exactly what happened.

Internally, the medical profession has been weakened through an oversupply of doctors and the fragmentation and lack of success in resisting government controls of its labor union, the AMA (McKinlay 1999). However, the greatest impact on the autonomy of the medical profession is external and largely due to the counter-vailing power of four sources: (1) government regulation, (2) the managed care system, (3) corporations in the health care business, and (4) changes in the tradi-tional doctor–patient relationship. As McKinlay (1999:1) points out, "A future sociology of the professions can no longer overlook pervasive macrostructural influences on provider behavior."

GOVERNMENT REGULATION

Rising costs of health care result in increased public demands for government inter-vention (Hollingsworth 1981). The response of the federal government to these de-mands has been to support improvements in health care delivery for all segments of the population, exert limited controls over physicians, and initiate efforts to reform the health care delivery system. The passage of legislation establishing Medicare and Medicaid public health insurance in the 1960s to provide for the medical needs of the elderly and the poor was accomplished despite the opposition of the AMA.

Other legislation (also initially opposed by the AMA) followed in the 1970s. Professional standards review organizations, as previously discussed, were estab-lished to evaluate the care given to Medicare and Medicaid patients. Even though PSROs were controlled by doctors, their function was a signal that the government wanted to ensure a standard of quality care. Support through planning grants and loan guarantees was also provided to encourage the development of health mainte-nance organizations (HMOs)—a form of prepaid group practice emphasizing preventive care. One-half of the funds earmarked for HMOs were allocated for areas that were medically underserved. Although doctors and hospitals still controlled the efforts of PSROs, the sum total of regulatory efforts, as Paul Starr (1982:403–404) notes, went far beyond what physicians and hospitals wanted. Planning was aimed not at expansion but at containment and was formally linked for the first time with regulation.

Further regulation came in the early 1980s with the establishment of diagnos-tic related groups by the federal government. DRGs are schedules of fees placing a ceiling on how much the government will pay for specific services rendered to Medicare patients by hospitals and doctors. This action continued the government's attempts to meet public demands to control the cost of health care, even though it was bitterly contested by hospitals and the AMA.

What is clear is that the medical profession was losing its partisan support from the government. As McKinlay (1999) explains, an important role of the state (local, state, and national governments) has been to sponsor professionalism. Medical doc-tors in particular were helped by regulating competitors, awarding a privileged status, and guaranteeing profits. That situation has now changed. During the last decades of the twentieth century, the state shifted its primary allegiance, observes McKinlay, from professional interests to private interests, especially those intended to better the health of the general public and contain costs. The medical profession, through the AMA, was a dominant institutional force in the corridors of government, but that is the case no longer as organized medicine has lost the power to determine health policy. A key factor in this situation is the loss of public trust that began during medicine's "golden age of fee for-service" (Light 2000:212).

MANAGED CARE

One of the most extensive changes in health care delivery reducing the authority of physicians has been the introduction of managed care. The failed health plan of the Clinton administration featured a reorganization of health care delivery in the United States into systems of managed care, but those systems emerged in the private sector anyway in response to market conditions and anticipated government controls. Managed care refers to health care organizations—health maintenance organizations or preferred provider organizations—that "manage" or control the cost of health care by monitoring how doctors treat specific illnesses, limit referrals to specialists, and require authorization prior to hospitalization, among other measures. As providers in managed care plans, doctors would have to work in accordance with the regulations and fee structure set by the plan that employs them.

At their best, managed care organizations organize and improve health care in a stable, reliable, and less costly manner, and combine prevention with patient education; at their worst, such organizations disrupt doctor–patient relationships, take deep discounts out of doctor and hospital fees, and produce large profits without developing good managed clinical care (Light 2000; Wholey and Burns 2000). In managed care systems, patients pay a set fee on a per capita basis every month and in return are entitled to whatever health care they require. Primary-care physicians, on their part, function both as "double agents" and "gatekeepers" (Waitzkin 2000, 2001). They are "double agents" because they look out for the interests of the patient but also look out for the interests of the managed care organization, and they have to consider the interests of both in the treatment they provide. Patients are required to consult with them first because they serve as "gatekeepers" to more expensive medical procedures and care by specialists. Primary-care practitioners are relied on to keep the "gates" closed unless it is absolutely necessary. "That is how physicians and their bosses keep enough of patients' capitation payments to break even," states Howard Waitzkin (2000:272), "or maybe come out a little ahead." Doctors in managed care systems are expected to generate a certain level of income for the organization, and if they fail to do so, they can be fired.

Furthermore, primary care physicians are forced to spend time as "patient advocates," convincing various bureaucrats that more specialized and expensive care is warranted, since they must secure the permission that patients need to receive the care. This process takes time and energy and is often frustrating (Waitzkin 2000). This situation also affects the patient's experience, as he or she is structurally constrained from simply going directly or being referred to a specialist. In some cases, patients have not been granted access to more expensive treatments or have experienced delays in obtaining such treatment while their health worsened, or in a few instances they died. Not surprisingly, some patients have voiced considerable dissatisfaction with managed care. Light (2000) complains that most managed care corporations do a better job of managing contracts and costs through discounts than managing the complex tasks of patient care. On balance, however, the managed care concept has reduced costs, and some managed care organizations have moved to less rigid controls on the delivery of medical treatment (Wholey and Burns 2000). Yet, for doctors, managed care also means a significant reduction in the authority to make referrals and choose modes of treatment.

THE COMING OF THE CORPORATION

The "Coming of the Corporation" is the title of a chapter in Paul Starr's influential book *The Social Transformation of American Medicine* (1982). In it, Starr describes how America was on its way to a major change in its system of health care delivery through the intervention of large health care conglomerates. Starr (1982:428) states:

> This transformation—so extraordinary in view of medicine's past, yet so similar to changes in other industries—has been in the making, ironically enough, since the passage of Medicare and Medicaid. By making health care lucrative for providers, public financing made it exceedingly attractive to investors and set in motion the formation of large-scale corporate enterprises. Nursing homes and hospitals had a long history of proprietary ownership, but almost entirely as small, individually owned and operated enterprises. One of the first developments in the corporate transformation was the purchase of these facilities by new corporate chains. This, in a sense, was the first beachhead of for-profit corporations in the delivery of medical care.

Next came a virtual wave of mergers, acquisitions, and diversifications by the health care corporations in which not only hospitals and nursing homes were acquired but also emergency-care centers, hospital supply companies, hospital restaurants, medical office buildings, alcohol and drug abuse centers, health maintenance organizations, health spas, psychiatric hospitals, home health care services, and hospital management systems. For the first time in the United States, health care became regarded as a major business arena. Profit-making corporations expanded either into markets that were underserved or into areas where their services could successfully compete with existing nonprofit-seeking institutions. The profit-seeking hospital chains, for example, would provide attractively furnished rooms, good food, a friendly staff, and more efficient services. With health insurance paying the majority of the cost for hospital care, some patients evidently prefer the surroundings and more expensive services of the for-profit hospital. In the context of corporate health care, the physician is an employee rather than an independent practitioner. The doctor is bound to the rules and regulations of the corporation which, in all probability, is managed by people trained in business, not medicine.

At present, about 13 percent of all U.S. hospitals are owned by profit-making organizations. What attracted corporations to health care delivery is that it is an area where sound business practices can realize profits. The federal government, through Medicare and Medicaid, has poured billions of dollars into health care since the mid-1960s. Much of this money went to pay for doctor and hospital services. The corporations, however, have not been as interested in this public money as they have in the private health insurance companies. Private insurance companies reduce the risk of nonpaying patients through the coverage they provide. Medicare and Medicaid, in recent years, have become financially strained, and limits have been set by the government on how much they would pay for specific health services. So the goal of the health care corporations is to attract patients with private health insurance that will cover the relatively higher charges of the profit-making hospitals.

Another new development has been the expansion of free-standing emergency centers that take business away from hospitals. Sometimes referred to as "Docs-in-a-Box" or "7-Eleven Medicine," these centers (called free-standing because they are not affiliated with a hospital) are typically open seven days a week, eighteen to twenty-four hours a day, and try to attend to their patients with a minimum of waiting time. They treat the cuts, broken bones, bruises, and minor ailments usually treated in doctors' offices or hospital emergency rooms. Sometimes these facilities are located in shopping centers or other convenient locations. They are generally open for business, accessible, and reasonably priced, and they provide fast service.

In an era of cost containment, cost-efficient innovations like the free-standing emergency centers and the multihospital corporate systems may have an advantage in attracting privately insured patients. They can offer quick and efficient service. In addition, the large multihospital systems can consolidate their resources and not duplicate services available elsewhere in the system, thereby saving them money. As not-for-profit hospitals find it increasingly difficult to contend with rising costs and limits on reimbursements from public health insurance, Starr suggests that there will be more pressure to sell out to the corporations with greater financial resources. There are, however, some limits to growth. Starr indicates that the large chains avoid owning hospitals in depressed areas with large numbers of Medicaid patients, nor do they seek to own teaching hospitals. The market for these chains is considered to be in the more attractive neighborhoods where the hospitals serve relatively affluent patients. What this means is that the poor will not generally benefit because the for-profit hospitals, with their higher prices, try to attract those who can afford their services. As Starr (1982:436) notes, "The for-profit chains have an undisguised preference for privately insured patients."

Physicians have not shown strong objections to being employed by the corporations or sending their patients to the for-profit hospitals. There are two major reasons for this development. One is the availability of doctors for such jobs. Second, health care corporations provide jobs, offices, equipment, hospital privileges, and perhaps even a salary guarantee. Starr points out that because of their dependence on doctors, the corporations will be generous in granting them rewards, including more autonomy than they give to most corporate employees. More part-time and intermittent employment may also be available, especially for women doctors who wish to spend time with their children. Starr (1982:445–446) comments:

> . . . the profession is no longer steadfastly opposed to the growth of corporate medicine. Physicians' commitment to solo practice has been eroding; younger medical school graduates express a preference for practicing in groups. The longer period of

residency training may cultivate more group-oriented attitudes. Young doctors may be more interested in freedom *from* the job than freedom *in* the job, and organizations that can provide more regular hours can screen out the invasions of private life that come with independent professional practice.

Nevertheless, there will be a loss in autonomy for those physicians who do corporate work. Starr explains that doctors will no longer control such basic issues as time of retirement and there will likely be more regulation of the pace and routines of work. There will also be standards of performance in which doctors will be evaluated and paid on the basis of the amount of revenues they generate or number of patients treated per hour. Physicians who do not meet corporate standards are likely to lose their jobs. Moreover, there is likely to be a close scrutiny of mistakes in order to not only ensure quality medical care but also to avoid corporate liability for malpractice. Corporate management, utilizing data supplied by statisticians monitoring quality-of-care programs, will probably not be particularly concerned about professional norms of etiquette when it comes to dealing with doctors who are careless or incompetent. The locus of control will be outside the immediate health care facility and in the hands of a management system that is primarily business oriented. In corporations, doctors are not as likely to always dominate decision making about policy, hospital budgets, capital investments, personnel appointments, salaries, and promotions.

To what extent the large health care corporations will be able to extend their control over the medical marketplace is not known. But it seems apparent that those doctors who practice corporate medicine will constitute a physician group with less control over the conditions of their practice than American physicians in the past. In successfully avoiding government regulation of their work, physicians may have established the circumstances for corporations to move in and dominate an unregulated area of the economy. This process is materially aided by a growing surplus of physicians desiring the benefits and work schedule a corporate practice can provide. As Starr (1982:445) explains, "The great irony is that the opposition of doctors and hospitals to public control of public programs set in motion entrepreneurial forces that may end up depriving both private doctors and voluntary hospitals of their traditional autonomy." Future studies of physicians may have to distinguish between owning, managing, employed, and independent physicians. Physicians who own hospitals and clinics or who are in independent private practice will have considerably more autonomy than physician managers of corporate facilities and doctors employed as practitioners by a corporation.

THE CHANGING PHYSICIAN–PATIENT RELATIONSHIP

Leo G. Reeder (1972) was among the first to show the changing relationship between physicians and their patients. He identifies three significant trends in contemporary society. One is the *shift in medicine away from the treatment of acute diseases toward preventive health services* intended to offset the effects of chronic disorders. Since the control of acute diseases has largely been accomplished, it is no longer the most important task for modern medical practice. Reeder (1972:407) explains:

> In a system dominated by curative or emergency care there is a "seller's market." The customer is suspect; client-professional relationships tend to be characterized by the traditional mode of interaction so well described in the literature. On the other hand, when prevention of illness is emphasized, the client has to be persuaded that he has a need for medical services such as periodic check-ups. The person has to be encouraged to come into the physician's office for medical care. Under these circumstances, there are elements of a "buyer's market"; in such situations there is more of a tendency for the "customer to be right."

The other two features of societal change noted by Reeder are the *growing sophistication of the general public with bureaucracy* and the *development of consumerism*. Reeder claims that the increased development of large-scale bureaucratic industrial systems has ensured a similarity of experiences and attitudes in contemporary society and this has tended to "level" or make more familiar the bureaucratic aspects of modern medicine. Also highly significant is the development of consumerism. Reeder states that during the 1960s, the concept of the person as a "consumer" rather than a patient became established; doctors were regarded as "health providers," so a new relationship of provider–consumer emerged in direct opposition to the old relationship of physician–patient with its emphasis upon patient dependency. The new concept places the consumer on a more equal basis with the physician in the health care interaction. It also provides the philosophy behind the increased consumer involvement in health legislation and other matters such as consumer interest health care groups.

In an age of consumerism, the social role of the physician and the overall physician–patient relationship can hardly escape modification. In general, this modification takes the form of physician and patient interacting on a more equal footing in terms of decision making and responsibility for outcome. There is evidence that the physician–patient relationship is turning into more of a provider–consumer relationship, especially among patients who are relatively well educated and have middle- and upper-class social backgrounds (Cockerham 2000a; Cockerham, Kunz, and Lueschen 1988a; Freidson 1989; McKinlay 1999). More affluent persons appear to be increasingly oriented toward taking control over their lives, including their health.

THE DEPROFESSIONALIZATION OF PHYSICIANS

Increased consumerism on the part of patients and greater government and corporate control over medical practice indicate that the professional authority of physicians is in a state of decline. That is, doctors are moving from being the absolute authority in medical matters toward having lessened authority. With many patients insisting on greater equality in the doctor–patient relationship and health organizations that employ doctors seeking to control costs, maximize profits, and provide efficient services that are responsive to market demand, physicians are caught in the middle.

George Ritzer and David Walczak (1988) indicate that medical doctors are experiencing a process of deprofessionalization. Ritzer and Walczak (1988:6) define

Physician adjusting an electron microscope. Some sources predict that the majority of physicians will be employees—rather than self-employed practitioners—in the near future.

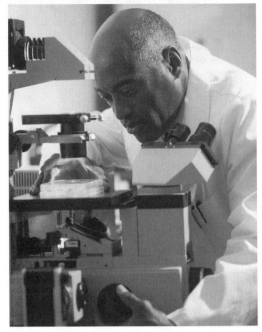

deprofessionalization as "a decline in power which results in a decline in the degree to which professions possess, or are perceived to possess, a constellation of characteristics denoting a profession." Deprofessionalization essentially means a decline in a profession's autonomy and control over clients. In the case of physicians, they still retain the greatest authority in medical affairs but that authority is no longer absolute and medical work is subject to greater scrutiny by patients, health care organizations, and government agencies. As Donald Light (1989:470) notes, buyers of health care "want to know what they are getting for their money" and it did "not take long for them to demand detailed accounts of what services are being rendered at what cost." This situation has led to greater control and monitoring systems by the government seeking to control costs, businesses attempting to constrain the expenses of employee health care, and insurance companies and profit-seeking health care corporations looking to maximize income.

Ritzer and Walczak argue that government policies emphasizing greater control over health care and the rise of the profit orientation in medicine identify a trend in medical practice away from substantive rationality (stressing ideals like serving the patient) toward greater formal rationality (stressing rules, regulations, and efficiency). Formal rationality, as discussed in Chapter 5, is defined by Max Weber (1978) as the purposeful calculation of the most efficient means to reach goals and substantive rationality, which, in turn, is an emphasis on ideal values and situations—rather than efficiency and practicality. Ritzer and Walczak join others (Ritchey 1981) in claiming that formal rationality has become dominant in medical practice. The result is that greater external control over physicians by the government and corporations now exists and lessens the professional power and authority of doctors.

Hence, pressure on physicians from below (consumers) and above (government and business corporations in the health field) forecasts a decline in their professional dominance. Doctors are still powerful in health matters but not to the extent they were in the 1950s and 1960s, which has been described as a "golden age" of medical power and prestige (Hafferty and Light 1995). Government policies, market forces, and consumerism have required greater accountability and placed constraints on the exercise of professional power in an ever-increasing manner. According to Frederic Hafferty and Donald Light (1995:138), "the basic overall thrust of professionalism is toward a loss and not a continuation or strengthening of medicine's control over its own work."

THE EVOLUTION OF THE ORGANIZATION OF MEDICAL PRACTICE

All of these factors—government regulation, corporate medicine, the contemporary physician–patient relationship, and deprofessionalization—forecast change in the manner in which health care is organized and delivered in the United States. Phillip Kletke, David Emmons, and Kurt Gillis (1996) examined trends in the organization of medical practice and predicted that the majority of physicians will be employees in the near future. This trend, which Kletke and his colleagues found was evident in virtually every segment of the patient care physician population, was especially characteristic of young physicians. However, the shift toward practicing medicine as an employee is not limited to younger doctors, but is evident among physicians at all stages of their careers. The trend is also seen among both male and female doctors, and in all medical specialties and regions of the country. Thus, the dominant pattern of medical practice in the United States is becoming one in which most doctors are employees.

What is promoting the trend away from self-employment, according to Kletke and his associates, is a general evolution in the health care delivery system toward greater size and complexity. The loss in autonomy, government and insurance regulations, cost controls, the growth of managed care, competition in the medical marketplace, the attraction of regular hours and guaranteed salaries, and the possibility of higher earnings than solo physicians anchored outside of large health care systems play an important role in this development. Whereas solo physicians are thought of as having greater clinical autonomy, Kletke and his associates note that such autonomy has declined for all doctors—not just those who are employees. Consequently, the opportunity for exercising autonomy in patient care is not overwhelmingly on the side of the self-employed.

Evidence from several sources shows that the dominance of the medical profession is weakening. In medical sociology, several studies show that medicine is no longer able to exercise exclusive control over the content and context of its work (Freidson 1993; Hafferty and Light 1995; Hafferty and McKinlay 1993; Light 1993, 2000; McKinlay 1999). Therefore, in comparison to physicians in the past, current and future generations of doctors are likely to have much lower levels of clinical autonomy and professional control. "Many of these physicians," state Kletke and colleagues (1996:560), "will be in the employ of what has been called the 'new medical-industrial complex,' with their practices subject to an increasing degree of bureaucratic rationalization." This situation represents a major shift in the organization of American health care delivery, since solo, self-employed, fee-for-service doctors have been the nation's traditional model of medical practitioner.

SUMMARY

There are increasing signs of influences outside the medical profession that the professional dominance of the physician is weakening. This change originates from four directions. First, there are signs of increasing government regulation. Second, managed care is reducing the authority of doctors. Third, corporations are taking over more of the medical market and hiring physicians as employees to provide medical services. In this situation, decision making is vested in the hands of corporate management and not physician practitioners. Just what type of role doctors will play in a corporate system of health care delivery is not fully established, but it seems likely that physicians will lose some of their autonomy. Last, more affluent and educated persons appear to be increasingly consumer oriented toward health care. That is, they are making decisions on their own about which steps are most appropriate for them in dealing with their health. In doing so, they are becoming less dependent on physicians and changing the traditional physician–patient relationship to one of provider–consumer. If current trends continue, most doctors in the near future will be employees, rather than self-employed practitioners.

THE PHYSICIAN IN A CHANGING SOCIETY
INTERNET SITES

1. The American Medical Association (homepage).
   http://www.ama-assn.org

2. The American Medical Association—Institute for Ethics.
   http://www.ama-assn.org/ama/pub/category/2558.html

   Provides access to empirical and scholarly research in biomedical and professional ethics.

3. The American Medical Association—Ethics Resource Center.
   http://www.ama-assn.org/ama/pub/category/2732.html

   A resource center providing content expertise and collegial assistance to the AMA and the medical profession.

4. The American Medical Association—SPEAK Initiative.
   http://www.ama-assn.org/ama/pub/category/2740.html

   The Soliciting Physicians' Ethical Attitudes and Knowledge (SPEAK) initiative is designed to promote evidence-based report writing and policy setting by identifying relevant issues confronting the ethical practice of medicine that are worthy of consideration.

5. The American Medical Association—Council on Ethical and Judicial Affairs (CEJA).
   http://www.ama-assn.org/ama/pub/category/2498.html

   Organization which sets ethics for the AMA. This site contains links to the AMA code of ethics and the fundamental elements of the patient–physician relationship.

6. Health Care Financing Administration—Medicare: Professional/Technical Information.
   http://cms.hhs.gov/medicare/default.asp

   Contains extensive links to all aspects of the Medicare program.

7. Health Care Financing Administration—Medicaid: Professional/Technical Information.
   http://cms.hhs.gov/medicaid/default.asp

   Contains extensive links to all aspects of the Medicaid program.

CHAPTER

12

Nurses, Physician Assistants, Pharmacists, and Midwives

Although the dominant form of social interaction in the health care relationship has traditionally been that of the one-to-one encounter between the physician and the patient, the technical complexity and range of contemporary medical care have evolved well beyond this exclusive two-person social system. Modern medical treatment has come to involve a great variety of health personnel who specialize in treatment, laboratory procedures, therapy, rehabilitation, and administration. More than four million people in the United States are currently employed in nonphysician health care tasks.

Other than a few consulting professions such as clinical psychology, the occupations performing tasks of patient care are organized around the work of the physician and are usually under the physician's direct control. Eliot Freidson (1970a:49) claims that these occupations—such as nurse, pharmacist, laboratory technician, physical therapist—reflect four characteristic features that account for their subordinate position in the practice of medicine. First of all, Freidson notes that the technical knowledge employed in health occupations needs to be approved by physicians. Second, these workers usually assist physicians in their work rather than replace the basic skills of diagnosis and treatment. Third, such workers are subordinate to the physician because their work largely occurs at the "request of" the physician; the "doctor's orders" provide them with their work requirements. And fourth, among the various occupational roles in the health field, physicians have the greatest prestige.

However, just as the physician–patient relationship appears to be moving toward less dependency and increased equality for the patient, a similar trend may be developing in the physician–registered nurse relationship. This development would take the form of greater autonomy for registered nurses (RNs) in their work role and a higher level of colleagueship with physicians (S. Porter 1992). To what extent this would be possible is uncertain because, as Robert Brannon (1994a, 1994b) points out, physicians continue to control the critical decisions of admitting and discharging hospital patients, diagnosing a patient's ills, and conceptualizing the overall treatment plan. Nurses do not decide on the medical problems to be addressed or the means of doing so. "Their observations, discretion, and continuous presence on [a] hospital's wards," states Brannon (1994b:170), "[are] essential to meeting a physician's medical objectives, but RNs [are] more likely to facilitate the production of care than to define what that care should be." Physicians are therefore retaining their dominant role in relation to other health workers, even though an expansion of responsibilities for registered nurses is emerging. But some changes already exist as nurse practitioners and physician assistants can make treatment decisions independently of doctors in some states and prescribe drugs. So inroads are being made on the authority once exclusively held by physicians.

NURSING: PAST AND PRESENT

Nursing represents the largest single group of health workers in the United States, with an estimated 2,271,300 people employed as licensed registered nurses in 1999; more than 200,000 people were estimated to be employed as licensed practical nurses. About 75 percent of all licensed registered and practical nurses in the United States work in hospitals and nursing homes, while the remainder are employed in doctors' offices, public health agencies, schools, industrial plants, and programs of nursing education, or as private duty nurses.

Registered nurses are responsible for the nature and quality of all nursing care patients receive, as well as for following the instructions of physicians regarding patients. In addition, they supervise practical nurses and other health personnel involved in providing patient care. The primary task of licensed practical nurses is the bedside care of patients; they may also assist in the supervision of auxiliary nursing workers such as certified nurse's aides (CNAs), orderlies, and attendants. These auxiliary nursing personnel, who number about 290,000 in the United States, assist registered and practical nurses by performing less skilled medical care tasks and by providing many services designed for the overall personal comfort and welfare of patients.

Whereas the licensed registered and practical nurses and nurse's aides are generally women, orderlies and attendants are usually men employed to care for male patients and perform whatever heavy duties are required in nursing care. Nursing tasks obviously occur in a system of social relationships that are highly stratified by sex. The registered nurse, who has the most advanced training and professional qualifications of any of the nursing workers, is generally a female who is matched occupationally with a physician, whose role is dominant and who, in the past, was likely to be a male. The registered nurse, in turn, supervises lesser trained females (practical nurses and nurse's aides) and lesser trained males (orderlies and attendants). Thus emerges the traditional stereotype of the physician as father figure and the nurse as mother figure.

The Early Development of Nursing as an Occupation

While males perform nursing tasks, the social role of the nurse has been profoundly affected by its identification with traditionally feminine functions (Carpenter 1993; F. Davis 1966, 1972; Freidson 1970a, 1970b; Mauksch 1972; Olesen and Whittaker 1968; S. Porter 1992). For instance, Hans Mauksch (1972:208) pointed out that in many European languages the very word *sister* not only refers to nuns but also generically identifies the nurse. In the English language, the word *nurse* carries with it a connotation of the mother's relationship to her child. Accordingly, the initial image of the nurse in Western society was that of a "mother-surrogate," in which nursing was equated with the mothering function (Schulman 1972).

Following the rise of Christianity in the Western world, the practice of nursing as a formal occupation was significantly influenced by the presence of large numbers of nuns who performed nursing services under auspices of the Roman Catholic church. Prior to the late nineteenth century, hospitals were generally defined as places for the poor and lower social classes, often little more than "flophouses"; anyone who could afford it was usually cared for at home. Nursing activities in hospitals were thus viewed as acts of charity because they were usually carried out under difficult and unpleasant circumstances, as nurses served the personal needs of patients who were usually dirty and illiterate as well as diseased. Nursing under these conditions was regarded by the church as a means by which those persons providing the services could attain spiritual salvation by helping those less fortunate. Hence, the original concept of nursing was not as a formal occupation with its own body of knowledge and specialized training procedures; rather, its primary focus as religious activity was in spiritual considerations. Nuns were not under the authority of doctors, and they could refuse any orders they did not believe appropriate for themselves or their patients. Nuns were also reported to have refused to treat certain categories of patients such as unwed mothers or persons with venereal disease (Freidson 1970a).

Besides nuns, there were secular nurses working in public hospitals. But these women were characterized as "women off the streets" or "of bad character," who were considered as little or no better than the low class of patients for whom they provided their services. Well into the nineteenth century, nursing could be described as an activity for women who lacked specialized training in medical care, a supportive work role that was not officially incorporated into the formal structure of medical services. Moreover, nursing was not an occupation held in high regard by the general public.

Florence Nightingale

The role of nursing in Western society was changed in the middle of the nineteenth century through the insight and effort of Florence Nightingale. Nightingale, an English Protestant from a respectable middle-class family, believed that God had called her to the service of Christianity as a result of a vision she had experienced in 1837. There was some confusion, however, on Nightingale's part as to exactly what service she was expected to render. Being a Protestant, she could not choose to become a Catholic nun. She solved her dilemma by deciding to become a nurse. Over the strong objections of her family and after a delay of several years, she was finally able to secure training as a nurse from a Protestant minister in Germany.

Returning to England in 1853, Nightingale established a hospital for "Sick Gentlewomen in Distressed Circumstances" and staffed it with trained nurses from good families. She insisted that nursing was intended to become an honorable and respected occupation, and she sought to achieve this purpose through a formal training program with recruits from upper- and middle-class social backgrounds. Good

Florence Nightingale, the founder of modern nursing. She started the first nursing school in Great Britain at St. Thomas's Hospital in London in 1860.

intentions notwithstanding, Nightingale's hospital was not entirely successful because of the role conflict between the duties of the nurse and the prevailing standards of proper behavior for "ladies." Some of her nurses, for example, were reluctant to view nudity or to be present at physical examinations (Freidson 1970a).

However, in 1854 the Crimean War afforded Nightingale a much better opportunity to establish nursing as a formal occupation. She organized a contingent of nurses, and, assisted by money raised by public subscription, she and her group sailed for the Crimea, where Great Britain, France, and Turkey were involved in war with Russia. Once there, Nightingale offered to the British military authorities the nursing services of her women for sick and wounded troops.

At first the military refused to employ her nurses, and she retaliated by refusing to allow any of the nurses to provide patient care on their own initiative. Instead the nurses worked only when their assistance was specifically requested by physicians. Eventually such requests were forthcoming and Nightingale's nurses received considerable publicity in the British press as "angels of mercy." In fact, Nightingale's nurses had captured the imagination of the British public, and when Nightingale returned to England after the war she found herself hailed as a heroine. Capitalizing upon her fame and popularity, she instigated a successful fund-raising effort that brought in enough money to organize a nursing school at St. Thomas Hospital in London. Other schools were also established, and within a few years the "Nightingale system" became the model for nursing education.

Nightingale's approach to nursing training emphasized a code of behavior that idealized nurses as being responsible, clean, self-sacrificing, courageous, cool headed, hard working, and obedient to the physician and possessing the tender qualities of the mother; this idealized portrayal of nurses saw them as nothing less than "disciplined angels" (Strauss 1966). In reality, Nightingale had incorporated the best attributes of the mother and the housekeeper into her ideal nurse. This image did little to establish the view of nurses as having the qualities of leadership and independence necessary for true professional status. Although Nightingale had been able to establish nursing as a distinct and honorable occupation, her philosophy perpetuated the traditional social role of the nurse as a female supervised and controlled by a male physician. Perhaps in her time there was no other way to gain access to an official position within the male-dominated field of medicine, but the overall effect of subordination to the physician's orders weakened nursing's efforts in its struggle to achieve professionalization.

Nursing Education

Florence Nightingale's ideas formed the basis for establishing the first accredited schools of nursing in the United States. These schools, founded in 1873, were located at Bellevue Hospital in New York City, the Connecticut Training School in New Haven, and the Boston Training School. Although they were intended to be separately administered, the new nursing schools were affiliated with hospitals that provided financial support and required, in turn, that the students furnish much of the nursing services on the hospital wards. During the late nineteenth and early twentieth centuries, the number of hospitals and hospital nursing schools grew rapidly. At the same time, increasing numbers of women entered the labor market as a result of immigration from abroad or migration from rural to urban areas. Nursing was an attractive occupation for many of these women because it afforded an opportunity for a woman to make a living and also to have a respectable position in the community.

But many of the students in these early nursing schools did not receive the training that the Nightingale system required. Since only a few trained nurses were available and money was often in short supply, many hospital administrators and physicians, perhaps also unaware of Nightingale's techniques for training nurses, used nursing students as inexpensive and exploitable sources of hospital labor. As a result, much of the effort of nursing educators during the first decades of the twentieth century was directed at securing less hospital service and more education for nursing students in hospital schools. They also sought a university-based nursing school, with the first one being formed at the University of Minnesota in 1909.

While nursing educators were able to improve the standards of education for their students, they failed to obtain centralized control over educational programs. Unlike medical schools, which follow a prescribed and generally similar program of education leading to the M.D., nursing has been characterized by different types of educational experiences—all of which can qualify the student as a registered nurse. For example, there are currently three types of programs available for RNs: (1) two-year associate degree programs usually located in junior or community colleges; (2) hospital-based diploma schools requiring two and one-half to three years of study; and (3) four-year and five-year university baccalaureate programs.

The most prestigious of the nursing education programs is the baccalaureate program, which is intended to provide training not only in nursing skills and theory, but also to provide the background for becoming a nursing educator or leader. But, as Mauksch (1972:211) makes clear, the graduates of any nursing program—despite the differences in time, money, effort and, supposedly, intellect demanded by their program—are virtually identical in terms of the basic skills required for their jobs.

The major source of nurses in the United States has traditionally been the hospital-based diploma school. College-based programs, with their combination of occupational training and liberal arts education, have become increasingly popular with nursing students in the last few years, although diploma schools provide more day-to-day experience with patients. As Table 12-1 shows, in 1961 diploma schools accounted for more than 80 percent of all nursing graduates, but by 1970 this percentage had declined to 52.3 percent, and the period between 1970 and 1996 witnessed a further rapid decline to 6.0 percent. Although the percentage of graduates from baccalaureate programs increased over the period covered by Table 12-1, the primary beneficiary of declining numbers of diploma graduates had been the associate degree (A.D.) programs. With only 3 percent of the total number of nursing graduates in 1961, A.D. programs produced 59.8 percent of the total by 1995–1996.

The A.D. programs are relatively inexpensive, require only two years of training, and yet place their graduates on the same career track as graduates of diploma and baccalaureate degree schools. Originally conceived as a middle-range level of nursing education somewhere between the training required to perform simple or assisting nursing tasks and that required for complex tasks, the work role of the A.D.

TABLE 12-1   Schools of Nursing (R.N.) by Types of School and Percentage of Graduates
(1961, 1970, 1983–1984, 1995–1996).

Type of School	1961 (N = 30,267)	1970 (N = 43,639)	1983–1984 (N = 80,312)	1995–1996 (N = 94,757)
Diploma	83.6	52.3	15.2	6.0
Associate Degree	3.0	26.8	55.3	59.8
Bachelor's Degree	13.4	20.9	29.5	34.2
TOTALS	100.0%	100.0%	100.0%	100.0%

Sources: National Center for Health Statistics, *Health Resources Statistics* (Washington, D.C.: U.S. Government Printing Office, 1978) and *Health, United States, 2002* (Washington, D.C.: U.S. Government Printing Office, 2002); *Nursing Data Review, 1998* (New York: National League of Nursing, 1997).

graduate has expanded into supervisory and management functions. Some controversy has arisen over this trend because it requires A.D. nurses to function beyond their intended level of training. Although problems regarding the work role persist, A.D. programs have become the largest single source of nurses in the United States.

Despite the remarkable growth of the A.D. programs and the growing acceptance of their graduates in nursing, their appearance has presented a special problem in terms of nursing's claims of professional status, since the A.D. programs are essentially vocational rather than professional. A strategy to avoid this situation was to designate A.D. nurses as "technical" nurses and baccalaureate degree nurses as "professional" nurses, while advocating that all nurses be graduates of college programs at some time in the future. Although this became the official position of the American Nurses' Association in 1965, it was not accepted by the majority of its membership, who had graduated from diploma schools. These nurses replied that it would be a hardship for them to quit work and return to college, and they pointed out that a liberal arts education did not help a nurse perform better nursing procedures (Olesen and Whittaker 1968). The end result was that among RNs the baccalaureate nurses are regarded as the *most* professional—leaders of organized nursing—yet associate degree and diploma nurses consider themselves to also be professionals.

In the late 1980s, however, nursing received a considerable boost in status and income with the development of a severe nursing shortage in American hospitals. The number of nursing school graduates declined significantly from more than 80,000 in 1983–1984 to fewer than 65,000 in 1987–1988. Long hours, stress, and low pay had reduced the attractiveness of nursing as a career field. In 1994–1995, as shown in Table 12-1, the number of graduates had increased to nearly 95,000. The enrollment in nursing schools had increased dramatically along with higher salaries. In 1980, starting salaries for nurses were $14,000; in 1999, the average salary for a nurse with three years or less of experience was $40,000 annually. In some large cities, experienced nurses earned over $60,000. As salaries and demand for nurses soared, nursing school enrollments increased. Although the nursing shortage has yet to ease, the image of nursing as a career has been enhanced.

Nursing Students

In 2000, 1,508 schools of nursing offered programs leading to the R.N. Nursing students have traditionally been characterized as having lower-middle-class and working-class social origins, often from small towns or rural areas, who are attracted to nursing as a means of upward social mobility (Hughes, MacGill, and Deutscher 1958). Although this pattern still persists today, there have been increasing numbers of students from upper- and upper-middle-class families and urban areas entering nursing schools (Davis 1972; Mauksch 1972), with the result that nursing, like teaching, has become a distinctly middle-class occupation.

There have been several studies of student nurses and their reasons for seeking training as a nurse. These studies, as summarized by Mauksch (1972), suggest that the objectives of a majority of nursing students are to be needed and to be engaged in personal helping relationships. However, some studies have suggested that a serious conflict often develops within new students concerning the lay image of the nurse as mother-surrogate (an image the students usually bring with them to the school) and the refusal of the nursing faculty to reinforce this image (Davis 1972; Olesen and Whittaker 1968; Psathas 1968; Warnecke 1973). Nursing faculties have tended to insist on students viewing their patients objectively, and this tendency has operated to deemphasize an intimate nurse–patient relationship. The prevailing reward system also places greater emphasis on removing the nurse from patient care and placing her in a supervisory position over auxiliary nursing workers.

In a major study of nursing students on the West Coast, Fred Davis (1972) observed six distinct stages of socialization. First was the stage of *initial innocence,* which consisted of the nursing students wanting to do things for patients within a secularized Christian-humanitarian ethic of care and kindness consistent with the lay (mother-surrogate) image of nursing. This stage was characterized, however, by feelings of inadequacy, worry, and frustration, as the nursing instructors failed to support the lay image of the nurse. Instead, the students were directed toward seemingly inconsequential tasks of patient care such as making beds and giving baths. These feelings of frustration, which usually came during the first semester of training, generated the second stage, which Davis called *labeled recognition of incongruity.* In this stage, the nursing students began collectively to articulate their disappointment and openly to question their choice of becoming a nurse. At this point a number of the students resigned from the school because they did not or could not adjust to the incongruity between lay expectations and actual training.

For those that remained, the third stage of "*psyching out*" began, in which the nursing students, like the medical students in the study by Howard Becker and his associates (1961), attempted to anticipate what their instructors wanted them to know and to concentrate upon satisfying these requirements. Whereas some students may have attempted to "psych out" the instructors from the very beginning, it now became a group phenomenon with the entire class collectively participating in the process. The fourth stage, termed *role simulation,* was characterized by students performing so as to elicit favorable responses from the instructors. The approved mode of behavior was the exhibition of an objective and "professional" (detached) attitude toward patient care, which included an understanding of the principles be-hind nursing techniques as well as mastery of those techniques. Many of the stu-dents felt they were "playing at acting like a nurse" and they questioned their lack of conviction about the role. But Davis points out that the more successful they be-came at convincing others that their performance was authentic, the more they began to gain confidence in themselves as nurses. This stage usually came at the end of the first year. The last two years of their program were characterized as the fifth stage of *provisional internalization* and the sixth stage of *stable internalization*. During these final two stages, the nursing students took on a temporary self-identity as a "professional" nurse, as defined by the faculty, and finally settled into a stable and consistent identification of self by the time of their graduation.

The Davis (1972) study ranks, with that of Virginia Olesen and Elvi Whittaker (1968), as perhaps one of the best known sociological studies of nursing education. Some of the findings, however, may not reflect conditions today. Davis found that unlike medical students who desire a medical education as a terminal career, not all nursing students, perhaps not even a majority, view a career in nursing as their pri-mary life goal. Davis, along with Olesen (Davis, 1972; Davis and Olesen 1963), ob-served that several nursing students did not, either upon entry into nursing school or upon graduation, see themselves as being fully committed to a career in nursing. Their major life goal was that of marriage and family. They held such views despite the influence of the women's movement and the encouragement of the nursing fac-ulty to view nursing as a lifelong career. Davis (1972:46) found that the majority of students sought nursing training "as a kind of life insurance," should marriage and having a family not occur or should the marriage be less than ideal and result in "childlessness, divorce, premature widowhood, excessive financial burdens, or boredom with the home."

Therefore, the contingency of marriage became the decisive factor upon which all other decisions were based. Davis noted that a student's announcement of an en-gagement to be married was a great occasion for both the student and her class-mates. Not only did it indicate that the major concern was resolved in a positive manner for the engaged student, but it also served to remind those not engaged of their less positive circumstances. Davis (1972:46) found that during the senior year there was "a veritable marital sweepstakes," in which the announcements of some engagements acquired the "theatrical overtones of a last minute rescue."

The overall image of nursing projected by such studies is that of an occupation dominated by a small group of older, career-oriented RNs who serve as leaders, policy makers, and educators for a large and transient mass of younger nurses whose career aspirations are often affected by outside influences such as marriage (Freidson 1970b).

Research by Sam Porter (1992) in Northern Ireland presents a different view. Porter, who worked as a nurse, conducted a participant observation study of the nursing staff at a large urban hospital in Belfast. He finds that, contrary to the con-clusions of previous studies, many nurses today regard their employment as a career. "A number of nurses," comments Porter (1992:523), "explicitly stated that, notwithstanding their desire to marry, they saw their job as a career which they expected to follow throughout their working lives." He concludes that with the increasing perception of nursing as a career in itself, the notion that nurses regard their first priority as finding a spouse is out of date.

National Associations

Nurses have sought to improve the conditions of nursing practice and move toward enhanced professionalism through the organization of national associations representing nursing interests. The most prominent of these organizations have been the National League for Nursing and the American Nurses' Association.

The National League for Nursing is composed mainly of nursing educators and formal agencies interested in nursing education. Its primary aim is to promote quality standards for nurses' training. The American Nurses' Association (ANA) has become the major organization for registered nurses and is the official representative of nursing in relations with outside organizations. The ANA has not been a powerful organization, nor has membership played an important role in the ability of individual nurses to establish professional relationships with nursing colleagues. Only during the last few years has the ANA enjoyed the increasing support of a number of concerned nurses, who see in it the potential to enhance the professional status of nurses.

Gender and "The Doctor–Nurse Game"

As Porter (1992) observes, issues of gender have been of considerable importance in explaining the role of nurses. Nursing has traditionally been one of the world's major occupations for women. But unlike other jobs dominated numerically by women—elementary school teachers, librarians, and secretaries—nursing is paired with a powerful male-dominated profession. Sociologists have long recognized that nursing, as a historically subordinated occupation, has been constrained in its development by the medical profession (Carpenter 1993; Freidson 1970b). However, there are signs that gender inequality is losing some of its power in nurse–doctor relationships. The changes appear to be the result of three developments: (1) greater assertiveness by nurses, (2) increased numbers of male nurses, and (3) the growing numbers of female doctors.

The formal lines of authority that exist in the medical setting operate to place nurses at a disadvantage in acting upon their judgments regarding medical treatment. Yet there are times when nurses do go ahead and exercise their own judgment in opposition to the orders of physicians. An example of this situation is found in the experiment conducted by Steven Rank and Cardell Jacobson (1977) in two hospitals in a large midwestern city. The experiment consisted of having an assistant, using the name of a little known staff surgeon at the hospital who had given permission to use his name, telephone eighteen nurses who were on duty and order them to administer a nonlethal overdose of Valium to appropriate patients. The call was made in a self-confident manner, using medical terminology and familiarity with hospital routine. None of the nurses questioned the telephone request, and all but one suspicious nurse entered the request on a medication chart. One of the experimenters, posing as a contractor working on a bid to install some new equipment on the ward, was present at the time of the call with the duty of terminating the experiment should the nurse actually proceed to administer the drug, refuse to comply, fail to take action after fifteen minutes, or try to call the "doctor" back. As a further safeguard, nursing supervisors were stationed in each of the patients' rooms to prevent the medication from being administered. Sixteen out of eighteen nurses refused to administer the Valium. One nurse (Rank and Jacobson 1977:191) said, "Whew! 30 mg—he [the doctor] doesn't want to sedate her [the patient]—he wants to knock her out." Twelve of these nurses tried to recontact the doctor; only two appeared ready to comply with the order. Rank and Jacobson suggest that the high rate of noncompliance was due to an increased willingness among hospital personnel to challenge a doctor's orders in contemporary medical practice (a 1966 study had found twenty-one out of twenty-two nurses willing to give an overdose), rising self-esteem among nurses, and a fear of lawsuits for malpractice.

However, rather than challenge physicians' orders directly, which can have unpleasant consequences for the nurse (being "chewed out," fired), most nurses have been able to develop an extremely effective informal interactional style with physicians. This interaction has been described by Leonard Stein (1967) as the "doctor–nurse game" because it has all the features of a game—an object, rules, and scores. The object of the game is for the nurse to be bold, show initiative, and make significant recommendations to the doctor in a manner, however, that appears passive and totally supportive of the "super-physician." The central rule of the game is to avoid open disagreement between the players. This requires the nurse to communicate a recommendation without appearing to do so, while the physician, in seeking a recommendation, must appear not to be asking for it. Stein notes that the greater the significance of the recommendation, the more subtly it must be conveyed. Both participants must therefore be aware of each other's nonverbal and verbal styles of communication.

Stein illustrates the doctor–nurse game with an example of a nurse telephoning and awakening a hospital staff physician who is on call with a report about a female patient unknown to the doctor. The nurse informs the doctor that the patient is unable to sleep and had just been informed that day about the death of her father. What the nurse is actually telling the doctor is that the patient is upset and needs a sedative in order to sleep. Since the doctor is not familiar with the patient, the doctor asks the nurse what sleeping medication has been helpful to the patient in the past. What the doctor is actually doing is asking the nurse for a recommendation; however, the sentence is phrased in such a way that it appears to be a question rather than a request for a recommendation. The nurse replies that phenobarbital 100 mg has been effective for this particular patient, which Stein interprets as a disguised recommendation statement. The doctor then orders the nurse to administer phenobarbital 100 mg as needed and the nurse concludes the interaction by thanking the doctor for the order. The nurse has been successful in making a recommendation without appearing to do so, and the doctor has been successful in asking for a recommendation without appearing to do so.

While all this may seem silly to persons unfamiliar with the physician–nurse relationship, it nonetheless represents a significant social mechanism by which the physician is able to utilize the nurse as a consultant and the nurse is able to gain self-esteem and professional satisfaction from her work. A successful game creates a doctor–nurse alliance and allows the doctor to have a good "score" by gaining the respect and admiration of the nursing staff; the nurse, in turn, scores by being identified by the physician as "a damn good nurse." If the doctor fails to play the game well, pleasant working relationships with the nurses may become difficult and the doctor may have problems of a trivial yet annoying nature when it comes to getting his work done. Nurses who do not play the game well (are outspoken in making recommendations) are either terminated from employment if they also lack intelligence, or are tolerated but not liked if they are bright. Nurses who do not play the game at all, according to Stein, are defined as dull and are relegated to the background in the social life of the hospital. The essence of the doctor–nurse game is that physicians and nurses agree that the physician is superior and this hierarchical structure must be maintained; however, nurses may make recommendations to doctors as long as they *appear* to be initiated by the physician and disagreement is avoided.

Stein, Watts, and Howell (1990) reexamined the doctor–nurse game several years later and determined that a different situation now exists. Stein and his colleagues and others (D. Allen 1997; Carpenter 1993; Porter 1992; Svensson 1996; Weiss and Lonnquist 2003) find that many nurses are no longer willing to be treated as mere subordinates by physicians. Several reasons are offered for this change. First is declining public esteem for doctors due to widespread questioning of the profit motive in medical practice and greater recognition that physicians make mistakes. Second is the increased number of women doctors. When female doctors and nurses interact, the stereotypical roles of male domination and female submission are missing. Third, the nursing shortage has emphasized to doctors the value of highly trained, competent nurses. Fourth, most nurses today are educated in academic settings. Nurses are recognizing that academic qualifications—as opposed to practical on-the-job training—mean enhanced skills and status. Fifth, the women's movement may be encouraging nurses to define their own roles with greater autonomy. Instead of trying to professionalize the entire occupation of nursing, nurses are turning to "clinical nursing" as an exclusive specialty within general nursing that emphasizes specific nursing procedures, management of basic-skill nurses, and the central role of the nurse as the responsible worker for groups of patients.

Besides more assertiveness by female nurses, nursing has attracted larger numbers of males in recent years with increasing pay. For years, men have comprised 4 to 6 percent of all registered nurses. However, in 1999–2000, some 12.5 percent of nursing students were male, attracted not only to the higher pay but also to availability of jobs. Greater numbers of male nurses disrupt the traditional gender role of submission for nurses, since male nurses are not as likely to play the doctor–nurse game. Liliane Floge and Deborah Merrill (1986) found that while female nurses were supposed to appear passive in making recommendations to physicians, this did not seem to be the case for male nurses. Floge and Merrill (1986:939) state:

> We found that male nurses were more likely to voice their opinions than female nurses and to have their opinions accepted by male physicians. One typical example was a male nurse saying to a physician, "You'll find that ____." . . . It was also common to hear a physician asking a male nurse for his opinion. In addition, one male nurse recalled a time when a female nurse was called a "bitch" after she pointed out a male physician's mistake to him, while the male nurse was thanked and told to change the medication when the same physician repeated the same mistake at a later time.

Male nurse holding a young girl in a
hospital corridor. Some 12.5 percent of all
nursing students were males in 1999–2000.

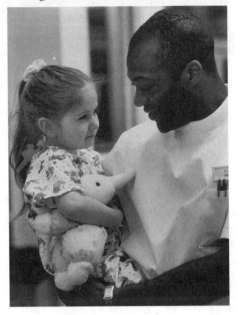

While male physicians tended to regard male nurses as more competent than
female nurses and to treat them accordingly, Floge and Merrill (1986) found that female
physicians were not as likely to play the doctor–nurse game with either male or female
nurses. But female physicians were also more likely than male physicians to have their
actions questioned by nurses. Consequently, when it comes to physician–nurse relationships, gender still plays a significant role in shaping the nature of the interaction.

While it might be inferred that gender issues have promoted poor relationships
between physicians and nurses, this does not appear to be the case. Extensive research shows considerable satisfaction among both groups and generally positive
working relations (Prescott and Bowen 1985). Nurses valued trust and respect on
the part of doctors and being regarded as intelligent participants in patient care; doctors, on their part, appreciated nurses who were competent and helpful and had
good communication skills.

NURSING: FUTURE TRENDS

Nurses have achieved status through their high standards and professional orientation toward their work role and the extension of nursing tasks beyond bedside care.
Typically, lower-echelon workers like nurse's aides provide the majority of bedside
care under the supervision of a registered nurse, while RNs, especially those with

baccalaureate degrees, have expanded their range of services to include hospital administration, primary-care healing, nurse anesthetists, cardiovascular nurse specialists, and other areas of specialization in nursing. Nurse specialists, like those in AIDS units, have enhanced status and greater autonomy in patient care than do non-specialists. According to Linda Aiken and Douglas Sloane (1997:218), who studied the effects of specialization on nurses providing care for AIDS patients, "Nurse specialization allows nurses to develop, demonstrate, and communicate to physicians their superiority in certain important spheres of patient care." This situation is promoted by the fact that nursing skills are critically important to AIDS patients for symptom control and comfort. Aiken and Sloane also found that the willingness of nurses in AIDS units to accept responsibility for patients with a stigmatized, fatal, and communicable disease enhanced their social standing in the hospital.

Hospital Administration

One significant change in the work role of nursing has been the evolution of the R.N. into an administrative role. Competent nurses cannot be rewarded by promotion to the higher rungs of the medical profession; in order to reach the top of the medical structure, the nurse is forced to leave nursing altogether and become a doctor. Since this is usually impractical, many nurses have sought a career in hospital administration. From the perspective of hospital administrators, registered nurses can be used more economically in managerial and supervisory positions because lower paid personnel are available for bedside tasks.

The paradox in this development, however, is that while it allows the nurse to gain a somewhat more secure claim of professional status, it greatly reduces or eliminates the contact with patients for which nursing was organized in the first place. Yet it has been suggested that patients usually cannot tell one type of nurse from another and generally do not overtly request emotional support (Elder 1963). Instead, patients typically request simple tasks—such as medications to ease pain, bedpans, or assistance in moving to a more comfortable body position—which can be accomplished by less qualified nursing aides. As Sam Schulman (1972:236) points out, in hospitals "mother-surrogateness is seldom encountered: in large measure, it is not asked for by patients nor is it given by nurses." Schulman concludes that, in an indirect sense, patients are supportive of the removal of most professional nurses from their bedsides because they want the most professional persons in charge of their care. Whether patients do approve of removing the best qualified nurses from their bedside is an arguable point; nevertheless, it is happening.

The Nurse Practitioner

The most recent change in nursing has been the emergence of another kind of nurse—the nurse practitioner or nurse clinician. This change is not intended to create a new type of health worker, but instead to use more fully the skills and capabilities of the well-trained nurse. The nurse practitioner is intended to occupy a work position similar to that of the physician assistant role. The nurse practitioner is trained to assume many of the primary and routine tasks of patient care normally handled by the physician, such as giving physical examinations, taking medical histories, ordering laboratory tests and X-rays, providing health education to patients and their families, and making the decision as to whether the patient needs to consult with a physician. This role for the nurse allows the physician to assume the more realistic position of a highly trained specialist. It frees physicians from the routine tasks of medical practice and allows them to concentrate more fully on the complex medical problems for which their training has prepared them.

Although the role of nurse practitioner has not been fully conceptualized in terms of the training, qualifications, and responsibilities, existing research (Light 1983) suggests that nurse practitioners have met with a high degree of acceptance among patients who have used their services, and that patient care can indeed be made more efficient by involving paramedical personnel.

Hence, a formal role for nurses who practice medicine as well as nursing is developing within the context of patient care. In the future, nurse practitioners may provide much of the primary care for patients. Although this development would not change nursing's subordinate work role, it would allow nurse practitioners a greater degree of decision making. A major concern, however, with this projection of an expanded role is that the nurse practitioner may simply be "consumed" by the medical profession as a "lesser" doctor or given only a more complex form of tasks delegated by the physician. Research in Great Britain by Anne Bowling (1981) found nurses generally no more in favor of performing clinical tasks delegated to them than doctors were of doing the delegating. Bowling suggests that, in striving for personal autonomy, nurses tend to reject performing part of the doctor's duties in favor of emphasizing the uniquely "caring" functions of the nurse. The basis of this attitude was a narrow professionalism on the part of both nurses and doctors. The nurses wanted to maintain their occupational identity by separating their work role from that of physicians.

Current trends suggest, however, that the new generation of RNs in the United States is playing an expanded role in medicine through increased decision making and direct responsibility for their decisions. Some twenty-six states in the United States allow nurse practitioners to work without supervision or collaboration with a physician[1] and sixteen states allow them to prescribe medications without the involvement of a physician[2]. With the exception of Illinois and Tennessee, which currently have no laws providing for nurse practitioners, all other states require them to have physician supervision or collaboration or allow physicians to limit what they

[1]States allowing nurse practitioners to provide health care without supervision by physicians are Alaska, Hawaii, Washington, Oregon, Montana, Wyoming, Utah, Colorado, North Dakota, Nebraska, Kansas, New Mexico, Texas, Oklahoma, Arkansas, Iowa, Indiana, Michigan, West Virginia, Delaware, New Jersey, Connecticut, Rhode Island, Vermont, New Hampshire, and Maine, and the District of Columbia.

[2]States allowing nurse practitioners to prescribe drugs without a physician's permission are Alaska, Washington, Oregon, Montana, Wyoming, South Dakota, Nebraska, Colorado, Arizona, New Mexico, Iowa, Wisconsin, South Carolina, Vermont, New Hampshire, and Maine, and the District of Columbia.

may do. Nurse practitioners may not prescribe drugs in Illinois, but all other states allow some degree of prescribing with physician involvement if they lack authorization to prescribe on their own.

PHYSICIAN ASSISTANTS

While the concept of the nurse practitioner derives from the expansion of a traditional occupation, that of physician assistant (PA) represents a new form of paramedical practitioner. This relatively new occupation results from the recognition by American physicians that specialization has reduced them to narrower and narrower competencies and that the pressure of increasing case loads has reduced the time available for attending to many minor and routine patient demands. It has been charged that some physicians have relied upon excessive use of laboratory and diagnostic tests (thus increasing the costs of medical treatment) as a partial substitution for physician–patient interaction. It has also been suggested that decreased physician–patient time per visit has contributed to patient dissatisfaction and thus to malpractice suits. Ideally physician assistants will handle many routine medical problems, thereby releasing the physician for increased physician–patient contact and more attention to difficult and complex problems. A general job description of the physician assistant would be to provide a level of primary patient care similar to or higher than that of nurse practitioners. Moreover, as James Cawley (1985:79) explains:

> A key corollary to the emergence of the PA was the notion that these providers could also bring new attributes to medical practice. Apart from the pressing reality of the shortage of physicians, there was also the problem that physicians were often too unconcerned with the routine illnesses of many patients. Patients tended to place little emphasis on important elements of primary care, such as counseling, patient education, and preventive service. A growing need was expressed for a new type of health provider, harking back to the days of the "old GP." These providers, working with physicians, could offer skills not only in medical diagnosis and management, but also in the caring and preventive aspects of practice.

By 2000, there were 37,821 physician assistants in the United States, nearly half of whom were women. Their training was either in primary care or in specialties, especially ophthalmology and orthopedics. Typically, they work directly for physicians, either in private medical practices or in hospitals providing in-patient services. They spend the largest part of their workday providing direct patient care, divided about equally between those tasks directly supervised and those indirectly supervised by physicians; considerably less time was spent in technical or laboratory work or in the supervision of other health workers. The physician assistant is becoming an established occupation within medicine (Cawley 1985; Hooker 1991). The District of Columbia and all states except Mississippi legally recognize PA practice. Forty-six states and the District of Columbia authorize PAs to prescribe medications. Most important for patient care, the physician assistant, in conjunction with the nurse practitioner, may be able to resolve the significant issue of providing more primary-care practitioners in the American system of health care delivery. It appears that the use of nurse practitioners and physician assistants will increase as long as they extend the medical functions of physicians without competing for or challenging their authority and autonomy (Ferraro and Southerland 1989:200).

PHARMACISTS

Pharmacy is another area of health care that expanded its role in the latter part of the twentieth century. Pharmacists no longer just prepare and dispense medication, but they also provide advice, information, and instructions about drug use (Pilnick 1999). Pharmacists, in fact, are the most accessible of all health care personnel as they practice in a wide range of settings, including community pharmacies, hospitals, and clinics, and also provide mail and telephone services. Whereas pharmacists cannot dispense prescription drugs without authorization from a physician or other legally sanctioned practitioner, they explain the effects of prescription drugs and levels of doses primarily to patients and at times to practitioners—as well as provide instructions for their use. They also explain and recommend over-the-counter drugs to customers with common ailments. Most importantly, they are the key source of medication information for the general public. Although pharmacists have considerably more expertise than customers or patients about medications, they reduce the social distance between them by using terms that a layperson can understand (Pilnick 1998).

There are approximately 185,000 pharmacists in the United States and eighty-one schools of pharmacy. Educational requirements are changing early in the twenty-first century in that pharmacy schools will only award the doctor of pharmacy (Pharm.D.) degree for six years of study beyond high school. Previously, a five-year bachelor of science in pharmacy (B.S. Pharmacy) degree was available, but it is being phased out in favor of greater professional preparation. This development reinforces the position of pharmacists as the most knowledgeable health care

---

BOX 12-1   The First Pharmacies

Arabs founded the first pharmacies. In fact, the word "drugs" is of Arab origin, as are the words alcohol, sugar, and syrup. Many drugs were introduced by the Arabs, including camphor, the painkiller laudanum, and medicinal alcohol. Roy Porter (1997:102) points out that since the time of the great Arab alchemist, Jabir ibn Hayyan, in the tenth century, the Arabs were developing the techniques of crystallization, filtration, and distillation in the making of drugs, and investigating their properties. The value of this Arab contribution to medicine, Porter finds, was not the novelty of their drugs, but the thoroughness with which they catalogued and preserved their knowledge. Latin translations of Arabic texts helped Western medicine revive after the Dark Ages and promoted the establishment of pharmacies in the West.

specialist about medicines and their use. Although the role of pharmacists is expanding to assume greater patient counseling, they supplement rather than challenge the patient care tasks of physicians and health care practitioners.

MIDWIVES

Midwives are women who assist a mother during childbirth. There are two types of midwives, nurse-midwives who deliver babies under the supervision of a physician and lay midwives who assist births on their own. Midwifery is one of the earliest forms of care available to women. As Rose Weitz and Deborah Sullivan (1986) describe the history of midwifery, midwives attended practically all births in colonial America. In fact, as late as the eighteenth century it was considered undignified for male physicians to care for pregnant women and attend to the delivery of babies. That function was considered "women's work." What changed this situation was a growing belief in scientific progress among the general population and the development of obstetrics as a new medical specialty. Births attended by midwives began to drop rapidly as physicians took over responsibility for delivering babies. In the meantime, the medical profession developed strong opposition to midwifery, arguing that surgical skills and knowledge of drugs, as well as more sanitary conditions found in hospital delivery rooms, were far superior to any service midwives could provide.

Midwife attending to a pregnant woman. Despite once powerful opposition from the medical profession, midwifery is slowly making a comeback in the U.S. Registered nurse-midwives are legally authorized to work throughout the country.

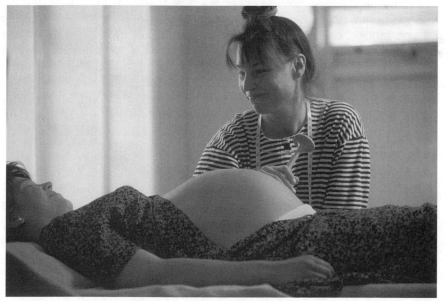

Weitz and Sullivan found that, by 1900, only about half of all births in the United States were attended by midwives; by 1950, midwifery ceased in all but remote areas.

However, midwifery has slowly made a comeback in American society despite the opposition of the medical profession. Midwives have become available to women in some locales who wish to have a natural childbirth, featuring breathing and relaxation techniques and emotional support in the place of pain-killing drugs. Many physicians, in turn, now practice many of the same techniques for women who opt for natural childbirth. Lay midwives have remained in existence because they deliver babies in the home, something that physicians typically refuse to do, and they have disproportionately served racial/ethnic minorities and people in rural areas (Hartley 1999, 2002). Midwives also serve women whose religious beliefs prevent them from using doctors (DeVries 1993). While opposition to midwifery by the medical profession continues, today some sixteen states license or register lay midwives. About 700 lay midwives practiced in the United States in 1999.

Weitz and Sullivan (1986) studied the development of midwifery in Arizona. They found that to become a midwife, a woman had to show evidence of formal training in midwifery, observations of live births, and supervised experience, as well as pass oral, written, and clinical examinations developed by a nurse-midwife in consultation with physicians. These rules were developed in Arizona in the late 1970s after controversy emerged over the legal requirements for licensing. Earlier requirements had not been stringent, but when the number of midwives in the state increased and began serving middle-class clients, physicians objected. The new rules, as Weitz and Sullivan point out, gave the medical establishment substantial control of the licensure process, but midwives are able to practice. Weitz and Sullivan characterize the conflict with doctors as a struggle for women's rights and note continued problems with physician acceptance of midwives.

Nurse-midwives, however, are registered nurses trained to deliver babies, often without a doctor's direct supervision (but legal arrangements to have a physician on call are required). Nurse-midwives are legally authorized to work in all fifty states and the District of Columbia. Approximately 6,700 certified nurse-midwives were practicing in the United States in 1999. According to Heather Hartley (1999, 2002), the use of nurse-midwives is increasing in urban managed care systems to meet the demands of consumers desiring a natural childbirth and reducing costs. Hartley suggests that the number of nurse-midwives will increase as the college-educated population continues to show a growing preference for less technology-oriented births.

SUMMARY

Nursing as an occupation has evolved from being an informal exercise of charity ("sisterhood") into a formal occupational role subordinate to the authority and control of the physician. Many social factors have contributed to the maintenance of this situation, especially the stereotype of the mother-surrogate. It has also been noted that in some cases nurse's training is not always viewed by nursing students as a means to a career but as a kind of "life insurance" should they be disappointed in their primary goals of marriage and family. Nevertheless, nurses have continually struggled to achieve formal colleagueship with physicians, and they have achieved professional-like status, especially through their roles in hospital administration and as nurse practitioners.

The role of nurse practitioner seems particularly promising because it enables nurses to gain some autonomy over what they do and to share more fully in medicine's specialized body of knowledge. Both the nurse practitioner and the physician assistant roles result from a trend toward physician specialization that has made doctors less accessible to patients with minor and generalized ailments who nonetheless require attention. These relatively new roles represent evidence that some health workers are displacing physicians. Pharmacists are not competing with physicians, but their role has expanded as well with greater involvement in discourse with laypersons about the use and effects of medications. Midwives, however, find their services constrained by doctors and their occupation relegated to a marginal role in medicine.

NURSES, PHYSICIAN ASSISTANTS, PHARMACISTS, AND MIDWIVES INTERNET SITES

Nursing

1. American Nurses' Association.
   http://www.nursingworld.org

   Homepage of the nation's largest full-service professional organization.

2. Health Resources and Services Administration: Division of Nursing.
   http://bhpr.hrsa.gov/nursing/

   Homepage of the key federal program for nursing education and practice.

3. National Institutes of Health: National Institute of Nursing Research.
   http://www.nih.gov/ninr

   The NINR supports clinical and basic research to establish a scientific basis for the care of individuals across the life span.

4. National League for Nursing
   http://www.nln.org

   Homepage of the National League for Nursing.

Physician Assistants

1. American Academy of Physician Assistants.
   http://www.aapa.org

   National organization that represents physician assistants in all specialties and all employment settings.

2. National Commission on Certification of Physician Assistants.
   http://www.nccpa.net

   Homepage of the only credentialing organization for physician assistants in the United States.

3. Yahoo! Health: Medicine: Physician Assistant: Schools, Departments, and Programs.
   http://www.dir.yahoo.com/Health/Medicine/Physician.Assistant

   A list with links to many physician assistant programs in the United States.

Pharmacists

1. American Pharmaceutical Association.
   http://www.aphanet.org

   A national professional society of pharmacists.

2. American Association of Colleges of Pharmacy.
   http://www.aacp.org

   Both sites provide information about pharmacists as well as links to pharmacy-related sites.

3. American Society of Health-System Pharmacists.
   http://www.safemedication.com

   Information about prescription drugs.

Midwives

1. American College of Nurse-Midwives.
   http://www.acnm.org

   Includes information on how to find a midwife, education, and certification.

2. Midwives Alliance of North America.
   http://www.mana.org

   MANA's central mission is to promote midwifery as a quality health care option for North American families.

CHAPTER 13

Hospitals

Since many health problems require a level of medical treatment and personal care that extends beyond the range of services normally available in the patient's home or in the physician's office, modern society has developed formal institutions for patient care intended to help meet the more complex health needs of its members. The hospital, the major social institution for the delivery of health care in the modern world, offers considerable advantages to both patient and society. From the standpoint of the individual, the sick or injured person has access to centralized medical knowledge and the greatest array of technology in hospitals. From the standpoint of society, as Talcott Parsons and Renée Fox (1952) suggest, hospitalization both protects the family from many of the disruptive effects of caring for the ill in the home and operates as a means of guiding the sick and injured into medically supervised institutions where their problems are less disruptive for society as a whole.

The purpose of this chapter is to consider the social role of the hospital. Besides serving the prescribed social function of providing medical treatment, hospitals can be viewed from the perspective of a functionally specific world. This chapter will examine the organizational aspects of that world in the following order: (1) development of the hospital as a social institution; (2) the hospital system in the United States; (3) social organization of hospital work, including its effect on the patient role; and (4) the rising cost of hospital services.

THE DEVELOPMENT OF THE HOSPITAL AS A SOCIAL INSTITUTION

The development of hospitals as institutions providing medical services for the general public proceeded in pace with the prevailing needs, beliefs, values, and attitudes of the societies they served (Coe 1978; R. Porter 1997; C. Rosenberg 1987; R. Stevens 1989). Historically, hospitals have passed through four distinct phases of development: (1) as centers of religious practice, (2) as poorhouses, (3) as deathhouses, and (4) as centers of medical technology.

Hospitals as Centers of Religious Practice

Although the Romans were the first to establish separate medical facilities (for economic and military reasons) that have been described as hospitals, the origin of the institution we know today as the hospital has usually been associated with the rise of Christianity. Christian theology emphasized that human beings were duty bound to provide assistance to the sick and needy; this belief was reinforced by the notion that spiritual salvation could be obtained by whoever provided such a service. Consequently, the Roman Catholic church encouraged its clergy to found hospitals and to locate these hospitals near churches as an integral feature of Christian religious endeavor. Furthermore, during the period of the Crusades between 1096 and 1291, many hospitals were established along the routes taken to the Holy Land by the Christian armies. Secular benefactors, such as kings, queens, and other members of the nobility, wealthy merchants, artisan and craftsmen's guilds, and municipalities also founded hospitals. By the end of the fifteenth century, an extensive network of hospitals existed throughout Western Europe.

The medieval hospital, however, was not a hospital by any modern standard. True, these hospitals were community centers for the care of the lower-class sick; yet the medical care, supervised and largely performed by clergy and nuns, consisted primarily of a rudimentary form of nursing. The primary functions of the medieval hospital were the exercise of religious practices and the extension of charity and welfare services to the poor, including both the able-bodied and the sick. These early hospitals, therefore, provided a wide spectrum of social tasks for the benefit of the lower classes, especially the provision of food, shelter, sanctuary, and prayer as well as nursing.

During the Renaissance and the Reformation, the religious character of the hospital began to disappear as increasing numbers of hospitals were placed under the jurisdiction of secular authorities. Nevertheless, as Rodney Coe (1978) has observed, three basic features of the modern hospital are derived from the influence of the church. First, the concept of a service oriented toward helping others has become a guiding principle for the manner in which hospital personnel are required to approach their work. Second, hospitals are supposed to have a "universalistic" approach—that is, to accept for treatment all people who may be sick or injured. And third, the custodial nature of hospital care has been facilitated by housing patients within the confines of a single location.

Hospitals as Poorhouses

The secular control of hospitals marked a period of decline for the development of Europe's hospital system. Even though monks and nuns continued to work in hospitals, the removal of the centralized authority of the church left hospitals under many separate administrations, usually those of municipal governments. Without general regulations pertaining to hospital administration, individual hospitals were free to pursue any course of action they desired. This situation encouraged abuse, particularly in regard to neglect of facilities, misappropriation of funds, and the lowering of prevailing standards of patient care. In England the suppression of the monastery system in the mid-1500s led to the collapse of the English hospital system as many hospitals, left without personnel or money, were forced to close. The few remaining hospitals limited their services to people who were actually sick and who could be cured. While this policy relegated the poor, both the incurably ill and the able-bodied, to poorhouses or to the streets for their support, it marked the beginning of a new definition of hospitals as institutions active in curing the sick and injured so that they could return to society.

However, by the end of the sixteenth century, the economic and social conditions of the poor worsened to a considerable degree. Unemployment, higher prices, and the loss of land created a serious problem of vagrancy throughout Europe. Many vagrants claimed to be sick or crippled, and they crowded whatever hospital facilities were available. In accordance with the new definition of social welfare as a community rather than a church responsibility, measures were eventually taken by city and national authorities to provide public assistance. Many hospitals were re-opened, but they soon acquired the characteristics of boarding houses because they offered food and shelter to the poor, regardless of whether they were sick or healthy. Those persons living in hospitals who could work were required to pay for their lodging, while hospitals received further financial support through public taxation. Hospitals became little more than social "warehouses," where invalids, the aged, orphans, and the mentally defective could be sent and thus removed from the mainstream of society. Even today in the United States, people with chronic health problems requiring long-term hospitalization—the insane, the incurable, and individuals suffering from highly infectious diseases—tend to be sent to public institutions, while private hospitals tend to accept patients with acute disorders. And some hospitals, like Cook County in Chicago, Philadelphia General, Bellevue and Kings County in New York, and San Francisco General, were established as institutions for the poor.

Hospitals as Deathhouses

Following the Renaissance and the Reformation, the outward character of hospitals appeared to change very little from that of public institutions whose purpose was to provide welfare services for the lower social classes on behalf of the communities in which they were located. Nonetheless, changes were taking place as physicians discovered that hospitals contained large numbers of sick and injured (and also

BOX 13-1   Mental Hospital Admissions

A legacy of the hospitals as poorhouses period of history are mental hospitals, the majority of which are operated by state or county governments. Mental hospital admissions are either voluntary or involuntary. Voluntary commitment results when individuals consent to be admitted and about 70 percent of all resident patients in psychiatric facilities enter voluntarily (Cockerham 2003). Involuntary commitment results when a state uses its legal authority to confine an individual in a mental hospital. Involuntary commitment proceedings are of two types: those dealing with criminal offenses, in which insanity is claimed as a defense, and those that are civil (non-criminal) in nature.

In criminal cases, the claim of mental disorder is used as an excusing condition that relieves the individual of criminal responsibility for his or her crime. The model for an excusing condition in Anglo-American law is the accident, and it defines a class of persons who fall outside the boundaries of blame. The defendant takes the position that he or she is guilty but attempts to shift the responsibility to a mental disorder. The culprit then becomes the mental disorder because *it* kept the person from acting in a reasonable manner under the circumstances. A finding of insanity by a judge or jury, based upon the testimony of psychiatrists as expert witnesses, is a matter of opinion as there are no objective standards for ascertaining mental disorder. A verdict of insanity in favor of the defendant, however, does not usually release the individual to return immediately to society, but instead commits the person involuntarily to a mental hospital for a time to be determined later by the hospital staff and the courts.

For involuntary civil commitment, the diagnosis of a mental disorder is not sufficient justification for the confinement of an individual to a mental hospital. There usually must also be a finding that the mental disorder is of such a degree or character that if the individual in question were allowed to remain at large, that person would constitute a danger to self, others, or property. Judges normally make decisions on a case-by-case basis, based on the opinion of psychiatrists who estimate the probability that the individual will commit a dangerous act. Actions ranging from murder to writing bad checks have been found to be sufficient evidence of dangerousness. To determine dangerousness, the courts look to the severity of the harm, the likelihood that the action will occur, and the past behavior of the person who provoked the prediction of dangerousness.

generally powerless) people whose health problems could be studied and upon whom the various evolving techniques of medical treatment could be practiced.

Physicians had first begun to associate themselves with hospitals during the fourteenth century; initially they had little influence because they were not members of the hospital staff and provided their services on a purely voluntary basis. By the seventeenth century, however, physicians acquired a virtual monopoly over the existing body of medical knowledge that placed them in the position of first advising and eventually directing all patient care within the hospital. As physicians became increasingly influential, nonmedical hospital tasks gradually disappeared. By the early nineteenth century, hospitals had clearly assumed their present-day role as institutions for medical care, for medical research, and for the education of medical students.

Although medical treatment was recognized as the primary function of the hospital in the eighteenth century, the primitive level of that treatment produced few cures. Trained physicians were unable to achieve consistent results with their techniques and, accordingly, neither they nor hospitals were held in high esteem by the general population. Because so few patients survived treatment despite occasional heroic efforts, hospitals acquired an image as places where the poor went to die.

According to Coe (1978), the high death rate in hospitals was also related to the appalling living conditions provided patients. Typically, hospitals were dirty, poorly ventilated, and filled to capacity. Often more than one patient was placed in a single bed regardless of the patient's disorder, and treatment was usually carried out publicly on the ward itself. Surgery, which Coe points out was limited at that time mostly to amputations and childbirth, plus the purging of fevers with various potions, bloodletting to eliminate "excess" blood, and the removal of the dead all occurred in the same general area where patients ate and slept. Nor did the attending physicians and surgeons practice even the most rudimentary standards of sanitation, moving from bed to bed and treating a great variety of diseases, including those that were infectious, without washing their hands or changing their clothes. Thus, it is not surprising that hospitals were regarded by most people as places where only the lower social classes went to die.

Hospitals as Centers of Medical Technology

Since the end of the nineteenth century, a new image of hospitals evolved as institutions where patients of all social classes could generally expect to find the highest quality medical care and could reasonably expect to be cured of their disorders. Three major factors were responsible for this change. First was the fact that medicine had indeed become a science in terms of employing the scientific method to seek out accurate medical knowledge and to develop successful techniques that could be employed in a consistent manner. Of particular importance were increased knowledge about human physiology and the development of the science of bacteriology; also important was the perfection of ether as an anesthetic, which allowed surgery to be performed in a relatively painless fashion. Since the new medical technology required extensive and often expensive facilities, these facilities were centralized in hospitals so that they could be available to most physicians. Hospitals eventually became places where physicians also referred their upper- and middle-class patients, since the most advanced medical technology was located there. While the poor generally remained in a charity status as hospital patients, a new type of patient came into being—the private patient—who required private accommodations, who usually had a private physician, and who paid for hospital services.

A second important factor, concomitant with the development of medical technology, was the discovery and use of antiseptic measures in the hospital to help curtail infection. Hospitals were not only properly cleaned and ventilated, but also patients with infectious diseases were isolated in special areas of the hospital, and hospital staffs were required to wash their hands and change their clothing after working with these patients. The use of such items as surgical masks, rubber gloves, and sterilized surgical instruments became commonplace. These procedures not only reduced the number of deaths among hospital patients but also reduced the amount of time required for patient recovery.

Third, there was a significant improvement in the quality of hospital personnel. Especially important was the entry on the scene of the trained nurse and the laboratory technician, whose specialized skills were able to support the physician in his or her primary role of diagnostician and practitioner. As Charles Rosenberg (1987) points out in his historical analysis of the development of American hospitals, no single change has transformed the day-to-day work in a hospital more than trained nurses. In the twentieth century, the hospital has become the major institutional resource available to society for coping with problems of health and illness.

HOSPITALS IN THE UNITED STATES

The first hospitals were founded in the United States more than two hundred fifty years ago. Generally their development paralleled that of Western European institutions in the 1700s. The first such hospital was established by William Penn in Philadelphia in 1713, with the care of the sick being incidental to the main purpose of providing shelter for the poor. Charity Hospital in New Orleans was founded by the Catholic church in 1737 for similar reasons. The first hospital to be established in the United States solely for the purpose of treating the sick was the Pennsylvania Hospital, founded by Benjamin Franklin and a group of interested citizens in 1751. These early hospitals were not governmental undertakings but were largely based

Founded in 1751, Philadelphia's Pennsylvania Hospital was the first general hospital in America.

on voluntary initiative by private citizens who wanted medical care available on a nonprofit basis. They were generally intended to provide treatment for patients who had curable disorders.

Federal government participation in health care did not actually begin until 1798 with the U.S. Public Health Service hospital program for merchant seamen. State governments did not enter into health care delivery until the 1800s, and their efforts were largely confined to the establishment of state mental institutions. By 1873 there were only 178 hospitals of all types in the United States; in 2000, the number of hospitals was 5,810.

Hospital Ownership

The ownership of hospitals in the United States may be classified into three major types: (1) nonprofit; (2) for profit, or (3) government (federal, state, or local).[1] Table 13-1 shows the number of hospitals for the years 1975 to 2000. The figures in Table 13-1 show that the total number of hospitals has fallen from 7,156 in 1975 to 5,810 in 2000. Table 13-1 indicates that 245 (approximately 4 percent) of the hospitals in 2000 were owned by the federal government, while 5,565 (or 96 percent) were nonfederal. Table 13-1 also shows that 4,915 or 85 percent of all hospitals are classified as community or short-stay hospitals in which patients are expected to stay for only a few days or weeks. The most common type of hospital in the United States is the nonfederal and nonprofit community hospital. Nonprofit hospitals numbered 3,003 in 2000, representing 52 percent of all American hospitals.

Controlled by a board of trustees, nonprofit hospitals are exempt from federal income taxes and many other forms of state and local taxes. These hospitals have generally been characterized as emphasizing high-quality care for the upper and middle social classes, while also allowing access to their facilities by lower-class patients. Nonprofit hospitals are highly dependent on community physicians for membership

TABLE 13-1   Types of Hospitals, United States, 1975–2000.

Type of Ownership	NUMBER			
	1975	1980	1990	2000
Total	7,156	6,965	6,649	5,810
Federal	382	359	337	245
Nonfederal	6,774	6,606	6,312	5,565
Community	5,875	5,830	5,384	4,915
Nonprofit	3,339	3,322	3,191	3,003
For profit	775	730	749	749
State-local government	1,761	1,778	1,444	1,163

Source: Adapted from American Hospital Association data.

[1]A hospital is defined as a facility with at least six beds that is licensed by the state as a hospital or that is operated as a hospital by a federal or state agency.

on their staffs and for the referral of patients. Large nonprofit hospitals, however, are somewhat less dependent than smaller hospitals on local physicians because of their greater prestige, more extensive facilities, and higher ratio of staff positions for doctors.

Table 13-1 shows that 797 community hospitals (13 percent of the total) were classified in 2000 as for profit. In the past, these hospitals have usually been small and highly dependent on local physicians for staff membership and patient referrals. However, Paul Starr's (1982) research demonstrated that the trend for profit-making hospitals is to merge into a multihospital chain owned by a large corporation. In this situation, physicians on the hospital staff are generally employees of the corporation, but doctors outside the hospital are encouraged to also place their patients in the profit-making hospitals through incentives like hospital staff privileges and higher-quality care for their patients by the hospital staff. The usual source of income for profit-making hospitals is internal and generated from patient care, especially payments from private insurance companies.

The number of state and local government-owned community hospitals in Table 13-1 for 2000 is 1,163, which is 20 percent of the total. Government hospitals tend to lack prestige in comparison to other hospitals. They are the major source of health care for people with low incomes, particularly in urban areas. Government hospitals place their emphasis on public access to their facilities. Yet the increased affiliation of government hospitals with medical schools portends a shift in emphasis toward quality care and modern facilities. Nevertheless, America's hospital system remains a two-class system of medical care—one primarily for the relatively affluent and the other generally serving the less affluent in state and local hospitals.

THE ORGANIZATION OF THE NONPROFIT COMMUNITY HOSPITAL

Certainly not all hospitals are alike in their organization of services, but nonprofit community hospitals, as the most common single type of hospital in the United States, exhibit the organizational features of many hospitals. Figure 13-1 shows the typical organization of large nonprofit community hospitals. These hospitals have been described as "multipurpose institutions" in that they provide a variety of health-related functions for society such as (1) treating patients; (2) conducting medical research; (3) training health practitioners; (4) providing laboratories and other medical facilities to the community; and (5) sponsoring health education and preventive medicine programs for the general public. Robert Wilson (1963), for example, describes the hospital as a hotel, a school, a laboratory, and a stage for treatment. The *primary* goal of the hospital, however, is that of providing medical treatment to its patients within the limits of contemporary medical knowledge and technology and the hospital's available resources.

To accomplish its tasks and coordinate its various activities, the hospital relies on a prescribed hierarchy of authority (as shown in Figure 13-1), which is operationalized through formal rules, regulations, and administrative procedures. The key

FIGURE 13-1 Typical large nonprofit community hospital organized into five divisions.

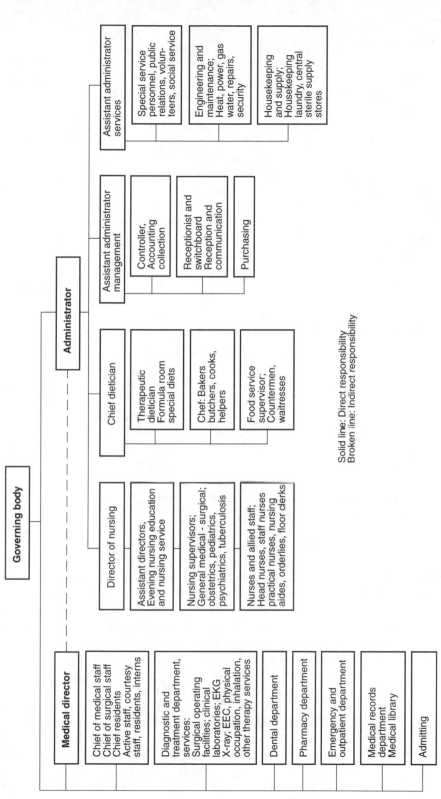

Solid line: Direct responsibility
Broken line: Indirect responsibility

Source: *Technology and Manpower in the Health Service Industry*, Manpower Research Bulletin, No. 14 (Washington, D.C.: U.S. Department of Labor, Manpower Administration, May 1967).

to hospital efficiency and overall effectiveness is coordination of the various departments and individuals. They represent a complex and highly specialized division of labor that is both interlocking and interdependent.

Consider what happens when a staff doctor prescribes medication for a patient. The doctor's order for medication is written in the patient's medical records by a floor clerk, and the clerk, or a nurse's aide or orderly, takes the request to the pharmacy. When the medication is sent by the pharmacy, it is most likely administered by a nurse. A record is then forwarded to the accounting office so that the proper charges for the drug can be entered on the patient's bill; another written order might be sent from the pharmacy to purchasing (through the appropriate administrative channels) to reorder the medication and replace it for future use by another patient. So the rather routine activity of one particular member of the hospital staff (in this case a doctor) initiates a chain of events that affects the work of several other hospital employees.

The Hospital: Dual Authority

According to Figure 13-1, the overall supervision of the general hospital comes under the auspices of its governing body. In most nonfederal hospitals, that governing body is a board of trustees. Figure 13-1 also shows that, whereas the medical director and the hospital administrator are linked to the governing body by a direct line of responsibility, they are only indirectly responsible to each other. What this type of arrangement indicates is that the authority system of the general hospital operates on a dual level. This system is an outgrowth of the organizational conflict in the hospital between bureaucracy and professionalism.

It has been noted that Max Weber's concept of bureaucracy is not totally compatible with the norms of hospital authority (Hillier 1987). Weber described bureaucracy as a rational and impersonal division of labor characterized by the principles of *office hierarchy* and levels of graded authority (lower offices are supervised by higher ones), and by *fixed and official areas of jurisdiction* governed by laws or administrative regulations. The essence of the conflict between bureaucracy and the professional consists of the professional's insistence on exercising an autonomous individual judgment within the limits prescribed by the profession itself. As Mary Goss (1963) points out, the work norms of the professional (in this case, the medical doctor) emphasize self-determination for each practitioner, that is, exclude control by those outside the profession. The bureaucrat (here, the hospital administrator), in contrast, seeks to follow a rationalistic management approach that favors the efficient coordination of the hospital's activities through formal rules and impersonal regulations applicable to all persons in all situations.

Charles Perrow (1963) has traced the evolution of this conflict in his study of one voluntary general hospital he believes to be representative of most other hospitals of this type. Perrow noted that in the late 1800s and early 1900s the voluntary general hospital was dominated by its board of trustees, because this was an era when securing capital funds and gaining community recognition were critical hospital goals. Since community involvement was the pivotal factor, individual members of boards of trustees were usually laypersons selected at large from the community. Legally they were responsible for protecting the community's interests, but they also sought to incorporate hospital services into the general pattern of community life. Perrow believes this approach ultimately derives from seventeenth-century attitudes toward hospitals as state institutions operated on public funds, that is, as community welfare agencies and poorhouses.

In the 1930s trustee domination succumbed to medical domination. Perrow cites three major reasons for this change: First, the emphasis on free care declined significantly as hospital services became oriented toward patients who could pay; second, the facilities to support a complex system of medical technology were developed, and the quality of care provided patients was improved; and third, the hospital sought prestige through medical research in terms defined by physicians. Hence, medical domination went hand in hand with increasing medical knowledge. During this period, however, Perrow also noted the appearance of several abuses that could be attributed to the great personal power of the medical director and department heads. Especially deficient was the outpatient care afforded to people with low incomes; also conspicuous was the favoritism shown toward certain physicians in the use of hospital facilities and staff promotions. Perrow (1963:123) observed:

> There was little to prevent such abuses. The doctor is an individual entrepreneur, selling his services for a profit. His income is affected by the facilities he commands in the hospital, his freedom from scrutiny, and by the price he must pay in the form of reciprocal duties such as teaching or committee work. Reliance upon professional ethics, even buttressed by the atmosphere created by teaching and research activities, is not sufficient in itself to guarantee a disinterested, ethical non-economic point of view. Nor will it prevent abuses stemming from the enormous concentration of power in the hands of the chief of staff and department heads who also control the hospital.

What was needed, said Perrow, was a system to limit these powers, to establish objective criteria for promotion and to provide for more effective representation of patient and organizational interests. That system gradually emerged during the 1940s and 1950s as the role of hospital administrator gained in importance; through a constitutional system, the administration was able to define the medical staff's official power, standardize the hospital's administrative procedures, and establish a level of quality for the hospital's medical services. These early administrators were often physicians who could be expected to further the interests of the medical staff, but in doing so began to curtail their power. As authority became centralized in the administrator's office, there often developed a blockage of communication between the staff and the board of trustees. This period, according to Perrow, was characterized by a complex power struggle that eventually led, in the 1950s, to a system of multiple leadership common among general hospitals today.

Multiple leadership, at least in its hospital version, is actually a system of dual authority, one administrative and the other medical. Perrow notes the high probability of such a system developing in the hospital, because goals are generally multiple (trustees, administration, and medical staff often have diverse interests), the criteria for achieving them are broad, and the power of each group to protect its interests is considerable. Since the physician's professional norms can set specific limits on the hospital administrator's authority and vice versa, the result has been to reconcile the physician-professional with the administrator-bureaucrat by establishing a system of dual authority.

The board of trustees still remains the nominal center of authority in the general hospital. It usually meets on a periodic basis, weekly or monthly, to review the hospital's operations and act upon matters that are brought to its attention. Generally the trustees themselves are people who are influential in the wider community. But despite their position as the hospital's ultimate source of authority, the trustees have only limited de facto authority over the medical staff, who usually make all health-related decisions. The board of trustees typically concerns itself with administrative matters and public relations while working closely with the hospital administrator, who acts as their agent in exercising authority and supervising the day-to-day routine of the hospital.

The occupational groups in the hospital most affected by its system of dual authority are the nurses and auxiliary nursing workers who perform health care tasks on the hospital's wards. Nurses are responsible to the physician for carrying out the physician's orders, but they also are responsible to the nursing supervisors and the upper echelons of the hospital's administration. Even though the communication and allegiance of ward personnel tend to be channeled along occupational lines within and toward the "administrative channel of command," medical authority can and does cut across these lines. While this system can at times cause interpersonal stress, inconsistency, overlapping of responsibility, and inadequate coordination, it also allows ward personnel to "play off" one authority against the other if one appears unreasonable (Wessen 1972) and acts to reduce organizational inflexibility and authoritarianism (Georgopoulos and Mann 1972). In fact, Georgopoulos and Mann further argue that the hospital's system of dual authority is virtually inevitable in light of its high degree of functional specialization and professionalism. Nonetheless, hospital personnel share a common goal of providing quality patient care through competency, devotion to duty, and hard work, qualities Georgopoulos and Mann suggest have had the effect of producing many common norms, values, and complementary expectations. The hospital's normative system, they argue, underlies its administrative structure and

> . . . enables the hospital to attain a level of coordination and integration that could never be accomplished through administrative edict, through hierarchical directives, or through explicitly formulated and carefully specified organizational plans and impersonal rules, regulations, and procedures. (Georgopoulos and Mann 1972:308)

In a separate study of a psychiatric hospital, Anselm Strauss and his associates (1963) noted a similar process wherein the hospital rules governing the actions of the professionals who worked within its setting were far from extensive, clearly stated, or clearly binding. These researchers contended that the social order of the hospital was not fixed or automatically maintained, but was the result of continual

Hospital administrators meeting around a conference table. Hospitals have a dual system of authority, one system is administrative and other is medical.

negotiation between the administration, the medical staff, other hospital employees, and patients. The individuals involved had varying degrees of prestige and power, were at different stages in their careers, and had their own particular goals, reference groups, and occupational ideologies. In addition, hospital rules governing physicians' conduct were not clearly stated, extensive, or binding. The hospital administration tended to take a tolerant position toward institutional rules in the belief that good patient care required a minimum of "hard and fast" regulations and a maximum of "innovation and improvisation." Thus, there was continual negotiation of the medical rules—what they were and whether they applied in a particular situation. What held the hospital staff together was the sharing of a common goal to return their patients to the outside world in a better condition than when they entered the hospital. Strauss and associates (1963:154) explained:

> This goal is the symbolic cement that, metaphorically speaking, holds the organization together: the symbol to which all personnel can comfortably, and frequently point— with the assurance that *at least* about this matter everyone can agree! Although this symbol . . . masks a considerable measure of disagreement and discrepant purpose, it represents a generalized mandate under which the hospital can be run—the public flag under which all may work in concert.

Although it might appear from the Strauss study that the hospital was in a state of chaos, held together by only a single, idealistic agreement, actually the process of negotiation was observed to have a definite pattern. In following their own particular approach to their work, the physicians were able to originate relatively stable understandings with the nurses and other hospital employees; this process resulted in efficient and standardized forms of behavior not dependent on special instructions for all contingencies. Consequently, the process of negotiation not only created new meanings, but also reinforced the significance of the more formalized rules through a process of periodic appraisal.

In summary, the hospital's organization consists of a varied group of professionals and allied health workers with different functions, training, and occupational values. To make this social organization function effectively, it has been necessary to construct a decentralized system of authority organized around a generally acceptable objective of service to the patient. While the administrator directs and supervises hospital policy, the medical staff retains control over medical decisions.

However, the dual system of authority that has existed in hospitals is in jeopardy as a result of the precedent-setting *Darling* case in Charleston, Illinois.[2] The *Darling* case involved a suit for damages sought by the plaintiff for alleged medical and hospital negligence. The patient, Dorrence Darling, broke his leg while playing football and was taken to the emergency room of Charleston Community Hospital. A general practitioner put the leg in the cast. The leg became discolored and pulseless, and a foul odor developed. The nursing staff complained to the administrator and the physician in charge. The cast was ventilated but the odor continued. Ultimately the leg was amputated. The physician settled out of court. The nurses were not held negligent because they followed the accepted guidelines and procedure. The hospital bylaws provided for the consultation of another physician upon the request of the administrator. The administrators maintained that the hospital had provided the "brick" and "mortar" (the facilities) in which health care took place and that they had acted as all other hospital administrators would have acted. The court found the administrators negligent in their relationship to the patient by not requiring a consultation as provided in the hospital bylaws. It held that hospitals do much more than just furnish treatment facilities; they also assume certain responsibilities for the care of the patient.

Therefore, if the hospital is going to be held liable for professional medical decisions, administrators will likely exercise greater control over the practice of medicine within its facilities. Liability for patient care will result in the hospital's imposing more of its rules and regulations on the physicians, raising the standards of qualification required for staff privileges, and generally reducing the amount of professional discretion and autonomy physicians have traditionally been allowed to exercise. Thus, control by hospital administrators may affect not only professional discretion, but also professional effectiveness as the practitioners within the hospital are provided with better coordination of services and staff support. Enhanced coordination and control of services are already being provided hospital administrators through the information systems made available by modern computer technology. In all probability, the hospital administration in both nonprofit and profit-making hospitals will have increased control over the staff in the future through computerization of information used as a basis for decision making.

[2]See *Darling* v. *Charleston Community Hospital* 33 Ill. 2d 326, 211 N.E. 253 (1965), 50 Ill. App. 2d 253, cert. denied, 383 U.S. 946 (1966).

THE HOSPITAL–PATIENT ROLE

While hospital services are oriented toward a supportive notion of patient welfare, hospital rules and regulations are generally designed for the benefit of hospital personnel so that the work of treating large numbers of patients can be more efficient and easier to perform. Consequently, the sick and the injured are organized into various patient categories (maternity-obstetrics, neurology, orthopedics, urology, pediatrics, psychiatry) that reflect the medical staff's definition of their disorder and are then usually subject to standardized, staff-approved medical treatment and administrative procedures.

While it can be argued that standardizing patient care results in increased organizational efficiency—and ultimately serves the best interest of the patient—a prominent theme of the hospitalization experience noted by medical sociologists has been that of depersonalization. Erving Goffman (1961), for example, describes the status of mental hospital patients as akin to being "nonpersons," while Coe (1978) believes that patients in general tend to be devalued by hospital personnel because they are sick and dependent. H. Jack Geiger (1975:13), an M.D., illustrates the feelings of depersonalization in hospital care by commenting on his own experience as a patient:

> I had to be hospitalized, suddenly and urgently, *on my own ward*. In the space of only an hour or two, I went from apparent health and well-being to pain, disability, and fear, and from staff to inmate in a total institution. At one moment I was a physician: elite, technically skilled, vested with authority, wielding power over others, affectively neutral. The next moment I was a patient: dependent, anxious, sanctioned in illness only if I was cooperative. A protected dependency and the promise of effective technical help were mine—If I accepted a considerable degree of psychological and social servitude.

Geiger was subsequently placed in the ward's only private room, which he believed was more for the benefit of the staff than for himself. He felt that had he been placed among the other patients, lending objective credence to physician "mortality," the patients might have used the situation to reduce status and role barriers between themselves and the staff. Furthermore, Geiger learned what he now believes is the major reason why physicians make such "notoriously terrible patients." It was not because their technical knowledge caused them to be more fearful of the consequences of their disorder or more critical of the way it was treated. Instead it was the loss of their professional role and authority in the medical setting, which Geiger surmises is an integral part of their self-concept.

The same situation is seen in a study by Christopher McKevitt and Myfanwy Morgan (1997) of doctors in Great Britain who had recently been ill. Being a patient was described as "difficult" and "embarrassing," and many resisted the idea of admitting they were ill. Physicians seemed to minimize their symptoms and those of other doctors. One doctor in a group practice said he was amazed that his colleagues did not take more notice that he was having trouble breathing. He told one doctor that he had a pain in his chest when he took a deep breath. The other doctor replied, "Don't take a deep breath" (McKevitt and Morgan 1977:649). Being so ill as being unable to cope with one's daily tasks was considered something to be avoided at all costs, especially if it led to hospitalization. As one female psychiatrist admitted to a hospital with a psychiatric illness put it:

> I was horrified, just horrified. I was working on the day I went into hospital. I was like, working in the bin—to being part of the bin! I found it hard to mix with other patients because, you know,—these are *patients*. It was hard to say "I'm a patient. I'm part of this group." Accepting that was like going lower and lower. (McKevitt and Morgan 1997:650)

Personnel in hospitals do not have the express goal of making their patients feel depersonalized, but the organization of the hospital's work does favor rules and regulations that reduce patient autonomy and encourage patient receptivity of the hospital routine. Yet it should be noted that the process of depersonalization is not just a result of the manner in which large numbers of patients are managed or the work conditions; it is also related to the patient's subjective experience of feeling sick. Howard Leventhal (1975) has explained that most reports of depersonalization commonly cite the experience of one's self as a physical object or thing. A second common experience is the feeling that one's own psychological self is isolated from other psychological selves (other people). Furthermore, Leventhal suggests that bodily symptoms such as pain can create a sense of separation within the individual of the physical self from the conscious psychological self. This inner alienation, in addition to the feeling of isolation from others, compounded by the doubt, uncertainty, and confusion that often accompany feelings of illness, can create for patients a sense of inadequacy and inability to control their lives. Leventhal's argument is that this attitude of incompetency is further intensified by the patient's having to assume an institutional role like the sick role, in which he or she is officially dependent and excluded from decision making. The process of depersonalization is undoubtedly enhanced by the need of the physician or nurse to have access to the patient's body. However legitimate this may be, Coe (1978) points out that the exposure and giving over of one's body to strangers can be a degrading and humiliating experience, even though it is intended to be therapeutic.

Stripping, Control of Resources, and Restriction of Mobility

Coe (1978) states that patients are alienated from their usual lives and reduced to a largely impersonal status in the hospital through three basic mechanisms of hospital processing: (1) stripping, (2) control of resources, and (3) restriction of mobility. Coe explains that when patients present themselves for treatment in a hospital, they bring with them a particular social identity, what Goffman refers to as a "face" (see Chapter 4); this represents their attitudes, beliefs, values, concept of self, and social status, all of which form the basis for their manner of presenting themselves to the world. *Stripping* occurs when the hospital systematically divests the person of these past representations of self. The patient's clothes are taken away and replaced with a set of pajamas; regardless of whether the pajamas are the property of the hospital or the patient, the simple fact of wearing pajamas serves as a uniform that identifies that person as sick and restricts movement to those areas of the hospital in which pajamas (patient dress) are authorized. Personal belongings of value are taken away and locked up for safekeeping by the staff. Visiting regulations control not only when patients are allowed to have visitors, but also who is allowed to visit (children under age fourteen are typically excluded). In addition, the staff supervises the patient's diet, decides when the patient should be asleep or awake, and in essence controls the general conduct of the patient's social life in the hospital. The hospital routine for one patient is very similar to the routine of others having the same or similar health problems.

Another important feature of hospitalization is the *control of resources* by the staff. Coe includes under the control of resources not only physical items, like bedclothes and toilet paper, but also the control of information about the patient's medical condition. Patients are normally not aware of their prognosis or the results of laboratory tests and X-rays unless the physician decides to inform them.

The third aspect of depersonalization outlined by Coe is the *restriction of mobility*. In most hospitals patients are not allowed to leave their wards without the permission of the head nurse, who is usually required to know the location of all patients at all times; when patients do leave the ward to travel to another area of the hospital, they are generally accompanied by a nurse, nurse's aide, or orderly. When patients are admitted to the hospital and also when discharged, they are taken in a wheelchair between the ward and the hospital entrance regardless of their ability to walk because the hospital is "responsible" for them whenever they are inside its walls. The result is that even the ability of patients to move about is supervised and controlled.

Conforming Attitudes

Some patients may be so seriously ill that feelings of depersonalization do not enter the picture. All they desire is to get well, and they are happy to do or experience whatever is necessary to accomplish that goal. That is, they are quite willing to conform to the situation.

Yet this assumption may not be entirely correct. In a study of hospital patients in New York City, Judith Lorber (1975) found that conforming attitudes were common among cancer patients but not among patients hospitalized for very serious surgery. Lorber suggests that the cancer patients may have been scared by the ambiguities of the information they received. One woman, for example, refused to believe her doctor was telling her the truth after she had a tumor removed and it was found to be benign. Serious surgery patients, however, were much better informed about their illnesses, yet they behaved more "deviantly" (were troublesome, uncooperative, and complaining) than the cancer patients. Their somewhat lengthy stays in the hospital had not generally resulted in their complete acceptance of the staff's model of the "good" (obedient) patient. Thus, seriousness of a patient's illness was not a good predictor of whether a patient would conform to hospital routine.

The best attitude predictors, according to Lorber, were age and education: the younger and better educated the patient, the less likely was the patient to express highly conforming attitudes. Conversely, the older and more poorly educated patients were the least likely to express deviant attitudes. Yet among college-educated patients, Lorber found those patients over sixty years of age to be moderately conforming, while those under sixty tended to adopt "deviant" attitudes. This latter finding is consistent with other studies (Cartwright 1964; Coser 1956), which suggest that younger patients tend to be more aggressive about seeking information in the hospital and less conforming, while older patients tend to be more submissive to hospital rules.

Lorber (1975:220) also examined the attitudes of the doctors and nurses toward the patients, and her analysis of staff evaluations suggested the important finding that "ease of management was the basic criterion for a label of good patient, and that patients who took time and attention felt to be unwarranted by their illness tended to be labeled problem patients. In short," Lorber (1975:220) says, "the less of a doctor's time the patient took, the better he or she was viewed." Patients who had a tendency to complain or be uncooperative or overemotional were generally considered to be a problem only by the particular staff member who had cause to interact with them. The key variable, therefore, in how the doctors and nurses defined the patients was the amount of time from the staff that the patient demanded. Interestingly enough, Lorber reported that some staff members labeled certain patients as "good" if they couldn't remember them very well.

A question remains as to what actions physicians and nurses take to deal with troublesome hospital patients. Some studies (B. Glaser and Strauss 1965; Green and Platt 1997) suggest that staff members tend to avoid patients who are not liked or who are uncooperative; sometimes particularly bothersome patients will be reprimanded or scolded. Lorber found that the usual method of handling difficult patients in a New York City hospital was to prescribe tranquilizers or sedatives. If drugs did not accomplish the desired cooperation, then disruptive patients might on occasion be sent home or transferred to a convalescent center with trained psychiatric nurses. Lorber's general impression was that the hospital staff tended to treat the short-term, paying patients in a permissive fashion and put up with the problems they caused. It remains to be seen if the staff would have been as tolerant had the patients been hospitalized on a long-term, charity basis.

The Sick Role for Hospital Patients

To Parsons's (1951) concept of the sick role, which emphasizes patient cooperation and striving to get well, we may now add that of the hospitalized sick role, which apparently includes an obligation to accept hospital routine without protest. Lorber (1975:214) notes the similarities between Parsons's sick role and the role of the hospital patient. Both are universalistic, affectively neutral, functionally specific, and collectivity oriented. However, a major difference between them, Lorber observes, is that the idea of voluntary cooperation, one-to-one intimacy, and conditional permissiveness (being temporarily excused from normal social activities on the condition of seeking medical advice and care) applies primarily to the relationship between an outpatient and a private physician. Inpatient care subjects the hospital patient to a role additionally characterized by submission to authority, enforced cooperation, and depersonalized status.

Coe (1978) has suggested that acquiescence is the most common form of patient adjustment to hospital routine and the most successful for short-stay patients in terms of the quality of their interaction with the hospital staff. Basically, all the attitudes of the hospitalized sick role are results of the necessity for a well-established work routine for hospital staff. As Rose Laub Coser (1956) has pointed out, in meeting the medical needs of patients, the hospital demands that its patients give up substantial rationality about the direction and nature of their personal activities in favor of the functional rationality of organizational life.

THE RISING COST OF HOSPITALIZATION

Any discussion of American hospitals would be incomplete without considering the financial cost of hospitalization, which has risen more sharply in recent years than any other aspect of medical care. For purposes of comparison, John Knowles (1973) indicates that in 1925 the cost of one day's stay as a patient at the Massachusetts General Hospital in Boston was $3.00, and the bill was paid entirely by the patient. By 2000, however, the average one-day cost of hospitalization had risen to $1,149, with most of the expense paid by a third party such as a private health insurance company—Blue Cross, Blue Shield, or some other hospital-medical plan—or Medicare, Medicaid, or a state welfare agency. Not only did costs increase significantly, but the manner of payment has also changed, as about 90 percent of all expenses for hospital services are now paid by third-party sources. In some cases, third-party coverage has led to increased hospital admission rates, since health needs that are met in the physician's office are often not covered by insurance. Hospitalization can therefore reduce the patient's direct cost of health care. But this does not mean that patients escape paying hospital bills. Government expenditures are paid out of tax revenues, while private health insurance costs must also be covered and private companies are set up to make a profit.

Overall health expenditures in the United States in 2000 amounted to $1,299.5 billion, of which $395.4 billion was spent on hospital care. Thus, about 30 percent of all the money spent on health in the United States is spent on hospital services. What does the hospital do with its income? Knowles explains that hospital expenses are categorized as either routine or ancillary costs. Routine costs are those expenses of providing room and board, including the provision of several different diets of three meals a day served in bed; the cost of nonmedical supplies and equipment; the salaries of all members of the hospital's nonmedical staff; and the salaries of medical technicians, nurses, auxiliary nursing workers, and residents who are available to patients on a twenty-four-hour basis, seven days a week. Ancillary expenses include the cost of laboratories, the pharmacy, operating rooms, X-ray rooms, cast rooms, and other specialized hospital facilities, plus the cost of all medical supplies. Even though patients do not get to see or even use all of a hospital's facilities, the cost of maintaining and operating these facilities for those patients who do use them continues regardless.

The most expensive hospitals in the United States are located in New England and on the Pacific Coast, while the least expensive are found in the South and in some of the Rocky Mountain states. Supposedly, regional differences in the cost of hospitalization are related to regional differences in the overall cost of living. Other factors that have been found to be important in determining hospital costs are the ratio of personnel to total expenses (the cost of labor is higher in high-cost hospitals) and the patient occupancy rate (low-cost hospitals tend to have relatively high occupancy rates). Hospital costs also rise from increased costs for labor, medical equipment, supplies, and new construction.

However, the cost of paperwork is also significant. Steffie Woolhandler and his associates (Woolhandler, Himmelstein, and Lewontin 1993) suggest that hospitals in the United States could save $50 billion annually if they required less paperwork and utilized one form for all health insurance claims as is done in Canada. For example, a hospital in the Canadian province of British Columbia employed one clerk to process insurance claims; a few miles away in an American hospital of the same size in the state of Washington, forty-five clerks were employed full time to handle insurance claims. Canada, with its system of national health insurance, uses a single claim form. Yet the United States—with government-sponsored Medicare and Medicaid health insurance programs and numerous private health insurance companies requiring various deductions and copayments and providing different levels of coverage—has a complex and administratively burdensome approach to filing claims.

Technological innovations have also been identified as an important cause of rising hospital costs. However, as William Rushing (1984) points out, innovations in technology are not always translated into higher hospital costs. New technology increases hospital costs when the innovations are used by only a few patients and require the training and employment of increased numbers of specialists and superspecialists. Furthermore, physicians are often dependent upon the technology based in hospitals, and the technology needs to be available for the hospital to support its relationships with doctors. Consequently, public expectations, the nature of hospital services, and physician–hospital relationships all combine to encourage a hospital to have the most recent innovations regardless of whether such innovations are cost effective.

What can be done about controlling hospital costs? One improvement would be a single uniform insurance claim form that would reduce the amount of paperwork and the need for armies of clerks to process claims. Another improvement would be basic health insurance coverage for everyone. If all patients carried a basic coverage, hospitals could rely on a steady stream of income and not suffer serious financial losses for treating the uninsured. Many of America's uninsured rely on hospital emergency rooms for primary care. Inappropriate use of costly emergency services contributes to the rising cost of health care—especially when the cost of care cannot be recovered. Federal law requires hospitals to accept patients in emergency rooms and prevents them from turning away emergency patients who cannot pay until their condition is stabilized. This requirement forces hospitals to accept acutely ill or injured patients through their emergency rooms regardless of insurance status. It also encourages the uninsured to use emergency rooms for primary care, since they know it is difficult or impossible to be treated at a private doctor's office without adequate funds or insurance coverage. With universal coverage, everyone could visit doctor's offices or use less expensive hospital facilities during normal working hours.

One measure, instituted in 1983, is federal legislation that establishes a fixed rate for each procedure (according to which DRG, or diagnostic related group, the procedure falls under) that the government will pay hospitals for patients insured by Medicare. In the past, Medicare, which covers the elderly, paid hospitals for whatever it reasonably cost them to treat Medicare patients. The more hospitals spent, the more the government paid. If the spending had continued unchecked, the Medicare hospital insurance trust fund would have been depleted by 1988. Some states passed legislation aimed at regulating hospital rates, limiting construction of hospitals and nursing homes, and encouraging doctors to lower their fees. Private insurance companies also took steps to set fixed rates so hospital expenses for publicly insured patients would not be passed on to them.

Hospitals responded by expanding services and controlling costs in ways that ensured their survival (Gay et al. 1989; Potter 2001; Stevens 1989). While some hospitals have been more successful than others in this regard, Rosemary Stevens (1989:324) points out that "hospitals naturally responded to DRGs, as they had to other government programs in the past, with an eye to maintaining their own income, expanding rather than contracting their overall services, and to solidifying their competitive position." Even not-for-profit hospitals have to buy new technology, replace worn equipment, and maintain or improve their physical plant—besides meeting rising labor and energy costs and dealing with inflation. Throughout the twentieth century, as Stevens observes, not-for-profit hospitals have been profit-maximizing enterprises, even though they viewed themselves as charities serving the community and still, to some extent, are charities in that they discount or write off some services for the poor. On balance, however, the record of American hospitals in meeting the health needs of the socially disadvantaged is not good, and Stevens explains that disparities in services between social classes is a major challenge to the ideals of hospital services today.

Whenever the prices of goods and services in general increase, the cost of health care and hospitalization can be expected to rise accordingly. The principal social policy issues today with respect to American hospitals are to limit costs in such a way that hospital care is kept within a reasonable relationship to the rest of the economy and the needs of all Americans for hospitalization are met.

SUMMARY

This chapter has reviewed the hospital's evolving role as a community institution intended to serve the needs of sick and injured people as a form of social responsibility. Passing through stages of being a center for religious practice, a poorhouse, and a deathhouse, the hospital has finally come to be a center for medical technology designed to handle the health problems of all members of society, not just the lower classes.

Today in the United States hospitals can be classified in terms of their type of ownership (voluntary or nonprofit, profit-making, or government owned) and by their type of service (general medical-surgical or specialty). The largest single type of hospital in the United States is voluntary and general medical-surgical. These hospitals are nominally supervised by a governing body, such as a board of trustees, but actually exhibit a dual system of authority: administrative and medical. Although hospitals are supposedly oriented toward the welfare of the patient, a significant body of literature in medical sociology is concerned with the fact that treating large numbers of people has resulted in organizational procedures that tend to depersonalize the individual patient. The final section of the chapter dealt with the rising cost of hospitalization, which has become a major social issue.

HOSPITALS INTERNET SITES

1. American Hospital Association.
   http://www.aha.org

   National organization that represents all types of hospitals, health care networks, and their patients and communities.

2. Health Research and Educational Trust.
   http://www.hospitalconnect.com/aha/hret

   HRET is a not-for-profit organization involved in research, education, and demonstration programs addressing health management and policy issues.

3. Institute for Diversity in Health Management.
   http://www.diversityconnection.org

   A nonprofit organization that collaborates with educators and health services organizations to make minority youth more aware that health services management is a viable career option.

4. American Hospital Directory.
   http://www.ahd.com

   Provides free information on any hospital in the United States regarding services provided, financial information, and utilization services.

5. Hospital Web.
   http://neuro-www2.mgh.harvard.edu/hospitalwebworld.html

   Links to hospitals throughout the world.

6. Blue Cross and Blue Shield (homepage).
   http://www.bluecares.com

7. Ultimate Insurance Links.
   http://www.barryklein.com

   Complete list with links to life and health insurance companies in the United States.

Health Care Delivery and Social Policy in the United States

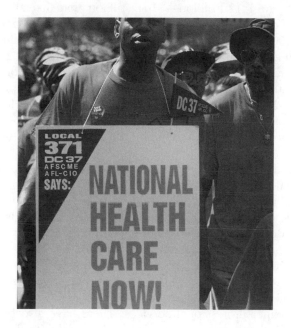

The central issues in the public debate about health care delivery in the United States are those of cost, equity, and the distribution of services. No other single issue in medicine has attracted more public attention in recent years than the rising cost of health care and the diminished ability of certain segments of American society to obtain health services adequate for their needs. Despite living in a wealthy country, a substantial portion of the American population does without even minimally adequate health care. The Americans most affected by the sharply escalating costs of medical services include not only the poor but also the near poor who are unable to contend with rising costs. Furthermore, the proportion of the population without health insurance has increased. About 13.9 percent of the population under the age of 65 did not have health insurance in 1990; this figure rose to 16.8 percent by 2000.

RISING COSTS

In 1980, an average of $1,063 per person was spent on health care in the United States; by 2000 this figure had risen to $4,637—the highest in the world by far. For comparative purposes, Switzerland (based upon 1998 figures) spent $2,853 per person on health which was second highest in the world that year, while Mexico spent $419 and Turkey $318 per capita. United States' figures for 1998 were $4,177 per person. Not only is health spending in the United States the highest in the world, but the jump to $4,637 per capita for 2000 also represents a sizeable increase over both 1998 and 1999 ($4,377). Moreover, health spending in 2001 soared to an average of $5,035 per person—the highest ever.

Also in 1980, Americans spent a total of $247.3 billion on health needs, as compared to expenditures of $1.3 trillion in 2000 and $1.4 billion in 2001. Hospital costs alone in 2000 were $412.1 billion—$164.8 billion more than all health expenditures in 1980. Hospital care and prescription drugs accounted for 45 percent of the increased spending in 2000. Spending on hospital care rose by $19.9 billion, or 5.1 percent, to $412.1 billion in 2000 and rose again by 8.3 percent to $451.2 billion in 2001. Drug spending increased $17.9 billion, or 16.4 percent, to $121.8 billion in 2000 and 15.6 percent to $140.6 billion in 2001. Total national spending on prescription drugs doubled between 1995–2000 and tripled between 1990–2000. Hospitals accounted for 31.7 percent of all health spending in 2000, down from 42 percent in 1982, while drugs were 9.4 percent of total spending on health in 2000. This is more than double the percentage spent in 1982.

The rapid increase in drug expenditures has been due not only to the aging of the population but also to the effects of prescription drug advertising, the wider availability of insurance to cover drug costs, an increase in the number of prescriptions written by doctors, and a shift toward greater use of new, high-price drugs. Some drugs can reduce health spending by lowering the need for hospital care, but that is not the case for all drugs. Figure 14-1 shows the annual health care spending in the United States between 1960 and 2000, adjusted for inflation in 1996 dollars, since 1996 is the base year set by the federal government. The greatest increases overall since 1960 shown in Figure 14-1 are for hospital care and doctors, dentists, and other professional services. There have also been recent significant increases in nursing homes and home health care due to the aging of the population and prescription drugs. Some $92.2 billion was spent in 2000 on nursing home care.

Another illustration of the increase and the magnitude of the cost of health care in American society can be found in an examination of the U.S. consumer price index. As in most other nations of the world, the cost of goods and services has been steadily rising. Table 14-1, however, shows that between 1982–1984 and 2001 the cost of medical care increased more (172.8 percent) than any other major category of personal expense. The increase in the cost of medical care exceeded the rise in cost of all items combined between 1982–1984 and 2001.

Within the general category of medical care, Table 14-2 shows the increase in the costs of various subcategories of items. The greatest single increase since 1982–1984 has been in the cost of hospital and related services (238.3 percent); this

FIGURE 14-1　Annual Health Care Spending, United States, 1960–2000.

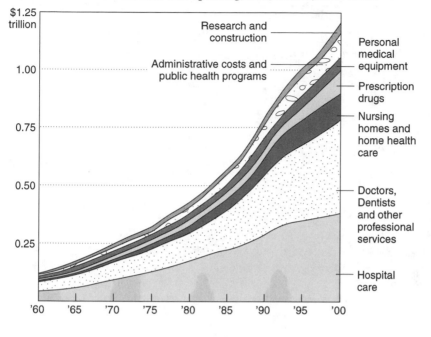

BOX 14-1　Health Spending in 2001

Spending on health care in the United States is increasing at the fastest rate in several years as the controls of managed care are loosening and there is greater use of hospitals and drugs by an aging population. In 2001, the most recent year figures are available, health spending rose 8.7 percent to a total of $1.4 trillion and represented 14.1 percent of the GDP. This is the largest share of the GDP on record. The United States devotes more of its economy to health care than any other country.

While there was some increase in the cost of medical care, the primary catalyst for spending was the *quantity* of care required by a population that is getting older. Medicare costs rose 7.8 percent in 2001 and Medicaid spending rose 10.8 percent. The fastest growing category of health spending was on prescription drugs. Some $140.6 billion was spent on drugs in 2001 that represents an increase of 15.7 percent over spending in 2000. This is a smaller percentage of increase than that shown for the year 2000 (16.4 percent) and 1999 (19.7 percent), as copayments were increased by managed care plans and the greater use of generic drugs was encouraged. Nevertheless, the cost of drugs is still high and not likely to be easily reduced as the demand continues, especially for the elderly. Spending for doctors rose 8.6 percent in 2001 to $313.6 billion, while the costs of hospitals was $451.2 billion for an increase of 8.3 percent. Measures to contain health care costs generally are likely to be major features of the nation's policy agenda in the coming years.

TABLE 14-1   Consumer Price Index, United States, Selected Years, 1950–2001.

Year	All Items	Medical Care	Food	Apparel and Upkeep	Housing	Energy
1950	24.1	15.1	25.4	40.3	—	—
1955	26.8	18.2	27.8	42.9	—	—
1960	29.6	22.3	30.0	45.7	—	22.4
1965	31.5	25.2	32.2	47.8	—	22.9
1970	38.8	34.0	39.2	59.2	36.4	25.5
1975	53.8	47.5	59.8	72.5	50.7	42.1
1980	82.4	74.9	86.8	90.9	81.1	86.0
1985	107.6	113.5	105.6	105.0	107.7	101.6
1990	130.7	162.8	132.4	124.1	128.5	102.1
1991	136.2	177.0	136.3	128.7	133.6	102.5
1992	140.3	190.1	137.9	131.9	137.5	103.0
1993	144.5	201.4	140.9	133.7	141.2	104.2
1994	148.2	211.0	144.3	133.4	144.8	104.6
1995	152.4	220.5	148.4	132.0	148.5	105.2
1996	156.9	228.2	153.3	131.7	152.8	110.1
1997	160.5	234.6	157.3	132.9	156.8	111.5
1998	163.0	242.1	160.7	133.0	160.4	102.9
1999	163.0	250.6	164.1	131.3	163.9	106.6
2000	172.2	260.8	167.8	129.6	169.6	124.6
2001	177.1	272.8	173.1	129.3	176.4	129.3

NOTE: 1982–1984 = 100.

Source: U.S. Department of Labor, as quoted in National Center for Health Statistics, *Health, United States, 2002* (Washington, D.C.: U.S. Government Printing Office, 2002).

category is followed by increases in prescription drugs (200.9 percent). Physician services rose 153.6 percent.

The greatest innovation in the delivery of health services during the 1980s and 1990s was in the area of cost containment, and little was accomplished with respect to problems of equity and distribution of services (L. Brown 1986; Grey 1991, 1997; Sleeper et al. 1998). In the public sector, the federal government instituted cost controls for services to Medicare patients by establishing set fees for diagnostic related groups (DRGs). As Mary Ruggie (1992) points out, the use of DRGs demonstrates the government's increasing role in controlling costs. "Government," states Ruggie (1992:939), "is no longer inclined to accept charges set by health care providers but is instead prepared to lead the pattern of funding in its own direction." In the private sector, business corporations increasingly turned to lower-cost health maintenance organizations and preferred provider organizations (PPOs) to provide health care to their employees. Some corporations required second opinions from other doctors before surgery could be scheduled, and some required data from insurance carriers to enable them to evaluate the performance of doctors and hospitals serving

TABLE 14-2 Consumer Price Index for All Items and Medical Care Components, United States, Selected Years, 1950–2001.

Item and Medical Care Component	CONSUMER PRICE INDEX										
	1950	1960	1965	1970	1975	1980	1985	1990	1995	1998	2001
CPI, all items	24.1	29.6	31.5	33.8	53.8	82.4	107.6	130.7	152.4	163.0	177.1
Less medical care	—	30.2	32.0	39.2	54.3	82.8	107.2	128.8	148.6	158.6	171.9
CPI, all services	16.9	24.1	26.6	35.0	48.0	77.9	109.9	139.2	168.7	184.2	203.4
All medical care	15.1	22.3	25.2	34.0	47.5	74.9	113.5	162.8	220.5	242.1	272.8
Medical care services	12.8	19.5	22.7	32.3	46.6	74.8	113.2	162.7	224.2	246.8	278.8
Professional medical services	—	—	—	37.0	50.8	77.9	113.5	156.1	201.0	222.2	246.5
Physicians' services	15.7	21.9	25.1	34.5	48.1	76.5	113.3	160.8	208.8	229.5	253.6
Dental services	21.0	27.0	30.3	39.2	53.2	78.9	114.2	155.8	206.8	236.2	269.0
Eye care[1]	—	—	—	—	—	—	—	117.3	137.0	144.1	154.5
Services by other medical professionals[1]	—	—	—	—	—	—	—	120.2	143.9	155.4	167.3
Hospital and related services	—	—	—	—	—	69.2	116.1	178.0	257.8	287.5	338.3
Hospital rooms	4.9	9.3	12.3	23.6	38.3	68.0	115.4	175.4	251.2	—	—
Inpatient hospital services[2]	—	—	—	—	—	—	—	—	—	104.0	121.0
Outpatient hospital services[1]	—	—	—	—	—	—	—	138.7	204.6	233.2	281.1
Medical care commodities	39.7	46.9	45.0	46.5	53.3	75.4	115.2	163.4	204.5	221.8	247.6
Prescription drugs	43.4	54.0	47.8	47.4	51.2	72.5	120.1	181.7	235.0	258.6	300.9
Nonprescription drugs and medical supplies[1]	—	—	—	—	—	—	—	120.6	140.5	147.7	150.6
Internal and respiratory over-the-counter drugs	—	—	39.0	42.3	51.8	74.9	112.2	145.9	167.0	175.4	178.9
Nonprescription medical equipment and supplies	—	—	—	—	—	79.2	109.6	138.0	166.3	174.9	178.2

NOTE: 1982–1984 = 100, except where noted.
[1]Dec. 1986 = 100.
[2]Dec. 1996 = 100.

Source: U.S. Department of Labor, as quoted in National Center for Health Statistics, *Health, United States, 2002* (Washington, D.C.: U.S. Government Printing Office, 2002).

their employees. Many firms also increased the amount that their employees had to pay out of their own pockets for health care.

Managed Care

Thus, in the early to mid-1990s, private health care in the United States experienced a dramatic reorganization into managed care plans. Changing from a largely office-based, fee-for-service system to an increasingly group or organization-based managed care system, American medical practice took on a dramatically different new structure (Pescosolido and Boyer 2001; Pescosolido, Tuch, and Martin 2002). Some of this restructuring was in response to the anticipated health reforms of the Clinton administration, and some was due to a "buyer's revolt" by business corporations and insurance companies seeking to control health care costs by controlling medical work (Budrys 2001; Hafferty and Light 1995; Sleeper et al. 1998; Stevens 2001). By 1998, some 61 percent of all Americans with health insurance were enrolled in managed care programs; in 1988, only some 29 percent of the insured were members of such plans. Managed care, as noted in Chapter 11, refers to health organizations, like HMOs and PPOs, that "manage" or control the cost of health care by monitoring the work of doctors and hospitals, limiting visits to specialists within a particular managed care network and to all physicians outside it, and requiring prior authorization for hospitalization.

Managed care alters the patient–physician relationship by introducing a third party—the case manager—to the decision-making process. The case manager represents the bill payer, usually an insurance company, who certifies that the care to be rendered is both effective and the least costly alternative. The case manager also authorizes hospitalization. Another feature of managed care is its reliance upon capitation financing. Capitation (per capita) financing is a fixed monthly sum paid by the subscriber and his or her employer that guarantees care to that person and the person's immediate family with little or no additional cost. Health care providers, in turn, must provide necessary care and are not paid for any additional services. This measure discourages inefficient and unnecessary treatment.

Patients are also allowed to see a specialist only after being screened by the primary care physician who routinely cares for them. Since specialist care is usually more costly, the primary care physician serves as a gatekeeper to the use of specialists and is usually rewarded by keeping referrals to a minimum. Finally, patients are required to use the physicians within the managed care network—unless the subscriber or a family member has a medical emergency outside the plan's geographical area.

The current cost containment effort in U.S. health care had its origins in the federal government's effort to control payments to providers of Medicare services by the introduction of DRGs. Hospitals, in turn, sought to shift some of their costs from government payers to private payers, primarily health insurance companies. The insurance companies responded by playing a more substantial role in the organization and management of the use of services through managed care programs. No longer is managed care the alternative health care delivery model that it once was, rather it has become the dominant model (Pescosolido and Boyer 2001).

Some medical sociologists now argue that the first "social contract" between medicine and American society for health care featuring fee-for-service reimbursement, physician dominance, and limited government intervention has been replaced by a second one (Hafferty and Light 1995; Pescosolido and Boyer 2001; Pescosolido, McLeod, and Alegría 2000). The second social contract involves third-party reimbursements, greater use of nonphysician providers, and direct government involvement in financing and regulation. As Bernice Pescosolido and Carol Boyer (2001:186) point out: "The nature of the second social contract has significantly altered the powerful position of physicians, making them more subject to limitations set by those who fund their services and the demands of those employers who purchase managed care plans." This situation has led to a dramatic decline of their influence in the private medical market in the United States (F. Stevens 2001).

Has managed care controlled costs? The answer appears to be that the system has kept rising costs in check until recently. Between 1993 and 1997, health care's portion of the GDP fluctuated around 13.5 percent. In 1995, the U.S. Department of Commerce estimated that national health expenditures would exceed 15 percent of the GDP; however, only 13.4 percent of the GDP was spent on health that year—the smallest increase in several years. And by 1997, the percentage of the GDP had fallen to 13.1 percent. But by 2001, the percentage of the GDP spent on health care had risen to 14.1 percent and the total amount of spending had soared to $1.4 trillion. If health spending continues to increase as it did in 2001, then the percentage of the GDP spent on health care is certain to rise if expenditures in other sectors decrease with the slowing of the economy. Moreover, pressure from patients, physicians, and employers to give patients more choice in obtaining services have, for example, ended the requirement to obtain approval from a primary care physician before seeing a specialist in some managed care programs. And rising costs within managed care plans have resulted in higher insurance premiums and copayments. It is therefore too early to ascertain whether managed care can keep a cap on costs—especially for the long term.

EQUITY IN HEALTH SERVICES

The problem of equity with respect to health services is and remains a serious problem in American society. In a free market system lacking national health insurance, those persons who are economically disadvantaged are also medically disadvantaged when it comes to obtaining quality services. As discussed in Chapter 6, the United States has a two-track system of health care delivery divided into a private track and a public track. The public track is a system of welfare medicine supported by public health insurance, especially Medicaid (for the poor) but also Medicare (for the elderly).

As Bruce Vladeck (1983) explained several years ago, public health insurance has provided access to the American health care delivery system for the poor, but the character of the services rendered—that of welfare medicine—has not changed dramatically. The urban poor have historically been dependent on public hospitals and clinics rather than private hospitals and practitioners for providing patient care. And that is still the case today for many of the poor and near poor as physicians, pharmacists, and hospitals have joined banks, supermarkets, and department stores in migrating out of inner-city areas where the poor are concentrated. Vladeck (1983:9) describes the situation as follows:

> Apart from whatever esthetic differences such a pattern might imply, the fact remains that the poor—and to an even greater extent, the near-poor, who lack even the limited access to private physicians Medicaid provides—have no continuing relationship with individual physicians. This means that access to other services resides in the hands of bureaucratic strangers. The poor and near-poor are more likely to be admitted to hospitals through emergency rooms than a scheduled admission, and more likely to be sicker when they are admitted. They are more likely to be treated by a foreign medical graduate, or a house staff physician still in training (or both) than a fully trained American graduate. Their drug prescriptions are written by physicians with less personal knowledge and understanding of the patients' characteristics and problems, and they are likely to be seen on a follow-up visit by a physician other than the one who treated them originally.

The rural poor likewise have problems of access to health care as medical facilities and health practitioners may not be available locally. And the rural poor (as other people living in rural areas) also may be more likely to be treated by foreign medical school graduates. This situation is brought on by the doctor shortage in these areas caused by a reluctance of many American-trained physicians to work in small communities. Another segment of society particularly affected by problems of equity is the large number of Americans—over 16 percent of the population—who do not have health insurance. The largest proportion of persons (67 percent) without health insurance in 2001 were those whose family income was less than $40,000. Most individuals and families without health insurance make too much money to qualify for Medicaid but still struggle financially.

Without health insurance or available cash, people can be and are turned away from hospitals and sent elsewhere. Ultimately, they may be sent to "hospitals of last resort," which are generally public hospitals under the jurisdiction of city, county, or state governments. These hospitals are the ones that accept patients other hospitals refuse to treat because of an inability to pay for services.

DISTRIBUTION OF SERVICES

Besides problems with rising costs and equity, the American system of health care delivery is not evenly distributed geographically, and primary care or family practitioners are underrepresented among physicians.

A major factor in obtaining adequate medical care for some people is the numerical shortage of physicians serving patients in rural areas and urban slums. Physicians generally prefer to practice medicine in urbanized settings where they are close to cultural, educational, and recreational facilities. Another advantage of an urban practice is its proximity to extensive technological resources in the form of well-equipped hospitals, clinics, and laboratories staffed by well-trained personnel. Also important are the relationships with colleagues, which tend to enhance professional life, and these relationships are more readily available in urban areas where there are greater opportunities for professional recognition. And finally, it should be recognized that the more financially rewarding medical practices are those in large cities.

The maldistribution of physicians in the United States can be illustrated by comparing differences between predominantly urban and rural states. Differences within states are even larger. One out of every twenty counties in the United States does not have a single doctor, and more than half of all counties do not have a pediatrician. Even though small communities often advertise and try actively to recruit physicians, many doctors remain attracted to urban life.

The physician shortage is not limited to rural areas, however; it also extends into certain urban locales. Physicians in private practice are seldom found in neighborhoods characterized by large numbers of poor and nonwhite residents. Areas whose residents have relatively low levels of education and income tend to have proportionately fewer medical doctors in private practice. Consequently, shortages of physicians may exist in parts of New York City as well as in rural Alaska and Texas.

But there are a few signs that the distribution of physicians is beginning to improve. Part of this development is due to market conditions. Some areas have an oversupply of doctors, which encourages others to look elsewhere for establishing their practice. Also, rural areas with only one physician for every 3,500 or more people and poverty areas with only one doctor per 3,000 or more are eligible to apply for doctors under the National Health Service Corps (NHSC), a federally funded program designed to recruit and help organize the practices of health providers such as physicians, osteopaths, dentists, and physician assistants for isolated and low-income areas. Physicians who volunteer for NHSC service are paid financial incentives for joining, and medical students are given scholarships in return for participation in the program after graduation. For every year of support, the medical student is required to serve a year in the corps. In addition, other programs exist, such as the Rural Practice Project funded by the Robert Wood Johnson Foundation and administered by the School of Medicine at the University of North Carolina. This project, which has pilot programs in several states, matches a physician in a rural area with a health care administrator to provide improved services to medically deprived people.

Another factor in the maldistribution of physicians is that of overspecialization, which has reduced the number of doctors engaged as general practitioners in primary care and family practice. The number of general and family practitioners declined substantially from 95,980 in 1949 to 60,049 in 1980; but, by 2000, there was an increase to 83,165.

A major reason for the trend in specialization has to do with the complexities of modern medicine. At Cornell Medical School, Patricia Kendall and Hanan Selvin (1957) noted years ago that as students progressed through medical school, more and more of them began to express a preference for specialized training. Kendall and Selvin found that the reason for the tendency to specialize was the students' desire to restrict themselves to a particular area of knowledge with which they could be highly skillful, rather than trying to deal with an insurmountable body of knowledge. In addition, a specialized and more manageable area of medicine may be less demanding of personal time, has more prestige, and provides a greater income.

There are more than thirty specialty boards affiliated with the AMA that certify physicians to practice in as many as eighty medical specialties such as internal medicine, pediatrics, anesthesiology, family practice, obstetrics, gynecology, dermatology, psychiatry, general surgery, orthopedic surgery, urology, ophthalmology, and neurology. While medical specialization has produced positive benefits by allowing physicians to concentrate their efforts upon treating certain parts of the body, it has produced negative side effects in that it made it more difficult to find a physician to take on continuing responsibility for the "whole" patient.

The relatively low number and availability of primary care practitioners inhibits the access of patients to the health care delivery system in the United States. Hospital emergency rooms thus become centers of primary care because of the lack of general practitioners, the reluctance of physicians to make house calls, and the unavailability of private physicians in the urban inner city. Also relevant is the fact that hospital emergency rooms are accessible, have a minimum of administrative barriers, and have the resources of an entire hospital behind them. The people who tend to utilize emergency rooms for primary care are the underprivileged who have minimal social ties and no other regular source of medical care.

OVERVIEW OF HEALTH CARE DELIVERY

The existing health care delivery system in the United States is a conglomerate of health practitioners, agencies, and institutions, all of which operate more or less independently. The greatest portion of all patient services, approximately 80 percent, is provided in the offices of private physicians, who sell their services on a fee-for-service arrangement. About two-thirds of the 690,128 active physicians are involved in direct patient care work in an office- or clinic-based practice, while the remainder are mostly residents in training, or full-time staff members of hospitals.

The next most prominent form of health care delivery consists of services provided by hospitals. With the exception of tax-supported government institutions, hospitals, like physicians, charge patients according to a fee-for-service system. Nonprofit hospitals charge patients for hospital services from the standpoint of recovering the full cost of services provided and meeting the hospital's general expenses. Proprietary hospitals not only calculate the cost of services rendered but also function to realize a profit from those services. Nonprofit and profit-making hospitals rely heavily on third-party sources, either private health insurance or government agencies, to pay most or all of a patient's bill.

Besides office-based medical practices and hospitals, the other types of organizations involved in the delivery of health care to the American public are official agencies, voluntary agencies, health maintenance organizations, preferred provider organizations, and allied health enterprises in the business community.

Official agencies are public organizations supported by tax funds, such as the U.S. Department of Health and Human Services, the Centers for Disease Control and Prevention, the U.S. Public Health Service, and the Food and Drug Administration, which are intended to support and conduct research, develop educational materials, and provide services designed to minimize public health problems. Official agencies also have the responsibility for the direct medical care and health services required by special populations like reservation Indians, the military, veterans, the mentally ill, lepers, tuberculosis patients, alcoholics, and drug addicts.

Voluntary agencies are charitable organizations, such as the Multiple Sclerosis Society, the American Cancer Society, and the March of Dimes, who solicit funds from the general public and use them to support medical research and provide services for disease victims.

Health maintenance organizations (HMOs) are managed care prepaid group practices in which a person pays a monthly premium for comprehensive health care services. HMOs are oriented toward preventive and ambulatory services intended to reduce hospitalization. Under this arrangement, HMOs derive greater income from keeping their patients healthy and not having to pay for their hospital expenses than they would if large numbers of their subscribers were hospitalized. There is evidence that HMOs and other managed care organizations reduce hospital use and produce lower overall medical costs than the traditional open-market fee-for-service pattern (Gold 1991; Wholey and Burns 2000). Most of the savings are due to lower rates of hospitalization, but surgical rates are also especially low for HMO populations. Physicians participating in HMOs may be paid according to a fee-for-service schedule, but many are paid a salary or on a capitation (set amount per patient) basis. Membership entitles patients to receive physicians' services, hospitalization, laboratory tests, X-rays, and perhaps prescription drugs and other health needs at little or no additional cost.

There are some disadvantages to HMOs, namely that patients (especially at night or on weekends) may be treated by whoever is on duty rather than their "own" doctors, and a patient may need a referral from his or her primary care practitioner to consult a specialist. HMOs have attracted considerable attention because of their cost control potential and emphasis on preventive care. The number of HMOs and their enrollment have been rapidly increasing in the last few years. In 1970 there were 37 HMOs serving 3 million people; in 2001 there were 541 HMOs enrolling 79.5 million people.

Preferred provider organizations (PPOs) are a relatively new form of managed care health organization in which employers who purchase group health insurance agree to send their employees to particular hospitals or doctors in return for discounts. PPOs have the advantage of being imposed on existing networks of hospitals and physicians without having to build clinics or convert doctors into employees. Doctors and hospitals associated with a PPO are expected to provide their usual services to PPO members, but lower charges are assessed against the members' group health insurance. Thus, the health care providers obtain more patients and in return charge less to the buyer of group insurance. Nationally, PPOs had 105 million members in 1998.

Allied health enterprises are the manufacturers of pharmaceuticals and medical supplies and equipment which play a major role in research, development, and distribution of medical goods.

The majority of Americans have health insurance benefits provided through their place of employment and paid for by contributions from both the employee and employer. In 1984, some 96 percent of all insured workers were enrolled in traditional health plans that allowed them to choose their own doctors and have most of their costs for physician and hospital services covered in an unmanaged fee-for-service arrangement. However, this situation changed dramatically because of soaring costs of health care and limitations being placed on the insurance benefits provided. By 1998, only 15 percent of all insured workers had unmanaged fee-for-service health plans, while the remainder had managed fee-for-service plans in which utilization was monitored and prior approval for some benefits, like hospitalization, was required. The day in which doctors and their patients decided just between themselves what care was needed without considering cost appears over, as financial concerns are increasingly influencing how patients are cared for.

Some features of the health care delivery system in the United States remain unchanged. As Marsha Gold (1999) points out, the system is still pluralist; that is, it is characterized by more than one major client: a substantial private sector, the elderly and the poor with government-sponsored health insurance, and a large uninsured population. But there has also been widespread change, with both government and private corporations (employers) dominating health policy as the major purchasers of health services and supporting managed care as the primary form of medical practice. This development means that more people with private health insurance are now limited in their use of health services to a particular managed care network, such as an HMO or PPO. Moreover, as Gold (1999:14) explains, "Physician practice is shifting away from its historical roots in self-employment toward group and salaried arrangements that are better positioned to meet the current demands on providers stemming from both the shift to managed care and growth of medical technology." Physician incomes are increasing less rapidly than in the past, and professional autonomy, as previously noted, is declining as well.

Given the magnitude of these changes—the reorganization of medical practice into managed care, along with constraints on income and autonomy—it is not surprising, as Gold (1999:14) points out, that the satisfaction of physicians with their work situation has decreased. However, as Mary Warren and her associates (Warren, Weitz, and Kulis 1998:364) explain, "Whereas physicians twenty years ago may have been horrified at the prospect of managed care, physicians now accept it as the rules of the game—at least in areas in which high percentages of patients belong to such plans—and recognize that the price of refusing to play by those rules is bankruptcy." Thus, many physicians have had to make the adjustment to managed care, and the revenue, especially capitation fees, from this type of practice now constitutes a growing percentage of physician incomes.

Traditionally, doctors and hospitals have been paid on a fee-for-service basis. This method of payment is consistent with the principle of the open market, in which the consumers of health care, like the consumers of other products, are free to choose which health care providers offer the best services at prices they can afford. High-quality services and affordable prices are supposed to result from competition among providers. Theoretically, physicians who are incompetent or who charge excessive fees and hospitals with lower-quality services would be driven out of the market by more competent, reasonably priced, and more effective physicians and better hospitals. To eliminate or reduce free choice would supposedly undermine the incentive of physicians and hospitals to satisfy patients.

The fee-for-service system is a highly attractive situation for doctors. It allows physicians to decide how much money they should charge for their services, how many patients they should have, how many hours they should work per week, what branch of medicine they should specialize in, and where they should practice medicine. The market, professional ethics, and sense of duty to their patients are supposed to block any desire to make as much money as possible.

Fee-for-service health care delivery, however, is not a good example of a competitive marketplace. The fundamental law of the marketplace is supply and demand. When the supply of a product exceeds the demand for it, prices should drop. However, that law does not apply to medicine because physicians define what patients need and provide their services at prices they set. Therefore, doctors and hospitals create their own demand. Organized medicine has traditionally opposed changing the fee-for-service system because of the advantages it provides the profession. Yet fee-for-service discriminates against those people who are unable to pay the fees, making them dependent on welfare or charity. It also contributes to increased costs through high fees and the unnecessary duplication of technology and services by various providers and hospitals seeking to gain or maintain income. Rising costs and lack of universal access to quality care finally forced changes, beginning with Medicare and Medicaid in the 1960s, and continuing today with the dominance of managed care systems charging a set capitation fee to patients each month.

SOCIAL LEGISLATION IN HEALTH CARE

The medical profession in the United States has had a consistent record of resistance to social legislation seeking to reduce the authority, privileges, and income of physicians (Marmor 1999; Skocpol 1995; D. Smith 2002; Starr 1982). With the exception of some individual doctors, the profession as a group has opposed workmen's compensation laws, social security and voluntary health insurance in their initial stages, Medicare and Medicaid, and the creation of professional standards review organizations (PSROs) to review the work of physicians involved in federally funded programs. The medical profession has also opposed the expansion of health maintenance organizations and strongly resisted proposals for national health insurance. "In short," Ernest Saward (1973:129) states, "the organized medical profession has repeatedly been on the negative side of social issues where the general public has been on the affirmative side."

Medicare and Medicaid: Passage and Programs

For more than forty years, the AMA fought successfully to block the passage of any federal health care legislation that threatened the fee-for-service system or that advocated national health insurance. By the early 1960s, however, it was clear to most segments of society that private health insurance had not met the needs of the aged and the poor (Budrys 1987, 2001; Marmor 1999; Starr 1982). A considerable portion of the literature in medical sociology during the 1950s and 1960s, for instance, documented the disadvantaged position of the elderly and the poor in obtaining adequate health care in American society. Several sociological and political factors thus combined to influence the drafting of laws to provide hospital insurance for the aged—the commitments of Presidents John F. Kennedy and Lyndon B. Johnson; the changed composition of the U.S. Senate in 1962 and the U.S. House of Representatives in 1964; the lack of past effective health care legislation; the continuing increase in the cost of medical care; and perhaps the lessening credibility of the AMA, which claimed that "physicians cared for the elderly" and "knew their health needs better than anyone else" or that federal health insurance was incompatible with "good" medicine (Stevens 1971:438–439).

Despite the strong resistance of the medical profession, Congress passed the Medicare and Medicaid amendments of the Social Security Act in 1965. Although these amendments were compromises between what was ideal and what was politically feasible, their passage marked a watershed in the history of medical politics in the United States as Congress for the first time emerged as a dominant voice in health care delivery and demonstrated that the direction of medical practice might no longer be the sole prerogative of organized medicine (Marmor 1999; Pescosolido and Boyer 2001; Skocpol 1995). In addition, the resistance of the medical profession to Medicare brought home the point to the general public and lawmakers that the medical profession could not always be relied upon to place the public's interest ahead of the profession's interest.

Medicare   Medicare is a federally administered program providing hospital insurance (part A) and supplemental medical insurance (part B) for people sixty-five years or older, regardless of financial resources; disabled people under the age of sixty-five who receive cash benefits from Social Security or railroad retirement programs; and certain victims of chronic kidney disease. Medicare offers two plans: the Original Medicare Plan and Medicare plus Choice. The hospital insurance benefits (part A) under the Original Medicare Plan in 2002 include (1) 150 days of hospitalization; (2) care in a skilled nursing facility (nursing home) for up to 100 days after three days of hospitalization; (3) home health care after hospitalization; and (4) hospice care. Supplementary Medicare insurance benefits (part B) include (1) physician services, certain non-routine services of podiatrists, limited services of chiropractors, and the services of independently practicing physical therapists; (2) certain medical and health services, such as diagnostic services, diagnostic X-ray tests, laboratory tests, and other services, including ambulance services, some medical supplies, appliances, and equipment; (3) outpatient hospital services; (4) home health services (with no requirement of prior hospitalization) for up to 100 visits in one calendar year; and (5) outpatient physical and speech therapy services provided by approved therapists.

There are specified deductible and coinsurance amounts for which the beneficiary is responsible. The deductible in 2002 on the hospital insurance (part A) was $792 for a hospital stay of 1–60 days, $198 per day for days 61–90, and $396 per day for days 91–150. All hospital costs are paid by the patient after 150 days. There is no cost for the first twenty days of nursing home care and copayments of $99 per day for days 21–100. Home health care services are covered and varying copayments are required for hospice care. The deductible on the medical insurance (part B) was $100, with a 20 percent coinsurance amount also required for most part B services. After a beneficiary pays the first $100 for part B services, Medicare pays 80 percent of the charges it approves. The hospital insurance is financed primarily through social security payroll deductions, while the medical insurance plan, whose participation is voluntary, is financed by premiums paid by the enrollees and from federal funds. The medical insurance premium was $50 a month.

Medicare plus Choice plans link Medicare benefits with either managed care plans like HMOs or private fee-for-service plans. Enrollees receive all of their Medicare benefits under the original plan, but may get extra benefits like prescription drugs or additional days in the hospital. However, there may be additional expenses of monthly premiums, higher and more frequent copayments, and additional charges for the type of care needed.

The Medicare program is under the overall direction of the Secretary of Health and Human Services and is supervised by the Bureau of Health Insurance of the Social Security Administration. Most of the day-to-day operations of Medicare are performed by commercial insurance companies and Blue Cross/Blue Shield plans that review claims and make payments. Requests for payment are submitted by the provider of services; reimbursement is made on the basis of reasonable charges as determined by the private insurance companies who issue the payments. In 2000, a total of $221.8 billion in Medicare benefits were paid under coverage that extends to 39.6 million elderly and disabled people.

Medicaid   Medicaid is technically a welfare program. It provides for the federal government's sharing in the payments made by state welfare agencies to health care providers for services rendered to the poor. Medicaid provides, to the states, federal matching funds ranging from 50 to 80 percent, depending on the per capita income of the states involved. Each state is required to cover all needy persons receiving cash assistance. Eligible health care services include inpatient and outpatient hospital services, laboratory and X-ray services, skilled nursing home services, and physicians' services, plus other forms of health care covered at the option of the individual states. For instance, it permits states to include not only the financially needy but also the medically needy, the aged, blind, and disabled poor, as well as their dependent children and families. In 1986, Congress passed legislation extending Medicaid coverage to children under five years of age and pregnant women with incomes below the poverty level, which in 1999 was $17,029 annually for a family of four.

In 2000, 40.6 million people received Medicaid benefits and the cost to federal and state governments was $142.3 billion. Medicaid was originally intended to cover people on welfare, but the extension of benefits to children and pregnant women from low-income families, who may or may not be on welfare, indicates that the insurance is also being used to cover people with medical expenses who have no other source of health insurance. However, since Medicaid is administered by the states, not the federal government, it is subject to variation in levels of benefits.

Medicare and Medicaid: Evaluation

Medicare and Medicaid were not designed to change the structure of health care in the United States. These programs did not place physicians under the supervision of the federal government nor attempt to control the distribution or quality of medical practice. Instead they were based on preexisting patterns of insurance coverage, involving the participation of private health insurance companies, and they allowed physicians to continue to set their own fees and conduct business as usual.

In fact, Medicare and Medicaid turned out to be a financial boon to organized medicine and to hospitals as they channeled billions of dollars into health care. It can also be argued that Medicare and Medicaid contributed to rising prices in health care as they provided the opportunity to pass excessive demands for payment on to insurance companies instead of to the patients themselves. Of course, the general public does not really escape from paying higher prices, as the costs of the programs have to be met through payroll deductions and tax revenues.

However, the problems in American health services are not just poor management and high incomes for physicians. The problems in fact go to the very core of medical practice—its purpose to provide quality medical care for the entire population. What Medicare and Medicaid have accomplished on a national scale is basically two highly important measures. First, these programs may have been expensive and may not have met all the needs of the aged and the poor for which they were intended, but they have provided needed health services for the old and those in poverty where these services were not previously available.

Second, Medicare and Medicaid established the precedent of the federal government's involvement in the administration of health care, and this involvement is the key to future health care planning and reorganization. And, according to Stevens, the time has long passed in the United States when the question of whether the federal government should intervene in health care delivery is debated. Federal government involvement in health care is now an important and substantial reality, and whatever happens in the future organization and scope of health care services in the United States is now dependent on federal government decisions.

One far-reaching measure is the 1983 federal legislation to curb Medicare spending by setting fixed amounts to be paid for services (DRGs) provided under its coverage. The new Medicare payment system was passed by Congress with relatively little debate as part of a plan to guarantee the financial status of the social security program. Hospitals make money if they keep costs below what Medicare pays, and they can lose money if their costs exceed the rate. Under the law, hospitals cannot collect additional money from Medicare patients if they find federal money does not pay the entire bill. This situation requires hospitals to be both cost conscious and more efficient when it comes to treating patients covered by Medicare.

A major overhaul of Medicare fees (the Physicians Payment Reform Act), passed in 1989, set fixed fees for physicians as well. This federal legislation lowered the amounts (by 20 percent) usually paid to doctors providing specialized services, such as those performed by surgeons and radiologists, while increasing amounts (by 40 percent) for general and family practitioners and internal medicine physicians for preventive care. A major goal was to focus Medicare more toward prevention and health maintenance than toward treatment per se, especially treatment involving very expensive medical procedures. The amount physicians can charge patients in excess of payments they receive from the government was also limited to 25 percent in 1992 and was 20 percent in 2000. Many physicians accept the amount paid by Medicare as payment in full.

Government spending for Medicare slowed until recently, but is now increasing. In the 1990s, spending had increased an average of $12.8 billion or 10 percent annually, but in 1998 it rose only $3.1 billion to $213.6 billion, and in 1999 Medicare spending fell for the first time in history to a total of $212 billion. Cuts mandated by Congress, low inflation, and efforts to eliminate fraud were the principal reasons for the decline. However, the continuing growth of the elderly population is expanding the number of persons eligible for Medicare, and this expansion makes future cost increases likely as the cost of care itself also rises. Rising costs caused Medicare expenditures to jump to $221.8 billion in 2000.

HEALTH REFORM

In the 1990s, the United States found itself the only First World country without national health insurance. The election of Bill Clinton to the United States presidency in 1992 marked the beginning of efforts to change this situation. All the problems of rising costs and increasing numbers of uninsured had pushed public demand for universal coverage to one of the top positions on the nation's political agenda. Previous presidential efforts had failed. Harry Truman had proposed a national health insurance program for all Americans in 1945 when health care costs consumed only 4 percent of GNP. But Truman's plan died in Congress after strong opposition from the AMA and concerns that such a program was a form of socialism. In 1974, Richard Nixon began pushing for a national health insurance scheme that was closely tied to the concept of HMOs, only to become politically crippled by the Watergate scandal that ultimately forced him to resign. Jimmy Carter suggested a plan during his first term in office but lost reelection in 1980. Only Lyndon Johnson had success with his limited reforms that established Medicare and Medicaid in 1965.

However, in the late 1980s and early 1990s, several new developments took place. First, large corporations like Chrysler, appalled by the rising costs of health care in conducting business, openly called for a national health insurance program. Second, Congress showed a willingness to expand Medicare benefits for the elderly and extend Medicaid benefits to children and pregnant women living below the poverty line, while considering legislation that would require small businesses to furnish health insurance to their employees. And third, several states took the lead in developing their own health insurance programs.

Hawaii was the first state to enact a health insurance program for its residents in 1974 that required all employers to contribute to an insurance program for their employees and provided financial assistance to small businesses in meeting the costs. The state plan, along with Medicare, Medicaid, and private insurance eventually resulted in 88 to 90 percent of the population in Hawaii—among the highest in the nation—having health insurance.[1] In 1994, Tennessee committed itself to becoming the first state to give health insurance to every uninsured person by converting its Medicaid program into the TennCare managed care program. For almost the same total cost, the new program provides health insurance to more residents by sharply limiting physician and hospital fees. Vermont provides health insurance to the poor for a nominal fee and guarantees free medical and dental care to all residents under the age of 18 with family incomes less than $50,000 annually. Programs to provide universal health coverage for low-wage workers and the uninsured have been enacted but not fully implemented for political or fiscal reasons in Florida, Massachusetts, Minnesota, Oregon, and Washington.

With most states turning their attention to cutting budget deficits, and not increasing expenditures on health care in the 1990s, the ranks of the uninsured under the age of 65, as previously noted, increased from 13.9 percent in 1990 to 16.8 percent in 2000. Particularly disadvantaged with respect to health insurance are racial/ethnic minorities, especially Mexican Americans, along with low-income workers (Seccombe and Amey 1995) and unmarried women (Meyer and Pavalko 1996). Rising costs and the growing numbers of uninsured persons resulted in greater public demands for the federal government to intervene to control costs and encouraged the Clinton administration to enact health reforms (Skocpol 1995).

The Clinton Plan

President Clinton announced his plan for national health insurance in 1993.[2] At the time, this plan or a modified version of it seemed likely to become reality. However, the proposal failed to clear Congress in 1994. Briefly stated, the Clinton plan provided a basic level of health insurance benefits to all legal residents of the United States. The proposed benefit package covered the services of physicians and other health care professionals, hospitals, emergency care, home health care, ambulances, outpatient laboratory tests, and other needs. Americans would have been enrolled in regional health alliances managed by the states. The alliances would have negotiated prices with health care networks and other providers, offered a range of programs, and collected premiums from employers and employees. The various health care networks would be organized and administered by insurance companies. Presumably, the majority of these health care networks would evolve into super HMOs in which physicians would be employees or under some contractual obligation to the network. All networks would be required to offer the

---

[1]States in 2000 with over 90 percent of population having some type of health insurance were Rhode Island (92.7), New Hampshire (92.1), and Pennsylvania (91.5). States with the lowest percentage of insured were New Mexico (73.3), Texas (76.4), Oklahoma (77.6), Louisiana (78.4), Montana (78.7), Florida (79.5), and Alaska (79.6).

[2]For details of the Clinton proposals, see Paul Starr, *The Logic of Health Care Reform*, rev. and enl. ed. (New York: Penguin Books, 1994); and White House Domestic Policy Council, *Health Security: The Official Text* (New York: Touchstone, 1993).

President Clinton holds up a proposed health security identification card while outlining his plan for health reform to a joint session of Congress in 1993. The plan was defeated.

same basic level of benefits but could compete for subscribers by offering lower prices and high quality.

The system would have been financed by health insurance premiums paid by individuals and families, with employers paying 80 percent of the premiums for their employees. Federal subsidies would have been available for small businesses, low-wage workers, and the unemployed to obtain coverage. A cap on out-of-pocket personal expenses would limit how much a family would have to pay for health care. All Americans would have been issued a national health identification card that would guarantee them access to needed services.

The financing of national health care would come not only from employers and employees but also from new taxes on items like cigarettes, savings from Medicaid, and spending limits on Medicare. Furthermore, in a major cost-reduction measure, there would be a standard medical claim form that would replace the hundreds of forms used by insurance companies today.

The effect of the Clinton administration proposals on the American health care delivery system would have been profound. These changes would involve the general population, federal and state governments, physicians, hospitals, and health insurance companies. First, all Americans and legal residents of the United States would have had guaranteed access to health care for the first time in history. Thus, the United States would join all other modern nations in providing universal or near-universal health care coverage. Second, the federal government would have become responsible for health care delivery for the nation as a whole. This would represent a major change in the function of the federal government and mean that access to health care had become a legal right for qualified persons. State governments, in turn, would be required to manage the regional health alliances within their jurisdiction.

When the plan was delivered to Congress in October, 1993, numerous interest groups lobbied legislators to adopt provisions favorable to them or to oppose it altogether. The issues and their solutions were complex, and delays in bringing the health reform bill forward through various congressional committees gave vested interests more time to mobilize. President Clinton also never successfully explained his plan to the American people and allowed his opponents to define it in negative terms (Skocpol 1996). The small business lobby strongly opposed measures requiring businesses with few employees to pay so much (80%) of the costs of health insurance for their workers. The AMA opposed government control over health care delivery and losses in income for doctors. Not only physicians, but hospitals, drug companies, and insurance companies were opposed to price controls or global caps on health spending; labor unions and the elderly were against losses or caps on health benefits they now have; and consumer groups were dissatisfied with the powerful position of insurance companies, copayments, deductibles, and the lack of immediate coverage for the uninsured. Lobbying efforts, lack of consensus between the Democrats and Republicans in Congress charged with drafting the legislation, and growing public uncertainty resulted in congressional inaction. In September 1994, the White House conceded there was no chance of passing national health insurance that year, but vowed to make it a priority again in 1995, which it did not do as the Republicans gained control of both the House and Senate in 1994. Weakened by a sexual scandal, leading to an unsuccessful impeachment trial, President Clinton was unable to advance national health care legislation as his term ended in early 2001.

The Clinton plan marks the most ambitious effort ever to bring national health insurance to the United States. However, some type of national health reform eventually seems likely. The reason is that the problems that brought on the struggle for national health insurance remain unresolved to date. As large numbers of people continue to go without health insurance coverage and those with insurance have benefits cut by employers and health insurance companies because of cost-saving measures, pressures to act are likely to resurface. To date, the Clinton plan appears to have had two major effects. First, it stimulated movement toward the massive reorganization of American health care into a delivery system in which managed care is now the dominant approach in the private sector. Second, it moved health to the forefront of domestic politics, with both the Democrats and Republicans in Congress recognizing that changes need to be made. One legacy of this situation is the passage by Congress in 1996 of the Health Insurance Reform Act, whose major provisions guarantee that workers in employer-sponsored health plans will be able to maintain their health insurance after changing or losing their jobs and bars insurance companies from denying coverage to people who have preexisting medical conditions.

HEALTH CARE: A RIGHT OR A PRIVILEGE?

According to Bryan Turner (1988), one way to understand politics in modern democracies is to view issues from the standpoint of conflict theory. Conflict theory takes the position that social inequality leads to conflict, which leads to change.

The conflict approach in sociology has its origins in the work of Karl Marx and Max Weber, but its modern focus is not just on class conflict but also on differences between interest groups as they maneuver for advantages in democratic political systems. Turner suggests that modern societies are characterized by conflict between democratic principles (which emphasize equality and universal rights) and the organization of economic services involving the production, exchange, and consumption of goods and services (which feature inequality). In other words, the ideology of advanced democracies promotes equality, but the reality of the capitalist economic system produces considerable inequality. Conflict, or tension, arises, states Turner, as democracies try to resolve this contradiction and bring equality to an economic system that is inherently unequal. It is therefore possible, concludes Turner (1988:52), "to conceptualize modern politics in terms of struggles by interest blocs and communities for political recognition of their needs and interests."

And this is exactly what is happening with respect to current measures at health reform. Several social scientists working in the tradition of conflict theory have argued that Americans would best be served by adopting a national health insurance system similar to those found in Europe (Navarro 1994, 1996; Waitzkin 1991, 2001). This argument is based on the traditional role of medical care as a commodity in the United States; that is, as a service to be bought and sold. Efforts to control costs are met with strong opposition because, as Paul Starr (1994) explains, the best organized interests in health benefit from the present system because the

About 16.8 percent of the American population did not have health insurance in 2000.

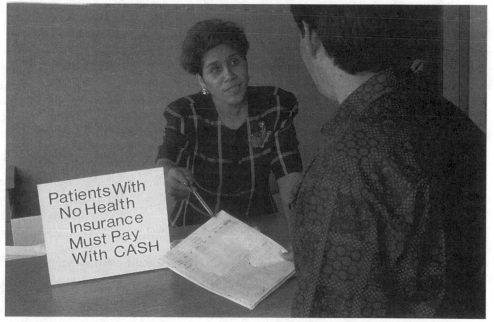

costs of health care equal incomes from health care. As Starr (1994: xxxvi–xxxvii) puts it:

> Rising costs have meant rising incomes; controlling costs means controlling incomes. The health care industry now represents a seventh of the U.S. economy, and the stakeholders in that industry—not just physicians, but hospitals, makers of medical equipment and pharmaceuticals, venture capitalists, and insurance companies—are not about to sit out a political battle that could so greatly affect their interests, in some cases their survival.

In the final analysis, what health reform is really about is the issue of whether medical care is a *right* of all Americans or whether it is a *privilege*. As a commodity, medical care is a privilege. One argument is that such care is indeed a privilege, not a right, and if people want medical treatment they should pay for it. The difficulty of the training and the high value of the skills required to become a physician, as well as the time and effort put into providing care, should entitle doctors to receive high incomes. Others in the health field should be appropriately reimbursed for their services, too. This argument should not necessarily be construed to mean that the poor are unworthy of receiving medical care. Behind this argument is a generalized opposition to the welfare state; it is felt that the best way to help the poor is to provide them with jobs so that they can *buy* medical care like everybody else. To give the poor the highest quality of medical care available without improving the conditions of poverty within which they live is thought to be an exercise in futility.

However, a more socially responsible argument is that medical care does represent a special case. More in the nature of an opportunity rather than a commodity, quality health care should be available as a right of all Americans, regardless of living conditions or financial status. Even though people have the ability through their choice of lifestyles and preventive measures to influence their health status, many health problems are beyond their control. For example, a person's health can be adversely affected by genetics, the environment, or even chance. While it seems reasonable for individuals to bear the responsibility for health outcomes based upon their informed and voluntary choice, people are not always fully informed about the consequences of their behavior, and some health problems arise that individuals are unable to contain on their own.

A society's commitment to health care reflects some of its most basic values about what it is to be a member of the human community. Therefore, it can be argued that society has an ethical obligation to ensure equitable access to health services by making that care a basic social right. This is because of health care's special importance to society in relieving suffering, preventing premature death, and restoring the ability to function to the people who live in it. The concept that the individual has a right to health care and society the ethical obligation to provide it has been accepted by those countries that have national health insurance coverage for its population.

Movement toward conceptualizing and establishing health care as a right in the capitalist economy of the United States is consistent with other measures associated with being a welfare state. The advent of the welfare state in Western society, as T. H. Marshall (1964) explained, is a culmination of processes that began in the eighteenth century. Marshall pointed out that the establishment of the welfare state is the latest phase in the evolution of citizens' rights in the West. To *civil* rights (gained in the eighteenth century), like freedom of speech and equality before the law, and *political* rights (acquired in the late eighteenth and nineteenth centuries), such as the right to vote and participate in the exercise of government, were added *social* rights (achieved in the late nineteenth and twentieth centuries) of protection from economic insecurity and the provision of at least a marginal level of economic welfare.

The emergence of these various rights of citizenship, all promoting equality, states Marshall, is a paradox, because they came during the same historical period as the rise of capitalism, which essentially is a system of inequality. Inequality in the capitalist system stems from the fact that it is based on private ownership of property and the gearing of economic activity to profit in the marketplace. Individuals are not equal in the amount of property they own or acquire, their position in relation to the production of goods and services in the marketplace, and the amount of profits (or losses) they derive from their work. As John Myles (1984:30) comments, "This marriage between a protective state and a capitalist economy was a union of opposites, for it required an accommodation between two opposing logics of distribution—one that attached rights to the possession of *property* and another that attached rights to *persons* in their capacity as citizens."

Essentially, what had taken place, in Marshall's (1964) view, was conflict between the rights of citizenship considered inherent in a democratic society by the general populace and the capitalist social class system. In the modern welfare state, individual rights of citizenship, not ownership and control of property, emerged as the basis for political representation and entitlement to public programs. Current efforts at health reform are an extension of the rights of citizenship to health care in the United States. Canada and the nations of the European Union have previously made health care a social right.

SUMMARY AND CONCLUSION

This chapter has examined the significant social debate regarding the rising cost of health care, problems in equity, and the unequal distribution of health services in the United States. These issues have been a focal point of concern in the interaction between medicine and society. Although organized medicine has consistently opposed social legislation that might affect the fee-for-service system of medical practice and the entrepreneurial role of the physician, the passage of Medicare and Medicaid signified the emergence of public awareness that the medical profession's interests were not always those of the general public. Efforts at health reform represent the beginning of a potentially profound change in the system of health care delivery in the United States—one that would guarantee access to health care for Americans and establish health as a social right.

HEALTH CARE DELIVERY AND SOCIAL POLICY IN THE UNITED STATES INTERNET SITES

1. Centers for Medicare and Medicaid Services (CMS).
   http://www.cms.hhs.gov

   The federal agency that administers the Medicare and Medicaid programs.

2. Medicare: The official U.S. government site for Medicare information.
   http://www.medicare.gov

3. CMS, Medicare.
   http://cms.hhs.gov/medicare

   Includes links to carrier directories, publications, eligibility, and enrollment.

4. CMS, Medicaid.
   http://cms.hhs.gov/medicaid

   Contains links with information to all aspects of Medicaid.

5. Medicaid, National Summary Statistics.
   http://cms.hhs.gov/medicaid/mcaidsad.asp

6. National Health Care Indicators and Expenditures, National Health Expenditures, 2000.
   http://cms.hhs.gov/statistics/nhe/historical/highlights.asp

   National Health Expenditures measure spending for health care in the United States by type of service delivered and source of funding for those services.

7. Physicians for a National Health Program.
   http://pnhp.org

   A network of more than 7,000 physicians and other health care workers that support universal access to health care.

Health Care in Developed Countries

To varying degrees, all nations of the world are faced with increased pressure of demands for quality health care and faced with rising costs of providing that care. This pressure has led to a renewed search for alternatives, among both developed and developing countries, with the result that interest and scholarship in the field of transnational studies of health systems have significantly increased (Cockerham 1999; Gallagher, Stewart, and Stratton 2000; Gallagher and Subedi 1995; Lassey, Lassey, and Jinks 1997; Lüschen et al. 1995; F. Stevens 2001; Subedi and Gallagher 1996; Wall 1996). In this chapter, the focus is on health care in developed countries other than the United States. Socialized forms of medicine common to Canada, Great Britain, and Sweden, will be discussed initially, followed by an examination of decentralized national health programs in Japan, Germany, the Netherlands, and France.

The value of studying the health care delivery systems of different countries is the insight provided into the norms, values, culture, and national outlook of those societies, as well as the lessons learned from their experiences. As Donald Light (1986) points out, medical care and health services are acts of political philosophy; therefore, social and political values underlie the choices made, the institutions formed, and the levels of funding provided. Consequently, a nation's approach to health care is based upon its historical experience, culture, economy, political ideology, social organization, level of education and standard of living, and attitudes toward welfare and the role of the state.

In Europe the provision of health services became an important component of government policy in the last half of the nineteenth century. Behind this development was the desire of various European governments for a healthy population whose productivity could be translated into economic and military power. In some countries, providing national health insurance was also a means to reduce political discontent and the threat of revolution from the working class. Compulsory health insurance was usually part of a larger program of social insurance intended to protect the income of workers when sick, disabled, unemployed, or elderly. Initially, protection was provided only to wage earners below a certain income level, but gradually benefits were extended to all or most of the population. Germany established the first system for national health insurance in 1883, followed by Austria in 1888, Switzerland and Great Britain in 1911, Russia in 1912, and the Netherlands in 1913.

Entitlements based on citizenship are aimed at providing people with welfare and health benefits, regardless of their position in society. The social welfare systems of Europe are more advanced in this direction than in the United States. Many Europeans receive comprehensive health insurance; protection of lost income due to illness, injury, or unemployment; and allowances to supplement family expenses for the maintenance of children, such as clothing and school lunches. These benefits are provided to all citizens, the affluent and the nonaffluent alike.

It was not until 1965 and the passage of Medicare and Medicaid that the United States provided health care benefits for some Americans—the aged and the poor. When European governments were introducing social insurance programs around the beginning of the twentieth century, the U.S. government was not deeply involved in regulating either the economy or health services, nor was there a significant threat of social revolution from discontented workers. Moreover, Americans have traditionally been less committed to government welfare programs and more in favor of private enterprise in dealing with economic and social problems. Except for the elderly, participation in the welfare system is not considered normative in the United States, and those Americans who do receive welfare tend to be stigmatized and socially devalued (L. Mead 1985). But in Europe, providing welfare and social security for the general population, not just the poor and elderly, is a normal feature of the state's role. This situation implies a fundamental difference in the social values of Americans and Europeans, with Americans stressing individualism and Europeans viewing government in a more paternalistic fashion.

The result is that European governments are typically responsible for the delivery of health care and most of its financing. For example, nearly 78 percent of all health costs in the European Union are financed from public sources, either through national health insurance or direct payments by the state (Schneider et al. 1994). The United States, in contrast, finances only some 40 to 45 percent of its health costs annually with public money, mostly in the form of payments from the federal government. The remaining 55 to 60 percent is privately financed through commercial insurance companies and out-of-pocket costs borne by patients. No European country nor Japan has such a high level of private financing as the United States.

Not only does the United States have a significantly higher level of private financing, but it also spends more on health than any other country in the world. Table 15-1 shows the total health expenditures as a percentage of gross domestic product for selected countries for 1960–1999. In 1960, the United States was second only to Canada in health spending but forged into a tie for first place in 1970 and has been first ever since—except for 1980 when Sweden spent a higher percentage of its GDP. Table 15-1 shows that for 1999, the United States spent 13.1 percent of its GDP on health, followed by France at 9.4 percent. The country with the lowest percentage of health expenditures among the countries shown in Table 15-1 for

TABLE 15-1   Total Health Expenditures as a Percentage of Gross Domestic Product: Selected Countries, Selected Years, 1960–1999.

Country	1960	1965	1970	1975	1980	1985	1990	1995	1999
Australia	4.3	4.9	5.4	5.7	7.0	7.5	7.9	8.2	—
Austria	4.3	5.0	5.3	7.3	7.6	6.6	7.1	8.5	8.2
Belgium	3.4	3.9	4.0	5.8	6.4	7.2	7.4	8.7	8.8
Canada	5.4	6.1	7.0	7.3	7.1	8.3	9.0	9.3	9.3
Czech Republic	—	—	—	—	3.8	4.5	5.0	7.3	7.4
Denmark	3.6	4.8	6.1	6.5	9.1	8.7	8.5	8.2	8.4
Finland	3.9	4.9	5.6	6.3	6.4	7.2	7.9	7.5	6.8
France	4.1	5.2	5.7	6.8	7.4	8.3	8.6	9.6	9.4
Germany	4.7	5.1	6.3	7.8	8.8	9.3	8.7	10.2	—
Greece	3.1	3.6	5.6	—	6.5	—	7.5	8.9	—
Hungary	—	—	—	—	—	—	6.6	7.5	—
Iceland	3.3	2.8	4.9	5.9	6.1	7.2	7.9	8.2	8.7
Ireland	3.6	4.4	5.1	7.7	8.4	7.6	6.7	7.3	—
Italy	3.6	4.0	5.1	5.8	7.0	7.0	8.1	7.9	8.2
Japan	3.0	4.3	4.6	5.5	6.5	6.7	6.1	7.2	—
Mexico	—	—	—	—	—	—	4.4	5.6	—
Netherlands	3.9	4.4	6.0	7.7	8.0	7.8	8.5	8.9	8.7
New Zealand	4.3	4.5	5.2	6.4	6.0	5.3	7.0	7.3	8.1
Norway	2.9	3.9	4.4	6.7	7.0	7.8	8.0	8.0	9.3
Poland	—	—	—	—	—	—	5.3	6.0	6.2
Portugal	—	—	—	6.4	5.6	6.1	6.2	7.6	—
Spain	1.5	2.7	3.6	5.1	5.4	5.4	6.6	7.0	—
Sweden	4.5	5.6	6.9	8.0	9.1	8.7	8.5	8.1	—
Switzerland	4.8	3.8	5.4	7.0	7.3	7.7	8.3	9.6	—
United Kingdom	3.9	4.1	4.5	5.5	5.6	5.9	6.0	6.9	6.9
United States	5.1	6.0	7.0	8.4	8.8	10.1	12.0	13.4	13.1

Source: National Center for Health Statistics, *Health, United States, 2002* (Washington, D.C.: U.S. Government Printing Office, 2002).

TABLE 15-2   Per Capita Health Expenditures: Selected Countries, Selected Years, 1960–1999.

Country	1960	1965	1970	1975	1980	1985	1990	1995	1999
Australia	$ 89	$125	$212	$443	$ 663	$ 998	$1,318	$1,792	—
Austria	64	92	159	377	663	816	1,205	1,834	2,014
Belgium	53	82	130	310	578	884	1,247	1,906	2,181
Canada	109	151	260	434	710	1,193	1,678	2,128	2,463
Czech Republic	—	—	—	—	—	—	576	901	983
Denmark	—	—	—	—	819	1,177	1,453	1,882	2,275
Finland	54	92	163	312	510	849	1,292	1,421	1,547
France	72	120	206	393	701	1,082	1,520	1,991	2,125
Germany	77	129	224	462	824	1,242	1,602	2,178	—
Greece	21	27	100	104	345	—	707	1,139	—
Hungary	—	—	—	—	—	—	—	678	
Iceland	50	85	137	294	576	947	1,376	1,823	2,287
Ireland	35	50	98	233	455	592	796	1,319	—
Italy	49	80	154	286	579	831	1,327	1,589	1,905
Japan	26	62	130	260	523	818	1,082	1,632	—
Mexico	—	—	—	—	—	—	260	388	—
Netherlands	—	101	207	414	715	961	1,403	2,714	2,543
New Zealand	90	—	174	359	456	587	937	1,244	1,506
Norway	46	75	131	311	632	915	1,363	1,864	2,612
Poland	—	—	—	—	—	—	258	420	535
Portugal	—	—	45	154	260	381	614	1,050	—
Spain	14	37	82	190	325	454	815	1,068	—
Sweden	89	146	270	477	850	1,172	1,492	1,622	—
Switzerland	132	137	279	522	854	1,251	1,782	2,477	—
United Kingdom	74	99	144	277	444	669	968	1,301	1,569
United States	141	202	341	582	1,052	1,735	2,688	3,637	4,377

Source: National Center for Health Statistics, *Health, United States, 2002* (Washington, D.C.: U.S. Government Printing Office, 2002).

1999 is Poland (6.2 percent). However, information for several countries for 1999 is missing but the pattern for 1995 is much the same with the United States showing the highest expenditures and Mexico and Poland the lowest.

Another measure of health costs is per capita health expenditures. Table 15-2 shows that the United States spent more per capita from 1960 to 1999 than any other country. For 1999, the most recent year shown in Table 15-2, the United States spent $4,377 per capita on health. Poland was last with expenditures of $535. More recent figures for the United States for 2001, not shown in Table 15-2, show health spending is 14.1 percent of the GDP and $5,035 per capita.

The American health care delivery system is clearly the most expensive in the world. Yet on the two most common measures of a country's overall level of health—infant mortality and life expectancy—the United States does not rank especially high. As shown in Table 15-3, Sweden had the lowest infant mortality rate in the

TABLE 15-3   Infant Mortality Rates: Selected Countries, 1990 and 1998.

Country	INFANT MORTALITY RATE	
	1990	1998
	Infant deaths per 1,000 live births	
Sweden	6.0	3.5
Japan	4.6	3.6
Norway	7.0	4.0
Finland	5.6	4.1
Singapore	6.7	4.2
France	7.3	4.6
Germany	7.0	4.6
Denmark	7.4	4.7
Switzerland	6.8	4.8
Austria	7.8	4.9
Australia	8.2	5.0
Czech Republic	10.1	5.2
Netherlands	7.1	5.2
Canada	7.7	5.3
Italy	8.0	5.3
Scotland	7.7	5.5
New Zealand	8.3	5.5
Belgium	7.9	5.6
England and Wales	7.9	5.7
Greece	9.3	5.7
Spain	7.6	5.7
Israel	9.8	5.7
Portugal	10.9	5.9
Ireland	8.2	6.2
Cuba	10.7	7.1
United States	9.2	7.2
Slovakia	13.5	8.8
Kuwait	17.3	9.4
Poland	16.0	9.5
Hungary	14.8	9.7
Puerto Rico	14.8	10.5
Chile	16.8	10.9
Costa Rica	—	12.6
Bulgaria	14.8	14.4
Russia	17.6	16.4
Romania	30.1	20.5

Source: U.S. National Center for Health Statistics, *Health, United States,* 2002 (Washington, D.C.: U.S. Government Printing Office, 2002).

world at 3.5 per 1,000 live births in 1998. Japan was second with a rate of 3.6 infant deaths per 1,000 live births. The United States was ranked twenty-eighth with an infant mortality in 1998 of 7.2 per 1,000 live births, which ranked the United States just behind Cuba and just ahead of Slovakia.

As for life expectancy, perhaps the best overall single measure of a nation's health, Table 15-4 shows that Japan had the highest life expectancy for males at 77.2

TABLE 15-4   Life Expectancy at Birth, According to Sex: Selected Countries, 1997.

MALE		FEMALE	
Country	Life Expectancy in Years	Country	Life Expectancy in Years
Japan	77.2	Japan	83.8
Sweden	76.7	France	82.2
Switzerland	76.3	Switzerland	82.1
Canada	75.8	Spain	81.9
Greece	75.6	Sweden	81.8
Australia	75.6	Canada	81.4
Norway	75.5	Italy	80.3
Netherlands	75.2	Australia	80.8
Italy	74.9	Norway	81.0
Spain	74.9	Greece	80.8
New Zealand	74.9	Belgium	80.6
United Kingdom	74.7	Netherlands	80.6
France	74.6	Austria	80.6
Finland	74.6	Germany	80.5
Belgium	74.3	Finland	80.5
Austria	74.3	New Zealand	80.1
Germany	74.0	United Kingdom	79.6
Costa Rica	74.0	Costa Rica	79.5
United States	73.6	United States	79.4
Denmark	73.6	Puerto Rico	79.3
Ireland	73.4	Portugal	78.8
Portugal	71.6	Ireland	78.6
Puerto Rico	71.4	Denmark	78.4
Czech Republic	70.5	Czech Republic	77.5
Slovakia	68.9	Poland	77.0
Poland	68.5	Slovakia	76.7
Bulgaria	67.0	Hungary	75.1
Hungary	66.4	Bulgaria	73.8
Romania	64.6	Romania	73.4
Russia	62.0	Russia	73.0

Source: U.S. National Center for Health Statistics, *Health, United States, 2002* (Washington, D.C.: U.S. Government Printing Office, 2002).

years in 1997. Next are Sweden, Switzerland, and Canada. The United States ranked nineteenth in male life expectancy at 73.6 years. Table 15-4 indicates that males in Costa Rica lived longer on average than their American counterparts. For females, Table 15-4 shows Japan with the highest life expectancy at 83.8 years for 1997. France was next at 82.2 years, followed by Switzerland and Spain. The United States is shown in Table 15-4 to have had a life expectancy of 79.4 years, which is the nineteenth highest ranking, behind Costa Rica and just ahead of Puerto Rico.

SOCIALIZED MEDICINE: CANADA, GREAT BRITAIN, AND SWEDEN

A summary of the key features of fee-for-service, socialized medicine, decentralized national health programs, and socialist medicine health care systems is shown in Table 15-5 (see also Field 1989). Socialist systems are undergoing massive changes in Russia and other ex-communist nations in Eastern Europe. At present, the former communist states appear headed more toward the socialized medicine approach. We will now examine socialized medicine, beginning with Canada.

Socialized medicine refers to a system of health care delivery in which health care is provided in the form of a state-supported consumer service. That is, health care is purchased, but the buyer is the government, which makes the services available at little or no additional cost to the consumer. There are several different forms of socialized medicine, and the types that exist in Canada, Great Britain, and Sweden will be discussed in this section. Despite some differences between countries, what is common to all systems of socialized medicine is that the government (1) directly controls the financing and organization of health service in a capitalist economy, (2) directly pays providers, (3) owns most of the facilities (Canada is an exception), (4) guarantees equal access to the general population, and (5) allows some private care for patients willing to be responsible for their own expenses.

TABLE 15-5   Types of Health Care Delivery Systems.

Role of Government	TYPES OF SYSTEMS			
	Fee-for-Service	Socialized Medicine	Decentralized National Health	Socialist Medicine
Regulation	limited	direct	indirect	direct
Payments to providers	limited	direct	indirect	direct
Ownership of facilities	private and public	private and public	private and public	public
Public access	not guaranteed	guaranteed	guaranteed	guaranteed
Private care	dominant	limited	limited	unavailable

Canada

The Canadian system of health care delivery is of particular interest to Americans because it is the system most often discussed as a future model for the United States (Bennett and Adams 1993; Bolaria and Dickinson 1994, 2001; Clarke 1996; Graig 1993; Lassey, Lassey, and Jinks 1997; Livingston 1998). Like the United States, physicians in Canada are generally private, self-employed, fee-for-service practitioners. Unlike in the United States, doctors' fees are paid by government-sponsored national health insurance according to a fee schedule negotiated between the provincial government and medical association. Most hospitals also operate on a budget negotiated with government officials at the provincial level. Thus, Canada does not have a single health care delivery system, but instead ten provincial and three territorial ones (Bolaria and Dickinson 2001). The federal government, however, influences health policy and the delivery of care through fiscal and budgetary mechanisms, so the Canadian system is not as decentralized as that of Germany or France where central governments exercise little direct control over health matters. Canada essentially has a private system of health care delivery paid for almost entirely by public money.

The publicly financed health care system is supported by taxes and premiums collected by the federal and provincial governments. Responsibility for providing health care rests with each province or territory, with federal government supplementary funds. Virtually every Canadian has comprehensive insurance coverage for hospital and doctor expenses. Dental care, prescription drugs for persons under age sixty-five, ambulance service, private hospital rooms, and eyeglasses are not covered.

Canada was late in adopting its version of socialized medicine. Universal hospital insurance was not provided until 1961, and coverage for physician fees was not passed until 1971 over the opposition of doctors. Prior to this period, Canadians paid their medical and hospital bills in a variety of ways—direct payments by patients, private health insurance, and municipal government payments. The health profile of Canadians with respect to infant mortality and life expectancy is somewhat better than for Americans. Table 15-3 shows that Canadians in 1998 had a lower rate of infant mortality than Americans (5.3 as compared to 7.2 deaths per 1,000 live births). Table 15-4 shows that Canadian males had a life expectancy of 75.8 years in 1997 compared to 73.6 years for American males; Canadian females had a life expectancy of 81.4 years compared to 79.4 years for American females.

Canada does have some striking differences in health within the country, however. Eastern Canadians, for example, are more likely to develop cancer and die from it than western Canadians. Mortality rates from cancer are approximately 10 percent below the national average in Saskatchewan, Alberta, and British Columbia, but are at least 13 percent higher than the national average in Nova Scotia and, except for Newfoundland, 5 percent higher in the other eastern provinces, such as Quebec. Government studies blame poorer diets in the eastern provinces and the high rate of smoking in Quebec (38 percent of the population over the age of 15 are smokers) as the principal reasons for the difference.

The major problem facing Canada with respect to health care delivery is, as in most other major countries, one of rising costs. During the 1970s Canada's expenditures for health remained constant at about 7 percent of GDP and rose to over

8 percent in the early 1980s. The federal government realized it had no control over spending and enacted Bill C-37 in 1977 that limited federal contributions to national health insurance and made them independent of provincial health spending. Federal income and corporate taxes were also reduced, thereby giving the provinces room to increase their taxes in order to balance spending without increasing the overall tax rate. So while federal taxes went down, provincial taxes went up and taxation in general stayed at about the same level. Currently, the federal government pays about 24 percent (4 percent in direct costs and 20 percent of provincial expenditures) of health care costs, the provinces 44 percent, private spending 30 percent, local governments 1 percent, and workers compensation 1 percent. Private health insurance, usually provided by employers, supplements public benefits with coverage for private or semiprivate hospital rooms, prescription drugs, dental and vision care, and other services (Lassey et al. 1997).

In 1984, the Canada Health Act was passed, which reaffirmed the principle of universal access to health care and imposed penalties on provinces that allowed physicians to charge patients fees above government limits. By 1987, all provinces had banned extra billing by doctors. However, as Laurence Graig (1993:52) points out: "Although Canadian health care is essentially free at the point of service (patients never see a bill), it is by no means *free* to the individual." Canadians pay 15 to 20 percent more in income taxes than Americans, with the result that some of the affluent pay over half of their income in taxes. Quebec, for example, has the highest income tax, and persons in the highest tax bracket pay 51.7 percent of their income in taxes. Canadians also pay a sales tax of about 15 percent on their purchases.

Canadian physicians, like their American counterparts, are also a profession whose power is in decline (Coburn 1993; Bolaria and Dickinson 2001). In 1986, doctors in Ontario conducted a major strike to protest the federal government's decision to curtail the extra billing of patients. The issue was over whether or not doctors could set their own fees. The medical profession in Ontario contended that the Canada Health Act changed their status from that of private practitioner to "public employee," since the government determined how much physicians could charge for their services (A. Williams et al. 1995). Many physicians supported the strike, but others did not, and the protest collapsed, leaving the government's position unchanged. Since the mid-1980s, there has been considerably less conflict between the government and the medical profession; most Canadian physicians today appear to have accepted the government's payment system (Williams et al. 1995). Virtually all Canadian doctors participate in provincial health plans and have no other major source of payment for most medical procedures (Lassey et al. 1997).

Many reports state that Canadians prefer their health care system—especially in contrast to the American model (Graig 1993; Livingston 1998). Major reasons for the greater satisfaction of Canadians with their health care delivery system are its quality and lower cost. Canadian patients pay virtually nothing directly to doctors and hospitals. Rather, the provincial governments are the nation's purchaser of health services, paying a set fee to doctors for patient care and providing a set budget for operating costs to hospitals. For example, Canadian hospitals, unlike American hospitals, cannot make more money by providing more services. The essential difference between the

---

BOX 15-1   SARS in Canada and China

In April 2003, the World Health Organization added Toronto to its list of cities that travelers should avoid because of the outbreak of the new, deadly, and infectious severe acute respiratory syndrome (SARS). Worldwide, some 7,000 persons had been infected and at least 495 died. The epidemic had struck Hong Kong and Beijing the hardest, but Hanoi, Singapore, and Toronto also had major outbreaks. SARS is a pneumonia-like mystery disease spread through close contact with infected persons. Many physicians and nurses in hospitals with SARS patients were infected and some died. Symptoms include fatigue, headache, body aches, chills, dry cough, and difficulty breathing. SARS first appeared in Quangdong Province in China in November 2002, from causes yet unknown. A businessman died of it and infected enough doctors and nurses to fill a hospital ward. An elderly doctor from Quangdong who had treated SARS patients traveled to Hong Kong in February 2003 for a wedding. He felt ill, and later died. He infected at least five other persons at his hotel, including a businessman who traveled to Hanoi and died spreading the disease, as did a 78-year-old Canadian grandmother from Toronto who infected her doctor and four family members after returning home. She died, along with her son and his wife. By late April, some 257 persons had been infected in Toronto and 22 had died.

The mayor of Toronto was upset about the adverse effect WHO's travel advisory was having on the city's economy. He believed the epidemic to be under control after no new cases appeared for more than a week and went on television to tell business travelers and tourists that Toronto was safe. Two fans at a Toronto Blue Jays home baseball game with the Kansas City Royals carried a sign saying "What SARS?" The Canadian prime minister also complained to WHO and the advisory was lifted two days later. Some people thought politics had overruled medicine. The fact remains that Toronto is the epicenter for SARS in North America (the United States had only 63 cases and no deaths), although this situation may change as the disease is still active as this book goes to press. The final story has yet to be told.

United States and Canada in health spending, as Robert Evans (1986) explains, is that the Canadian system combines universal comprehensive coverage for the population combined with cost controls. "Universal coverage," as Evans (1986:597) points out, "is a necessary condition for government to engage in bilateral negotiations to exercise the leverage whereby cost escalation can be controlled." Since the government buys essentially all the care provided, it has the leverage to control the costs of that care. The biggest drawback to the Canadian system is long waits for some medical procedures, like certain types of surgery, cancer radiation, and some diagnostic tests. When such delays are a problem for individual patients, sometimes they cross the border into the United States to obtain private care (Brooke 2000).

In the 1990s, Canada experienced a crisis in health care as spending outstripped the government's ability to pay. Rising costs drove spending on health to 10.2 percent of the GDP in 1993, the second highest in the world (after the United States) that year. Aggravating the situation were an economic recession and lower tax revenues that reduced federal government contributions and caused the provinces to run up deficits to finance health care. About 30 percent of the total budget for Canada's provinces and territories is spent on health care. Some provinces instituted cost-saving measures such as limiting hospital budgets and doctor's fees and significantly reducing amounts paid for Canadians obtaining health care abroad, such as in the United States. Some provinces also allowed a few private clinics to open to reduce government costs. Cuts in health care spending, as shown in Table 15-1, resulted in a decline to 9.3 percent of the GDP in 1995 and 1999. Several hospitals closed or merged, spaces for students in medical schools were reduced, and many older doctors and nurses were offered early retirement (Brooke 2000). The long-term outlook remains serious. Because Canada's population is aging, fewer people will be working and paying taxes to support the health care system. At the same time, demands on the system will be increasing because older people need more care. Canada faces a major challenge in maintaining the quality of its health care in the twenty-first century.

Great Britain

The British National Health Service (NHS) was formed in 1948 after it was recognized that attempts spanning more than thirty years had failed to finance health care by means of a national health insurance program that had limited benefits and covered only manual workers. A national health service is created by a government's nationalizing or taking over the responsibility for a nation's health care. Thus, the government becomes the employer for health workers, maintains facilities, and purchases supplies and new equipment through the use of funds collected largely by taxation. Little or no money is exchanged between the patient and the provider of services. Except for paying taxes, health services are essentially free to those who use them.

Although Germany was the first country to enact national health insurance, Britain established the first health care system in any Western society to offer free medical care to the entire population. Prior to 1948, the quality of care one received in Britain clearly depended on one's financial resources; the poor suffered from a decidedly adverse situation. Thus, the Labor Party, which was in power after World War II, undertook to ensure that everyone would be able to receive medical treatment free of charge. To accomplish this purpose the government had to take over privately owned hospitals. The National Health Service Act of 1948 reorganized British health care into three branches: (1) the Executive Councils, which are responsible for administering the system; (2) the Local Health Authority Services Branch, which is responsible for public health, outpatient care, home nursing, community care for the mentally ill, and homes for the aged; and (3) the Hospital and Specialist Services Branch, which is responsible for the management of all hospitals (except for a few private speciality hospitals) and physician specialists, who constitute the medical staff in British hospitals.

The first line of medical care in Great Britain remained the general practitioner who worked out of an office or clinic as part of either a solo or group practice. General practitioners are paid an annual capitation fee for each patient on their patient list as part of a contractual arrangement with the National Health Service. The average number of patients on a general practitioner's list is about 2,000. With special permission, a general practitioner may have up to 3,500 patients on his or her list if a solo practitioner. Group practices can have even larger patient lists, depending on the number of doctors involved. The general practitioner is required to provide medical services free of charge. The patient (if over the age of sixteen) has the right to select his or her doctor, and the doctor is free to accept or reject anyone as a full-time patient. But if a potential patient is rejected from joining a doctor's list, the doctor must still provide treatment if the person is not on any other physician's list or if the person's physician is absent. A higher capitation fee is paid for patients who are sixty-five years of age or older, and additional sums are paid by the government to meet certain basic office expenses, to join a group practice, for additional training, for seniority, and for practicing medicine in areas that are underserved by physicians.

Except for emergencies, if treatment by a specialist (called "consultant" in the British system) or hospitalization is warranted, the general practitioner must refer the patient to a specialist. Generally, specialists are the only physicians who treat patients in hospitals. Specialists are paid a salary by the government. About 11 percent of the funds to support the National Health Service are derived from payroll deductions and employer's contributions; most of the revenue comes from general taxation. The average worker pays about 9 percent of his or her earnings for national health insurance, which is matched by employers.

Because of strong opposition from physicians when the National Health Service was first organized, physicians are also allowed to treat private patients and a certain number of hospital beds ("pay" beds) are reserved for this type of patient. Private patients are responsible for paying their own bills, and most of them have health insurance from private insurance companies. The advantage of being a private patient is prestige, less time spent in waiting rooms and obtaining appointments, and, of course, privacy.

In addition to the medical care provided by the National Health Service, the British have a sickness benefit fund to supplement income while a person is sick or injured, death benefits paid to survivors, and maternity benefits.

The British Medical Association (BMA) had initially opposed both the enactment of national health insurance between 1911 and 1913 and the formation of the National Health Service after World War II, but each became law as the government was determined to institute the programs and enough inducements were offered to physicians to reduce the strength of their opposition (Kingdom 1996; Larkin 1993; Lassey et al. 1997). In the face of strong government determination and skillful politics by the prime ministers at the time (Lloyd George in 1912 and Aneurin Bevan in 1946), the BMA was rendered ineffective. Both prime ministers managed to divide the loyalties of the BMA. Bevan, for example, refused to be drawn into lengthy negotiations with the BMA but provided concessions to teaching hospitals and consultants (specialists) and permitted the treatment of private patients in state hospitals to gain the support of many in the medical establishment. It also became increasingly clear to the medical profession that the government was going to turn the measure into law either with or without the support of the BMA.

In the end, the BMA became a partner with the government in instituting changes. Sentiment for cooperation with the government on the part of British physicians was established in the nineteenth century when the greatest threat to the BMA came from private organizations. These organizations were the medical aid institutions (commercial businesses) and the so-called friendly societies (insurance companies) that hired doctors as employees to provide less expensive medical services to their clients. In an effort to eliminate these external medical organizations, the BMA willingly worked with government agencies to control standards of medical practice. Consequently, it was through the involvement of the government in the medical market that the BMA became the most powerful and influential medical organization in Great Britain.

Initially, the National Health Service (NHS) was marked by controversy and subject to considerable criticism. The mode of capitation payments to general practitioners meant that the more patients seen by a physician, the more money the physician was able to make. Hence, there was a serious concern and some evidence that medical care was being provided in quantity rather than quality. A measure was introduced to pay physicians less for treating more patients, but as the population has increased the doctors have found it difficult to reduce their patient load. Also, the government and physicians have disputed the amount paid for capitation fees, with the physicians arguing that it is not enough. Disputes have taken place between general practitioners and specialists as well. Specialists have higher prestige and draw higher incomes, and general practitioners have claimed that the NHS favors specialists not only in regard to income but also to fringe benefits (vacations, retirement, and so on), while demanding that politicians and government administrators be more sensitive to their needs.

Consequently, conflict and problems concerning health care delivery in Britain are largely between health care providers and the government; there is little direct involvement by the general public (Gill 1994; Ham 1992; Klein 1992; Light 1997; S. Williams et al. 1993). As Derek Gill (1994) explains, it is the state's role to act as the protector of patients' rights and interests, but the structure of the NHS provides few channels for the public to voice its concerns directly.

The central problem faced by the British NHS is its lack of financial resources. Great Britain is not overly affluent and therefore is unable to spend as much money on welfare and medical services as some other countries. Moreover, the NHS has worked hard to hold down medical costs, and only about 6.9 percent of Britain's GDP was spent on health care in 1999. This is well below the level of expenditures in the United States and Canada and less than that of most European countries. Though relatively successful in combating rising expenses, this policy has had its drawbacks. British doctors and nurses are paid considerably less, on the average, than their American counterparts. British physicians average about 60 percent less in pay than American doctors. Occasionally British doctors, nurses, or other health workers will go out on strike in order to increase their salaries. Many doctors, especially consultants, do a considerable amount of private work in order to increase their income.

British patients have become increasingly dissatisfied with waiting for long periods of time in doctors' offices and for appointments to see them, as well as for long delays in obtaining elective surgery and what they perceive are low staffing levels in hospitals. Nationwide surveys in the late 1980s indicated that satisfaction with the NHS was seriously declining (Bosanquet 1988). In order to improve the situation, the British government, led by Prime Minister Margaret Thatcher, initiated reforms intended to create a competitive "internal market" within the nation's health care delivery system (Annandale 1998; Annandale and Field 2001; Gill 1994; Graig 1993; Hughes and Griffiths 1999; Kingdom 1996; Klein 1992; Lassey et al. 1997; Light 1997; Mechanic 1995b; Nettleton 1995; S. Williams et al. 1993).

The most important measure was enactment of the National Health Service and Community Care Act of 1990. The provisions of this act made the NHS more responsive to the needs of patients by delegating greater power and responsibility down to local health districts and hospitals. Hospitals can now be self-governing as NHS hospital trusts and can finance themselves by contracting directly for their services with district health authorities. District health authorities (DHAs) are responsible for paying for health care in their area, managing the provision of that care, and planning in accordance with regional and national guidelines. The DHAs are managed and receive their resources from NHS executive regional offices who are funded, in turn, by the central government. Additionally, general practitioners in group practices with at least 5,000 patients can apply for a budget, as general practitioner fund holders (GPFH), to purchase services from hospitals for their patients. General practitioners were also given higher incomes from capitation fees and encouraged to compete for patients. Patients, in turn, were allowed to choose and change general practitioners more readily. And finally, the work of specialists is to be audited and reviewed regularly to determine satisfactory performance.

Furthermore, hospitals providing services to private patients were allowed to make a profit from those services instead of providing them at cost. Hospitals were also allowed to market their services to make them more attractive to private patients, and NHS patients could be admitted by their doctors to the best hospitals available—not just those in their district. These measures were intended by the government to improve efficiency, reduce delays in receiving treatment, and assist doctors and hospitals to increase their incomes by attracting more patients. Although these new measures signified the application of free-market methods to a state-financed system, public opinion polls show that support for the principle of state health care and greater government expenditures for health has risen since the early 1980s (Graig 1993). In addition to reforming the health care marketplace, a *Patient's Charter* was provided that assured patients of ten basic rights, including the right to receive care, be referred to a consultant if necessary, be given a clear explanation of treatment, have access to health records and have the confidentiality of those records maintained, receive detailed information on local health services, be guaranteed admission to treatment by a specific date, and have any complaints about the NHS investigated.

Despite these reforms, however, serious problems remained. Conditions in hospitals, many of them old and in need of renovation, worsened; waiting lists for surgery lengthened beyond a year; different regions of the country had different standards of care; and there was deepening dissatisfaction among doctors, nurses, and other health care workers over government budget cuts. Market reforms did not eliminate shortages caused by government underfunding. In 1997, the Labor Party came to power (after an eighteen-year absence) under its prime minister Tony Blair, who proposed to reorganize the health care system and abolish the internal market of the NHS established by the Conservatives. However, the internal market has largely remained intact with its emphasis on primary care, contracts, and NHS trusts. Yet there have been changes under Blair as new Primary Care Groups consisting of local networks of general practitioners and community health nurses were replacing the fundholding and nonfundholding general practices in purchasing care from hospitals and specialists; three new medical schools were established to alleviate doctor shortages; one-stop, drop-in medical centers were authorized; a twenty-four hour medical hot line (NHS Direct) staffed by doctors and nurses was established; and medical information was being posted on the Internet for both doctors and patients.

Although reforms have been found necessary, the NHS has accomplished what it set out to do: provide free comprehensive medical care to the residents of Great Britain. It has shown significant results: The general health profile of Britain is among the highest in the world. Tables 15-3 and 15-4 show, for example, that the infant mortality rates for England and Wales are lower than in the United States, while life expectancy for males and females is higher. On balance, health care in Britain is of a high quality despite problems. While significant inequalities in health remain between social classes (Adonis and Pollard 1997; Arber 1993, 1997; Borooah 1999; Chandola 2000; Hart 1986, 1989, 1991; Lahelma et al. 2000, 2002; Marmot 1996; Marmot, Bobak, and Smith 1995; Marmot and Wilkinson 1999; Rahkonen, Arber, and Lahelma 1995; Reid 1998; Townsend, Davidson, and Whitehead 1990, Wilkinson 1996), these differences are not as substantital as those in Third World countries. Poor health among the lower classes in Britain is due more to the unhealthy lifestyles and living environment associated with poverty, rather than a lack of access to quality health care (Jarvis and Wardle 1999; Hart 1986, 1991; Reid 1998; Shaw, Dorling, and Smith 1999; Wilkinson 1996).

Sweden

Sweden, along with Great Britain, has demonstrated that a socialized system of health care delivery can be effective in a capitalist country through the formation of a national health service. The Swedish National Health Service is financed through taxation. Taxes in Sweden have been the highest in the world. Tax reform in 1991 reduced the highest income tax rate from 72 to 51 percent, but the top tax bracket was temporarily increased to 56 percent in 1995. Sweden remains one of the world's most egalitarian countries when it comes to the provision of welfare benefits to the general population, and inequities in living conditions have been reduced to a level that is more equal than in most other countries. Universal health insurance, old-age pensions, unemployment insurance, and job retraining programs protect employed Swedes and their families from serious concern about being pushed into poverty by poor health, old age, and unemployment. There are social class differences in health in Sweden with the lower class showing a less positive health profile than more affluent Swedes, but the difference is less pronounced than in most other countries (Blank and Diderichsen 1996; Diderichsen 1990; Hemström 1999, 2001; Lundberg 1992; Sundquist and Johansson 1997). Sweden, along with the other Nordic countries, has the lowest proportion of poor people in Europe (Hemström 2001).

On practically every measure, the Swedes must be considered one of the world's healthiest populations overall. As shown in Table 15-3, Sweden has the lowest infant mortality rate in the world (3.5 deaths per 1,000 live births). Table 15-4 shows that Sweden has the second highest life expectancy for males (76.7 years) and fifth highest for females (81.8 years).

The Swedish National Health Service is the responsibility of the Ministry of Health and Social Affairs, which was established in its present form in 1964. Only particularly important health issues are decided by the ministry. Most decisions pertaining to health policy are made by the National Board of Health and Welfare, which was established in 1968. This board plans, supervises, and regulates the delivery of health services at the county level. Physicians are employed by county councils and are paid according to the number of hours worked rather than the number of patients treated. Physicians are obligated to work a fixed number of hours per week, usually about forty to forty-two. It is generally left up to the doctor to decide what percentage of his or her time is to be spent on treating patients, doing research, or teaching. Physicians' salaries are standardized by specialty, place and region of work, and seniority.

A major characteristic of the National Health Service in Sweden is that general hospitals are owned by county and municipal governments. These local governments are responsible for maintaining and providing services. The state pays the general hospitals a relatively small amount of money from a health insurance fund, leaving the balance to be paid from local tax revenues. Enrollment in the government-sponsored health insurance program is mandatory for the entire population. Most of the money to support the insurance program comes from the contributions of employers and payroll deductions of employees. This insurance, a form of national health insurance, is used primarily to pay the salaries of physicians and other health workers. There are also some general practitioners in private practice whose fees are paid by the insurance fund and token payments from patients. Fees for all physicians, however, are set by the government and paid according to their schedule.

The Swedish health care system has some additional benefits other than generally free medical treatment. Excessive travel expenses to visit physicians and hospitals are paid by the government, and there is a cash sickness fund designed to protect a person's standard of living against losses of income due to illness or injury. Under this program people may receive up to 80 percent of the income they would be earning if they were able to work at their job. Drugs are either free or inexpensive, and financial supplements are paid to each woman giving birth to a child and to families with children under the age of sixteen regardless of income.

It would be somewhat misleading to consider the funding of Sweden's health care delivery system as an example of national health insurance, since most of the revenues come from county councils. The total health bill in Sweden is met by contributions of approximately 61 percent from county taxes, 27 percent from the national government, 8 percent from the health insurance system, and 4 percent from patient fees. In 1995, health costs were 8.1 percent of the GDP, down from 9.1 percent in 1985. Pressure on government budgets had intensified during the early 1990s because of a slowdown in the economy, rising unemployment, and tax reform. As Bernard Jones (1996:104) explains, Sweden, for the first time in living memory, had to worry about finances, and the resources of the welfare state— previously provided on a generous scale—began to be rationed. The county councils, who allocate about 75 percent of their budgets to health care, reduced their expenditures. Patients spent less time in hospitals than in the past and are now treated more often as outpatients. In 1994, the county councils also introduced a new financial system of payments to hospitals based on the actual number of patients treated instead of a traditional fixed annual budget, and competition between hospitals was allowed with the goal of improving quality and lowering costs. Consequently, Sweden, like Great Britain, has moved toward a purchaser-provider model within its own government-run health system, and maintained this approach even when the economy improved in the late 1990s.

Sweden remains committed to universal and equal access to health services paid by public funding. County councils have been directed by the national legislature to remain responsible for health care delivery but pass the responsibility for nursing homes to municipalities and transfer part of their budgets to local health districts. This measure will allow the districts to purchase services from different primary care centers and hospitals, a development intended to promote competition between providers and greater freedom of choice for patients. These changes in Sweden's health services are not extreme; rather, they are intended to improve a highly successful system by introducing limited aspects of a free market.

DECENTRALIZED NATIONAL HEALTH PROGRAMS: JAPAN, GERMANY, THE NETHERLANDS, AND FRANCE

Decentralized national health programs differ from systems of socialized medicine in that government control and management of health care delivery is more indirect. The government acts primarily to regulate the system, not operate it. Often the government functions in the role of a third party mediating and coordinating health care delivery between providers and the organizations involved in the financing of services. In decentralized national health programs, the government (1) indirectly controls the financing and organization of health services in a capitalist economy, (2) regulates payments to providers, (3) owns some of the facilities, (4) guarantees equal access to the general population, and (5) allows some private care for patients willing to be responsible for their own expenses. In this section, the decentralized national health care systems in Japan, Germany, the Netherlands, and France will be discussed.

Prenatal Intensive Care Unit in Japan. The Japanese have the highest life expectancy in the world for both males and females.

Japan

Japan spent 7.3 percent of its GDP on health care in 1995 (more than half of that of the United States), but the Japanese have achieved striking results over the last thirty years. For example, in 1955 the average life expectancy of a Japanese was more than four years less than that of an American. By 1967, Japan's life expectancy had passed that of the United States and currently, as shown in Table 15-4, is the highest in the world for both males (77.2 years) and females (83.8 years). Japanese rates for infant mortality, listed in Table 15-3, are the second lowest in the world (3.6 per 1,000 live births in 1998).

Japan has a national health insurance plan, introduced in 1961, but its benefits are relatively low by Western standards. Japanese patients pay 30 percent of the cost of health services, with the national plan paying the remainder. However, patients are reimbursed by the plan for expenses over 60,000 yen ($580) for medical care during any given month; low-income patients are reimbursed for amounts spent over 33,600 yen ($325) monthly. People over seventy years of age have all of their costs covered. Patients are allowed to choose their own doctors and encouraged to visit them regularly, and these policies more than likely promote the longevity of the Japanese, since health problems can be diagnosed during early stages. About one-third of Japanese doctors are in private practice and are paid on a fee-for-service basis; all the rest are full-time, salaried employees of hospitals. Physicians not on a hospital staff cannot treat their patients once they are hospitalized.

Physician fees for office visits and examinations are quite low because the government sets fees. Regardless of seniority or geographical area, all Japanese doctors in private practice are paid the same amount for the same procedures according to the government's uniform fee schedule. Fee revisions are negotiated by the Central Social Medical Care Council in the Ministry of Health and Welfare comprised of eight providers (doctors, dentists, and a pharmacist), eight payers (four insurers, two from the government, and two from management and labor), and four who represent public interests (three economists and a lawyer); however, any changes in fees are ultimately decided by the Ministry of Finance because government subsidies must be kept within general budgetary limits. In effect, the government virtually determines fees for doctors and hospitals. Hospital costs tend to be low because the government refuses to pay high costs in that area as well.

The government fee schedule is the primary mechanism for cost containment. Providers are prohibited by law from charging more than the schedule allows. Japanese doctors do receive a substantial supplementary income from the drugs they prescribe (25 or more percent of the price of the drug), and the Japanese use more prescription drugs than patients anywhere (Graig 1993; Ikegami and Campbell 1995; Powell and Anesaki 1990). Private practitioners in Japan earn significantly more (about four times as much) than hospital-based doctors.

The Japanese national health insurance plan does not cover all Japanese. Instead, the government encouraged private organizations to keep government involvement at a minimum by setting up their own welfare programs. Part of the normative structure of the Japanese business world is that companies are responsible for taking care of their own employees. In Japan this responsibility includes providing retirement plans, helping retired employees find postretirement work, arranging vacations, offering low cost loans for housing, and providing medical care. Consequently, there are separate programs of health services for employees of large companies, small and medium-sized companies, and public and quasi-public institutions. Some large companies even employ doctors and own hospitals. There is also a program for citizens who are not covered under other plans. Consequently, the entire Japanese population is covered by some type of health insurance plan, and the average Japanese has a much greater measure of security concerning health care than the average American (Anderson, Oscarson, and Yu 1995; Anesaki and Munakata 2001; Garland 1995; Graig 1993; Ikegami 1991, 1992; Ikegami and Campbell 1995; Powell and Anesaki 1990).

The concept of having a decentralized system of health care based largely on occupation is supported by Japanese businessmen, who generally provide more benefits than are required by law. Business leaders oppose a heavy welfare burden for government; they want to pay less in taxes and avoid the governmental administrative overhead required for a large public welfare system. The tax burdens in welfare states like Sweden and Great Britain are undesirable, as is the type of welfare system in the United States. Also important is the desire of Japanese businesses to provide security to their employees in exchange for employee loyalty and productivity. This policy gives large Japanese corporations an advantage in attracting workers because of the greater benefit packages they can offer. As a result, of course, some Japanese have better health care benefits than others, although the overall provision of health benefits in Japan is highly equitable.

Naoki Ikegami (1992) notes that it can be argued that the excellent health of the Japanese population and relatively low medical costs are more a reflection of lifestyles and economic conditions than the health care delivery system. Ikegami says that this argument may well be accurate, but he calls attention to the fact that universal coverage without rationing care is a major achievement. While no health system can be perfect because demands can easily exceed resources, the Japanese have established the most efficient system in the world: It is relatively low cost, effective, and equitable.

However, there are problems. Some 80 percent of all Japanese hospitals are privately owned by physicians, but many facilities are old and lack space. Because the Japanese government limits how much they can charge, Japanese hospitals are often required to admit more and more patients in order to meet their expenses. Overcrowding has therefore become common in most hospitals. The average length of hospitalization in Japan is also longer than in the West. Hospital administrators complain that it is difficult to finance updated facilities or hire additional personnel without increases in the amounts charged to patients.

There are typically long waits at doctors' offices and clinics as well because Japanese physicians do not use an appointment system. Basically, it is a case of first come, first served, and some patients begin lining up outside the doctor's office before it opens. Furthermore, relationships between doctors and patients in Japan tend to be more impersonal than in the United States. Patients are told little about their diagnoses, the treatment prescribed, or types of drugs being administered. "Doctors," state Margaret Powell and Masahira Anesaki (1990:174), "tend to explain away the problem in soothing terms without necessarily providing precise information about what exactly the problem is." The doctor–patient relationship is based on trust and the traditional Japanese cultural value of deference to authority. A patient requesting information directly would be seen as questioning the physician's authority, judgment, and knowledge. Therefore, patients are to rely on what doctors tell [or usually do not tell] them.

According to Hiroyuki Hattori and his colleagues (1991), doctors will disclose the fact that a patient has terminal cancer to the patient's family (as a form of substitute consent) but not to the patient. As few as 5 percent of all patients dying of cancer may be aware they have the disease (Powell and Anesaki 1990). This situation may be changing somewhat because of court decisions verifying patient rights, the possibility of malpractice suits, and growing public concern about full disclosure of information (Hattori et al. 1991; Powell and Anesaki 1990). In the meantime, the Japanese medical profession remains highly self-regulated and adverse to public scrutiny (Powell and Anesaki 1990).

Other problems are due to changes in disease patterns. Heart disease is on the rise and is now the second leading cause of death after cancer. Historically, Japan has had low mortality rates from heart disease in comparison to Western societies. This trend undoubtedly influences higher levels of life expectancy among the Japanese, especially among males. The traditional low-fat, low-protein and high carbohydrate Japanese diet of fish, rice, and green vegetables is a major factor in this situation (Cockerham, Hattori, and Yamori 2000; Powell and Anesaki 1990). Also, the stress-reducing aspects of Japanese culture, such as strong group solidarity and cooperation in dealing with problems and after-work socializing by males on a regular basis with close friends in bars or noodle shops, may be important. These drinking places are often designed to encourage relaxation and allow a temporary escape from the tensions of modern living. After-work socializing with co-workers seems to have become a routine activity in the lifestyles of many men in industrial Japan.

Nevertheless, a more Westernized lifestyle and increase in the consumption of animal fats and proteins—associated with Western diets—have promoted more heart disease, along with the stresses of living in a dynamic, hard-working, and densely populated society (Anesaki and Munakata 2001; Powell and Anesaki 1990). The shift toward higher fat in Japanese diets has also contributed to a rise in colon and pancreatic cancers, and heavy smoking among Japanese males has led to an acceleration in mortality rates from lung cancer (Wynder et al. 1991). The Japanese also have the highest rates of stomach cancer in the world. Increases in death rates from cancer and heart disease, as well as the highest mortality rates from stroke of any advanced country, suggest that increases in life expectancy for the Japanese may be slowing down and perhaps reaching a limit.

These changes, combined with the rapid growth of Japan's elderly population, are likely to place tremendous pressure on Japan's health care delivery system in the future. The proportion of people living to old age is increasing in Japanese society faster than in any other country in the world, and this situation is going to require a significant response from Japan's system of health care delivery.

Germany

The structure of health care delivery in the Federal Republic of Germany has not changed significantly since 1883 and the reforms instituted by Bismarck's administration in imperial Germany. The program established at that time was based on three principal components: (1) compulsory insurance, (2) free health services, and (3) sick benefits. Employees, self-employed, unemployed, old-age pensioners, and certain categories of domestic workers providing infant and child care, home help, and the like are all required to be insured by one of Germany's public health insurance organizations. There are 1,317 public health insurance groups, and membership in a particular health plan is typically determined by such factors as occupation or place of employment. For example, there are plans for miners, craftsmen, seamen, and farmers, and some large business corporations sponsor their own program for the people they employ. Germany's largest public health insurance organization, consisting of several local sickness funds, is the Allgemeine Ortskrankenkassen (AOK), which insures about half the population. The AOK originally insured only blue-collar workers but broadened its membership base to include the general population.

As John Myles (1984) pointed out, Bismarck's welfare measures in the late nineteenth century were both a response to democratization and an attempt to suppress it. That is, Bismarck wanted to defuse the demands for political rights from an increasingly well-organized and leftist-oriented working class by providing them with social rights that linked workers to the state rather than to labor unions or socialist political parties. Included in Bismarck's plan was the first national health insurance program ever. David Childs and Jeffrey Johnson (1981:99) summarize the outcome: "Whatever view we might now take of Bismarck's motives in introducing these schemes, there can be no doubt that they were excellent for their time and they became a model for both subsequent German governments and for foreign governments."

Following Germany's defeat in World War II and the incorporation of its eastern lands into a separate communist state, West Germany became a multiparty republic in 1949. The Federal Republic's constitution, the Basic Law, guarantees the social welfare of its citizens, continues the comprehensive social welfare system developed by Bismarck, and now includes the East Germans after unification in 1990. The program that currently exists includes health insurance, old-age pensions, sickness benefits for income lost to illness or injury, unemployment insurance, and family assistance in the form of allowances for children, rent (especially for the elderly), and public funds for the construction of low-income housing.

Approximately 90 percent of all Germans participate, involuntarily or voluntarily, in the nation's public health insurance program. The remainder consist mainly of civil servants, who have their own insurance, and high-income earners who can take out private insurance. In the state plan, health care is free to the individual except for small copayments and covers medical and dental treatment, drugs and medicines, and hospital care as needed. In the event of illness, the employer must continue to pay the employee's full wages for six weeks, and then the health insurance fund provides the individual with his or her approximate take-home pay for up to seventy-eight weeks. If the illness is more protracted, benefits are continued under a welfare plan unless the person is permanently incapacitated and is entitled to a disability pension. About 13.3 percent of a worker's monthly gross earnings goes to pay for health insurance, with half the contribution made by the employee and half by the employer.

The welfare system in Germany made it possible for its citizens to demand the most in all welfare programs. Thus, Germans, on the average, appear to have a different mentality about the welfare state than Americans. All Germans can use its services whenever and as long as it is necessary; therefore, they can approach the social welfare system for health care, pensions, and other benefits with an exceptionally strong sense of personal entitlement. A distinctive psychological orientation on the part of Germans, in comparison to Americans, helps us to understand the different approaches to welfare. The German word *anspruchsdenken* cannot be translated literally into English, but essentially means a "mentality of entitlement." It signifies a readiness on the part of the individual to claim and use the welfare benefits to which he or she is entitled by law. The fact that *anspruchsdenken* has no equivalent in English underscores the lack of a corresponding mentality in American society (Cockerham, Kunz, and Lueschen 1988a).

Public health insurance plans are coordinated by the National Federation of Health Insurance. The insurance plan will issue a medical certificate to members and their dependents periodically. This certificate is presented to a physician when services are rendered. The physician then submits the certificate to his or her association of registered doctors, which all physicians are required to join. Payment is made to the physician through the doctors' association according to a fee schedule agreed upon by the association and the public health insurance plans. Hospital fees and payments are handled in the same manner (Inglehart 1991; Jost 1998; Kirkman-Liff 1991; Knox 1993; Lassey et al. 1997; Schulenberg 1995; Wysong and Abel 1991).

As the preceding discussion indicates, the German government does not play a major role in the financing of health services. The government's primary function is one of administration. The Federal Ministry of Labor and Social Affairs exercises general supervision of the health care delivery system through state ministries and local health boards. According to Donald Light (1986; Light and Schuller 1986), this form of health service organization is one of corporatism and represents a unique contribution by Germany to the provision of health care. Corporatism in the German context consists of (1) compulsory membership on the part of the population in a national health plan and (2) a set of institutions situated between the government and its citizens with the authority to manage health care under government auspices.

Approximately 50 percent of Germany's physicians are general practitioners, which is a relatively high percentage compared to the United States. Most German doctors practice medicine in private offices or clinics on a solo basis. Few work in a group practice. German physicians are well paid, earning somewhat more, on average, than American doctors. Health care costs rose significantly during the 1970s and the government put pressure on physicians and hospitals to keep down costs. Table 15-1 shows that between 1985 and 1990, health costs decreased, from 9.3 to 8.7 percent of the GDP. The Health Care Reform Act of 1989 helped limit costs by increasing the amounts paid by persons insured voluntarily in the public health plan, adding a small copayment for prescription drugs, establishing price ceilings for most drugs, and other measures. The Health Structure Act of 1993 mandated price cuts for drugs; lower incomes for doctors and dentists, along with compulsory retirement at age sixty-eight; increased copayments for patients; and limits on hospital budgets. Germans have been able to choose their own public health insurance fund since 1997.

By the late 1990s, however, many Germans considered their health care system to be in a crisis (Jost 1998). Health care costs had risen from 8.7 percent of the GDP in 1990 to 10.2 percent in 1995, the second highest in the world after the United States. By 1998, health costs had further increased to 10.4 percent of the GDP (Knesebeck and Siegrist 2001). Moreover, the economy slowed, and Germans in the west paid additional taxes to modernize the east. Germany also has a high rate of unemployment (about 11 percent overall), especially in the east (where the rate was over 17 percent). The German population is also aging. Some 19.3 percent were age 60 and over in 2000; by 2040, the proportion of Germans in this age group will be 24.5 percent (or one in four Germans). Also in 2000, there were 26 persons age 65 and older, for every 100 adults between the ages of 20 and 65; however, by 2040, German insurance companies are projecting there will be 56 persons age 65 and older for every 100 younger adults. High unemployment and younger adults of working age in relation to the number of eldery persons means fewer potential tax revenues to support health care and the social welfare system. In order to generate more income without raising taxes, health ordinances that went into effect in 1997 further increased copayments by patients for prescription drugs, hospitalization, physical therapy, and other services. Future changes in the German health policy are uncertain at present, but inevitable as Germany continues to provide generous benefits to its citizens and permanent residents (Jost 1998).

The general level of health of the German population, however, is good. Table 15-3 shows that Germany had a lower infant mortality rate than the United States in 1998. The U.S. infant mortality rate was 7.2 per 1,000 compared to 4.6 for Germany. Table 15-4 indicates that both German men and women had a higher life expectancy. For men, the Germans showed a life expectancy of 74.0 years in 1997 and American men were listed at 73.6 years; for women, the German figures were 80.5 years versus 79.4 years for Americans. Almost half of all deaths are due to diseases of the heart and circulatory system. The prevalence of heart disease in eastern Germany is higher than in the western lands, with eastern men showing higher levels of cigarette smoking, hypertension, cholesterol, and obesity (Häussler, Hempel, and Reschke 1995; Heinemann, Barth, and Hoffmeister 1995; Knesebeck and Siegrist 2001; Nolte et al. 2002). The unfavorable trend in heart disease in eastern Germany appears to be primarily caused by a less healthy lifestyle involving differences in smoking, alcohol consumption, diet, exercise, and possibly stress (Cockerham 1999; Häussler et al. 1995; Heinemann, Dinkel, and Görtler 1996). Not surprisingly, life expectancy is higher in the west at 73.5 years for men and 79.8 years for women in 1993–1995, compared to 70.7 years for men and 78.2 years for women in the east during the same period. Unification should eventually produce a greater convergence in health and life expectancy in Germany. There are already signs that the change in the health care delivery in eastern Germany is helping improve life expectancy (Nolte et al. 2002).

The Netherlands

Health care delivery in the Netherlands is based on the German system, which was imposed on the Dutch when their country was occupied by German forces during World War II. After the war, the Dutch kept the health care system with a few modifications. About 60 percent of the Dutch population receives health care through public health insurance funds similar to those in Germany. The funds are organized on a regional basis, membership is compulsory for individuals and families below a certain income, and the insured is not entitled to choose among the various funds. The insurance funds receive revenue from a single national fund, which is supported by state subsidies and contributions of 2.85 percent from employees and 4.95 percent from employers—an amount equal to 8 percent of an employee's wages. Sickness benefits for payment of wages when ill for a period of six weeks are provided, after which 70 percent of wages are paid up to twelve months. Dental care, eyeglass lenses, drugs, and hospital care are provided. There is also a compulsory health insurance plan for local and regional (but not national) civil servants, who comprise 5 percent of the population.

The remaining 35 percent of the Dutch population has private health insurance. As in Germany, these are civil servants, the self-employed, and people with the highest incomes. Employees who purchase private insurance receive a contribution from their employers equal to what would be paid for public insurance. There are several different private health insurance companies, both profit and nonprofit, and various types of health plans. Physicians are divided into general practitioners (GPs) and specialists, with GPs providing a "gatekeeper" role, since all referrals to specialists and hospitals come through them (Kirkman-Liff 1991; Lassey et al. 1997). Patients have limited choice of a GP, since they usually register with one in their area. GPs have an average of 2,350 registered patients; they are paid on a fee-for-service basis for patients with private insurance and on a per capita basis for patients with public insurance. Specialists are paid on a fee-for-service basis from both private and public insurers. Hospitals are all nonprofit and receive an operating budget annually from both private and public health insurance funds.

The population of the Netherlands is relatively small (some 16 million people), but the country is one of the most densely populated in the world (about 438 persons per square kilometer). The Dutch have distinct social classes, but differences are not extreme. By taxing wealth heavily and providing generous welfare benefits to the less affluent, there has been a redistribution of income to reduce class distinctions. The lowest income tax rate is 38.4 percent and the highest 60 percent; there is also a net wealth tax of 0.8 percent for persons earning large amounts. Egalitarianism is expressed not only in material goods, but in welfare benefits. People living on welfare or unemployment insurance receive 80 percent of their previous salary for six months, then 75 percent for up to two years and an extra month's allowance for holidays.

Consequently, the Netherlands has achieved a degree of socioeconomic equity beyond that of most nations. Yet the Dutch upper and middle classes still have lower mortality rates, higher life expectancy, and better health than the lower class (Kunst, Looman, and Mackenbach 1990; Spruit 1990). They are also more likely to live a healthy lifestyle (F. Stevens et al. 1995). Positive changes in the health of the Dutch begin first in the upper classes, such as smoking cessation and favorable changes in diet; as a result, lung cancer and heart disease are less prevalent at the top of society and more prevalent at the bottom (Kunst, et al. 1990). Still, on every measure, the Netherlands has one of the healthiest populations in the world. Table 15-3 shows infant mortality to be thirteenth lowest in the world at 5.5 infant deaths per 1,000 live births, while Table 15-4 shows life expectancy to be eighth highest for men at 75.2 years and twelfth highest for women at 80.6 years.

France

Unlike Germany, which began its social welfare system in the 1880s, France did not have similar developments until 1930. A law passed in 1901 did authorize numerous private organizations to offer health plans on a nonprofit basis to specific occupational

The "French paradox" refers to the relatively low rate of heart disease in a country known for its rich diet, heavy smoking, and high alcohol consumption. Regular and moderate wine drinking appears to be an important protective factor.

groups, but the 1930 legislation laid the legal foundation for a national welfare system by subsidizing health care, housing, and old-age benefits for low-income families. The entire system, known as the Sécurité Sociale, was reorganized in 1945 after World War II and expanded to include practically the entire population.

However, there is no single organization providing health insurance on a nationwide basis. Rather, the French insurance system is divided between occupational groups. Professionals, businessmen, craftsmen, civil servants, farmers, and other occupations have their own organizations. For family and old-age benefits, a similar system exists. Unlike Germany, where the several public health insurance plans are regulated by a single administrative system, France has nineteen channels of regulation and administration for the financing and provision of welfare services, including health care. Consequently, there is a minimum level of centralization in France's social welfare system. All of the various insurance organizations are nonprofit, supervised by a particular government agency (one among many), and responsible just to their members. According to Bruno Dumons and Gilles Pollet (1999:227), the French health care system is difficult to regulate because of its complexity and the influence of its history. The historical legacy of the division of responsibilities for health care persists, and attempts to change this situation have failed. As Isidor Wallimann (1986:1307) points out:

It must be concluded, therefore, that the French welfare system is very unique in that it covers the entire population against such things as old age and illness by means of an insurance system which is not only more decentralized but also organized around occupational or class location of individuals.

How can uniformity and equality in covering the entire population be achieved with so many different insurance organizations? The answer is that the French welfare system is neither uniform nor equal (Corbett 1994; Dumons and Pollet 1999; Lassey et al. 1997; Orfali 2001; Rodwin and Sandier 1993)—but everyone does receive a level of health benefits adequate to meet hospital and most physician costs. The French health insurance system provides universal coverage, freedom of choice in doctors and hospitals, and diversity (Fielding and Lancry 1993; Orfali 2001; Rodwin and Sandier 1993).

The major differences are in pension, not health, plans. Everyone is required to belong to a national health insurance plan, and all such plans are supervised by various government agencies. The Department of Agriculture, for example, manages the health insurance organization for farmers and agricultural workers, and the Department of Social Affairs and National Security controls the salary and wage earner's health plan. These agencies all follow national policy, which provides some uniformity and coordination; otherwise, there are many differences and inequalities. Different organizations have different rates of contributions and levels of benefits. Persons in well-paid occupations pay more in contributions and receive more in benefits, particularly in old-age pensions. Consequently, France's social welfare system is divided along socioeconomic lines and subject to greater class conflict than found in most other Western states.

Some 70 percent of all French hospitals are in the public sector, and hospital bills for serious illnesses in both public and private hospitals are completely covered by the patient's national health insurance plan, and most of the bills for less serious problems are also met. Patients pay doctors directly for their services and are then reimbursed for 75 percent of their costs by their insurance. Physician and hospital fees are negotiated with the government and paid according to a fixed schedule. In 1996, in a major effort at reform, the French Parliament, that previously had no direct authority over the health care system except indirectly through the national budget—took direct control over the nation's health budget (Orfali 2001). The Parliament now sets a ceiling on health expenditures that is binding for all participants in the health insurance system. The portion of France's GDP spent on health in 1999 was 9.4 percent which is below that of the United States, but ranks toward the high end of spending for the European Union.

France differs from other Western states in its method of financing social insurance, including health benefits. The French depend less on taxes on personal income to meet their social needs than any other Western country. About 42 percent of the funds come from contributions made by employers and employees, 39 percent from property tax, and 19 percent from income tax. Employees contribute 6.9 percent of their wages and salaries, while employers pay 12.8 percent of their payrolls for health benefits. Thus, France is unique in that employers pay an unusually high share of contributions into the social insurance system. Other countries, like the United States, Canada, Great Britain, and Germany, have equal percentages of contributions from employers and employees. But in France, employers are required to contribute heavily to social welfare because of the political success of socialists and labor unions in attempting to reduce or eliminate altogether the contributions of workers.

The French government has placed a strong emphasis upon health education and the promotion of healthy lifestyles. Such programs are in line with the fact that a significant gap in health and mortality continues to persist between the social classes in France. Per capita spending on health care has risen, however, and French hospitals are, on the average, more modern than those in Britain. The French also spend more on medication than other Europeans, with the government reimbursing 70 percent of their costs.

The overall profile of French health is positive. Table 15-3 shows that infant mortality in 1998 was 4.6 deaths per 1,000 live births, which is far better than the rate of 7.2 deaths in the United States. Table 15-4 shows that, in 1997, life expectancy for French men stood at a high level (74.6 years), while French women had the second highest longevity in the world (82.2) for their gender. Discussions of health in France, however, are incomplete without mentioning the famous "French paradox." France is a country famous for its rich diet, along with heavy smoking and alcohol consumption—yet it has relatively low rates of heart disease. Why? One major contributing factor is regular and moderate alcohol use, notably red wine, that provides protection against arteriosclerosis (Orfali 2001). Another factor is the low proportion of people who are overweight. Yet there are still major challenges for the French health system. There is a gap of eight years in life expectancy between women and men, there are over 13.5 million smokers, alcoholism is high, and significant class differences in health and mortality persist (Lostao et al. 2001; Orfali 2001).

CONCLUSION

This review of the organization and social policy of health care in selected developed countries suggests that no nation has an ideal system of dealing with health problems. All nations are faced with rising demands for quality health care in the face of limited resources, and the high cost of care has presented special problems in achieving desired outcomes. Exact comparisons between nations in terms of the effectiveness of their respective health care delivery systems are difficult because of varying political structures, diet, degree of technological advancement, social commitment to national health care, and cultures, which have an impact on the overall health profile of a particular country. Sweden, for example, appears to have a much more effective approach to the provision of medical care than the United States as measured in terms of infant mortality and life expectancy. Yet Sweden has a much smaller and more homogeneous population than the United States and fewer social class differences. It is much easier for the Swedes to focus on health care and mobilize their financial resources to cope with it. Nevertheless, it can be said that the

United States has an overall level of health that places it among the world's healthiest nations but not near the top.

Japan has been particularly successful in its approach to health; health care is both low-cost and readily accessible to the general public. The Japanese have the highest life expectancy for both men and women in the world. Economic conditions in Japan and Japanese lifestyles may be the primary factors in this development, but the health care delivery has undoubtedly made a major contribution. Yet the Japanese situation is one that other capitalist countries may not necessarily want, since large business corporations have the expense of providing their own health benefits, people under 70 years of age in the national plan are responsible for up to 30 percent of the cost of their care monthly, and the use of prescription drugs is the highest in the world.

It is clear from the discussion in this chapter that the governments of developed nations are under increasingly greater pressure to contain health care costs and yet maintain high-quality coverage for the entire population. One approach in Western Europe, influenced by the "internal market" measure introduced by Britain, has been to allow limited competition between providers within government-run health care systems to contract their services to purchasers, such as a regional health agency. These agencies, in turn, allocate the care to the people in their areas. Efforts at reform are likely to continue in the twenty-first century as the numbers of elderly increase and place greater demands on health care systems, with fewer workers in the economy paying taxes to support those systems.

For the present, several general trends are appearing in developed societies which are likely to have an effect on health care policy in the future. These trends are the following: (1) Considerable attention is being paid to the cost of health care, and controls over such costs are an important aspect of health policy; (2) preventive medical services are receiving increasing emphasis in developed countries as more attempts are being made to keep well people healthy; (3) efforts are being made to design a more effective administration of large health care systems, and (4) there is more demand and increased responsiveness on the parts of governments and policymakers to provide a health care system that meets national needs. While different countries are taking different approaches to solve health problems, all countries appear to be moving toward a system that will reduce inequities and control costs.

HEALTH CARE IN DEVELOPED COUNTRIES
INTERNET SITES

Canada

1. Canadian Institute for Health Information.
    http://www.cihi.ca

2. Canadian Ministry of Health.
    http:.//www.hc-sc.gc.ca

Great Britain

1. The British Medical Association.
   http://www.bma.org.uk

2. Highlights on Health in Great Britain.
   http://www/who.dk/eprise/main/who/countryinformation/country?

   Area Code = UNK

Sweden

The Swedish Government, Ministry of Health and Social Affairs.
http://social.regeringen.se/inenglish/

Japan

Japanese Ministry of Health, Labour, and Welfare.
http://www.mhlw.go.jp/english/index.html

Germany

1. The German Ministry of Health.
   http://www.bmgesundheit.de

2. Highlights on Health in Germany.
   http://www.who.dk/eprise/main/who/countryinformation/country?

   Area Code = DEU

The Netherlands

1. National Institute of Public Health and the Environment.
   http://www.rivm.nl/en/

2. Highlights on Health in the Netherlands.
   www.who.dk/eprise/main/who/countryinformation/country?

   Area Code = NET

France

Highlights on Health in France.
www.who.dk/eprise/main/who/countryinformation/country?

Area Code = FRA

Health Care in Former Socialist, Socialist, and Developing Countries

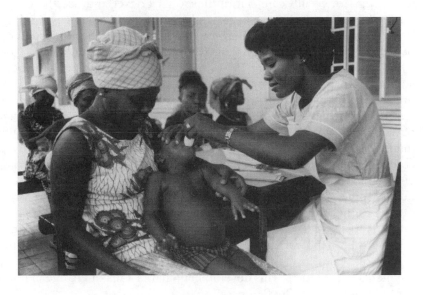

To have a more complete appreciation of the various approaches to health care, it is necessary to look beyond North American, European, and Japanese delivery systems. In this chapter we will discuss changes in the former socialist medical systems of Russia, Poland, and Hungary, as well as in the present-day socialist country of China. Next we will review socialized medicine in Saudi Arabia and Kenya, the decentralized system in Mexico, and the mixed fee-for-service system in South Africa.

SOCIALIST MEDICINE: ALTERATIONS IN RUSSIA, POLAND, HUNGARY, AND CHINA

The socialist model of health care delivery has slowly disappeared since 1989–91 when communism collapsed in Eastern Europe and the former Soviet Union. Centralized planning, rigid control of the economy, unrealistic quotas for the production of goods, and shoddy products, along with a lack of incentives for workers and a relatively low standard of living, marked the economic failure of communism (Skidelsky 1995). A lack of public confidence and the desire of various national groups to break away from Russian domination were other major problems. When the Soviet Union's last president, Mikhail Gorbachev, opened the door to reform, the communist system in Europe fell apart—changing much of socialist medicine in the process. In this section we will review the situation in Russia, Poland, and Hungary, and then review the changes in China, which retains its socialist identity in politics.

Russia

The old Soviet system of health care delivery is disappearing. Comprehensive health care remains free to the general population. However, people who can afford it pay for health care out of their own pocket and use the best doctors and hospitals; they also receive faster and higher quality services. In 1991 and 1993, Russia passed legislation establishing a new system of health insurance, consisting of compulsory and voluntary plans (Curtis, Petukhova, and Taket 1995; McKeehan 1995; Sheiman 1994; Twigg 1999, 2000, 2002). The compulsory social health insurance plan is financed by central government subsidies for pensioners and the unemployed, along with contributions (3.6 percent of payrolls) from employers to cover workers. Health insurance is mandatory for all employees, provides the same basic benefits without choice, and is administered by eighty-nine regional government health insurance funds that make payments to participating private insurance companies. Individuals or employers have a choice of insurance companies, and competition between these companies is expected to control costs and ensure quality services. There is also a voluntary plan of private insurance that anyone can purchase out of his or her own pocket which provides supplemental benefits. The intent is to move away from the former Soviet method of paying for health care directly out of the central government's budget and replacing it with a universal system of health insurance providing basic benefits for all citizens in the form of payments to providers. This development marks a major change in financing health care delivery for the Russian people.

Prior to the collapse of communism in the former Soviet Union and Eastern Europe, the health care delivery systems in the region were philosophically guided by Marxist–Leninism programs for reshaping capitalism into socialism. The ultimate goal of Marxist–Leninism was the establishment of a classless society, featuring an end to class oppression, private property, worker alienation, and economic scarcity. However, Marxist-Leninist ideology pertaining to health was never developed in depth.

The new Soviet state established in the aftermath of the 1917 revolution nevertheless faced serious health problems, including large-scale epidemics and famine. More out of practical than theoretical necessity, the Fifth All-Russian Congress of Soviets outlined some fundamental principles of Marxist-Leninist health policy in 1918. The congress mandated that health care would be (1) the responsibility of the state, (2) provided without direct cost to the user, (3) controlled by a central authority, and (4) allocated priority for care to workers, with (5) an emphasis on preventive care (Cassileth, Vlassov, and Chapman 1995; Light 1986). Because of the critical need for doctors and a shortage of manpower resulting from industrial and military demands, large numbers of women, especially nurses with working-class backgrounds, were sent to medical schools where they were given cram courses and certified as physicians. William Knaus (1981:83) explains:

> Many had no ambitions beyond a weekly paycheck. The Soviet government responded in kind with a low wage scale and a social status for medicine that treated the new physician with no more respect given a factory worker. Professionalism was not rewarded nor even encouraged. Medicine became a job and women were the ones chosen to do it.

Russia has more doctors per capita than any major nation (about 4.7 physicians for every 1,000 people), and some three-fourths are women (Cassileth et al. 1995; Lassey et al. 1997). However, men hold the majority of academic positions in medicine and medical posts in the Ministry of Health. Thus, Russian women are more likely to be medical practitioners than medical professors, administrators, and policymakers. A strong sense of professionalism for the majority of doctors in the former Soviet medical system was neither encouraged, nor rewarded. The Soviet government provided low wages (about $24 a month, less than what a bus driver would make) and their status was equivalent to that of a high school teacher (Cassileth et al. 1995; Field 1995).

In 1987, a few years before the collapse of the Soviet regime, the average salary for health care providers was 71 percent of the national average (Mezentseva and Rimachevskaya 1992). Prominent physicians, however, had access to special stores, preferred apartments, good schools for their children, special vacation benefits, and other privileges. In order to receive personal attention and access to better care, patients typically provided gifts or bribes to health care personnel, which evolved into a second economy within the overall health care system. Mark Field (1993:167), in fact, referred to the bribery system as the "commercialization of Soviet medicine" and noted that it was paradoxical that payments by patients were reintroduced in a system designed to remove financial incentives from the patient–physician relationship. Russian doctors now have a payment structure based on income from insurance and patients for services rendered.

A hierarchical system of health care delivery facilities provided services, with local polyclinics (multiple service clinics) the initial point of entry for primary care and the source of referrals to specialists and higher level hospital care. The general public did not have a choice of physicians, but assignment to a medical practitioner was made on the basis of residence. There were differences in the quality of care provided in that a stratified arrangement of clinics and hospitals existed, with separate closed systems for elite groups, such as top government officials, miners, and other high-priority industrial workers, and open systems for cities and rural areas (Davis 1989). Yet despite shortcomings in financing, technology, and public access to quality care, the Soviets nevertheless established a nationwide health care delivery system providing free treatment.

The former Soviet health care system is now part of history, as the Russian Federation's new insurance-based structure is being established. Nevertheless, serious problems remain including low financing and declining life expectancy. As late as 1989, only some 3.4 percent of the GDP was spent on health care in the former Soviet Union as a whole (Rowland and Telyukov 1991), but in the Russian Federation in the mid-1990s that figure was less than 2 percent of the GDP (Field 1995) and stood at 2.2 percent of the GDP in 1997 (Cockerham 1999). This is a low percentage in comparison to other industrialized countries and less than one would expect, given the magnitude of health problems in the country. According to Elena Mezentseva and Natalia Rimachevskaya (1992), health care costs have typically been financed on the basis of the so-called *residual principle,* that is from funds left over after providing for the needs of the sectors of the economy which were given priority.

From the end of World War II until the mid-1960s, health progress in the former Soviet Union was rapid and consistent. For example, Table 16-1 shows that in Russia (the former Russian Soviet Federated Socialist Republic) life expectancy for males was 40.4 years in 1938 but reached 64.0 years in 1965; for females, life expectancy

A Russian nurse attends to a patient in a Moscow hospital. Men and women in Russia had a longer life expectancy in 1965 than they did in 2000.

TABLE 16-1   Life Expectancy at Birth in Russia, 1896-2000.

Year	Males	Females
1896	30.9	33.0
1910	—	—
1926	39.3	44.8
1938	40.4	46.7
1958	61.9	69.2
1965	64.0	72.1
1970	63.0	73.4
1980	61.4	73.0
1984	61.7	73.0
1985	62.7	73.3
1986	64.8	74.3
1987	64.9	74.3
1988	64.8	74.4
1989	64.2	74.5
1990	63.8	74.3
1991	63.5	74.3
1992	62.0	73.8
1993	58.9	71.9
1994	57.6	71.2
1995	58.3	71.7
1996	59.8	72.5
1997	60.8	72.9
1998	61.8	72.8
1999	59.9	72.0
2000	58.9	71.8

Source: Russia State Committee on Statistics, 2002.

increased from 46.7 years to 72.1 over the same period. However, in the mid-1960s, life expectancy began a downward trend, largely brought on by rising mortality from heart disease among middle-age working-class males. With the collapse of the former Soviet Union in 1991 and the continued decline of Russia's standard of living in the 1990s, the decrease in life expectancy for both men and women accelerated.

This situation is depicted in Table 16-1 showing life expectancy in Russia for selected years between 1896 and 2000. Table 16-1 shows that male life expectancy in Russia fell from 64.0 in 1965 to 61.4 in 1980, but improved to 64.9 in 1987. Russian demographers credit this brief rise in male longevity to Gorbachev's anti-alcohol campaign in the mid-1980s, which significantly curtailed both the production and consumption of alcohol. For example, Vladimir Shkolnikov and Alexander Nemtsov (1994) calculated the difference between observed and expected deaths by sex and age and found that longevity increased 3.2 years for males and 1.3 years for females during the campaign's duration, with the greatest advances occurring in 1986.

Shkolnikov and Nemtsov (1994:1) concluded that "the rapid mortality decrease in the years 1984 to 1987 can be assumed to reflect a pure effect of reduced alcohol abuse on mortality, because there were no other significant changes in conditions of public health in that short period." But the campaign was discontinued in late 1987 because of its widespread unpopularity, and both alcohol consumption and male mortality correspondingly increased. As shown in Table 16-1, average life expectancy for Soviet men had declined to 64.2 years by 1989.

Following the 1991 demise of the former Soviet Union, we see in Table 16-1 that life expectancy for Russian males dropped from 63.5 years to a low of 57.6 in 1994. For females, Table 16-1 shows a relatively slow but consistent upward trend between 1965 and 1989 from 72.1 years to 74.5 years. In 1991, in the new Russian Federation, females lived 74.3 years on average, but by 1994 life expectancy for women had fallen to 71.2 years. Consequently, both Russian men and women had a lower life expectancy in 1994 than their counterparts in 1965. Between 1995 and 1998, however, there was a slight increase in life expectancy for both Russian men and women due to a reduction in alcohol-related deaths (Shkolnikov, McKee, and Leon 2001). The most vulnerable people had died and their premature deaths had less effect on life expectancy as a result. This was not a genuine improvement in longevity as Table 16-1 shows life expectancy figures resumed their downward movement from 61.8 years for males in 1998 to 58.9 years in 2000. Males averaged nearly two years less longevity in 1998 compared to 2000. Life expectancy for females fell a full year from 72.8 years to 71.8 years during the same period.

There has been a fluctuation in infant mortality for reasons that are unexplained. In 1971, infant mortality in Russia was 21.2 deaths per 1,000 live births; by 1975 infant mortality had risen to 28.2 deaths per 1,000 births, but it dropped to 18.3 in 1990, only to rise to 21.4 in 1993. Since 1993, infant mortality has consistently declined and reached its lowest point ever in 2001 of 14.7 infant deaths per 1,000 births. Possible risk factors are the use of cigarettes and alcohol during pregnancy, as well as a diet low in animal protein but high in grains, potatoes, and fat causing low birth weights; also the long Russian winters may reduce the availability of fresh vegetables and other sources of vitamins for the diets of pregnant women. The relationship of low birth weight to high infant mortality is important because undernourished babies are particularly at high risk for pneumonia, which accounted for about half of all infant deaths in the former Soviet Union.

Other health-related developments in Russia are the rising death rate and falling birth rate. As depicted in Figure 16-1, Russia's birth rate dropped from 17 births per 1,000 people in 1984 to 9.1 per 1,000 in 2001. Between 1984 and 1994, Russia's death rate rose from 11.5 to 15.7 deaths for every 1,000 persons. In 2001 the death rate was 15.6 per 1,000 persons. Declining birth rates are not unusual in today's world; increasing death rates, however, are highly unusual for a major country. Russian society clearly has serious problems as it struggles with forging a democratic political system and strong free market economy. Without an economic recovery, health reforms will continue to be difficult.

The decline of life expectancy in Russia and elsewhere in the former Soviet bloc countries was one of the most significant developments in world health in the late

FIGURE 16-1 Birth and death rates in the former Soviet Union and Russian Federation, 1984–1997 (per 1,000 people).

Source: Russia State Committee on Statistics, 1998.

twentieth century. This situation is without precedent in modern history. Nowhere else has health worsened so seriously in peacetime among industrialized nations. Ironically, the former Soviet Union and Eastern Europe espoused an ideology of social equality that theoretically should have promoted health for all. However, the reverse occurred, and life expectancy turned downward in the region for more than three decades. This is a surprising development. That an entire group of industrialized countries under a stable administrative system would experience such a prolonged decline in public health was completely unexpected.

The rise in mortality was greatest in Russia and came very late to East Germany, but virtually all former Soviet bloc countries were affected to varying degrees. The deaths largely stemmed from higher rates of heart disease and to a lesser extent from alcohol abuse and alcohol-related accidents. An unhealthy lifestyle appears to be the primary cause of the increase in heart disease and other health problems leading to the downturn in life expectancy (Cockerham 1997b, 1999, 2000; Cockerham, Snead, and DeWaal 2002). This lifestyle was characterized by extremely heavy alcohol and cigarette consumption, high-fat diets, and little or no leisure-time exercise, and was, as noted, particularly common among middle-aged working-class males who were the principal victims of the rise in premature deaths. Thus, gender (male), age (middle age), and class (working class) were the key sociological variables in this health crisis. Medical treatment could not compensate for the damage to the circulatory system caused by unhealthy lifestyle practices, and the pathological effects they engendered overshadowed the contributions of infectious diseases, environmental pollution, and medically avoidable deaths to the increase in mortality. A health policy that failed to cope with the rise in heart disease and stress was also an important causal factor. The Soviet system lacked the flexibility administratively and structurally to adjust to health problems that could not be handled by the mass measures successful in controlling infectious ailments (Field 2000). Ultimately the unhealthy

BOX 16-1   State Socialism and Health Lifestyles

The author and his colleagues (Cockerham, Snead, and DeWaal 2002) investigated whether Soviet-style state socialism had the potential to induce passivity on the part of some Russians toward health promotion. The research strategy to investigate this situation in present-day Russia was to examine the health practices of a national sample of Russian respondents who wish to return to socialism as it was before Gorbachev's reforms and the collapse of the Soviet Union. They compared this group with those who do not wish to return to socialism and favor staying with the present political and economic course or adopting some other measures. They wanted to determine if respondents favoring a return to a socialist state have less healthy lifestyles than those who reject socialism, or whether political ideology does not matter.

The investigators thought a heritage of state socialism could influence passivity among pro-socialists in adopting an active health lifestyle. This is because the choices of individuals in Soviet society were confined to a singular social and political ideology and expected to conform to it. This ideology ranked the interests of the state and the collective (units of colleagues in factories, farms, offices, and schools) much higher than those of the individual, while solidarity with the state was considered far more important than individualism and personal autonomy. The state provided for the needs of the individual and the individual, in turn, was expected to give up considerable personal reliance and freedom. To many, the state was a shelter. It provided free education and health care, old-age pensions, and low-cost housing and food, along with guaranteed employment. Health was the responsibility of the state, not the individual. A political and social environment constraining innovation and creativity, may also have promoted feelings of apathy, alienation, and low sense of personal control. Such apathy could extend to neglecting good health practices. After all, if a person got sick, the state was supposed to take care of them.

The data show that pro-socialists consume alcohol much more frequently, while anti-socialists are largely doing what little exercise and preventive checkups are being carried out. Anti-socialists also rank their health status significantly higher than pro-socialists. Thus those in favor of returning to state socialism did indeed live less healthy lifestyles—although neither group collectively practices good health measures. In fact, the extent of negative health practices is so widespread that it can be argued that the health lifestyles of anti-socialists is only marginally better than that of pro-socialists, but it is better nonetheless.

lifestyle of a particular segment of the population was the major social determinant of the downturn in life expectancy.

For example, Russian historian Roy Medvedev (2000) finds that the high mortality rate cannot be explained by economic factors alone; rather, he ranks national peculiarities of diet and lifestyle as particularly important causes. Peder Walberg and his colleagues (Walberg et al. 2000) found that the steep decrease in life expectancy in the early 1990s was not due to impoverishment since the greatest rises in mortality were in the wealthiest regions (i.e., Moscow, St. Petersburg, Murmansk, Pskov) of

Russia which experienced the smallest declines in household income. They also observed that alcohol consumption was far more important than the rapid pace of change and high unemployment in explaining regional differences in mortality. In fact, Martin Bobak et al. (1999) state that drinking behavior in Russia seems unrelated to individual perceptions of recent societal changes. The number of binge drinkers appears to be large regardless of the economy and the acute effects of binge drinking in particular have been identified as responsible for a substantial number of cardiovascular deaths among young men (Bobak et al. 1999; Chenet et al. 1998).

While the amount of taxed alcohol consumed in Russia is about 7 liters of pure alcohol per capita, the real figure is at least 14 to 15 liters when the consumption of unregistered imports and home distilled beverages are taken into account (Treml 1997). This is the highest per capita consumption of alcohol in the world. When it is noted that adult males consume 90 percent of the alcohol, yet comprise 25 percent of the population, it is apparent that the drinking practices of males far exceed per capita consumption and reflect a tremendous concentration of drinking. Not only is per capita consumption extraordinarily high, but the type of alcohol typically consumed (vodka) and the drinking style (oriented toward drunkenness and binge drinking) are considerably more harmful than the moderate drinking of wine. Cigarette consumption is also higher in Russia than in the West, and male deaths from lung cancer are extremely high by international standards (Lopez 1998; McKee et al. 1998). About 53 percent of all Russian men and 20 percent of women smoke. As for nutrition, the Russian diet has changed considerably since the 1960s, moving away from the consumption of cereals and potatoes toward much greater consumption of sugar and red meat. By 1990, over 36 percent of Russian food provided energy from fat, making it one of the fattiest diets in the world (Popkin et al. 1997). Furthermore, men consume about 50 percent more fat than women (Shapiro 1995). There are few data on healthy exercise, but what there are show exercise to be minimal (Palosuo 2000; Palosuo et al. 1998). As Russian medical sociologist Elena Dmitrieva (2001) concludes, Russia lacks a self-protective health culture.

Poland

Poland is another former socialist country that experienced a deteriorating state of health (Cockerham 1999). Life expectancy declined and morbidity rates for heart disease and cancer rose. Rates for tuberculosis were twice the average for Europe. There were also were significant increases in the incidence of influenza and hepatitis. Official Polish government figures show that life expectancy in 1989 was 66.7 years for men and 75.5 years for women; by 1991, life expectancy had dropped to 66.1 years for men and 75.3 years for women. The rise of mortality was especially severe for men and was largely due to premature deaths from heart disease of males in the 45- to 64-year-old age group. By 2000, however, improvement was noted as life expectancy recovered to 69.7 years for men and 77.9 years for women.

Poland is in the forefront of the rapid social, economic, and political changes taking place in the former Soviet bloc countries. Poland is a member of NATO, has been accepted into European Union in 2004, and has strived for a strong economy with Western Europe as its major trading partner. The GDP per capita rose from

$1,000 in 1990 to $9,900 in 2001. Although economic problems remain and Poland has suffered through a recent recession, the nation appears on the path to the ordinary problems of the free market.

As in the West, health inequalities are greatest in the lower class and have worsened in recent years as the market economy produced a growing impoverishment among those at the bottom of society who were unable to take advantage of the new economic conditions (Ostrowska 1993, 1998, 2001). Studies of household nutrition and health, for example, show that less affluent families are eating more foods of reduced quality (Bakken, Jezewska-Zychowicz, and Winter 1999). However, alcohol consumption has declined among the heaviest drinkers, and the diet of the population as a whole is healthier than under communism (the lower class is an exception). The consumption of cigarettes is remaining stable, as Poland has experienced novel and aggressive commercials in the media from Western tobacco companies intended to increase sales in a new market of smokers, while public health campaigns try to reduce the number of smokers.

Given the rise in male life expectancy from 66.1 years in 1991 (the last year of decline) to 69.7 years in 2000 (the highest longevity ever) and the increase in female life expectancy from 75.3 years to 77.9 years (the highest ever) during the same period, Poland's health situation is returning to a positive state. Since 1998, Poland has had a national health insurance system similar to the German model that is based on payroll deductions (7.1 percent) of the wages and salaries of workers. This is an important development providing access to health care for the entire population in a market economy.

Hungary

Health conditions in the former socialist state of Hungary are also improving. In 1966, Hungarian men reached an all-time high of 67.5 years in life expectancy followed by a consistent decline to 64.5 years in 1992 and 1993. Since 1994 male life expectancy has risen to 66.1 in 2000, but is still below the level reached in 1966. For women life expectancy has continued to increase to a 2000 level of 74.4 years. The downturn in longevity for Hungarian men has been due largely to increased death from heart disease during middle age, especially among blue-collar workers, with heavy smoking and alcohol serving as significant risk factors (Cockerham, 1999; Józan 1996). Hungarian government data show that the percentage of regular smokers increased between 1984 and 1994, while the number of alcoholics doubled between 1987 and 1993. In 1998, 44 percent of the men and 27 percent of the women smoked. Trends such as these translate into higher mortality rates in the future, so it is not clear if the current improvement in male life expectancy is temporary or long term. We do know that lung cancer from smoking among Hungarian males is the highest in Europe (Levi et al. 1995) and the diet is high in saturated animal fats (Biro, Antal, and Zajkas 1996).

A nationwide health behavior survey conducted by the Hungarian Central Statistical Office (1995) not only found that the percentage of smokers had increased, but some 72 percent of the sample of over five thousand households drank alcohol regularly and 11.6 percent of the respondents were characterized as "excessive drinkers." Only 21.4 percent of the men and 13.5 percent of the women reported regular physical exercise, while less than 10 percent of the men and 12.5 percent of the women ate vegetables almost every day in the winter. Furthermore, over half of all visits to physicians were made by just 10 percent of the respondents. Hungary's health profile is among the worst in Europe, and these data help us to understand why.

Between 1948 and 1989, Hungary operated a Soviet-style health care delivery system characterized by central planning and control, subsidized by the state, and providing free health care to the general population under the Uniform State Health Service Act of 1950. This act officially eliminated health insurance and made free health care a right of all citizens. Private practice was not forbidden but in reality existed only in dentistry. The health system was financed by the government's central budget.

With the fall of communism, Hungary has revamped its health care delivery system. Most people are enrolled in a compulsory national health insurance plan that is supported by contributions from workers, employers, and government funds. Only individuals and families with substantial incomes can remain outside the national health plan. Patients are allowed free choice of health care providers. General practitioners are paid by the insurance fund on a per capita basis; specialists are paid on a fee-for-service basis. Hospitals are paid on a service-rendered basis according to a fee schedule of diagnostic related groups (DRGs)—similar to the DRG system used for Medicare in the United States. Private health insurance is available for the affluent, and private medical care has been legalized. Hungary is still undergoing the transformation of its health services, and its short-term goal is to increase efficiency while the country moves more fully into a capitalist economic system.

China

The People's Republic of China remains a socialist country politically, but its economic transition from socialism to a market-driven economy has been accompanied by dramatic changes in its health care delivery system. China no longer has a socialist system of health care in which the state controls, organizes, finances, and allocates health care directly to all citizens free of charge. The Chinese health care system is now financed largely by fees paid by patients, employers, and health insurance companies (Chen 2001; Hesketh and Zhu 1997b; Hsiao 1995).

Prior to the 1949 revolution that brought the communists to power, there were few Western-trained physicians in China and these doctors generally lived in major cities where they commanded high fees for their work. Except for a few missionary doctors in the countryside, the bulk of the Chinese population received medical care from folk practitioners. There was a heavy death toll from disease, poor sanitation, and widespread ignorance about health matters. In 1949, the average life expectancy of a Chinese was only thirty-five years.

Improvement in health became one of the major goals of the Communist Chinese government after it came to power following the civil war with Nationalist forces. One of the first public health measures was the "Patriotic Health Movement," in which millions of Chinese killed flies, removed trash, and worked to improve sanitation. Two other measures were also important. First, traditional Chinese medicine was revived, featuring the use of herbal medicines and techniques like acupuncture, in which pain is controlled by the insertion of needles into certain designated points in the body. Even though its therapeutic value is not fully understood, traditional Chinese medicine is still used today throughout China with considerable effectiveness for many health problems. Often traditional medicine is used in conjunction with Western medicine, and while Chinese physicians are trained largely in either the traditional or the Western approach, all receive some training in both disciplines. China is the only country that consistently treats traditional and scientific medicine equally, making both of them legally available and requiring Western-style physicians to learn traditional methods (Hesketh and Zhu 1997a).

Second, the so-called barefoot doctors movement was begun, in which 1.8 million paramedical personnel were eventually trained in rudimentary medicine and sent to rural areas to provide basic medical treatment and assist in efforts at preventive medicine and public health (Lassey et al. 1997; Sidel 1993). Through this movement, the majority of the population was able to have at least some routine access to medical care.

China's attempts at improving its health care system suffered a serious setback during the Cultural Revolution of 1966 to 1977. The Cultural Revolution was intended by China's leaders to be a mass movement of the people that would expose corruption and rid the government of unnecessary bureaucracy. Many influential people were subjected to severe public criticism and even persecuted by revolutionary groups such as the Red Guards, whose membership included thousands of young students. Schools and universities were closed as young people abandoned their studies to participate in revolutionary activities. Factions developed within the movement itself, and this period of Chinese history is marked with chaos as power struggles were waged within the hierarchy of the government and the Communist party. There was a widespread disruption of work and education, and many people lost their lives in the street fighting, torture, and pressure to commit suicide that followed. For nearly four years, there was virtually no medical research or training of medical students. Thousands of doctors were forced to leave their positions and were sent into the countryside to work with peasants in agricultural communes. When medical education was resumed in 1970, the time for training was cut from eight years after high school to three years, with emphasis on practical and applied medicine. Almost anyone could gain admission to medical school, and few or no examinations were given during training. The quality of Chinese doctors declined accordingly, and the old system has now returned, but many valuable years were lost in regard to both medical education and research.

Today an extensive network of health care facilities exists in China. Clinics providing preventive medicine, birth control measures, and first aid are readily available in both rural areas and urban neighborhoods. People with serious illnesses or injuries are referred to district and regional hospitals. Many factories have their own clinics and hospitals. Medical care for factory workers is paid for by insurance that state-owned and some collectively owned factories have established with money obtained from the sale of goods (Grogan 1995; G. Henderson et al. 1995).

In rural areas, China's transition from a communal (collective farm) agricultural system in the 1980s to a household-centered approach (on state-owned land) led to the collapse of the collective farm health care system (Chen 2001; Grogan 1995; Henderson et al. 1995). Without collective farming income, farm health clinics were dissolved, and many barefoot doctors left health care altogether or went into private practice (Y. Liu et al. 1995; Xueshan et al. 1995). The financial burden in rural areas was shifted to individual households who have to pay for health care out of their pockets. Those who cannot afford to pay may go without care—as the Chinese government struggled to find an equitable and efficient way to deliver health services to rural areas (Bloom and Tang 1999; Liu et al. 1995; Xueshan et al. 1995). Only 155 million out of a total of 1.2 billion people are covered by social health insurance (X. Liu and Hsiao 1995). A new health reform plan has been introduced to provide universal insurance coverage with comprehensive benefits in the cities and later in the countryside. The new plan is financed by contributions from employees, employers, and local governments.

At present the central government provides less than 1 percent of all health expenditures; the responsibility for providing services was delegated to the provincial and county governments (Hesketh and Zhu 1997b). But the amount of money available covers only minimum wages for health care workers and capital investments for the construction of new facilities. The remaining expenses are to be covered by patient fees. Basic levels of health care tend to be provided below cost, but profits can be made from the sale of drugs and use of technology. Hospitals and health centers have to generate their own incomes from the services they provide to patients, but they control the allocation of profits. The result is the end of China's system of universal access to free health care and its replacement by a fee-for-service model. Although incomes have risen throughout China in recent decades, the urban and especially the rural poor are the most disadvantaged in obtaining health services (Hesketh and Zhu 1997b; Y. Liu, Hsiao, and Eggleston 1999).

In 2001, the average life expectancy in China for males was 70.0 years and for females 73.9 years. The infant mortality rate was 27.2 infant deaths per 1,000 live births. Acute infectious diseases were largely brought under control or eliminated, but the recent global SARS epidemic started in China and caused considerable problems in Hong Kong and Beijing (see Box 15-1). Heart disease and cancer, however, remain the major health problems in most parts of the country. An increasingly important health problem now and in the future is lung cancer. China has an estimated 300 million smokers who account for 30 percent of the world's tobacco consumption. Some 70 percent of China's adult male population smokes, and the proportion of adult female smokers is about 7 percent. Lung cancer rates are increasing 4.5 percent a year, and smoking-related deaths are expected to reach around two million annually by 2025. Already some 800,000 Chinese die annually from smoking-related causes (Lin et al. 1998). The government has initiated a nationwide campaign against smoking, but this effort is counter to the interests of the vast state-owned tobacco monopoly, which is the world's largest producer of cigarettes. Tax revenues from tobacco sales are the government's single largest source of income. Consequently, the Chinese government is faced with an important dilemma: if smoking declines, its greatest single source of income will be reduced.

SOCIALIZED MEDICINE: SAUDI ARABIA AND KENYA

Socialized medicine, as noted in Chapter 15, is a system of health care delivery in which care is provided in the form of a state-supported consumer service. Socialized medicine is practiced in different environments, and this section discusses socialized health care in a relatively wealthy country (Saudi Arabia) and a relatively poor nation (Kenya).

Saudi Arabia

Saudi Arabia is a desert kingdom whose native population, as Eugene Gallagher (2001) and others (Mackey 1987) explain, is Arab and Islamic to a degree extreme even for the Middle East. Ruled by a king who is an absolute monarch, Saudi Arabian society is characterized by the traditional segregation of women from public life and strong extended family relationships. Saudi Arabia is included in this chapter as an example of a form of socialized medicine provided by an affluent nation. As late as 1945, Saudi Arabia was a poor country largely inhabited by nomadic Bedouin tribes. Sandra Mackey (1987) points out that most Saudis lived in tents or small, poorly ventilated houses made of straw and mud. There was no electricity, education, or medical care. But in the 1950s, money from oil revenues began pouring into the country, and during the 1970s Saudi Arabia became an economic power because of its wealth and reserves of oil. Between 1970 and 1979, revenues increased from $1.2 billion to $65 billion annually and reached $125 billion in the early 1980s before oil prices declined. Currently, oil brings about $25 billion in revenues. With so much money coming into the country earlier in such a relatively short period of time, Saudi Arabia experienced an unprecedented spurt of economic growth and modernization. In the 1990s and early 2000s, Saudi Arabia found itself with a considerably lower income, but the nation is still more affluent than most developing countries.

The oil revenues are paid to the king who distributes funds to manage the nation. Although the exact population of Saudi Arabia is not known, it probably numbers around 22 million people (17 million Saudis and 5 million foreign nationals). Saudis pay no income tax and are assured an adequate standard of living by their government. Any higher living standard is to be earned by the individual, with the government ready to guarantee grants and loans for housing and business ventures. Mackey (1987:217–218) describes the situation as follows:

> The oil boom made the Saudis rich. They were not only statistically rich, as reckoned by dividing oil revenues by the number of people, but also in the sense that the Saudis commanded high disposable incomes and lived in one of the world's most benevolent welfare states. Huge oil revenues coupled with Saudi Arabia's small population enabled the House of Saudi to give every Saudi citizen a share of prosperity on a scale few rulers have ever matched. Through careful management, there would have been enough money to make every citizen a ward of the state. King Faisal early rejected this idea, choosing instead to press Saudis into the work force while cushioning them against serious need with grants, loans, subsidies, and government services.

Massive amounts of money were channeled into housing, education, and medical care (Gallagher 1995). Where in 1970 there had been 47 hospitals, 7,165 hospital beds, and 789 physicians, by 1995 there were 175 modern hospitals, nearly 26,737 beds, and 15,476 physicians and the figures are higher today. The King Faisal Medical City in the capital of Riyadh, opened in 1975, was intended to be the best equipped medical center in the world. In addition, there were four medical schools, five nursing schools, and other institutions for training dentists, pharmacists, and medical technicians. Health care in government hospitals is free, and if it is necessary for a Saudi citizen to go abroad for specialized medical treatment, the expenses for that person and at least one other family member will be paid by the government.

Saudi Arabia, however, has both a public and private system of health care delivery. Yet as Gallagher and Maureen Searle (1985) observe, Saudi affluence provides two important contrasts with most other developing nations. First, the re-sources of government medicine are of a high quality and are well distributed throughout the urban and vast desert areas of the kingdom. Second, with the spread of wealth in the population, more families are able to become medical consumers in the private sector, thereby reducing the number of people dependent upon pub-lic health care. While private and public medicine may not provide the same stan-dard of care, the gap between "first-class" private care and "second-class" govern-ment medicine, in Gallagher and Searle's view, is substantially narrower than that found in other developing nations. Providing high-quality medical care to those in need is one way in which the government, with its wealth, can benefit the public in a manner consistent with Saudi political culture and the teachings of Islam. Gallagher and Searle (1985:259) state:

> Citizens are entitled to receive modern health services within the public sector without such services becoming the object of political contention, such as occurs increasingly in Western nations. Public provision for health care has strong popular appeal. Anyone can become ill, need health care, and benefit from its application. When, as in Saudi Arabia, it is provided in a monarchic system of government, health care can be en-dowed with a sense of patrimonial solicitude for the ill and ailing. This imagery has strong meaning within the symbolic context of extended-family concern for kinsmen, which is very powerful in Saudi Arabia.

Consequently, unlike other aspects of modernization involving Western cul-ture such as bureaucracy, structure, and the Protestant work ethic, the provision of Western-style health care to Saudi Arabia's population has not produced severe strains in Saudi society. But the transition to a modern medical system has not been without challenges, despite ample funding. Two problems in particular are not typ-ical of Western societies. One is the lack of trained Saudi medical professionals, and the other is health care for women. While there are over 15,000 physicians in Saudi Arabia, about 85 percent of them are foreigners. There are also equally high per-centages of foreigners working as nurses. It will be several years before enough Saudi physicians and other health personnel are able to provide Saudi Arabia with medical self-sufficiency.

The position of females in Saudi society presents some special considerations for health care providers. Women are segregated from men in educational institutions and hospitals; women are also not allowed to drive automobiles, nor can they travel abroad without the permission of the senior male member of their family. While separate hospital facilities and clinics can be established for women or different hours arranged for medical consultations if separate facilities are not available, female patients may have to be treated by foreign male physicians because of the shortage of Saudi doctors. To meet the health needs of women and avoid dependence on male physicians, about 50 percent of all Saudi medical students are female. Thus, medicine is one of the few professions open to women in Saudi Arabia. As Gallagher and Searle (1985) note, females are segregated in varying degrees throughout the Middle East for pre-Islamic reasons of male honor and female virtue, but this practice is more strictly observed in Saudi Arabia than in most other societies in the region. As a result, Saudi medicine is confronted with the requirement to comply with the culture's division of the sexes wherever possible. This is seen in Saudi medical education where medical schools have both a male and female campus; even though English is the language of instruction, Western textbooks are used, and many of the faculty are neither Saudi nor Muslim—Saudi and Islamic values prevail. As Gallagher (1988b) observed, all students dress conservatively, participate in daily prayers, and shun the consumption of pork and alcohol. The students are rigidly segregated by sex in the same school. Gallagher (1988b:391–392) provides an example:

> Several male students asked that the main (male) library curtain off the windows facing the central campus courtyard so that they would not be able to view female students crossing the yard en route to lab sessions. Although the females always wore the full black cloaks (*abbayas*) that were required when they moved off the female campus, the complainants said that the female students were too much of a distraction from their studies. The library installed curtains in response. The curtains were moveable, however, so that students could open or close them according to the sensibilities of whoever was in the library.

Gallagher provides other examples, such as students complaining that the non-Muslim faculty did not understand Islam, demanding the library cancel subscriptions to magazines if they contained liquor ads and articles about sex, and refusing to perform clinical clerkships outside of Saudi Arabia in other Arab states they felt were too permissive. Opposition to Western culture is also seen in conflict over the use of English as the language of instruction, since the students and their patients all speak Arabic (Gallagher 2001). But virtually all written material is in English, making it impossible to adopt Arabic.

Infant mortality rates in Saudi Arabia are still somewhat high with 2000 rates of 52.9 infant deaths per 1,000 live births. In comparison to other countries in the region, Saudi Arabia shows lower infant mortality rates than countries like Yemen, where 2000 rates were 70.3 per 1,000, but has much higher rates than countries like Kuwait at 11.5 per 1,000. Therefore, Saudi Arabia still has some distance to cover before becoming one of the world's healthiest nations. Nevertheless, progress in health is being made. In 1976, the average life expectancy of a Saudi was 45 years; by 1981 life expectancy had risen to 54 years, and in 2001 life expectancy reached 68.4 years for males and 73.5 years for females.

Kenya

Kenya is located in East Africa and covers an area approximately the size of France. As a result of one of the highest birth rates in the world (29.3 births per 1,000 persons in 2000) and declining mortality, the population of Kenya increased from 5.4 million in 1948 to 30.3 million in 2000. With a rapidly rising population and a depressed agricultural economy, based largely on the production of coffee and tea, Kenya has serious economic and social problems—although the economy is somewhat better than other nations in the region. Kenya is included in this chapter as an example of the type of socialized health care delivery system developed by a relatively poor Third World country.

Kenya has a national health service that employs physicians and other health personnel and owns hospitals, but private practitioners, mission clinics run by church organizations, and traditional native folk healers are also available. The Kenyan national health care system was established in the early 1950s under a colonial administration and includes regional and district hospitals and a network of rural health clinics. Modern, Western-style health care in Kenya, as elsewhere in Africa, is primarily provided by the state, concentrated almost exclusively in major urban centers, and inherited largely without modification from a former colonial power, which, in Kenya's case, was Great Britain. This is the situation not only in Kenya, but throughout Africa south of the Sahara (Rensburg and Ngwena 2001).

Despite good intentions, Kenyan health policy is typical of other African states in that most of the national health budget is spent in the capital of Nairobi. S. Ogoh Alubo (1990) notes, for example, a period when Kenya spent 40 percent of its entire health budget on Nairobi's National Kenyatta Hospital and only 2 percent went to rural health clinics. On the average, urban health institutions in Kenya receive 80 to 85 percent annually of the total national health budget. Almost every hospital is located in an urban center. The best educated and most wealthy members of Kenyan society also live in urban areas, especially in Nairobi and Mombassa, and they demand and receive the highest quality public health services in the country (Mwabu 1984).

Consequently, there is a considerable disparity between urban and rural health care. Some 85 percent of Kenya's population lives in rural areas where dispensaries and clinics are poorly equipped and understaffed by trained personnel. Kenya has one doctor for every 20,000 persons, but less than 10 percent of Kenya's physicians are located in rural settings. As a result, few medical doctors are available for rural residents. Another major problem that rural residents face is that they must often travel great distances to reach a health clinic; even though care is free—as it is for all Kenyans who use public facilities—travel expenses, a lack of transportation and roads in rural areas, and the time involved are major considerations in making the decision to seek medical care. In some areas, professional health care is simply not available.

Cheryl Bentsen (1991) studied the Maasai tribe in Kenya and found they rarely get sick. When they do, they treat themselves with home remedies, cauterize wounds with hot ash, drink medicinal soups made from roots and bark, or, if these measures fail, visit a herbalist or traditional healer. Physicians are visited only for emergencies unless a clinic is nearby. She reports on the case of one Maasai warrior who did visit a medical doctor. The man had been severely gored by a water buffalo but had managed to make his way to a remote clinic. The doctor, a novice, feeling that the man would not survive the long drive over back roads to Nairobi, where modern medical care was available, performed surgery. He lacked experience, anesthesia, and blood for transfusion. The only painkiller was aspirin, and the doctor propped a textbook in front of him so he could refer to it during the operation. The next morning, when the doctor went to check on his patient, he was gone. But months later, the man returned in good health with the gift of a goat. Despite a lack of experience and equipment, the surgery was successful.

Many people turn to traditional folk healers, even in large cities, not only for treatment, but also to find out why they contract certain illnesses and who or what is responsible (Fosu 1989). Traditional healers are widely available to the African public, although their popularity varies, and they remain the most common source of health care in rural Africa. Traditional healers are inexpensive, effective in reducing anxiety and stress, and embedded in the culture of the groups they serve; consequently, they are likely to persist as health providers in a developing country like Kenya where there is an acute shortage of trained health professionals.

Although the Kenyan health care system is financed by revenues from the country's general budget and public services are provided at no cost, there are sometimes small fees for physician consultations and charges for drugs. However, even small fees as low as 50¢ have been barriers to health care for rural Kenyans living in poverty (Mbugua, Bloom, and Segall 1995). Private care is also available to those persons who want it and can afford it. Kenya has a medical school and nursing schools for the training of their own health professionals, and health care delivery remains an important government priority in the nation's development. Infant mortality has increased in Kenya from 64 deaths per 1,000 births in 1978 to 68.7 per 1,000 in 2000, which is significantly lower than in neighboring countries like Ethiopia, where the rate was 125 per 1,000. Life expectancy in Kenya in 1998 was 46.6 years for males and 47.5 years for females, which reflects the impact of AIDS on the population. As Kenya enters the twenty-first century, it confronts increasingly serious problems in public health. Many people, perhaps a majority in rural areas, are infected with malaria. But the most life-threatening epidemic at present is AIDS, which, while not as prevalent in Kenya as in nearby Rwanda and Uganda, is nevertheless extensive and spreading throughout the population. About 2 million people are believed to be HIV-infected in Kenya.

DECENTRALIZED NATIONAL HEALTH: MEXICO

Mexico has a decentralized national health system covering most of the general population through a variety of programs that fall into one of three broad categories. First, there are the public social security organizations that provide both health insurance and old-age benefits for specific groups of private and government employees. Second is the health care provided through the government's Secretariat of Health and Welfare or SSA (Secretaria de Salubridad y Asistencia), which is the primary source of care for the majority of persons not covered by a social security organization—especially the urban poor. And third is the private health care system, which consists of various private practitioners, hospitals and clinics, and charitable organizations.

The largest health plan in Mexico covers workers in the private sector and is administered by the Mexican Social Insurance Institute or IMSS (Instituto Mexicano de Seguro Social). The IMSS was established in 1943 as a compulsory government-sponsored social security program for salaried workers in Mexico City and surrounding areas and is financed by contributions from workers, employers, and the state. The program was extended to other metropolitan areas during 1943–45; salaried agricultural workers were added in 1954; and, in 1973, legislation was enacted that provided for the extension of IMSS social insurance to everyone with jobs in the private sector, including those who could not afford to contribute financially. Known as the IMSS Social Solidarity Program, health services are provided free of charge to low-income workers and their families in return for approximately ten days of work in public projects. The level of benefits available for low-income members, however, is not comprehensive and is limited to general medical and maternity care. Furthermore, despite efforts to expand the IMSS program to rural areas, more than 90 percent of the IMSS membership is urban.

Another health plan, which provides the most extensive and generous benefits of any social security program, was established in 1960 for government workers and is administered by the Social Insurance Institute of State Employees (ISSSTE or Instituto de Seguridad y Servicios Sociales Para los Trabajadores del Estado). The IMSS and ISSSTE programs are by far the largest health insurance plans in Mexico. Other social security programs with health insurance are available to members of the armed forces (ISSSFAM) and the state-run oil industry (PEMEX). Approximately 45 percent of Mexico's population is covered by these various social security plans.

The Secretariat of Health and Welfare (SSA), created in 1943, is responsible for Mexico's overall health policy and provides health care directly to the urban poor through its own hospitals and clinics. Nearly 20 percent of the population is dependent on the SSA to meet their health needs. Another 15 percent of the population utilizes the private sector. According to Peter Ward (1985), private medicine is not just for the wealthy. "The poor make extensive use of the private sector," states Ward (1985:111), "for 'lightweight' consultations, and they may also receive private treatment paid by their employer—a feature of patronage that remains widespread throughout Mexico."

In theory, Mexico has a national health system; yet in reality, not everyone has access to it (Castro 2001; Hunt 1996; Lassey et al. 1997; Sherraden 1995; Warner 1991). Exact figures are not known, but some 15 to 20 percent of the population lacks ready access to modern health care. Most of these persons live in rural areas, including highly isolated sections of the country. Many of them have no health insurance, or if they do have some type of coverage, physicians and clinics are not available locally. Consequently, they turn to a variety of sources, either public health care, private doctors and hospitals, nuns, or folk healers, or they rely on self-treatment (Nigenda et al. 2001).

Despite its nationwide program of social insurance, Mexico has a serious problem of maldistribution of services. More than 35 percent of all doctors are located in the Mexico City area, which has only 20 percent of the population; consequently, Mexico City has a surplus of physicians, while other parts of the country have a shortage. Even though health clinics are established throughout the country, rural areas are likely to be served by a nurse. For the country as a whole, there are approximately eighty physicians per 100,000 people, and about 75 percent of all doctors are employed in some type of government-sponsored health program— although some have both a public and private practice. The remaining 25 percent are private fee-for-service practitioners. In border areas near the United States, affluent Mexicans and others covered by some type of U.S. health insurance visit American doctors; some Americans, in turn, seek the services of less expensive Mexican physicians and buy drugs at cheaper prices in Mexican pharmacies. Many drugs in the United States requiring prescriptions, including some antibiotics and painkillers, are sold over the counter in Mexico. Crossing the U.S.-Mexico border from one side or the other to obtain health services is a fact of life for some people (Warner 1991).

The overall health of the Mexican population is improving. Life expectancy in 2000 was 68.5 years for males and 74.7 years for females; infant mortality was 26.1 deaths per 1,000 births in 2000 compared with 80 per 1,000 in 1965. Some 4.7 percent of Mexico's GDP was spent on health in 1997. Health care delivery in major urban centers in Mexico is often of high quality, especially in the national medical institutes in Mexico City; in rural areas, however, access to modern medicine is limited and difficult to obtain. Overall, Mexico has established a generally effective national system of health care delivery, despite being a developing nation and having an often troubled economy that has affected public spending on health care.

But significant problems remain. As is the case in Africa, Mexican health care is oriented toward curative rather than preventive medicine; hence, there has not been a large-scale effort to prevent illness through public health programs intended to improve nutrition, water, sewage systems, and training in hygiene (Ward 1985). In addition, the various social health insurance plans differ in the levels of benefits provided, and the decentralized system of health care delivery promotes a lack of coordination, planning, and fiscal control in a country that lacks great national wealth. And, most importantly, a significant segment of the population in rural areas lacks access to modern health services.

However, as Ward (1985:110) explains, "at least, [health care] coverage has . . . been extended to the not so powerful, and specifically to wider sections of the working population that includes both blue- and white-collar workers." Mexico's health policy emphasizes continued improvement in the health of the general population, with a particular focus on meeting the basic health needs of the underprivileged. Health care for the urban poor seems to be Mexico's highest priority at this point in the development of its health care delivery system. According to Mexican medical sociologist Roberto Castro (2001), health conditions in Mexico significantly changed in the last century, but this change was not the same for all social classes and regions in the country.

FEE-FOR-SERVICE: SOUTH AFRICA

The Republic of South Africa has been experiencing massive social change in recent years, with the end of white rule coming in 1994. According to South African medical sociologist H. C. J. van Rensburg (1991; Rensburg, Fourie, and Pretorius 1992; Rensburg and Ngwena 2001), the major features of South African health care up to the present result from a lengthy molding process of more than three centuries. While various native tribes in the region had their own system of traditional healers, the first Western medical care arrived shortly after 1652 when the Dutch East India Company established a resupply station at what later became Capetown. In 1795 the British occupied the Cape area, and the descendants of the early Dutch—the Boers who later became known as Afrikaners—moved into the hinterlands. Eventually, the British obtained control over the region after defeating the Zulus in the late nineteenth century and the Boers in the early twentieth century. The new country that was set up in 1910—the Union of South Africa—sealed cooperation between whites. Other racial and ethnic groups were not consulted.

The health care system that had developed in the meantime was unplanned, uncoordinated, and fragmented along racial lines. As Rensburg explains, political unification had little meaning in terms of a unified health care system. The structure of health care delivery was divided in several ways. First, there was a dominant Western and scientific component which existed largely in urban areas and traditional healing which mostly took place in rural regions. The former served whites and some urban blacks, while the latter is used exclusively by blacks. Even today, many South African blacks use traditional healing or a combination of traditional and Western medicine. Second, a racially differentiated Western system arose that divided health care providers and hospitals. Whites were given health care by whites, blacks by blacks, Asians by Asians, and so forth. Each racial group had its own practitioners, but whites controlled the official health care system for the nation as a whole. Third, a mixed funding system came into being that featured a private fee-for-service system, similar to that of the United States, and a public system financed by the government that served the poor and elderly. Again, the former approach was principally for whites and those who could afford private care at the hands of physicians of their own race, and the latter was largely for blacks and other racial minorities.

Efforts to establish a nonracial, national health service failed in the 1940s, and, in 1948, a nationwide policy of apartheid, or separation of the races, officially divided the entire society—including health care. Whites maintained power through an all-white government that controlled the police and armed forces and imposed a strict system of racial segregation in jobs, schools, townships, and health care delivery. People were registered with the government according to race and classified as either white, Asian, coloured (mixed race), or black. Ten separate departments of health for the nation were initially established, but reforms in 1983 reduced the number to three (Rensburg and Benatar 1993; Rensburg and Ngwena 2001).

Considerable inequality in levels of health care still exist among the races in South Africa. The highest quality care is in the fee-for-service private sector and is used principally by whites (Benatar and Rensburg 1995; Rensburg 1996; Rensburg and Ngwena 2001). Inequality in health care is matched with inequality in employment, education, housing, and overall quality of life, although some blacks have moved into positions of power and wealth since the mid-1990s. When it comes to unemployment, for example, blacks had the highest rates by far in 1999 of 24.5 percent, followed by Indians (14.5), coloureds (13.5), and whites (4.4). The poverty rate for 1995 shows that 67.8 percent of blacks live in poverty compared to 35.3 percent of coloureds, 14.3 percent of Indians, and 8.4 percent of whites. It is therefore not surprising that racial differences in health and access to health care persist. Rensburg and Benatar (1993) have noted that the tendency to separate people of different races for decades and even centuries has undeniably left race-differentiated imprints on the organization and distribution of health services in South Africa. As Rensburg and Charles Ngwena (2001:378) state: "Despite the dismantling of apartheid, race and gender distortions in health care are bound to persist for decades to come, partly due to the backlogs created by the previous system, and partly as a result of the continuation of typically race-based provision in a class-segregated system, with the more wealthy catered for by the private sector, while the less wealthy have to rely on a less effective public health sector."

Data for 1998 show that white males and females had higher life expectancy than (in order) Asians, blacks, and coloureds. White males lived 69 years on average compared to 60 years for blacks, while white females lived 76 years compared to 67 years for blacks. Indian males lived 64 years and females 70 years, while the coloured population had the lowest life expectancy of all racial groups with males

HIV/AIDS demonstration in South Africa which had the highest number (4.7 million) of HIV-infected people in the world in 2000. Almost one-fourth of the entire population is HIV positive.

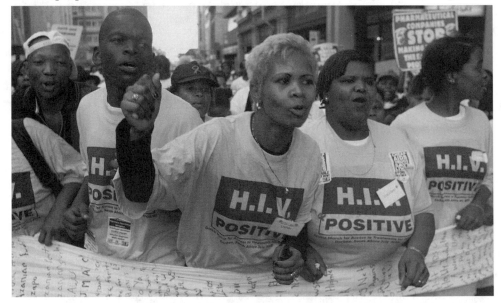

living to 59 years and females to 65 years. Infant mortality rates were 7.3 deaths per 1,000 births for whites, 9.9 for Indians, 36.3 for coloureds, and 54.3 for blacks. However, these figures are rapidly changing for the worse, especially for the black African population, because of the high prevalence of HIV/AIDS. Overall life expectancy in South Africa is estimated to have fallen from 66 years in 1998 to 56 years in 2001, and may drop to as low as 41 years by 2010. Some estimates already place life expectancy in South Africa to less than 50 years for both men and women.

The AIDS epidemic is clearly a health crisis of major proportions in South Africa. By the end of the year 2000, for example, some 4.7 million people in South Africa were estimated to have HIV/AIDS, *more than any other country in the world* (Rensburg et al. 2002). This figure represents some 24.5 percent—almost one-fourth—of the entire population. AIDS-related mortality comprised 40 percent of all deaths in 2000. About 1,700 people are infected daily. Some 56 percent of HIV/AIDS victims are women, and people living in poverty are especially vulnerable although those in higher social strata are not exempt from infection. Generally, the epidemic is taking the path of least resistance through socially and economically disadvantaged groups (Gilbert and Walker 2002). HIV/AIDS numbers and future projections for South Africa are shown in Table 16-2. Not only does Table 16-2 show that in 2008–10 the average life expectancy of women is expected to fall between 37 and 48 years, but population growth will be less than one percent (0.4 percent), and a million people may die from AIDS annually.

TABLE 16-2   HIV/AIDS Numbers and Projections for South Africa.

Indicator	1999–2000	2005	2008–2010
Total number of HIV+ people (millions)	4.3–5.3	6.0	7.5
HIV prevalence rate (20–64 age group)	14–15%	20–23%	22–27%
HIV prevalence rate (15–49 age group)	19.9%		
HIV prevalence rate (antenatal)	24.5%	31.0%	
Number of people living with AIDS	200,000–236,000	500,000–600,000	1 million
Annual number of deaths due to AIDS	120,000–250,000	380,000–700,000	635,000–1 million
Infant mortality rate	41		>60
Population growth rate	2.09%		0.4% (1.4% without AIDS)
Average life expectancy (female)	54–56	43	37–48
Proportion of workforce HIV+	11%–11.5%	20%	21%–22.5%
Proportion of workforce with AIDS	0.4%	1.65%	2.7%
Number of public servants HIV+	100,000		270,000
Current living AIDS orphans (under 15 years)	371,000–600,000	1 million	2 million

Source: D. van Rensburg et al., 2002.

As for other health problems, the 1998 South Africa Demographic and Health Survey found that blacks generally had the greatest prevalence of infant mortality, diarrhea, and sexually transmitted diseases, but white males had the highest prevalence of chronic illnesses like heart disease, hypertension, stroke, and diabetes. White men and black women were the most overweight. Rural blacks were most disadvantaged in health, as many do not live long enough to develop a chronic disease.

One important measure undertaken in 1996 was the provision of free health care at public health facilities. South African hospitals are also racially integrated for the first time, but private hospitals that serve the affluent are of much higher quality than hospitals in the public sector (Benatar and Rensburg 1995). Although the reforms in health care have been significant steps in bringing equity to the public health system and providing greater accessibility to disadvantaged groups, Rensburg and Ngwena (2001) observe that in many respects the introduction of free care was not adequately planned or budgeted. In many locales there was serious overcrowding and deterioration in the quality of care. There is currently no national health insurance program and the management of health care has been delegated to the various provinces, with few signs of strengthening the public sector. As Rensburg and Ngwena (2001:178) point out: "Little has as yet materialized of the intention to rid the health system of its notorious two-class character, that is, a weak public sector that caters 'second-class' services to the majority of the population dependent upon the state, and a strong private health sector providing 'first-class' service for the wealthy and [privately] insured minority." As it heads into the twenty-first century, South Africa remains burdened by its history of apartheid in the face of an unprecedented challenge to the health and well-being of its population from HIV/AIDS.

CONCLUSION

Countries throughout the world are confronted with major challenges in providing health care, as is indicated by this discussion of selected countries that are not developed nations. Rising costs and demand in excess of resources are common almost everywhere. Countries like Saudi Arabia, which have wealth, are obviously in a better position than less affluent nations in meeting the health needs of citizens. Developing countries that lack resources, which is the case for the great majority, find it especially hard to meet needs as seen in the case of Kenya. However, the health situation in Kenya is better than in most other African countries south of the Sahara—which speaks to the fact that health services for most Africans are inadequate or nonexistent.

In many developing countries, modern health care is concentrated in urban areas, and rural residents are often left to cope with illness on their own or seek out traditional healers. Modern medical care may be an unaffordable luxury. In such countries, health policy is usually oriented toward meeting basic health needs (curing), rather than prevention or the expansion of specialized services. Whereas levels of health are much worse in some countries than in others, life expectancy in developing nations has generally improved. Widespread use of immunizations and the effective treatment of diarrhea with oral fluids have saved millions of lives. Successes, however, can be diminished by the rise of new and deadly problems, such as AIDS, drug-resistant forms of malaria and tuberculosis, and the growing consumption of tobacco in developing countries. Waste, inefficiency, and theft hamper the delivery of health services in some countries as well. Consequently, the world has considerable distance to travel before health for all can be a global certainty.

As discussed in this chapter, the former socialist countries of Russia, Poland, and Hungary experienced a period of decreasing life expectancy and increasing mortality—especially for men. The emergence of this East-West health division left Europe with a difficult public health challenge for the 1990s and beyond. The search for an optimal form of health care delivery goes on. The fee-for-service approach, like that of the United States, South Africa, and now China, has a tradition of inequality. Since the collapse of socialist-style health systems in Europe and their failure to promote high levels of health, the influence of these models in the world has been significantly reduced. Only Cuba still operates a purely socialist system, but it is a relatively poor country with a shortage of drugs, equipment, and high-quality facilities. Most of the countries of the world appear to be moving toward some type of socialized or decentralized national health system—incorporating various forms of universal coverage and limited or managed competition.

HEALTH CARE IN FORMER SOCIALIST, SOCIALIST, AND DEVELOPING COUNTRIES INTERNET SITES

Russia

State Committee of the Russian Federation on Statistics (Goskomstat).
http://www.gks.ru/eng/bd.asp

Poland

Poland: Health Services and Care.
http://poland.pl/health

Hungary

Hungarian Central Statistical Office.
http://www.ksh.hu/pls/ksh/does/index.eng.html

China

Chinese Medical Association.
http://www.chinamed.com.cn

Saudi Arabia

Saudi Arabia Ministry of Health.
http://www.saudinf.com/main/start.htm

Kenya

Africa Online—Kenya: Health.
http://www.africaonline.com/site/africa/health.jsp

Mexico

Ministry of Health (SSA) [in Spanish with English links].
http://www.ssa.gob.mx

South Africa

Medical Research Council of South Africa.
http://www.mrc.ac.za./

References

ABEL, THOMAS. 1991. "Measuring health lifestyles in a comparative analysis: Theoretical issues and empirical findings." *Social Science and Medicine,* 32:899–908.

ABEL, THOMAS, and WILLIAM C. COCKERHAM. 1993. "Lifestyle or lebensführung? Critical remarks on the mistranslation of Weber's 'class, status, party.'" *Sociological Quarterly,* 34:551–556.

ABEL, THOMAS, WILLIAM C. COCKERHAM, GUENTHER LUESCHEN, and GERHARD KUNZ. 1989. "Health lifestyles and self-direction in employment among American men: A test of the spillover effect." *Social Science and Medicine,* 28:1269–1274.

ABEL, THOMAS, ESTHER WALTER, STEFFEN NIEMANN, and ROLF WEITKUNAT. 1999. "The Berne-Munich lifestyle panel." *Sozial- und Präventivmedizin,* 44:91–106.

ABERCROMBIE, NICHOLAS, ALAN WARDE, KEITH SOOTHILL, JOHN URY, and SYLVIA WALBAY. 1988. *Contemporary British Society.* Oxford, U.K.: Polity Press.

ABRUMS, MARY. 2000. "Jesus will fix it after awhile: Meanings and health." *Social Science and Medicine,* 50:89–105.

ADLER, ISRAEL, and JUDITH T. SHUVAL. 1978. "Cross pressures during socialization for medicine." *American Sociological Review,* 43:693–704.

ADLER, NANCY E., THOMAS BOYCE, MARGARET A. CHESNEY, SHELDON COHEN, SUSAN FOLKMAN, ROBERT L. KAHN, and S. LEONARD SYME. 1994. "Socioeconomic status and health." *American Psychologist,* 49:15–24.

ADONIS, ANDREW, and STEPHEN POLLARD. 1997. *A class act: The myth of Britain's classless society.* London: Penguin.

AIKEN, LINDA H., and DOUGLAS M. SLOANE. 1997. "Effects of specialization and client differentiation on the status of nurses: The case of AIDS." *Journal of Health and Social Behavior,* 38:203–222.

ALI, JENNIFER, and WILLIAM R. AVISON. 1997. "Employment transition and psychological distress: The contrasting experiences of single and married mothers." *Journal of Health and Social Behavior,* 38:345–362.

ALLEN, DAVINA. 1997. "The nursing-medical boundary: A negotiated order?" *Sociology of Health and Illness,* 19:398–498.

ALLEN, GILLIAN, and ROY WALLIS. 1976. "Pentecostalists as a medical minority," pp. 110–137 in *Marginal medicine,* R. Wallis and P. Morley (eds.). New York: The Free Press.

ALLMAN, RICHARD M., WILLIAM C. YOELS, and JEFFREY MICHAEL CLAIR. 1993. "Reconciling the agendas of physicians and patients," pp. 29–48 in *Sociomedical perspectives on patient care,* J. Clair and R. Allman (eds.). Lexington: University of Kentucky Press.

ALUBO, S. OGOH. 1990. "Debt crisis, health and health services in Africa." *Social Science and Medicine,* 31:639–648.

ANDERSEN, RONALD, and LUANN ADAY. 1978. "Access to medical care in the U.S.: Realized and potential." *Medical Care,* 16:533–546.

ANDERSEN, RONALD, and ODIN W. ANDERSON. 1979. "Trends in the use of health services," pp. 371–391 in *Handbook of medical sociology,* 3rd ed., H. Freeman, S. Levine, and L. Reeder (eds.). Englewood Cliffs, N.J.: Prentice Hall.

ANDERSEN, RONALD, SANDRA ZELMAN, AIDA L. GIACHELLO, LUANN ADAY, and GRACE CHIU. 1981. "Access to medical care among the Hispanic population of the southwestern United States." *Journal of Health and Social Behavior,* 22:78–89.

ANDERSON, JAMES G., RENEE OSCARSON, and YIAN YU. 1995. "Japan's health care system: Western and east Asian influences," pp. 32–44 in *Global perspectives on health care,* E. Gallagher and J. Subedi (eds.). Englewood Cliffs, N.J.: Prentice Hall.

ANESAKI, MASAHIRA, and TSUNETSUGU MUNAKATA. 2001. "Health, illness, and health policy in Japan," pp. 441–455 in *The Blackwell companion to medical sociology,* W. Cockerham (ed.). Oxford, UK: Blackwell.

ANGEL, RONALD, and JACQUELINE L. ANGEL. 1996a. "The extent of private and public health insurance coverage among adult Hispanics." *Gerontologist,* 36:332–340.

————. 1996b. *Who will care for us? Aging and long-term care in multicultural America.* New York: New York University Press.

ANNANDALE, ELLEN C. 1989. "The malpractice crisis and the doctor–patient relationship." *Sociology of Health and Illness,* 11:1–23.

————. 1998. *The sociology of health and medicine.* Cambridge, U.K.: Polity Press.

ANNANDALE, ELLEN C., and DAVID FIELD. 2001. "Medical sociology in Britain," pp. 180–198 in *The Blackwell companion to medical sociology,* W. Cockerham (ed.). Oxford, UK: Oxford University Press.

ANSPACH, RENEE R. 1993. *Deciding who lives: Fateful choices in the intensive-care nursery.* Berkeley: University of California Press.

ANTONOVSKY, AARON. 1979. *Health, stress, and coping.* San Francisco: Jossey-Bass.

APPLE, DORRIAN. 1960. "How laymen define illness." *Journal of Health and Social Behavior,* 1:219–225.

ARBER, SARA. 1989. "Gender and class inequalities in health: Understanding the differentials," pp. 250–279 in *Health inequalities in European countries,* J. Fox (ed.). Aldershot, U.K.: Gower.

————. 1993. "Chronic illness over the life course: Class inequalities among men and women in Britain," pp. 39–64 in *Medical sociology: Research on chronic illness,* T. Abel, S. Geyer, U. Gerhardt, J. Siegrist, and W. van den Heuvel (eds.). Bonn: Informationszentrum Sozialwissenschaften.

————. 1997. "Comparing inequalities in women's and men's health: Britain in the 1990s." *Social Science and Medicine,* 44:773–787.

ARBER, SARA, and HILARY THOMAS. 2001. "From women's health to a gender analysis of health," pp. 94–113 in *The Blackwell companion to medical sociology,* W. Cockerham (ed.). Oxford, UK: Blackwell.

ARDAGH, JOHN. 1987. *France today.* London: Penguin.

ARLUKE, ARNOLD, LOUANNE KENNEDY, and RONALD C. KESSLER. 1979. "Reexamining the sick-role concept: An empirical assessment." *Journal of Health and Social Behavior,* 20:30–36.

ARMSTRONG, DAVID. 1989. *An outline of sociology as applied to medicine,* 3rd ed. London: Wright.

ASELTINE, ROBERT H., JR., and RONALD C. KESSLER. 1993. "Marital disruption and depression in a community sample." *Journal of Health and Social Behavior,* 34:237–251.

ASKENASY, ALEXANDER R., BRUCE P. DOHRENWEND, and BARBARA S. DOHRENWEND. 1977. "Some effects of social class and ethnic group membership on judgments of the magnitude of stressful life events: A research note." *Journal of Health and Social Behavior,* 18:432–439.

ATKINSON, PAUL. 1995. *Medical talk and medical work.* London: Sage.

ATKINSON, THOMAS, RAMSAY LIEM, and JOAN H. LIEM. 1986. "The social costs of unemployment: Implications for social support." *Journal of Health and Social Behavior,* 27:317–331.

AUERBACH, JUDITH, and ANNE FIGERT. 1995. "Women's health research: Public policy and sociology." *Journal of Health and Social Behavior,* extra issue:115–131.

AVERY, CHARLENE. 1991. "Native American medicine: Traditional healing." *Journal of the American Medical Association,* 265:2271, 2273.

AVISON, WILLIAM R., and R. JAY TURNER. 1988. "Stressful life events and depressive symptoms: Disaggregating the effects of acute stressors and chronic strains." *Journal of Health and Social Behavior,* 29:253–264.

BACKETT, KATHRYN C., and CHARLIE DAVISON. 1995. "Lifecourse and lifestyle: The social and cultural location of health behaviours." *Social Science and Medicine,* 40:629–638.

BAER, HANS A. 2001. *Biomedicine and alternative healing systems in America: Issues of class, race, ethnicity, and gender.* Madison, WI: University of Wisconsin Press.

BAER, HANS A., CINDY JEN, LUCIA M. TANASSI, CHRISTOPHER TSIA, and HELEN WAHBEH. 1998. "The drive for professionalization in acupuncture: A preliminary view from the San Francisco Bay Area." *Social Science and Medicine,* 46:537–553.

BAKER, PATRICIA S., WILLIAM C. YOELS, and JEFFREY M. CLAIR. 1996. "Emotional processes during medical encounters: Social disease and the medical gaze," pp. 173–199 in *Health and the sociology of emotions,* V. James and J. Gabe (eds.). Oxford, U.K.: Blackwell.

BAKKEN, ROSALIE, MARZENA JEZEWSKA-ZYCHOWICZ, and MARY WINTER. 1999. "Household nutrition and health in Poland." *Social Science and Medicine,* 49:1677–1687.

BAKX, KEITH. 1991. "The 'eclipse' of folk medicine in western society." *Sociology of Health and Illness,* 13:20–38.

BARBOZA, DAVID. 2000. "Rampant obesity, a debilitating reality for the urban poor." *New York Times* (December 26):D5.

BARNARTT, SHARON N. 1990. "A review of medical sociology textbooks." *Teaching Sociology,* 18:372–376.

BARNETT, TONY, and PIERS BLAIKE. 1992. *AIDS in Africa.* New York: Guilford.

BARON-EPEL, ORNA, and GIORA KAPLAN. 2001. "General subjective status or age-related subjective health: Does it make a difference?" *Social Science and Medicine,* 53:1373–1381.

BARTLEY, MEL, DAVID BLANE, and GEORGE DAVY SMITH. 1998. "Introduction: Beyond the Black Report." *Sociology of Health and Illness,* 20:563–577.

BARTLEY, MEL, and IAN PLEWIS. 1997. "Does health-selective mobility account for socioeconomic differences in health? Evidence from England and Wales, 1971–91." *Journal of Health and Social Behavior,* 38:313–429.

BAUMANN, BARBARA. 1961. "Diversities in conceptions of health and physical fitness." *Journal of Health and Social Behavior,* 2:39–46.

BECKER, HOWARD S. 1973. *Outsiders: Studies in the sociology of deviance.* 2nd ed. New York: The Free Press.

BECKER, HOWARD S., and BLANCHE GREER. 1958. "The fate of idealism in medical school." *American Sociological Review,* 23:50–56.

BECKER, HOWARD S., BLANCHE GREER, EVERETT C. HUGHES, and ANSELM STRAUSS. 1961. *Boys in white: Student culture in medical school.* Chicago: University of Chicago Press.

BECKER, MARSHALL H. 1979. "Psychosocial aspects of health-related behaviors," pp. 253–274 in *Handbook of medical sociology,* H. Freeman, S. Levine, and L. Reeder (eds.). Englewood Cliffs, N.J.: Prentice Hall.

BECKER, MARSHALL H. (ed.). 1974. *The health belief model and personal health behavior.* San Francisco: Society for Public Health Education, Inc.

BECKER, MARSHALL H., and LOIS A. MAIMAN. 1975. "Sociobehavioral determinants of compliance with health and medical care recommendations." *Medical Care,* 13:10–24.

BECKER, MARSHALL H., LOIS A. MAIMAN, JOHN P. KIRSCHT, DON P. HAEFNER, and ROBERT H. DRACHMAN. 1977. "The health belief model and prediction of dietary compliance: A field experiment." *Journal of Health and Social Behavior,* 18:348–366

BECKER, MARSHALL H., and IRWIN M. ROSENSTOCK. 1989. "Health promotion, disease prevention, and program retention," pp. 284–305 in *Handbook of medical sociology,* 4th ed., H. Freeman and S. Levine (eds.). Englewood Cliffs, N.J.: Prentice Hall.

BELL, SUSAN E. 2000. "Experiencing illness in/and narrative," pp. 184–199 in *Handbook of medical sociology,* 5th ed., C. Bird, P. Conrad, and A. Fremont (eds.). Upper Saddle River, NJ: Prentice Hall.

BENATAR, SOLOMON R., and H. C. J. VAN RENSBURG. 1995. "Health care services in a new South Africa." *Hastings Center Report,* 25:16–21.

BENDIX, REINHARD. 1960. *Max Weber: An intellectual portrait.* New York: Doubleday.

BENNETT, ARNOLD, and ORVILL ADAMS (eds.). 1993. *Looking north for health: What we can learn from Canada's health care system.* San Francisco: Jossey-Bass.

BEN-SIRA, ZEEV. 1976. "The function of the professional's affective behavior in client satisfaction: A revised approach to social interaction theory." *Journal of Health and Social Behavior,* 17:3–11.

———. 1980. "Affective and instrumental components in the physician–patient relationship: An additional dimension of interaction theory." *Journal of Health and Social Behavior,* 21:170–180.

BENTSEN, CHERYL. 1991. *Maasai days.* New York: Anchor.

BERGER, PETER L., and THOMAS LUCKMANN. 1967. *The social construction of reality.* New York: Anchor.

BERKANOVIC, EMIL. 1972. "Lay conceptions of the sick role." *Social Forces,* 51:53–63.

BERKMAN, LISA F., and LESTER BRESLOW. 1983. *Health and ways of living: The Alameda County study.* Fairlawn, N.J.: Oxford University Press.

BIRD, CHLOE E. 1999. "Gender, household labor, and psychological distress: The impact of the amount and diversion of housework." *Journal of Health and Social Behavior,* 40:32–45.

BIRD, CHLOE E., PETER CONRAD, and ALLEN M. FREMONT. 2000. "Medical sociology at the millenium," pp. 1–10 in *Handbook of medical sociology,* 5th ed., C. Bird, P. Conrad, and A. Fremont (eds.). Upper Saddle River, N.J.: Prentice Hall.

BIRD, CHLOE E., and ALLEN M. FREMONT. 1991. "Gender, time use, and health." *Journal of Health and Social Behavior,* 32:114–129.

BIRD, CHLOE E. and PATRICIA P. RIEKER. 1999. "Gender matters: An integrated model for understanding men's and women's health." *Social Science and Medicine,* 48:745–755.

BIRO, G., M. ANTAL, and G. ZAJKAS. 1996. "Nutrition survey of the Hungarian population in a randomized trial between 1992–1994." *European Journal of Clinical Nutrition,* 50:201–208.

BLACK REPORT. 1980. *Inequalities in health: Report on a research working group.* London: Department of Health and Social Services.

BLACKWELL, ELIZABETH. 1902. *Essays in medical sociology.* London: Bell.

BLANK, NELSON, and FINN DIDERICHSEN. 1996. "Social inequalities in the experience of illness in Sweden: A 'double suffering'." *Scandinavian Journal of Social Medicine,* 24:81–89.

BLAXTER, MILDRED. 1990. *Health and lifestyles.* London: Tavistock.

BLAXTER, MILDRED, and RICHARD CYSTER. 1984. "Compliance and risk-taking: The case of alcohol liver disease." *Sociology of Health and Illness,* 6:290–310.

BLOOM, GERALD, and SHENGLAN TANG. 1999. "Rural health prepayment schemes in China: Towards a more active role of government." *Social Science and Medicine,* 48:951–960.

BLOOM, SAMUEL W. 1973. *Power and dissent in the medical school.* New York: The Free Press.

———. 1986. "Institutional trends in medical sociology." *Journal of Health and Social Behavior,* 27:265–277.

———. 1990. "Episodes in the institutionalization of medical sociology: A personal view." *Journal of Health and Social Behavior,* 31:1–10.

———. 2000. "The institutionalization of medical sociology in the United States, 1920–1980," pp. 11–31 in *Handbook of medical sociology,* 5th ed., C. Bird, P. Conrad, and A. Fremont (eds.). Upper Saddle River, N.J.: Prentice Hall.

———. 2002. *The word as scalpel: A history of medical sociology.* New York: Oxford University Press.

BOBAK, MARTIN, HYNER PIKHART, CLYDE HERTZMAN, RICHARD ROSE, and MICHAEL MARMOT. 1998. "Socioeconomic factors, perceived control and self-reported health in Russia: A cross-sectional survey." *Social Science and Medicine,* 47:269–279.

BOBAK, MARTIN, MARTIN McKEE, RICHARD ROSE, and MICHAEL MARMOT. 1999. "Alcohol consumption in a national sample of the Russian population." *Addiction,* 94:857–866.

BOLARIA, B. SINGH, and HARLEY D. DICKINSON (eds.). 1994. *Health, illness, and health care in Canada,* 2nd ed. Toronto: Harcourt Brace.

———. 2001. "The evolution of health care in Canada: Toward community or corporate control?" pp. 199–213 in *The Blackwell companion to medical sociology,* W. Cockerham (ed.). Oxford, UK: Blackwell.

BOOTH, ALAN, and PAUL AMATO. 1991. "Divorce and psychological stress." *Journal of Health and Social Behavior,* 32:396–407.

BOROOAH, VANI K. 1999. "Occupational class and the probability of long-term limiting illness." *Social Science and Medicine,* 49:253–266.

BOSANQUET, NICK. 1988. "An ailing state of national health," pp. 93–108 in *British social attitudes, the 5th report,* R. Jowell, S. Witherspoon, and L. Brook (eds.). Aldershot, U.K.: Gower.

BOSK, CHARLES L. 1979. *Forgive and remember: Managing medical failure.* Chicago: University of Chicago Press.

BOSK, CHARLES L., and JOEL E. FRADER. 1990. "AIDS and its impact on medical work: The culture and politics of the shop floor." *Milbank Quarterly,* 68:257–279.

BOSMA, HANS, RICHARD PETER, JOHANNES SIEGRIST, and MICHAEL MARMOT. 1998. "Two alternative job stress models and the risk of coronary heart disease." *American Journal of Public Health,* 88:68–74.

BOULTON, MARY, DAVID TUCKETT, CORAL OLSON, and ANTHONY WILLIAMS. 1986. "Social class and the general practice consultation." *Sociology of Health and Illness,* 8:325–350.

BOURDIEU, PIERRE. 1984. *Distinction: A social critique of the judgement of taste,* R. Nice (trans.). Cambridge, MA: Harvard University Press.

BOURNE, PETER. 1970. *Men, stress, and Vietnam.* Boston: Little, Brown.

BOWLING, ANNE. 1981. *Delegation in general practice: A study of doctors and nurses.* London: Tavistock.

BRAITHWAITE, RONALD L., and SANDRA E. TAYLOR (eds.). 1992. *Health issues in the black community.* San Francisco: Jossey-Bass.

BRANNON, ROBERT L. 1994a. *Intensifying care: The hospital industry, professionalization, and the reorganization of the nursing labor process.* Amityville, N.Y.: Baywood.

———. 1994b. "Professionalization and work intensification." *Work and Occupations,* 21:157–178.

BRAVEMAN, PAULA, and ELEUTHER TARIMO. 2002. "Social inequalities in health within countries: Not only an issue for affluent nations." *Social Science and Medicine,* 54:1621–1635.

BRENNER, M. HARVEY. 1973. *Mental illness and the economy.* Cambridge, Mass.: Harvard University Press.

———. 1987a. "Economic change, alcohol consumption and disease mortality in nine industrialized countries." *Social Science and Medicine,* 25:119–132.

———. 1987b. "Relation of economic change to Swedish health and social well-being, 1950–1980." *Social Science and Medicine,* 25:183–196.

BRENNER, M. HARVEY, and ANNE MOONEY. 1983. "Unemployment and health in the context of economic change." *Social Science and Medicine,* 17:1125–1138.

BROADHEAD, ROBERT S. 1983. *The private lives and professional identity of medical students.* New Brunswick, N.J.: Transaction.

BROOKE, JAMES. 2000. "Full hospitals make Canadians wait and look south." *New York Times,* January 16, p. 3.

BROOKS-GUNN, JEANNE, and FRANK F. FURSTENBERG. 1990. "Coming of age in the era of AIDS: Puberty, sexuality and contraception." *Milbank Quarterly,* 68, (1):59–84.

BROWN, CAROLYN M., and RICHARD SEGAL. 1996. "Ethnic differences in temporal orientation and its implications for hypertension management." *Journal of Health and Social Behavior,* 37:350–361.

BROWN, E. RICHARD. 1979. *Rockefeller medicine men: Medicine and capitalism in America.* Berkeley: University of California Press.

BROWN, GEORGE W., and TIRRIL HARRIS. 1978. *Social origins of depression: A study of psychiatric disorder in women.* New York: The Free Press.

BROWN, JULIA S., and MAY E. RAWLINSON. 1977. "Sex differences in sick role rejection and in work performance following cardiac surgery." *Journal of Health and Social Behavior,* 18:276–292.

BROWN, LAWRENCE D. 1986. "Introduction to a decade of transition." *Journal of Health Politics, Policy and Law,* 11:569–584.

BROWN, PHIL. 1995. "Naming and framing: The social construction of diagnosis and illness." *Journal of Health and Social Behavior,* extra issue:34–52.

———. 2000. "Environment and health," pp. 143–158 in *Handbook of Medical Sociology,* C. Bird, P. Conrad, and A. Fremont (eds.). Upper Saddle River, N.J.: Prentice Hall.

BUDRYS, GRACE. 1987. *Planning for the nation's health: A study of twentieth-century developments in the United States.* Westport, Conn.: Greenwood Press.

BUNTON, ROBIN, and ROGER BURROWS. 1995. "Consumption and health in the 'epidemiological' clinic of late modern medicine," pp. 206–222 in *The sociology of health promotion,* R. Bunton, S. Nettleton, and R. Burrows (eds.). London: Routledge.

———. 2001. *Our unsystematic health care system.* Lanham, MD: Rowman and Littlefield.

BURTON, RUSSELL P. D. 1998. "Global integrative meaning as a mediating factor in the relationship between social roles and psychological distress." *Journal of Health and Social Behavior,* 39:201–215.

BURY, MICHAEL. 1991. "The sociology of chronic illness: A review of research and prospects." *Sociology of Health and Illness,* 13:451–468.

———. 1997. *Health and illness in a changing society.* London: Routledge.

———. 2000. "On chronic illness and disability," pp. 173–183 in *Handbook of medical sociology,* 5th ed., C. Bird, P. Conrad, and A. Fremont (eds.). Upper Saddle River, N.J. Prentice Hall.

BUTLER, JAY C., MITCHELL L. COHEN, CINDY R. FRIEDMAN, ROBERT M. SCRIPP, and CRAIG G. WATZ. 2002. "Collaboration between public health and law enforcement: New paradigms and partnerships for bioterrorism planning and response." *Emerging Infectious Diseases,* 8:1–9.

CALNAN, MICHAEL. 1987. *Health & illness: The lay perspective.* London: Tavistock.

———. 1989. "Control over health and patterns of health-related behaviour." *Social Science and Medicine,* 29:131–136.

CAMPBELL, JOHN D. 1978. "The child in the sick role: Contributions of age, sex, parental status, and parental values." *Journal of Health and Social Behavior,* 19:35–51.

CANNON, WALTER B. 1932. *The wisdom of the body.* New York: W. W. Norton.

CANTOR, NORMAN F. 2001. *In the wake of the plague: The black death and the world it made*. New York: Free Press.

CARLSON, ELWOOD. 1989. "Concentration of rising Hungarian mortality among manual workers." *Sociology and Social Research*, 73:119–127.

CARLSON, ELWOOD, and SERGEY TSVETARSKY. 1992. "Concentration of rising Bulgarian mortality among manual workers." *Sociology and Social Research*, 76:81–84.

CARPENTER, MICK. 1993. "The subordination of nurses in health care: Towards a social divisions approach," pp. 95–130 in *Gender, work and medicine*, E. Riska and K. Wegar (eds.). London: Sage.

CARTWRIGHT, ANN. 1964. *Human relations and hospital care*. London: Routledge & Kegan Paul.

CASSELL, ERIC J. 1985. *Talking with patients*, Vol. 2. Cambridge, Mass.: MIT Press.

———. 1986. "The changing concept of the ideal physician." *Daedalus*, 115:185–208.

CASSILETH, BARRIE R., VASILY V. VLASSOV, and CHRISTOPHER C. CHAPMAN. 1995. "Health care, medical practice, and medical ethics in Russia today." *Journal of the American Medical Association*, 273:1569–1622.

CASTRO, ROBERTO. 2001. "Medical sociology in Mexico," pp. 214–232 in *The Blackwell companion to medical sociology*, W. Cockerham (ed.). Oxford, UK: Blackwell.

CATALANO, RALPH, and C. DAVID DOOLEY. 1977. "Economic predictors of depressed mood and stressful life events in a metropolitan community." *Journal of Health and Social Behavior*, 18:292–307.

CAWLEY, JAMES F. 1985. "The physician assistant profession: Current status and future trends." *Journal of Public Health Policy*, 6:78–99.

CHALFANT, H. PAUL, and RICHARD KURTZ. 1971. "Alcoholics and the sick role: Assessments by social workers." *Journal of Health and Social Behavior*, 12:66–72.

CHANDOLA, TARANI. 2000. "Social class differences in mortality using the new UK National Statistics Socio-Economic Classification." *Social Science and Medicine*, 50:641–649.

CHAPMAN, ELIZABETH. 2000. "Conceptualization of the body for people living with HIV. Issues of touch and contamination." *Sociology of Health and Illness*, 22:840–857.

CHARMAZ, KATHY. 1983. "Loss of self: A fundamental form of suffering in the chronically ill." *Sociology of Health and Illness*, 5:168–195.

———. 1991. *Good days, bad days: The self in chronic illness and time*. New Brunswick, N.J.: Rutgers University Press.

CHEN, MEEI-SHIA. 2001. "The great reversal: Transformation of health care in the People's Republic of China," pp. 456–482 in *The Blackwell companion to medical sociology*, W. Cockerham (ed.). Oxford, UK: Blackwell.

CHENET, LAURENT, MARTIN MCKEE, DAVID LEON, VLADIMIR SHKOLNIKOV, and SERGEI VASSIN. 1998. "Alcohol and cardiovascular mortality in Moscow: New evidence of a causal association." *Journal of Epidemiology and Community Health*, 52:772–774.

CHILDS, DAVID, and JEFFREY JOHNSON. 1981. *West Germany: Politics and society*. London: Croom Helm.

CIAMBRONE, DESIRÉE. 2001. "Illness and other assaults on the self: The relative impact of HIV/AIDS on women's lives." *Sociology of Health and Illness*, 23:517–540.

CLAIR, JEFFREY MICHAEL. 1993. "The application of social science to medical practice," pp. 12–28 in *Sociomedical perspectives on patient care*, J. Clair and R. Allman, (eds.). Lexington: University of Kentucky Press.

CLARK, MARGARET. 1959. *Health in the Mexican-American culture*. Berkeley: University of California Press.

CLARKE, ADELE E., and VIRGINIA L. OLESEN. 1999. *Revisioning women, health, and healing*. London: Routledge.

CLARKE, JUANNE NANCARROW. 1996. *Health, illness, and medicine in Canada*. Toronto: Oxford University Press.

CLEARY, PAUL D., DAVID MECHANIC, and JAMES R. GREENLEY. 1982. "Sex differences in medical care utilization: An empirical investigation." *Journal of Health and Social Behavior*, 23:106–119.

COBURN, DAVID. 1993. "Professional powers in decline: Medicine in a changing Canada," pp. 92–103 in *The changing medical profession: An international perspective*, F. Hafferty and J. McKinley (eds.). New York: Oxford University Press.

COCKERHAM, WILLIAM C. 1983. "The state of medical sociology in the United States, Great Britain, West Germany, and Austria." *Social Science and Medicine*, 17:1513–1527.

———. 1988. "Medical sociology," pp. 575–599 in *Handbook of sociology*, N. Smelser (ed.). Newbury Park, Calif.: Sage.

————. 1990. "A test of the relationship between race, socioeconomic status, and psychological distress." *Social Science and Medicine*, 31:1321–1326.

————. 1997a. *This aging society*, 2nd ed. Upper Saddle River, N.J.: Prentice Hall.

————. 1997b. "The social determinants of the decline of life expectancy in Russia and Eastern Europe: A lifestyle explanation." *Journal of Health and Social Behavior*, 38:117–130.

————. 1999. *Health and social change in Russia and Eastern Europe*. London: Routledge.

————. 2000a. "The sociology of health behavior and health lifestyles," pp. 159–172 in *Handbook of medical sociology*, 5th ed., C. Bird, P. Conrad, and A. Fremont (eds.). Upper Saddle River, N.J.: Prentice Hall.

————. 2000b. "Medical sociology at the millennium," pp. 420–441 in *The international handbook of sociology*, S. Quah and A. Sales (eds.). London: Sage.

————. 2000c. "Health lifestyles in Russia." *Social Science and Medicine*, 51:1313–1324.

————. 2001. "Medical sociology and sociological theory," pp. 3–22 in *The Blackwell companion to medical sociology*, W. Cockerham (ed.). Oxford, UK: Blackwell.

————. 2003. *Sociology of mental disorder*, 6th ed. Upper Saddle River, N.J.: Prentice Hall.

COCKERHAM, WILLIAM C., ALFRED RÜTTEN, and THOMAS ABEL. 1997. "Conceptualizing health lifestyles: Moving beyond Weber." *Sociological Quarterly*, 38:601–622.

COCKERHAM, WILLIAM C., and FERRIS J. RITCHEY. 1997. *The dictionary of medical sociology*. Westport, Conn.: Greenwood.

COCKERHAM, WILLIAM C., GERHARD KUNZ, and GUENTHER LUESCHEN. 1988a. "Social stratification and health lifestyles in two systems of health care delivery: A comparison of America and West Germany." *Journal of Health and Social Behavior*, 29:113–126.

————. 1988b. "Psychological distress, perceived health status, and physician utilization in America and West Germany." *Social Science and Medicine*, 26:829–838.

COCKERHAM, WILLIAM C., GUENTHER LUESCHEN, GERHARD KUNZ, and JOE L. SPAETH. 1986a. "Social stratification and self-management of health." *Journal of Health and Social Behavior*, 27:1–14.

————. 1986b. "Symptoms, social stratification, and self-responsibility for health in the United States and West Germany." *Social Science and Medicine*, 22:1263–1271.

COCKERHAM, WILLIAM C., HIROYUKI HATTORI, and YUKIO YAMORI. 2000. "The social gradient in life expectancy: The contrary case of Okinawa in Japan." *Social Science and Medicine*, 51:115–122.

COCKERHAM, WILLIAM C., KIMBERLY SHARP, and JULIE WILCOX. 1983. "Aging and perceived health status." *Journal of Gerontology*, 38:349–355.

COCKERHAM, WILLIAM C., M. CHRISTINE SNEAD, and DEREK F. DeWAAL. 2002. "Health lifestyles in Russia and the socialist heritage." *Journal of Health and Social Behavior*, 43:42–55.

COCKERHAM, WILLIAM C., MORTON C. CREDITOR, UNA K. CREDITOR, and PETER B. IMREY. 1980. "Minor ailments and illness behavior among physicians." *Medical Care*, 18:164–173.

COCKERHAM, WILLIAM C., THOMAS ABEL, and GUNTHER LÜSCHEN. 1993. "Max Weber, formal rationality, and health lifestyles." *Sociological Quarterly*, 34:413–425.

COE, RODNEY M. 1978. *Sociology of medicine*, 2nd ed. New York: McGraw-Hill.

COLE, STEPHEN. 1986. "Sex discrimination and admission to medical school, 1929–1984." *American Journal of Sociology*, 92:529–567.

COLE, STEPHEN, and ROBERT LEJEUNE. 1972. "Illness and the legitimation of failure." *American Sociological Review*, 37:347–356.

COLEMAN, DAVID, and JOHN SALT. 1992. *The British population: Patterns, trends, and processes*. Oxford, UK: Oxford University Press.

COLUMBOTOS, JOHN. 1969. "Social origins and ideology of physicians: A study of the effects of early socialization." *Journal of Health and Social Behavior*, 10:16–29.

CONGER, RAND D., FREDERICK O. LORENZ, GLEN H. ELDER, JR., RONALD L. SIMONS, and XIAOJIA GE. 1993. "Husband and wife differences in response to undesirable life events." *Journal of Health and Social Behavior*, 34:71–88.

CONRAD, PETER. 1975. "The discovery of hyperkinesis: Note on the medicalization of deviant behavior." *Social Problems*, 23:12–21.

————. 1986a. "The social meaning of AIDS." *Social Policy*, 21:51–56.

————. 1988a. "Health and fitness at work: A participant's perspective." *Social Science and Medicine*, 26:545–550.

——. 1988b. "Worksite health promotion: The social context." *Social Science and Medicine,* 26:545–550.

——. 1994. "Wellness as a virtue: Morality and the pursuit of health." *Culture, Medicine, and Society,* 18:385–401.

——. 1999. "A mirage of genes." *Sociology of Health and Illness,* 21:228–241.

——. 2000. "Medicalization, genetics, and human problems," pp. 322–334 in *Handbook of medical sociology,* 5th ed., C. Bird, P. Conrad, and A. Fremont (eds.). Upper Saddle River, N.J.: Prentice Hall.

CONRAD, PETER, and JONATHAN GABE. 1999. "Introduction: Sociological perspectives on the new genetics: An overview." *Sociology of Health and Illness,* 21:505–516.

CONRAD, PETER, and JOSEPH W. SCHNEIDER. 1980. *Deviance and medicalization: From badness to sickness.* St. Louis: Mosby.

COOLEY, CHARLES H. 1964. *Human nature and the social order.* New York: Schocken.

COOMBS, ROBERT H. 1978. *Mastering medicine: Professional socialization in medical school.* New York: The Free Press.

COOMBS, ROBERT H., SANGEETA CHOPRA, DEBRA R. SCHENK, and ELAINE YUTAN. 1993. "Medical slang and its functions." *Social Science and Medicine,* 36:987–998.

COOPER-PATRICK, LISA, JOSEPH J. GALLO, J. J. GONZALES, HONG THI VU, NEIL R. POWE, CHRISTINE NELSON, and DANIEL E. FORD. 1999. "Race, gender, and partnership in the patient–physician relation." *Journal of the American Medical Association,* 282:583–589.

CORBETT, JAMES. 1994. *Through French windows.* Ann Arbor: University of Michigan Press.

COSER, ROSE L. 1956. "A home away from home." *Social Problems,* 4:3–17.

COX, SUSAN M., and WILLIAM MCKELLIN. 1999. "'There's this thing in our family': Predictive testing and the construction of risk for Huntington Disease." *Sociology of Health and Illness,* 21:622–646.

CRAWFORD, ROBERT. 1984. "A cultural account of health: Control, release, and the social body," pp. 60–103 in *Issues in the politicial economy of health care,* J. McKinley (ed.). New York: Tavistock.

CROOG, SYDNEY H., and DONNA F. VER STEEG. 1972. "The hospital as a social system," pp. 274–314 in *Handbook of medical sociology,* 2nd ed., H. Feeman, S. Levine, and L. Reeder (eds.). Englewood Cliffs, N.J.: Prentice Hall.

CROSSLEY, MICHELE. 1998. "'Sick role' or 'empowerment'? The ambiguities of life with an HIV positive diagnosis." *Sociology of Health and Illness,* 20:507–531.

CUNNINGHAM-BURLEY, SARAH, and ANNE KERR. 1999. "Defining the 'social': Towards an understanding of scientific and medical discourses on the social aspects of the new genetics." *Sociology of Health and Illness,* 21:647–668.

CURTIS, SARAH, NATASHA PETUKHOVA, and ANN TAKET. 1995. "Health care reforms in Russia: The example of St. Petersburg." *Social Science and Medicine,* 40:755–765.

DAHRENDORF, RALF. 1979. *Life chances.* Chicago: University of Chicago Press.

——. 1990. *Reflections on the revolution in Europe.* New York: Random House.

DAVIDSON, LAURIE, and LAURA KRAMER GORDON. 1979. *The sociology of gender.* Chicago: Rand McNally.

DAVIS, FRED. 1966. "Problems and issues in collegiate nursing education," pp. 138–175 in *The nursing profession,* F. Davis (ed.). New York: John Wiley.

——. 1972. *Illness, interaction, and the self.* Belmont, Calif.: Wadsworth.

DAVIS, FRED, and VIRGINIA OLESEN. 1963. "Initiation into a women's profession: Identity problems in the status transition of coed to student nurse." *Sociometry,* 26:89–101.

DEAN, ALFRED, BOHDAN KOLODY, and PATRICIA WOOD. 1990. "Effects of social support from various sources on depression in elderly persons." *Journal of Health and Social Behavior,* 31:148–161.

DEAN, KATHRYN. 1989. "Self-care components of lifestyles: The importance of gender, attitudes and the social situation." *Social Science and Medicine,* 29:137–152.

DENTON, JOHN A. 1978. *Medical sociology.* Boston: Houghton Mifflin.

DESJARLAIS, ROBERT, LEON EISENBERG, BYRON GOOD, and ARTHUR KLEINMAN. 1995. *World mental health: Problems and priorities in low-income countries.* New York: Oxford University Press.

DEVRIES, RAYMOND G. 1993. "A cross-national view of the status of midwives," pp. 131–146 in *Gender, work and medicine,* E. Riska and K. Wegar (eds.). London: Sage.

D'HOUTAUD, A., and MARK G. FIELD. 1984. "The image of health: Variations in perception by social class in a French population." *Sociology of Health and Illness,* 6:30–59.

———. 1986. "New research on the image of health," pp. 233–258 in *Concepts of health, illness and disease,* C. Currer and M. Stacey (eds.). Leamington Spa, U.K.: Berg.

DIDERICHSEN, FINN. 1990. "Health and social inequities in Sweden." *Social Science and Medicine,* 31:359–367.

DILL, ANN. 1994. "Institutional environments and organizational reponses to AIDS." *Journal of Health and Social Behavior,* 35:349–369.

DMITRIEVA, ELENA. 2001. "The Russian health care experiment: Transition of the health care system and rethinking the sociology of medicine," pp. 320–333 in *The Blackwell companion to medical sociology,* W. Cockerham (ed.). Oxford, UK: Blackwell.

DOHRENWEND, BARBARA S., LARRY KRASNOFF, ALEXANDER R. ASKENSASY, and BRUCE P. DOHRENWEND. 1978. "Exemplification of a method for scaling life events: The PERI life events scale." *Journal of Health and Social Behavior,* 19:205–229.

DOHRENWEND, BRUCE P. 1975. "Sociocultural and social-psychological factors in the genesis of mental disorders." *Journal of Health and Social Behavior,* 16:365–392.

DOOLEY, DAVID, and RALPH CATALANO. 1984. "Why the economy predicts help-seeking: A test of competing explanations." *Journal of Health and Social Behavior,* 25:160–176.

DRENTEA, PATRICIA. 2000. "Age, debt, and anxiety." *Journal of Health and Social Behavior,* 41:437–450.

DRENTEA, PATRICIA, and PAUL J. LAVRAKAS. 2000. "Over the limit: The association among health, race, and debt." *Social Science and Medicine,* 50:517–529.

DUBOS, RENÉ. 1959. *Mirage of health.* New York: Harper & Row.

———. 1969. *Man, medicine, and environment.* New York: Mentor.

———. 1981. "Health and creative adaptation," pp. 6–13 in *The nation's health,* P. Lee, N. Brown, and I. Red (eds.). San Francisco: Boyd & Fraser.

DUFF, RAYMOND S., and AUGUST B. HOLLINGSHEAD. 1968. *Sickness and society.* New York: Harper & Row.

DUMONS, BRUNO, and GILLES POLLET. 1999. "Healthcare," pp. 216–234 in *Modern France,* M. Cook and G. Davie (eds.). London: Routledge.

DUNN, ANDREA L., BESS H. MARCUS, JAMES B. KAMPERT, MELISSA E. GARCIA, HAROLD W. KOHL III, and STEVEN N. BLAIR. 1999. "Comparison of lifestyle and structured interventions to increase physical activity and cardiorespiratory fitness." *Journal of the American Medical Association,* 281:327–334.

DURKHEIM, EMILE. 1950. *The rules of sociological method.* New York: The Free Press.

———. 1951. *Suicide.* New York: The Free Press.

———. 1956. *The division of labor in society.* New York: The Free Press.

DUTTON, DIANA B. 1978. "Explaining the low use of health services by the poor: Costs, attitudes, or delivery systems?" *American Sociological Review,* 43:348–368.

———. 1986. "Social class, health, and illness," pp. 31–62 in *Applications of social science to clinical medicine and health policy,* L. Aiken and D. Mechanic (eds.). New Brunswick, N.J.: Rutgers University Press.

DWYER, JEFFREY W., LESLIE L. CLARKE, and MICHAEL K. MILLER. 1990. "The effect of religious concentration and affiliation on county cancer mortality rates." *Journal of Health and Social Behavior,* 31:185–202.

EBERSTADT, NICHOLAS. 1994. "Health and mortality in Central and Eastern Europe: Retrospect and prospect," pp. 198–225 in *The social legacy of communism,* J. Millar and S. Wolchik (eds.). New York and Cambridge, UK: Woodrow Wilson Center and Cambridge University Press.

EHRENREICH, BARBARA, and DIERDRE ENGLISH. 1979. "The 'sick' women of the upper classes," pp. 123–143 in *The cultural crisis of modern medicine,* J. Ehrenreich (ed.). New York: Monthly Review Press.

EITINGER, L. 1964. *Concentration camp survivors in Norway and Israel.* London: Allen & Unwin.

———. 1973. "A followup of the Norwegian concentration camp survivors." *Israel Annals of Psychiatry and Related Disciplines,* 11:199–209.

ELDER, R. G. 1963. "What is the patient saying?" *Nursing Forum,* 2:25–37.

ELLISON, CHRISTOPHER G. 1991. "Religious involvement and subjective well-being." *Journal of Health and Social Behavior,* 32:80–99.

ELSTON, MARY ANN. 1993. "Women doctors in a changing profession: The case of Britain," pp. 27–61 in *Gender, work and medicine,* E. Riska and K. Wegar (eds.). London: Sage.

ENGELS, FRIEDRICH. [1845] 1973. *The condition of the working class in England.* Moscow: Progress Publishers.

ENGLE, GEORGE L. 1971. "Sudden and rapid death during psychological stress: Folklore or folkwisdom?" *Annals of Internal Medicine,* 74:771–782.

———. 1977. "The need for a new medical model: A challenge for biomedicine." *Science,* 196:129–135.

ENSEL, WALTER M., and NAN LIN. 1991. "The life stress paradigm and psychological distress." *Journal of Health and Social Behavior,* 32:321–341.

EPSTEIN, HELEN. 1998. "Life and death on the social ladder." *New York Review of Books,* (July 16):26–30.

ETTORRE, ELIZABETH. 1999. "Experts as 'storytellers' in reproductive genetics: Exploring key issues." *Sociology of Health and Illness,* 21:539–559.

EVANS, ROBERT G. 1986. "Finding the levers, finding the courage: Lessons from cost containment in North America." *Journal of Health Politics, Policy and Law,* 11:585–616.

———. 1994. "Introduction," pp. 3–26 in *Why are some people healthy and others not? The determinants of the health of populations,* R. Evans, M. Barer, and T. Marmor (eds.). New York: Aldine de Gruyter.

EVANS, ROBERT G., MORRIS L. BARER, and THEODORE R. MARMOR (eds.). 1994. *Why are some people healthy and others not? The determinants of the health of populations.* New York: Aldine de Gruyter.

EVERETT, MARGARET. 2003. "The social life of genes: Privacy, property and the new genetics." *Social Science and Medicine,* 56:53–65.

EZZY, DOUGLAS. 2000. "Illness narratives: Time, hope and HIV." *Social Science and Medicine,* 50:605–617.

FAIRBANKS, DIANNE TIMBERS, and RICHARD L. HOUGH. 1981. "Cross-cultural differences in perceptions of life events," pp. 63–84 in *Stressful life events and their contexts,* B. Dohrenwend and B. Dohrenwend (eds.). New York: Prodist.

FARIS, ROBERT E., and H. WARREN DUNHAM. 1939. *Mental disorders in urban areas.* Chicago: University of Chicago Press.

FEATHERSTONE, MIKE. 1987. "Lifestyle and consumer culture." *Theory, Culture and Society,* 4:5–70.

FENWICK, RUDY, and MARK TAUSIG. 1994. "The macroeconomic context of job stress." *Journal of Health and Social Behavior,* 35:266–282.

FERRARO, KENNETH F. 1980. "Self-ratings of health among the old and old-old." *Journal of Health and Social Behavior,* 21:377–383.

———. 1993. "Are black older adults health-pessimistic?" *Journal of Health and Social Behavior,* 34:201–214.

FERRARO, KENNETH F., and MELISSA M. FARMER. 1996. "Double jeopardy to health hypothesis for African Americans: Analysis and critique." *Journal of Health and Social Behavior,* 37:27–43.

———. 1999. "Utility of health data from social surveys: Is there a gold standard for measuring morbidity?" *American Sociological Review,* 64:303–315.

FERRARO, KENNETH F., MELISSA M. FARMER, and JOHN A. WYBRANIEC. 1997. "Health trajectories: Long-term dynamics among black and white adults." *Journal of Health and Social Behavior,* 38:38–54.

FERRARO, KENNETH F., and TAMMY SOUTHERLAND. 1989. "Domains of medical practice: Physicians' assessment of the role of physician extenders." *Journal of Health and Social Behavior,* 30:192–205.

FIELD, MARK G. 1985. "Soviet life, 1985: In sickness and health." *Wilson Quarterly,* Autumn:1–14.

———. (ed.). 1989. *Success and crisis in national health systems.* London: Routledge.

———. 1991. "The hybrid profession: Soviet medicine," pp. 43–62 in *Professions and the state,* A. Jones (ed.). Philadelphia: Temple University Press.

———. 1993. "The physician in the Commonwealth of Independent States: The difficult passage from bureaucrat to professional," pp. 162–183 in *The changing medical profession,* F. Hafferty and J. McKinley (eds.). New York: Oxford University Press.

———. 1995. "The health crisis in the former Soviet Union: A report from the 'post-war' zone." *Social Science and Medicine,* 41:1469–1478.

———. 2000. "The health and demographic crisis in post-Soviet Russia. A two-phase development," pp. 11–42 in *Russia's torn safety nets: Health and social welfare during the transition,* M. Field and J. Twigg (eds.). New York: St. Martin's Press.

FIELDING, JONATHAN E., and PIERRE-JEAN LANCRY. 1993. "Lessons from France—'Vive la différence.'" *Journal of the American Medical Association,* 270:748–756.

FIFE, BETSY L., and ERIC R. WRIGHT. 2000. "The dimensionality of stigma: A comparison of its impact on the self of persons with HIV/AIDS and cancer." *Journal of Health and Social Behavior,* 41:50–67.

FILLENBAUM, GERDA G. 1979. "Social context and self-assessment of health among the elderly." *Journal of Health and Social Behavior,* 20:45–51.

FIORENTINE, ROBERT. 1987. "Men, women, and the premed persistence: A normative alternatives approach." *American Journal of Sociology,* 92:1118–1139.

FISHER, SUE. 1984. "Doctor–patient communication: A social and micro-political performance." *Sociology of Health and Illness,* 6:1–27.

FISHER, SUE, and ALEXANDRA DUNDAS TODD. 1990. *The social organization of doctor–patient communication,* 2nd ed. Norwood, N.J.: Ablex.

FITTON, FREDA, and H. W. K. ACHESON. 1979. *The doctor/patient relationship: A study in general practice.* London: Department of Health and Social Security.

FLOGE, LILIANE, and DEBORAH M. MERRILL. 1986. "Tokenism reconsidered: Male nurses and female physicians in a hospital setting." *Social Forces,* 64:925–947.

FOSU, GABRIEL B. 1989. "Access to health care in urban areas of developing societies." *Journal of Health and Social Behavior,* 30:398–411.

FOUCAULT, MICHEL. 1973. *The birth of the clinic.* London: Tavistock.

FOX, A. J. (ed.). 1989. *Health inequalities in European countries.* Aldershot, U.K.: Gower.

FOX, JOHN W. 1980. "Gore's specific sex-role theory of mental illness: A research note." *Journal of Health and Social Behavior,* 21:260–267.

FOX, RENÉE. 1957. "Training for uncertainty," pp. 207–241 in *The student-physician,* R. K. Merton, G. Reader, and P. L. Kendall (eds.). Cambridge, Mass.: Harvard University Press.

FOX, RENÉE C., LINDA H. AIKEN, and CARLA MESSIKOMER. 1990. "The culture of caring: AIDS and the nursing profession." *Milbank Quarterly,* 67:226–258.

FRASER, CAROLINE. 1999. *God's perfect child: Living and dying in the Christian Science Church.* New York: Metropolitan Books/Henry Holt.

FRANK, ARTHUR W. 1991. *At the will of the body: Reflections on illness.* Boston: Houghton Mifflin.

FREIDSON, ELIOT. 1960. "Client control and medical practice." *American Journal of Sociology,* 65:374–382.

———. 1970a. *Profession of medicine.* New York: Dodd, Mead.

———. 1970b. *Professional dominance.* Chicago: Aldine.

———. 1975. *Doctoring together.* New York: Elsevier North-Holland.

———. 1989. *Medical work in America: Essays on health care.* New Haven, Conn.: Yale University Press.

———. 1993. "How dominant are the professions?" pp. 54–66 in *The changing medical profession: An international perspective,* F. Hafferty and J. McKinley (eds.). New York: Oxford University Press.

FREUND, PETER E. S., and MEREDITH B. MCGUIRE. 1999. *Health, illness, and the social body,* 3rd ed. Englewood Cliffs, N.J.: Prentice Hall.

FROHLICH, KATHERINE L., ELLEN CORIN, and LOUISE POTVIN. 2001. "A theoretical proposal for the relationship between context and disease." *Sociology of Health and Illness,* 23:776–797.

FROHLICH, NORMAN, and CAM MUSTARD. 1996. "A regional comparison and health indices in a Canadian province." *Social Science and Medicine,* 42:1273–1281.

FUCHS, VICTOR R. 1974. *Who shall live?* New York: Basic Books.

———. 1986. *The health economy.* Cambridge, Mass.: Harvard University Press.

FULLER, THEODORE D., JOHN N. EDWARDS, SANTHAT SERMSRI, and SAIRUDEE VORAKITPHOKATORN. 1993. "Gender and health: Some Asian evidence." *Journal of Health and Social Behavior,* 34:252–271.

FUNCH, DONNA P., and JAMES R. MARSHALL. 1984. "Measuring life stress: Factors affecting fall-off in the reporting of life events." *Journal of Health and Social Behavior,* 25:453–464.

GALLAGHER, EUGENE B. 1976. "Lines of reconstruction and extension in the Parsonian sociology of illness." *Social Science and Medicine,* 10:207–218.

———. 1988a. "Modernization and medical care." *Sociological Perspectives,* 31:59–87.

———. 1988b. "Convergence or divergence in third world medical education? An Arab study." *Journal of Health and Social Behavior,* 29:385–400.

———. 1995. "Culture and technology in health care, as exemplified in Gulf Arab medicine," pp. 83–93 in *Global perspectives on health care,* E. Gallagher and J. Subedi (eds.). Englewood Cliffs, N.J.: Prentice Hall.

———. 2001. "Health, health care, and medical education in the Arab world," pp. 393–409 in *The Blackwell companion to medical sociology,* W. Cockerham (ed.). Oxford, UK: Blackwell.

GALLAGHER, EUGENE B., and C. MAUREEN SEARLE. 1984. "Cultural forces in the formation of the Saudi medical role." *Medical Anthropology,* 8:210–221.

———. 1985. "Health services and the political culture of Saudi Arabia." *Social Science and Medicine,* 21:251–262.

———. 1989. "Content and context in health professional education," pp. 437–454 in *Handbook of medical sociology,* 4th ed., H. Freeman and S. Levine (eds.). Englewood Cliffs, N.J.: Prentice Hall.

GALLAGHER, EUGENE B., THOMAS J. STEWART, and TERRY D. STRATTON. 2000. "The sociology of health in developing countries," pp. 389–397 in *Handbook of medical sociology,* 5th ed., C. Bird, P. Conrad, and A. Fremont (eds.). Upper Saddle River, N.J.: Prentice Hall.

GALLAGHER, EUGENE B., and JANARDAN SUBEDI (eds.). 1995. *Global perspectives on health care.* Upper Saddle River, N.J.: Prentice Hall.

GARLAND, T. NEAL. 1995. "Major orientations in Japanese health care," pp. 255–267 in *Global perspectives on health care,* E. Gallagher and J. Subedi (eds.). Englewood Cliffs, N.J.: Prentice Hall.

GARRETT, LAURIE. 1994. *The coming plague.* New York: Farrar, Straus and Giroux.

GAY, E. GREER, JENNIE J. KRONENFELD, SAMUEL L. BAKER, and ROGER L. AMIDON. 1989. "An appraisal of organizational response to fiscally constraining regulation: The case of hospitals and DRGs." *Journal of Health and Social Behavior,* 30:41–55.

GEERTSEN, REED, MELVILLE R. KLAUBER, MARK RINDFLESH, ROBERT L. KANE, and ROBERT GRAY. 1975. "A reexamination of Suchman's views on social factors in health care utilization." *Journal of Health and Social Behavior,* 16:226–237.

GEIGER, H. JACK. 1975. "The causes of dehumanization in health care and prospects for humanization," pp. 11–36 in *Humanizing health care,* J. Howard and A. Strauss (eds.). New York: Wiley-Interscience.

GEORGOPOULOS, BASIL F., and FLOYD C. MANN. 1972. "The hospital as an organization," pp. 304–311 in *Patients, physicians and illness,* 2nd ed., E. Jaco (ed.). New York: Macmillan.

GERHARDT, UTA. 1989a. *Ideas about illness: An intellectual and political history of medical sociology.* London: Macmillan.

———. 1989b. "The sociological image of medicine and the patient." *Social Science and Medicine,* 29:721–728.

———. 1989c. "Sociology on medicine: Understanding medical sociology's critical standpoint," pp. 31–48 in *Health and illness in America and Germany,* G. Lüschen, W. Cockerham, and G. Kunz (eds.). Munich: Oldenbourg.

GERTH, H. H., and C. WRIGHT MILLS (eds.). 1946. *From Max Weber: Essays in sociology.* New York: Oxford University Press.

GIBBS, JACK. 1971. "A critique of the labeling perspective," pp. 193–205 in *The study of social problems,* E. Rubington and M. S. Weinberg (eds.). New York: Oxford University Press.

GILBERT, LEAH, and LIZ WALKER. 2002. "Treading the path of least resistance: HIV/AIDS and social inequalities—A South African case study." *Social Science and Medicine,* 54:1093–1110.

GILL, DEREK. 1994. "A national health service: Principles and practice," pp. 480–494 in *The sociology of health and illness: Critical perspectives,* 4th ed., P. Conrad and R. Kern (eds.). New York: St. Martin's Press.

GILLICK, MURIEL R. 1984. "Health promotion, jogging, and the pursuit of a moral life." *Journal of Health Politics, Policy and Law,* 9:369–387.

GISSLER, MIKA, OSSI RAHKONEN, MARJO-RIITTA-JÄRVELIN, and ELINA HEMMINKI, 1998. "Social class differences in health until the age of seven years among the Finnish 1987 birth cohort." *Social Science and Medicine,* 46:1543–1552.

GLASER, BARNEY G., and ANSELM M. STRAUSS. 1965. *Awareness of dying.* Chicago: Aldine.

GLASS, JENNIFER, and TETSUSHI FUJIMOTO. 1994. "Housework, paid work, and depression among husbands and wives." *Journal of Health and Social Behavior,* 35:179–191.

GLASSNER, BARRY. 1988. *Bodies.* New York: G. P. Putnam.

———. 1989. "Fitness and the postmodern self." *Journal of Health and Social Behavior,* 30:180–191.

GLIK, DEBORAH C. 1990. "The redefinition of the situation: The social construction of spiritual healing experiences." *Sociology of Health and Illness,* 12:151–168.

GOCHMAN, D. S. 1971. "Some correlates of children's health care beliefs and potential behavior." *Journal of Health and Social Behavior,* 12:148–154.

GOFFMAN, ERVING. 1959. *The presentation of self in everyday life.* New York: Anchor.

———. 1961. *Asylums.* New York: Anchor.

———. 1963. *Stigma: Notes on the management of a spoiled identity.* Englewood Cliffs, NJ: Prentice-Hall.

GOLD, MARSHA R. 1991. "HMOs and managed care." *Health Affairs,* 10:189–206.

———. 1999. "The changing US health care system: Challenges for responsible public policy." *Milbank Quarterly,* 77:3–37.

GOLDBERG, DAVID M. 1995. "Does wine work?" *Clinical Chemistry,* 41:14–16.

GOLDBERG, KENNETH C., ARTHUR J. HARTZ, STEVEN J. JACOBSEN, HENRY KRAKAUER, and ALFRED A. RIMM. 1992. "Racial and community factors influencing coronary artery bypass graft surgery rates for all 1986 Medicare patients." *Journal of the American Medical Association,* 267:1473–1477.

GOLDSTEIN, MICHAEL S. 1992. *The health movement: Promoting fitness in America.* New York: Twayne.

———. 2000. "The growing acceptance of complementary and alternative medicine," pp. 284–297 in *Handbook of medical sociology,* 5th ed., C. Bird, P. Conrad, and A. Fremont (eds.). Upper Saddle River, N.J.: Prentice Hall.

GOODE, WILLIAM J. 1957. "Community within a community." *American Sociological Review,* 22:194–200.

———. 1960. "Encroachment, charlatanism, and the emerging profession: Psychology, sociology, and medicine," *American Sociological Review,* 25:902–914.

GORDON, GERALD. 1966. *Role theory and illness.* New Haven, Conn.: College and University Press.

GORE, SUSAN. 1989. "Social networks and social supports in health care," pp. 306–331 in *Handbook of medical sociology,* 4th ed., H. Freeman and S. Levine (eds.). Englewood Cliffs, N.J.: Prentice Hall.

GORE, SUSAN, ROBERT H. ASELTINE, JR., and MARY ELLEN COLTEN. 1992. "Social structure, life stress, and depressive symptoms in a high school-aged population." *Journal of Health and Social Behavior,* 33:97–113.

GORTMAKER, STEVEN L., JOHN ECKENRODE, and SUSAN GORE. 1982. "Stress and the utilization of health services: A time series and cross-sectional analysis." *Journal of Health and Social Behavior,* 23:25–38.

GOSS, MARY E. 1963. "Patterns of bureaucracy among hospital staff physicians," pp. 170–194 in *The hospital in modern society,* E. Freidson (ed.). New York: The Free Press.

GOULDNER, ALVIN. 1970. *The coming crisis of western sociology.* New York: Basic Books.

GOVE, WALTER R., MICHAEL HUGHES, and CAROLYN BRIGGS STYLE. 1983. "Does marriage have positive effects on the psychological well-being of the individual?" *Journal of Health and Social Behavior,* 24:122–131.

GRAIG, LAURENCE A. 1993. *Health of nations,* 2nd ed. Washington, D.C.: Congressional Quarterly, Inc.

GREEN, GILL. 1995. "Attitudes towards people with HIV: Are they as stigmatizing as people with HIV perceive them to be?" *Social Science and Medicine,* 41:557–568.

GREEN, GILL, and STEPHEN PLATT. 1997. "Fear and loathing in health care settings reported by people with HIV." *Sociology of Health and Illness,* 19:70–92.

GREEN, HARVEY. 1986. *Fit for America: Health, fitness, sport, and American society.* New York: Pantheon.

GREENLEY, JAMES R., and RICHARD A. SCHOENHERR. 1981. "Organization effects on client satisfaction with humaneness of service." *Journal of Health and Social Behavior,* 22:2–18.

GREGSON, SIMON, TOM ZHUWAU, ROY M. ANDERSON, and STEPHEN K. CHANDIWANA. 1998. "Is there evidence for behaviour change in response to AIDS in rural Zimbabwe?" *Social Science and Medicine,* 46:321–330.

GREY, BRADFORD H. 1991. *The profit motive and patient care: The changing accountability of doctors and hospitals.* Cambridge, Mass.: Harvard University Press.

———. 1997. "Trust and trustworthy care in the managed care era." *Health Affairs,* 16:34–49.

GROGAN, COLLEEN M. 1995. "Urban economic reform and access to health care coverage in the People's Republic of China." *Social Science and Medicine,* 41:1073–1084.

GRZYWACZ, JOSEPH G., and NADINE F. MARKS. 2001. "Social inequalities and exercise during adulthood: Toward an ecological perspective." *Journal of Health and Social Behavior,* 42:202–220.

HAAS, JACK, and WILLIAM SHAFFIR. 1977. "The professionalization of medical students: Developing competence and a cloak of competence." *Symbolic Interaction,* 1:71–88.

————. 1982. "Taking on the role of doctor: A dramaturgical analysis of professionalization." *Symbolic Interaction,* 5:205–222.

HAFFERTY, FREDERIC. 1991. *Into the valley: Death and the socialization of medical students.* New Haven, Conn.: Yale University Press.

————. 2000. "Reconfiguring the sociology of medical education: Emerging topics and pressing issues," pp. 238–257 in *Handbook of medical sociology,* 5th ed., C. BIRD, P. CONRAD, and A. FREMONT (eds.). Upper Saddle River, N.J.: Prentice Hall.

HAFFERTY, FREDERIC W., and DONALD W. LIGHT. 1995. "Professional dynamics and the changing nature of medical work." *Journal of Health and Social Behavior,* extra issue:132–153.

HAFFERTY, FREDERIC W., and JOHN B. McKINLAY. 1993. "Conclusion: Cross-cultural perspectives on the dynamics of medicine as a profession," pp. 210–226 in *The changing medical profession: An international perspective,* F. Hafferty and J. McKinlay (eds.). New York: Oxford University Press.

HAINES, VALERIE A., and JEANNE S. HURLBERT. 1992. "Network range and health." *Journal of Health and Social Behavior,* 33:254–266.

HAINES, VALERIE A., JEANNE S. HURLBERT, and JOHN J. BEGGS. 1996. "Exploring the determinants of support provision: Provider characteristics, personal networks, community contexts, and support following life events." *Journal of Health and Social Behavior,* 37:252–264.

HALL, OSWALD. 1946. "The informal organization of the medical profession." *Canadian Journal of Economics and Political Science,* 12:30–44.

————. 1948. "The stages of a medical career." *American Journal of Sociology,* 53:327–336.

HALLOWELL, NINA. 1999. "Doing the right thing: Genetic risk and responsibility." *Sociology of Health and Illness,* 21:597–621.

HAM, CHRISTOPHER. 1992. *Health policy in Britain,* 3rd ed. London: Macmillan.

HAMILTON, V. LEE, CLIFFORD L. BROMAN, WILLIAM S. HOFFMAN, and DEBORAH S. RENNER. 1990. "Hard times and vulnerable people: Initial effects of plant closing on autoworkers' mental health." *Journal of Health and Social Behavior,* 31:123–140.

HAMMOND, JUDITH. 1980. "Biography building to insure the future: Women's negotiation of gender relevancy in medical school." *Symbolic Interaction,* 3:35–49.

HARDEY, MICHAEL. 1998. *The social context of health.* Buckingham, U.K.: Open University Press.

————. 1999. "Doctor in the house: The Internet as a source of lay health knowledge and the challenge to expertise." *Sociology of Health and Illness,* 21:820–835.

HARRIS, DANIEL M., and SHARON GUTEN. 1979. "Health-protective behavior: An exploratory study." *Journal of Health and Social Behavior,* 20:17–29.

HART, NICKY. 1991. "The social and economic environment and human health," pp. 151–180 in *Oxford Textbook of Public Health,* Vol. 1, W. Holland, R. Detels, and G. Knox (eds.). Oxford, U.K.: Oxford University Press.

HARTLEY, HEATHER. 1999. "The influence of managed care on supply of certified nurse-midwives: An evaluation of the physician dominance thesis." *Journal of Health and Social Behavior,* 40:87–101.

————. 2002. "The system of alignments challenging physician professional dominance: An elaborated theory of countervailing powers." *Sociology of Health and Illness,* 24:178–207.

HATTORI, HIROYUKI, STEPHEN M. SALZBERG, WINSTON P. KIANG, TATSUYA FUJIMIYA, YUTAKA TEJIMA, and JUNJI FURUNO. 1991. "The patient's right to information in Japan—Legal rules and doctor's opinions." *Social Science and Medicine,* 32:1007–1016.

HAUG, MARIE, HIROKO AKIYAMA, GEORGEANN TRYBAN, KYOICHI SONODA, and MAY WYKLE. 1989. "Self-care: Japan and the U.S. compared." *Social Science and Medicine,* 33:1011–1022.

HAUG, MARIE, and BEBE LAVIN. 1981. "Practitioner or patient—Who's in charge?" *Journal of Health and Social Behavior,* 22:212–229.

————. 1983. *Consumerism in medicine.* Beverly Hills, Calif.: Sage.

HÄUSSLER, B., ELKE HEMPEL, and P. RESCHKE. 1995. "Die Entwicklung von Lebenswartung und Sterblichkeit in Ostdeutschland nach der Wende (1989–1992)" ["Life expectancy and mortality in East Germany after the fall of the Berlin Wall (1989–1992)"]. *Gesundheitswesen,* 7:365–372.

HAYES, DIANE, and CATHERINE E. ROSS. 1987. "Concern with appearance, health beliefs, and eating habits." *Journal of Health and Social Behavior,* 20:17–29.

HAYES-BAUTISTA, DAVID E. 1976a. "Modifying the treatment: Patient compliance, patient control, and medical care." *Social Science and Medicine,* 10:233–238.

————. 1976b. "Termination of the patient-practitioner relationship: Divorce, patient style." *Journal of Health and Social Behavior,* 17:12–21.

HAYWARD, MARK D., EILEEN M. CRIMMINS, TONI P. MILES, and YU YANG. 2000. "The significance of socioeconomic status in explaining the racial gap in chronic health conditions." *American Sociological Review,* 65:910–930.

HEINEMANN, L., W. BARTH, and H. HOFFMEISTER. 1995. "Trend of cardiovascular risk factors in the East German population." *Journal of Clinical Epidemiology,* 48:787–795.

HEINEMANN, L., R. DINKEL, and E. GÖRTLER. 1996. "Life expectancy in Germany: Possible reasons for the increasing gap between East and West Germany." *Reviews on Environmental Health,* 11:15–26.

HELZER, JOHN E. 1981. "Methodological issues in the interpretations of the consequences of extreme situations," pp. 108–129 in *Stressful life events and their contexts,* B. Dohrenwend and B. Dohrenwend (eds.). New York: Prodist.

HEMSTRÖM, ÖRJAN, 1999. "Explaining differential rates of mortality decline for Swedish men and women: A time-series analysis, 1945–1992." *Social Science and Medicine,* 49:1759–1777.

————. 2001. "Society, health, and health care in Sweden," pp. 298–318 in *The Blackwell companion to medical sociology,* W. Cockerham (ed.). Oxford, UK: Blackwell.

HENDERSON, GAIL, JIN SHUIGAO, JOHN AKIN, LI ZHIMING, WANG JIANMIN, MA HAIJIANG, HE YUNAN, ZHANG XIPING, CHANG YING, and GE KEYOU. 1995. "Distribution of medical insurance in China." *Social Science and Medicine,* 41:1119–1130.

HENDERSON, LAWRENCE J. 1935. "Physician and patient as a social system." *New England Journal of Medicine,* 212:819–823.

HENIG, ROBIN W. 1993. "Are women's hearts different?" *New York Times Magazine,* 58, (October 3): 58–61.

HERZLICH, CLAUDINE. 1973. *Health and illness.* London: Academic Press.

HERZLICH, CLAUDINE, and JANINE PIERRET. 1986. "Illness: Causes to meaning," pp. 71–96 in *Concepts of health, illness and disease,* C. Currer and M. Stacey (eds.). Leamington Spa, U.K.: Berg.

————. 1987. *Illness and self in society,* E. Forster (trans.). Baltimore: Johns Hopkins University Press.

HESKETH, THERESE, and WEIXING ZHU. 1997a. "Health in China: Traditional Chinese medicine: one country, two systems." *British Medical Journal,* 314:115–117.

————. 1997b. "Health in China: The healthcare market." *British Medical Journal,* 314:1616–1618.

HILDRETH, CAROLYN J., and ELIJAH SAUNDERS. 1992. "Heart disease, stroke, and hypertension in blacks," pp. 90–105 in *Health issues in the black community,* R. Braithwaite and S. Taylor (eds.). San Francisco: Jossey Bass.

HILLIER, SHEILA. 1987. "Rationalism, bureaucracy, and the organization of the health services: Max Weber's contribution to understanding modern health care systems," pp. 194–220 in *Sociological theory and medical sociology,* G. Scambler (ed.). London: Tavistock.

HINES, RALPH. 1972. "The health status of black Americans: Changing perspectives," pp. 40–50 in *Patients, physicians and illness,* 2nd ed., E. Jaco (ed.). New York: The Free Press.

HINZE, SUSAN W. 1999. "Gender and the body of medicine or at least some body parts: (Re)constructing the prestige hierarchy of medical specialties." *Sociological Quarterly,* 40:217–240.

HJERMANN, I., K. VELVE BYRE, I. HOLME, and P. LEREN. 1981. "Effect of diet and smoking intervention on the incidence of coronary heart disease." *Lancet,* 8259:1303–1310.

HOLLINGSHEAD, AUGUST B. 1973. "Medical sociology: A brief review." *Milbank Memorial Fund Quarterly,* 51:531–542.

HOLLINGSHEAD, AUGUST B., and FREDERICK C. REDLICH. 1958. *Social class and mental illness: A community study.* New York: John Wiley.

HOLLINGSWORTH, J. ROGERS. 1981. "Inequality in levels of health in England and Wales, 1891–1971." *Journal of Health and Social Behavior,* 22:268–283.

HOLLMANN, W., H. LIESEN, R. ROST, H. HECK, and J. SATOMI. 1985. "Präventive Kardiologie: Bewegungsmangel und körperliches Training aus epidemiologischer und experimenteller Sicht." ["Preventive cardiology: Movement impairment and physical training as an epidemiological and experimental field."] *Zeitschrift für Kardiologie,* 74:46–54.

HOLLOWAY, JOSEPH E. (ed.). 1990. *Africanisms in American culture.* Bloomington: Indiana University Press.

HOLMES, T. H., and M. MASUDA. 1974. "Life change and illness susceptibility," pp. 45–72 in *Stressful life events: Their nature and effects,* B. S. Dohrenwend and B. P. Dohrenwend (eds.). New York: John Wiley.

HOLMES, T. H., and R. H. RAHE. 1967. "The social readjustment rating scale." *Journal of Psychosomatic Research,* 11:213–225.

HOOKER, RODERICK S. 1991. "The military physician assistant." *Military Medicine,* 156:657–660.

HORWITZ, ALLAN V., HELENE RASKIN WHITE, and SANDRA HOWELL-WHITE. 1996. "The use of multiple outcomes in stress research: A case study of gender differences in response to marital dissolution." *Journal of Health and Social Behavior,* 37:278–291.

HOUGH, RICHARD L., DIANNE TIMBERS FAIRBANKS, and ALMA M. GARCIA. 1976. "Problems in the ratio measurement of life stress." *Journal of Health and Social Behavior,* 17:70–82.

HOUSE, JAMES S. 1974. "Occupational stress and coronary heart disease." *Journal of Health and Social Behavior,* 15:12–27.

———. 2002. "Understanding social factors and inequalities in health: 20th century progress and 21st century prospects." *Journal of Health and Social Behavior,* 43:125–142.

HOUSE, JAMES S., JAMES M. LEPKOWSKI, ANN M. KINNEY, RICHARD P. MERO, RONALD C. KESSLER, and A. REGULA HERZOG. 1994. "The social stratification of aging and health." *Journal of Health and Social Behavior,* 35:213–234.

HOWARD, JAN, and ANSELM STRAUSS (eds.). 1975. *Humanizing health care.* New York: Wiley-Interscience.

HRABA, JOSEPH, FREDERICK O. LORENZ, ZDENKA PECHAĈOVÁ, and QIANG LIU. 1998. "Education and health in the Czech Republic." *Journal of Health and Social Behavior,* 39:295–318.

HSIAO, WILLIAM C. L. 1995. "The Chinese health care system: Lessons for other nations." *Social Science and Medicine,* 41:1047–1055.

HUGHES, DAVID, and LESLEY GRIFFITHS. 1999. "On penalties and the Patient's Charter: Centralism v. decentralised governance in the NHS." *Sociology of Health and Illness,* 21:71–94.

HUGHES, EVERETT C., HELEN MACGILL, and IRWIN DEUTSCHER. 1958. *Twenty thousand nurses tell their story.* Philadelphia: Lippincott.

HUIE, STEPHANIE A. BOND, ROBERT A. HUMMER, and RICHARD G. ROGERS. 2002. "Individual and contextual risks of death among race and ethnic groups in the United States." *Journal of Health and Social Behavior,* 43:350–381.

HUMMER, ROBERT A. 1993. "Racial differences in infant mortality in the U.S.: An examination of social and health determinants." *Social Forces,* 72:529–554.

HUMPHRIES, KARIN H., and EDDY VAN DOORSLAER. 2000. "Income-related health inequality in Canada." *Social Science and Medicine,* 50:663–671.

HUNGARIAN CENTRAL STATISTICAL OFFICE. 1995. *Preliminary report on the health behavior survey—94.* Budapest: Hungarian Ministry of Health.

HUNT, CHARLES W. 1989. "Migrant labor and sexually transmitted disease: AIDS in Africa." *Journal of Health and Social Behavior,* 30:353–373.

———. 1996. "Social vs. biological: Theories on the transmission of AIDS in Africa." *Social Science and Medicine,* 42:1283–1296.

HUNT, LINDA M. 1996. "Inequalities in the Mexican national health care system: Problems in managing cancer in southern Mexico," pp. 130–147 in *Society, health, and disease,* J. Subedi and E. Gallagher (eds.). Upper Saddle River, N.J.: Prentice Hall.

HYDE, DAVID R., and PAYSON WOLFF. 1954. "The American Medical Association: Power, purpose and politics in organized medicine." *Yale Law Journal,* 63:938–1022.

IDLER, ELLEN L. 1987. "Religious involvement and the health of the elderly: Some hypotheses and an initial test." *Social Forces,* 66:226–238.

———. 1995. "Religion, health, and nonphysical senses of self." *Social Forces,* 74:683–704.

IDLER, ELLEN L., and YAEL BENYAMINI. 1997. "Self-rated health and mortality: A review of twenty-seven community studies." *Journal of Health and Social Behavior,* 38:21–37.

IDLER, ELLEN L., and STANISLAV V. KASL. 1992. "Religion, disability, depression, and the timing of death." *American Journal of Sociology,* 97:1052–1079.

INGLEHART, JOHN K. 1991. "Health policy report: Germany's health care system." *New England Journal of Medicine,* 324:503–508, 1750–1756.

IKEGAMI, NAOKI. 1991. "Japanese health care: Low cost through regulated fees." *Health Affairs,* Fall:87–109.

———. 1992. "The economics of health care in Japan." *Science,* 258:614–618.

IKEGAMI, NAOKI, and JOHN C. CAMPBELL. 1995. "Medical care in Japan." *New England Journal of Medicine,* 333:1295–1299.

ILLSLEY, R., and P. G. SVENSSON (eds.). 1986. *The health burden of social inequities*. Copenhagen: World Health Organization Regional Office for Europe.

JACKSON, PAMELA BRABOY. 1997. "Role occupancy and mental health." *Journal of Health and Social Behavior*, 38:237–255.

JALLINOJA, PIIA. 2001. "Genetic screening in maternity care: Preventive aims and voluntary choices." *Sociology of Health and Illness*, 23:286–307.

JANZ, NANCY K., and MARSHALL H. BECKER. 1984. "The health belief model: A decade later." *Health Education Quarterly*, 11:1–47.

JARVIS, GEORGE K., and HERBERT C. NORTHCOTT. 1987. "Religion and differences in morbidity and mortality." *Social Science and Medicine*, 25:813–814.

JARVIS, MARTIN J., and JANE WARDLE. 1999. "Social patterning of individual health behaviours: The case of cigarette smoking," pp. 240–255 in *The social determinants of health*, M. Marmot and R. Wilkinson (eds.). Oxford, UK: Oxford University Press.

JASPERS, KARL. 1988. *On Max Weber*, J. Dreijmans (ed.). New York: Paragon House.

JEWKES, RACHEL K., JONATHAN B. LEVIN, and LOVEDAY A. PENN-KEKANA. 2003. "Gender inequalities, intimate partner violence and HIV preventive practices: Findings of a South African cross-sectional study." *Social Science and Medicine*, 56, 125–134.

JOHNSON, MALCOLM. 1975. "Medical sociology and sociological theory." *Social Science and Medicine*, 9:227–232.

JONES, BERNARD. 1996. "Sweden," pp. 104–126 in *Health systems in liberal democracies*, A. Wall (ed.). London: Routledge.

JOOSTEN, J. 1989. "The structure of the concept of 'health' in the Dutch population." *Colloque INSERM*, 178:71–84.

JOST, TIMOTHY. 1998. "German health care reform: The next steps." *Journal of Health Policy and Law*, 23:697–711.

JÓZAN, PÉTER. 1996. "Health crisis east of the Elbe: A consequence of death-ended modernization." Paper presented to the Sawyer-Mellon Conference on increasing adult mortality in Eastern Europe, University of Michigan, Ann Arbor (March).

JYLHÄ, MARIA. 1994. "Self-rated health revisited: Exploring survey interview episodes with elderly respondents." *Social Science and Medicine*, 39:983–990.

KAGAWA-SINGER, MARJORIE. 1993. "Redefining health: Living with cancer." *Social Science and Medicine*, 37:295–304.

KARLSEN, SAFFRON, and JAMES Y. NAZROO. 2002. "Agency and structure: The impact of ethnic identity and racism on the health of ethnic minority people." *Sociology of Health and Illness*, 24:1–20.

KASL, S., and S. COBB. 1966. "Health behavior, illness behavior, and sick role behavior." *Archives of Environmental Health*, 12:246–266.

KASSEBAUM, G., and B. BAUMANN. 1965. "Dimensions of the sick role in chronic illness." *Journal of Health and Social Behavior*, 6:16–27.

KASTELER, JOSEPHINE, ROBERT L. KANE, DONNA M. OLSEN, and CONSTANCE THETFORD. 1976. "Issues underlying prevalence of 'doctor-shopping' behavior." *Journal of Health and Social Behavior*, 17:328–339.

KATZ, PEARL. 1999. *The scalpel's edge: The culture of surgeons*. Boston: Allyn and Bacon.

KELLETT, ANTHONY. 1982. *Combat motivation*. Boston: Kluwer.

KELLY, MICHAEL P., and DAVID FIELD. 1996. "Medical sociology, chronic illness and the body." *Sociology of Health and Illness*, 18:241–257.

KELNER, MERRIJOY, BEVERLY WELLMAN, BERNICE PESCOSOLIDO, and MIKE SAKS. 2000. *Complementary and alternative medicine: Challenge and change*. Amsterdam: Harwood.

KENDALL, PATRICIA, and GEORGE G. READER. 1988. "Innovations in medical education of the 1950s contrasted with those of the 1970s and 1980s." *Journal of Health and Social Behavior*, 29:279–293.

KENDALL, PATRICIA L., and HANAN C. SELVIN. 1957. "Tendencies toward specialization in medical training," pp. 153–174 in *The student-physician*, R. Merton, G. Reader, and P. Kendall (eds.). Cambridge, Mass.: Harvard University Press.

KESSLER, RONALD C., and JAMES A. MCCRAE. 1981. "Trends in the relationship between sex and psychological distress: 1957–1976." *American Sociological Review*, 46:443–452.

———. 1982. "The effect of wives' employment on the mental health of married men and women." *American Sociological Review*, 47:217–227.

KESSLER, RONALD C., KATHERINE A. McGONAGLE, SHANYANG ZHAO, CHRISTOPHER B. NELSON, MICHAEL HUGHES, SUZANN ESHLEMAN, HANS-ULRICH WITTCHEN, and KENNETH S. KENDLER. 1994. "Lifetime and 12-month prevalence of DSM-III-R psychiatric disorders in the United States." *Archives of General Psychiatry,* 51:8–19.

KESSLER, RONALD C., and JANE D. McLEOD. 1984. "Sex differences in vulnerability to undesirable life events." *American Sociological Review,* 49:620–631.

KESSLER, RONALD C., and HAROLD W. NEIGHBORS. 1986. "A new perspective on the relationships among race, social class, and psychological distress." *Journal of Health and Social Behavior,* 27:107–115.

KESSLER, RONALD C., J. BLAKE TURNER, and JAMES S. HOUSE. 1989. "Unemployment, reemployment, and emotional functioning in a community sample." *American Sociological Review,* 54:648–657.

KIEV, ARI. 1968. *Curanderismo: Mexican-American folk psychiatry.* New York: The Free Press.

KING, GARY, and DAVID R. WILLIAMS. 1995. "Race and health: A multidimensional approach to African-American health," pp. 93–130 in *Society and health,* B. Amick, S. Levine, A. Tarlov, and D. Walsh (eds.). New York: Oxford University Press.

KINGDOM, JOHN. 1996. "The United Kingdom," pp. 127–162 in *Health care systems in liberal democracies,* A. Wall (ed.). London: Routledge.

KINNELL, ANN MARIE KOFMEHL. 2001. "'So why are you here?' Assessing risk in HIV prevention and test decision counseling." *Sociology of Health and Illness,* 23:447–477.

KIRKMAN-LIFF, BRADFORD L. 1991. "Health insurance values and implementation in the Netherlands and the Federal Republic of Germany." *Journal of the American Medical Association,* 265:2496–2502.

KLEIN, RUDOLF. 1992. "In search of the perfect health care system: Britain's pursuit of the global mirage." *International Journal of Health Services,* 3:187–194.

KLETKE, PHILLIP R., DAVID W. EMMONS, and KURT D. GILLIS. 1996. "Current trends in physicians' practice arrangements." *Journal of the American Medical Association,* 276:555–560.

KNAUS, WILLIAM A. 1981. *Inside Russian medicine.* Boston: Beacon Press.

KNESEBECK, OLAF VON DEM, and JOHANNES SIEGRIST. 2001. "Medical sociology in Germany," pp. 287–297 in *The Blackwell companion to medical sociology,* W. Cockerham (ed.). Oxford, UK: Blackwell.

KNIGHT, ROSEMARY A., and DAVID A. HAY. 1989. "The relevance of the health belief model to Australian smokers." *Social Science and Medicine,* 28:1311–1314.

KNOWLES, JOHN H. 1973. "The hospital," pp. 91–102 in *Life and death and medicine,* San Francisco: W. H. Freeman & Company Publishers.

KNOX, RICHARD. 1993. *Germany's health system.* New York: Faulkner & Gray.

KOLKER, ALIZA, and B. MEREDITH BURKE. 1998. *Prenatal testing: A sociological perspective.* Westport, Conn.: Bergin and Garvey.

KOOIKER, SJOERD, and TERKEL CHRISTIANSEN. 1995. "Inequalities in health: The interaction of circumstances and health-related behaviour." *Sociology of Health and Illness,* 17:495–524.

KOOS, EARL. 1954. *The health of Regionville.* New York: Columbia University Press.

KOSA, JOHN, AARON ANTONOVSKY, and IRVING K. ZOLA (eds.). 1969. *Poverty and health.* Cambridge, Mass.: Harvard University Press.

KOTARBA, JOSEPH A., and PAMELA BENTLEY. 1988. "Workplace wellness participation and the becoming of self." *Social Science and Medicine,* 26:551–558.

KREBS-SMITH, SUSAN M. 1998. "Progress in improving diet to reduce cancer risk." *Cancer,* 83:1425–1432.

KRONENFELD, JENNIE J., KIRBY L. JACKSON, KEITH E. DAVIS, and STEVEN N. BLAIR. 1988. "Changing health practices: The experience from a worksite health promotion project." *Social Science and Medicine,* 26:515–524.

KUGELMANN, ROBERT. 1999. "Complaining about chronic pain." *Social Science and Medicine,* 49:1663–1676.

KUNST, ANTON E., FEIKJE GROENHOF, JOHAN P. MACKENBACH, and the EU WORKING GROUP ON SOCIOECONOMIC INEQUALITIES IN HEALTH. 1998. "Mortality by occupational class among men in 11 European countries." *Social Science and Medicine,* 46:1459–1476.

KUNST, A. E., C. W. N. LOOMAN, and J. P. MACKENBACH. 1990. "Socio-economic mortality differences in the Netherlands in 1950–1984: A regional study of cause-specific mortality." *Social Science and Medicine,* 31:141–152.

LAGASSE, RAPHAEL, PERRINE C. HUMBLET, ANN LENAERTS, ISABELLE GODIN, and GUIDO F. G. MOEN. 1990. "Health and social inequities in Belgium." *Social Science and Medicine,* 31:237–248.

LAHELMA, EERO. 2001. "Health and social stratification," pp. 64–93 in *The Blackwell companion to medical sociology*, W. Cockerham (ed.). Oxford, UK: Blackwell.

LAHELMA, EERO, SARA ARBER, KATARINA KIVELA, and EVA ROOS. 2002. "Multiple roles and health among British and Finnish women: The influence of socioeconomic circumstances." *Social Science and Medicine*, 54:727–740.

LAHELMA, EERO, SARA ARBER, OSSI RAHKONEN, and KARRI SILVENTOINEN. 2000. "Widening or narrowing inequalities in health? Comparing Britain and Finland from the 1980s to the 1990s." *Sociology of Health and Illness*, 22:110–136.

LAHELMA, EERO, and TAPANI VALKONEN. 1990. "Health and social inequities in Finland and elsewhere." *Social Science and Medicine*, 31:257–266.

LAI, GINA. 1995. "Work and family roles and psychological well-being in urban China." *Journal of Health and Social Behavior*, 36:11–37.

LAKKA, T. A., J. M. VENALAINEN, R. RAURAMAA, R. SALONEN, R. TUOMILEHTO, and J. SALONEN. 1994. "Relation of leisure-time physical activity and cardiorespiratory fitness to the risk of acute myocardial infarction in men." *New England Journal of Medicine*, 330:1549–1554.

LARKIN, GERALD V. 1993. "Continuity in change: Medical dominance in the United Kingdom," pp. 81–91 in *The changing medical profession: An international perspective*, F. Hafferty and J. McKinley (eds.). New York: Oxford University Press.

LAROCCO, JAMES M., JAMES S. HOUSE, and JOHN R. P. FRENCH, JR. 1980. "Social support, occupational stress, and health." *Journal of Health and Social Behavior*, 21:202–218.

LAROSA, JOHN C., DONALD HUNNINGHAKE, DAVID BUSH, MICHAEL H. CRIQUI et al. 1990. "The cholesterol facts: A summary of the evidence relating dietary fats, serum cholesterol, and coronary heart disease." *Circulation*, 81:1721–1733.

LASSEY, MARIE L., WILLIAM R. LASSEY, and MARTIN J. JINKS (eds.). 1997. *Health care systems around the world*. Upper Saddle River, N.J.: Prentice Hall.

LAU, RICHARD R., MARILYN JACOBS QUADREL, and KAREN A. HARTMAN. 1990. "Development and change of young adults' preventive health beliefs and behavior: Influence from parents and peers." *Journal of Health and Social Behavior*, 31:240–259.

LAUER, ROBERT. 1974. "Rate of change and stress." *Social Forces*, 52:510–516.

LAUFER, ROBERT S., M. S. GALLOPS, and ELLEN FREY-WOUTERS. 1984. "War stress and trauma: The Vietnam veteran experience." *Journal of Health and Social Behavior*, 25:65–85.

LAUMANN, EDWARD O., JOHN H. GAGNON, ROBERT T. MICHAEL, and STUART MICHAELS. 1994. *The social organization of sexuality*. Chicago: University of Chicago Press.

LAUMANN, EDWARD O., and ROBERT T. MICHAEL (eds.). 2001. *Sex, love, and health in America: Private choices and public policies*. Chicago: University of Chicago Press.

LAUMANN, EDWARD O., and YOOSIK YOUM. 2001. "Racial/ethnic group differences in the prevalence of sexually-transmitted diseases in the United States: A network explanation," pp. 327–351 in *Sex, love, and health in America: Private choices and public policies*, E. Laumann and R. Michael (eds.). Chicago: University of Chicago Press.

LAURIER, DOMINIQUE, MARGUERITE GUIGUET, NGUYEN PHONG CHAU, JAMES A. WELLS, and ALAIN-JACQUES VALLERON. 1992. "Prevalence of obesity: A comparative survey in France, the United Kingdom and the United States." *International Journal of Obesity*, 16:565–572.

LAVEIST, THOMAS A., and AMANI NURU-JETER. 2002. "Is doctor-patient race concordance associated with greater satisfaction with care?" *Journal of Health and Social Behavior*, 43:296–306.

LAVIN, BEBE, MARIE HAUG, LINDA LISKA BELGRAVE, and NAOMI BRESLAU. 1987. "Change in student physicians' views on authority relationships with patients." *Journal of Health and Social Behavior*, 28:258–272.

LEAR, DANA. 1996. "Women and AIDS in Africa: A critical review," pp. 276–301 in *Society, health, and disease*, J. Subedi and G. Gallagher (eds.). Upper Saddle River, N.J.: Prentice Hall.

LEBLANC, ALLEN J. 1993. "Examining HIV-related knowledge among adults in the U.S." *Journal of Health and Social Behavior*, 34:23–36.

LECLERE, FELICIA B., RICHARD G. ROGERS, and KIMBERLY PETERS. 1998. "Neighborhood social context and racial differences in women's heart disease mortality." *Journal of Health and Social Behavior*, 39:91–107.

LEE, I-MIN, CHUNG-CHENG HSIEH, and RALPH S. PAFFENBARGER. 1995. "Exercise intensity and longevity in men." *Journal of the American Medical Association*, 273:1179–1184.

LEE, SING. 1996. "Reconsidering the status of anorexia nervosa as a Western culture-bound syndrome." *Social Science and Medicine,* 42:21–34.

LEFTON, MARK. 1984. "Chronic disease and applied sociology: An essay in personalized sociology." *Sociological Inquiry,* 54:466–476.

LENNON, MARY CLARE. 1987. "The psychological consequence of menopause: The importance of timing of a life stage event." *Journal of Health and Social Behavior,* 23:353–366.

———. 1994. "Women, work, and well-being: The importance of work conditions." *Journal of Health and Social Behavior,* 35:235–247.

LENNON, MARY CLARE, and SARAH ROSENFIELD. 1992. "Women and mental health: The interaction of job and family conditions." *Journal of Health and Social Behavior,* 33:316–327.

LESHO, EMIL P. 1999. "An overview of osteopathic medicine." *Archives of Family Medicine,* 8:477–484.

LEVENTHAL, HOWARD. 1975. "The consequences of personalization during illness and treatment: An information-processing model," pp. 119–162 in *Humanizing health care,* J. Howard and A. Strauss (eds.). New York: Wiley-Interscience.

LEVI, F., C. LA VECCHIA, F. LUCCHINI, and E. NEGRI. 1995. "Cancer mortality in Europe, 1990–92." *European Journal of Cancer Prevention,* 4:389–417.

LEVINE, CAROL. 1990. "AIDS and changing concepts of family." *Milbank Quarterly,* 68:33–58.

LEVY, JERROLD E. 1983. "Traditional Navajo health beliefs and practices," pp. 118–178 in *Disease change and the role of medicine: The Navajo experience,* J. Kunitz (ed.). Berkeley: University of California Press.

LIGHT, DONALD W. 1979. "Uncertainty and control in professional training," *Journal of Health and Social Behavior,* 20:310–322.

———. 1983. "Medical and nursing education: Surface behavior and deep structure," pp. 455–478 in *Handbook of health, health care, and the health professions,* D. Mechanic (ed.). New York: The Free Press.

———. 1986. "Comparing health care systems: Lessons from East and West Germany," pp. 429–443 in *The sociology of health and illness,* 2nd ed., P. Conrad and R. Kern (eds.). New York: St. Martin's Press.

———. 1988. "Toward a new sociology of medical education." *Journal of Health and Social Behavior,* 29:307–322.

———. 1989. "Social control and the American health care system," pp. 456–474 in *Handbook of medical sociology,* 4th ed., H. Freeman and S. Levine (eds.). Englewood Cliffs, N.J.: Prentice Hall.

———. 1992. "The practice and ethics of risk-related health insurance." *Journal of the American Medical Association,* 267:2503–2508.

———. 1993. "Countervailing power: The changing character of the medical profession in the United States," pp. 69–79 in *The changing medical profession: An international perspective,* F. Hafferty and J. McKinley (eds.). New York: Oxford University Press.

———. 1994. "Life, death, and the insurance companies." *New England Journal of Medicine,* 330:498–500.

———. 1997. "From managed competition to managed cooperation: Theory and lessons from the British experience." *Milbank Quarterly,* 75:297–341.

———. 2000. "The medical profession and organizational change: From professional dominance to contervailing power," pp. 201–216 in *Handbook of medical sociology,* 5th ed., C. Bird, P. Conrad, and A. Fremont (eds.). Upper Saddle River, N.J.: Prentice Hall.

LIGHT, DONALD W., and ALEXANDER SCHULLER (eds.). 1986. *Political values and health care: The German experience.* Cambridge, Mass.: MIT Press.

LIGHT, DONALD W. and FREDERIC W. HAFFERTY (eds.). 1993. *The changing medical profession: An international perspective.* New York: Oxford University Press.

LIN, BOQI, RICHARD PETO, ZHENG-MING CHEN, JILLIAN BOREHAM, YA-PING WU, JUN-YAO LI, T. COLIN CAMPBELL, and JUN-SHI CHEN. 1998. "Emerging tobacco hazards in China: 1. Retrospective proportional mortality study of one million deaths." *British Medical Journal,* 317:1411–1422.

LIN, NAN, XIAOLAN YE, and WALTER W. ENSEL. 1999. "Social support and depressed mood: A structural analysis." *Journal of Health and Social Behavior,* 40:344–359.

LINK, BRUCE. 1983. "Reward system of psychotherapy: Implications for inequities in service delivery." *Journal of Health and Social Behavior,* 24:61–69.

LINK, BRUCE G., and JO PHELAN. 1995. "Social conditions as fundamental causes of diseases." *Journal of Health and Social Behavior,* extra issue:80–94.

———. 2000. "Evaluating the fundamental cause explanation for social disparities in health," pp. 33–47 in *Handbook of medical sociology,* 5th ed., C. Bird, P. Conrad, and A. Fremont (eds.). Upper Saddle River, N.J.: Prentice Hall.

LINN, BERNARD S., and MARGARET W. LINN. 1980. "Objective and self-assessed health in the old and very old." *Social Science and Medicine,* 14:311–315.

LIPOWSKI, Z. J. 1970. "Physical illness, the individual and the coping process." *Psychiatry in Medicine,* 1:91–101.

LIU, XINGZHU, and WILLIAM C. L. HSIAO. 1995. "The cost escalation of social health insurance plans in China: Its implication for public policy." *Social Science and Medicine,* 41:1095–1101.

LIU, YUANLI, WILLIAM C. HSIAO, and KAREN EGGLESTON. 1999. "Equity in health and health care: The Chinese experience." *Social Science and Medicine,* 49:1349–1356.

LIU, YUANLI, WILLIAM C. L. HSIAO, QUING LI, XINGZHU LIU, and MINGHUI REN. 1995. "Transformation of China's rural health care financing." *Social Science and Medicine,* 41:1085–1093.

LIVINGSTON, MARTHA. 1998. "Update on health care in Canada: What's right, what's wrong, what's left." *Journal of Public Health Policy,* 19:267–288.

LOPEZ, ALAN D. 1998. "Mortality from tobacco in the new independent states," pp. 262–274 in *Premature mortality in the new independent states,* J. Bobadilla, C. Costello, and F. Mitchell (eds.). Washington, D.C.: National Academy Press.

LORBER, JUDITH. 1975. "Good patients and problem patients: Conformity and deviance in a general hospital." *Journal of Health and Social Behavior,* 16:213–225.

———. 1984. *Women physicians: Careers, status, and power.* New York: Tavistock.

———. 1993. "Why women physicians will never be true equals in the American medical profession," pp. 62–76 in *Gender, work, and medicine,* E. Riska and K. Wegar (eds.). London: Sage.

———. 1997. *Gender and the social construction of illness.* Thousand Oaks, Calif.: Sage.

LOSCOCCO, KARYN A., and GLENNA SPITZE. 1990. "Working conditions, social support, and the well-being of female and male factory workers." *Journal of Health and Social Behavior,* 31:313–327.

LOSTAO, LOURDES, ENRIQUE REGIDOR, PIERRE AÏACH, and VICENTE DOMÍNGUEZ. 2001. "Social inequalities in ischaemic heart and cerebrovascular disease mortality in men: Spain and France, 1980–1982 and 1988–1990." *Social Science and Medicine,* 52:1879–1887.

LOWENSTEIN, J. 1997. *The midnight meal and other essays about doctors, patients, and medicine.* London: Yale University Press.

LUDMERER, KENNETH. 1985. *Learning to heal.* New York: Basic Books.

LUNDBERG, OLLE. 1992. "Health inequalities in Sweden: Levels and trends." *International Journal of Health Services,* 3:167–174.

LUPTON, DEBORAH. 1997. Psychoanalytic sociology and the medical encounter: Parsons and beyond." *Sociology of Health and Illness,* 19:561–579.

LÜSCHEN, GÜNTHER, WILLIAM C. COCKERHAM, and GERHARD KUNZ. 1987. "Deutsche und amerikansiche Gesundheitskultur—oder what they say when you sneeze." ["German and American health culture—or what they say when you sneeze."] *Mensch Medizin Gesellschaft,* 12:59–69.

———. 1989. *Health and illness in Germany and America.* Munich: Oldenbourg.

LÜSCHEN, GÜNTHER, WILLIAM COCKERHAM, JOUKE VAN DER ZEE, FRED STEVENS, JOS DIEDERIKS, MANUAL GARCIA FERRANDO, ALPHONSE D'HOUTAUD, RUUD PEETERS, THOMAS ABEL, and STEFFEN NIEMANN. 1995. *Health systems in the European Union: Diversity, convergence, and integration.* Munich: Oldenbourg.

MACDONALD, DAVID S. 1996. "Notes on the socioeconomic and cultural factors influencing the transmission of HIV in Botswana." *Social Science and Medicine,* 42:1325–1333.

MACINTYRE, SALLY. 1986. "The patterning of health by social position in contemporary Britain: Directions for sociological research." *Social Science and Medicine,* 23:393–415.

———. 1989. "The role of health services in relation to inequalities in health in Europe," pp. 317–332 in *Health inequalities in European countries,* J. Fox (ed.). Aldershot, U.K.: Gower.

———. 1997. "The Black Report and beyond: What are the issues?" *Social Science and Medicine,* 44:723–745.

MACKEY, SANDRA. 1987. *The Saudis: Inside the desert kingdom.* Boston: Houghton Mifflin.

MADSEN, WILLIAM. 1973. *The Mexican-Americans of south Texas,* 2nd ed. New York: Holt, Rinehart, & Winston.

MAKOFSKY, DAVID. 1977. "Malpractice and medicine." *Society,* 14:25–29.

MALAT, JENNIFER. 2001. "Social distance and patients' rating of healthcare providers." *Journal of Health and Social Behavior,* 42:360–372.

MANNING, PHILIP. 1992. *Erving Goffman and modern sociology.* Stanford, Calif.: Stanford University Press.

MARANG–VAN DE MHEEN, PERLA, GEORGE DAVEY SMITH, and CAROLE L. HART. 1999. "The health impact of smoking in manual and non-manual social class men and women: A test of the Blaxter hypothesis." *Social Science and Medicine,* 48:1851–1856.

MARMOR, THEODORE R. 1999. *The politics of Medicare,* 2nd ed. Hawthorne, N.Y.: Aldine de Gruyter.

MARMOT, MICHAEL, and RICHARD G. WILKINSON (eds.). 1999. *Social determinants of health.* Oxford, UK: Oxford University Press.

MARMOT, MICHAEL. 1996. "The social pattern of health and disease," pp. 42–70 in *Health and social organization,* D. Blane, E. Brunner, and R. Wilkinson (eds.). London: Routledge.

MARMOT, MICHAEL, MARTIN BOBAK, and GEORGE DAVY SMITH. 1995. "Explanations for social inequalities in health," pp. 172–210 in *Society and health,* B. Amick, S. Levine, A. Tarlov, and D. Walsh (eds.). New York: Oxford University Press.

MARMOT, MICHAEL, REBECCA FUHRER, SUSAN L. ETTNER, NADINE F. MARKS, LARRY L. BUMPASS, and CAROL D. RYER. 1998. "Contribution of psychosocial factors to socioeconomic differences in health." *Milbank Quarterly,* 76:403–448.

MARMOT, M. G., M. J. SHIPLEY, and GEOFFREY ROSE. 1984. "Inequalities in death—Specific explanations of a general pattern." *Lancet,* 83:1003–1006.

MARMOT, M. G., GEORGE DAVEY SMITH, STEPHEN STANSFELD, CHANDRA PATEL, FIONA NORTH, JENNY HEAD, IAN WHITE, ERIC BRUNNER, and AMANDA FEENEY. 1991. "Health inequalities among British civil servants: The Whitehall II study." *Lancet,* 337:1387–1392.

MARSHALL, T. H. 1964. *Class, citizenship, and social development.* Chicago: University of Chicago Press.

MARTIN, LINDA G. 1988. "The aging of Asia." *Journal of Gerontology,* 43:S99–S113.

MARTIN, PAUL. 1999. "Genes as drugs: The social shaping of gene therapy and the reconstruction of genetic disease." *Sociology of Health and illness,* 21:517–538.

MARTIN, STEVEN C., ROBERT M. ARNOLD, and RUTH M. PARKER. 1988. "Gender and medical socialization." *Journal of Health and Social Behavior,* 29:333–343.

MATT, GEORG E., and ALFRED DEAN. 1993. "Social support from friends and psychological distress among elderly persons: Moderator effects of age." *Journal of Health and Social Behavior,* 34:187–200.

MATTHEWS, SHARON, CLYDE HERTZMAN, ALECK OSTRY, and CHRIS POWER. 1998. "Gender, work roles, and psychosocial work characteristics as determinants of health." *Social Science and Medicine,* 46:1417–1424.

MAUKSCH, HANS. 1972. "Nursing: Churning for a change?" pp. 206–230 in *Handbook of medical sociology,* 2nd ed., H. E. Freeman, S. Levine, and L. G. Reeder (eds). Englewood Cliffs, N.J.: Prentice-Hall.

MBUGUA, J. KARANJA, GERALD BLOOM, and MALCOLM SEGALL. 1995. "Impact of user charges on vulnerable groups: The case of Kibwezi in rural Kenya." *Social Science and Medicine,* 41:829–835.

MCDONOUGH, PEGGY, DAVID R. WILLIAMS, JAMES S. HOUSE, and GREG J. DUNCAN. 1999. "Gender and the socioeconomic gradient in mortality." *Journal of Health and Health Behavior,* 40:17–31.

MCFARLANE, ALLAN H., GEOFFREY R. NORMAN, DAVID L. STREINER, and RANJAN G. ROY. 1983. "The process of social stress: Stable, reciprocal, and mediating relationships." *Journal of Health and Social Behavior,* 24:160–173.

MCKEE, MARTIN, MARTIN BOBAK, RICHARD ROSE, VLADIMIR SHKOLNIKOV, LAURENT CHENET, and DAVID LEON. 1998. "Patterns of smoking in Russia." *Tobacco Control,* 7:22–26.

MCKEEHAN, IRINA V. 1995. "Planning of national primary health care and prevention programs: The first health insurance law of Russia, 1992–1993," pp. 174–197 in *Global perspectives on health care,* E. Gallagher and J. Subedi (eds.). Englewood Cliffs, N.J.: Prentice Hall.

MCKEOWN, THOMAS. 1979. *The role of medicine.* Oxford, U.K.: Blackwell.

MCKEVITT, CHRISTOPHER, and MYFANWY MORGAN. 1997. "Anomalous patients: The experiences of doctors with an illness." *Sociology of Health and Illness,* 19:644–667.

McKinlay, John B. 1996. "Some contributions from the social system to gender inequalities in heart disease." *Journal of Health and Social Behavior,* 37:1–26.

———. 1999. "The end of the golden age of doctoring." *New England Research Institutes Newsletter,* (Summer):1, 3.

McKinlay, John B., Sonja M. McKinlay, and Robert Beaglehole. 1989. "Trends in death and disease and the contribution of medical measures," pp. 14–45 in *Handbook of medical sociology,* 4th ed., H. Freeman and S. Levine (eds.). Englewood Cliffs, N.J.: Prentice Hall.

McLanahan, Sara, and Jennifer L. Glass. 1985. "A note on the trend in sex differences in psychological distress." *Journal of Health and Social Behavior,* 26:328–336.

McLeod, Jane D., and Ronald C. Kessler. 1990. "Socioeconomic status differences in vulnerability to undesirable life events." *Journal of Health and Social Behavior,* 31:162–172.

McLeod, Jane D., and James M. Nonnemaker. 2000. "Poverty and child emotional and behavioral problems: Racial/ethnic differences in processes and effects." *Journal of Health and Social Behavior,* 41:137–161.

Mead, George Herbert. 1934. *Mind, self, and society.* Chicago: University of Chicago Press.

Mead, Lawrence M. 1985. *The social obligations of citizenship.* New York: The Free Press.

Mechanic, David. 1962a. "The concept of illness behavior." *Journal of Chronic Diseases,* 15:189–194.

———. 1962b. *Students under stress: A study of the social psychology of adaptation.* New York: The Free Press.

———. 1964. "The influence of mothers on their children's health attitudes and behavior." *Pediatrics,* 33:444–453.

———. 1972. *Public expectations and health care.* New York: Wiley-Interscience.

———. 1978. *Medical sociology,* 2nd ed. New York: The Free Press.

———. 1979. "Correlates of physician utilization: Why do major multivariate studies of physician utilization find trivial psychosocial and organizational effects?" *Journal of Health and Social Behavior,* 20:387–396.

———. 1989. "Medical sociology: Some tensions among theory, method, and substance." *Journal of Health and Social Behavior,* 30:147–160.

———. 1995a. "Sociological dimensions of illness behavior." *Social Science and Medicine,* 41:1207–1216.

———. 1995b. "The Americanization of the British National Health Service." *Health Affairs,* 14:51–67.

Mechanic, David, and Ronald J. Angel. 1987. "Some factors associated with the report and evaluation of back pain." *Journal of Health and Social Behavior,* 28:131–139.

Mechanic, David, and Edmund H. Volkart. 1961. "Stress, illness behavior, and the sick role." *American Sociological Review,* 25:51–58.

Medvedev, Roy. 2000. *Post-soviet Russia,* G. Shriver (trans. and ed.). New York: Columbia University Press.

Meitlin, Curt, and Joseph Woelfel. 1974. "Interpersonal influence and symptoms of stress." *Journal of Health and Social Behavior,* 15:311–319.

Merton, Robert K., George G. Reader, and Patricia Kendall. 1957. *The student-physician.* Cambridge, Mass.: Harvard University Press.

Meyer, Madonna Harrington, and Eliza K. Pavalko. 1996. "Family, work, and access to health insurance among mature women." *Journal of Health and Social Behavior,* 37:311–325.

Mezentseva, Elena, and Natalia Rimachevskaya. 1992. "The health profile of the population in the republics of the former Soviet Union: An analysis of the situation in the 70s and 80s." *International Journal of Health Sciences,* 3:127–142.

Mielck, Andreas, Adrienne Cavelaars, Uwe Helmert, Karl Martin, Olaf Winkelhake, and Anton E. Kunst. 2000. "Comparison of health inequalities between East and West Germany." *European Journal of Public Health,* 10:262–267.

Miller, Michael H. 1973. "Who receives optimal medical care?" *Journal of Health and Social Behavior,* 14:176–182.

———. 1974. "Work roles for the associate degree graduate." *American Journal of Nursing,* 74:468–470.

Miller, Stephen J. 1970. *Prescription for leadership: Training for the medical elite.* Chicago: Aldine.

MILLMAN, MARCIA. 1977a. "Masking doctors' errors." *Human Behavior,* 6:16–23.

———. 1977b. *The unkindest cut.* New York: Morrow.

MIROWSKY, JOHN. 1985. "Depression and marital power: An equity model." *American Journal of Sociology,* 91:557–592.

———. 1999. "Subjective life expectancy in the U.S.: Correspondence to actuarial estimates by age, sex, and race." *Social Science and Medicine,* 49:967–979.

MIROWSKY, JOHN, and CATHERINE E. ROSS. 1989. *Social causes of psychological distress.* New York: Aldine de Gruyter.

———. 1995. "Sex differences in distress: Real or artifact?" *American Sociological Review,* 60:449–468.

MIROWSKY, JOHN, CATHERINE E. ROSS, and JOHN REYNOLDS. 2000. "Links between social status and health status," pp. 47–67 in *Handbook of medical sociology,* 5th ed., C. Bird, P. Conrad, and A. Fremont (eds.). Upper Saddle River, N.J.: Prentice Hall.

MORA, GEORGE. 1985. "Historical and theoretical trends in psychiatry," pp. 1–75 in *Comprehensive textbook of psychiatry,* Vol. 1, 4th ed., A. Freedman, H. Kaplan, and B. Sadock (eds.). Baltimore: Williams & Wilkins.

MORRIS, J. N., D. G. CLAYTON, M. G. EVERITT, A. M. SENNENCE, and E. H. BURGESS. 1990. "Exercise in leisure time: Coronary attack and death rates." *British Heart Journal,* 63:325–334.

MORSE, JANICE M., DAVID E. YOUNG, and LISE SWARTZ. 1991. "Cree Indian healing practices and Western health care: A comparative analysis." *Social Science and Medicine,* 32:1361–1366.

MOSKOS, CHARLES C., JR. 1970. *The American enlisted man.* New York: Russell Sage.

MOSS, GORDON E. 1973. *Illness, immunity, and social interaction.* New York: John Wiley.

MULATU, MESFIN SAMUEL, and CARMI SCHOOLER. 2002. "Causal connections between socioeconomic status and health: Reciprocal effects and mediating mechanisms." *Journal of Health and Social Behavior,* 43:22–41.

MULLEN, PATRICIA D., JAMES C. HERSEY, and DONALD C. IVERSON. 1987. "Health behavior models compared." *Social Science and Medicine,* 24:973–981.

MUNAKATA, TSUNETSUGU. 1994. *AIDS in Japan.* Tokyo: Akashi Shoten.

MUNAKATA, TSUNETSUGU, and KAZUO TAJIMA. 1996. "Japanese risk behaviors and their HIV/AIDS-preventive behaviors." *AIDS Education and Prevention,* 8:115–133.

MURRAY, CHRISTOPHER J. L., and ALAN D. LOPEZ. 1996. "Evidence-based health policy—Lessons from the global burden of disease study." *Science,* 274:740–743.

MUSICK, MARC A. 1996. "Religion and subjective health among black and white elders." *Journal of Health and Social Behavior,* 37:221–237.

MUTCHLER, JAN E., and JEFFREY A. BURR. 1991. "Racial differences in health and health care service utilization in later life: The effect of socioeconomic status." *Journal of Health and Social Behavior,* 32:342–356.

MWABU, GERMANO MWIGA. 1984. "A model of household choice among medical treatment alternatives in rural Kenya." Unpublished Ph.D. dissertation, Boston University.

MYLES, JOHN F. 1984. *Old age in the welfare state.* Boston: Little, Brown.

NATIONAL CENTER FOR HEALTH STATISTICS. 1985. *Health, United States, 1985.* Washington, D.C.: U.S. Government Printing Office.

———. 1986. *Health, United States, 1986.* Washington, D.C.: U.S. Government Printing Office.

———. 1999a. *Health, United States, 1999.* Washington, D.C.: U.S. Government Printing Office.

———. 1999b. *United States life tables, 1997. National vital statistics report.* No. 28. Hyattsville, Md.: U.S. Department of Health and Human Services.

———. 2002. *Health, United States, 2002.* Washington, D.C.: U.S. Government Printing Office.

NAVARRO, VICENTE. 1994. *The politics of health policy.* Oxford, UK: Blackwell.

———. 1996. "Why Congress did not enact health reform." *Journal of Health Politics, Policy and Law,* 20:455–462.

NETTLETON, SARAH. 1995. *The sociology of health and illness.* Cambridge, U.K.: Polity Press.

———. "The sociology of the body," pp. 43–63 in *The Blackwell companion to medical sociology,* W. Cockerham (ed.). Oxford, UK: Blackwell.

NIGENDA, GUSTAVO, LEJEUNE LOCKETT, CRISTINA MANCA, and GERARDO MORA. 2001. "Non-biomedical health care practices in the state of Morelos, Mexico: Analysis of an emergent phenomenon." *Sociology of Health and Illness,* 23:3–23.

NISBET, L. A., and D. V. MCQUEEN. 1993. "Anti-permissive attitudes to lifestyles associated with AIDS." *Social Science and Medicine,* 36:949–955.

NOLEN, WILLIAM A. 1970. *The making of a surgeon.* New York: Random House.

NOLTE, ELLEN, REMBRANDT SCHOLZ, VLADIMIR SHKOLNIKOV, and MARTIN MCKEE. 2002. "The contribution of medical care to changing life expectancy in Germany and Poland." *Social Science and Medicine,* 55:1905–1921.

OBBO, CHRISTINE. 1993. "HIV transmission through social and geographical networks in Uganda." *Social Science and Medicine,* 36:949–955.

OLESEN, VIRGINIA L., and ELVI W. WHITTAKER. 1968. *The silent dialogue.* San Francisco: Jossey-Bass.

ORFALI, KRISTINA. 2001. "The French paradoxes," pp. 263–286 in *The Blackwell companion to medical sociology,* W. Cockerham (ed.). Oxford, UK: Blackwell.

ORNISH, DEAN, S. E. BROWN, L. W. SCHERWITZ, J. H. BILLINGS, W. T. ARMSTRONG, T. A. PORTS, S. M. MCLANAHAN, R. L. KIRKEEIDE, R. J. BRAND, and K. L. GOULD. 1990. "Can lifestyle changes reverse coronary heart disease?" *Lancet,* 336:129–133.

OSTROWSKA, A. 1993. "From totalitarianism to pluralism in Poland: Problems of transformation of the health system." *European Journal of Public Health,* 3:43–47.

———. 1998. "Health-promoting lifestyles." *Dialogue and Universalism,* 9:97–110.

———. 2001. "In and out of Communism: The macrosocial context of health in Poland," pp. 334–346 in *The Blackwell companion to medical sociology,* W. Cockerham (ed.). Oxford, UK: Blackwell.

OTTEN, MAC W., STEVEN M. TEUTSCH, DAVID F. WILLIAMSON, and JAMES S. MARKS. 1990. "The effect of known risk factors on the excess mortality of black adults in the United States." *Journal of the American Medical Association,* 268:845–850.

PAFFENBARGER, RALPH S., JR., ROBERT T. HYDE, ALVIN L. WING, and CHUNG-CHENG HSIEH. 1986. "Physical activity, all-cause mortality, and longevity of college alumni." *New England Journal of Medicine,* 314:605–613.

PAFFENBARGER, RALPH S., JR., ROBERT T. HYDE, ALVIN WING, I-MIN LEE, DEXTER L. JUNG, and JAMES KAMPERT. 1993. "The association of changes in physical-activity level and other lifestyle characteristics with mortality among men." *New England Journal of Medicine,* 32:538–545.

PALOSUO, HANNLE. 2000. "Health-related lifestyles and alienation in Moscow and Helsinki." *Social Science and Medicine,* 51:1325–1341.

PALOSUO, HANNELE, ANTTI UUTELA, IRINA ZHURAVLEVA, and NINA LAKOMOVA. 1998. "Social patterning of ill health in Helsinki and Moscow." *Social Science and Medicine,* 46:1121–1136.

PANDEY, SANJAY K., JOHN J. HART, and SHEELA TIWARY. 2003. "Women's health and the Internet: Understanding emerging trends and issues." *Social Science and Medicine,* 56:179–191.

PAPPAS, GREGORY, SUSAN QUEEN, WILBUR HADDEN, and GAIL FISHER. 1993. "The increasing disparity in mortality between socioeconomic groups in the United States, 1960 and 1986." *New England Journal of Medicine,* 329:103–109.

PARSONS, GENEVIEVE NOONE, SARA B. KINSMAN, CHARLES L. BOSK, PAMELA SANKAR, and PETER A. UBEL. 2001. "Between two worlds: Medical student perceptions of humor and slang in the hospital setting." *Journal of General Internal Medicine,* 16:544–554.

PARSONS, TALCOTT. 1951. *The social system.* Glencoe, Ill.: The Free Press.

———. 1975. "The sick role and role of the physician reconsidered." *Milbank Memorial Fund Quarterly,* 53:257–278.

———. 1979. "Definitions of health and illness in light of American values and social structure," pp. 120–144 in *Patients, physicians, and illness,* 3rd ed., E. Jaco (ed.). New York: The Free Press.

PARSONS, TALCOTT, and RENÉE FOX. 1952. "Illness, therapy and the modern urban American family." *Journal of Social Issues,* 8:31–44.

PAVALKO, ELIZA K., GLEN H. ELDER, JR., and ELIZABETH C. CLIPP. 1993. "Worklives and longevity: Insights from a life course perspective." *Journal of Health and Social Behavior,* 34:363–380.

PAVALKO, ELIZA K., and BRAD SMITH. 1999. "The rhythm of work: Health effects of women's work dynamics." *Social Forces,* 77:1162–2241.

PEARLIN, LEONARD I. 1989. "The sociological study of stress." *Journal of Health and Social Behavior,* 30:241–256.

PEARLIN, LEONARD I., CAROL S. ANESHENSEL, and ALLEN J. LEBLANC. 1997. "The forms and mechanisms of stress proliferation: The case of AIDS caregivers." *Journal of Health and Social Behavior,* 38:223–236.

PEARLIN, LEONARD I., MORTON A. LIEBERMAN, ELIZABETH G. MENAGHAN, and JOSEPH T. MULLAN. 1981. "The stress process." *Journal of Health and Social Behavior,* 22:337–356.

PERROW, CHARLES. 1963. "Goals and power structures: A historical case study," pp. 112–146 in *The hospital in modern society,* E. Freidson (ed.). New York: The Free Press.

PESCOSOLIDO, BERNICE A. 1992. "Beyond rational choice: The social dynamics of how people seek help." *American Journal of Sociology,* 97:1096–1138.

PESCOSOLIDO, BERNICE A., and CAROL A. BOYER. 2001. "The American health care system: entering the twenty-first century with high risk, major challenges, and great opportunities," pp. 180–198 in *The Blackwell companion to medical sociology,* W. Cockerham (ed.). Oxford, UK: Blackwell.

PESCOSOLIDO, BERNICE A., and JENNIE J. KRONENFELD. 1995. "Health, illness, and healing in an uncertain era: Challenges from and for medical sociology." *Journal of Health and Social Behavior,* extra issue:5–35.

PESCOSOLIDO, BERNICE A., JANE McLEOD, and MARGARITA ALEGRÍA. 2000. "Confronting the second social contract: The place of medical sociology in research and policy for the twenty-first century," pp. 411–426 in *Handbook of medical sociology,* 5th ed., C. Bird, P. Conrad, and A. Fremont (eds.). Upper Saddle River, N.J.: Prentice-Hall.

PESCOSOLIDO, BERNICE A., STEVEN A. TUCH, and JACK K. MARTIN. 2001. "The profession of medicine and the public: Examining Americans' changing confidence in physician authority from the beginning of the 'health care crisis' to the era of health care reform." *Journal of Health and Social Behavior,* 42:1–16.

PETER, RICHARD, and JOHANNES SIEGRIST. 1997. "Chronic work stress, sickness absence, and hypertension in middle managers: General or specific sociological explanations?" *Social Science and Medicine,* 45:1111–1120.

PETO, RICHARD, ALAN D. LOPEZ, JILLIAN BOREHAM, MICHAEL THUN, and CLARK HEATH, JR. 1992. "Mortality from tobacco in developed countries: Indirect estimation from national vital statistics." *Lancet,* 339:1268–1278.

PHIFER, JAMES F., KRZYSZTOF Z. KANIASTY, and FRAN H. NORRIS. 1988. "The impact of natural disaster on the health of older adults: A multiwave prospective study." *Journal of Health and Social Behavior,* 29:65–78.

PILNICK, ALISON. 1998. "'Why didn't you say just that?' Dealing with issues of asymmetry, knowledge and competence in the pharmacist/client encounter." *Sociology of Health and Illness,* 20:29–51.

———. 1999. "'Patient counseling' by pharmacists: Advice, information, or instruction?" *Sociological Quarterly,* 40:587–612.

———. 2002. *Genetics and society: An introduction.* Buckingham, UK: Open University Press.

PINKSTONE, J. 2000. *Ways of knowing: A new science, technology and medicine.* Manchester, UK: University of Manchester Press.

PIPERNO, ALDO, and FERDINANDO DI ORIO. 1990. "Social differences in health and utilization of health services in Italy." *Social Science and Medicine,* 31:305–312.

PITTS, MARIAN, MARGARET BOWMAN, and JOHN McMASTER. 1995. "Reactions to repeated STD infections: Psychosocial aspects and gender issues in Zimbabwe." *Social Science and Medicine,* 40:1299–1304.

POLEDNAK, ANTHONY P. 1989. *Racial and ethnic differences in disease.* New York: Oxford University Press.

POLLNER, MELVIN. 1989. "Divine relations, social relations, and well-being," *Journal of Health and Social Behavior,* 30:92–104.

POPKIN, BARRY, NAMVAR ZOHOORI, LENORE KOHLMEIER, ALEXANDER BATURIN, ARSENI MARTINCHIK, and ALEXANDER DEEV. 1997. "Nutritional risk factors in the former Soviet Union," pp. 314–334 in *Premature death in the new independent states,* J. Bobadilla, C. Costello, and F. Mitchell (eds.). Washington, D.C.: National Academy Press.

POPPIUS, ESKO, LEENA TENKANEN, RAIJA KALIMO, and PERTTI HEINSALMI. 1999. "The sense of coherence, occupation, and risk of coronary heart disease in the Helsinki Heart Study." *Social Science and Medicine,* 49:109–120.

PORTER, ROY. 1997. *The greatest benefit to mankind: A medical history of humanity.* New York: Norton.

PORTER, SAM. 1992. "Women in a women's job: The gendered experience of nurses." *Sociology of Health and Illness,* 14:510–527.

POTTER, SHARYN J. 2001. "A longitudinal analysis of the distinction between for-profit and not-for-profit hospitals in America." *Journal of Health and Social Behavior,* 42:17–44.

POWELL, MARGARET, and MASAHIRA ANESAKI. 1990. *Health care in Japan.* London: Routledge.

POWER, C., and C. HERTZMAN. 1997. "Social and behavioral pathways linking early life and adult disease." *British Medical Bulletin,* 53:210–221.

PRESCOTT, PATRICIA A., and SALLY A. BOWEN. 1985. "Physician–nurse relationships." *Annals of Internal Medicine,* 103:127–133.

PRESIDENT'S COMMISSION FOR THE STUDY OF ETHICAL PROBLEMS IN MEDICINE AND BIOMEDICAL AND BEHAVIORAL RESEARCH. 1983. *Securing access to health care,* Vol. 1. Washington, D.C.: U.S. Government Printing Office.

PRESTON, RICHARD. 1994. *The hot zone.* New York: Anchor Books.

———. 1999. "West Nile mystery." *New Yorker,* (Oct. 18 & 25):90–108.

PRETORIUS, ENGELA, G. W. DE KLERK, and H. C. J. VAN RENSBURG. 1993. *The traditional healer in South African health care.* Pretoria: Human Sciences Research Council.

PROHASKA, THOMAS R., GARY ALBRECHT, JUDITH A. LEVY, NOREEN SUGRUE, and JONG-HWA KIM. 1990. "Determinants of self-perceived risk for AIDS." *Journal of Health and Social Behavior,* 31:384–394.

PSATHAS, GEORGE. 1968. "The fate of idealism in nursing school." *Journal of Health and Social Behavior,* 9:52–64.

QUAH, STELLA R. 1989. "The social position and internal organization of the medical profession in the third world: The case of Singapore." *Journal of Health and Social Behavior,* 30:450–466.

———. 2001. "Health and culture," pp. 23–42 in *The Blackwell companion to medical sociology,* W. Cockerham (ed.). Oxford, UK: Blackwell.

RADLEY, ALAN. 1989. "Style, discourse and constraint in adjustment to chronic illness." *Sociology of Health and Illness,* 11:230–252.

———. (ed.). 1993. *Worlds of illness: Biographical and cultural perspectives on health and disease.* London: Routledge.

———. 1994. *Making sense of illness: The social psychology of health and disease.* London: Sage.

———. 1999. "The aesthetics of illness: Narrative, horror and the sublime." *Sociology of Health and Illness,* 21:778–796.

RADLEY, ALAN, and MICHAEL BILLIG. 1996. "Accounts of health and illness: Dilemmas and representations." *Sociology of Health and Illness,* 18:220–240.

RADO, S. 1949. "Pathodynamics and treatment of traumatic war neurosis (traumatophobia)." *Psychosomatic Medicine,* 43:363–398.

RAHKONEN, OSSI, SARA ARBER, and EERO LAHELMA. 1995. "Health inequities in early adulthood: A comparison of young men in Britain and Finland." *Social Science and Medicine,* 41:163–171.

RANK, STEVEN G., and CARDELL K. JACOBSON. 1977. "Hospital nurses' compliance with medication overdose orders: A failure to replicate." *Journal of Health and Social Behavior,* 18:188–193.

RANSFORD, H. EDWARD. 1986. "Race, heart disease worry, and health protective behavior." *Social Science and Medicine,* 12:1355–1362.

RASMUSSEN, HOWARD. 1975. "Medical education—Revolution or reaction." *Pharos,* 38:53–59.

REEDER, LEO G. 1972. "The patient-client as a consumer: Some observations on the changing professional-client relationship." *Journal of Health and Social Behavior,* 13:406–412.

REGIDOR, ENRIQUE, JUAN L. GUTIÉRREZ-FISAC, and CARMEN RODRIGUEZ. 1995. "Increased socioeconomic differences in mortality in eight Spanish provinces." *Social Science and Medicine,* 41:801–807.

REID, IVAN. 1998. *Social class differences in Britain.* Cambridge, U.K.: Polity Press.

REMENNICK, LARISSA I. 1998. "The cancer problem in the context of modernity: Sociology, demography, politics." *Current Sociology,* 46:1–150.

RENAUD, SERGE, and MICHEL DE LORGERIL. 1992. "Wine, alcohol, platelets, and the French paradox for coronary heart disease." *Lancet,* 339:1523–1526.

RENSBURG, DINGIE VAN, IRWIN FRWIN FRIEDMAN, CHARLES NGWENA, ANDRÉ PELSER, FRANCOIS STEYN, FREDERIK BOOYSEN, and ELIZABETH ADENDORFF. 2002. *Strengthening local government and civic responses to the HIV/AIDS epidemic in South Africa.* Bloemfontein, South Africa: Centre for Health Systems Research & Development.

RENSBURG, H. C. J. VAN. 1991. "South African health care in change." *South African Journal of Sociology,* 22:1–10.

———. 1996. "Demographic transition, social security, and health care: The South African case." *Demographic transition, health care and social security,* W. Yang and M. Lee (eds.). Taipei: Academia Sinica.

RENSBURG, H. C. J. VAN, A. FOURIE, and E. PRETORIUS. 1992. *Health care in South Africa: Structure and dynamics.* Pretoria: Academia.

RENSBURG, H. C. J. VAN, and CHARLES NGWENA. 2001. "Health and health care against an African background," pp. 365–391 in *The Blackwell companion to medical sociology,* W. Cockerham (ed.). Oxford, UK: Blackwell.

RENSBURG, H. C. J. VAN, and S. R. BENATAR. 1993. "The legacy of apartheid in health and health care." *South African Journal of Sociology,* 24:99–111.

REYNOLDS, JOHN R. 1997. "The effects of industrial employment conditions on job related distress." *Journal of Health and Social Behavior,* 38:105–116.

RIEKER, PARTRICIA P., and CHLOE E. BIRD. 2000. "Sociological explanations of gender differences in mental and physical health," in *Handbook of medical sociology,* 5th ed., C. Bird, P. Conrad, and A. Fremont (eds.). Upper Saddle River, N.J.: Prentice Hall.

RIER, DAVID A. 2000. "The missing voice of the critically ill: A medical sociologist's first-person account." *Sociology of Health and Illness,* 22:68–93.

RISKA, ELIANNE. 2001. "Health professions and occupations," pp. 144–158 in *The Blackwell companion to medical sociology,* W. Cockerham (ed.). Oxford, UK: Blackwell.

RISKA, ELIANNE, and KATARINA WEGAR. 1993. "Women physicians: A new force in medicine?" pp. 77–93 in *Gender, work and medicine,* E. Riska and K. Wegar (eds.). London: Sage.

RITCHEY, FERRIS J. 1981. "Medical rationalization, cultural lag, and the malpractice crisis." *Human Organization,* 40:97–112.

RITZER, GEORGE, and DAVID WALCZAK. 1988. "Rationalization and the deprofessionalization of physicians." *Social Forces,* 67:1–22.

ROBERT, STEPHANIE A. 1998. "Community-level socioeconomic status effects on adult health." *Journal of Health and Social Behavior,* 39:18–37.

ROBERT, STEPHANIE A., and JAMES S. HOUSE. 2000. "Socioeconomic inequalities in health: An enduring sociological problem," pp. 79–97 in *Handbook of medical sociology,* 5th ed., C. Bird, P. Conrad, and A. Fremont (eds.). Upper Saddle River, N.J.: Prentice Hall.

ROBERTS, ROBERT E., and EUN SUL LEE. 1980. "Medical care use by Mexican-Americans: Evidence from the human population laboratory studies." *Medical Care,* 43:266–281.

ROBERTS, ROBERT E., and STEPHEN J. O'KEEFE. 1981. "Sex differences in depression reexamined." *Journal of Health and Social Behavior,* 22:394–400.

ROBINSON, BEVERLY J. 1990. "Africanisms and the study of folklore," pp. 211–224 in *Africanisms in American culture,* J. Holloway (ed.). Bloomington: Indiana University Press.

RODENSTEIN, MARIANNE. 1987. "Wandlüngen des gesundheitsverstandnisses in der moderne." ["The transformation of health understanding in modernity."] *Mensch Medizin Gesellschaft,* 12:292–298.

RODRÍGUEZ, JOSEP A., and LOUIS LEMKOW. 1990. "Health and social inequities in Spain." *Social Science and Medicine,* 31:351–358.

RODWIN, VICTOR G., and SIMONE SANDIER. 1993. "Health care under French national health insurance." *Health Affairs,* Fall:111–131.

ROEBUCK, JULIAN, and ROBERT QUAN. 1976. "Health-care practices in the American Deep South," pp. 141–161 in *Marginal medicine,* R. Wallis and P. Morely (eds.). New York: The Free Press.

ROGERS, RICHARD G. 1996. "The effects of family composition, health, and social support linkages on mortality." *Journal of Health and Social Behavior,* 37:326–338.

ROGERS, RICHARD G., and EVE POWELL-GRINER. 1991. "Life experiences of cigarette smokers and nonsmokers in the United States." *Social Science and Medicine,* 32:1151–1159.

ROGERS, RICHARD G., ROBERT A. HUMMER, and CHARLES B. NAM. 2000. *Living and dying in the USA: Behavioral, health, and social differentials of adult mortality.* New York: Academic Press.

ROGLER, LLOYD H., and AUGUST B. HOLLINGSHEAD. 1965. *Trapped: Families and schizophrenia.* New York: Wiley.

ROGOFF, NATALIE. 1975. "The decision to study medicine," pp. 109–129 in *The student-physician,* R. K. Merton, G. Reader, and P. L. Kendall (eds.). Cambridge, Mass.: Harvard University Press.

ROOS, EVA, EERO LAHELMA, MIKKO VIRTANEN, RITVA PRÄTTÄLÄ, and PIRJO PIETINEN. 1998. "Gender, socioeconomic status and family status as determinants of food behaviour." *Social Science and Medicine,* 46:1519–1529.

ROSENBERG, CHARLES E. 1987. *The care of strangers: The rise of America's hospital system.* New York: Basic Books.

ROSENBERG, EMILY J., and BARBARA S. DOHRENWEND. 1975. "Effects of experience and ethnicity on ratings of life events as stressors." *Journal of Health and Social Behavior,* 16:127–129.

ROSENFIELD, SARAH. 1980. "Sex differences in depression: Do women always have higher rates?" *Journal of Health and Social Behavior,* 21:33–42.

———. 1989. "The effects of women's employment: Personal control and sex differences in mental health." *Journal of Health and Social Behavior,* 30:77–91.

———. 1992. "The costs of sharing: Wives' employment and husbands' mental health." *Journal of Health and Social Behavior,* 33:213–225.

———. 1999. "Gender and mental health: Do women have more pathology, men more, or both the same (and why)?" pp. 348–360 in *A handbook for the study of mental health: Social contexts, theories, and systems,* A. Horwitz and T. Scheid (eds.). Cambridge, UK.: Cambridge University Press.

ROSENSTOCK, IRWIN. 1966. "Why people use health services." *Milbank Memorial Fund Quarterly,* 44:94–127.

ROSS, CATHERINE E., and CHLOE E. BIRD. 1994. "Sex stratification and health lifestyle: Consequences for men's and women's perceived health." *Journal of Health and Social Behavior,* 35:161–178.

ROSS, CATHERINE E., and RAYMOND S. DUFF. 1982. "Returning to the doctor: The effect of client characteristics, type of practice, and experiences with care." *Journal of Health and Social Behavior,* 23:110–131.

ROSS, CATHERINE E., and CHIA-LING WU. 1995. "The links between education and health." *American Sociological Review,* 60:719–745.

———. 1996. "Education, age, and the cumulative advantage in health." *Journal of Health and Social Behavior,* 37:104–120.

ROSS, CATHERINE E., and JOHN MIROWSKY. 1979. "A comparison of life-event-weighting schemes: Change, undesirability and effect-proportional indices." *Journal of Health and Social Behavior,* 20:166–177.

———. 2001. "Neighborhood disadvantage, disorder, and health." *Journal of Health and Social Behavior,* 42:258–276.

ROSS, CATHERINE E., JOHN MIROWSKY, and PATRICIA ULBRICH. 1983. "Distress and the traditional female role: A comparison of Mexicans and Anglos." *American Journal of Sociology,* 89:560–682.

ROTH, JULIUS, and PETER CONRAD (eds.). 1987. *The experience and management of chronic illness.* Newbury Park, Calif.: Sage.

ROTHMAN, ELLEN LERNER. 1999. *White coat: Becoming a doctor at Harvard Medical School.* New York: HarperCollins.

ROWLAND, DIANE, and ALEXANDRE V. TELYUKOV. 1991. "Soviet health care from two perspectives." *Health Affairs,* Fall:71–86.

ROXBURGH, SUSAN. 1996. "Gender differences in work and well-being: Effects of exposure and vulnerability." *Journal of Health and Social Behavior,* 37:265–277.

RUCH, LIBBY O. 1977. "Multidimensional analysis of the concept of life change." *Journal of Health and Social Behavior,* 18:71–83.

RUCH, LIBBY O., and SUSAN MEYERS CHANDLER. 1983. "Sexual assault trauma during the acute phase: An exploratory model and multivariate analysis." *Journal of Health and Social Behavior,* 24:174–185.

RUCH, LIBBY O., SUSAN MEYERS CHANDLER, and RICHARD A. HARTER. 1980. "Life change and rape impact." *Journal of Health and Social Behavior,* 21:248–260.

RUESCHMEYER, DIETRICH. 1972. "Doctors and lawyers: A comment on the theory of professions," pp. 5–19 in *Medical men and their work,* E. Freidson and J. Lorber (eds.). Chicago: Aldine.

RUGGIE, MARY. 1992. "The paradox of liberal intervention: Health policy and the American welfare state." *American Journal of Sociology,* 97:919–944.

RUNDALL, THOMAS G. 1978. "Life change and recovery from surgery." *Journal of Health and Social Behavior,* 20:418–427.

RUNDALL, THOMAS G., and JOHN R. C. WHEELER. 1979. "The effect of income on use of preventive care: An evaluation of alternative explanations." *Journal of Health and Social Behavior,* 20:397–406.

RUSHING, WILLIAM A. 1984. "Social factors in the rise of hospital costs," pp. 27–114 in *Research in the sociology of health care,* Vol. 3, J. Roth (ed.). Greenwich, Conn.: JAI.

———. 1995. *The AIDS epidemic: Social dimensions of an infectious disease.* Boulder, Colo.: Westview Press.

SAKANO, JUNKO, and YOSHIHIKO YAMAZAKI. 1990. *Survey of the role of white-collar workers as family members in the Tokyo area.* University of Tokyo: Department of Health Sociology.

SAWARD, ERNEST W. 1973. "The organization of medical care," pp. 129–135 in *Life, death, and medicine.* San Francisco: W. H. Freeman.

SCAMBLER, GRAHAM. 2002. *Health and social change: A critical theory.* Buckingham, UK: Open University Press.

SCAMBLER, GRAHAM, and ANTHONY HOPKINS. 1986. "Being epileptic: Coming to terms with stigma." *Sociology of Health and Illness,* 8:26–43.

SCHEFF, THOMAS J. 1966. *Being mentally ill.* Chicago: Aldine.

SCHEUCH, ERWIN K. 1987. "Entwicklung der Bevölkerungsstruktur and unser Gesundheitswesen." ["The structural development of the population and our public health"]. *Mensch Medizin Gesellschaft,* 12:135–143.

SCHIEMAN, SCOTT, and HEATHER A. TURNER. 1998. "Age, disability, and the sense of mastery." *Journal of Health and Social Behavior,* 39:169–186.

SCHNEIDER, MARKUS, PETER BIENE-DIETRICH, MONIKA GABANYI, UWE HOFMANN, MANFRED HUBER, AYNUR KÖSE, and JÜRG H. SOMMER. 1994. *Gesundheitssysteme in internationalen Vergleich [Health systems in international comparison].* Augsburg, Germany: BASYS.

SCHNEIROV, MATTHEW, and JONATHAN DAVID GECZIK. 1996. "A diagnosis for our times: Alternative health's submerged networks and the transformation of identities." *Sociological Quarterly,* 37:627–644.

SCHOENBAUM, MICHAEL, and TIMOTHY WAIDMANN. 1997. "Race, socioeconomic status, and health: Accounting for race differences in health." *Journal of Gerontology,* 52B:61–73.

———. 2002. *Health and social change.* Buckingham, UK: Open University Press.

SCHOR, EDWARD L., and ELIZABETH G. MENAGHAN. 1995. "Family pathways to child health," pp. 18–45 in *Society and health,* B. Amick, S. Levine, A. Tarlov, and D. Walsh (eds.). New York: Oxford University Press.

SCHULENBURG, J. MATTHIAS VON. 1995. "Forming and reforming the market for third-party purchasing of health care: A German perspective." *Social Science and Medicine,* 39:1473–1481.

SCHULMAN, SAM. 1972. "Mother surrogate—After a decade," pp. 233–239 in *Patients, physicians and illness,* E. Jaco (ed.). New York: The Free Press.

SCHUTT, RUSSEL K., TATJANA MESCHEDE, and JILL RIERDAN. 1994. "Distress, suicidal thoughts, and social support among homeless adults." *Journal of Health and Social Behavior,* 35:134–142.

SECCOMBE, KAREN. 1989. "Ethnicity or socioeconomic status? Health differences between elder Alaska natives and whites." *Gerontologist,* 29:551–556.

SECCOMBE, KAREN, and CHERYL AMEY. 1995. "Playing by the rules and losing: Health insurance and the working poor." *Journal of Health and Social Behavior,* 36:168–181.

SEEMAN, M., and J. W. EVANS. 1962. "Alienation and social learning in a reformatory." *American Journal of Sociology,* 69:270–284.

SEEMAN, MELVIN, and TERESA E. SEEMAN. 1983. "Health behavior and personal autonomy: A longitudinal study of the sense of control in illness." *Journal of Health and Social Behavior,* 24:144–160.

SEGALL, ALEXANDER. 1976. "The sick role concept: Understanding illness behavior." *Journal of Health and Social Behavior,* 17:162–168.

SEGALL, ALEXANDER, and JAY GOLDSTEIN. 1989. "Exploring the correlates of self-provided health care behaviour." *Social Science and Medicine,* 29:153–161.

SELYE, HANS. 1956. *The stress of life.* New York: McGraw-Hill.

SERMSRI, SANTHAT. 1999. *Socio-cultural perspectives in health.* Bangkok, Thailand: Panich.

SHAPIRO, JUDITH. 1995. "The Russian mortality crisis and its causes," pp. 149–178 in *Russian economic reform at risk,* A. Aslund (ed.). London: Pinter.

SHAPIRO, MARTIN. 1978. *Getting doctored*. Kitchener, Ontario, Canada: Between the Lines.

SHARMA, URSULA M. 1990. "Using alternative therapies: Marginal medicine and central concerns," pp. 127–139 in *New directions in the sociology of health,* P. Abbott and G. Payne (eds.). London: Taylor & Francis.

SHARP, KIMBERLY, CATHERINE E. ROSS, and WILLIAM C. COCKERHAM. 1983. "Symptoms, beliefs, and use of physician services among the disadvantaged." *Journal of Health and Social Behavior,* 24:255–263.

SHAW, MARY, DANNY DORLING, and GEORGE DAVEY SMITH. 1999. "Poverty, social exclusion, and minorities," pp. 211–239 in *The social determinants of health,* M. Marmot and R. Wilkinson (eds.). Oxford, UK: Oxford University Press.

SHEIMAN, IGOR. 1994. "Forming the system of health insurance in the Russian Federation." *Social Science and Medicine,* 39:1425–1432.

SHEPARD, JAMES, STUART M. COBBE, IAN FORD, CHRISTOPHER G. ISLES, A. ROSS LORIMER, PETER W. MACFARLANE, JAMES H. MCKILLOP, and CHRISTOPHER J. PACKARD. 1995. "Prevention of coronary heart disease with pravastatin in men with hypercholesterolemia." *New England Journal of Medicine,* 353:1301–1307.

SHERRADEN, MARGARET S. 1995. "Development of health policy and services for rural Mexico," pp. 122–140 in *Global perspectives on health care,* G. Gallagher and J. Subedi (eds.). Englewood Cliffs, N.J.: Prentice Hall.

SHKOLNIKOV, VLADIMIR. 1995. "Recent trends in Russian mortality." Paper presented at the USAID Conference, Moscow (October).

SHKOLNIKOV, VLADIMIR M., DAVID A. LEON, SERGEY ADAMETS, EUGENIY ANDREEV, and ALEXANDER DEEV. 1998. "Educational level and adult mortality in Russia: An analysis of routine data 1979 to 1994." *Social Science and Medicine,* 47:357–369.

SHKOLNIKOV, VLADIMIR M., and FRANCE MESLÉ. 1996. "The Russian epidemiological crisis as mirrored by mortality patterns," pp. 113–162 in *Russia's demographic crisis,* J. DaVanzo (ed.). Santa Monitca, Calif.: RAND.

SHKOLNIKOV, VLADIMIR, and ALEXANDER NEMTSOV. 1994. "The anti-alcohol campaign and variations in Russian mortality." Paper presented to the workshop on mortality and adult health priorities in the New Independent States, Washington, D.C. (November).

SHKOLNIKOV, VLADIMIR, MARTIN MCKEE, and DAVID A. LEON. 2001. "Changes in life expectancy in Russia in the mid-1990s." *Lancet,* 357:917–927.

SHORTELL, STEPHEN M. 1973. "Patterns of referral among internists in private practice." *Journal of Health and Social Behavior,* 14:335–348.

SHORTER, EDWARD. 1991. *Doctors and their patients*. New Brunswick, N.J.: Transaction.

SHUVAL, JUDITH T. 1990. "Health in Israel: Patterns of equality and inequality." *Social Science and Medicine,* 31:291–304.

———. 2001. "Migration, health, and stress," pp. 126–143 in *The Blackwell companion to medical sociology,* W. Cockerham (ed.). Oxford, UK: Blackwell.

SHUVAL, JUDITH T., NISSIM MIZRACHI, and EMMA SMETANNIKOV. 2002. "Entering the well-guarded fortress: Alternative practitioners in hospital settings." *Social Science and Medicine,* 55:1745–1755.

SIDEL, VICTOR W., and RUTH SIDEL. 1982b. *The health of China*. Boston: Beacon Press.

———. 1993. "New lessons from China: Equity and economics in rural health care." *American Journal of Public Health,* 83:1665–1666.

SIEGEL, KAROLYN, and BEATRICE J. KRAUSS. 1991. "Living with HIV infection: Adaptive tasks of seropositive gay men." *Journal of Health and Social Behavior,* 32:17–32.

SIEGRIST, JOHANNES. 1989. "Steps toward explaining social differentials in morbidity: The case of West Germany," pp. 353–371 in *Health inequalities in European countries,* J. Fox (ed.). Aldershot, U.K.: Gower.

———. 1995. *Medizinische soziologie* 5th ed. Munich: Urban & Schwarzenberg.

———. 1996a. "High cost–low gain conditions at work as a determinant of cardiovascular disease mortality," pp. 169–185 in *East-west differences in life expectancy: Environmental and non-environmental determinants,* S. Kelly and M. Bobak (eds.). Dordrecht, the Netherlands: Kluwer.

———. 1996b. "Adverse health effects of high-effort/low-reward conditions." *Journal of Occupational Health Psychology,* 1:27–41.

————. 2001. "Work stress and health," pp. 114–125 in *The Blackwell companion to medical sociology*, W. Cockerham (ed.). Oxford, UK: Blackwell.

SIEGRIST, JOHANNES, and RICHARD PETER. 1996. "Threat to occupational status control and cardiovascular risk." *Israel Journal of Medical Science*, 32:179–184.

SIEGRIST, J., R. PETER, P. CREMER, and D. SEIDEL. 1997. "Chronic work stress is associated with atherogenic lipids and elevated fibrinogen in middle-aged men." *Journal of Internal Medicine*, 242:149–156.

SIEGRIST, JOHANNES, RICHARD PETER, ASTRID JUNGE, PETER CREMER, and DIETER SEIDEL. 1990. "Low status control, high effort at work and ischemic heart disease: Prospective evidence from blue-collar men." *Social Science and Medicine*, 31:1127–1134.

SIHVONEN, ARI-PEKKA, ANTON E. KUNST, EERO LAHELMA, TAPANI VALKONEN, and JOHAN P. MACKENBACH. 1998. "Socioeconomic inequalities in health expectancy in Finland and Norway in the late 1980s." *Social Science and Medicine*, 47:303–315.

SIMMONS, L., and H. WOLFF. 1954. *Social science in medicine*. New York: Russell Sage.

SIMON, ROBIN W. 1992. "Parental role strains, salience of parental identity and gender differences in psychological distress." *Journal of Health and Social Behavior*, 33:25–35.

————. 1995. "Gender, multiple roles, role meaning, and mental health." *Journal of Health and Social Behavior*, 36:182–194.

————. 1997. "The meanings individuals attach to role identities and their implications for mental health." *Journal of Health and Social Behavior*, 38:256–274.

————. 2000. "The importance of culture in sociological theory and research on stress and mental health: A missing link?" pp. 68–78 in *Handbook of medical sociology*, 5th ed., C. Bird, P. Conrad, and A. Fremont (eds.). Upper Saddle River, N.J.: Prentice Hall.

————. 2002. "Revisiting the relationships among gender, marital status, and mental health." *American Journal of Sociology*, 1065–1096.

SINGER, ELEANOR, AMY D. CORNING, and TONI ANTONUCCI. 1999. "Attitudes toward genetic testing and fetal diagnosis." *Journal of Health and Social Behavior*, 40:429–445.

SINGH, GOPAL K., and STELLA M. YU. 1995. "Infant mortality in the United States: Trends, differentials, and projections, 1950 through 2010." *American Journal of Public Health*, 85:957–964.

SKIDELSKY, ROBERT. 1995. *The road from serfdom: The economic and political consequences of the end of communism*. New York: Penguin Press.

SKOCPOL, THEDA. 1995. *Social policy in the United States*. Princeton, N.J.: Princeton University Press.

————. 1996. *Boomerang: Clinton's health security effort and the turn against government in U.S. politics*. New York: Norton.

SLEEPER, SALLY, DOUGLAS R. WHOLEY, RICHARD HARMER, SHAWN SCHWARTZ, and VITO INOFERIO. 1998. "Trust me: Technical and institutional determinants of health maintenance organizations shifting risk to physicians." *Journal of Health and Social Behavior*, 39:189–200.

SMAJE, CHRIS. 2000. "Race, ethnicity, and health," pp. 124–128 in *Handbook of medical sociology*, 5th ed., C. Bird, P. Conrad, and A. Fremont (eds.). Upper Saddle River, N.J.: Prentice Hall.

SMITH, ALLEN C., and SHERRYL KLEINMAN. 1989. "Managing emotions in medical school: Students' contacts with the living and the dead." *Social Psychology Quarterly*, 52:56–69.

SMITH, DAVID G. 2002. *Entitlement politics: Medicare and Medicaid 1995–2001*. Hawthorne, NY: Aldine de Gruyter.

SMITH, JAMES P. 1999. "Healthy bodies and thick wallets: The dual relation between health and economic status." *Journal of Economic Perspectives*, 13:145–166.

SNOW, LOUDELL F. 1977. "Popular medicine in a black neighborhood," pp. 19–25 in *Ethnic medicine in the Southwest*, E. Spicer (ed.). Tucson: University of Arizona Press.

————. 1978. "Sorcerers, saints and charlatans: Black folk healers in urban America." *Culture, Medicine, and Psychiatry*, 2:69–106.

————. 1993. *Walkin' over medicine*. Boulder, CO: Westview Press.

SONTAG, SUSAN. 1978, *Illness as metaphor*. New York: Farrar, Straus, and Giroux.

SPLAWSKI, I., K. TIMOTHY, M. TATEYAMA, C. CLANCY, A. MALHORTA, A. BEGGS, F. CAPPUCCIO, G. SAGNELLA, R. KASS, and M. KEATING. 2002. "Variant of SCN5A Sodium Channel implicated in risk of cardiac arrhythmia." *Science*, 297:1333–1336.

SPRUIT, INGEBORG P. 1990. "Health and social inequities in the Netherlands." *Social Science and Medicine*, 31:319–329.

SROLE, LEO, T. S. LANGNER, S. T. MICHAEL, M. K. OPLER, and T. A. C. RENNIE. 1962. *Mental health in the metropolis: The midtown Manhattan study,* Vol. 1. New York: McGraw-Hill.

STARR, PAUL. 1982. *The social transformation of American medicine.* New York: Basic Books.

———. 1994. *The logic of health care reform,* rev. and enl. ed. New York: Penguin Books.

STEIN, LEONARD I. 1967. "The doctor–nurse game." *Archives of General Psychiatry,* 16:699–703.

STEIN, LEONARD I., DAVID T. WATTS, and TIMOTHY HOWELL. 1990. "The doctor–nurse game revisited." *New England Journal of Medicine,* 322:546–549.

STERN, BERNARD F. 1927. *Social factors in medical progress.* New York: Columbia University Press.

STEVENS, FRED. 2001. "The convergence and divergence of modern health care systems," pp. 139–176 in *The Blackwell companion to medical sociology,* W. Cockerham (ed.). Oxford, UK: Blackwell.

STEVENS, FRED, JOS DIEDERIKS, JOUKE VAN DER ZEE, and GÜNTHER LÜSCHEN. 1995. "Health lifestyles, health concern, and social position in the Netherlands and Germany." *European Journal of Public Health,* 5:46–49.

STEVENS, ROSEMARY. 1971. *American medicine and the public interest.* New Haven, Conn.: Yale University Press.

———. 1989. *In sickness and in wealth: American hospitals in the twentieth century.* New York: Basic Books.

STOLLER, ELEANOR PALO. 1984. "Self-assessments of health by the elderly: The impact of informal assistance." *Journal of Health and Social Behavior,* 25:260–270.

STRAUS, ROBERT. 1957. "The nature and status of medical sociology." *American Sociological Review,* 22:200–204.

STRAUSS, ANSELM. 1966. "Structure and ideology of the nursing profession," pp. 60–104 in *The nursing profession,* F. Davis (ed.). New York: John Wiley.

———. 1970. "Medical ghettos," pp. 9–26 in *Where medicine fails,* A. Strauss (ed.). Chicago: Aldine.

———. 1975. *Chronic illness and the quality of life.* St. Louis: C. V. Mosby.

STRAUSS, ANSELM, and JULIET M. CORBIN. 1988. *Shaping a new health care system.* San Francisco: Jossey-Bass.

STRAUSS, ANSELM, LEONARD SCHATZMAN, DANUTA EHRLICH, RUE BUCHER, and MELVIN SABSHIN. 1963. "The hospital and its negotiated order," pp. 147–169 in *The hospital in modern society,* E. Freidson (ed.). New York: The Free Press.

SUBEDI, JANARDAN, and EUGENE B. GALLAGHER (eds.). 1996. *Society, health, and disease: Transcultural perspectives.* Upper Saddle River, N.J.: Prentice Hall.

SUCHMAN, EDWARD A. 1963. *Sociology and the field of public health.* New York: Russell Sage.

———. 1965a. "Social patterns of illness and medical care." *Journal of Health and Social Behavior,* 6:2–16.

———. 1965b. "Stages of illness and medical care." *Journal of Health and Social Behavior,* 6:114–128.

SUNDQUIST, JAN, and SVEN-ERIK JOHANSSON. 1997. "Indicators of socio-economic position and their relation to mortality in Sweden." *Social Science and Medicine,* 45:1757–1766.

SUSSER, MERVYN, and EZRA SUSSER. 1996a. "Choosing a future for epidemiology: I. Eras and paradigms." *American Journal of Public Health,* 86:668–673.

———. 1996b. "Choosing a future for epidemiology: II. From black box to Chinese boxes and eco-epidemiology." *American Journal of Public Health,* 86:674–677.

SUSSER, M. W., and W. WATSON. 1971. *Sociology in medicine,* 2nd ed. New York: Oxford University Press.

SVARSTAD, BONNIE L. 1986. "Patient-practitioner relationships and compliance with prescribed medical regimens," pp. 438–459 in *Applications of social science to clinical medicine and health policy,* L. Aiken and D. Mechanic (eds.). New Brunswick, N.J.: Rutgers University Press.

SVENSSON, ROLAND. 1996. "The interplay between doctors and nurses—A negotiated order perspective." *Sociology of Health and Illness,* 18:379–398.

SWISHER, RAYMOND R., GLEN H. ELDER, JR., FREDERICK O. LORENZ, and RAND D. CONGER. 1998. "The long arm of the farm: How an occupation structures exposure and vulnerability to stressors across role domains." *Journal of Health and Social Behavior,* 39:72–89.

SYTKOWSKI, PAMELA A., WILLIAM B. KANNEL, and RALPH B. D'AGOSTINO. 1990. "Changes in risk factors and the decline in mortality from cardiovascular disease." *New England Journal of Medicine,* 322:1635–1641.

SZASZ, THOMAS S. 1974. *The myth of mental illness,* rev. ed. New York: Harper & Row.

SZASZ, THOMAS, and MARC HOLLENDER. 1956. "A contribution to the philosophy of medicine: The basic models of the doctor–patient relationship." *Journal of the American Medical Association,* 97:585–588.

TAIRA, DEBORAH, DANA GELB SAFRAN, TODD B. SETO, WILLIAM H. ROGERS, and ALVIN R. TARLOV. 1997. "The relationship between patient income and physician discussion of health risk behaviors." *Journal of the American Medical Association,* 278:1412–1417.

TAUSIG, MARK, and RUDY FENWICK. 1999. "Recession and well-being." *Journal of Health and Social Behavior,* 40:1–16.

TESSLER, RICHARD, DAVID MECHANIC, and MARGARET DIMOND. 1976. "The effect of psychological distress on physician utilization: A prospective study." *Journal of Health and Social Behavior,* 17:353–364.

THOITS, PEGGY A. 1987. "Gender and marital status differences in control and distress: Common stress versus unique stress explanations." *Journal of Health and Social Behavior,* 28:7–22.

———. 1994. "Stressors and problem-solving: The individual as psychological activist." *Journal of Health and Social Behavior,* 35:143–159.

———. 1995. "Stress, coping, and social support processes: Where are we? What next?" *Journal of Health and Social Behavior,* extra issue:53–79.

THOMPSON, JAMES. 1984. "Compliance," pp. 109–131 in *The experience of illness,* R. Fitzpatrick, S. Newman, G. Scambler, and J. Thompson (eds.). London: Tavistock.

THOROGOOD, NICKI. 1990. "Caribbean home remedies and their importance for black's health care in Britain," pp. 140–152 in *New directions in the sociology of health,* P. Abbott and G. Payne (eds.). London: Taylor & Francis.

TIERNEY, KATHLEEN J., and BARBARA BAISDEN. 1979. *Crisis intervention programs for disaster victims: A source book and manual for smaller communities.* Rockville, Md.: National Institute of Mental Health.

TIMMERMANS, STEFAN. 2000. "Technology and medical practice," pp. 309–321 in *Handbook of medical sociology,* 5th ed., C. Bird, P. Conrad, and A. Fremont (eds.). Upper Saddle River, N.J.: Prentice Hall.

TIMMERMANS, STEFAN, and ALISON ANGELL. 2001. "Evidence-based medicine, clinical uncertainty, and learning to doctor." *Journal of Health and Social Behavior,* 42:342–359.

TOWNSEND, PETER, and NICK DAVIDSON (eds.) and MARGARET WHITEHEAD. 1990. *Inequalities in health.* London: Penguin Books.

TREML, VLADIMIR. 1997. "Soviet and Russian statistics on alcohol and abuse," pp. 220–238 in *Premature death in the new independent states,* J. Bobadilla, C. Costello, and F. Mitchell (eds.). Washington, D.C.: National Academy Press.

TREVIÑO, FERNANDO M., M. EUGENE MOYER, R. BURCIAGA VALDEZ, and CHRISTINE A. STROUP-BENHAM. 1991. "Health insurance coverage and utilization of health services by Mexican Americans, mainland Puerto Ricans, and Cuban Americans." *Journal of the American Medical Association,* 265:233–237.

TROVATO, FRANK. 1994. "Mortality trends in Canada," pp. 22–64 in *Health, illness, and health care in Canada,* B. Bolaria and H. Dickinson (eds.). Toronto: Harcourt Brace Canada.

TSENG, SHU-FEN, and LIANG-MING CHANG. 1999. "Virtual and reality: A comparison of doctor–patient relationship to the Internet and face-to-face medical encounter." Paper presented to the International Conference on Socio-cultural and Policy Dimensions of Health Care, Singapore, November.

TUCHMAN, BARBARA W. 1978. *A distant mirror: The calamitous 14th century.* New York: Random House.

TULCHINSKY, THEODORE H., and ELENA V. VARAVIKOVA. 1996. "Addressing the epidemologic transition in the former Soviet Union: Strategies for health system and public health reform in Russia." *American Journal of Public Health,* 86:313–320.

TURNER, BRYAN S. 1988. *Status.* Milton Keynes, U.K.: Open University Press.

———. 1992. *Regulating bodies: Essays in medical sociology.* London: Routledge.

———. 1995. *Medical power and social knowledge,* 2nd ed. London: Sage.

———. 1996. *The body and society,* 2nd ed. Oxford, U.K.: Blackwell.

TURNER, HEATHER, ROBERT B. HAYS, and THOMAS J. COATES. 1993. "Determinants of social support among gay men: The context of AIDS." *Journal of Health and Social Behavior,* 34:37–53.

TURNER, J. BLAKE. 1995. "Economic context and the health effects of unemployment." *Journal of Health and Social Behavior,* 36:213–229.

TURNER, R. JAY, and WILLIAM R. AVISON. 1992. "Innovations in the measurement of life stress: Crisis theory and the significance of event resolution." *Journal of Health and Social Behavior,* 33:35–50.

TURNER, R. JAY, and DONALD A. LLOYD. 1995. "Life-time traumas and mental health: The significance of cumulative adversity." *Journal of Health and Social Behavior,* 36:360–376.

———. 1999. "The stress process and the social distribution of depression." *Journal of Health and Social Behavior,* 40:374–404.

TURNER, R. JAY, BLAIR WHEATON, and DONALD A. LLOYD. 1995. "The epidemiology of social stress." *American Sociological Review,* 60:125–140.

TUXWORTH, W., A. M. NEVILL, C. WHITE, and C. JENKINS. 1986. "Health, fitness, physical activity, and morbidity of middle aged male factory workers." *British Journal of Industrial Medicine,* 43:733–753.

TWADDLE, ANDREW. 1969. "Health decisions and sick role variations: An exploration." *Journal of Health and Social Behavior,* 10:105–114.

———. 1973. "Illness and deviance." *Social Science and Medicine,* 7:751–762.

TWIGG, JUDYTH L. 1999. "Obligatory medical insurance in Russia: The participants' perspective." *Social Science and Medicine,* 49:371–382.

———. 2000. "Unfilled hopes: The struggle to reform Russian health care and its financing," pp. 43–64 in *Russia's torn safety nets: Health and welfare during the transition,* M. Field and J. Twigg (eds.). New York: St. Martin's Press.

———. 2002. "Health care reform in Russia: A survey of head doctors and insurance administrators." *Social Science and Medicine,* 55:2253–2265.

ULBRICH, PATRICIA M., GEORGE J. WARHEIT, and RICK S. ZIMMERMAN. 1989. "Race, socioeconomic status, and psychological distress: An examination of differential vulnerability." *Journal of Health and Social Behavior,* 30:131–146.

UMBERSON, DEBRA, CAMILLE B. WORTMAN, and RONALD C. KESSLER. 1992. "Widowhood and depression: Explaining long-term gender differences in vulnerability." *Journal of Health and Social Behavior,* 33:10–24.

U.S. CENSUS BUREAU. 1996. *Population projections of the United States by age, sex, race and Hispanic origin, 1995 to 2050.* Washington, D.C.: U.S. Government Printing Office.

———. 1999. *Statistical Abstract of the United States, 1999.* Washington, D.C.: U.S. Government Printing Office.

VALKONEN, TAPANI. 1987. "Social inequality in the face of death." Unpublished manuscript. Helsinki: Department of Sociology, University of Helsinki.

———. 1989. "Adult mortality and level of education: A comparison of six countries," pp. 142–162 in *Health inequalities in European countries,* J. Fox (ed.). Aldershot, U.K.: Gower.

VEGA, WILLIAM A., and HORTENSIA AMARO. 1994. "Latino outlook: Good health, uncertain prognosis." *Annual Review of Public Health,* 15:39–47.

VERBRUGGE, LOIS M. 1983. "Multiple roles and physical health of women and men." *Journal of Health and Social Behavior,* 24:16–30.

———. 1985. "Gender and health: An update on hypotheses and evidence." *Journal of Health and Social Behavior,* 26:156–182.

———. 1986. "From sneezes to adieus: Stages of health for American men and women." *Social Science and Medicine,* 22:1195–1212.

———. 1989. "The Twain meet: Empirical explanations of sex differences in health and mortality." *Journal of Health and Social Behavior,* 30:282–304.

VLADECK, BRUCE C. 1983. "Equality, access, and the costs of health services," pp. 1–18 in *Securing access to health care,* Vol. 3, President's Commission for the Study of Ethical Problems in Medicine and Biomedical and Behavioral Research. Washington, D.C.: U.S. Government Printing Office.

VOLKART, E. H. (ed.). 1951. *Social behavior and personality.* New York: Social Science Research Council.

WAITZKIN, HOWARD. 1985. "Information giving in medical care." *Journal of Health and Social Behavior,* 26:81–101.

———. 1991. *The politics of medical encounters.* New Haven, Conn.: Yale University Press.

———. 2000. "Changing patient–physician relationships in the changing health-policy environment," pp. 271–283 in *Handbook of medical sociology,* 5th ed., C. Bird, P. Conrad, and A. Fremont (eds.). Upper Saddle River, N.J.: Prentice Hall.

————. 2001. *At the front lines of medicine: How the medical care system alienates doctors and mistreats patients . . . and what we can do about it.* Lanham, MD: Rowman and Littlefield.

WAITZKIN, HOWARD, THERON BRITT, and CONSTANCE WILLIAMS. 1994. "Narratives of aging and social problems in medical encounters with older persons." *Journal of Health and Social Behavior,* 35:322–348.

WALBERG, PEDER, MARTIN MCKEE, VLADIMIR SHKOLNIKOV, LAURENT CHENET, and DAVID A. LEON. 1998. "Economic change, crime, and mortality crisis in Russia." *British Medical Journal,* 317:312–318.

WALDRON, INGRID, CHRISTOPHER C. WEISS, and MARY ELIZABETH HUGHES. 1998. "Interacting effects of multiple roles on women's health." *Journal of Health and Social Behavior,* 39:216–236.

WALL, ANN (ed.). 1996. *Health systems in liberal democracies.* London: Routledge.

WALLIMANN, ISIDOR. 1986. "Social insurance and the delivery of social services in France." *Social Science and Medicine,* 23:1305–1317.

WALSH, DIANA CHAPMAN, GLORIAN SORENSEN, and LORI LEONARD. 1995. "Gender, health, and cigarette smoking," pp. 131–171 in *Society and health,* B. Amick, S. Levine, A. Tarlov, and D. Walsh (eds.). New York: Oxford University Press.

WAN, THOMAS T. H., and SCOTT J. SOIFER. 1974. "Determinants of physician utilization: A causal analysis." *Journal of Health and Social Behavior,* 15:100–108.

WARBASSE, JAMES. 1909. *Medical sociology.* New York: Appleton.

WARD, PETER. 1985. *Welfare politics in Mexico.* London: Allen & Unwin.

WARNECKE, RICHARD B. 1973. "Non-intellectual factors related to attrition from a collegiate nursing program." *Journal of Health and Social Behavior,* 14:153–167.

WARNER, DAVID C. 1991. "Health issues in the U.S.-Mexican border." *Journal of the American Medical Association,* 265:242–247.

WARREN, MARY GUPTILL, ROSE WEITZ, and STEPHEN KULIS. 1998. "Physician satisfaction in a changing health care environment: The impact of challenges to professional autonomy, authority, and dominance." *Journal of Health and Social Behavior,* 39:356–367.

WEBER, MAX. 1958. *The Protestant ethic and the spirit of capitalism.* New York: Scribner.

————. 1978. *Economy and society,* 2 vols, G. Roth and C. Wittich (eds.). Berkeley: University of California Press.

WEBSTER, ANDREW. 2002. "Innovative health technologies and the social: Redefining health, medicine, and the body." *Current Sociology,* 50: 443–457.

WEINER, HERBERT. 1985. "Schizophrenia: Etiology," pp. 650–651 in *Comprehensive textbook of psychiatry,* Vol. 1, 4th ed., H. Kaplan and B. Sadock (eds.). Baltimore: Williams & Wilkins.

WEISS, GREGORY L., and LYNNE E. LONNQUIST. 2003. *Sociology of health, healing, and illness,* 4th ed. Englewood Cliffs, N.J.: Prentice Hall.

WEITZ, ROSE. 1999. "Watching Brian die: The rhetoric and reality of informed consent." *Health,* 3:209–227.

WEITZ, ROSE, and DEBORAH SULLIVAN. 1986. "The politics of childbirth: The reemergence of midwifery in Arizona." *Social Problems,* 33:163–175.

WELCH, SUSAN, JOHN COMER, and MICHAEL STEINMAN. 1973. "Some social and attitudinal correlates of health care among Mexican–Americans." *Journal of Health and Social Behavior,* 14:205–213.

WENGER, NANETTE K. 1982. "Coronary heart disease in women: Myth and fact." *Hospital Practice,* 17:114A–X.

WERMUTH, LAURIE. 2003. *Global inequality and human needs.* Boston: Allyn and Bacon.

WESSEN, ALBERT F. 1972. "Hospital ideology and communication between ward personnel," pp. 325–342 in *Patients, physicians and illness,* 2nd ed., E. Jaco (ed.). New York: Macmillan.

WEST, CANDACE. 1984. "When the doctor is a 'lady': Power, status and gender in physician-patient encounters." *Symbolic Interaction,* 7:87–106.

WHEATON, BLAIR. 1980. "The sociogenesis of psychological disorder: An attributional theory." *Journal of Health and Social Behavior,* 21:100–124.

WHITEHEAD, MARGARET. 1990. "The health divide," pp. 222–356 in *Inequalities in health,* P. Townsend and N. Davidson (eds.) and M. Whitehead. London: Penguin Books.

————. 1998. "Diffusion of ideas on social inequalities in health: A European perspective." *Milbank Quarterly,* 76:469–492.

WHOLEY, DOUGLAS R., and LAWTON R. BURNS. 2000. "Tides of change: The evolution of managed care," pp. 217–237 in *Handbook of medical sociology*, 5th ed., C. Bird, P. Conrad, and A. Fremont (eds.). Upper Saddle River, N.J.: Prentice Hall.

WICKRAMA, K. A. S., RAND D. CONGER, LORA EBERT WALLACE, and GLEN H. ELDER, JR. 1999. "The intergenerational transmission of health-risk behaviors: Adolescent lifestyles and gender moderating effects." *Journal of Health and Social Behavior*, 40:258–272.

WICKRAMA, K. A. S., FREDERICK O. LORENZ, RAND D. CONGER, and GLEN H. ELDER, JR. 1997. "Linking occupational conditions to physical health through marital, social, and intrapersonal processes." *Journal of Health and Social Behavior*, 38:363–375.

WIGHT, DANIEL. 1999. "Cultural factors in young heterosexual men's perception of HIV risk." *Sociology of Health and Illness*, 21:735–758.

WILDMAN, RICHARD C., and DAVID RICHARD JOHNSON. 1977. "Life change and Langner's 22-item mental health index: A study and partial replication." *Journal of Health and Social Behavior*, 18:179–188.

WILKINSON, RICHARD G. 1996. *Unhealthy societies*. London: Routledge.

WILLIAMS, A. PAUL, EUGENE VAYDA, MAY L. COHEN, CHRISTEL A. WOODWARD, and BARBARA M. FERRIER. 1995. "Medicine and the Canadian state: From the politics of conflict to the politics of accommodation?" *Journal of Health and Social Behavior*, 36:303–321.

WILLIAMS, DAVID R. 1990. "Socioeconomic differentials in health: A review and redirection." *Social Psychology Quarterly*, 53:81–99.

———. 1996. "Race/ethnicity and socioeconomic status: Measurement and methodological issues." *International Journal of Health Services*, 26:483–505.

WILLIAMS, DAVID R., and CHIQUITA COLLINS. 1995. "U.S. socioeconomic and racial differences in health: Patterns and explanations." *Annual Review of Sociology*, 21:349–386.

WILLIAMS, DAVID R., DAVID T. TAKEUCHI, and RUSSELL K. ADAIR. 1992. "Socioeconomic status and psychiatric disorder among blacks and whites." *Social Forces*, 71:179–194.

WILLIAMS, DAVID R., and MICHELLE HARRIS-REID. 1999. "Race and mental health: Emerging patterns and promising approaches," pp. 295–314 in *A handbook for the study of mental health: Social contexts, theories, and systems*, A. Horwitz and T. Scheid (eds.). Cambridge, U.K.: Cambridge University Press.

WILLIAMS, GARETH H. 1984. "The genesis of chronic illness: Narrative re-construction." *Sociology of Health and Illness*, 6:175–200.

WILLIAMS, RORY. 1983. "Concepts of health: An analysis of lay logic." *Sociology*, 17:187–205.

WILLIAMS, SIMON J. 1995. "Theorising class, health and lifestyles: Can Bourdieu help us?" *Sociology of Health and Illness*, 17:577–604.

———. 1999. "Is anybody there? Critical realism, chronic illness and the disability debate." *Sociology of Health and Illness*, 21:797–819.

———. 2000. "Chronic illness as biographical disruption or biographical disruption as chronic illness?" *Sociology of Health and Illness*, 22:40–67.

WILLIAMS, SIMON J., MICHAEL CALNAN, SARAH L. CANT, and JOANNE COYLE. 1993. "All change in the NHS? Implications of the NHS reforms for primary care prevention." *Sociology of Health and Illness*, 15:19–43.

WILSON, ROBERT N. 1963. "The social structure of a general hospital." *Annals of the American Academy of Political Science*, 346:67–76.

———. 1970. *The sociology of health*. New York: Random House.

WILSON, WILLIAM JULIUS. 1991. "Studying inner-city social dislocations: The challenge of public agenda research." *American Sociological Review*, 56:1–14.

———. 1996. *When work disappears: The world of the new urban poor*. New York: Knopf.

WINKLEBY, MARILYN A., DARIUS E. JATULIS, ERICA FRANK, and STEPHEN P. FORTMANN. 1992. "Socioeconomic status and health: How education, income, and occupation contribute to risk factors for cardiovascular disease." *American Journal of Public Health*, 82:816–820.

WINKLEBY, MARILYN A., HELENA C. KRAEMER, DAVID K. AHN, and ANN N. VARADY. 1998. "Ethnic and socioeconomic differences in cardiovascular disease risk factors: Findings for women from the Third National Health and Nutrition Examination." *Journal of the American Medical Association*, 280:356–362.

WNUK-LIPINSKI, EDMUND. 1990. "The Polish country profile: Economic crisis and inequalities in health." *Social Science and Medicine,* 31:859–866.

WOLINSKY, FREDERIC D. 1988. *The sociology of health: Principles, professions, and issues,* 2nd ed. Belmont, Calif.: Wadsworth.

WOLINSKY, FREDERIC D., and SALLY R. WOLINSKY. 1981. "Expecting sick-role legitimation and getting it." *Journal of Health and Social Behavior,* 27:229–242.

WOOLHANDLER, STEFFIE, DAVID U. HIMMELSTEIN, and JAMES P. LEWONTIN. 1993. "Administrative costs in U.S. hospitals." *New England Journal of Medicine,* 329:400–403.

WORLD HEALTH ORGANIZATION. 1986. "Lifestyles and health." *Social Science and Medicine,* 22:117–124.

WRAY, LINDA A., A. REGULA HERZOG, ROBERT J. WILLIS, and ROBERT W. WALLACE. 1998. "The impact of education and heart attack on smoking cessation among middle-age adults." *Journal of Health and Social Behavior,* 39:271–294.

WYNDER, ERNST L., YASUYUKI FUJITA, RANDALL E. HARRIS, TAKESHI HIRAYAMA, and TOMOHIKO HIYAMA. 1991. "Comparative epidemiology of cancer between the United States and Japan." *Cancer,* 67:746–763.

WYSONG, JERE A., and THOMAS ABEL. 1991. "Universal health insurance and high-risk groups in West Germany: Implications for U.S. health policy." *Milbank Quarterly,* 68:527–560.

XUESHAN, FENG, TANG SHENGLAN, GERALD BLOOM, MALCOLM SEGALL, and GU XINGYUAN. 1995. "Cooperative medical schemes in contemporary rural China." *Social Science and Medicine,* 41:1111–1118.

YOSHIDA, KAREN K. 1993. "Reshaping of self: A pendular reconstruction of self and identity among adults with traumatic spinal cord injury." *Sociology of Health and Illness,* 15:217–245.

ZBOROWSKI, MARK. 1952. "Cultural components in responses to pain." *Journal of Social Issues,* 8:16–30.

ZOLA, IRVING K. 1966. "Culture and symptoms—An analysis of patients' presenting complaints." *American Sociological Review,* 31:615–630.

———. 1972. "Medicine as an institution of social control." *Sociological Review,* 20:487–504.

———. 1982. *Missing pieces: A chronicle of living with a disability.* Philadelphia: Temple University Press.

———. 1989. "Toward the necessary universalizing of a disability policy," *Milbank Quarterly,* 67, Supp. 2:401–428.

Photo Credits

Chapter 1 Joel Gordon Photography, p. 1; David Jennings/AP/Wide World Photos, p. 9; AP/Wide World Photos, p. 12.

Chapter 2 Keith Brofsky/Getty Images, Inc.—Photodisc, p. 19; Peter Southwick/Stock Boston, p. 25; Bruce Ayres/Getty Images Inc.—Stone Allstock, p. 37.

Chapter 3 Elizabeth Crews/The Image Works, p. 40; Lester Sloan/Woodfin Camp & Associates, p. 54; Spencer Grant/PhotoEdit, p. 48.

Chapter 4 Digital Vision Ltd., p. 72; Natalie Fobes/Getty Images Inc.—Stone Allstock, p. 76; Spencer Grant/PhotoEdit, p. 87.

Chapter 5 Spencer Grant/Photo Researchers, Inc., p. 94; Mark Lennihan/AP/Wide World Photos, p. 106; Michael Newman/PhotoEdit, p. 101.

Chapter 6 Michael Siluk/The Image Works, p. 118; Mark Richards/PhotoEdit, p. 129; Bill Aron/PhotoEdit, p. 136.

Chapter 7 Michael Weisbrot/Stock Boston, p. 141; EyeWire Collection/Getty Images/ EyeWire, Inc., p. 145; Tom Levy/Lonely Planet Images/Photo 20-20, p. 156.

Chapter 8 Art Stein/Photo Researchers, Inc., p. 167; David Lissy/Network Aspen, p. 169; Roger Ressmeyer/Corbis, p. 174.

Chapter 9 Larry George/Index Stock Imagery, Inc., p. 185; Steve Dunwell/Getty Images, Inc.—Liaison, p. 188; M. Meadows/Photo Researchers, Inc., p. 203.

Chapter 10 Jeffry W. Myers/Getty Images, Inc.—Taxi, p. 207; Mayo Foundation/Getty Images Inc.—Image Bank, p. 213; Stewart Cohen/Getty Images Inc.—Stone Allstock, p. 221.

Chapter 11 Tim Brown/Getty Images Inc.—Stone Allstock, p. 229; Mark Richards/PhotoEdit, p. 233; ADAMSMITH/Getty Images, Inc.—Taxi, p. 242.

Chapter 12 Michael Newman/PhotoEdit, p. 246; Bassano/Camera Press London/Globe Photos, Inc., p. 249; Telegraph Colour Library/Getty Images, Inc.—Taxi, p. 258; Eriksson, Per/ Getty Images Inc.—Image Bank, p. 263.

Chapter 13 Joseph Nettis/Photo Researchers, Inc., p. 267; Getty Images Inc.—Hulton Archive Photos, p. 272; Charles Gupton/Stock Boston, p. 279.

Chapter 14 Bob Strong/The Image Works, p. 289; Ron Edmonds/AP/Wide World Photos, p. 307; Michael Newman/PhotoEdit, p. 309.

Chapter 15 Jiro Ose/Jiro Ose, p. 313; Richard Passmore/Getty Images Inc.—Stone Allstock, p. 338; Wagner/Corbis/Saba Press Photos, Inc., p. 330.

Chapter 16 B. Wolff/United Nations, p. 343; Juda Ngwenya/Getty Images Inc.—Hulton Archive Photos, p. 364; Charles Steiner/The Image Works, p. 346; Elvee Regine/Stock Illustration Source, Inc., cover page.

Name Index

Abel, T., 16, 97, 101, 106, 335
Abercrombie, N., 67
Abrums, M., 174–175
Acheson, H., 191
Adair, R., 61
Adams, O., 320
Adler, I., 217
Adler, N., 63, 91
Adonis, A., 67, 108, 327
Aiken, L., 30, 36, 37, 259
Alegría, M., 295
Alexander, F., 147
Alexander, J., 276
Ali, J., 51
Allen, D., 257
Allen, G., 171–172
Allman, R., 190
Alubo, S., 359
Amaro, H., 57
Amato, P., 72, 82
Amey, C., 125, 306
Andersen, R., 126, 197
Anderson, J., 331
Anderson, O., 128
Anderson, R., 128
Anesaki, M., 69, 331, 332–333
Aneshensel, C., 30, 37
Angel, J., 126, 127
Angell, A., 217
Annandale, E., 16, 67, 233, 326
Anspach, R., 192
Antal, M., 352
Antonovsky. A., 85–86, 157
Antonucci, T., 204
Apple, D., 135
Arber, S., 51, 63, 67, 327
Ardagh, J., 109
Arluke, A., 132, 133, 151, 157
Arnold, R., 196
Aseltine, R., 72, 82, 91
Askenasy, A., 90
Atkinson, P., 192

Atkinson, T., 78
Auerbach, J., 47
Avery, C., 182
Avison, W., 51, 90

Backett, K., 100
Baer, H., 167, 168, 169, 170, 175–176, 179, 182
Baisden, B., 85
Baker, P., 217
Bakken, R., 352
Bakx, K., 175–176
Barboza, D., 55
Barer, M., 66, 91
Barnett, T., 34, 35
Baron-Epel, O., 42
Barth, W., 336
Bartley, M., 67
Baumann, B., 135, 155, 157
Beaglehole, R., 5
Becker, H., 15, 102, 113, 114, 115, 116, 135, 158, 160, 166, 215–217, 220, 253
Beggs, J., 78
Bell, S., 163
Benatar, S., 363–364, 366
Bendix, R., 98
Bennett, A., 320
Ben-Sira, Z., 220, 231
Bentley, P., 95, 103
Bentsen, C., 359
Benyamini, Y., 42
Berger, P., 123
Berkanovic, E., 154
Berkman, L., 104
Bernard, C., 209
Billig, M., 137
Bird, C., 14, 16, 47, 50, 51, 100–101
Biro, G., 352
Blackwell, E., 12, 195
Blaike, P., 34, 35

Blane, D., 67
Blank, N., 63, 328
Blaxter, M., 2, 67, 108, 198
Bloom, G., 355, 360
Bloom, S., 13, 14, 216
Bobak, M., 62, 63, 327, 351
Bolaria, B., 320, 321
Borooah, V., 63, 67, 327
Booth, A., 72, 82
Bosanquet, N., 326
Bosk, C., 30, 37, 232–233
Bosma, H., 81
Boulton, M., 192
Bourne, P., 86
Bourdieu, P., 99
Bowen, S., 258
Bowling, A., 260
Bowman, M., 35
Boyer, C., 294–295, 302
Braithwaite, R., 52, 57, 60
Brannon, R., 247
Braveman, P., 60, 62
Brenner, M., 77
Breslow, L., 104
Britt, T., 192
Broadhead, R., 217
Brooke, J., 322–323
Brooks-Gunn, J., 30
Brown, C., 115
Brown, E., 209
Brown, G., 88
Brown, J., 154
Brown, L., 292
Brown, P., 24, 163
Brown, R., 209
Budrys, G., 294, 302
Bunton, R., 109
Burke, B., 203
Burns, C., 237–238
Burns, L., 299
Burr, J., 42, 57, 60
Burrows, R., 109

Burton, R., 51, 82
Bury, M., 2, 67, 163
Butler, J., 11

Calnan, M., 108, 135
Campbell, J., 154, 331
Cannon, W., 79
Cantor, N., 22
Carlson, E., 63
Carpenter, M., 248, 255, 257
Cartwright, A., 284
Cassell, E., 161, 190–191,
    199–200
Cassileth, B., 345
Castro, R., 361–362
Catalano, R., 78
Cawley, J., 261
Chalfant, H., 150
Chandler, S., 78, 88
Chandola, T., 63, 67, 327
Chang, L., 201
Chapman, C., 345
Chapman, E., 30, 36, 37,
    161, 163
Charmaz, K., 161, 163
Chen, M., 353, 355
Chenet, L., 351
Childs, D., 334
Christiansen, T., 108
Ciambrone, D., 36, 161, 163
Clair, J., 190, 217
Clark, M., 159
Clarke, A., 194
Clarke, J., 320
Clarke, L., 100, 102, 175
Clinton, B., 212, 237, 305–308
Clipp, E., 72, 82
Coates, T., 36
Cobb, S., 94, 116, 118
Coburn, D., 321
Cockerham, W., 1, 14, 16, 42,
    44, 50, 61–63, 67, 69,
    91–92, 94–95, 97, 101,
    106–107, 110–113, 121,
    126, 132–133, 151, 155,
    186–187, 189, 241, 270,
    313, 333–334, 336, 346,
    349–352
Coe, R., 138, 268, 271,
    281–283, 285
Cole, S., 150, 157

Coleman, D., 108
Collins, C., 54
Colten, M., 91
Columbotos, J., 216
Comer, J., 126
Conger, R., 91
Conrad, P., 14, 16, 95, 103, 149,
    161, 203, 205, 217
Cooley, C., 73
Coombs, R., 217–220
Cooper-Patrick, L., 196
Corbett, J., 109, 339
Corbin, J., 163
Corin, E., 16
Corning, A., 204
Coser, R., 284–285
Cox, S., 203
Crawford, R., 96, 103, 134
Crossley, M., 155
Cunningham-Burley, S., 203
Curtis, S., 344
Cyster, R., 198

D'Agostino, R., 25, 104
Dahrendorf, R., 97
Davidson, N., 63, 67, 113, 327
Davis, C., 346
Davis, F., 190, 248, 253–254
Davison, C., 100
Dean, A., 78, 84, 90
Dean, K., 95, 101, 109, 119–120
DeLorgeril, M., 109
Denton, J., 171
Desjarlais, R., 50
DeVries, R., 264
DeWaal, D., 16, 110, 349–350
D Houtaud, A., 97, 135
Dickinson, H., 320–321
Diderichsen, F., 63, 328
Dill, A., 30
Dimond, M., 88, 186
Dinkel, R., 336
DiOrio, F., 63, 109
Dmitrieva, E., 351
Dohrenwend, B. P., 86, 90
Dohrenwend, B. S., 87, 90
Dooley, C., 78
Doorslaer, E., 63
Dorling, D., 327
Drentea, P., 72, 82
DuBos, R., 2, 3, 5

Duff, R., 224–225
Dumons, B., 338–339
Dunham, H., 13
Dunn, A., 29
Durkheim, E., 13, 15, 75, 76, 147
Dutton, D., 113, 126, 129–132
Dwyer, J., 100, 102, 175

Earickson, R., 30
Eckenrode, J., 88
Eggleston, K., 355
Ehrenreich, B., 194
Eitinger, L., 85
Elder, G., 72, 82
Elder, R., 259
Ellison, C., 174
Elston, M., 195
Emmons, D., 243
Engle, G., 4, 72
Engels, F., 13
English, D., 194
Ensel, W., 78, 84, 90
Epstein, H., 64, 66
Etorre, E., 203
Evans, J., 133
Evans, R., 66, 91–92, 322
Everett, M., 203–204
Ezzy, D., 161, 163

Fairbanks, D., 90
Faris, R., 13
Farmer, M., 42, 60, 163
Featherstone, 98, 108
Fennell, M., 276
Fenwick, R., 16, 72, 78
Ferraro, K., 42, 60, 163, 262
Field, D., 163, 326
Field, M., 97, 135, 319,
    345–346, 349
Fielding, J., 339
Fife, B., 164
Figert, A., 47
Fillenbaum, G., 42
Fiorentine, R., 195
Fisher, S., 190, 193
Fitton, F., 191
Flexner, A., 214
Floge, L., 257–258
Fosu, G., 359
Foucault, M., 4, 18
Fourie, A., 363

Fox, A., 15, 63
Fox, J., 51
Fox, R., 30, 36, 37, 216–217, 267
Frader, J., 30, 37
Frank, A., 189, 233
Fraser, C., 173
Fremont, A., 14, 16, 47
Freidson, E., 15, 122, 132,
    149–150, 158–160,
    185–186, 199, 211, 224,
    226, 231–235, 241, 244,
    246–247, 248, 250, 254–255
Freud, S., 147
Freund, P., 162–163
Frey-Wouters, E., 86
Frohlich, N., 16, 63
Fuchs, V., 102
Fujimoto, T., 50
Fuller, T., 50
Funch, D., 90
Furstenberg, F., 30

Gabe, J., 203, 205
Gallagher, E., 104, 157, 222,
    313, 356–358
Gallops, M., 86
Garcia, A., 90
Garland, N., 331
Garrett, L., 10–11
Gay, E., 287
Geczik, J., 170
Geertsen, R., 122–123
Geiger, H., 281
Georgopoulos, B., 278
Gerhardt, U., 147
Gibbs, J., 160
Gilbert, L., 365
Gill, D., 325–326
Gillick, M., 102
Gillis, K., 243
Gissler, M., 63
Glaser, B., 284
Glass, J., 50
Glassner, B., 103–104
Glik, D., 172
Gochman, D., 115
Goffman, E., 15, 74, 164,
    281–282
Gold, M., 299, 300
Goldberg, D., 109
Goldberg, K., 56
Goldstein, J., 119

Goldstein, M., 95, 102, 169
Goode, W., 208, 231
Gordon, G., 152
Gore, A., 212
Gore, S., 88, 91, 118, 123
Görtler, E., 336
Gortmaker, S., 88
Goss, M., 276
Gouldner, A., 14
Gove, W., 51
Graig, L., 320–321, 326, 331
Green, G., 30, 36–37, 284
Green, H., 102
Greer, B., 220
Gregson, S., 34
Grey, B., 233, 292
Griffiths, L., 326
Grogan, C., 354–355
Grzywacz, J., 55
Guten, S., 103, 107
Gutiérrez-Fisat, J., 63

Haas, J., 217, 218
Hafferty, F., 169, 212, 217, 222,
    227, 235–243, 244, 294–295
Haines, V., 78, 84, 90
Hall, O., 215, 222–227
Hallowell, N., 203
Ham, C., 325
Hamilton, V., 88
Hammond, J., 195
Hardey, M., 67, 201
Harris, D., 98, 103, 107
Harris, T., 88
Harris-Reid, M., 61
Hart, C., 100
Hart, J., 201
Hart, N., 44, 60, 63, 327
Harter, R., 88
Hartley, H., 264
Hartman, K., 123
Hattori, H., 67, 92, 120,
    332–333
Haug, M., 115, 119–120, 134,
    187, 189
Häussler, B., 336
Hay, D., 115
Hayes, D., 103
Hayes, R., 36
Hayes-Bautista, D., 187, 231
Haywood, M., 54, 55, 57
Heinemann, L., 336

Helzer, J., 86
Hempel, E., 336
Hemström, D., 63, 328
Henderson, G., 354
Henderson, L., 13
Henig, R., 194
Hersey, J., 116
Hertzman, C., 67
Herzlich, C., 109, 135
Hesketh, T., 353–354
Hildreth, C., 53
Hillier, S., 276
Himmelstein, D., 286
Hines, R., 126
Hinze, S., 195–196
Hjermann, I., 26, 27
Hoffmeister, H., 336
Hollender, M., 186–187, 205
Hollingshead, A., 13, 14, 87,
    124, 224–225
Hollingsworth, J., 68, 236
Hollman, W., 28
Holloway, J., 179
Holmes, T., 89–90
Hooker, R., 261
Hopkins, A., 161
Horwitz, A., 72, 82
Hough, R., 90
House, J., 54, 57, 60, 62–63, 80,
    88, 92
Howard, J., 190
Howell, T., 257
Hraba, J., 63
Hsiao, W., 353, 355
Hsieh, C., 27, 104
Hughes, D., 326
Hughes, Ma., 51, 82
Hughes, Mi., 51, 58
Hummer, R., 54, 57
Humphries, K., 63
Huie, S., 57
Hunt, C., 34–35
Hunt, L., 361
Hurlbert, J., 78, 84, 90
Hyde, D., 211–212
Hyde, R., 27

Idler, E., 42, 100, 174
Ikegami, N., 331–332
Illsley, R., 63
Inglehart, J., 335
Iverson, D., 116

Jackson, P., 82
Jacobson, C., 255–256
Jallinoja, P., 204
Janz, N., 116
Jarvis, M., 327
Jewkes, R., 35
Jezewska-Zychowicz, M., 352
Jinks, M., 313, 320
Johansson, S., 63, 328
Johnson, D., 88
Johnson, J., 334
Johnson, M., 14
Jones, B., 329
Joosten, J., 135
Jost, T., 335–336
Józan, P., 352
Jylhä, M., 42

Kagawa-Singer, M., 136
Kaniasty, K., 85
Kannel, W., 25, 104
Kaplan, G., 42
Karlsen, S., 16, 55
Kasl, S., 94, 116, 118, 174
Kasteler, J., 231
Kassebaum, G., 155, 157
Katz, P., 189
Kellett, A., 86
Kelly, M., 163
Kelner, M., 169
Kendall, P., 217, 222, 297
Kennedy, L., 132, 151, 157
Kerr, A., 203
Kessler, R., 50–51, 61, 69, 72,
    82, 88, 91, 132, 151, 157
Kiev, A., 179–181
King, G., 52
Kingdom, J., 324, 326
Kinnell, A., 30
Kirkman-Liff, B., 335, 337
Klein, R., 325, 326
Kleinman, S., 217
Kletke, P., 243–244
Knaus, W., 345
Knesebeck, O., 335–336
Knight, R., 115
Knowles, J., 285
Koch, R., 209
Kolker, A., 203
Kolody, B., 90
Kookier, S., 108
Koos, E., 127–128, 131

Kosa, J., 157
Kotarba, J., 95, 103
Krauss, B., 36, 162
Krebs-Smith, S., 27
Kronenfeld, J., 16, 107
Kugelmann, R., 136
Kulis, S., 189, 300
Kunst, A., 63, 337
Kunz, G., 106, 186, 241, 334
Kurtz, R., 150

Laennec, R., 209
Lagasse, R., 63
Lahelma, E., 60, 62–63, 327
Lai, G., 50
Lakka, T., 28
Lancry, P., 339
Larkin, G., 324
LaRosa, J., 27
Lassey, M., 313, 320–321, 324,
    326, 335, 337, 339, 345,
    354, 361
Lassey, W., 313, 320–321, 324,
    326, 335, 337, 339, 345,
    354, 361
Lau, R., 123
Lauer, R., 87–88
Laufer, R., 86
Laumann, E., 11, 56
Laurier, D., 109
LaVeist, T., 193
Lavin, B., 134, 187, 189, 220
Lavrakas, P., 72
Lear, D., 34, 35
LeBlanc, A., 30, 37
LeClere, F., 55
Leclerc. A., 63
Lee, E., 126
Lee, I., 27, 104
Lee, S., 137
Lefton, M., 161
LeJeune, R., 150, 157
Lemkow, L., 63
Lennon, M., 50
Leon, D., 348
Leonard, L., 48
Lesho, E., 167, 168
Leventhal, H., 282
Levi, F., 352
Levin, J., 35
Levine, C., 30, 37
Levy, J., 181–182

Lewin, K., 113
Lewontin, J., 286
Liem, J., 78
Liem, R., 78
Light, D., 2, 169, 212, 220, 222,
    227, 234–235, 237, 242,
    243–244, 260, 294–295,
    314, 325–326, 335, 345
Lin, N., 78, 84, 90, 355
Link, B., 7, 55, 60, 62, 192, 225
Linn, B., 42
Linn, M., 42
Lipowski, Z., 158
Lister, J., 210
Liston, R., 209
Liu, Y., 355
Livingston, M., 320–321
Lloyd, D., 87, 91
Long, C., 209
Lonnquist, L., 120, 257
Looman, C., 63, 337
Lopez, A., 43, 351
Lorber, J., 121, 195–196, 226,
    283–284
Loscocco, K., 78
Lostao, L., 63, 340
Lowenstein, J., 189, 233
Luckmann, T., 123
Ludmerer, K., 213
Lueschen, G., 97, 100–101,
    106–107, 109, 186, 241,
    313, 334
Lundberg, O., 63, 328
Lupton, D., 147

MacDonald, D., 34–35
MacIntyre, S., 63, 67, 113
Mackenbach, J., 63, 337
Mackey, S., 356
Madsen, W., 126, 176, 180,
    197–198
Maiman, L., 116, 135
Malat, J., 193
Mann, F., 278
Manning, P., 75
Marang-van de Mheen, P.,
    99, 101
Marks, N., 55
Marmor, T., 66, 91, 301–302
Marmot, M., 60, 62–65, 67,
    92, 327
Marshall, J., 90, 294

Marshall, T., 311
Martin, J., 229
Martin, L., 44
Martin, P., 203
Martin, S., 196
Marx, K., 13, 96, 97, 111–112
Masuda, M., 90
Matt, G., 78, 84, 90
Matthews, S., 50
Mauksch, H., 248, 251, 253
Mbugua, J., 360
McDonough, P., 63
McFarlane, A., 89
McGuire, M., 162–163
McIntire, C., 12
McKee, M., 348, 351
McKeehan, I., 344
McKellin, W., W., 203
McKeown, T., 2, 5
McKevitt, C., 281–282
McKinlay, J., 5, 194, 235–236,
    241, 244
McKinlay, S., 5
McLanahan, S., 50
McLeod, J., 51, 91, 295
McMaster, J., 35
McQueen, D., 36
McRae, J., 50
Mead, G., 73
Mead, L., 314
Mechanic, D., 42–43, 74, 82–83,
    88, 116, 118, 135–136, 186,
    212, 225, 326
Medvedev, R., 350
Merrill, D., 257–258
Meitlin, C., 90
Menaghan, E., 62
Merton, R., 15, 217
Meschede, T., 78
Mesle, F., 110
Messikomer, C., 30, 36–37
Meyer, M., 306
Mezentseva, E., 345–346
Michael, R., 11
Mielck, 63
Miller, M., 100, 102, 175, 225
Miller, S., 223
Millman, M., 232–234
Mirowsky, J., 42, 50–51, 55, 60,
    62, 88, 111
Mizrachi, N., 169
Mooney, A., 77

Morgan, M., 281–282
Morris, J., 28
Morse, J., 181–183
Morton, W., 209
Moskos, C., 86
Moss, G., 79, 83
Mulatu, M., 60, 62
Mullen, P., 116
Munakata, T., 36, 331–333
Murray, C., 43
Musick, M., 100, 102, 174
Mustard, C., 63
Mutchler, J., 42, 57, 60
Myles, J., 311

Nam, C., 57
Navarro, V., 111–112, 309
Nazroo, J., 16, 55
Neighbors, H., 61
Nemtsov, A., 348
Nettleton, S., 16, 67, 326
Ngwena, C., 359, 363–364, 366
Nigenda, G., 361
Nisbet, L., 36
Nolen, W., 220
Nolte, E., 336
Norris, F., 85
Nuru-Jeter, A., 193

Obbo, C., 34, 35
Olesen, V., 194, 248, 252–254
Orfali, K., 339–340
Ornish, D., 104
Oscarson, R., 331
Ostrowska, A., 352
Otten, M., 55, 60, 184

Paffenbarger, R., 27, 104
Palosuo, H., 351
Pandey, S., 201
Pappas, G., 63
Parker, R., 196
Parsons, G., 217–19
Parsons, T., 14–15, 18, 132,
    142, 145–161, 165–166,
    185–186, 188, 267, 284
Pasteur, L., 5, 24
Pavalko, E., 50, 72, 82, 306
Pearlin, L., 30, 37, 72, 75,
    78, 82
Penn-KeKana, L., 35
Perrow, C., 276–277

Pescosolido, B., 16, 123–124,
    169, 229, 294–295, 302
Peter, R., 81
Peters, K., 55
Peto, R., 49
Petukhova, N., 344
Phelan, J., 55, 60, 62
Phifer, J., 85
Pierret, J., 109, 135
Pinkstone, J., 200
Piperno, A., 63, 109
Pitts, M., 35
Platt, S., 30, 36–37, 284
Plewis, I., 67
Polednak, A., 52–54, 57
Pollard, S., 67, 108, 327
Pollet, G., 338–339
Pollner, M., 174
Popkin, B., 351
Poppius, E., 63
Porter, R., 3, 6, 214, 230, 235,
    262, 268
Porter, S., 247–248,
    254–255, 257
Potter, S., 287
Potvin, L., 16
Powell, M., 69, 331–333
Powell-Griner, E., 99
Power, C., 67
Preston, H., 8
Preston, R., 10
Pretorius, E., 363
Prohaska, T., 32
Psathas, G., 253

Radley, A., 136–137, 155, 163
Rado, S., 86
Rahe, R., 89
Rahkonen, O., 63, 327
Ransford, H., 103, 107
Rasmussen, H., 230
Rawlinson, M., 154
Reader, G., 217, 222
Redlich, F., 13, 124
Reeder, L., 240–241
Regidor, E., 63
Reid, I., 64, 67, 108–109, 327
Renennick, L., 136
Renaud, S., 109
Rensburg, D., 34, 359, 363–366
Reschke, P., 336
Reynolds, J., 60, 62, 78

Rieker, P., 47
Rier, D., 152, 188, 190
Rierdan, J., 78
Rimachevskaya, N., 345–346
Riska, E., 195, 197
Ritchey, F., 1, 14, 243
Ritzer, G., 241–243
Robert, S., 54, 57, 60, 62–63
Roberts, R., 126
Robinson, B., 179, 198
Rodenstein, M., 103
Rodriguez, C., 63
Rodriguez, J., 63
Rodwin, V., 339
Roebuck, J., 178–179
Roentgen, W., 210
Rogler, L., 87
Rogers, R., 55, 57, 78, 99
Roos, N., 101
Rose, G., 65
Rosenberg, C., 90, 268, 272
Rosenfield, S., 50, 51
Rosenstock, I., 102, 113, 115
Ross, C., 42, 50–51, 55, 60,
    62–63, 88, 99, 100–102,
    111, 126, 132
Ross, R., 210
Roth, J., 161
Rothman, E, 221–222
Rowland, D., 346
Roxburgh, S., 50
Ruch, L., 78, 88, 90
Rueschmeyer, D., 231
Ruggie, M., 292
Rundall, T., 88, 127, 131
Rushing, W., 30, 35, 286
Rütten, A., 16

Saks, M., 169
Salt, J., 108
Sandier, S., 339
Saunders, E., 53
Saward, E., 301
Scambler, G., 16, 161
Scheff, T., 186
Scheuch, E., 107
Schieman, S., 163
Schneider, I., 149
Schneider, M., 314
Schneirov, M., 170
Schoenbaum, M., 54
Schooler, C., 60, 62

Schor, E., 62
Schulenberg, J., 335
Schuller, A., 2, 335
Schulman, S., 248, 259
Schutt, R., 78, 84
Searle, M., 222, 357, 358
Seccombe, K., 58, 125, 306
Segal, R., 115
Segall, A., 119, 155
Segall, M., 360
Seeman, M., 133
Seeman, T., 133
Selvin, H., 297
Selye, H., 80, 87
Sermsri, S., 35
Shaffir, W., 217–218
Shapiro, J., 351
Shapiro, M., 217
Sharma, U., 170
Sharp, K., 42, 126, 132
Shaw, M., 327
Sheiman, I., 344
Shepard, J., 27, 104
Sherraden, M., 361
Shipley, M., 65
Shkolnikov, V., 63, 110, 348
Shortell, S., 225
Shorter, E., 199
Shuval, J., 63, 72, 169, 217
Sidel, V., 354
Siegel, K., 36, 162
Siegrist, J., 72, 80–81, 113,
    335–336
Sihvonen, A., 63
Simmons, L., 13
Simon, R., 50–51, 82
Singer, E., 204
Singh, G., 60
Skidelsky, R., 344
Skocpol, T., 16, 301–302,
    306, 308
Sleeper, S., 292, 294
Sloane, D., 259
Smaje, C., 60
Smetannikov, E., 169
Smith, A., 217
Smith, B., 50
Smith, D., 301
Smith, G., 62–63, 67, 99, 327
Smith, J., 63, 66
Snead, C., 16, 110, 113,
    349, 350

Snow, J., 23–24
Snow, L., 176–179
Soifer, S., 120
Sontag, S., 162
Sorensen, G., 48
Southerland, T., 262
Spitze, G., 78
Splawski, I., 54
Spruit, I., 63, 337
Srole, L., 13
Starr, P., 16, 224, 236, 238–240,
    274, 301–302, 306, 309–310
Stein, L., 256–257
Steinman, M., 126
Stern, B., 13
Stevens, F., 295, 313, 337
Stevens, R., 210, 213–214, 225,
    234, 268, 287, 294, 302
Stewart, T., 313
Stoller, E., 42
Stratton, T., 313
Straus, R., 15, 16
Strauss, A., 6, 130–131, 163,
    190, 250, 278–279, 284
Style, C., 51
Subedi, J., 313
Suchman, E., 13, 121–122,
    131–132, 137–139
Sullivan, D., 263–264
Sundquist, J., 63, 328
Susser, E., 24
Svarstad, B., 198
Svensson, P., 63
Svensson, R., 257
Swartz, L., 181–182
Swisher, R., 72
Sytkowski, P., 25, 104
Szasz, T., 149–150,
    186–187, 205

Taira, D., 192
Tajima, K., 36
Taket, A., 344
Takeuchi, D., 61
Tang, S., 355
Tarimo, E., 60, 62
Tausig, M., 16, 72, 78
Taylor, S., 52, 57, 60
Telyukov, A., 346
Tessler, R., 88, 186
Thoits, P., 50–51, 83–84, 87,
    90–91

Thomas, H., 51
Thompson, J., 198–199
Thorogood, N., 176, 179
Tierney, K., 85
Timmermans, S., 202, 217
Tiwary, S., 201
Todd, A., 190
Townsend, P., 63, 67, 113, 327
Treml, V., 351
Trevino, F., 127
Trovato, F., 63
Tseng, S., 201
Tsvetarsky, S., 63
Tuch, S., 229, 294
Tuchman, B., 22–23
Turner, B., 72, 88, 103, 150, 308
Turner, H., 36, 163
Turner, R., 87, 90–91
Tuxworth, W., 28
Twaddle, A., 135, 149–150, 152
Twigg, J., 344

Ulbrich, P., 50, 61
Umberson, D., 72

Valkonen, T., 62–63
Vega, W., 57
Verbrugge, L., 44, 47, 120, 121
Virchow, R., 209
Vladeck, B., 295–296
Vlassov, V., 345
Volkart, E., 73, 82, 135

Waidmann, T., 54
Waitzkin, H., 111, 190, 192,
    230, 237, 309
Walberg, P., 350
Walczak, D., 241–243
Waldron, I., 51, 78
Walker, L., 365
Wall, A., 313
Walliman, I., 338
Wallis, R., 171–172

Walsh, D., 48
Wan, T., 120
Warbasse, J., 12
Ward, P., 361
Wardle, J., 327
Warheit, G., 61
Warnecke, R., 253
Warner, D., 361–362
Warren, M., 189, 300
Watson, W., 63, 131–132
Watts, D., 257
Weber, M., 13, 15, 96–101,
    103–104, 107, 116–117,
    147, 242, 276
Webster, A., 200
Wegar, K., 195
Weiner, H., 91
Weiss, C., 51
Weiss, G., 82, 120, 257
Weitz, R., 188–189, 190–192,
    263–264, 300
Welch, S., 126
Welch, W., 210
Wellman, B., 169
Wenger, N., 26
Wermuth, L., 60, 62
Wessen, A., 278
West, C., 194–195
Wheaton, B., 87, 133
Wheeler, J., 127, 131
White, H., 72
White, S., 72
Whitehead, M., 63, 67, 113, 327
Whittaker, E., 248, 252–254
Wholey, D., 237–238, 299
Wickrama, K., 50, 100–101, 123
Wight, D., 30
Wilcox, J., 42
Wildman, R., 88
Wilkinson, R., 60, 62–63, 64,
    66–67, 113, 327
Williams, A., 321
Williams, C., 192

Williams, D., 54, 60–62
Williams, G., 163, 192
Williams, R., 135
Williams, S., 163, 325–326
Wilson, R., 148, 274
Wilson, W., 56
Wing, A., 27
Winkleby, M., 7, 55, 60, 62
Winter, M., 352
Wnuk-Lupinski, E., 63
Woelfel, J., 90
Wolff, H., 13
Wolff, P., 211–212
Wolinsky, F., 15, 132,
    151, 174
Wolinsky, S., 132, 151
Wood, P., 90
Woolhandler, S., 286
Wortman, C., 72
Wray, L., 63, 99
Wright, E., 164
Wu, C., 42, 62, 63, 99
Wybraniec, J., 163
Wynder, E., 333
Wysong, J., 335

Xueshan, F., 355

Yamori, Y., 67, 92, 333
Ye, X., 78, 84
Yoels, W., 190, 217
Yoshida, K., 163
Youm, Y., 56
Young, D., 181, 182
Yu, S., 60
Yu, Y., 331

Zajkas, G., 352
Zborowski, M., 137, 153–154
Zhu, W., 353–354
Zimmerman, R., 61
Zola, I., 131, 137, 149, 154, 157,
    161, 163, 196–197

Subject Index

Activity-passivity model, 186, 188
Acquired Immune Deficiency Syndrome. *See* AIDS
Acupuncture, 168–169
Africa, 3, 8, 10, 22, 159
   AIDS, 30, 31, 34–36
African Americans, 45, 51–57, 61, 124–127, 176–179, 198
   AIDS, 20, 32–34, 43, 46, 51, 53
   life expectancy, 51–52
   smoking, 49
Age. *See also* Aging
   health and life expectancy, 40–44
Aging, 40–44
AIDS, 7, 30–39, 43, 51, 53, 57, 59, 96, 105, 161, 162, 164
Alcohol, 46, 48, 55, 57–59, 60, 62, 77, 95, 99, 100–101, 104–105, 108–109, 110–112, 116, 143, 150, 164, 175, 198–199, 340, 347–349, 351–352
Alternative medicine, 119, 123, 167, 168–170, 184, 201. *See also,* Complementary and alternative medicine
American Academy of Physician Assistants, 265
American Chiropractic Association, 184
American Heart Association, 39
American Hospital Association, 288
American Indians/Native Alaskans. *See* Native Americans
American Medical Association, 39, 168, 170, 210–214, 227–228, 234–236, 244–245, 298, 301, 308

American Medical Student Association, 228
American Medical Women's Association, 211
American Nurses Association, 255, 265
American Osteopathic Association, 168, 183
American Pharmaceutical Association, 266
American Psychological Association, 93
American Sociological Association, 17–18
American Stroke Association, 39
Anorexia nervosa, 137
Argentina, AIDS, 36
Asia, 8, 22
   AIDS, 35, 36
Asian/Pacific Islander Americans, 51, 53, 57, 59–61
   AIDS, 32–33, 58
Association of American Medical Colleges, 228
Australia, 22, 49, 115, 170
   AIDS, 36
Austria, 209

Bangladesh, 44
Belarus, 111
Belgium, 63, 107
Bernard, Claude, 209
Bioterrorism, 10–12, 18
Black Americans. *See* African Americans
Black Report, 64, 67
Blackwell, Elizabeth, 12, 195
Botswana
   AIDS, 34
Bowditch, Henry, 209

Brazil
   AIDS, 36
British Medical Association, 324–325, 342
British Sociological Association, 17–18
Bubonic plague, 22–23
Bulgaria, 63, 111
Bureau of Labor Statistics, 46

Cambodia
   AIDS, 36
Canada, 49, 63, 88, 119, 163, 170, 181–182, 217, 218, 313, 341
   health care delivery, 320–323
   SARS, 322
Cancer, 6, 19, 20, 29–30, 43–44, 46, 48, 50–53, 58–60, 65, 96, 99, 102, 105, 118, 136, 139, 155, 159, 162, 164, 173, 175, 218, 221, 320
Carnegie Foundation, 214
Catholic Church, 4
Centers for Disease Control and Prevention (CDC), 9, 10, 11, 16, 18, 29, 31–32, 38–39, 56, 71, 117, 140, 298
Central America
   AIDS, 36
Central Intelligence Agency (CIA), 9, 10
China, 22, 322, 343, 353–355
   AIDS, 36
   SARS, 322, 355
Chiropractors, 167, 168, 170–171, 183
Christian Science Church, 173
Chronic disease, 6, 20, 24–25, 46–47, 55, 96, 119, 148, 155, 162–163, 187
Chrysler Corporation, 305

Clinton Administration, 212, 237, 294, 306–308
Cloning, 204–205
Complementary and alternative medicine (CAM), 167, 168–170
Conflict Theory, 308–309
Congo, 7
    AIDS, 34
Consumer Price Index. *See* U.S. Consumer Price Index
Cooley, Charles H., 72–75, 78
Coronary heart disease. *See* Heart Disease
    complexity, 25–29
    diet, 26–27
    exercise, 27–29
Cuba, 179, 367
Cuban Americans, 58, 125–126
Curanderos, 179–181
Czech Republic, 63, 111

Darling case, 280
Darling, Dorrence. *See* Darling case
Decentralized national health programs, 319, 329–340
Democratic Republic of the Congo, 7, 8
    AIDS, 34
Denmark, 62, 108–109, 119
    AIDS, 35
Deprofessionalization. *See* Physicians, deprofessionalization
Deviance, 142–145, 158–160, 161–162, 165
Diabetes, 25–26, 46, 53, 55, 57–60, 95–96, 118–119, 161–162, 173, 187
Diagnostic Related Groups (DRGs), 236, 287, 292, 294, 304, 353
Diet, 26–28, 95, 98–99, 101–104, 110, 320, 333, 336, 340, 348–349, 351–352
Dietary Supplement Health and Education Act, 169
Disabled persons. *See* Physical disability

Disease. *See also* Chronic disease and Infectious disease
    germ theory, 5–6, 24
    modernization, 29–38
Doctor-nurse game, 255–258
Doctor-patient interaction, 185–206
Durkheim, Emile, 13, 15, 72, 75–78, 147

Eastern Europe, 319
Ebola, 7–8
Eddy, Mary Baker, 173
Egypt, 8
Engels, Friedrich, 13
England. *See* Great Britain
Epidemiology, 19–39
    AIDS, 30–38
    definition, 19–20
    development, 22–24
    measures, 20–22
Estonia, 111
Europe, 5, 10, 22, 27, 35, 44, 63, 106–107, 110–111, 113, 208–210, 213, 268–271, 314
    AIDS, 34–35
European Society for Health and Medical Sociology, 17
European Union, 49–50, 108, 314
Evidence-based medicine (EBM), 217
Exercise, 26, 27–29, 55, 62, 100–104, 109, 110–112, 116, 134, 150, 336, 349, 351, 353

Faith healers, 167, 168, 170, 171–175, 183
Family. *See* Social networks
Finland, 17, 28, 62–63, 204
Flexner report, 214, 226–227
Folk healers, 167, 168, 170, 175–183
Formal rationality, 104, 242–243
France, 4, 63, 97, 107, 109, 116, 135, 209, 313, 342
    AIDS, 35
    health care delivery, 337–340
French paradox, 338, 340

Freud, Sigmund, 147
Functionalism, 75–78, 144–152

Gabon, 7, 34
General Adaptation Syndrome, 80
Gender, 35, 44–51, 71, 119, 121, 193–196, 197
    and heart disease, 25–26
    and mental health, 50–51
Genetics, 52, 54–55, 78, 202–205
Germ theory. *See* Disease, germ theory
German Society for Medical Sociology, 17
German Sociological Association, 17
Germany, 5, 8, 17, 28, 63, 80–81, 103, 106–107, 110–113, 116, 209, 313, 342
    AIDS, 35
    health care delivery, 323–327
Great Britain, 8, 17, 22–23, 27–28, 62–68, 81, 108–109, 110, 113, 116, 131–132, 135, 170, 197, 201, 208
    AIDS, 35
Greece,
    AIDS, 35
Guidance-cooperation model, 186–188
Goffman, Erving, 15, 72–75, 78, 164, 281, 282

Habitus, 99
Haiti, 179
    AIDS, 31, 36
Handicapped. *See* Physical disability
Hayyan, Jabir ibn, 262
Health
    definition, 2
Health behavior, 94–117
    definition, 94
Health Belief Model, 113–116
Health care, 47, 229–245, 289–368
    consumerism, 241–243
    rights, 308–311
    social legislation, 301–305

Health care delivery, 41, 119, 289–368
  corporations, 238–240
  costs, 290–295
  distribution of services, 296–298
  equity, 295–296
  overview, 298–301
Health insurance.
  See Insurance, health
Health Lifestyles, 3, 6–7, 24, 63, 66, 68–69, 94–117, 119, 123
  definition, 94–95
  gender, 101
  Japan, 333
  Marxist critique, 111–112
  motivation, 101–104
  religion, 100, 102
  Russia and Eastern Europe, 110–111, 349–350
  Weber, 96–101
  Western society, 97–101, 104–110
Health maintenance organizations (HMOS), 236–237, 292, 298–299
Health reform, 305–311
Heart disease, 6–7, 19, 25–29, 43–44, 46, 51–53, 58–59, 60, 65, 68–69, 77, 80–81, 96, 99, 104, 109–110, 118, 155, 162, 187, 332, 336
Hippocrates, 3, 180
Hispanic Americans, 51, 53–55, 57–58, 61, 124–127, 197.
  See also Cuban Americans, Mexican Americans, Puerto Rican Americans
  AIDS, 32–33, 57
HIV, 7, 11, 30–38, 43, 155, 162, 164
Homeopathy, 168
Hong Kong, 8, 322
Hospitals, 222–224, 227, 267–288, 298, 329
  as social institutions, 268–272
  authority, 276–280
  cost of services, 285–287
  organization, 274–280
  ownership, 273–274
  United States, 272–274

Hospital patient role, 281–285
Hospital sick role, 284–285
Human Genome Project, 202
Hungary, 62, 63, 111, 343, 352–353
Hypertension, 25–27, 44, 46, 52–53, 55, 57, 60, 69, 80, 115, 168

Illness
  definition, 141–142
  as deviance, 141–145, 161–162
  experience, 135–139, 162–163
Illness behavior, 118–140, 142, 159–160
  age, 120–121
  definition, 94, 118
  ethnicity, 121–127
  self care, 95, 119–120
  sex, 120–121
  social psychological models, 135–139
Incidence
  definition, 20
India, 8, 22, 23, 24
  AIDS, 36
Infant mortality rates, 5, 21–22, 77
  Canada, 317, 320
  Cuba, 317–318
  France, 317, 340
  Germany, 317, 356
  Great Britain, 317, 327
  Japan, 317–318, 330
  Kenya, 317, 360
  Mexico, 317, 362
  Netherlands, 317, 337
  Russia, 317, 348
  Saudi Arabia, 317, 358
  selected countries, 317
  Slovakia, 317–318
  South Africa, 317, 365
  Sweden, 316–317, 328
  United States, 21–22, 54, 58–60, 317–318, 320, 356
Indonesia
  AIDS, 36
Infectious disease, 5–12, 22, 24, 46

Insurance
  health, 124–126
  national health, 295, 305–309
International Sociological Association, 17
Internet, 200–202
International Chiropractors Association, 184
Israel, 8, 63, 152, 217, 220
Italy, 63, 109
  AIDS, 35

Jamaica, 30
Japan, 8, 11, 17, 22, 49, 68, 76, 115, 119–120, 313, 342
  AIDS, 36
  health care delivery, 330–333
Japanese Society for Health and Medical Sociology, 17
Journal of the American Medical Association (JAMA), 210–211

Kenya, 8, 343, 359–360
Koch, Robert, 5, 209

Labeling theory, 158–161, 165–166
Laennec, Rene, 209
Lassa fever, 7
Latin America, 8, 10
  AIDS, 36
Lay referral system, 121–122, 132, 137, 224, 231
Lesotho
  AIDS, 34
Lewin, Kurt, 113
Life chances, 95
Life changes. *See* Stress, life changes
Life events. *See* Stress, life events
Life expectancy, 27, 28, 40–42, 45–48, 318
  black females, 45, 51, 60
  black males, 45, 48, 51, 60
  Botswana, 34
  Canada, 318–320
  China, 353, 355
  Costa Rica, 318–319
  Europe, 44
  Females, 41, 44–48, 318

Life expectancy (*cont.*)
  France, 318–319, 340
  Germany, 318, 336
  Great Britain, 44, 318, 327
  Hungary, 318, 352
  Japan, 318, 330
  Kenya, 360
  males, 41, 44–48, 318
  Mexico, 362
  Netherlands, 318, 337
  Poland, 318, 351–352
  preindustrial society, 44
  Puerto Rico, 318–319
  Russia, 346–348, 349
  Saudi Arabia, 358
  selected countries, 318
  South Africa, 364–365
  sub-Saharan Africa, 34
  Sweden, 318–319, 328
  Switzerland, 318–319
  United States, 40–41, 45,
    51–52, 318–320, 327,
    330, 336
  Wales, 44
  white females, 45, 51–52, 60
  white males, 45, 51, 60
  women, 41, 44–48
Lifestyles. *See* Health lifestyles
Lister, Joseph, 210
Liston, Robert, 209
Lithuania, 111
Locus of control, 133
Long, Crawford, 209
Looking Glass Self, 73
Lung cancer, 48–49. *See also*
  Cancer

Magic, 3
Malaria, 8
Malaysia
  AIDS, 36
Malpractice. *See* Medicine,
  malpractice
Managed care, 237–238, 294–295
Marburg virus, 7–8
McIntire, Charles, 12
Marx, Karl, 13, 96, 96, 111–112
Mead, George Herbert, 73
Medicaid, 61, 107, 125, 128, 130,
  132, 140, 234, 236, 238,
  291, 295, 301–305, 312, 314

Medical decision rule, 186
Medical schools, 7, 208–210,
  213–222, 224, 227, 323
Medical slang, 219
Medical sociology
  definition, 1
  development, 12–18
  practical application and
    theory, 13–17
Medical students, 215–222
  admission, 215, 222
  female, 215, 222
  idealism, 216, 220
  male, 215, 222
  minorities, 215, 222
  social class, 215
Medicare, 41, 61, 107, 121, 125,
  128, 132, 140, 170, 212,
  234, 236, 238, 291–292,
  295, 301–305, 312, 314
Medicine
  countervailing power,
    235–236
  corporate control, 238–240
  government regulation,
    236–237
  malpractice, 233–234
  power structure, 222–227
  primitive, 3
  social control, 149–150,
    231–235
Mental disorder, 29, 50–51, 92,
  143, 270
  gender differences, 50–51
  race, 61
  social class differences,
    61, 69
  stress, 77–78
Mexican Americans, 125–127,
  159, 179–181, 197, 306
Mexico, 290, 316, 343, 360–362
Middle Ages, 3, 23, 141
Midwives, 263–264
Morbidity rates
  and gender, 46–51
Mortality rates, 21–22, 49
  and gender, 45–51
  and race, 51–60
Morton, William, 209
Mutual participation model,
  187, 188, 205

Myanmar
  AIDS, 36

Namibia
  AIDS, 34
National Association for
  Chiropractic Medicine, 184
National Center for
  Complementary and
  Alternative Medicine,
  169, 184
National Center for Health
  Statistics (NCHS), 29, 45,
  46, 47, 48, 49, 52, 53, 59,
  100, 120, 121, 125, 128,
  207, 252, 292, 293, 315
National Football League, 28
National health insurance. *See*
  Insurance, national health
National Health Service
  British, 68, 323–327
  Swedish, 327–329
National Heart, Lung, and
  Blood Institute, 39
National Institute for
  Occupational Safety and
  Health (NIOSH), 28
National Institutes of Health,
  14, 39, 117, 169, 184, 265
National Institute of Mental
  Health, 13, 14, 93
National League for Nursing,
  255, 265
Native Americans, 51, 53,
  58–59, 181–183
  AIDS, 32–33
  life expectancy, 58
Naturopathy, 168
Nepal, 44
Netherlands, 8, 17, 63, 107,
  110, 135, 313, 342
  health care delivery, 336–337
New Zealand, 49
  AIDS, 36
Nightingale, Florence, 249–250
Norway, 26, 62, 63, 108
  AIDS, 35
Nurses. *See* Nursing
Nursing, 247–261
  associations, 255
  education, 250–255

future trends, 258–261
history, 247–250
hospital administration, 259
nurse practitioner, 259–261
schools. *See* Nursing,
    education
students, 253–255

Obesity, 25, 26, 27, 29, 46, 55,
    56, 64, 69, 101, 102, 104,
    105, 109, 115
Office of Alternative
    Medicine, 169
Osteopaths, 167–168, 183

Palmer, Daniel, 170
Parsons, Talcott, 13, 14–15, 18,
    145–158, 159, 160, 161,
    165, 166, 185, 186, 188,
    267, 284
Pasteur, Louis, 5, 24
Patient-physician relationship,
    147–152, 155–156, 240,
    241, 243
    communication, 190–198
    future, 199–200
    new technology, 200–202
Paracelsus, 4
Pharmacists, 262–263
Philippines, 8
    AIDS, 36
Physical disability, 44–45,
    162–163
Physicians, 147, 207–245
    deprofessionalization,
        241–243
    peer regulation, 231–235
    professionalization, 207–215
    socialization, 215–222
    specialization, 225
Physician assistants, 261–262
Pima Indians, 58
Pneumonic plague, 23, 24
Poland, 63, 111, 316, 343,
    351–352
Poverty, 22–23, 24, 35, 56–57,
    64, 96, 108, 112–113,
    127–134, 156–157, 160,
    295–296
    and health, 7, 54, 55, 60–62,
        68–69, 99, 327

Preferred provider
    organizations (PPOs), 292,
    294, 298, 299
Prevalence
    definition, 20
Preventive care, 112–116, 131
Professional dominance, 235
Professional standard review
    organizations (PSROs),
    234, 236, 301
Protestant ethic, 98, 104, 107
Public health, 4–7
Puerto Rican Americans, 58,
    125–126
Puerto Rico, 87
    AIDS, 32

Race, 21, 40, 42, 45, 49, 51–61,
    71, 124–127
Religion, 100, 102
Renaissance, 3, 268
Research Committee on the
    Sociology of Health, 17
Roentgen, Wilhelm, 210
Roman Catholic Church.
    See Catholic Church
Roman Empire, 4
Romania, 8, 111
Ross, Ronald, 210
Russia, 8, 49–50, 63, 110–111,
    319, 343–352
    AIDS, 35

Saudi Arabia, 8, 355, 356–358
Self-care. *See* Illness behavior,
    self-care
Selye, Hans, 80
Severe Acute Respiratory
    Syndrome (SARS), 8,
    322, 355
Sexually transmitted diseases
    (STDS), 10–11, 55–56, 57,
    58, 105, 164
Sick role, 14–15, 47, 132, 137,
    141–166, 185, 186, 188
Singapore, 22
Smoking, 25–28, 46, 48–50,
    55, 58, 62, 64, 67, 69,
    77, 95–96, 99, 101–102,
    104–105, 108–109,
    110–112, 115, 134, 150,

156, 175, 187, 336–337,
    340, 351–352, 355
Social class. *See* Socioeconomic
    status
Social environment, 24
Social networks, 122–124
Social Readjustment Rating
    Scale, 89–91
Social support, 67, 78,
    83–84, 90
Social Security Administration,
    41–42, 303
Socialist medicine, 319
Socialized medicine, 319–329
Socioeconomic status, 24, 40,
    52, 54–55, 57, 60, 61–69,
    71, 78, 97–101, 111–113,
    116, 124, 126, 154,
    156–157, 170, 187,
    192–193, 197–199, 205, 225
    concept, 62
    health and life expectancy,
        61–69
    illness behavior, 127–134
    mental disorders, 61
Sociology
    definition, 1
    medical. *See* Medical
        sociology
    in medicine, 15–16
    of medicine, 15–16
South Africa, 343, 363–366
    AIDS, 34, 364–366
South America
    AIDS, 36
South Asia, 22, 44
    AIDS, 35
Soviet Union. *See* Russia
Spain, 63
    AIDS, 35
Stern, Bernard, 13
Stigma, 164
Still, Andrew Taylor, 167
Stress, 45, 46, 52, 55, 64, 66, 69,
    72–93, 95, 104, 110, 116,
    160
    adaptation, 81, 82–83
    credit card debt, 72, 82
    definition, 72
    extreme situations, 84–87
    life changes, 84–91

Stress (*cont.*)
  life events, 78, 82, 87–91
  physiological responses, 79–81
  social groups, 83–84
  social stressors, 82
  socioeconomic status, 91–92
Substantive rationality, 242–243
Suicide, 13, 19, 43, 53, 59–60, 65, 76, 92, 105, 160, 164
Sweden, 62–63, 313, 342
  AIDS, 35
  health care delivery, 327–329
Switzerland, 4, 290
  AIDS, 35
Symbolic interaction, 72–75
Swaziland
  AIDS, 34

Taiwan, 201
TennCare, 306
Thailand
  AIDS, 35–36
Thomas, William I., 72–75, 78, 82
Trepanation, 3
Turkey, 290

Uganda, 7, 8
Ukraine, 111
  AIDS, 35
United States, 12, 14–15, 17, 21–22, 25–26, 29, 35, 40–42, 45–46, 48–49, 50–61, 63, 101–103, 105, 106–107, 110, 112–113, 115–116, 119, 121, 124–127, 132, 135, 150–154, 159, 167–184, 197, 204, 205, 207–227, 272–287, 289–312, 314–316, 318–320, 322, 327, 330, 340
  AIDS, 30–34, 35, 38
  infant mortality rates.
    See Infant mortality rates, United States
  life expectancy. *See* Life expectancy, United States
  mortality rates, 21
U.S. Consumer Price Index, 290, 292, 293
U.S. Department of Health and Human Services, 16, 38, 71, 140, 206, 298

Veterans Administration, 125
Virchow, Rudolf, 5, 209

Wales, 62, 68
Warbasse, James, 12–13
Weber, Max, 13, 15, 96–101, 103–104, 107, 116–117, 147, 242, 276
Welch, William, 209, 210
West Indies, 179
Western Europe, 4, 17, 22
West Nile virus, 8–10
Whitehall Studies, 64–66, 81, 92
Wholism, 6–7
World Health Organization, 2, 18, 95, 96, 322

Yemen, 8

Zambia
  AIDS, 34
Zimbabwe
  AIDS, 34